To Mary Lee —

    Whose editorial discretion
and all-round competence
constantly amazes me.

    With much affection,

        David Martin

The Web of Disinformation

The Times Friday August 6 1971
London

GENERAL MIHAILOVIĆ
From Colonel S. W. Bailey

Sir. Circumstances regrettably prevented me from appending my signature to Brigadier Armstrong's letter (July 17). As the Brigadier's predecessor, and political adviser for some months after his arrival at General Mihailović's headquarters, I warmly endorse the feelings expressed therein, and wish to add my tribute to the memory of Draža Mihailović.

It cannot be disputed that Mihailović was a sensitive and complex character, or that his actions and motives during the war were accordingly surrounded by much mystery and misgivings; which partly accounts for the remorseless way in which he and his memory were treated by many of his countrymen.

Today there are signs that their hostility is weakening, and that some of them now understand that he was, to use the words he spoke at his trial, "caught up in the whirlwind of the world", and that, although an arrant traitor in their eyes, he yet remained true to what he believed to be the proper precepts and loyalties.

This change of climate, together with the release in Yugoslavia of documents from the General's archives and those of the then Yugoslav Government in exile, and in Britain of the state papers for 1941-45, should at last make possible an objective account of the events of the time.

Although I fear that archives have been too severely pruned, and that the release of official documents may prove to be too selective, for the full truth ever to be known, I do believe that everything must now be done to give Mihailović his rightful, honourable place in history. He and his Cetniks did more than is generally appreciated for the Allied cause.

Yours faithfully,

S. W. BAILEY.
Lou Castelas,
13–Maussane-lès-Alpilles,
France
July 31.

DAVID MARTIN

THE WEB
OF
DISINFORMATION

*Churchill's Yugoslav
Blunder*

HARCOURT BRACE JOVANOVICH, PUBLISHERS

San Diego   New York   London

Grateful acknowledgment is made for permission to reprint portions
from David Martin's essay "James Klugmann, SOE Cairo, and the
Mihailovich Deception," which appears in *Deception Operations:
Studies in the East-West Context,* edited by David Charters and Maurice
Tugwell (Pergamon Press, 1990).

Library of Congress Cataloging-in-Publication Data
Martin, David, 1914–
The web of disinformation: Churchill's Yugoslav blunder/
David Martin — 1st ed.
p.   cm.
Includes bibliographical references.
ISBN 0-15-180704-3
1. World War, 1939–1945 — Diplomatic history.   2. Great
Britain — Foreign relations — Yugoslavia.   3. Yugoslavia — Foreign
relations — Great Britain.   4. Yugoslavia — Politics and
government — 1918–1945.   5. Churchill, Winston, Sir, 1874–
1965.   6. Great Britain. Special Operations
Executive.   7. Klugmann, James.   I. Title.
D754.Y9M37   1990
940.53'2241 — dc20   90-30029

Maps by Sven Dolling
Designed by G. B. D. Smith
Printed in the United States of America

First edition
A B C D E

This book is dedicated to the memory of
George S. ("Gov") Musulin

An American of Serbian parentage, George served as a member of the first OSS mission to General Draža Mihailović in 1943–44. He was instrumental in persuading the US Army Air Force to undertake the evacuation of some hundreds of American airmen who had been forced down over Yugoslavia and was the first commander of the American Air Crew Rescue Unit (Halyard mission), which carried out the evacuation. George was a man of great moral courage and rare integrity. At his funeral his former CIA superior remarked, "If there had been a medal for integrity, George would have deserved two of them."

George died on February 21, 1987, and is buried in Arlington National Cemetery.

I have read and reread your letter . . . with great interest, and with a certain measure of astonishment . . . If, of course, as now seems more than possible, our information re Mihailovich's activities were incomplete, to say the least, then the whole affair changes color . . . If the information contained in your work had been available to us at the time, our whole policy might and probably would, have been very different.

From a letter to David Martin by Sir Douglas Howard, wartime head, British Foreign Office Southern Department. *(Howard was in charge of Yugoslav affairs, read all the incoming message traffic, and briefed Anthony Eden on Yugoslavia on an almost daily basis.)*

Contents

List of Maps

Note on the Spelling and Pronunciation of Serbo-Croat Words and Names

s = s as in sink
š = sh as in shift
c = ts as in mats
č = ch as in charge
ć = similar to, but lighter than, č—as in arch
ž = j as in French *jour*
z = z as in zodiac
j = y as in yell
nj = ni as in minion
g = g as in go
dj = g as in George
lj = li as in million

Acknowledgments

There are many people whose assistance in preparing this manuscript I would like to acknowledge. Chronologically they divide into three categories. The first consists of those who gave their assistance in 1944, 1945, and early 1946, when I was preparing my first book on Mihailović, *Ally Betrayed*. Many more gave their assistance in 1976 and 1977, when I was gathering material for my second book, *Patriot or Traitor: The Case of General Mihailovich*. Since that book appeared in 1978, the list of acknowledgments I must make has grown substantially, as a result of further research on the history of the Tito-Mihailović conflict, including two trips to England and France.

I would like to start off with a special tribute to the memory of Dr. Miloš Sekulić, former chief physician at the Belgrade General Hospital and an official of the Serbian Agrarian Party. Dr. Sekulić gave me indispensable assistance in writing *Ally Betrayed*. When it came to documents that might be useful in researching the Yugoslav civil war, he was probably the world's foremost "pack rat." Most of the first draft of that book was written in his apartment.

Then there were the many British and American liaison officers who had been attached to either Mihailović or Tito.

Let me deal first with the officers who served on the Mihailović side. Among those I was able to interview—some on several occasions—were, on the British side, Colonel S. William Bailey, Lt. Colonel Duane Hudson, Brigadier C. D. Armstrong, and Majors Peter Solly-Flood, Jasper Rootham, Kenneth Greenlees, Erik Greenwood, Rupert Raw, Robert Wade, Edgar C. S. Hargreaves, Michael Lees, and Archie Jack—in the last two cases for many, many hours. Also on the British side were a number of individuals who were part of SOE Cairo or part of SOE London or officials in the Foreign Office. In particular I wish to express my gratitude for lengthy interviews to Sir Douglas Howard, wartime head of the Southern Department of the Foreign Office (which was in charge of Yugoslav affairs), and Peter Boughey, who was in charge of the Yugoslav section of SOE London until shortly before the abandonment of Mihailović.

I am grateful, too, to Ms. Elisabeth Barker, head of the Yugoslav divi-sion of the Political Warfare Executive (PWE), for two lengthy conversa-tions, which were all the more interesting because she had been one of Tito's earliest enthusiasts in the wartime military-political bureaucracy. While we did not agree on the key facts, we at least demonstrated to each other's satisfaction that civilized discussion was possible between people who hold diametrically opposed views on the Tito-Mihailović conflict.

In addition, I am indebted to David Erskine and Sir William Crawshay, both of whom were associated with SOE Cairo, for submitting to my ques-tions.

Let me also acknowledge the very great debt I owe to the Right Honor-able Julian Amery, MP, for vital information conveyed in the course of many trans-Atlantic telephone calls and a vigorous correspondence over a period of time. Amery at age twenty-one was deputy chief of the Balkan Section of SOE, in which capacity he had a number of meetings with then Colonel Mihailović before the March 26 revolution and the German invasion.

On the American side, I am indebted for information and advice to Gen-eral William J. Donovan, the head of the Office of Strategic Services; to Captain George Vujnovich, operations officer for OSS in Bari, Italy; to Lt. Colonel Albert B. Seitz, the head of the first mission to Mihailović, and to his aides in this assignment, Captain Walter R. Mansfield and Captain George S. Musulin; to Colonel Robert H. McDowell and the other members of the McDowell mission—John Milodragovich, Mike Rajachich, and Ellsworth Kramer—and to Nick Lalich, who headed up the American Air Crew Res-cue Unit after taking over from George Musulin.

I am grateful, too, for the insights I was able to derive from conversa-tions with a number of British and American officers who served with the Partisans—on the British side, Sir William Deakin, Sir Fitzroy Maclean, Lord Henneker, and Sir Alexander Glen; and on the American side, Joe Veselinovich and Eli Popovich, who served as deputy to Lt. Colonel Linn M. (Slim) Farish, the head of the American mission to Tito.

I also wish to thank the American airmen who had been rescued by Mihailović and who moved heaven and earth seeking permission to testify at his trial in Belgrade. After all these years I still retain contact with a signif-icant number of them. In the pages that follow I tell the story of two of them, Major General Donald J. Smith, USAF (Ret.) and Major Richard L. Felman, USAF (Ret.). Others who belong in the front rank are Lieutenant

Colonel Charles L. Davis, USAF (Ret.), Lieutenant Colonel Milton Friend, USAF (Ret.), Dave LaBissoniere, Mike McKool, George Salapa, Jr., and Lt. Colonel John E. Scroggs, USAF (Ret.).

Then there are the several score officers of the Mihailović movement whom I interviewed in England, France, Germany, and the United States. Without listing them, I thank them all. Equally, I would like to express my gratitude to my many American, Yugoslav, and British friends who encourged me and contributed in various ways to my research.

In a separate category are the scholars on whose assistance I was able to call for specialized information. Prominent in this category are Dr. Walter R. Roberts of Washington, D.C., Dr. Kosta St. Pavlowitch of Cambridge University, Professor Stevan Pavlowitch of Southampton University, Dr. Milorad M. Drachkovitch of the Hoover Institution, Dr. Ivan Avakumovic of the University of British Columbia, and Dr. Thomas Kirkwood Ford, Jr. of Mississippi College.

In a special category is my good friend Vane Ivanović of London, who served as a British officer in PWE Bari, Italy. Vane was able to throw light on situations that defied the understanding of ordinary Westerners, combining as he did the wisdom of the Balkans with the sophistication of a man educated at the best of English schools. It is characteristic of his fidelity to the nation of his birth that, although he has not been back to postwar Yugoslavia, to this day he remains a Yugoslav citizen.

My special thanks goes to Robert T. Crowley, a very sage former CIA official and coauthor of *The New KGB: Engine of Soviet Power,* who provided me with early information about James Klugmann and served as an adviser while my manuscript was being written.

I also wish to acknowledge, with thanks, the cooperation I received from Michael Straight, whose book *After Long Silence* is without question the only frank account yet written by someone who was actually a member of the Cambridge Communist conspiracy. His testimony provided me with an intimate personal picture of Klugmann as a young man.

I am grateful, too, to Mrs. Mirjana Vujnovich for undertaking the thankless but essential task of checking and inserting the proper accents on all Yugoslav names, and to Alexander Radichevich and Nicholas Pasić for checking my manuscript for accuracy, and to Arne Steinberg for his research assistance.

At this point I wish to mention the enormous debt I owe to my wife, Virginia Worek Martin, for her steadfast assistance over the period of almost fifteen years that this book was gestating. She was more than an assistant. She traveled with me to England four times, to Germany once, and to France twice in gathering the material that appears in these pages. She took notes and sat in on virtually all my interviews. She made many valuable suggestions and recommendations in putting together the manuscript; and she did a highly conscientious job of proofreading.

I also wish to express my gratitude to my part-time secretary, Valerie Johnson, for her infinite patience and good humor, which enabled me, at age seventy-five and slowed down by nine years of Parkinsonism, to complete this one last book on the Tito-Mihailović conflict. A few more acknowledgments, and then I shall be through.

I have never before gone into the case of James Klugmann in such depth, nor have I before this characterized him as a Soviet mole. In a previously published article on Klugmann I said that "the jury is still out." Inevitably, on the way to my present conclusions, I have done some writing on the decisive role played by James Klugmann in bringing about the abandonment of Mihailović; and inevitably, there is some repetition, especially of documentation.

I wish to thank the Hoover Institution Press and the Board of Trustees of the Leland Stanford Jr. University for permission to reprint important segments of my 1978 book, *Patriot or Traitor: The Case of General Mihailovich*, in particular the "Chronological Compendium" and the section dealing with the sabotage of the Mihailović operation. Similarly, I would like to thank the Center for the Study of Conflict of New Brunswick University for permission to reproduce some key documents and quotations that originally appeared in a chapter entitled "James Klugmann, SOE-Cairo, and the Mihailović Deception" in a symposium on Soviet disinformation published under the auspices of the Center. I would also like to thank *The Washington Times* for permission to reproduce, as part of the much larger chapter on the subject in this book, my article on the rescue of the American airmen that appeared in July 1976.

Finally, I also wish to thank the Controller of Her Britannic Majesty's Stationery Office for permission to quote from the files of the Public Record Office.

Thesis and Introduction

Of all the changes in Allied policy that occurred during World War II, there is nothing even remotely comparable to the dramatic switch that took place just before the end of 1943 in British policy toward Yugoslavia. This book attempts to explain how and why this change came about.

During 1941 and 1942 and the first part of 1943, Britain gave all-out support to General Draža Mihailović as the leader of the national resistance movement in Yugoslavia. By the end of 1943, for all practical purposes, Mihailović had been abandoned, ostensibly because it was believed that his forces were inactive against the enemy and had engaged in collaboration with them. At this point Britain and the United States (which had conceded British primacy in determining Balkan policy) began to extend unqualified support to the Communist resistance movement of Marshal Josip Broz Tito, apparently oblivious to the danger this posed to the Yugoslav peoples and to the future of Western policy in the Balkans.

I have spent a large part of my life since 1944 in attempting to establish the truth about General Mihailović and the movement he headed in Yugoslavia during World War II. This has been no easy task, because reports coming from the field were outrageously and systematically falsified and even suppressed by a person or persons in the Yugoslav Section of the British Special Operations Executive (SOE) in Cairo (and later Bari, Italy), which was charged with responsibility for relaying intelligence about Yugoslavia to the Foreign Office and SOE London.

That there was falsification on a very large scale is beyond challenge, as I shall establish in the ensuing pages, and as is confirmed by the quotation from Sir Douglas Howard that precedes this introduction. It can also be established that relations between Mihailović and the British government were sabotaged in many ways by SOE Cairo, flying in the face of general directives from the Foreign Office.

Who was responsible for the falsification and sabotage? Falsification, perhaps inevitably, became routine during the latter part of the war, when it was a matter of justifying the switch from Mihailović to Tito. But the campaign of disinformation and sabotage launched before mid-1943, that is, a good six to eight months before the policy switch was finalized by Churchill, theoretically took place at a time when the British intelligence apparatus was supposed to be providing the leaders of the British government with objective information that would be of use in assessing their options.

After ploughing through many thousands of pages at the British Public Record Office and after interviewing in depth over 100 people who served in the British government and on both the Mihailović and Tito sides, I have been led to the conclusion that James Klugmann (later Major James Klugmann and deputy chief of the SOE Yugoslav Section) was the person primarily responsible.

The name of James Klugmann is not widely known to British or American readers—in fact, it is probably known only to a small minority who have devoted themselves to a study of Soviet intelligence operations in the Western world.

Who was James Klugmann? At Cambridge in the 1930s he played a central role in the Communist grouping that produced such notorious Soviet agents as Kim Philby, Guy Burgess, Donald Maclean, and Anthony Blunt. Indeed, by common consent he was the most brilliant member of the group.

Writing approximately three years ago, I described James Klugmann as an ''agent of influence.'' This implied that while he used his influence to achieve Soviet objectives, he did not do so under direction or as a member of the Soviet apparatus. Further research and further thought, however, have now brought me to the point where I am prepared to describe Klugmann without equivocation as a Soviet agent. Admittedly, the proof of this is based on circumstantial evidence. But when all that evidence, without a single deviation, points to a single conclusion, I believe one is justified in stating this conclusion in unmistakable terms.

Klugmann was what is technically known as a ''mole,'' as opposed to a conventional spy. Because most cases that have attracted headlines in recent years involved men or women who have become spies for mercenary reasons, there is a tendency to think of all spies or agents in these terms. The mole, however, enters the game for ideological reasons. It may take months or years, but in order to prepare the ground for future activities, he first entrenches himself in a key portion of the government apparatus.

Kim Philby, Donald Maclean, Guy Burgess, and Anthony Blunt were also moles. Indeed, considered as a whole and recalling that they all originated in a single left-wing group on the Cambridge campus, they would have to be put down as the most remarkable family of moles that ever gnawed at the security of a major Western nation.

The function of the mole is twofold. It can be espionage in the classical sense, as was the case with Klaus Fuchs and Julius Rosenberg. Far more often than not, however, moles have been used for policy perversion. Their task has been to use the craft of disinformation to persuade key people in the Free World, primarily Britons and Americans, to do those things which best serve Soviet interests. Thus, Alger Hiss was a mole; and the evidence is that he did many things, having won the trust of his superiors, that greatly advanced the Soviet cause. Klugmann was a mole whose great accomplishment was to falsify information in a manner that resulted in handing over a nation of 15 million people to Communist control.

I do not say that Klugmann did this all by himself, but I do believe that he was *primarily* responsible. I emphasize the word "primarily," because, obviously, Klugmann did not accomplish his objective completely unaided. He was aided in the first instance by certain developments inside Yugoslavia, such as the frightful massacre of the Serb minority in the Independent State of Croatia and the inhuman scale of the reprisals imposed by the Nazis for all acts of resistance. These matters will be dealt with in the pages that follow. But apart from the assistance he received from historical developments—which, obviously, he could not control and for which he had no responsibility—Klugmann was assisted in many ways by compatriots who, for a variety of reasons, shared his enthusiasm for Tito, if not his enthusiasm for a Communist Great Britain.

There were many other officers in the armed forces and officials in the wartime bureaucracy—in particular the British Broadcasting Corporation (BBC), the Political Warfare Executive (PWE), and the Secret Intelligence Service (MI6)—who belonged to one sector or another of the pro-Soviet spectrum and who believed that they were serving the cause of progress by promoting Tito.

Although Guy Burgess headed the special Talks department of BBC, actual members of the Communist movement were a tiny minority, and Soviet agents could have been counted on the fingers of two hands. They were there, however, and they were of critical importance. Fitzroy Maclean, who headed up the British mission to Tito, told me when I saw him London in November 1977 that he was convinced—as I was—that the Soviets had penetrated MI6. This perception was reinforced by other information, which I had received previously from my old friend Vane Ivanović, a prominent member of the Yugoslav community, much sought after by Britons concerned with Yugoslavia. Vane had been with PWE in Bari. According to him, there was one office in Bari to which his chief, Archie Lyall, refused to circulate classified documents, "on the ground that everything he might write would be known to Yugoslav Partisan HQ by the following day."[1] The "forbidden" office was the office of MI6.

Far more numerous than the Communists, and infinitely more numerous than the committed agents, were the muddle-headed liberals who shared a nebulous feeling that they, too, were serving the cause of progress. Also numerous were conservatives afflicted with pro-Tito mania, who were moved by the conviction that the support of Tito served British interests in the prosecution of the war against the Nazis. Although they rendered invaluable assistance in the making of the Yugoslav tragedy, none of the individuals in these categories was as knowledgeable as Klugmann or had as much input into the shaping of policy.

Over the past ten years roughly, the word "disinformation" has entered the political vocabulary. Entire books have been written about it, including, notably, the books by Ilya Dzerkvilov and Stanislav Levchenko, defectors who had been professionals in the field of KGB disinformation. There is still a tendency to equate disinformation with propaganda—but propaganda can be basically truthful, while disinformation is never truthful.

There is nothing new, of course, about the phenomenon of disinformation. The Allies in World War II were practicing disinformation when they mounted elaborate deceptions to persuade the Germans that the invasion fleet they were assembling on the south coast of England would strike at points other than Normandy. But when it comes to political deception, or disinformation, the Communist regimes are in a league by themselves. First of all, as an indication of the importance they attach to it, the Soviets have made disinformation a specific responsibility of one of the principal bureaus of the KGB. Second, they have at their disposal in all democratic countries select cadres of moles, some of whom have risen to high positions in virtually every department concerned with national security. Third, they are armed with by far the most formidable propaganda apparatus in history. Fourth, their machinery of disinformation disposes of entire legions of intellectuals, including members of the media, whose innocence and naïveté virtually invite manipulation.

Although Winston Churchill never seemed to realize that he and the rest of the Free World had been the objects of a classic Communist disinformation operation in the case of Yugoslavia, in dealing with the Communist uprising in Greece under the EAM (National Liberation Front) in September 1944 he expressed his clear conviction that the British press, and the American press in their overwhelming majority, as well as the US State Department, had been grievously misled. Although he did not mention the Communist propaganda apparatus or Soviet disinformation machinery, it is obvious that this is what he had in mind when he wrote:

Now that the free world has learned so much more than was then understood about the Communist movement in Greece and elsewhere, many readers will be astonished at the vehement attacks to which His Majesty's Government, and I in particular as its head, were subjected. The vast majority of the American Press violently condemned our action, which they declared falsified the cause for which they had gone to war. If the editors of all these well-meaning organs will look back at what they wrote then and compare it with what they think now, they will, I am sure, be surprised. The State Department, in the charge of Mr. Stettinius, issued a markedly critical pronouncement, which they in turn were to regret, or at least reverse, in after-years. In England there was much perturbation. *The Times* and *The Manchester Guardian* pronounced their censures upon what they considered our reactionary policy.[2]

As the story in this book unfolds, we shall have occasion to examine in detail the machinations of the two principal military bureaucracies involved in the Yugoslav tragedy: the Yugoslav desk of the Special Operations Executive (Cairo), which was in charge of all resistance activities in Yugoslavia, and "Most Secret Source," as MI6 was known in the wartime records.

"Special Operations Executive" and "Most Secret Source"—the very names inspire awe and respect, even in foreign ministers and prime ministers. They suggest a careful and systematic gathering of intelligence from many secret sources and the dispassionate analysis of the totality of information received. That is why a desk officer with an ideological commitment who was part of the machinery of SOE Cairo or of "Most Secret Source" had almost unlimited possibilities when it came to misdirecting those responsible for the conduct of national policy.

Whatever the explanation for the bias and lack of balance displayed by SOE Cairo and "Most Secret Source" in reporting on both the Tito and Mihailović movements, there can be no question that these reports, which figure prominently in the files of the Prime Minister's Office and the Foreign Office, had great influence and played a major role in persuading Churchill and Foreign Secretary Anthony Eden that they had no alternative but to abandon Mihailović.

With the propaganda apparatus at their disposal, the Soviets, since they were established in 1917, have on occasion had remarkable success in manipulating popular opinion in the democratic countries. Minor confidence games they had played quite skillfully before World War II. Their hoodwinking of Churchill on the question of Tito and Mihailović marked the first instance where they had been able to extend their manipulation to a leading Western statesman on a matter of strategic moment.

There remain two questions to be resolved. Was Klugmann in a position to mastermind such a campaign of disinformation and sabotage? There can be no doubt that he was. The one remaining question is: Could this campaign have been the work of someone else attached to SOE Cairo, thus far not identified as a Soviet agent? Again, this possibility has to be ruled out when the SOE personnel roster for the period is carefully examined.

THE CAMPAIGN AGAINST MIHAILOVIĆ

Communist authorities have published hundreds of documents which, they charged, prove that the entire Mihailović movement was engaged in massive and systematic collaboration with the enemy. Two books have been published in the United States, based in part on the Belgrade documentation but also in part on captured German and Italian documents, which can be interpreted as pointing to the same conclusion.

On the other hand, it is clear that the thirty-odd British officers who served with Mihailović at various times from October 1941 to June 1944, as well as the eight American officers who served with him—again, for various periods of time—from August 1943 to December 1944, were convinced from their own experience that the Mihailović forces represented a genuine and vitally important resistance movement. These opinions were echoed by some 500 American airmen who bailed out or crashed over a very wide territory in Yugoslavia from the beginning of 1944 until the late fall of that year and who were rescued by the forces of General Mihailović.

On the surface there appears to be a direct and irreconcilable contradiction between the facts testified to by these many British and American officers and American airmen and the several volumes of documents published in Belgrade and the United States.

It would be patently absurd to believe that the British and American officers and the hundreds of American airmen had engaged in a gigantic conspiracy to conceal the real facts about Mihailović. These officers told the truth about their personal experiences and personal observations in Yugoslavia—and their collective testimony represents a body of evidence that must enter into any objective historical assessment. This testimony includes the numerous entries into the Operational Log of SOE Cairo based on reports by the British and American officers attached to Mihailović, the long report filed by Colonel S. William Bailey (chief of the British mission to Mihailović from Christmas Day 1942 to September 25, 1943) after his return to England, which depicted an unbroken state of hostilities between the Germans and Yugoslav Home Army forces, and the reports filed with OSS (Office of Strategic Services) by Colonel Albert B. Seitz, Captain Walter R. Mansfield, and the other American officers attached to Mihailović.

But it would be equally absurd to hold that all of the published documents are fraudulent or of no significance. (Incidentally, it is certainly not stretching supposition impermissibly to suggest that if the civil war had wound up with Mihailović triumphant, there would have been many more documents available than there are today dealing with Partisan "collaboration.")

Can these two apparently contradictory bodies of evidence be reconciled? The fact is that they can easily be reconciled—if viewed within the context of the forbiddingly complex situation that existed in Yugoslavia during World War II.

It is a misleading oversimplification to explain what happened in Yugoslavia during World War II as the product of a two-sided struggle between the Partisan resistance movement under the leadership of Marshal Tito, on the one hand, and, on the other hand, the occupying powers and their "collaborators."

First, there was the religious-political war launched by the quisling Ante Pavelić and his so-called "Independent State of Croatia" against the Serbian people living in its confines. Within the first few months of the German occupation this war had resulted in the massacre of at least 500,000 Serbs— men, women, and children—and had laid the basis for a continuing struggle between Pavelić's Ustaše formations and the Serbian formations on the periphery of the Independent State of Croatia, a conflict that was marked by massacres and countermassacres.

Second, there was the conflict between the occupying powers and the two major resistance forces—the Mihailović movement, which was essentially nationalist and dynastic, and the Partisan movement, which was committed to a Communist Yugoslavia.

Third, there was the conflict in Serbia between the forces of General Mihailović and the collaborationist "Četnik" forces of Kosta Pećanac, the followers of the Serbian fascist Dimitrije Ljotić, and—intermittently—the forces of General Milan Nedić, the Serbian Pétain.

Finally, there was the civil war that the Tito and Mihailović forces waged against each other, alongside or within the framework of the resistance movement.

Each side in this civil war regarded the other side with as much hatred as it did the Germans, because they both felt, with reason, that this conflict held the entire future of their country at stake. The Communists were committed to the goal of a Communist Yugoslavia, while the Mihailović movement was monarchist and strongly anti-Communist, with a generally democratic and peasant orientation.

The conflict between the followers of Tito and the followers of Mihailović was as merciless as only a Balkan civil war can be. When the Partisans captured Mihailović territory, they publicly executed known or even suspected sympathizers of Mihailović (it would perhaps be more accurate to say that they executed everyone suspected of any kind of opposition or potential opposition to a Communist regime); and the followers of Mihailović, when they captured leading Partisans, reciprocated in kind—although they were never quite as ruthless or arbitrary or murderous. Mihailović units engaged in actions against the Partisan units when they found them fighting the Germans and the Ustaše; Partisan units acted similarly against the Mihailović forces when they found them involved in combat with the common enemy. Both sides engaged in certain "accommodations" with the enemy, mostly such limited ones as historically occur between guerrilla forces and their enemies—exchanges of prisoners, temporary nonaggression pacts when the guerrillas needed a respite, and agreements that, in certain areas, were designed to leave the Mihailović forces and the Partisans free to fight each other. And sometimes there were agreements—on both sides—that exceeded, or appeared to exceed, the traditional limits of accommodations between resistance forces and occupiers.

There is a fundamental difference between "accommodations" and "collaboration," but this difference is not generally understood. "Accommodations" in the context of guerrilla warfare implies temporary and limited arrangements between adversaries that in no way alter their basic hostility toward each other. "Collaboration," on the other hand, signifies a total alliance between the collaborators and the occupation forces in the interest of common objectives. The language used in the accommodationist documents signed by both sides in Yugoslavia sometimes lends itself to unpleasant and sinister interpretations. In most cases, however, the documents were simply intended as guerrilla tricks designed to buy time or survival. For this reason these documents *by themselves* give a completely distorted picture of the reality of the situation. In the opinion of the author, this reality on the Mihailović side is more accurately attested to by the numerous eyewitness accounts reported in the pages that follow.

The campaign against Mihailović was launched in July 1942, when the Soviet Union, which had publicly supported Mihailović until that time, openly turned against him and charged that he was collaborating. This should have been the signal that the Soviet Union was, from that point on, implacably committed to the destruction of Mihailović and the installation of Tito in power. It is to be noted that the open change in Soviet policy coincided with the recruitment of the first group of Canadian-Yugoslav Communists, most of them Croats, almost certainly by design, to serve as British intelligence officers in Yugoslavia.

The campaign against Mihailović rested on three basic charges: first, that his forces were inactive and ineffectual against the Axis; second, that many of his followers were engaged in active collaboration with the Italians and the Germans against the Partisans; third, that Mihailović had lost most of his popular support, whereas Tito had overwhelming support among the anti-Axis Yugoslavs. In a remarkably short time the Soviets, by the simple device of feeding material to friendly or gullible press contacts in the Western world, had the Western press parroting their new line on Yugoslavia.

After nine or ten months of such softening up, this was the gist of the reports sent out beginning April 1943 by the several intelligence teams of Canadian-Yugoslav Communists recruited to serve with the Tito forces; and it constituted the gist, as well, of the reports sent out shortly afterward by the first British liaison officers (BLOs) with Tito's forces, Captain (later Lt. Colonel) William Deakin and Brigadier Fitzroy Maclean, who parachuted into Yugoslavia on May 27, 1943, and September 15, 1943, respectively.

Deakin, despite his junior rank, commanded considerable influence because he had, as a young history don at Oxford, assisted Churchill in writing his life of Marlborough. Maclean, who had served as first secretary in the British embassy in Moscow, was fluent in Russian and, as a conservative MP, was known to Churchill and respected by him. Because of their personal relationship with Churchill, the reports of Deakin and Maclean at that stage had a far greater impact than did the reports of Colonel Bailey and the thirty-odd other British liaison officers who served at Mihailović's headquarters or in the fifteen or more sub-missions scattered over the face of Serbia.

By the end of November 1943 there were entries in the records of the Foreign Office and the prime minister indicating that Churchill had completely lost confidence in Mihailović and that he had, for all practical purposes, decided to sever relations.

In the report he filed on November 6, 1943, Fitzroy Maclean spoke of a Partisan army of some 220,000 men, of which 30,000 were in Serbia and Macedonia. This roughly confirmed the prior reports of William Deakin. Mihailović was credited with having 10,000 armed men in Serbia.

There could be no more effective illustration of the power of propaganda to destroy the critical faculty of decent and intelligent people than the uncritical manner in which the completely impossible accounts of Partisan strength were accepted as gospel by politicians and the media during World War II.

Božidar Purić, at the time prime minister of the Yugoslav government in exile, related to me a conversation he had had with Anthony Eden during the first part of 1944. Purić said to Eden that he considered the estimate of 220,000 armed followers in the Tito movement to be a gross exaggeration. He said that from a simple logistical standpoint it would be utterly impossible in a country the size of Yugoslavia to find sufficient food for a permanent force of guerrillas of this magnitude. Eden, who had indicated more than a little skepticism about the Maclean report, admitted to Purić that he considered the figures contained in the report to be inflated. He said that he personally believed that Tito had an army of somewhere between 100,000 and 125,000 men.

"But 100,000 to 125,000 is not even remotely comparable to 220,000," said Purić. "Why does the British government lend its authority to such ridiculous estimates?"

Purić was right. The logistical problem of providing for a guerrilla army of 220,000 armed men would have been insuperable in the case of a country the size of Yugoslavia—it would be comparable to the United States, with a population of 250,000,000, fielding a guerrilla army of over 4 million in the event of an enemy occupation. Actually; the size of the guerrilla army as a percentage of the total population from which it was recruited would have had to be far greater in the case of wartime Yugoslavia for the simple reason that Tito had virtually zero following in Serbia proper, the most populous region of the Yugoslav state.

It is interesting to compare Maclean's estimate of Partisan strength with that of Colonel Bailey. Bailey, after 14 months in Yugoslavia, said when he got back to London that he did not

. . . believe that Tito himself controls more than 120,000 men, of whom perhaps half are territorially tied to the Northwest of area A. [Slovenia, Croatia, Slavonia, Vojvodina west of the Ticza, Bosnia north and west of the Drina, Dalmatia north of the Neretva, and the Adriatic Islands.] Of this 120,000, not more than 10,000 come from Serbia proper. *These estimates are based on careful personal interrogations of Partisan prisoners and deserters with all due allowance for prejudices of latter*[3] [author's emphasis].

It is to be noted that Mihailović, on the basis of his own intelligence, estimated Partisan strength at roughly 75,000. This figure was almost certainly on the low side because Mihailović, for obvious reasons, was seeking to downplay the size of Tito's following.

The Maclean report credited the Mihailović movement with having 10,000 armed men in Seriba. (This compares with an estimate of 35,000 men in the ready Mihailović forces, which was the estimate of Captain Walter T. Mansfield of the American mission after conducting an extensive tour of inspection of Mihailović units in northern and central Serbia.) In no area was the Maclean report more remote from the mark than in its estimates of Partisan and Mihailović strength. But this report was taken as gospel by the media, by political leaders, and by intelligence officers.

Both Maclean and Deakin, writing in the fall of 1944, admitted in effect that their 1943 estimates of Partisan strength in Serbia were grossly exaggerated. "At the beginning of 1944," said Maclean, "Partisan forces in Serbia were limited to a few scattered, ill-equipped detachments of a few hundred men each, who were all that had been left to carry on the struggle after the Partisan defeat and withdrawal of 1941. . . . ''[4]

But the gross overestimation of Partisan strength in Serbia in the fall of 1943 had been of critical importance in justifying the decision to abandon Mihailović. Despite Maclean's belated admission, Churchill took the figures of Partisan strength that Maclean had used in his November 6, 1943 report and further enlarged upon them in reporting to the British public.

There was no question that Serbia was the heartland of Yugoslavia. Nor was there any question of the martial valor of the Serbian people, or of their passionate opposition to the Nazi regime, or of the central role they had played in the revolution of March 27, 1941. But among those caught up in the pro-Tito mania of 1943 and 1944 apparently no one stopped to consider how passing strange it was that this people had overnight become ''collaborators'' and traitors.

Time and time again during the period preceding the final abandonment of Mihailović at the end of 1943, Colonel Bailey, and later Bailey and Brigadier Charles D. Armstrong, who succeeded Bailey as chief of mission on September 25, 1943, reported to their government that in Serbia proper, which contained the critical north-south communication lines the British would want sabotaged, the Tito forces amounted to nothing and the Mihailović forces were everywhere paramount.

Colonel Bailey returned to Britain in early March 1944 for the express purpose of trying to impart his information to Churchill. On March 15 he had a first meeting with Churchill and Foreign Secretary Eden, followed by a second meeting in early April. After his second meeting Bailey told his colleague Major Archie Jack that Churchill had said he now saw that he had been badly misinformed about the situation in Yugoslavia.[5]

That Churchill was enormously impressed by Bailey's account of the situation in Serbia is apparent from a statement he made shortly thereafter in a letter to Marshal Tito. The letter, dated May 17, 1944, said:

> We do not know what will happen in the Serbian part of Yugoslavia. Mihailović certainly holds a powerful position locally as Commander-in-Chief, and it does not follow that his ceasing to be Minister of War will rob him of his influence. We cannot predict what he will do. There is also a very large body, amounting perhaps to two hundred thousand, of Serbian peasant proprietors who are anti-German but strongly Serbian, and who naturally hold the views of a peasant ownership community, contrary to the Karl Marx theory.[6]

Where did Churchill get the information contained in this paragraph? Certainly not from Maclean and Deakin, who were still talking about Tito's overwhelming strength in all parts of the country. Certainly, too, this kind of lecturing was not likely to ingratiate him with Tito. It almost appears that Churchill was so impressed by the new information he had received from Bailey that he was willing to risk Tito's ire by at least raising the possibility of a compromise with Mihailović and Serbia.

There were a few partial inaccuracies in the Churchill letter. In the first place, it is very certain that Bailey never told him, or implied to him, that unlike the Serbian peasant proprietors, the Croatian and Slovenian and Moslem peasants found communism acceptable. The fact is that they were just as strongly opposed to it as their Serbian compatriots. It is clear also that Bailey, in reporting to the prime minister, was talking about the Serbian people as a whole and not just 200,000 Serbian peasant proprietors. This figure, which Bailey almost certainly did use, conforms roughly to both British and American estimates of Mihailović's military strength, counting both regular and territorial forces.

But what really stands out from the paragraph I have quoted is that suddenly it must have dawned on Churchill that one could not begin to discuss Yugoslavia without discussing Serbia, and that neither Deakin nor Maclean had ever set foot in Serbia at the time they submitted their reports recommending the abandoment of Mihailović.

Churchill virtually repeated the remarks he had made in his letter to Tito in a statement in the House of Commons on May 25, 1944. He repeated them once again in a second letter to Tito dated August 12, 1944. In this letter he said, "His Majesty's Government, while regarding Marshal Tito and his brave men with the utmost admiration, are not satisfied that sufficient recognition has been given to the power and rights of the Serbian people."[7] Churchill seemed tormented by the realization that *he himself* had not given "sufficient recognition . . . to the power and rights of the Serbian people" and driven by a desire at that late hour to do something to moderate the disastrous consequences of his policy.

Despite the massive support they now received in arms and ammunition, the Partisans, in accordance with the predictions of Bailey and Armstrong, accomplished remarkably little over the next six months to harass and sabotage the critical north-south lines of communication. As matters turned out, the British, having abandoned Mihailović at the turn of the year, found themselves in August 1944 in the invidious position of having to supply an undisguised Partisan invasion of Serbia, directed overwhelmingly against the Mihailović forces.

About this time there was growing evidence that the prime minister had become worried and pessimistic. The official account *British Foreign Policy in the Second World War*, written by Sir Llewellyn Woodward, has this to say about the change that came over Churchill's attitude:

The Prime Minister was not favourably impressed with Marshal Tito or his demands. He wrote a minute to Mr. Eden on August 31 that a great responsibility would rest on us after the war when all the arms in Yugoslavia—supplied by us—would be in Marshal Tito's possession, and could be used by him to subjugate the country. Mr. Eden noted on this minute that the Foreign Office hardly needed a reminder of this danger, and that, in spite of their warnings, the Prime Minister himself had persistently 'pushed Tito.'[8]

A WORD ABOUT SOURCES

In writing about so contentious a subject, a word about sources perhaps would be in order.

Obviously, the British and American liaison officers who were in Yugoslavia during 1943 and 1944 must be considered primary sources of information. The liaison officers on the Tito side have by and large shaped the writing of modern history (a) because of their personal relationship with Churchill, (b) because they have written several best-selling books, and (c) because their version of history came to coincide with the official position. Foremost among these officers were Captain Deakin and Brigadier Maclean. Their writings were reinforced by a number of other British officers who served with Partisan units in various parts of Yugoslavia during 1943 and 1944, and who made an apparently confirmatory contribution to the pro-Tito literature of the postwar period.

The eight American and roughly thirty British officers attached to the Mihailović forces during this period counted among them many men of quite extraordinary quality. If anything, they were substantially more qualified as intelligence officers than most of the British or American officers attached to Tito—despite the fact that the most senior of them did not write books about their experiences. Because of this lapse, their observations and experiences remain largely unknown.

How many of those who have read books or articles about World War II, for example, are familiar with the names of Lt. Colonel Duane T. ("Marko") Hudson, who joined the Mihailović forces during the latter part of 1941, or Colonel S. William Bailey, who joined Hudson on Christmas Day 1942 as chief of an enlarged British mission, or Brigadier Charles D. Armstrong, who joined Hudson and Bailey in late September 1943 as chief of a further enlarged British mission? How many are familiar with the names of U.S. Army officers Lt. Colonel Albert B. Seitz and Captain Walter R. Mansfield, who teamed up as the first American mission to Mihailović in August-September 1943, or Lt. Colonel (later Colonel) Robert H. McDowell, who headed up an OSS intelligence mission to Mihailović's headquarters from August 26 to November 1, 1944?

It is entirely understandable and proper that, in writing the history of wartime Yugoslavia, the British and American officers who were with Tito should be quoted as eyewitnesses. What is not understandable is that the British and American officers on the Mihailović side, who were in Yugoslavia on the average much longer than those on the Tito side, and many of whom had become tolerably fluent in Serbo-Croat, have thus far been virtually ignored in writings about this period of Yugoslav history. Over the years I have sought to close this gap by systematically interviewing these British and American officers and, whenever possible, tape-recording their statements.

This difference in historical treatment is all the more difficult to understand because the Allied officers who served with Mihailović are unanimous on the point that they could go wherever they wished and speak to whomever they wished without being followed or monitored, whereas most of those who served with Tito found themselves severely restricted in their movements and their contacts, and in some cases were confined under conditions that resembled house arrest.

Most of the documentation dealing with the operations of SOE Cairo is still sealed from public scrutiny. An important part of it was lost in a fire at SOE headquarters in Cairo in 1943. However, another important part of this documentation, the so-called "Operational Log," based on messages to and from the field, has been open for public inspection at the British Public Record Office since the mid-1970s.

By the fall of 1977, when I came across the first volume of the Operational Log, I had gone through many thousands of pages of records taken from the War Office, the Foreign Office, and the Prime Minister's Office. These had been valuable in reconstructing the diplomatic and political history that culminated in the abandonment of Mihailović. They had also thrown a good deal of light on the record of military activities on both sides. But in terms of providing firsthand confirmation of military actions, big and small, by the Mihailović forces, the Operational Log was uniquely useful. Despite its very much abbreviated style, through it one could frequently obtain the precious contemporaneous testimony of the British and American officers on the Mihailović side, which has until recently been ignored by historians and thus, in effect, suppressed. (Incidentally, I have found no one who could explain how the Operational Log became declassified while all the rest of SOE's records remained cloaked in secrecy.)

The Log, which was at that time in practically virginal condition, had clearly not been consulted by the many scholars who had conducted research on Yugoslavia prior to 1977. There were many, many volumes of the Log, consisting for the most part of one- or two- or three-sentence quotes from reports received from the British missions with both Mihailović and Tito.

Occasionally, however, it reproduced extensive excerpts and even the complete text of important messages received from the British liaison officers. It was clear that the purpose of the Log was to provide a quick, concise rundown on activities of which the British missions to both Tito and Mihailović had knowledge. Each Log entry carried with it a notation indicating which offices had received a copy of that entry. The Log, or at least the portion of it in the Public Record Office, begins chronologically on September 1, 1943.

Thus, there existed three levels of information concerning wartime Yugoslavia. There was the original text of the messages received from the BLOs, which has not yet been made public. There was the compilation of brief excerpts from the communications sent out by the BLOs, which are to be found in the Operational Log. And there was the information transmitted by SOE Cairo to SOE London and the Foreign Office, the content of which can in part be determined by comparing the Foreign Office records in London with what is revealed by the Operational Log. Such a comparison is most instructive.

For a more orderly recital of the facts that led Sir Douglas Howard to make the statement preceding this introduction, the reader is referred to the chronological compendium of reports by British and American officers of military activities and sabotage by the Mihailović forces.

I have decided that to tell the story of James Klugmann intelligently, one must tell it within the context of the larger story of what happened in Yugoslavia during World War II. As the case of Klugmann so dramatically demonstrates, the KGB can accomplish wonders if it has the right man in the right place at the right time. There can be no question that Klugmann was the right man. His implantation in the Yugoslav Section of SOE Cairo in February 1942 could scarcely have been more properly timed. It got him off to a very early start on an undertaking where his expertise and erudition were of critical importance.

To avoid confusion, I have, more or less consistently, referred to the Mihailović forces as the Yugoslav Home Army, rather than as the Četniks, admittedly a more popular appellation in the literature of the Western countries and in the Mihailović movement itself.

In his report to OSS, Colonel McDowell pointed out that the Mihailović movement really was "the sum total of a large number of local movements, each of which developed in 1941 and 1942 as a spontaneous local uprising against Axis occupation and atrocities." General Mihailović, said McDowell, was considered the nominal head of the movement. "He leads the movement only insofar as the local district leaders and the people are willing to follow . . ."

The use of the term "Četnik" resulted in a good deal of confusion.

Historically it meant in Serbia a guerrilla fighter. The term was used by the pre–World War II Četnik Association led by Kosta Pećanac, who fought bravely as a guerrilla against the Central Powers in World War I but openly collaborated with the Germans during World War II. Against the Četniks of Kosta Pećanac the Mihailović units fought many bitter battles.

Further confusion resulted from the existence of other Četnik formations completely outside the Mihailović organization or only nominally a part of it. Many of these formations acquitted themselves honorably, some heroically. Others did not. For these reasons, and because he looked upon his forces as the army of the legal government of Yugoslavia, Mihailović referred to his armed followers as the Yugoslav Home Army, or Yugoslav Army in the Homeland. While the great majority of his followers, especially in the early stages of the movement, were Serbs, by 1943 his forces already incorporated a significant number of Slovene and Moslem detachments, and Mihailović looked forward to the day when Croatian anti-Nazis would also join his movement in strength. The term "Četniks" had an honorable history in Serbia, but in the eyes of Yugoslavia's other ethnic groupings it was too distinctly Serbian. This, unquestionably, was also a consideration.

Christie Lawrence, an escaped British prisoner of war who joined the Četniks and was an eyewitness to many of the events of the great national uprising that swept Serbia in the fall of 1941, relates that just after Christmas of that year a courier arrived from Mihailović. "His chief news was that Mihailović no longer wanted any of his men to be known as Četniks. They were to be called '*Jugoslovenska Vojska u Otadžbini*,' which means 'the Jugoslav Army in the Fatherland'; and shortly after this, the British radio started to call us that, too." [9]

Popular usage, however, more or less overwhelmed the logic of Mihailović's position. To the Serbian peasants Mihailović's forces were known as Četniks because historically that had been the name given to Serbian guerrillas since the war of independence against Turkish rule during the nineteenth century. In addition, Mihailović's own followers referred to themselves, in both prose and song, as Četniks. The language of the Serbian peasants at this point invaded the language used by members of the British and American missions, so that Colonels Hudson and Bailey of the British mission and Colonel Seitz and Captain Mansfield of the American mission frequently spoke of "Četniks" in their communications and reports.

Colonel McDowell, in his report to OSS, sought to get around this difficulty by referring, consistently, to the Mihailović movement as the "Yugoslav Nationalist Movement." McDowell's argument was valid: the Mihailović movement *was* a nationalist movement, and to refer to it as such avoided the confusion caused by referring to it as "Četnik." However, Mihailović himself did not use the expression "Yugoslav Nationalist Movement'' in referring to his own forces, whereas he frequently used the expression ''Yugoslav Home Army'' or ''Yugoslav Army in the Homeland.'' I have sought to follow this procedure myself, but, obviously, one cannot tamper with the word usage of people one quotes. For these reasons the Mihailović forces are generally referred to as the ''Yugoslav Home Army'' when I am speaking, and more often than not as ''Četniks'' when others are speaking.

Let me make it clear at this point that I consider Winston Churchill, on the basis of his performance in World War II, to be one of the truly great figures of human history. Certainly, he brought the British people together as no other man could have done to confront the mortal threat to their liberties at the time of Dunkirk. It may be no exaggeration to say that he was instrumental in saving the entire free world from Nazi subjugation. But even the greatest men commit blunders, especially when they are dependent on others for information and advice. It is in this limited sense that I propose to examine Churchill's Yugoslav blunder.

The Web of Disinformation

1

James Klugmann: The Fifth Man?

When Guy Burgess and Donald Maclean took flight in May 1951 and sought refuge in the Soviet Union, there was speculation that they had been tipped off by a third man. Those who were knowledgeable about the situation believed that this third man was Kim Philby, former head of the Soviet counterespionage section of MI6. When Philby defected in 1963, there was further speculation that there might be another member of the group, still undisclosed, hiding somewhere in the interstices of British society. In 1978 this fourth man was revealed to be Sir Anthony Blunt, an art historian who had served the Royal Household as Surveyor of the Queen's Pictures. All four men had belonged to the same Communist group in Cambridge in the 1930s.

In the epilogue to his epic study *The Climate of Treason,* Andrew Boyle says, "We can only trust that the Americans have learned from the melancholy experience of the British, who perhaps have less worth spying for." [1]

Although the details remain speculative, it has been more or less taken for granted that there was a fifth member of the Cambridge conspiratorial group that produced Kim Philby, Guy Burgess, Donald Maclean, and Anthony Blunt. Who was this fifth man? The evidence that I have gathered to date points strongly to James Klugmann, who was not only the ideological mentor of Donald Maclean but by far the most brilliant of the Communist group at Cambridge.

There has been speculation that the fifth man may have been Sir Roger Hollis, the one-time director general of MI5, or one of several other people. (MI5 has responsibility in the fields of domestic security and counterespionage.) This, however, ignores the requirement that the fifth man had to be one of the same conspiratorial group that produced Burgess, Maclean, Philby, and Blunt. It is an assumption based partly on ignorance of the strategic importance of the operation in which Klugmann was engaged and of the major contribution he made thereby to the Soviet cause.

James Klugmann was born in Hampstead, London, in February 1912, the son of prosperous Jewish parents. His father was a city merchant. He was educated at Gresham School, Holt, Norfolk, and then went to Trinity College, Cambridge. He became a leader of the British and European Communist youth movements in the 1930s, a member of the Executive Committee of the British Communist Party in the postwar period, and the editor of its theoretical and historical organ, *Marxism Today*. He also served as an intelligence and coordinating officer in the Yugoslav Section of SOE Cairo and then in Bari, Italy, rising to the rank of major and deputy director of the Yugoslav Section by March 1944. If Klugmann was indeed the fifth man, it was obviously in his position in the Yugoslav Section of SOE, and not as a sometime recruiter of Soviet agents, that he made his most important contribution to the policy objectives of the Soviet empire.

Klugmann died on September 14, 1977. An initialed obituary article—obviously written by a political colleague—in *The* (London) *Times* of September 26, 1977, said about him:

> His commitment was to the international working class movement and the Communist Party, which he joined in 1933 and remained in until his death on September 14 . . . He was the main architect and organizer of the left-wing student movement of the thirties, and not only in Cambridge. As secretary of the *Rassemblement Mondial des Étudiants,* based in Paris but with affiliations all over the world, he travelled widely and was among the most distinguished leaders of the vast anti-Fascist student movement which in so many countries played an important part in resistance and liberation movements and contributed significantly to the victory of 1945.

> After the war he devoted himself to historical, theoretical and educational work for the Communist Party and became assistant editor and then editor of *Marxism Today* . . .

Remarkably enough, the article says not a word about Klugmann's outstanding record of service with the Yugoslav Section of SOE during World War II. It is difficult to avoid the suspicion that the obituary writer, whoever it was, thought it prudent not to mention Klugmann's role in bringing Tito to power. In this he may have been motivated to protect Klugmann against the suspicion that he might have been involved in Tito's anti-Moscow heresy. But it is also possible that the writer may have been motivated by a desire to mute any reference that might have led to an inquiry into the precise nature of the role Klugmann played in Yugoslav affairs during World War II.

An obituary photograph that appeared in *The* (London) *Morning Star* (a Communist paper) showed a genial Klugmann, with bald pate and curly fringe—a kind of middle-aged cherub—conversing warmly with some young Communists. Why was Klugmann so popular with Communist youth? According to the obituary article in *The Morning Star,* "he possessed exceptional ability in showing people how problems might be solved. He was always bubbling over with humour, and could hold audiences enthralled as a tutor and lecturer."

The geniality conveyed by this photograph—hardly the impression of a Soviet master agent—is reinforced by descriptions of Klugmann during his student days. Michael Straight, the scion of a distinguished American family, who was one of the Kim Philby–Anthony Blunt–James Klugmann group at Cambridge, told me that he recalls Klugmann as a stooped, bespectacled, warm-hearted, and compassionate intellectual whose commitment to communism left him no time for such minor preoccupations as taking a bath or cleaning his fingernails.

I sent Michael Straight the preliminary draft of what I had written, because I wanted the account checked for accuracy. In this account I had described Straight as "a very close friend" of Klugmann's. Straight wrote back:

> It would be accurate, I suppose, to say that 'very close friend' describes the world that we know rather than the world of James Klugmann. In that world, 'friendship' was, I think, seen as a personal luxury, appropriate for more stable times. I mean that James had no time to spare for personal relations *as such.* He was my immediate neighbor in Whewell's Court; he recruited me into the student communist movement; he spent no time in sharing his personal life or inquiring into mine; he had no personal life, in his own view, apart from the Communist Party.

Straight told me that he is also convinced that Klugmann served as principal adviser to Anthony Blunt on potential student recruits, because Blunt did not know the students personally whereas Klugmann knew them well. For that matter, it is widely believed that it was Klugmann and Burgess who had originally won Blunt over to the Communist cause.

JAMES KLUGMANN AS SEEN BY HIS CONTEMPORARIES

The political identity of James Klugmann during World War II and in the prewar period was no secret. He flaunted his communism. In his early teens he was a student at Gresham's, a highly reputable boys' school. There he formed a particularly close attachment to Donald Maclean, for whom he served as both model and ideological mentor. He was warm-hearted, affable, and caring, qualities that gave him entrée to his fellow students, who affectionately referred to him as "Kluggers." With all this, he was a brilliant student who at Cambridge had the rare distinction of winning a double first in modern languages.

At Gresham's he liked shocking people by referring to himself as "the Communist." "My commitment to the cause was for life," he said in an interview, "and it was an exhilarating moment to be alive and young. We simply *knew*, all of us, the revolution was at hand. If anyone had suggested that it wouldn't happen in Britain for, say, 30 years, I would have laughed myself sick."[2]

It was characteristic of Klugmann that even aboard the troopship that took him out from England, "he started holding shipboard classes about fascism, the causes of the war, dialectics, and the social and economic justification for socialism"—this according to *The Days of the Good Soldiers,* a book written by a British Communist about Communists in the armed forces during World War II.[3]

A prescient appreciation of Klugmann was written by Maurice Oldfield in 1939, just before World War II after hearing Klugmann address a mass anti-war rally in Boulogne, France. (Oldfield later became head of MI6.) "It is one thing to shout for peace," said Oldfield in a letter, "but quite another to encourage the obvious enemy by saying in advance that you won't fight in any circumstance . . . There was a very brilliant man at the rally, James Klugmann, who was the secretary of the *Rassemblement Mondial des Étudiants* . . . My assessment of him was that he is a Communist first and foremost, not like some of our other friends, who may be Communist third, but put home and country first and second, or second and first, if you prefer it that way."[4]

Klugmann was first identified as a Soviet agent on February 26, 1975, when Lord Clifford, speaking on a motion in the House of Lords that dealt with "subversive and extremist elements," named Klugmann as "an example of an intelligent, highly educated, and dedicated agent of a foreign power." In recent years the evidence that Klugmann was a Soviet agent has grown substantially, to the point where he has by now thus been identified by some half-dozen writers who had knowledge of specialized situations.

In 1981 Chapman Pincher, in his book *Their Trade Is Treachery,* referred to Klugmann as "a sinister figure" and reported that Klugmann, while still at Cambridge, had recruited John Cairncross, who later confessed that he was an agent for the Soviet apparatus. MI5 decided to use Cairncross to try to get a confession from Klugmann that might uncover other Soviet spies. Armed with a guarantee that he would not be prosecuted if he visited England for this purpose, Cairncross returned from Italy and went to see his old friend Klugmann. On MI5 instructions, he asked Klugmann to leave the Party, threatened to expose him if he did not, and promised to say nothing if Klugmann cooperated with MI5. Klugmann, however, proved a very hard nut to crack. He refused point-blank to give his cooperation to MI5, and because of his stubborn resistance, nothing came of the effort.[5]

In the same book Chapman Pincher charged that Klugmann was also instrumental in recruiting Bernard Floud, a Labour MP and suspected Soviet agent who committed suicide in 1967 while being interrogated by British intelligence.

On July 29, 1984, *The* (London) *Observer* reported that Anthony Blunt had confessed to inviting Sir Stuart Hampshire to a dinner in Paris, hosted by "James Klugmann, the Russian spy," to vet Hampshire as a possible recruit. Blunt's story was that they were simply considering Hampshire as a potential recruit for the British Communist Party, and that the entire incident had taken place in 1934, before he started recruiting for the KGB. However, according to *The Observer,* MI5 had firm information that the dinner took place in 1938, when Blunt was very busy indeed as a recruiter of Soviet agents.

Even Klugmann's very close friend of the period, Michael Straight, who admits to having performed some minor chores for Soviet intelligence during and after the war, found it difficult—and finally impossible—to resist the circumstantial evidence that Klugmann was already a Soviet agent and a recruiter of Soviet agents before World War II. In retrospect Straight was convinced that the purpose of a meeting he had in 1935 with Burgess, Blunt, and Klugmann, at their invitation, was to recruit him into the Soviet apparatus. Apparently hurt by the thought, he asks, "And James, whom I loved, did he know what was going on that evening? And was he a part of the snare?"[6] Straight relates that he found it "difficult to accept that Klugmann was a Soviet agent," but after discussing the matter with fellow students who had been Communists at Cambridge, he came to the conclusion that the charges were essentially correct, and that Klugmann, "in his gentle way," would have justified his deception as a "historical necessity."[7]

Anthony Blunt, after his exposure and the revocation of his knighthood, wrote an article in which he described Klugmann as "the pure intellectual of the Party." He said also that Klugmann "ran the administration of the Party with great skill and energy and it was primarily he who decided what organizations and societies in Cambridge were worth penetrating and what were not."[8]

According to Michael Straight, liberals and one-time radicals who knew Klugmann at Cambridge and afterward were almost unanimous—belatedly—in their suspicions about Klugmann's involvement as a Soviet agent.

Since World War II it had become fashionable to believe that the Soviets, because of security considerations, do not use members of the Communist Party, or people who have been publicly close to it, as intelligence agents.

From this premise it is only one step to the argument that Klugmann's prominence as a Communist virtually ruled out the possibility that he could have been a knowing agent operating under Soviet control. But this assumes that the rules governing the selection of Soviet agents are the same today as they were in Klugmann's day.

Actually, during the 1930s and 1940s the Communist parties of the world frequently used their own members and trustworthy sympathizers as agents because up until that time there was virtually zero awareness of the dangers posed by Soviet espionage and subversion. In the United States Alger Hiss, Frank Coe (later head of the International Monetary Fund), Julius and Ethel Rosenberg, and numerous other people who figured prominently in the postwar period were all either identifiable Communists or very close sympathizers of the Party. Britain had its Klaus Fuchs, its Bruno Pontecorvo—and its James Klugmann. Actually, it can be argued that Klugmann's overt communism served as a screen for his more nefarious activities as a Soviet agent.

Hugh Seton-Watson, who was, according to his own statement, a Soviet sympathizer at the time he shared an office with Klugmann in Cairo in 1942–43, had, long before his death in 1986, evolved into a philosophic and political conservative. But he wrote about Klugmann in a manner which indicated that, while he had no doubt about the latter's ideological proclivities, he retained a lingering admiration and affection for him. In 1980 Seton-Watson wrote:

> Of Klugmann's absolute devotion to the Communist cause there was no doubt. He proved it in a painfully humiliating manner years later by twice eating his own words about Yugoslavia . . . If in different circumstances the Party had instructed him to order my execution, or to execute me in person, I don't suppose that he would have hesitated. Nevertheless, though I did not see him for thirty years, I cherish his memory as a brilliant man who was once my friend, and as a person of selfless, almost saintlike, character.[9]

Seton-Watson was only one of a number of political conservatives who considered Klugmann saintlike and whose affection for him was unshaken even though they were convinced that he would slit their throats if under orders to do so. Klugmann's first boss when he joined the Yugoslav Section of SOE Cairo in February 1942 was Major Kenneth Greenlees. In February 1943 Greenlees was sent in to Mihailović as a liaison officer, in which capacity he served for much of the time as a personal aide to Colonel Bailey, the head of the British mission. By the common consent of his fellow BLOs, there was a good deal of the saint in Greenlees. A conservative and an ardent Catholic, Greenlees prayed every night that God should help his friends to find their way to the true faith. When Klugmann died, Greenlees wrote an

impressively generous letter to the editor of the Special Forces Club newsletter, in which he said:

> I was saddened by the news of James Klugmann's death. Though we were poles
> apart in politics and religion, I recognised the sincerity of his beliefs.
>
> I first met James in Cairo, in 1942, when he was posted to me, then GSO 3,
> SOE, as, I think, Lance Corporal Klugmann. I soon realised his sterling quali-
> ties—conscientious, a glutton for work, much travelled; speaking several lan-
> guages, a double first in modern languages at Cambridge; of an intellect way
> ahead of myself and many of those around me.
>
> I recommended him for Sergeant and, before I left for Yugoslavia, for a Com-
> mission. I was not surprised on my return in 1944 when he had been appointed
> GSO 2, Balkan Intelligence.
>
> After the war we met several times in London and once over a lunch at my Club
> he recounted frankly and amusingly his experiences at Cambridge before the
> war, his actions and plans during the war with SOE, his plans for the future
> based with the [Communist] Party in King Street . . . His last crack as we were
> leaving my Club was that, much as he had enjoyed our lunch, it wouldn't help
> me much, if and when the Party took over! I felt sure he meant it, but I simply
> couldn't take offence.[10]

On one occasion Klugmann came close to admitting an NKVD connection. After World War II he became deputy director of the United Nations
Relief and Rehabilitation Administration in Yugoslavia. He returned to England in 1946. One day on the streets of London he bumped into Kenneth
Greenlees. Greenlees was the kind of man who had only friends, Klugmann
was loquacious and affable—and so, despite their diametrically opposed views
on Mihailović, the two of them wound up having lunch together. According
to Greenlees, Klugmann related that when he had finished his UNRRA assignment in Yugoslavia, the Cominform (established after World War II as
the successor to the Communist International) had ordered him back to England to help orchestrate the series of rolling strikes at that time plaguing the
British economy.[11]

On November 30, 1987, I interviewed Michael Straight for the second
time at his home in Bethesda, Maryland. Straight had known Klugmann extremely well. Apart from being enormously fond of Klugmann, he had seen
a lot of him because Klugmann, in dormitory K1, was immediately under
Straight in K5. Looking back on the invitation to meet with Blunt, Klugmann, and Burgess, Straight said that the only reason he remembered what
might otherwise have passed as a meaningless incident is that he had written
to his mother that night, after thinking about the day's events. In a flash

Straight had realized that Blunt, Klugmann, and Burgess "were working together. They were setting me up—they had marked me out as a victim and they were setting me up. Otherwise, I would have no concrete evidence that they were working together . . . James knew Blunt was recruiting for the KGB in Cambridge and that Burgess was behind him." [12]

When asked if he had any knowledge of the Blunt-Klugmann approach to Stuart Hampshire in Paris, Straight replied, "I have no doubt in my own mind that Klugmann was a knowing recruiter for the KGB, or for both the KGB and the GRU [Red Army Intelligence]."

Although it was obvious that Straight's affection for Klugmann had not completely died, there was an element of bitterness in his voice when he reflected on one aspect of their relationship. He said that Klugmann was a very loving and gentle person who never raised his voice. "He had a very soft voice, a very endearing voice—in fact, it was almost like a caress when he spoke to you." And he asked, "How could James knowingly and consciously have brought people into a situation where they would be led by Burgess, Blunt, and others into a life of deceit?" The answer could only be, he said, that Klugmann was totally committed, totally convinced that capitalism was finished, and that deceit was essential at that juncture of history in order to ensure the victory of communism.

It is a truism that spies are never recognizable by their appearance. Many of them, in fact, appear to be quite ordinary people. But in Klugmann we have a new phenomenon: a spy who makes not the least effort to mute or disguise his ideological views; who is gentle, caring, and saintlike in his everyday behavior; who speaks with an endearing, caressing voice; and who retains the admiration and affection even of his political opponents. Such people are very rare. As spies, especially as moles inside key wartime bureaucracies, they can be formidably dangerous.

Klugmann's genial and relaxed attitude, combined with his brilliance and wide erudition, concealed the fact that he was essentially a rigid apparatchik. His blind adherence to Soviet communism survived intact the Hitler-Stalin Pact, the persecution of the Soviet Jews in the postwar period (including the mass execution of Jewish writers, which should have moved Klugmann because it resulted in mass defections internationally among Jewish members of the Communist parties), Khrushchev's denunciation of the crimes of the Stalin era (which caused many lifetime Communists to open their eyes a bit wider than Khrushchev had intended), Khrushchev's bloody suppression of the Hungarian revolution in 1956, and Brezhnev's 1968 suppression of Czechoslovakia's brief experiment with "communism with a human face."

Despite strong emotional ties to the Yugoslav Communists—after all, he had helped them come to power—Klugmann sided with Stalin at the time of the break with Tito and wrote a book denouncing Tito, his wartime hero.

The book, *Trotsky to Tito,* published in 1951, was couched in Stalinist rhetoric and spoke about the "treachery" of the Tito group having been "long and carefully concealed." When Stalin died, Klugmann lauded him as "the world's greatest working class leader" and as "the man of peace, of international fraternity."

While there is today no doubt that Klugmann was part of the Soviet apparatus, his activities thus far have not been the subject of a major study. What is known about him is primarily that, with Blunt, he played an important role in recruiting agents for the Soviet espionage apparatus.

In recent years a few writers have suggested that Klugmann was responsible in some way for the switch from Mihailović to Tito. The proof of this is admittedly circumstantial, since Klugmann's name appears only two or three times in the many thousands of pages I went through in the Public Record Office. But the last thing in the world that can be assumed is that Klugmann's impact on British policy vis-à-vis Yugoslavia was directly proportional to the frequency with which his name appears in those documents. If Klugmann was "conscientious, a glutton for work," as Greenlees described him, and if the period in question may be called "the Klugmann period," in the words of Basil Davidson, his commanding officer, obviously Klugmann must have left his imprint—a very big imprint—on Yugoslav policy. Presumably, documentary evidence of this will be found in the many more thousands of pages of SOE records that are still classified.

CHAPTER

2

The Kingdom of the Serbs, Croats, and Slovenes

At the time World War II erupted, there were in Yugoslavia roughly 7,000,000 Serbs, 3,750,000 Croats, 1,250,000 Slovenes, and approximately 2,000,000 of sundry minority peoples. Serbs, Croats, and Slovenes come of the same South Slav stock. Serbs and Croats speak the same language, but the Serbs write it in Cyrillic script, the Croats in Roman. As the situation in Ireland again demonstrates dramatically, however, common blood and a common language do not automatically result in a common understanding or a common political attitude.

The Yugoslav state was born in 1918 as a consequence of the Treaty of Versailles. There were solid reasons—economic, geographic, and political—in favor of the creation of a united South Slav state. So long as the Croats and Slovenes were under Hapsburg rule, there had, moreover, been a real and very strong desire for union with the Serbs. In the years before World War I there had even been militant student demonstrations in Zagreb, the capital of Croatia, in favor of unity with the Serbs, and many Croats committed to the ideal of unity with the Serbs even fought on the Salonika front with the Serbian army. The one difficulty was the unavoidable clash of religions, ideologies, and national temperaments once unity was attained.

In November 1918, with the encouragement of the Western Allies, there took place in Belgrade a historic conference attended by prominent delegates from Serbia, Croatia, and Slovenia. On December 1 the conference voted unanimously in favor of committing the three Yugoslav peoples to come together in "the Kingdom of the Serbs, Croats and the Slovenes" under the Karadjordjević dynasty.

At that moment it would have been difficult to foresee or predict the unavoidable clashes of religions, ideologies, and national temperaments that were bound to occur once unity was attained.

The ultimate differences between Serbs and Croats are probably rooted deep in physical environment. The Serbs are a people of the mountains. The Croats are, to a far greater extent, people of the plains.

The Serbs are Eastern Orthodox. The Croats and Slovenes have been subject to the somewhat more authoritarian influence of the Roman Catholic Church.

For 500 years the Serbs were ruled by the Turks, against whom their unremitting revolt culminated in the heroic uprising of Karadjordje in 1804 and the final victorious insurrection under Miloš Obrenović in 1815. The twentieth century made many demands on them. Their spirit steeled in two Balkan wars, they refused to flinch before the ultimatum of the Central Powers in 1914. Their suffering in World War I was terrible beyond description—it is questionable whether any other Allied nation suffered as much. The Serbs purchased their independence dearly, and they were compelled to defend it dearly. And out of their turbulent history has emerged a proud and soldierly people, uncompromising to the point of fanaticism.

In the Serbian epic poem that tells the story of the battle of Kosovo, Car Lazar, confronted on the one hand with the choice between an earthly kingdom and destruction on the battlefield, and on the other hand with the promise of a heavenly kingdom, chooses the heavenly alternative. Kosovo is more than a part of Serbian literature. It is a mystique—an expression of national spirit.

The history of the Croats, in contradistinction to that of the Serbs, is that of an oppressed people who tried to regain their freedom but failed. Forced into a union with Hungary in the year 1102, they were not liberated from the Hapsburg yoke until 1919, by the Treaty of Versailles. They had revolted several times and (apart from their aristocracy) had never fully accepted the overlordship of the Hapsburgs. But after the bloody suppression of the great rebellion under Matija Gubec in the sixteenth century they were never again strong enough to challenge the power of the Austro-Hungarian Empire.

Justly proud of the part they had played in World War I, the Serbs were inclined to take full credit for the liberation of Croatia and to consider the Yugoslav state their own private creation. Toward the Croats they had the inevitably paternalistic attitude of a people who had succeeded in emancipating themselves toward a people who had tried but failed. Nor did it occur to the average Serb that it was much easier for a mountain people to cope with the decaying power of the Ottoman Empire than for a people of the plains to cope with the relatively virile power of Austro-Hungary.

The Croats, for their part, manifested a superiority complex on other grounds. Having lived for centuries as a part of Europe while the Serbs were subjects of an Asiatic empire, they were prone to consider themselves the bearers of European culture and to look down upon the Serbs as little better than demicivilized. This conviction of their own superiority made it all the more difficult for the Croats to accept the rule of the Serb politicians.

Had the Yugoslav state been constituted on a federated basis from the beginning, much of the subsequent trouble might have been avoided. Unfortunately, those who brought the infant South Slav state into being saw greater advantages in a strong centralized government. In such a strong government, it goes without saying that the Serbs were always in a position to dominate the other two national groups, the Croats and the Slovenes. The Croats under these circumstances developed a highly sensitive minority complex. Though many of the Croat complaints were exaggerated, the Serb politicians, it must be said, were guilty of a number of actions that lent substance to these charges.

The outstanding figure in Serbian politics during this early period was Nikola Pašić, head of the Radical Party—a party that was approximately as "radical" as the French Radical Party. Pašić was a bearded patriarch of magnificent presence and great persuasive powers, a cunning and not always scrupulous politician but, with all his vices, a great man who believed wholeheartedly in strong government. It was Pašić who had led the Serbian people through the Balkan wars and World War I, and among his fellow Serbs he enjoyed an almost legendary reputation as a warrior-statesman. With the exception of a few brief interludes, he and his Radical Party held power uninterruptedly until the final dissolution of Parliament in January 1929.

The Croatian counterpart of Pašić was Stepan Radić, head of the Croatian Peasant Party—a talented man, passionately devoted to his peasantry, but narrowly nationalistic in his outlook, as most Croat politicians had become.

The difficulty of coping with the Serb majority in the centralized legislature had a solidifying effect on the Croats. To give their vote maximum effect, they united behind the Peasant Party. In terms of program, the Peasant Party was slightly to the left of the Radical Party. Its great weakness, paradoxically, sprang from its enormous strength in Croatia proper: like all parties that enjoy a near-monopoly on popular support, it became increasingly ossified internally, less tolerant of dissident opinion, less democratic in its methods. The development of this monopoly further crystalized the division between Serbs and Croats and strengthened the agitation for an independent Croatian state.

Radić's assassination in the Yugoslav Parliament by a young Montenegrin deputy on June 20, 1928, provoked a near-break in the young Yugoslav state. Shortly before the incident, Pašić had died and a host of minor politicians had immediately begun to vie for his position. Parliament remained in a state of chronic crisis bordering on paralysis. On January 6, 1929, King

Alexander, a courageous and gifted but politically unwise man, suspended both Parliament and the constitution and proclaimed himself the supreme ruler. He announced to the people that he had acted thus because the crisis between the various national parties had become a menace to Yugoslav unity, to which cause he had dedicated his life.

The dictatorship of King Alexander bore as heavily on the Serb masses as it did on the Croat masses. But to the Croats it was more than a dictatorship—it was an alien dictatorship, a Serb dictatorship. Nor did the fact that the regime did its utmost to appease the Croats by providing for proportionately heavier public expenditures in Croatia than in Serbia seem to have any effect. The flames of national resentment grew higher, and tempers reached the boiling point.

The division between Serb and Croat was exploited by Yugoslavia's neighbors, and especially by Fascist Italy, which was at that time pressing its claim for the Dalmatian littoral. The Italians were able to enlist the services of the Croat Ustaše terrorist organization headed by the fascist Ante Pavelić. It was a hireling of Pavelić's who assassinated King Alexander and French Foreign Minister Barthou in Marseilles on October 9, 1934.

The regency set up in consequence of the assassination of Alexander was nominally a triumvirate, but it soon became apparent that the effective power lay with one man—Prince Paul, first cousin of the king.

Prince Paul was a weak man whose chief capital consisted of a reputation for being pro-British. For Yugoslavia's internal problems he had no effective solution to offer. Confronted with the imminent threat of a European war, he was anxious to consolidate the Yugoslav state by forcing an understanding between Serbs and Croats. In August 1939, with the regent's approval, Premier Dragiša Cvetković, nominally representing the Serbian people, and Dr. Vladko Maček, who had succeeded Radić as head of the Croat Peasant Party, negotiated an entente for the ostensible purpose of settling the differences between the Serb and Croat peoples. Though it served to appease the Croat extremists, it is questionable whether the Maček-Cvetković entente produced any tangible improvement in national unity.

In the elections of 1938, Maček collaborated with the Democrats, Agrarians, and the old Radicals in the United Opposition. In order to purchase his support, Prince Paul and Cvetković were compelled to make concessions that the majority of the Serbs considered unjust to them. The Yugoslav state, which had previously been organized on a territorial basis, was now reorganized on a seminational basis; the Croats were removed from the direct aegis of the central government and given a province, or *banovina*, of their own—with boundaries that coincided with the demands of the more extreme Croat nationalists. Bitterly the Serbs complained that there were now more than twice as many Serbs in Croatia as there were Croats in Serbia. The total population of the new Croatian *banovina* was in excess of 4,000,000. Of this number, 1,300,000 were Serbs.

There is reason to believe that in sponsoring the Maček-Cvetković entente, Prince Paul was thinking in terms of collaboration with Britain and France. Even later in 1940, when he dispatched Dr. Milan Gavrilović as ambassador to Moscow, he seemed to have been disposed to resist Axis pressure. But the Allied position was disastrous, and when the Germans began to tighten the screws, Prince Paul was too weak a man to resist further. Early in March 1941 it was announced that Foreign Minister Cincar-Marković was going to meet for talks with representatives of the German government.

3

Revolution and Invasion

Lazarus, Prince of a race that I love,
Which empire choosest thou?
That of the heaven above?
Or that of the earth below?

But if rather a heavenly crown thou cherish
At Kosovo build ye a temple fair

Range ye the army in battle array
And let each and all full solemnly
Partake of the blessed sacrament there.
For then of a certainty know
Ye shall utterly perish, both thou,
And thine army all; and the Turk shall be
Lord of the land that is under thee.

from *Kosovo:*
TRANSLATION BY OWEN MEREDITH

With the fall of France in 1940 it appeared that nothing could prevent the establishment of the Nazi New Order in Europe. Czechoslovakia had surrendered without a fight. Poland had fallen before a military onslaught. Denmark, Norway, Holland, and Belgium had also been overwhelmed. Greece was fighting for its life against a massive Italian invasion. Hungary, Bulgaria, and Rumania had joined the New Order. Of the many countries that constituted Western Europe only Yugoslavia, Sweden, and Switzerland remained completely free.

In early 1941 the Nazis began to apply diplomatic pressure on the Yugoslavs. By March it was already evident that the negotiations between Yugoslav Foreign Minister Cincar-Marković and the Germans were going to lead to something. Up until that time the German press had been careful to avoid any intimation of the purpose of the discussions. The comings and goings had been described merely as "courtesy visits."

Ribbentrop was insisting on a full-fledged entente that would harness the Yugoslav economy to the Nazi New Order and guarantee freedom of movement through Yugoslavia for German troops and military equipment. In return the Germans were prepared to offer an enlargement of Yugoslav territory in the direction of Salonika. The Regent, Prince Paul, was pro-British, and he was uneasy about the heavy pressures from the Nazi side. The Serbian people were openly hostile to any suggestion of compromise with the Germans. The army was in a particularly truculent mood. In defiance of the government's wishes, and in complete contradiction of its policy, the army had already begun to mobilize. Several top-ranking officers had informed Prince Paul in no uncertain terms that the army would not tolerate an agreement which made Yugoslavia a vassal of Germany.

Prince Paul would have liked to delay. But Hitler's timetable called for the invasion of Russia in early May, and before he moved he had to make sure that his southern flank was secure.

On March 24 Yugoslav Premier Cvetković and Foreign Minister Cincar-Marković left for Vienna.

Serbia was seething with anger. In Belgrade the university students declared a state of siege on the campus. High-school students banged their desks during their German classes and shouted, "No more German! No more German!" In the villages the peasants came together, as had been their wont for centuries when danger threatened, to discuss what was to be done. The alternative to a pact with Germany was war with Germany; on this score not even the simplest peasant harbored any illusions. But among these people, steeped for centuries in the legend of Kosovo and schooled in a merciless struggle for freedom, there was scarcely a man who hesitated. If one must choose between certain destruction and the loss of one's soul, then the Serb peasant has his mind made up in advance. He must do as Car Lazar had done at Kosovo.

During the last fateful days of March a nameless Serbian uttered the words *"Bolje rat nego pakt. Bolje grob nego rob."* — "Rather war than the pact. Rather a grave than a slave." The slogan swept Serbia overnight. The words were heard wherever people came together. The spirit of Kosovo had come to life again.

It was the army that acted to implement the will of the people. On March 24 a small group of conspirators met at the headquarters of the Yugoslav Army Air Force. The leading spirit in this conspiracy was General Borivoje

Mirković, the bull-chested, energetic head of the air force. At this meeting it was decided to take immediate action if the pact with Germany were signed. An effort was made to enlist the participation of General Simović, the commander in chief. Simović was in favor of the venture, but he was afraid that things might not turn out as planned. With tears in his eyes he embraced the conspirators, wished them success, and told them that it would be better if he himself were not actively involved so that he could intervene on their behalf if the coup miscarried.

On the morning of March 25 it was announced that the so-called Tripartite Pact had been signed in Vienna by Germany, Italy, and Yugoslavia.

At 2:00 the next morning the units of the Yugoslav army began to move. Everything went according to plan. They occupied police headquarters, the post office, army headquarters, and the offices of the prime minister and foreign minister. Premier Cvetković was arrested at 2:30 A.M. Prince Paul was apprehended later in the morning aboard a train in Zagreb and was exiled to Greece.

The entire regime of Prince Paul and Cvetković and Cincar-Marković was overthrown in less than one hour, and at the cost of not a single life and fewer than one dozen cartridges.

One of the active British observers of the March 27 revolution was Julian Amery, the son of Leopold Amery, a distinguished conservative who served as colonial secretary. Amery was only twenty-one years old at the time, and it says something about the caliber of the man that he was appointed deputy director of the Balkan Division of SOE, serving under Colonel Bailey. When Colonel Bailey, on Christmas Day 1942, was dropped into Mihailović's headquarters as the new chief of mission, he asked for Julian Amery to be assigned as his deputy. This request, unfortunately, was not granted. Some of Amery's observations on the events of March 27 deserve quoting.

First, Amery proudly notes the fact that his father, as the only member of the British government who spoke Serbian, had made a stirring appeal over BBC, urging the Yugoslavs to be worthy of the traditions of Kosovo and to follow the path of honor rather than that of capitulation. He observes, however, that the revolution was not made by the limited number of Yugoslavs who may have known his father or who had contacts with SOE. "There has never been a more spontaneous revolt in history," he says.[1]

Who was responsible for this revolt? There have been various accounts, some of which gave the military a more important role, some a less important role. According to Amery, three men deserve the prime credit: Major Živan Knežević of the Royal Guards, General Mirković of the Yugoslav Air Force, and Voivoda Ilya Trifunović Birčanin, who retained a great national reputation thanks to his leadership of the Serbian guerrillas in World War I.

By Amery's account, Birčanin contributed 400 men, veterans who belonged to the *Narodna Odbrana* (National Defense) organization, to the task of seizing key positions in Belgrade.[2]

Having taken power out of the hands of those responsible for the Tripartite Pact, the armed forces acted to hand it back to the people. Early on the morning of March 27 the leaders of the various political parties were called together, and a government of national resistance was set up under the premiership of General Simović. Simultaneously it was announced that King Peter had come of age and assumed the responsibilities of the throne. The youthful king broadcast to his people, solidarizing himself with the revolution and calling upon them to be disciplined and courageous.

In Belgrade and throughout Serbia the revolution was greeted with delirious joy. The people felt as if a heavy stone had been removed from their hearts. All day long the people thronged the streets, singing, shouting, garlanding soldiers. *Bolje rat nego pakt!* The Serbian people, to use Churchill's phrase, had "found their soul."

In Croatia the news of the revolution of March 27 was greeted with unease or sullenness. The Ustaše quislings began to demonstrate openly, urging the Croats to break with the Serb warmongers. Even those who were not pro-German were uneasy. The Croat mentality is more logical, less romantic than that of the Serb. "How can we possibly hope to resist?" asked democratic Croats. "If we provoke war, we'll be crushed, and then the Ustaše will take power. At all costs we must avoid war with Germany."

This was substantially the stand of Dr. Vladko Maček, the head of the Croat Peasant Party, who had originally cast his vote for the pact. Dr. Maček's enormous popularity extended to all sectors of the Croatian population, with the exception of the far right and the far left. In order to patch together an effective Yugoslav government of national unity, it was essential to include Maček and the Croat Peasant Party. Confronted with so critical a diplomatic problem, Maček realized the need for national unity, but at the same time he was afraid that the impetuosity of the Serbs might plunge the country into the disaster of war with Germany. For several days he hesitated. Finally he agreed to enter the Cabinet, on two conditions: (1) that the negotiations with the Germans be continued, and (2) that no action be taken that might provoke German aggression.

Momčilo Ninčić, the new minister of foreign affairs, found himself in an extremely anomalous position. On the one hand, he was supposed to assure the Germans that the new Yugoslav government was prepared to negotiate in the spirit of the Tripartite Pact. On the other hand, it was obvious that the government of the revolution, whatever other concessions it might be willing to make, would never tolerate German army movements through Yugoslav territory and would enter into no deal at the expense of its Greek ally. The Germans understood this well, and they immediately began to make the necessary dispositions.

Meanwhile the Yugoslav army was finding itself increasingly hamstrung by political exigencies. In the first place, it had to delay general mobilization for five days for fear of provoking the Germans. But even more disastrous than this delay was the strategy forced upon it. The General Staff favored abandoning the less defensible terrain of Slovenia and Croatia and concentrating their forces in the mountains of Serbia, Bosnia, and Montenegro. Militarily, this was the obvious thing to do. The difficulty was that the Croat and Slovene politicians were suspicious of the Serbs; they consequently opposed a strategy that left their lands to the mercy of the enemy. They demanded that the plains of Slovenia and Croatia be defended equally with the mountain areas of Serbian Yugoslavia. "If we must fight," they said, "we wish to fight for our own lands." For the sake of maintaining national unity, the army committed itself to a disastrous policy of territorial defense. It was compelled to dissipate its strength along the vast stretches of the Albanian, Bulgarian, Rumanian, Hungarian, and Austrian frontiers. The debacle that followed was, under the circumstances, inevitable.

On April 6 the Luftwaffe, without any previous declaration of war, bombed Belgrade, which had previously been declared an open city. The Heinkels and Stukas swarmed over the undefended city, dropping their bombs without hindrance. Simultaneously the Wehrmacht invaded. It threw into the attack thirty-three divisions, of which six were Panzers and four were motorized. Against this might, the ill-prepared, ill-armed, and ill-deployed Yugoslav army could do very little. Despite heroic resistance at certain points, the battle for Yugoslavia was over in twelve days.

The debacle was accelerated by the wholesale defection of the Croat units of the army and by the activity of the quisling Ustaše militia, which sprang up in thousands on the day of the German invasion.

How will history evaluate the revolution of March 27? Will it be regarded as a rash political act that brought down on the Yugoslav peoples a calamity that could have been avoided? Or will it find some larger historical justification for it in terms of its overall political impact?

As things turned out, there can be no question that the Yugoslav peoples did not benefit from the revolution of March 27. The first step Hitler took after vanquishing the Yugoslav army was to divide Yugoslavia in a manner calculated to reward the Axis satellites—and, of course, reward Germany and Italy—and to create optimum conditions for controlling the resistance of the Yugoslav peoples. Germany and Italy divided up Slovenia, the northernmost province, Germany taking the larger northern portion and Italy the southern portion. The territory of Croatia was enormously enlarged, primarily at the expense of Serbia and Montenegro, and the establishment of an

Yugoslavia boundaries at the outset of World War II

Independent State of Croatia (NDH) was proclaimed, under the leadership of Ante Pavelić, without question the most barbarous quisling of World War II. The borders of the NDH were enormously expanded to include all of Bosnia and Herzegovina. The southern half of the NDH, including most of the Dalmatian coast, was marked off as an Italian zone of occupation, and the northern half as a German zone of occupation. The major portion of southeast Serbia, which had a large Macedonian population, was incorporated into Bulgaria as a reward for Bulgaria's participation in the war on the side of the Axis. Similarly, a generous portion of the territory of Vojvodina was annexed by the Hungarian satellite regime of Admiral Horthy, and southwestern Serbia was incorporated into the state of Albania, which had been under the control of an Italian army of occupation since April 1939. This was only the beginning of the wartime travail of the Yugoslav peoples.[3]

But while they did not benefit from the revolution of March 27, there can be no question, either, that this revolution constituted a rare act of national heroism. When Belgium and Holland resisted, they did so with the knowledge that the French and British armies stood at their borders. But

Yugoslavia boundaries during World War II, showing territory (shaded areas)
administered by Axis powers and satellites

when the Serbian people overthrew the regency of Prince Paul and hurled the Tripartite Pact back into the faces of Ribbentrop and Hitler, they did so with the examples of Warsaw, Rotterdam, Antwerp, and London fresh in their memories, and with the almost certain knowledge that their act meant war. They knew that they could look for no help from the hard-pressed British, and that the Germans would exact a terrible vengeance for their "betrayal." Poland, Norway, Belgium, and Holland were not given the alternatives of compromise. Yugoslavia, if it had wished, could have compromised with the Germans on terms no more degrading than those accepted by Sweden and Turkey. No one could have blamed the Yugoslav government if it had done so; strategically, its position was utterly impossible. But the Serbs said no to compromise. *"Bolje rat nego pakt!"* they shouted. The consequences were far-reaching.

At one stroke the revolution of March 27 disrupted Germany's economic hinterland, invalidated her dispositions, disorganized her timetable, and destroyed the myth of the Nazi New Order. And, what is perhaps most important, the example of this small nation defying the might of the unconquered

Wehrmacht—preferring all the horrors of war and subjugation to the loss of its spiritual freedom—did more than anything else up until that time to inspire the conquered peoples of Europe to resist.

Instead of incorporating Yugoslavia peacefully into the New Order, the Nazis were compelled to deal with it as an enemy nation. Instead of adding to their reserves of available manpower, they were compelled to divert thirty-three divisions for the conquest of Yugoslavia and to maintain an army of occupation that included eight or nine German divisions and a somewhat larger number of satellite divisions. Instead of launching their attack on Russia in mid-May, as soon as the roads had hardened, they were compelled to postpone it for almost five whole weeks of the strategically priceless dry-weather season. According to Göbbels, Hitler had decided to invade Greece for the purpose of extricating his Italian partner. This, of course, would have resulted in a certain delay. But even if the invasion of Yugoslavia set back Hitler's European timetable by two or three weeks, it may very well have saved Moscow.

The Germans were able to overcome the Yugoslav army in twelve days. But the revolution of March 27 may have cost them the war.

CHAPTER

4

The Occupation of Yugoslavia:
The Beginning of Soviet Deception

On May 4, 1941, Hitler proclaimed to the world that the Yugoslav state no longer existed.

On May 10 Draža Mihailović, then a colonel in the Yugoslav army, hoisted the Yugoslav flag on the mountain of Ravna Gora in Serbia and announced the continuation of the war against Germany.

The Yugoslav Communists, who were at that time captives of the Hitler-Stalin pact, did nothing to resist the Nazi army until the Soviet Union itself was invaded on June 22, 1941. Actually, there is evidence that they actively sabotaged the defense of Yugoslavia.

On the afternoon that Hitler invaded Russia, Josip Broz Tito, the secretary general of the Yugoslav Communist Party and a professional revolutionary who had somehow survived Stalin's massive purges of the leadership of foreign Communist parties, issued this proclamation: "A fateful hour has struck! . . . The precious blood of the heroic peoples is being shed. This is also our struggle, which we are obliged to support with all our strength . . ."[1]

The Nazi invasion of his own country had produced no comparable statement from Tito. It was the invasion of the Soviet Union that moved him to action.

The followers of Tito and the followers of Mihailović initially collaborated, but this fragile political alliance disintegrated when the Communists insisted on keeping their own military command and on establishing miniature Soviet republics wherever they temporarily came to power, replete with mass executions of prominent citizens. (It must be remembered that the communism we are dealing with at this point in history was not the cruel yet relatively bloodless totalitarianism of today but the communism of Josef Sta-

23

lin, with its total disregard for human life, with its endless executions and its Gulag Archipelagos.)

Milovan Djilas, Tito's chief lieutenant during the war, was very frank on the point that the Communists' goal was from the beginning the establishment of a Communist dictatorship, and that they used the resistance movement as an instrument to achieve this objective. Said Djilas, "The military operations which we Communists launched were motivated by our revolutionary ideology . . . A revolution was not feasible without a simultaneous struggle against the occupation forces."[2]

Speaking about the first phase of Communist resistance, Djilas admits frankly that the Communists antagonized the Yugoslav peasantry because they "killed far too many people."[3] In a gruesome commentary Djilas reported, "Communists confirmed their devotion by killing their own fathers, and there was dancing and singing around the bodies."[4]

During the closing months of 1941 Draža Mihailović became the toast of the Allied press. Nothing was said about Tito or the Partisans, for three reasons: first, there was no direct information about them or their activities; second, the British and American governments were bound to be somewhat more sympathetic to a traditionalist movement, such as the Mihailović movement, than they would be to a revolutionary Communist movement; third, the Soviets said nothing about Tito. With a monopoly on the media, it was natural that Mihailović should have become internationally known as the leader of the Yugoslav resistance.

Western ignorance of the existence of the Tito movement was in very large measure due to the fact that Stalin at that time, in the interest of receiving generous aid from the Allies, was deliberately muting all information that suggested revolutionary intentions by the Soviet Union for the postwar period. To this end, Stalin engaged in repeated deceptions.

In a speech on November 6, 1941, Stalin denied that the Soviets had expansionist ambitions toward the non-Communist states or intentions of interfering in their internal affairs. Noninterference in the affairs of other nations was reaffirmed in a twenty-year Anglo-Soviet treaty signed on May 26, 1942. Stalin's commitment to the Atlantic Charter and the United Nations Pact was followed by a speech on November 6, 1942, promising "liberation" of countries overrun by Hitler's troops and the "restoration of their democratic liberties." The deception operation reached its climax in May 1943 when the Communist International was formally "abolished."

The Yugoslav policy of the Soviet government was guided by the same caution about offending Churchill by suggesting that the Soviet government harbored revolutionary intentions. According to Edvard Kardelj, prime minister of Yugoslavia under Tito, Stalin exerted pressure on the Partisans "to reach an understanding with the Četniks at all costs and set up a joint army under the command of Mihailović . . . Obviously, as in many other questions, Stalin did not trust our information.''[5]

This round of Soviet deception was spectacularly successful in both Britain and the United States. The British Foreign Office agreed with its Moscow embassy that in abolishing the Comintern, the Soviets were abandoning an outdated and embarrassing institution. While the obvious tactical advantages to the Soviets were noted and considerable reservations expressed, nevertheless the official view was that ''the old idea of world revolution is dead and the expectation now is that the success of socialism or communism in the USSR will serve as an example to foreign countries . . .'' *The* (London) *Economist* welcomed the news, seeing it as ''the first steps in a campaign to eliminate the suspicions and mistrust which have hung like a damp pall over Russia's relations with the outside world,''[6] an assessment that was extraordinarily accurate but in a way the author may not have intended.

Americans as a nation reacted less enthusiastically to this deception campaign, although many in government were apparently impressed.

In mid-1942, however, something strange happened to change Soviet policy toward Yugoslavia. In one way or another the supercautious Stalin must have received intelligence that it had become safe to break with Mihailović without endangering the relationship with Churchill. Indeed, the abrupt and dramatic manner in which the change occurred strongly suggests that the Soviet government must have possessed information leading it to believe, even at that early date, that Churchill could be persuaded to throw his own backing to Tito. Certainly, Stalin was in no position, and would be in no position before the Red Army entered Yugoslavia, to assist Tito materially.

Here is a chronology of the events that marked this historic shift in Soviet policy.[7]

On July 6, 1942, at a reception held in honor of King Peter, at the official Information Center in New York, Mirko Marković, editor of the Communist newspaper *Slobodna Reč,* presented King Peter with a check for $1,000 ''to help the Četniks and their heroic leader Draža Mihailović.'' Both Serb and Croat Communists who were present at the reception assured King Peter of their unwavering support.[8]

On July 18, 1942, *Inprecor,* the international Communist organ published in London, editorialized, ''The forces of Mihailović, the patriot leader, are growing stronger and bolder, until they are raiding over the Italian border toward the great port of Trieste.'' Until approximately the same date, *The Daily Worker,* organ of the Communist Party USA, was also supporting Mihailović as the leader of the Yugoslav resistance forces.

Four days later, on July 22, the BBC monitoring service recorded a broadcast emanating from an apparently clandestine transmitter calling itself Radio Free Yugoslavia. There is evidence that Radio Free Yugoslavia had gone on the air some months before the July 22 broadcast, but if so, even the Communist press paid little or no attention to it. (The site of Radio Free Yugoslavia was subsequently identified as the Tiflis region.) The broadcast said that it was untrue that the Mihailović forces had been fighting against the Axis; that, in fact, Mihailović and his chief lieutenants had been collaborating with the enemy; and that all the fighting against the occupying forces during the previous year had been done by the Partisans.

On July 28, 1942, *The Daily Worker* carried an article stating that Mihailović had been labeled a fascist and a collaborator by Radio Free Yugoslavia.

On August 3, 1942, Stanoje Simić, the Yugoslav minister in Kuibyshev, protested strongly to the Soviet foreign minister, S. A. Lozovsky, over the attacks on Mihailović by Soviet and Communist sources. (Kuibyshev had become the wartime capital of the Soviet Union as a result of the Nazi threat to Moscow.)

On August 5, 1942, the Yugoslav minister in Washington, D.C., Constantin Fotitch, visited Undersecretary of State Sumner Welles to lodge a parallel protest.

Also on August 5, 1942, the Soviet Foreign Ministry presented to the Yugoslav legation in Kuibyshev a detailed memorandum supporting the charges that had been made of collaboration by Mihailović. This was the first time the Soviet government itself had made the charge.

On August 7, 1942, Soviet ambassador Ivan Maisky presented to the British Foreign Office a copy of the memorandum that had been given to the Yugoslav legation.

On August 19, 1942, the Yugoslav legation delivered a memorandum to the Soviet Foreign Office repudiating the charges against Mihailović.

On August 20, 1942, Foreign Secretary Anthony Eden replied to Maisky that Britain believed the charges were not based on accurate and objective intelligence. Eden proposed a discussion of the matter. If there was a Soviet reply to the proposal, there is no record of it.

Having reversed itself in a manner that must have completely satisfied Edvard Kardelj and his comrades, the Soviet government from that point on embarked on a merciless campaign of character assassination and disinformation directed against Mihailović. In retrospect it is possible to identify three main themes in the Soviet-Yugoslav campaign: first, that all the fighting against the Germans was being done by the Partisans; second, that the Četniks, and Mihailović personally, were collaborating with the Nazis; and third, that the dispute between Četniks and Partisans arose only as a result of Mihailović's intransigence.

From the standpoint of chronology it is worth noting that the new Soviet position on Yugoslavia was announced only a few days after SOE had embarked on the suicidal policy of recruiting Canadian-Yugoslav Communists to serve as intelligence officers in Yugoslavia. Their recruitment was supposed to be secret—but it was not a secret from Moscow, especially since the Canadian Communist Party had been asked to assist in the recruitment.

It can be taken for granted that one of the factors of Stalin's decision was the almost irresistible prospect of bringing Soviet power to the shores of the Adriatic, thus achieving the age-old Russian dream of access to the warmwater seas. One would have imagined that an old war-horse like Winston Churchill, no admirer of Bolshevism and accustomed to think in strategic terms, would have understood the basic implication of this switch in Soviet policy. But he did not. For this reason he was taken by surprise when the Partisans, toward the end of May 1945, occupied Trieste and embarked on the organized execution of thousands of their enemies. And he was also taken by surprise when Tito's Yugoslavia served as the cutting edge of the Cominform's massive postwar efforts to annex Greece to the Communist empire. And the question arises: Would he have supported Tito if he had foreseen these contingencies?

It is cause for reflection that some of those who supported Tito at the time prided themselves on their foresight when Tito broke with Moscow in 1948. They acted as though they had known all along that Tito would strike out for an independent Yugoslavia. They knew no such thing. Indeed, the entire history of communism up until that time pointed in the opposite direction. The least one would have expected of those responsible for British policy at the time is that they would have made some allowance for a worstcase scenario—indeed, it appeared for a time to be an inevitable scenario—in which a Titoist Yugoslavia would have cooperated with Moscow in the subversion of the adjoining countries and would have provided the Soviets with naval basing rights on the Adriatic. As matters turned out, the installation of Tito in power in Belgrade came within a hairsbreadth of resulting in a Communist takeover in Greece. Had Greece gone Communist, the survival of Italy would automatically have been called into question. Had Italy fallen to communism, the momentum would almost certainly have affected the delicately balanced situation in France.

In short, in the worst-case scenario, which should have been taken into account, the imposition of Communist rule in Yugoslavia might very well have led to the communization of much of Europe.

Fortunately, Europe was saved from this catastrophe by Tito's 1948 break with Moscow. But even this has not been an unqualified plus from the democratic side. As Laurence Silberman, former American ambassador to Belgrade, has pointed out, Tito, as one of the architects and patrons of the Third World "neutralist" movement, consistently made diplomatic difficulties for the United States. We need only recall that in recent years Yugoslavia has been uniformly uncooperative in apprehending anti-Western terrorists known to be on its territory.

Perhaps during the course of the war the Tito forces killed 1,000 or 2,000 or 3,000 more Germans than the Mihailović forces. The first question that must be asked is whether this unimpressive mortality statistic was worth the additional danger incurred by the Free World as a result of the elevation of Tito to power. The really important question, however, is whether there can be any moral justification, especially given the information now available, for a policy that made Britain morally responsible for the communization of Yugoslavia.

CHAPTER

5

Draža Mihailović: Myth and Reality

It was several months before news of Mihailović and of the resistance movement launched by him reached the Allied world. Radio contact with the Yugoslav government in exile in London was not established until September 13, 1941. The first articles about Mihailović appeared in the press a few months later. The reaction of the Allied public was electric. The German armies were driving toward Moscow and Leningrad, and the resistance movements in other countries were still in gestation—from every side the news was black. The knowledge that at least one people whose army had been defeated was refusing to make peace with Nazi Germany—that there was armed resistance on a substantial scale in the heart of Nazi Europe—came like a tonic after an unbroken diet of disaster.

The Allied press took up the story of Draža Mihailović and played it in crescendo, with minor variations, week after week. After Churchill and Roosevelt, Draža Mihailović was perhaps the most popular figure in the Anglo-American world. His name, indeed, became an international symbol of resistance to Nazi tyranny. The readers of *Time* magazine voted him "Man of the Year." But most lavish of all in its praise of Mihailović was the Communist press.

There was not a newspaper or magazine in England or the United States that did not run a feature on Draža Mihailović and his movement. The many biographies printed described him as a man of medium height and wiry frame, with a thoughtful forehead and blue eyes, sometimes pensive, sometimes twinkling, almost pedagogic behind their horn-rimmed glasses. He was modest in his manner, humble in his relations with the peasants, most abstemious in his personal habits—and one of the most prodigious marchers in the Yugoslav army.

He had been a soldier from his earliest youth, said his biographers. As for his family background, there was the word of Milivoj J. Sudjić, who

29

went over to Tito during the war and served for a period of time as a pro-Tito publicist, that Mihailović was "a man of the people, as were almost all of the officers of the old Serbian Army."[1] He had fought through both Balkan wars preceding World War I, had been wounded several times, and had received the highest decorations at his country's disposal. As a lecturer on military strategy at the General Staff College in Belgrade, he had done much to mold the younger officer cadres of the Yugoslav army. His revolutionary views on modern warfare had won the displeasure of the Yugoslav Colonels Blimp, and on one occasion he had been sentenced to a period of detention for advocating drastic changes in his country's defensive preparations.

Although Mihailović was not widely known in the Western world at the time his country was invaded by the Nazis, he was very well known to a limited number of people concerned with the security of the Balkan countries.

Sir Alexander Glen, who served as British naval attaché in Belgrade before the German invasion, told me that he and Colonel Clark, head of the British military mission in Yugoslavia, had cultivated Mihailović as one of the most promising junior officers in the Yugoslav army. Glen was obviously proud of his early friendship with Mihailović, despite the fact that he had wound up as a liaison officer with Tito. Indeed, when I saw him at his home in Worcestershire, England, in December 1977, he was still strongly pro-Tito in the sense that he felt that Tito had commanded a much more effective military force than Mihailović, and that in terms of serving Britain's immediate interests, Churchill had done the right thing in switching support to Tito. At the same time, however, it was obvious that he treasured the memory of the bright and dedicated young army officer he had known in Belgrade. About Mihailović, Glen wrote to Nora Beloff:

> A man whom I am proud to have known; a man of honour; serious, well-informed, a good listener, articulate when he spoke, and I found him broad in his understanding, with loyalty to the whole of Yugoslavia and not to a narrow Serb hegemony.[2]

Julian Amery had more to say about meetings involving "Sandy" Glen and Mihailović. Shortly before the coup of March 27, Amery and Glen had invited Colonel Mihailović to dinner "for the specific purpose of telling us something of his plans for fighting a guerrilla war if the Germans should overrun Yugoslavia." It was natural that they should do so, because Mihailović was then chief of the Operations Bureau of the General Staff, and also a recognized expert on guerrilla warfare. In this second capacity they had met with him more than once to hear his views on Albania. Amery relates that "when we asked him [Mihailović] how his plans for guerrilla warfare were going, he replied acidly that they all depended on fighting a regular campaign first. As things were going, the country seemed to be heading, not for resistance but for capitulation."[3]

Mihailović was also well known to important political elements in the Balkan countries. Dr. George M. Dimitrov, exiled leader of the Bulgarian Peasant Party, who knew Mihailović well when he served as military attaché in Sofia, told me that he had received a highly favorable impression of this serious and farsighted young officer. Dimitrov's one criticism of Mihailović during this period—and it must be remembered that Dimitrov himself was considered the next thing to a Communist by right-wing Bulgarians—was that he was somewhat too naïvely sympathetic to Russia and to the Balkan Communists.[4]

Transferred to a command in Slovenia shortly before the outbreak of the war, Mihailović had used his position to scourge the Volksdeutsch and quisling organizations that, with Nazi encouragement, had become brazenly active. Even in advance of the war, therefore, Mihailović commanded a certain notoriety among the Nazi élite concerned with Yugoslavia.

Although not an officer of high rank, he had established a considerable reputation as a theoretician by the time war broke out. Mihailović was never one to avoid taking controversial positions. He argued that large sums of money were being wasted on the fortification of the Slovenian frontier. He proposed a defensive plan that would have abandoned Slovenia and most of Croatia, with the Yugoslav army following back on redoubts in the mountainous areas of Bosnia and southwestern Serbia.

Mihailović's ability as a soldier was conceded even by his enemies. "Mihailovic . . . as is generally acknowledged, was a brilliant staff officer," said Michael Padev, a Bulgarian-American journalist who was pro-Tito at the time he wrote this in 1945 but finally turned violently anti-Communist and anti-Tito.[5] Officers who had served under Mihailović or with him all reported that he had an uncanny knowledge of the intricate topography of Yugoslavia. "He knew the mountains of Yugoslavia like he knows the inside of his pocket," said one of them. "Even in making the most difficult journey he rarely consults a map."

In the late summer of 1940, after the fall of France, Mihailović demonstrated where his sympathies lay by attending a reception at the British embassy in Belgrade in full uniform, without obtaining permission. For this he was punished by General Nedić, who was then minister of war, with twenty-four days' house arrest.[6]

Before hoisting the flag of continued resistance on Ravna Gora, Mihailović resisted the Germans with desperation. His motorized detachment was overwhelmed, losing all of its vehicles and most of its men. After the news of the Yugoslav capitulation was received on April 20, he made a fighting

speech to some eighty of the men he still had around him, saying that he
would not recognize the surrender, and that he intended to wage guerrilla
warfare.[7]

In the course of the war the available descriptive literature about Mihailović was enormously enhanced by the media and by the hundreds of American airmen who lived with him for a period of months before their evacuation
to safety in Italy. The accounts of the British and American officers who
came to know him well had to wait until after the war.

One thing that impressed all who came to know him was his remarkable
natural personal dignity, all the more impressive because it was combined
with an unaffected peasant egalitarianism. He would have his meals sitting
on the ground with Allied officers or American airmen or local peasants. On
the march he would always carry his own knapsack.

Lt. Colonel Robert H. McDowell, who headed up the US intelligence
mission to Mihailović in the fall of 1944, was in Yugoslavia for only two
months. However, during this period Mihailović was retreating through western Bosnia, where his position was still strong, and on the many marches
they made together and the many meals they shared and the many evenings
they warmed themselves at the campfire, McDowell had more than ample
opportunity to explore a wide range of subjects with Mihailović and to get
to know him on an intimate personal basis. It would be no exaggeration to
say that by the time McDowell parted with Mihailović, he had come to know
him better than any other officer, British or American.

What was his impression of Mihailović? McDowell summed him up as
"a very fine gentleman"—using the word "gentleman" in a broad, inclusive Southern sense of a man who possessed all the basic virtues. McDowell
told me that he considered Mihailović one of the three most impressive personalities he had met during his long and highly active career, the other two
being Mustafa Kemal Ataturk, the father of modern Turkey, and Pop Sava
Božić, a venerable Orthodox priest who commanded a large Mihailović formation in western Bosnia in which Serbs, Croats, and Moslems served harmoniously together. This evaluation was all the more impressive coming from
a man who was himself enormously impressive.

The German Lt. Colonel Kogard, who met with Mihailović in the village
of Divci on November 11, 1941, for negotiations that led to no result (see
Chapter 11), wrote the following memorandum about his impression of Mihailović:

His appearance makes a good impression. He is of middle height, self-confident,
and has an extraordinary capacity for self-control. Even when greatly disappointed, his expression does not change. He came [to the conference] believing
we would negotiate with him; when he was enjoined unconditionally to capitu-

late, the expression on his face did not change. His request for ammunition had to be refused. This must have been for him a very great disappointment, yet he showed it in no way.

He appears also very fit. In the morning of Tuesday [viz., the 11th of November] he was with his troops which were fighting in the area of Požega, departed at 10 a.m. and arrived at 1900 hours. He gave the impression of a trained mountain fighter.[8]

Some of the descriptions belonged to a later period, but so far as they went, the media's early descriptions of Mihailović the man were tolerably accurate. In describing his accomplishments, however, the press inflated the story to legendary proportions. The Allied public wanted to hear about Draža Mihailović and his resistance movement in the heart of Europe; and good news was so rare that those in charge of the Ministry of Information and BBC could hardly be blamed for passing a few exaggerations and some bits of apocrypha to boost public morale.

Mihailović was aware of the exaggerations in the Allied press and was personally unhappy about them. But the matter was not in his hands. His accomplishments were, without exaggeration, of epic significance. In attributing to him accomplishments that were under the circumstances impossible, his enthusiasts abroad actually rendered the general a great disservice. His activities during the initial period were on a large military scale; so far as this period is concerned, the Allied press did not exaggerate greatly. But when the uprisings in Serbia and Montenegro had been crushed, and Mihailović out of necessity had reverted to guerrilla fighting on a limited scale, the repeated accounts of open warfare between the mighty Wehrmacht and a Mihailović army of 200,000 men were, to say the least, a trifle flamboyant.

The uprisings in Serbia and Montenegro during the summer and fall of 1941 were militarily uneconomical but psychologically inevitable. The war had been so brief and the capitulation so unexpected that the Serbs still did not consider themselves a conquered people. Hitler's invasion of Russia, moreover, aroused all the old pan-Slav sympathies. Mother Russia was in danger! Without pausing to think of the consequences, the Serbs declared open war on the occupying powers.

The movement was fundamentally spontaneous. In a space of weeks the rebellion had swept from one end of Montenegro and Serbia to the other. Though there had been no time to create a centralized organization, the news of Ravna Gora had spread throughout the country, and in a general way the Serb peasants, as well as the many scattered groups of the Yugoslav army, already recognized this Colonel Mihailović as the senior officer of His Majesty King Peter.

In the case of the Montenegrin uprising, the Communists played an even more significant role than the nationalists, who subsequently came under Mihailović's command. In the case of the Serbian uprising, the Communists and the Mihailović nationalists probably played coequal roles, overall. The Titoites complain—with justice—that the Free World press said nothing about their activities during this period. But this is understandable, because the vast propaganda apparatus controlled by the Kremlin said absolutely nothing about the Partisans at this time.

On December 7, 1941, as the Germans were seeking to destroy the Mihailović movement through "Operation Mihailović," Mihailović was appointed brigadier general by King Peter. A month later, on January 11, 1942, he was appointed a full general and was named minister of the army, navy, and air force.

For almost three months, in the summer and fall of 1941, the better part of Montenegro, Serbia, and Bosnia was in the hands of the insurgents. When the German and Italian authorities realized how serious the situation had become, they embarked on the most ruthless suppression. It is said that up until the beginning of October, Hitler was not aware of the scope of resistance offered by the Mihailović forces and the Communists. He was informed only when the casualties in the anti-guerrilla operations had reached 1,000 German dead. Upon receiving this information, Hitler instructed his commanders to announce that for every German soldier killed, 100 Serbs would be shot, and for every German soldier wounded, 50 Serbs would be shot. He also ordered that every house from which shots were fired at German soldiers would be razed to the ground, and all male inhabitants over the age of fifteen would be executed.

This declaration was implemented with Teutonic precision.

6

Factors Involved in the Abandonment of Mihailović

I. German Reprisals: The Massacre of Kragujevac

Many thousands of Mihailović's followers were being taken prisoner by the Nazis, virtually up until the final withdrawal of the Germans from Yugoslavia in April 1945, and many thousands more were executed or killed in mass reprisals. This, regrettably, is an area that has not yet been exhaustively researched. The bits and pieces of evidence that are already a matter of record suggest that scores of thousands might not be an exaggeration of the number of Mihailović followers killed by the Germans. The paragraphs that follow deal with such bits and pieces, covering the years 1941 through 1944.

On October 29, 1941, Felix Benzler, German foreign minister plenipotentiary in Serbia, reported, "In the past week there have been executions of a large number of Serbs, not only in Kraljevo, but also in Kragujevac, as reprisals for the killing of members of the Wehrmacht, in the proportion of 100 Serbs for one German. In Kraljevo, 1,700 male Serbs were executed, in Kragujevac, 2,300 . . ."[1]

Walter Roberts, in *Tito, Mihailović and the Allies,* quotes two small items from the German *Kriegstagebuch,* or official war diary, for December 1942. "December 16: In Belgrade, 8 arrests, 60 Mihailović supporters shot." "December 27: In Belgrade, 11 arrests, 250 Mihailović supporters shot as retaliation."[2]

Colonel William Bailey of the British mission to Mihailović, in a message to SOE Cairo dated January 21, 1943, stated, "Have today seen original German placards of the following content brought from Belgrade: (1) In reprisal for demolition of railway bridge between Petrovac and Požarevac on December 13th, 1942, 50 hostages were shot. (2) Germans attribute sabotage to Mihailovich's organization and all shot are described as his supporters."[3] On May 28, 1943, Bailey sent this message: "150 hostages shot May 25th in Kraljevo as result of Keserović's clashing."[4]

A former British liaison officer, Jasper Rootham, in his book *Miss Fire,* described an action the Četniks undertook against Danube shipping on October 24, 1943. A few days later, Rootham related, the Germans announced that in retaliation for this action 150 Serbs had been shot in Belgrade.[5]

One of Rootham's fellow officers, Major Edgar C. S. Hargreaves, a New Zealander, was captured by the Germans in eastern Serbia in early December 1943 and taken to the Gestapo prison in Belgrade, where he stayed until September 1944. Rootham wrote that Hargreaves's window was "not far from the place where the shootings took place, and he saw hundreds of civilians shot."[6]

Perhaps the most dramatic evidence of the scale of German reprisals against Mihailović Serbs is to be found in *The Tourist Encyclopedia of Yugoslavia.* The section dealing with the Belgrade area relates that on the highway to Kragujevac, just before the mountain of Avala, at the village of Jajinci, there is a group sculpture, *Executions,* by Lojze Dolinar, with a plaque bearing these words: "Here in Jajinci 80,000 fighters for the freedom of Yugoslavia met their death at the hands of the German fascist occupiers."[7]

The Yugoslavs killed in Belgrade and at the execution grounds near Jajinci were, with rare exceptions, Mihailović Serbs—for the simple reason that Serbia was Mihailović territory. This is a point on which all of the British and American officers attached to Mihailović were agreed. The Partisans, from the time they were driven out of Serbia in late 1941 until September–October 1944, when they returned to Serbia as the Soviet army was driving on Belgrade, had only a few isolated pockets of strength in the Serbian countryside.

THE MASSACRE OF KRAGUJEVAC

While incidents like the massacre of Kragujevac were known to every Serb in Yugoslavia, for some reason they never achieved one one-hundredth of the notoriety of the burning of the Czechoslovak village of Lidice in 1944. The massive scale of the German reprisals played a key role in the subsequent history of the Yugoslav civil war. To the followers of Mihailović the reprisals meant that in order to protect their people, they would have to lie low until the signal was given for the national uprising that would bring national liberation. Reprisals were to be risked only when the military objective was important enough to justify the loss of human life. To the Partisans, on the other hand, the massacres at Kragujevac and elsewhere were grist for the mill of their recruiters, who would pick up young Serbs fleeing into the woods. The massacre of Kragujevac entered into the folk history of the period and unquestionably fed the differences between the followers of Mihailović and the Partisans.

The following account of the massacre is based on the report of a Slovene Catholic priest who happened to be in the town at the time, supplemented by the account of a survivor, Alexander Petrović, of London, England, who was a fifteen-year-old schoolboy in 1941. It is also substantiated by official Nazi records. On one point these records are challenged by subsequent historians. The official German report, already quoted, said that 2,300 Serbs were executed in Kragujevac in reprisal for an attack on German soldiers. Yugoslav historians place that number at close to 7,000. I shall hereafter use the figure of 7,000 because it is used by Tito, by Colonel Hudson, and by the respected historian Stevan Pavlowitch of the University of Southhampton.

The initial report by the Slovene Catholic priest and the report I received from Alexander Petrović in London in 1987 agreed in all fundamentals. According to these reports, during the second week of October 1941 a German military formation left Kragujevac, a town of some 35,000, on a punitive expedition to the town of Gornji Milanovac, the populace of which was alleged to have supported the Četniks. The expedition burned Gornji Milanovac to the ground, leaving only the Orthodox cathedral standing. Those inhabitants who escaped the German execution squads fled into the woods. On the way back, only a few miles from Kragujevac, the Germans were attacked by guerrillas, who killed ten and wounded twenty-six.

The Germans acted immediately to take reprisals. At dawn on October 20, German soldiers surrounded the town of Kragujevac and then went from door to door, dragging all the male inhabitants out of their houses.

No one knew what all this was about. General opinion had it that the Germans were trying to round up those who lacked identity cards—or that the men would be commandeered for work. So prevalent was this conviction that one unemployed worker, a Slovene, quarreled with his wife because she had used her knowledge of German to save him from being sent off to the barracks with his neighbors.

Not one of the men suspected the fate the Germans had prepared for them. "We have done no harm to anyone," they reasoned among themselves. "They can't prove anything against us—therefore, they can't do anything to us."

During that day the Germans collected in all some 7,000 men. They took the newspaper vendors from the streets and the cab drivers from their cabs. They entered the secondary school, ordered the lectures abruptly terminated, and took out all the pupils from the fifth to the eighth grade, together with their teachers and the headmaster, Pantelić. They raided the local court and marched out judges, prosecutors, prisoners, attorneys, and witnesses—all in one batch. They collected all the men who were at their daily labors. They took all the local merchants, artisans, waiters, apprentices, all the Jews who still remained in town, and, finally, they took one band of Gypsies. They marched to the barracks all the Orthodox priests, as well as the local Catholic priest, Father Zalar, who protested in vain that he was a Catholic and not a Serb.

That night almost the entire male population of the town—boys of fifteen and men of fifty—slept huddled together in the crowded Topovske Šupe barracks.

It was characteristic of the Nazis that, even on the eve of the massacre, they obeyed rules that placed certain limits on their inhumanity. For example, in their raid on the local high school they took all students who appeared to exceed the age of sixteen. Alexander Petrović, who was a high-school junior, recalls that the Nazis came to his classroom interrupting a German lesson. Their teacher appealed to the Nazis, in fluent German, on the ground that most of her students were not yet sixteen. Her intervention, combined with the fact that they had been in the midst of a German lesson, was enough to save Alexander and his classmates from the massacre that followed.

Tuesday, October 21, dawned. In the early morning the Nazis began to separate the imprisoned men into groups of forty. This done, they were escorted out of town by armed guards. Some groups were taken to the bushes, others to the greens, others to the roadside ditches. Then the machine guns opened up.

The military commander of Kragujevac who was responsible for the order was a Nazi officer by the name of Zimmerman. The Serbian people will not forget his name.

Like sheep they went to the slaughter, one group after another. Forty . . . then forty more . . . then forty again . . . And so they went, all day long. Some of them went more like lambs than like sheep: among the groups who were marched out to the machine guns were over a hundred schoolboys, their books still in their hands. With them went twelve teachers and their headmaster, Pantelić, who went down on his knees and implored the Nazis to spare the lives of his pupils. With them also went seven Serb Orthodox priests and a number of judges.

Before the actual shooting started, the major in command called for volunteers for the firing squads. When no volunteers stepped forward, the major resorted to peremptory orders. One German sergeant, to his eternal credit, refused to obey.

"Deprive me of my rank—do anything you wish to me," he said, "but I refuse to shoot down innocent and unarmed civilians."

The major ordered him arrested. And then the shooting began. All day the slaughter lasted. When an NCO informed the major that the "quota" had already been filled—the "quota" consisted of 1,000 Serbs for the 10 German soldiers killed, and 1,300 for the 26 Germans wounded, 2,300 in all—the major ordered the shooting to continue. Then all counting stopped. A massacre unsurpassed in history for its cold brutality took place. When the killing was over, the bodies of some 7,000 male inhabitants of the town of Kragujevac awaited burial.

When, on Tuesday morning, those who were left in Kragujevac awoke to the distant staccato of machine guns, horror fell like a pall upon the town. As Alexander Petrović relates, no one had to be told that each note in that terrible staccato stood for one Serbian life. Soon there arose from houses, and then from whole streets, the heart-rending wailing of Serbian women mourning for their men and of children crying for their fathers. Through every street the sound spread. Evening came. Night descended. And as the night wore on, the sound grew in volume and intensity, until by morning the whole town seemed to be roaring with anguish.

The streets that day were deserted. Shops, cafés, restaurants were empty. According to Alexander Petrović, Kragujevac appeared to be a place of the dead. From the houses there came only the sounds of crying and suppressed rage.

Not until Thursday did women, girls, and children venture to appear in the streets, dressed in mourning for their fathers, their sons, and their other dear ones. There was even one household that lost the father, two sons, the son-in-law, and the brother-in-law—all who remained were widows and orphans.

All of the victims had money on their persons because it had become customary for Serbian men to carry money wherever they went, in case they were sent unexpectedly out of their native towns. According to estimates, the victims had about 3 or 4 million dinars on them. The Nazis stripped them of all the money on their persons—and then, after the massacre, generously presented the town council of Kragujevac with 380,000 dinars for the poor of the town!

Out of all those whom the Germans had arrested, only a few hundred returned home—some on Monday, the others on Tuesday. About 600 were retained as hostages, to be executed in case more German soldiers were killed. These hostages were compelled to bury all those who had been shot. From

Wednesday until Sunday they dug. The massacred were buried where they had fallen, in common graves in groups of 40. Relatives were not allowed to see their loved ones for the last time nor to arrange for proper burial. Some of the graves were so shallow that during the night the dogs burrowed into them and carried away limbs and other fragments of human bodies.

THE CONFLICT OVER STRATEGY

The massacre of Kragujevac became a symbol of the differences over strategy that divided the Partisans from the followers of Mihailović. The question was not *whether* to fight but *how* and *when* to fight.

Mihailović's army contained a few mobile corps, but in the main it was a territorial army based on the resident peasantry of Serbia, Bosnia, Herzegovina, and Montenegro. When the Germans burned villages or massacred villagers or confiscated cattle, the peasant irregulars, as the ones immediately affected, were therefore inclined to weigh the advantages to be gained from any action against the cost in human life and villages destroyed. Their strategy of resistance consisted in doing as much damage as possible to the enemy while keeping reprisals to a minimum. As a national leader, Mihailović felt it his duty to protect the Yugoslav peoples from the very real and always present danger of reprisals.

The Partisans, on the other hand, had no such qualms about provoking reprisals, because it was not their lives, their villages, and their cattle at stake.

Mihailović explained his position to his government in London in a communication received on March 31, 1943. (Mihailović's communications with his own government were picked up and retransmitted by a British station in Malta under the code name "Villa Resta." There were scandalous and inexplicable delays in forwarding "Villa Resta" communications in both directions; at one point Malta had a backlog of more than a hundred waiting to be forwarded. The communication quoted below was, according to a note in the files, received in London on March 31, 1943, but had been dispatched by Mihailović apparently much earlier.)

> Our tactics differ basically from those adopted by the communists. The communists strive to occupy definite areas and to fully establish therein their bloody authority. They settle down in the towns and commence wide propaganda full of the most shameless lies.
>
> This provokes the occupiers into taking action to destroy the Soviet Republic and the communists either offer a certain amount of resistance by endeavouring to form a front or retire without resistance and leave the people to the mercies

of the occupiers, who apply the most terrible reprisals. They, the communists, retire with practically the whole of their forces in order to, in so far as they are not broken up or destroyed, set up in a new place a new Republic.

Otherwise they would be destroyed by the people. This happened (so it was done), in the republic of Užice, again in the republic of Durmitor, and now in the republic of Bihać. Once they lose an area they lose it forever and their strength decreases continually. Our tactics consist of holding the mountains and from there carrying out sorties against the occupying forces and their servants, or against points of importance to those forces, grouping the necessary forces. As soon as the units complete their tasks they disperse at once and return to their bases; when we held liberated territory in Western Serbia neither the Četnik units nor my staff stayed in the towns.[8]

There was another and perhaps more fundamental aspect to the conflict over strategy. Inherent in it was the ultimate struggle for political power. An intact village added to the strength of Mihailović. A destroyed village added to the strength of Tito. When his farm buildings had been burnt and his cattle driven off, there was little the peasant could do but take to the forests, where the Partisan recruiting agents were quick to round him up. Having already lost everything that mattered to him, the dispossessed peasant made an excellent Partisan, recklessly desirous of getting back at the Germans and all too frequently oblivious of the cost of his activities to other peasants. Quite apart from the assistance it gave the Soviet Union, Tito's strategy was one that actively invited reprisals. The destruction of villages, the fear of massacres, the impoverishment of the population were all grist for his political mill.

Even though I had no illusions about the fraudulent humanitarianism preached by the Communists at this period in history, I recall finding it difficult to accept that the Yugoslav Communists deliberately provoked the destruction of villages and the execution of villagers. But this strategy was spelled out in so many words by Edvard Kardelj, one of Tito's closest associates. Nora Beloff quotes Kardelj as saying:

We must at all costs push the Croatian as well as the Serb villages into the struggle. Some commanders are afraid of reprisals and that fear prevents the mobilization of Croat villages. I consider the reprisals will have the useful result of throwing Croatian villages on the side of Serb villages. In war we must not be frightened of the destruction of whole villages. Terror will bring about armed action.[9]

Wherever the Partisans went, they left behind a swath of desecrated and depopulated villages—and an undying legacy of hatred for them.

Over a long period of time the Partisans were constantly capturing centers that they were compelled to evacuate as soon as the enemy approached in force. The capture of Užice, Žabljak, Ostrog, Bihać, Split, Sušak, Fiume—the list could be expanded almost indefinitely—was followed almost immediately by their recapture and in most cases by mass reprisals on the German scale. The innocent inhabitants had no alternative but to stay and suffer the reprisals, or else take to the woods with the Partisans. To the local populace, these ephemeral Partisan occupations were disastrously costly. To the Partisan movement, they were excellent economy.

The conflict between those who had land and those who had no land also found its expression within the Mihailović movement. The student youth who adhered to Mihailović were above all anxious for activity. They had nothing to lose but their own lives, and these they were only too willing to risk. Of reprisals they had no personal fear, and therefore they were inclined to be impatient with the more conservative attitude of the peasant masses. Because youth is made that way, it did not occur to them that perhaps a man with a bit of property and a few cattle and a family of six had considerably more to fear from reprisals than they had. In the fall of 1943 the proponents of greater activity, most of whom were students, banded themselves into a faction. For a while there was talk of an open rupture in the Mihailović movement, but it all came to naught because the students could have taken none of the peasants with them.

The strategy of limited activity was not without its pitfalls. The morale of the peasant masses of the territorial army remained unaffected because when they were not training or fighting, they had their diurnal duties to attend to. But the prolonged spells of inactivity inevitably affected the morale of certain of the permanent units and of the weaker members of the officer corps. The state of affairs in several of the permanent units was justly criticized by the British mission. By itself, however, this no more condemns the strategy of Mihailović than the parallel demoralization among the Canadian troops in Britain condemns the postponement of the Second Front until the summer of 1944. If the strategy of Mihailović was correct, then a degree of demoralization had to be accepted as an unpleasant but quite unavoidable consequence.

By the beginning of 1943, however, the British were prodding Mihailović to emulate the Partisans in the hope that this would take some pressure off the British forces in North Africa and add to the pressure on the German forces in Europe.

It must be said that although Nazi reprisal policy continued to exact many thousands of victims, it underwent dramatic moderation, at least for a limited time, when Hermann Neubacher, the onetime mayor of Vienna, became special plenipotentiary southeast at the end of August 1943. Neubacher was a Nazi but, by Nazi standards, a relative moderate whose opposition to mass reprisals brought him into open conflict with August Meissner, who was in charge of military security in Serbia and the direction of all Serbian police units. Meissner's ruthlessness in carrying out the Nazi reprisal policy had earned for him the nickname "the blood-hound." [10]

The first falling out between Meissner and Neubacher came in October 1943, when Neubacher was angered to learn that in reprisal for the murder of 17 policemen, Meissner had ordered the execution of 850 political prisoners and the destruction of three villages. Neubacher's intervention secured the cancellation of Meissner's order. A few weeks later Meissner ordered the execution of 300 hostages in reprisal for the shooting of 6 Serbian policemen. Once again Neubacher was able to have the order countermanded. Such differences between Meissner and Neubacher continued to be repeated, and in early 1944 rumor had it in Belgrade that the two men would fight a duel. Neubacher appealed to Berlin and as a result was successful in having Meissner removed. [11]

There is reason to believe that Neubacher was truly horrified by the scale of the reprisals that had taken place in Serbia. However, it may be argued that he was motivated in part by a secret admiration for the Serbs—just as his counterpart in Croatia, the minister plenipotentiary Kasche, admired and was personally close to the Ustaše. Neubacher expressed the belief that Serbian nationalism was the most vital force in the Balkans and the only force capable of opposing Tito's communism. In line with this, he presented a plan to Ribbentrop in 1943 that proposed the political and economic union of Serbia, Montenegro, and the Sandžak, which, he held, would "establish a bloc of anti-Communist mountain people cutting across Tito's political territory." Although the plan was endorsed by Field Marshal von Weichs, it was firmly rejected by Hitler on July 20, 1944. [12] Apparently, the führer suffered from an incurable anti-Serbian complex that made him fear, more than anything else, the revival of Yugoslavia under Serbian national leadership.

While the emergence of Neubacher in September 1943 moderated somewhat the policy of reprisals, it did not, as has been pointed out, mean an end to it. The many activities in which Mihailović units were involved from August to October 1943 took advantage of this moderation. In the opinion of Brigadier Armstrong of the British mission, these activities would have led to further and more systematic anti-German actions if Mihailović had received supplies in any quantity worth mentioning, and if BBC had not converted itself into a spokesman for the Partisan cause, repeatedly crediting the Partisan army with military victories for which the Mihailović forces were actually responsible. This opinion was reinforced by the opinions of Colonel Seitz and Captain Mansfield of the American mission, who were confident that an expansion of the American presence with Mihailović would have resulted in stepped-up action against the Germans.

CHAPTER

7

Factors Involved in the Abandonment of Mihailović
II. The Ustaše Massacres

Tito had to postpone his bid for power until he could enlist the support of certain émigré politicians, the more impressionable sectors of the British and the American press, and persuadable elements in the British Foreign Office. In achieving these objectives, Tito and his helpers in British intelligence, from James Klugmann down, were aided in many ways by the Ustaše massacres.

Knowing that they could never purchase the support of the Serbs, the Nazis exerted themselves to purchase that of the Croats. The first act of the Nazi occupiers was to set up the Independent State of Croatia, with its territories enlarged to include the largely Serbian provinces of Bosnia and Herzegovina and the districts of Srem and Lika. Of the total population of some 6 million, in Croatia almost a third were now Serbs.

On the heels of the German occupation the news reached the Allied world that there had been extensive massacres of the Serb minority in the newly created Independent State of Croatia. The perpetrators were the Ustaše militia of the quisling Croat führer, Ante Pavelić. Some reports had it that 150,000 Serbs had been massacred; others said the figure was nearer 300,000; and soon reports began to arrive boosting the total to 500,000 and 600,000. All reports were replete with details of such psychopathic fiendishness that on first reading they seemed almost incredible.

The facts of the massacres would indeed be incredible if they had not been authenticated from so many different sources. In quantity the Ustaše massacres rivaled the worst of the Nazi crimes, and for sheer cruelty they surpassed anything that Himmler ever devised.

The massacres become understandable only against the background of Serb-Croat relations between the wars and in the light of the very special character of the Ustaše militia. This militia bore the same relationship to the Croatian army as the German SS Guard bore to the Wehrmacht. Its personnel were recruited from the most viciously anti-Serb and most depraved and sadistic elements in Croatia. Imbued with the Nazi concept of "racial" superiority and with the Nazi approach to the problem of ethnic minorities, the Ustaše cold-bloodedly adopted a program calling for the liquidation of the Serb community in Pavelić's Croatia. As some of their theorists put it: "We shall kill off a third of the Serbs, we shall drive a third of them out of Croatia, and the remaining third we shall compel to accept our religion." In line with this commitment, proclamations addressed to the Serb minority spoke not of "Serbs" but of "former Serbs."

There were a number of reports of entire Serb communities being locked in their churches and burned alive. There were reports that the Ustaše were making necklaces of Serbian eyes and adorning themselves with them. So fiendish were the reports that one simply cannot blame civilized Westerners for initially disbelieving them or at least having doubts about them. But the reports did not exaggerate. One member of the American mission to Tito, Lieutenant Joe Veselinovich, reported seeing a well filled with the remains of Serbian children.[1] Internationally famous Italian journalist Curzio Malaparte, in his best-selling book *Kaputt*, made this report on his interview with Ante Pavelić:

> "The Croatian people," said Ante Pavelić, "wish to be ruled with goodness and justice. And I am here to provide them."
>
> While he spoke, I gazed at a wicker basket on the Poglavnik's desk. The lid was raised and the basket seemed to be filled with mussels, or shelled oysters— as they are occasionally displayed in the windows of Fortnum and Mason in Piccadilly in London. Casertano looked at me and winked, "Would you like a nice oyster stew?"
>
> "Are they Dalmatian oysters?" I asked the Poglavnik.
>
> Ante Pavelić removed the lid from the basket and revealed the mussels, that slimy and jelly-like mass, and he said smiling, with that tired good-natured smile of his, "It is a present from my loyal Ustashis. Forty pounds of human eyes."[2]

It must be stressed that only a small minority of the Croat people were actively involved in the massacres. But the news of the Ustaše massacres, following hard on the German invasion, created bitterness in the most moderate of Serb hearts, and from the less moderate hearts hatred poured over with volcanic fury.

If some Serb nationalists went to one extreme in talking about the massacres, some Croatian nationalists—who were by no means sympathetic to the Ustaše—went to the opposite extreme. For many months they were inclined to deny that the massacres had taken place. Some of them even went so far as to suggest that the whole story was a Gestapo frame-up aimed at the unity of the Yugoslav peoples. And having committed themselves to this position, they were compelled by pride to go still further. When letters substantiating the original reports were received from a prominent Croat politician still in Yugoslavia, the letters were suppressed. When a Croat businessman arrived in London bringing with him an eyewitness account of what had happened, his account, too, was suppressed. At last, when it was no longer possible to deny that the massacres had taken place, it became customary to accuse the Serbs of exaggerating, or to say simply that "brothers were killing brothers." One particularly fatuous description of the situation in Yugoslavia stated that "Croats were killing Croats, Croats were killing Serbs, Serbs were killing Serbs, Serbs were killing Croats." After a very long delay, some of the Croat politicians got around to denouncing the Ustaše massacres. But by this time it was too late to make much impression on the embittered Serbs.

Today no one denies that the massacres did take place. It is of interest to note that in *The Yugoslav Peoples Fight to Live* Tito states that "during three months of 1941, with the aid of the Ustaše villains, the Nazis succeeded in exterminating more than half a million Serbs in Croatia, Bosnia, Herzegovina, and Voyvodina."[3]

Had the Croatian members of the Yugoslav government in exile immediately solidarized themselves with the Serbs when the fact of the massacres was established; had they broadcast to Yugoslavia condemning the Ustaše and appealing to the Croat people to give every assistance to their Serb brothers; had they taken the lead in organizing a campaign of protest—had they done these things, even the most embittered Serb nationalist would have felt gratitude for such a display of brotherly solidarity. Instead, they remained silent, and their silence was interpreted as acquiescence.

The Serb cabinet ministers urged that the government address an immediate appeal to world opinion in order to stop the massacres, making whatever reservations it considered necessary as to the details of the memorandum on the massacres submitted by the Serbian Orthodox church. The Croat ministers took the stand that until confirmation was received, the memorandum had to be considered suspect and nothing should be said about the massacres for fear of provoking bloodshed between the Serb and Croat peoples.

By the fall of 1941 reports began to arrive from various sources, Serb and Croat, substantially confirming the facts that had been received in previous reports. In line with the attitude they had taken, however, the Croatian ministers in the Yugoslav government in exile refused to permit publication or distribution of these reports.

In May 1942 a Croat businessman by the name of Ante Jerić arrived in London from Yugoslavia. From Lisbon, Jerić had forwarded to London an account of what he himself had seen in Croatia. Because of the objections of the Croat ministers, this account was not published. Below are a few excerpts from the testimony of Mr. Jerić:

All those [Croats] who live along the Adriatic coast or anywhere near have nothing in common with the Ustaše. A major exception to this rule are the Franjevci, and a minor exception the clergy and all who were brought up in a clerical atmosphere as members of the Croatian Catholic "Brotherhood." It is astonishing how coldly indifferent to the murders these persons proved to be. Some of them were even morally responsible for them. Such, for instance, was the friar, Dr. Belobrk of Metković, the Governor there, who must answer for several hundred victims. Besides him, the Ustaše "official," Professor Jelavić, was equally responsible.

Thus it was that on June 20 [1941] three men arrived in Metković from Zagreb, with Slavoljub Jurišić at their head.

The order was given that the killings were to start immediately. That same night fifty Serbs and one Croat—the solicitor Bosnić—were arrested and thrown into the Metković gaol, where some men had also been brought in lorries from Herzegovina. On the nights of the 26th and 27th June, they were taken away from Metković along the river Neretva, and they were slaughtered in the most bestial manner on its left bank, somewhere between Opuzen and Komina. Seventy-two men were killed on the first night and about three hundred on the second—all of them guiltless of any offence.

When, in the morning, I travelled on the steamer "Vardar" down the Neretva, I saw with my own eyes the bodies of the victims thrown together into four piles . . . I shall never forget this experience. The murderers returned to Metković, their daggers bloody and adorned with flowers . . .

Honest Croatians have said: "For twenty-three years we dinned our thousand-year-old culture into Serbian ears, but when the time came to demonstrate it to them, we offered them nothing except fire and the sword" . . .[4]

In Yugoslavia, and in Dalmatia particularly, a number of Croats did what they could to help the victims of the massacres, even at the risk of their own lives. In London the situation was not so fortunate. Several Croats holding minor positions, of whom Dr. Grga Andjelinović was perhaps the most notable, did speak of the massacres over BBC, condemning the Ustaše murderers and offering the Serb people their sympathy and solidarity. But Juraj Krnjević, Juraj Šutej, and Ivan Šubašić, the recognized leaders in exile of the Croat Peasant Party, remained silent. Whenever the subject was touched upon in London, they spoke not of "massacres" but of "fratricidal strife." Finally, on November 16, 1942, almost fifteen months after the arrival of the original reports, Dr. Krnjević got around to making the following broadcast to his countrymen:

. . . Among other outrages there is one for which we shall seek a special reckoning. I refer to forced catholicization. To force someone by the sword to change his faith is even more repugnant than physical violence. I do not appeal to Dr. Sharić [the Right Reverend Dr. Sharić, archbishop of Sarajevo], who is one of those who have lost both soul and conscience, but to the other authorities of the Catholic Church in Croatia, that they should ask themselves: Have I done my duty one hundred percent? It is not enough to maintain an embarrassed aloofness from Ustaše outrages such as forced conversion, or to make obscure pronouncements. What is necessary is that strong voices should speak in condemnation— which would be in keeping with the sentiments of the Croat people and with the dogma of the Catholic Church itself.

There can be no question of condemning the Croat people as a people as some Serbs did in the heat of the first reaction. But if some Serbs must be criticized for reacting in this way, so must the Croat ministers for their tardiness in appealing to their people in connection with the massacres. "Go and cry a little over the radio," said a prominent Serb to one of the Croat ministers. "Only in this way can you preserve Yugoslav unity." It was because the Croat leaders in London (obviously, those living in Croatia could not do so) took so long to "cry over the radio" that the hearts of the Serb people hardened against them and, through them, against the Croat people.

Many more Croats than the Serbs were aware opposed or protested against the massacres. For example, while certain members of the Croatian hierarchy failed to live up to the requirements of their calling, Archbishop Stepinac— not a Croatian extremist but a moderate who, as a youthful Yugoslav idealist, had fought as a volunteer with the Serbian army on the Salonika front in World War I—conducted himself with credit, especially when the very difficult circumstances that existed in Pavelić's Croatia are taken into consideration. As early as May 14, 1941, the archbishop wrote a letter to Pavelić protesting the massacre of 260 Orthodox Serbs at Glina. On October 3, 1943, he declared in a sermon in Zagreb, "We are striving with all our power to proclaim in public life, as strongly as we can, the principles of divine and eternal law—whether it concerns Croats or Serbs, Jews or Gypsies, Catholics, dissidents or Mohammedans." The archbishop's declarations, not surprisingly, were given no currency by the Axis-controlled media. Many Serbs who were inclined to blame him because they saw or heard no tangible evidence of his protests during the war now agree that he did use his influence to stay the massacres. They still say, however, that he did not speak loud enough or protest as vigorously as he should have.

It is incontestable that the Partisans owed much of their early accretion of strength, especially in Bosnia and Herzegovina, primarily to the Ustaše— for it was from the tens of thousands of Serbian peasants driven into the mountains by the Ustaše massacres, and prepared to grasp at any leadership offered to them, that the Partisans recruited a large part of their following.

Second, fearing a Serb vengeance—and there were a number of instances of Serb vengeance—many thousands of Croats who themselves had had no part in the massacres turned to Tito. This was especially true following the Italian capitulation in September 1943. As a fellow Croat, they reasoned, Tito would protect them from Mihailović, whom Partisan propaganda cleverly and unscrupulously depicted as the bearer of Serb vengeance. The Partisans not only did their best to promote the fear of vengeance but, taking advantage of the situation, accepted into their ranks thousands of Ustaše, officers and soldiers, whose mere action in joining the Partisans miraculously transformed them from fascist butchers into progressive humanitarians.

There were repeated protests about this situation from British and American officers with Mihailović. On the heels of the Italian surrender, the Partisans announced that a number of Ustaše units had come over intact to the Partisan army, and these announcements were duly repeated by BBC in its broadcasts to Yugoslavia. During this period Tito appealed frequently to the Ustaše to come over to his side, and he rewarded Ustaše officers who joined him with high commands in his army. Many of these were men who had betrayed Yugoslavia at the time of the German invasion, had fought with the Nazis on the Russian front, and had been decorated by both Hitler and Pavelić.

All this was something that Mihailović and his followers found repugnant and utterly incomprehensible. Mihailović had never abandoned hope for a reborn Yugoslavia after the war—he referred to his army always as the "Yugoslav Army in the Homeland." He had also taken the stand that only the guilty would be punished for the Ustaše massacres. In line with these attitudes, he did appeal to the Croatian *domobranci,* or home guard, to come over to his side. But he refused to appeal to the Ustaše as a matter of principle. In the eyes of Mihailović and his followers, there could be only one reward for the Ustaše murderers, especially for their officers—immediate execution. They took this stand because it was the Ustaše movement that had acted as Hitler's fifth column during the invasion of Yugoslavia; it was the Ustaše militia that was responsible for the terrible massacres of 1941; and it was from the ranks of the Ustaše that most of the volunteers for the Croat contingents on the Russian front came. For such men, said Mihailović and his followers, there could be no forgiveness and no redemption.

In appealing to the Ustaše, the Partisans argued that everyone who came over to their side was one less enemy to fight. Unquestionably, this policy did augment their numbers. But it also provided a fair element of truth to the charge made by Mihailović and his followers that in clashes with Partisan units they often found themselves fighting against ex-Ustaše contingents under well-known ex-Ustaše officers who, though they had changed their uniforms for Partisan uniforms, were still fighting the war as a war of Croat extremists against the Serbs.

When BBC replayed Partisan communiqués about entire Ustaše units joining the Partisan army, it was, in effect, reinforcing Tito's efforts to encourage Ustaše enlistment in his forces. Commenting on one such BBC broadcast, Colonel Bailey sent the following message to SOE Cairo on September 18, 1943:

> This clearly shows Ustaše intention take refuge so as evade responsibility their atrocities VS SERBS [of] CROATIA. Also shows TS [Tito's] intention increase numbers [by] all means to impose authority on people by force. Please inform me if the above took place with agreement [and] approval senior BLO with PSERDA[?].[5]

In subsequent months there were repeated references by both Bailey and Armstrong to this situation. Armstrong even suggested in one message that, in the interest of making the task of the BLOs with Mihailović less difficult, BBC should either pretend that the Ustaše, who were beginning at that time to come over to the Partisans in large numbers, were really *domobranci,* or else refer to them simply as "Croats."

The difference between the Ustaše and the *domobranci* was not a minor matter. The Ustaše militia occupied the same position with regard to Ante Pavelić as the German SS occupied with respect to Adolf Hitler. They were fascists. Pavelić had used the Ustaše in perpetrating the massacres and had sent units of them as a token of Croatian support to the Russian front, where they participated in the fighting at Stalingrad. The *domobranci,* on the other hand, were simple village home guards who fought primarily to protect their villages from the Communists. The Mihailović forces appealed repeatedly to the *domobranci* to come over to their side. They never appealed to the Ustaše.

The Partisans made much of the fact that certain Serb formations claiming to be under the command of Mihailović took vengeance for the Ustaše massacres by staging countermassacres of Croat and Moslem communities. It is true that such countermassacres did take place. But rather than condone or encourage them, Mihailović did everything in his power to prevent them, and otherwise to curb the extremists. To this end he strove to bring the independent Serb formations that had taken part in these countermassacres under his discipline. The task was not an easy one. Serb fathers whose children had been killed before their eyes by the Ustaše were not inclined to listen to arguments distinguishing between Ustaše and Croats; the Croats had killed their children, they would kill Croats. If the countermassacres were small in scale compared with the original massacres, it was thanks in no small measure to the efforts of Mihailović.

The matter of the countermassacres was frankly dealt with by Dr. Živko Topalović, the new head of Mihailović's Central National Committee, in his address to the Congress of Saint Sava on January 27, 1944. "One evil leads to another," said Dr. Topalović, adding:

> The truth is that these independent Serbian formations answered terror with terror and avenged themselves upon the Catholics and Moslems for the massacres. The Italian invader, in his desire to dominate completely the Adriatic Coast, and as much as possible the hinterland, systematically encouraged conflicts between Serbs and Croats and prompted their mutual destruction. This chaotic state of affairs would have been brought to an end through the introduction of discipline by General Mihailović's agents, who did what they could to prevent the fratricidal war.[6]

Though Partisan propaganda did its best to convey the impression that Mihailović's followers were fanatical pan-Serbians perennially thirsting for Croat blood, Mihailović's stand always was that Yugoslavia must be reconstituted, and that only the guilty would be held to account for the massacres.

Mihailović, at his bitterest, spoke thus of the problem: "I am often asked, Am I for Serbia or for Yugoslavia? If you ask my heart, it will answer: I am for a great and powerful Serbia; but if my reason, I would answer that the Serbs have made many sacrifices for Yugoslavia in two wars, but never have the Croats shown the least gratitude . . . . They [the Serbs] would have the right to say: We no longer want Yugoslavia. But there are higher interests which compel us to remake this country . . . ."

For some time after the massacres Mihailović's heart had the upper hand over his head. Though he refused to listen to the urgings of the ultranationalists who demanded a complete break with the Yugoslav ideal, whenever he was called upon to speak, it was Serbia that came first, and when he brought in Yugoslavia, it was obvious that he was speaking against his heart.

During this period the chiefs of Mihailović's political committee were, first, Dragiša Vasić, and next, Dr. Stevan Moljević. Both of them were repeatedly described by Bailey as pan-Serb extremists. From Vladimir Predavec, son of the first vice-president of the Croat Peasant Party, and the only surviving member of Mihailović's Central National Committee, I have received a letter that throws some doubt on Bailey's characterization of Moljević. Predavec said that he spent much time with Moljević and had numerous discussions with him, and that he considers it his duty to defend Moljević against this one charge. He said that it was quite true that Dragiša Vasić was pan-Serb and anti-Croat, but Dr. Moljević, who succeeded Vasić, was certainly a "good Serb" but not an extremist. Though he had seen his family killed by the Ustaše, says Predavec, Moljević was never anti-Croat. His position was that he "considered Yugoslavia a federation of three peoples: Serbs, Croats, and Slovenes. He was in no way a Serbian hegemonist." Colonel Bailey, however, was convinced otherwise and on several occasions expressed the opinion that Moljević was a great Serb influence, a bad influence, on Mihailović.

On December 19, 1943, Mihailović was celebrating the feast of his patron saint, Saint Nicholas. The festival was attended by representatives from all over Yugoslavia. In a speech delivered at the luncheon, Vladimir Predavec, as a Croat participant, said the following:

. . . As a Croat, I thank you, General Mihailović, for your three great achievements.

Firstly, for having preserved the Yugoslav ideal among the Serbs even after it had been stained by the blood of 700,000 Serb martyrs who were slain by the Ustaše terrorists. It was you who had the boldness to hoist the Yugoslav colours at Ravna Gora under the most difficult circumstances, and at a time when many Serbs thought that reconciliation could never be possible between them and the Croats.

Secondly, for having refused to preach the principle of vengeance against the Croats, demanding instead the punishment only of those who were guilty of the crimes committed.

Thirdly, for having taken, in the name of all the Yugoslavs, an energetic attitude to defend democracy against dictatorship of every kind, whether it came from the right or the left.[7]

In the government in exile in London the massacres and the fear of countermassacres together created an ever-widening chasm between the Serb and Croat ministers. Men like Šutej and Šubašić began to turn to Tito, not because they sympathized with his politics or believed that Mihailović was collaborating with the Germans but simply because they feared for their people and thought that Tito could protect them from the Serb extremists.

While the representatives of the Croat people in London were turning against Mihailović as "the national enemy of the Croat people," a parallel development was taking place in certain circles of the British Foreign Office. In all good faith the Foreign Office believed that the accounts of the massacres were grossly exaggerated. It was still early in the war, the facts of Belsen and Auschwitz had not yet been established, and to the Anglo-Saxon mentality it seemed altogether incredible that Croat fascists should have massacred 300,000 to 600,000 Serbs in cold blood. Some of the Foreign Office experts were, consequently, not inclined to be overly patient with the Serb "exaggerators," and by way of corollary they tended to side with the Croat politicians in the conflict that ensued in the Yugoslav government.

One other factor entered into the attitude of the Foreign Office. Having helped to bring together the South Slav peoples after World War I, certain of the Foreign Office experts were not disposed to see this unity disrupted. However, for some time after the Ustaše massacres there were knowledgeable members of the Foreign Office who despaired of a rapprochement between the Serbs and Croats. While multinational states may be desirable in many ways, they reasoned, it is not a matter of abstract principle. If both Serbs and Croats preferred to govern themselves, then a mutual separation might be the best solution. This, it might be added, was substantially the position of President Roosevelt, who on several occasions declared that he favored a homogeneous, united Serbia to a heterogeneous and disunited Yugoslavia.

But within the Foreign Office the apostles of Yugoslav unity were more numerous and more influential. Professor Arthur Seton-Watson, who had played a major role in creating the Yugoslav state after World War I, and whose opinion was still much consulted even though he had retired from the Yugoslav desk, reacted to the threatening rupture between Serbs and Croats with all the fury of a tigress protecting her cubs. "Mihailović," wrote Professor Seton-Watson, "has been gradually unmasked as one whose hatred of Soviet Russia and Pan-Serb hostility to the Croats outweighed the crying need for cooperation against the German invader."[8]

It was on the soil of this antipathy to Mihailović and the Serbs that the seeds of Tito's propaganda to the British and Croatian peoples, in particular, took root. To woo those elements in the Foreign Office who had thus turned against Mihailović was the simplest of tasks for an accomplished Machiavellian. In this task he was ably assisted by the pro-Tito elements in British intelligence—some of them pro-Tito on ideological grounds, others because they were caught up in the epidemic mania of pro-Titoism, still others because they were victims of disinformation.

First of all, it was necessary to weaken whatever influence Mihailović still retained by means of a campaign of calumny and minimization, in which the charge of collaboration played a central role. Concomitant with this, it was necessary to convince the British government that Tito had the Yugoslav peoples behind him. Finally, since the great majority of British officials who were anti-Mihailović were at the same time anti-Communist, it was necessary to assure them that the Partisan movement was not a Communist but a national movement, that Tito had no intention of introducing a Soviet regime, and that he was quite prepared to collaborate in a government with certain unobjectionable members of other parties.

So Tito smiled blandly and gave the requisite assurances. And, from Churchill down, many in the British government, their prejudices sharpened by reports that Mihailović was collaborating with the Axis and that Tito had far more followers than Mihailović, took him at his word. That they should have done so passes comprehension, because there was ample evidence available, even without access to wartime intelligence, that Tito's movement from the beginning until the end was neither national nor democratic.

Mention must be made, too, of the role played in the British abandonment of Mihailović by the constant internal squabbling of the Yugoslav government in exile in London. Much of this had to do with the Serbo-Croat antagonism and the Ustaše massacres. But not all of it. Although there were honorable and capable men, both Serbs and Croats, in the London government, by and large it had necessarily been set up on an ad hoc basis from the human material then available in London, without the benefit of distillation such as normally occurs in a democracy. There can be no question that this constant factionalism and backbiting repeatedly irritated the Foreign Office and embarrassed its efforts to support the Yugoslav government in exile. Nor can there be any doubt that this irritation severely damaged relations between the British government and Mihailović.

The slanting and falsification of British intelligence in favor of Tito and the Partisans at this juncture were unquestionably made easier by objective factors such as the Ustaše massacres and German reprisals and the difficulties created by the Yugoslav government in exile. But this slanting and falsification would never have taken place if not for James Klugmann and his like-minded helpers in British intelligence, abetted by a large number of other officers who were not in the least pro-Communist but who had been seriously infected by the pro-Tito mania that swept England in the wake of the Deakin and Maclean missions. The most celebrated victim of this mania, of course, was Churchill himself, who was all the more prone to suffer misdirection because of his incurably romantic regard for martial heroism and his big-power cynicism, which he would sometimes express with shattering frankness.

Early phase of the civil war in Serbia and Montenegro

CHAPTER

8

The Civil War

As the civil war in Yugoslavia grew in intensity, both the Partisans and the Mihailović forces were increasingly inclined to think more in terms of postwar Yugoslavia, and they consequently came to regard the other side as the chief enemy. In this, each side, according to its own lights, was behaving logically. The Communists wanted a Communist Yugoslavia affiliated with the Soviet Union. All those who were opposed to this were to be ruthlessly annihilated. Mihailović and his followers wanted an independent and democratic peasant Yugoslavia. They were prepared to resist to the death any attempt by the Communists to establish their regime.

Both sides sent out troikas (squads of three) to assassinate marked individuals on the other side. Both sides sometimes used their intelligence agents in German and quisling headquarters as an instrument of civil war; Partisan intelligence agents did their utmost to set German authorities on the trail of local Mihailović supporters, who reciprocated in kind. Both sides indulged in a fair amount of lying and a good deal of exaggeration—but in this respect the Communists had it all over the Mihailović movement.

Civil wars are not fought according to the Marquis of Queensbury's rules. The Mihailović movement and the Partisan movement, in addition to opposing the occupiers, were out to destroy each other. If a Partisan formation found a Mihailović formation engaged with the Germans or the Ustaše, one could hardly expect it to mark time until the Mihailović forces had finished with the enemy so that they would have a sporting chance of resisting when the Partisans attacked. And the same consideration applied to the Yugoslav Home Army.

There can be no doubt that the Mihailović forces engaged in certain ''parallel actions'' against the Partisans—or that the Partisans engaged in ''parallel actions'' against the Mihailović units. In October 1941 the Partisans abandoned the siege of Kraljevo and attacked the Mihailović forces from the rear while the latter were desperately battling with the Germans. During the offensive by units of the Home Army against the Višegrad-Sarajevo railway in October 1943, the Partisans hit the Mihailović troops on the flank shortly after the latter had occupied Rogatica, compelling them to abandon their projected attack on Sarajevo. Again, in September 1944 the personnel of an American intelligence mission sent in to Mihailović under Lt. Colonel McDowell saw how the Partisan armies invaded Serbia, bypassing the Germans and concentrating all their efforts against the Mihailović forces, who, for their part, were engaging the Germans.

All of this does not add up to a very pretty picture. But this is how civil wars are fought.

THE ONUS OF RESPONSIBILITY

When a clash of diametrically opposed ideologies makes civil war inevitable, it matters very little who fires the first shot. Confronted with a pragmatic choice, the question that each man must ask himself is which ideology he prefers.

Partisan propagandists charged that it was the Mihailović units who were responsible for initiating the civil war, and the Allied press seemed to have accepted this charge as true. Allied intelligence, however, had much evidence that the responsibility lay with the Partisans.

During the summer and fall of 1941 several efforts were made to achieve an agreement between the Partisan and the Mihailović commands, but after brief periods of collaboration all of the agreements reached broke down. Tito and Mihailović met on three separate occasions in an endeavor to iron out their differences. Tito claimed that it was he who took the initiative in arranging these meetings, and that even though he commanded the greater part of the resistance movement while Mihailović "had no armed forces whatever at his command," he did not stand on his dignity but presented himself personally at Mihailović's headquarters all three times. Mihailović, for his part, claimed that the meetings took place at his invitation, and that at the time Tito disposed of a comparatively small following. Each side accused the other of violating the terms of the several agreements reached by their commanders.

At the first meeting, in September 1941, no definite agreement was reached. When the second took place, in early October near the town of Gornji Milanovac, both sides were fighting against the Germans and the need for common action was more imperative than ever before. An agreement was reached covering joint actions at a number of points and providing for sharing the output of the munitions factory at Užice, which lay in the sphere of

Partisan control. The one matter on which they were unable to achieve an understanding was the question of authority. The Partisans took the stand that, though they were prepared to cooperate, they wished to retain their own distinct units under the control of their political commissars. Mihailović was adamantly opposed to the incorporation of political commissars in a unified army under his command. It was necessary, he said, to have a united Yugoslav army under a single command, without political commissars.

M. Deroc, basing himself on German and British as well as Yugoslav documentary sources, has written a fascinating history of the combined Partisan-Četnik attack on Gornji Milanovac.[1] The attack took place on the night of September 28–29, 1941. The Mihailović detachment was under the command of Lieutenant (later Captain) Zvonimir ("Zvonko") Vučković.[2] The Mihailović forces, Deroc said, were attacking from the northwest along the Takovo Highway and the Partisans from the plain of Ržanik on the south. According to Partisan accounts, only sixty Mihailović soldiers participated in this joint operation and it was the Partisans who did the bulk of the fighting in defeating the German garrison. However, notes Deroc, both Partisan and Mihailović sources are agreed that on September 29 the captured German garrison was escorted from Gornji Milanovac by Yugoslav Home Army soldiers. This was the first time that an entire Wehrmacht company had surrendered to a guerrilla unit. Captain Maurice Vitou, an escaped British POW who joined the Mihailović forces in the area, has described how these 200 German prisoners, "prisoners of war in their own territory," were treated in accordance with the Geneva Convention.[3]

Colonel Hudson, the first British officer attached to Mihailović, in a presentation made at a conference at St. Anthony College, Oxford, in December 1962, related how a short while later Mihailović took him to inspect the battlefield of Valjevo. Hudson recounted:

> During the siege of Valjevo in October-November 1941, when I went with Mihailović, his troops were half way round the town, the other half surrounded by Partisans (Tito's men) and I saw the engagement of Četnik tanks, I saw the wounded coming up—all Četniks—and I went down to the space where the tanks were withdrawn after the engagement and I went over the terrain.[4]

By mid-October the Mihailović forces and the Partisans together had succeeded in liberating large areas of Serbia, Bosnia, and Montenegro. The Partisans were in control of Užice and Čačak; Mihailović units were in control of Požega and Loznica; joint Mihailović and Partisan forces were besieging the German garrisons in Kraljevo and Valjevo. On October 22 the Partisans asked the Mihailović command to hand Loznica over to them. Mihailović refused. The Partisans launched an immediate attack on Loznica, which was beaten off after three days of fighting. But on October 28, at dusk, they attacked the heavily outnumbered Mihailović forces at Zajača and routed them.

After the attacks on Loznica and Zajača there was a series of aggressions by both sides. The followers of Mihailović claimed that toward the end of the month the Partisans unexpectedly abandoned the siege of Valjevo, leaving their flank completely unprotected. Seizing the opportunity, the Germans attacked around the uncovered flank, inflicting very heavy losses and finally compelling the Mihailović units to withdraw. At Kraljevo, according to the Mihailović claim, Home Army forces had succeeded in fighting their way into the center of the town when suddenly they found themselves attacked from the rear by the very Partisan forces that until then had been collaborating with them.

The Partisans, on the other hand, claimed that it was Mihailović units who were responsible for the original stab in the back. This is how Tito told the story:

> We came into possession of important documents, instructing all mobilized Četniks to report on November 2nd at 5:00 A.M. at a forest 10 kilometers from Užice. At once it became clear to us that Mihailović was preparing an armed attack on Užice . . . *We in turn were obliged to withdraw one of our units from the front of Valjevo* [author's italics] to defend Užice and Čačak . . . Aware of the exact movement of the Četniks in the direction of Užice, we ordered our troops to deliver a counter-attack on November 2nd at 4 A.M. Eight kilometers from Užice . . . our units met 800 Četniks and after a few hours fighting completely crushed them. Several hundred Četniks, including their commander, were killed. We then issued orders for a general attack on Užička-Požega, the Četniks' principal base. After an extremely bloody battle which lasted all day our units occupied Užička-Požega and rapidly began to press the Četniks towards Ravna Gora.[5]

What is most interesting in this declaration is the admission that Partisan forces were withdrawn from Valjevo. Only a few paragraphs previously, Tito had declared that "as early as October some 1,200 of Mihailović's Četniks participated jointly with our units in the military operations at Kraljevo and Valjevo." Since Tito nowhere charges that the Četniks had previously abandoned the siege of Valjevo, his account on the whole tends to bear out the Mihailović version that the Partisans withdrew without warning, leaving them to the mercy of the numerically superior Germans. It is also worth noting that although Tito charges Mihailović with a planned aggression against the Partisans at Užice, it was the Partisans, on Tito's own word, who launched a surprise attack on the Mihailović units outside Užice, killing 800 of them.

The fighting that began with the attacks on Loznica and Zajača went on over three weeks, until another agreement was drawn up. "Upon finding that strong German forces were approaching us," said Mihailović, "I again proposed an agreement and it was made just before five German divisions attacked both us and the Partisans." The Partisan version of this final agreement differs in one respect. "Upon seeing that he was encircled," says Tito, "Mihailović urgently dispatched liaison officer Mitić to our headquarters, imploring us to stop this bloody struggle."[6]

Representatives of the two factions met on November 21 in the presence of Captain Hudson and after one week of wrangling drew up an agreement calling for the return of prisoners taken by both sides, for a joint court of inquiry into "the stab in the back," and for a joint operational staff. Again, the major snag was the question of political commissars.

The ink on this agreement was hardly dry when fighting broke out again. The breakdown of the agreement was apparently definitive; an attempt in April 1943 to patch it up proved completely abortive. Every once in a while the two hostile factions would forget their quarrel and collaborate against the common enemy. In March 1942 troops under the Home Army commander, Major Keserović, were desperately battling units of the Prinz Eugen Division on the banks of the Drina River. Along came a Partisan contingent, took the Germans and the Ustaše from the rear, and helped the Mihailović forces to liquidate them. Once during the spring 1943 campaign in Montenegro, according to Mihailović sources, Peter Baćević gave similar assistance to a Partisan army in difficulty. Again, in the defense of Split in September 1943, followers of Tito and followers of Mihailović battled side by side for a week or more before fighting broke out between them. But instances of collaboration were the exception. On the whole, relations deteriorated progressively after November 1941.

As for the later stages of the civil war, the simple fact is that attacks and counterattacks were delivered on both sides. But the very nature of the Mihailović movement confined it to the defensive. The permanent militia, which numbered approximately 30,000 to 40,000, was never strong enough for major incursions into Partisan territory; the 150,000 to 200,000 peasants of the territorial militia were tied to their farms and not interested in staging expeditions into Croatia and Slovenia to reduce Partisan concentrations there. But when the Partisans attempted to invade their territory, it was a different matter. The villages mobilized and fought back.

The Partisan army, on the other hand, was a permanent force, its strength varying from 10,000 to 75,000 after the surrender of Italy. The Communist command was always extremely worried about its failure to achieve any hold on Serbia, because Serbia still remained the heart of Yugoslavia. The large forces of troops it repeatedly threw against this bastion of Mihailović strength were beaten back every time. Elsewhere in Yugoslavia, however, Tito massed his forces for successive drives against isolated Mihailović commands during 1943 and 1944. He ultimately obtained the upper hand in Lika, Montenegro, Herzegovina, and Bosnia.

The very nature of the Partisan army endowed it with an important advantage over the Mihailović army. As a permanent force composed of uprooted peasants and city proletarians, equally at home in all parts of Yugoslavia, it had no limits on its mobility. The Mihailović forces, on the other hand, fought heroically in defense of their own locales, but—like all territorial forces, such as the Continental army in the American Revolution—they were not easily persuaded to leave their lands and assist other units in difficulty. Although the Mihailović movement enjoyed a far more widespread popular influence than did the Partisan movement, the Partisans were generally able to outnumber them in battle simply because of the inability of the Mihailović command to concentrate its territorial units.

At least twice the superior mobility of the Partisan army saved it from possible extinction. In February 1942 it was driven from Montenegro by pro-Mihailović forces under the leadership of Pavle Djurišić. In a battle near Novi Pazar the Partisans were so decisively routed that, had Djurišić pursued them, he might have put an end there and then to the Partisan movement. Instead, when his Montenegrin peasants got to the Neretva River, they dropped the pursuit and returned to their farms, while the Partisans retreated into western Bosnia and there, unmolested, rebuilt their strength. Again, at the end of April 1943, when the Partisans invaded Montenegro, Lukačević met them near Konjic on the Neretva River and routed them in one of the bloodiest battles of the civil war. In this single engagement the Partisans, according to Mihailović intelligence, suffered some 4,000 casualties. Lukačević followed the retreating Partisans as far as Prozor, but his men were becoming restive, and there he gave up the pursuit. Regrouping their forces, the Partisans again attacked. This time they obtained the strategic advantage and defeated Lukačević badly.

By their own account the Partisans organized many full-scale offensives against the forces of Mihailović. Marshal Tito, in the brochure already quoted, describes his Montenegrin offensive thus:

> In addition, the High Command decided after the retreat across the Neretva river to undertake a major operation in pursuit of Draža Mihailović Četniks and to clear the vile henchmen of the invader out of Montenegro and Sandžak as well as Herzegovina.[7]

The fighting in Montenegro in the spring of 1943 was perhaps the most confused and bloody of the entire civil war. Moving their forces out of western Bosnia before the so-called fifth German offensive, the Partisans threw some 10,000 men against the Mihailović troops in Montenegro. Bloodily defeated in their first encounters with Lukačević at Konjic and Jablanica, the Partisans withdrew, regrouped, and attacked again. While all this was going on, the Axis moved six divisions—three German, two Italian, and one Ustaše—into position so that they surrounded the entire area.

So long as the Axis forces were not attacking, both Partisans and Mihailović units tried to peg their flanks and maneuver so as to take advantage of enemy movements. For fifteen bloody days the two Yugoslav factions battled each other along the Drina River between Goražde and Foča. During the first phase the Axis troops closed in and contentedly watched the two sides wear each other down. Then they moved in for the kill.

In the files of the British War Office there exists a memorandum dated June 3, 1943, which displays a remarkably astute understanding of Axis tactics at this stage of the civil war. Though unsigned, it was obviously written by someone at desk position in SOE Cairo, basing himself on intelligence received from the field. After the opening paragraph the report says:

> As a result of the German offensive which commenced in the early spring, the Partisans were driven south into the territory which we have always considered to be under the control of General Mihailović and his followers. This move on the part of the Germans was a clever one, as they knew that the Partisans had incurred the bitter hatred of the people in Montenegro and the Sandjak during the winter of 1941/42 when they were driven into this area, and it was certain therefore that whilst the Axis were attacking in the north, they could rely on the populace to oppose the entry of the Partisans into their territory.

> This, in fact, happened, and throwing the whole weight of their attack against a section of Mihailović's lines in order to escape, one portion of the Partisans succeeded in breaking through, while another portion went down south to the Northern Albanian frontier and yet another temporarily dispersed.

> . . . The result of this manoeuvre was to weaken both Mihailović's forces and the Partisans with a view to cleaning up finally both groups.[8]

First, the Axis forces surrounded a substantial Mihailović contingent at Kolašin and forced the surrender of Pavle Djurišić and some 3,000 troops. Virtually at the same time, they moved in and surrounded the Partisans on Mount Durmitor. For the Partisans this was one of the most desperate moments of the war. They fought with great heroism, but the ring of steel had closed around them so tightly that it seemed as though they were doomed.

Both the Home Army and the Partisans suffered disastrous losses in the Montenegrin fighting. The Partisans lost 5,000 men by their own admission—many more, according to Mihailović intelligence. Home Army units in Montenegro lost the better part of their permanent force. When the Partisans attacked Montenegro again later in the year—this time with British and American assistance—they managed to obtain the upper hand.

There is good evidence, even in their own official writings, that over the course of the entire war the Partisans did the bulk of their fighting not against the Germans or the Italians or the Ustaše but against the Mihailović forces. "In actual practice," said General Radoljub Čolaković, one of Tito's commanders, "more men fell on both sides in that fratricidal struggle begun by the Četniks in the service of the Germans, than in the struggle against the invaders and the Ustaše."

An interesting commentary on the final stages of the civil war is provided by P.I.C. Paper No. 53, entitled "A Brief Outline of the Position in Serbia 10 July 1944."[9] The paper says that the Partisans originally intended to fight their way into Serbia via the Ibar Valley. "British supplies," it said, "would then have been poured into Serbia and would have allowed them to consolidate their gains. This plan was frustrated by the failure of their two thrusts into Serbia in the winter of 1943 and the spring of 1944."

Let us pause to note that this sentence by itself provides an adequate answer to all those who defended the superior martial qualities of the Partisan army and those who held to the thesis that the Home Army ceased to exist as an effective military force after the battle of Neretva.

P.I.C. Paper No. 53 continues:

> British arms and supplies were, however, dropped on an effective scale to the Partisan detachments operating inside Serbia. These supplies have resulted in a marked local growth of Partisan strength and have meant that Partisan influence is being re-established from *within* Serbia, as a direct consequence of British support, and not from *outside*, through the liberating advance of the main Partisan forces. The consequence of this has been to raise British prestige in Serbia and to link the Serb Partisans more closely with the Western Allies rather than with the Russian armies in the East. The political implications of this as affecting the character of the new Yugoslavia which will emerge after the war are clear.

How tragically naïve were the conclusions reached by the writer of P.I.C. Paper No. 53 is demonstrated by the manner in which the war for Yugoslavia was actually concluded.

THE PARTISAN REGIME

It is an oversimplification to say that the Partisans were our Allies and that, ipso facto, those who attacked them were our enemies. After all, what is an enemy? An enemy is someone who incurs your hatred because he attempts to impose his rule on you or else, having imposed his rule, governs brutally. Accepting this definition, it is hardly surprising that the Serb peasants were sometimes inclined to regard the Partisans as their chief enemies, equally with the Germans and the Ustaše.

Whenever the Partisans entered a town, their first act was to set up a soviet and establish a commissar as local dictator. To terrorize the populace, they executed not only known members of the political opposition but even potential oppositionists. The British and American governments time and again received reports of the terroristic methods of the Partisans in the towns "liberated" by them.

The actual quislings were treated somewhat differently from the political opposition. In between the peasant who "collaborated" by giving a German soldier a drink of water and the mercenary who enlisted in the enemy forces, there were many degrees of "collaboration." When the Partisans entered a town, they would execute a few of the 100 percent collaborationists for appearances' sake. But in addition they would execute a substantial number of 5 and 10 and 15 percent collaborationists—people whose only crime was that they had done some small personal favor for enemy personnel. In the small villages every peasant knew to what degree his neighbors had been compromised with the Germans. When they saw these petty "collaborationists" being led away to execution, all the 75 and 90 and 100 percent collaborationists became panic-stricken. "If the Partisans can execute a man for merely offering food to a German soldier," reasoned the big-time collaborationist, "what chance do I stand when they find out about me?" The worst collaborators were generally the first to volunteer with the Partisans, and feeling themselves to be constantly under suspicion, they became, not very surprisingly, the most devoted and ruthless Partisans.

In the summer of 1944 an American OSS officer, Lieutenant Joe Veselinovich, who had emigrated to America as a boy some fifteen years before, found himself in the village of his birth, one of the many Serbian villages which had been included in Pavelić's Independent State of Croatia. He looked about him for familiar faces. Almost every male sported a red star on his cap. But there were no familiar faces, and all the voices he heard spoke with marked Croatian accents. The original Serb population—his friends, his relatives—had disappeared. Finally he discovered a group of old Serb women, among them his own aunt. She told him that the population of the village had been virtually exterminated during the Ustaše massacres, and that the Ustaše had brought in their own families and settled themselves on the lands of the murdered Serbs. She led him to a well that was full of the remains of Serbian children. On the way back his aunt nodded in the direction of a Partisan soldier.

"That man with the red star on his cap," she said, "is the man who murdered your uncle. The Ustaše come here and massacre us. Then the Partisans arrive, and the Ustaše put on red stars, and they become 'liberators.' "[10]

The Serb peasant hated the Partisans because of the terrible reprisals provoked by their activities. He hated them because they were accepting into their ranks the worst collaborators, including Ustaše officers. He hated them because of their brutal methods. That was why he considered the Partisans his enemies.

Captain Maurice Vitou who spent several weeks in the short-lived Čačak soviet in October 1941, gave this description of the regime:

> The town of Čačak was now under a new regime. A red flag with a five-pointed star was hoisted in the market place . . . We were given our liberty but were told that we must not leave the town without permission. House-to-house searches were conducted. Propaganda entertainment was enforced. The inhabitants told us that they were considerably better off when the town was under German occupation.[11]

In England and America it was called "liberation" when the Partisans momentarily occupied another Yugoslav town. In Yugoslavia they had another word for it.

"Many of those in America who criticized us for fighting the Partisans," said the followers of Mihailović, "would have done the same thing if they had been in our position. Suppose that America were occupied by an enemy power. Suppose that two resistance movements came into existence—one of them dominated by the Communist Party, the other one containing elements of the various other parties. Suppose that wherever the Communists went they insisted on imposing a miniature Soviet regime. Would Americans who were Republicans and Democrats and liberals and socialists accept such a regime in the interest of 'unity' against the enemy? Or would they fight against it? It is precisely this choice which confronted us."

PROGRAMMATIC SIMILARITIES AND DIFFERENCES

One of many mysteries surrounding Tito's takeover in Yugoslavia concerns the political snow job that Tito was able to do in selling his movement to the Western world as democratic and non-Communist.

Tito's Anti-Fascist Council of National Liberation held a number of conferences—there were youth conferences, women's conferences, Croat conferences, and so forth—before the Congress of Jajce in November 1943, at which it finally constituted itself a provisional government. All of these were conducted according to the traditional procedure of totalitarian parliaments. Resolutions were passed unanimously. Executives were elected unanimously. The opposition, if it did exist, manifested corpselike vitality. At the Congress of Jajce, Tito nominated Ivan Ribar as the president of the assembly. Ribar was elected unanimously. His motion that the congress confer the title "Marshal" on Tito was carried unanimously. The proceedings of these conferences were available to Allied intelligence and, therefore, to the press. Yet the story was given currency that the Partisan movement was a democratic, united-front movement politically controlled by moderate elements. Perhaps it was due to the zeitgeist.

Actually, between the enunciated program of the Council of National Liberation (Tito) and that of the Yugoslav Democratic National Committee (Mihailović) there was little visible difference. Tito shouted, "Long live our new democratic federal, prosperous Yugoslavia! . . . Death to fascism! Freedom to the people!" The National Congress convoked by Mihailović on January 26, 1944, declared in favor of "a democratically organized federal state" and proclaimed the need for "radical reforms . . . by which the fundamental principles of democracy will be applied not only to the political but also to the economic, social and cultural life of the nation."

The political regime within the Mihailović movement had many weaknesses, but in its favor it must be said that it always tolerated differences of opinion. In August 1941, four months after the Yugoslav capitulation, Mihailović set up a Central National Committee that embraced representatives of the various political parties. The Central National Committee continued to function throughout the occupation, concerning itself with a number of problems of postwar reconstruction. The committee was, however, hampered by lack of contact with the Yugoslav government in London, and also tardy in broadening its base and expanding its activities. Not until after Tito had set up a provisional government at the Congress of Jajce did the Central National Committee take steps to enlarge its authority by convoking a congress representing all parts of the country and all parties.

The National Congress convoked by the committee took place in the village of Ba near the mountain of Suvobor in Serbia, from January 25 to 28, 1944. It came to be called "the Congress of Saint Sava," after the saint with whose festival it coincided. Defying the Gestapo, 274 delegates attended the congress, many of them traveling for days across the mountains in order to reach Suvobor.

The congress witnessed a showdown between the die-hard pan-Serbs and other conservative elements, led by Dr. Dragiša Vasić and Dr. Stevan Moljević, and the more moderate elements then coming to the fore. During the earlier period Vasić and Moljević had played a dominant role in the Central

National Committee because they reflected the violent anti-Croat sentiment then prevalent among the Serbs. But by the time of the Congress of Saint Sava, feelings had subsided considerably on both sides. The Croats were beginning to come over to the resistance movement, while the Serbs were becoming increasingly aware of the need for collaboration with them. "It is well to be Serbs," said the moderate orators at the congress, "but we must also be Yugoslavs. What we must strive for is a new, federated Yugoslavia. What we must avoid is the domination by a centralized Belgrade Government which made Yugoslavia impossible in the past." After a lengthy debate the moderates won out. Živko Topalović, head of the Socialist Party of Yugoslavia, was elected president of the Central National Committee. Moljević was also elected to it, but he was no longer kingpin.

Despite the early prominence of Drs. Vasić and Moljević, the Mihailović movement from the beginning was strongly identified with the Serbian Agrarian Party, a liberal peasant party that had close ties with other peasant movements in Central Europe. Before the war Mihailović had served as army attaché in Sofia, where he established a very friendly relationship with Dr. George M. Dimitrov, the leader of the Bulgarian Agrarian Union. When he returned to Yugoslavia, Mihailović engaged in a continuing correspondence with Dr. Dimitrov, who regarded him as spiritually an agrarian.[12]

The program adopted by the congress made a general declaration in favor of democracy, came out for a federal state structure, and specified certain radical reforms. Its chief weakness was its defensive ideology. But if the decisions adopted suffered from vagueness on many points, they were certainly no more vague than those adopted by the Partisan congress at Jajce. While making it clear that they did not want to return to the bad political ways of the past, the participants in the congress at Ba were frankly and unanimously pro-monarchist—even for the consistently anti-monarchist Republicans the king had become the symbol of resistance to Tito. The Partisan conference, on the other hand, gave an augury of things to come in voting that the question of the monarchy should be submitted to a popular referendum.

Apart from this, there was only one vital difference between the program adopted by the Partisans at Jajce and that adopted by the Mihailović congress at Ba. The Mihailović resolution envisaged a Yugoslavia divided into three federal units: Serbia, Croatia, and Slovenia. The "Serbia" referred to was a Greater Serbia combining the four predominantly Serb provinces of Serbia, Montenegro, Bosnia, and Herzegovina with the Macedonian areas in the south. The Partisan resolution, on the other hand, envisaged a federal Yugoslavia in which Serbia, Montenegro, Bosnia, Herzegovina, and Macedonia would be included as separate units.

The Partisan position was obviously calculated to break up the Serb influence and to allay the fears of the Croats. In the projected federal state structure Croatia was to be the largest single unit. Though by its very nature highly acceptable to the Croats, the proposal had little to recommend it to the Serbs. The Bosnian, Herzegovinian, and Montenegrin Serbs share a common culture with the Serbs of Serbia proper; the regional differences between them are no greater than those found among that most variegated and most united of all peoples, the British. No matter what part of Yugoslavia they were found in, there has always been a strong desire for unity among the Serbs.

On the other hand, it is far from certain that the Bosnian and Montenegrin peoples would have welcomed a strongly centralized Belgrade administration. Their interwar experience had inclined them to be suspicious of Belgrade politicians, and they had reverted in defense to their old local loyalties. The average Bosnian peasant, for example, owed his chief loyalty to the village in which he lived. Next he was a Bosnian Serb. Next he was a Serb. And at a much more remote distance, he thought of himself as a Yugoslav. At the same time that he wished to be associated with the Serb people, he desired at least some regional autonomy. His desires, however, corresponded far more closely to the Mihailović concept of a federal Yugoslavia than to the Partisan concept. If it had been possible, within the proposed Serb federal unit, to arrange for a degree of autonomy in certain regional matters, such an arrangement would have met both the desires and the fears of the Bosnians and Montenegrins.

As for the Macedonians, the problem was admittedly complicated by the extensive interpenetration of Serb and Macedonian areas. The Macedonian peasants harbored a deep resentment against Belgrade and its several attempts to Serbify them, and they were hardly enthusiastic at the prospect of inclusion in a federal Greater Serbia. On this one point the Tito program was perhaps superior to the Mihailović program.

And so the Yugoslav resistance movement was divided down the middle, with both sides laying claim to remarkably similar programs. The difficulty in knowing whom to believe embraced much besides political programs. As Lt. Colonel Linn M. Farish, chief of the American mission to Tito, said in a report submitted to OSS in June 1944:

> Both sides proclaim as their aim a Free, United, and Democratic Yugoslavia with a form of government determined by a free electorate of the people after the country has been freed of the occupier. Both sides tell the people that the other side is not sincere. The Četniks say, and undoubtedly believe, that the aim of the Partisans is to force the indoctrinated communism of a minority on all the

people. The Partisans say that the Četniks are fighting to return the government of a few, which they claim is corrupt, fascist and dictatorial. At the same time, as stated above, both sides proclaim almost identical aims for the future of Yugoslavia.

Both sides attribute to the other the lack of effective resistance to the Germans. The Partisans say that they were betrayed by elements of the Government which are now included in the government-in-exile and the forces of General Mihailović. The Četniks claim that the Communists, many of whom are now the leaders of the Partisans, particularly the Croats, committed acts of sabotage and prevented the effective mobilization of the Yugoslav Army.

Both sides claim that they have been attacked by the other in collaboration with the Germans and will cite time and places as evidence.

Both sides claim that they have not been supported by the Allies, and that in order to fight the enemy they have had to first face arms in the hands of traitorous countrymen placed there by the Allies.

Both sides believe that their first enemy is the other, with the Germans and Bulgarians second.[13]

The political character of an organization is not determined by its paper program alone—least of all, probably, in circumstances such as those which existed in Yugoslavia. In attempting an assessment, it is more important to compare internal regimes, to determine the governing ideologies, and finally to weigh the ultimate motivations of those who stand at the helm.

The congress of Ba on January 25–28, 1944, may have come a bit late because old loyalties and habits invariably die hard, but the remarkable thing is that it came at all. The congress was, in effect, an effort to provide the movement with an in-country political authority as an alternative to the government in exile in London.

There was no British observer at the Ba congress, because SOE Cairo instructed the BLOs still in Yugoslavia that they were to have nothing to do with it. Fortunately, Captain George Musulin of the American mission was under no such restraint from OSS, and it is thanks to his attendance that the Free World possesses an objective account of what transpired. The Foreign Office received an account of the congress and the program adopted by it from Živko Topalović of the Yugoslav Socialist Party, who had been elected president of the Central National Committee. Topalović also wrote letters to Labour members of the British War Cabinet who had been his colleagues in the Socialist International. But, as the Foreign Office records reveal, there was no acknowledgment and no reply, as a matter of deliberate policy.

The Gestapo did not find out about the congress at Ba until after it had dispersed. Angered that such an assembly should have taken place under its very nose, the Gestapo staged mass arrests in many centers—over 500 in Belgrade alone—in order to get at its organizers. But the Partisans sought to denigrate the congress by charging that all the delegates had traveled with visas issued by the Gestapo.

9

Accommodations with the Italians

Mihailović's position was further bedeviled by the contentious issue of accommodations with the Italians, which was easy enough to understand but somewhat more difficult to explain.

Certain peripheral Mihailović commanders did enter into accommodations with the Italians fairly early in the war. They did so under the immediate impact of the terrible massacres of the Serbian population in the so-called Independent State of Croatia in the summer and autumn of 1941. Whereas the Germans gave carte blanche to the Croatian Ustaše and even instigated the killings of the Serb population, the Italians in their own area of occupation adjoining Croatia gave refuge to Serbs fleeing from the Ustaše, fed them, provided them with weapons for self-defense, and even disarmed and executed some Ustaše troops caught in the act of massacring Serbs. I have spoken with one former Italian officer, Professor Salvatore Loi, whose commander attached him, in civilian clothes, to a Serbian nationalist resistance organization in Lika that engaged the Ustaše in numerous fierce encounters. According to Professor Loi, tens of thousands of Serbs and Jews and even a few bands of Gypsies who fled from the Ustaše were able to find refuge in the Italian zone of occupation. Indeed, at an early stage in the massacres Italian troops actually marched into the southern zone of Pavelić's Croatia to put an end to the bloodshed.[1]

The Italians had their own private motivations for defending the Serbs. Underneath the pompous declarations about the complete unity of purpose of the Axis powers there existed a bitter rivalry between the Germans and the Italians in Yugoslavia. Because Mussolini had originally planned to convert the Independent State of Croatia into an Italian satellite, he had given early support to the Ustaše movement. Instead, the Germans were able to elbow out the Italians and convert Croatia into a vassal of Germany.

The Germans sought to strengthen their hold and enlarge their sphere by encouraging the expansion of the Independent State of Croatia. This the Italians resisted. The underhanded rivalry found the Germans disposed to back the Croats against the Serbs and the Italians inclined to back the Serbs against the Croats. But in fairness to the Italians it must be said that many of them were genuinely horrified by the bestiality of the Ustaše. (The gas chambers of Auschwitz were, after all, an invention peculiar to the Nazi genius.) In the circumstances, it was only natural that the Serbs should have regarded the Italians and the Germans differently.

While the battle against the Ustaše was in full swing, the civil war with the Partisans broke out. The Serbian peasant masses, many of whom had experienced the terror of temporary Communist rule, were inclined to regard the Communists not as liberators but as enemies to be opposed equally with the Germans and the Ustaše. Local Mihailović commanders, confronted with this complex of enemies, were disposed to reason that if the Italians, for their own private reasons, sought an armistice with them and were willing to provide food and arms in return, then there was nothing morally wrong with such an arrangement. As they saw it, what was at stake was the survival of their people and the prevention of a Communist takeover.

In certain regions the terror imposed by the Partisan commissars played a large part in inducing the peasants to accept arms from the Italians, whom they really hated as invaders. In Montenegro, for example, the Communists had always had a strong following, even before the war, and won new prestige for themselves by participating in the uprising of July 1941, which temporarily liberated the better part of Montenegro. After the July uprising, in fact, they were one of the few strong parties in Montenegro. And yet the Partisans, by their own admission, were driven out of Montenegro in February 1942.

They claimed that they were driven out by Italian arms. But they did not deny that these Italian arms were wielded by Montenegrin peasants. In one place Tito explained that the Mihailović officers "compelled the people by terror" to take arms from the Italians in order to fight against "the forces of liberation."[2] He admitted further that Bajo Stanišić, one of Mihailović's commanders, "succeeded in bringing a considerable number of guerrillas under his influence and transforming them into Četniks," and that "in Vasojevići, Djurišić succeeded in mobilizing fairly strong forces and equipped them with Italian arms."[3]

"The peasants of Montenegro had no love for the Italians," Montenegrin nationalists have told me. "There was always a great sympathy for communism in Montenegro, especially after the July revolt. If, despite all this, the Montenegrin people accepted Italian arms in order to drive out the Partisans, then it is up to the Partisans to explain how this change in attitude came about. They cannot complain of propaganda, because as propagandists they far surpassed any of their enemies. And the argument that within six months of the great rebellion the Montenegrin people could be induced to fight for the Axis against their own will is so feeble that it defeats itself. Our own explanation is that the regime of the Partisan commissars not only instituted no social reforms, but was infinitely more ruthless than the Italian regime had ever been. All those who opposed them, whether they were fascists or Montenegrin patriots, were sent before the firing squad. And even those who had not opposed them but were considered potential opponents were liquidated by way of precaution.''

The accommodations that existed varied in scope and quality from one locality to another. Although Mihailović was never involved in these accommodations—there is much evidence that he found them distasteful—for a period of time he tacitly accepted them so long as the officers in question did not subordinate themselves to Italian command. However, certain commanders of Četnik units that nominally accepted Mihailović's authority, but over which he had in practice very little control, did cross the line from "accommodations" to subordination. Several of them were repudiated by Mihailović because of this.

An entire historical literature has grown up in Italy on the subject of the accommodations between the Italian forces and the local Mihailović units. Not very surprisingly, the Italian officers argued that they were using the Mihailović followers—who, in turn, were convinced that they were using the Italians.

A vital commentary on this tortured situation is contained in Hitler's letter to Mussolini of February 16, 1943, which Ribbentrop personally delivered when he visited Rome toward the end of February 1943. Here are a few excerpts from this letter:

> The situation in the Balkans, Duce, preoccupies me greatly. However useful it might seem to play opposing factions off against one another, I hold it to be extremely perilous as long as the parties involved . . . agree unconditionally on one point: their limitless hatred of Italy and Germany . . . I detect a special danger, Duce, . . . in the way the Mihailović movement has been developing. The great mass of the coordinated and trustworthy data in my possession reveals clearly that this movement, which is ably organized and energetically directed from the political point of view, awaits only the moment in which it can turn against us . . . Mihailović seeks to obtain the arms and supplies for the execution of these plans by pretending to assist your troops . . . My conscience bids me, Duce, to put you on your guard against the further prosecution of such a policy . . .
>
> In the interests of our common aims I consider it desirable that your Second Army regard Mihailović and his movement as uncompromising enemies of the

Axis powers and I ask you, Duce, to give orders to this end to your higher commanders . . . [It] is essential that the furnishing of arms and supplies to his forces stop immediately . . . [It] will be necessary to disarm his units [and] to eliminate resistance . . . through determined concentric attacks . . . If this is not done, Duce, if the Communists and Četniks are not disarmed . . . a revolt will certainly break out in the case of an [Anglo-American] invasion . . . I believe, Duce, that there are obligations of which one cannot relieve oneself through political shrewdness but only through the full commitment of one's forces . . . The correctness of my views is amply confirmed by the incontrovertible evidence resulting from our surveillance of telegraphic and radio traffic.[4]

On March 9 Mussolini replied to Hitler's letter of February 16 in these terms:

We are fully in agreement that both Četniks and Partisans are enemies of the Axis and that tomorrow, in case of a landing [of the Allies] would make common front against us . . . General of the Army Pirzio Biroli has been charged with working out a coordinated agreement with the German High Command concerning future actions to be taken in respect to the movement of General Mihailović who, irrespective of whether he is treated as a traitor in the transmissions of the Partisan radio, is in any case our enemy by reason of his being the Minister of War of the Yugoslav Government in London.[5]

Hitler's letter to Mussolini followed almost immediately after General Gehlen's top-secret report of February 9, in which, as chief of Nazi intelligence for eastern Europe, he credited the Mihailović movement with having the support of 80 percent of the Serbian population. The letter preceded by roughly a month the series of high-level meetings between the Germans and the Partisans described in subsequent pages. These, in turn, preceded by less than three months the first urgent representations by Captain Deakin charging the Mihailović movement with collaboration and, implicitly but unmistakably, calling for its abandonment.

Colonel Hudson, as the first British officer with Mihailović, knew a good deal about the accommodations with the Italians from his observations, and he sent out a series of messages dealing with this matter. His reports were objective, but he was not, by background, a political analyst, and as we have pointed out, the situation confronting him was without precedent or analogue in the history of warfare. Through no fault of his own, therefore, Hudson's reports failed to convey the enormous political complexity of the situation. Unfortunately, they lent themselves to disinformation by the judicious selection of paragraphs. In 1944 when he got back to Cairo, he was infuriated by the manner in which SOE had edited some of his reports.[6]

On August 8, 1942, the Soviet ambassador to London had given Foreign Secretary Anthony Eden a document listing cases of alleged collaboration by

the Mihailović forces with the Italians during the course of 1942. Hudson's
reports appeared to confirm these allegations, at least in part. For Eden, who
had a particular contempt for the Mussolini regime, this raised some serious
questions about the Mihailović movement. He was disposed to agree with
his principal aides on Yugoslavia—Sir Alexander Cadogan, the permanent
undersecretary of state for foreign affairs; Sir Orme Sargent, Cadogan's deputy; and Sir Douglas Howard, the head of the Southern Department—that it
was in Britain's long-term interest to support Mihailović. However, Eden's
entries in the Foreign Office files make it clear that he disliked the idea of
any arrangement with the Italians for any purpose.

THE INCIDENT OF "THE SPEECH"

In March 1943 Colonel Bailey reported to the British government, through
SOE Cairo, on a speech that Mihailović supposedly made in his presence.
The report created a first-rate crisis in the relations between the British and
the Yugoslav governments. Prime Minister Churchill addressed a lengthy
communication to Premier Jovanović, in which he reproduced Bailey's report
on the speech:

> In the course of this speech, General Mihailović said that the Serbs were now
> completely friendless, that the English, to suit their own strategic ends, were
> urging them to undertake operations without the slightest intention of helping
> them either now or in the future, and that the English were now fighting to the
> last Serb in Yugoslavia. He continued that the English were trying to purchase
> Serbian blood at the cost of an insignificant supply of arms, but that he would
> never be a party to this 'shameful commerce typical of English traditional per-
> fidy.' Far from being guests, the Yugoslav King and Government were virtual
> prisoners of the English. They were forgotten and confined by His Majesty's
> Government who shamelessly violated Yugoslav sovereignty by negotiating di-
> rect with the Soviet Government on internal Yugoslav problems. The B.B.C.,
> with revolting cynicism, had dropped its support for the sacred Serbian cause.
> The Allies' lust for fraud was satisfied by the untimely, hypocritical, and anti-
> Yugoslav activities of the Partisans—but let the Allies realize that nothing they
> could do or threaten could turn the Serbs from their avowed and sacred duty of
> exterminating the Partisans. As long as the Italians remained his sole adequate
> source of benefit and assurance generally, nothing the Allies could do would
> make him change his attitude towards them. His enemies were the Partisans, the
> Ustaše, the Moslems, and the Croats. When he had dealt with them, he would
> turn to the Germans and the Italians. In conclusion, he said that he needed no
> further contact with the Western democracies, whose sole aim was to win the
> war at the expense of others.[7]

There followed a voluminous correspondence between the British government, the Yugoslav government, and General Mihailović on the subject of this speech. The Yugoslav government informed Mihailović by letter that the views imputed to him conformed to those of neither the British nor the Yugoslav governments. Mihailović in reply did not deny that he had used some strong words about the British in the presence of Colonel Bailey, but he insisted that certain portions of his speech had been inaccurately reported. He denied point-blank the statement attributed to him that the Italians were his "sole source of benefit." His wire said:

> It is not in the least necessary to emphasize that my only enemy is the Axis. I avoid battle with the communists in the country, and fight only when attacked. I am ready to establish the closest and most sincere co-operation with the British Supreme Command in the Middle East, and it is through no fault of mine that this co-operation has not already been established. Colonel Bailey has been with my staff for many months now, but the British Command has taken no special steps in regard to this, even though Colonel Bailey has stressed a number of times that he was waiting for instructions on this matter . . . I consider all inference that co-operation with the Italians must cease, and that there should be no contact or co-operation with former General Nedic to be superfluous, since I have repudiated with contempt all attempts at such co-operation.[8]

Though the British government seemed to have accepted the general's explanation in part, the incident unquestionably damaged relations and helped to provoke bitter recriminations in May and June of that year. Indeed, from that point on, the whole of 1943 was characterized by one crisis after another.

In Churchill's staunch old imperialist eyes, Britain's virtue was above all suspicion. The tone of his letters to the Yugoslav government on the subject of the speech, their length, and their insistence all suggest that he was stung to the quick by the audacity of this Balkan underling who had dared to speak of "Britain's perfidy" and suggested that Britain was attempting to use other peoples to promote her own interests.

It is altogether tragic that what was in itself an incident of third-rate importance should have been magnified out of all proportion by misunderstandings and by the intensity of personal feelings. Certainly, the Foreign Office's violent reaction to this report bore no relation to the intentions of the British mission in submitting it or to their own estimate of its importance. Unfortunately, in forwarding their account of the speech, it was difficult for Colonels Bailey and Hudson to provide the Foreign Office with a proper conception of the context in which it was delivered.

Mihailović made the speech in question on February 28, 1943, while officiating at the baptism of a peasant child in the Montenegrin town of

Lipovo, after his patience had been worn thin by two months of vexations and provocations since the arrival of Colonel Bailey on Christmas Day, 1942. The aid which the British mission had repeatedly promised was still a trickle. Of the scores of Yugoslav army officers waiting in Cairo to be parachuted into Mihailović's territory, only a bare half-dozen had been delivered. Colonel Bailey had brought with him demands for actions and more actions—and this despite the very heavy reprisals of September–December 1942. And now BBC was beginning to promote the cause of the Partisans. Ordinarily a man of considerable restraint, Mihailović had let his vexation accumulate to the bursting point. The baptism of the peasant child triggered the inevitable explosion.

That the speech was a momentary outburst of wrath and that Mihailović said a number of things he did not really mean was appreciated by both Colonel Bailey and Colonel Hudson. Indeed, its vehemence only indicated the familial intimacy with which Mihailović regarded Britain. Had he really been anti-British in the fundamental sense that Tito was, he never would have permitted himself the luxury of such an outburst. The Foreign Office, unfortunately, did not display a familial understanding of Mihailović's intemperance.

Bailey and Hudson knew the Serbian language well and would have had no reason to distort Mihailović's speech deliberately. There is, however, reason to believe that their report on it was inaccurate on several points. This is not very surprising, considering that the report was composed from memory some time after the event, that slivovitz (Serbian plum brandy) was freely available at the baptism, and that both Hudson and Bailey, in the spirit of the occasion, had imbibed freely. Mihailović also imbibed, but by all accounts he was, by both British and Serbian standards, an abstemious to moderate drinker.

Obviously, a few slight modifications in emphasis could have completely altered the significance of this speech. One of Mihailović's chief advisers, Colonel Mladen Žujović, who claims to have immediately written an aide-mémoire of the speech as he recalled it, had the general making some very strong remarks about the British, but his version was nowhere near as explosive as that of the BLOs.[9]

It is easy to understand how James Klugmann and the other pro-Tito elements in SOE Cairo and in British intelligence were able to use the speech to promote the growing official antagonism toward Mihailović. It is easy also to understand Churchill's personal resentment. But even if Mihailović had said all that he was reported to have said, it still is not easy to understand how those in charge of British policy could have been led to the conclusion that they must abandon Mihailović and turn Yugoslavia over to communism.

Eden might conceivably have acted a bit more tolerantly if more had been known at the time about the murderous record of the "Soviet republics" established temporarily in Montenegro and other areas, or about the Ustaše massacres and the role of the Italians in protecting the Serbs from the Ustaše. And it might also have thrown a different light on the situation if British intelligence had provided Eden with copies of some of the exchanges between Hitler and Mussolini on the subject of Mihailović in early 1943. It was clear, however, from Eden's attitude that in this one area British intelligence failed to produce.

The Serbian peasants in the areas occupied by the Italians were struggling for physical survival. They were disposed to look upon the Italians as the least of the three evils they had to contend with—all the more so because the Allied victory, in which they believed implicitly, would put an end to the Italian evil, but an Allied victory could not reverse the consequences of the Ustaše massacres or save them from a Communist dictatorship once it was established. They were "accommodating" with the Italians while fighting vigorously against their major enemies, the Ustaše and the Communists, and conducting some quiet sabotage against the Axis war machine. Some Mihailović commanders likened their accommodations with the Italians to Churchill's historic "accommodation" with the Soviet Union at the time of Hitler's invasion.

On one occasion when Churchill was asked to explain how he could reconcile his military embrace of the Soviet Union with his bitter hostility toward Bolshevism over the years, he replied in approximately these words: "If I were locked in mortal combat with a tiger, and a crocodile came along and bit the leg of the tiger, I should welcome the assistance of the crocodile—even though I have no love for crocodiles." Rightly or wrongly, this is also how some of the peripheral Mihailović commanders in Bosnia, Montenegro, and Herzegovina viewed the situation. But again, it must be emphasized that, with rare exceptions, this situation did not exist in Serbia proper, which was the principal bastion of the Mihailović movement.

Using Churchill's wartime policy vis-à-vis the Soviet Union as a justification for the peripheral Mihailović forces' accommodations with the Italians no doubt has some validity. Instances of accommodation, however, even when justifiable on political grounds, can easily merge into a semblance of collaboration. As followers of Mihailović themselves conceded, certain independent Četnik formations—or formations that invoked his name and called themselves Četniks—over which Mihailović had very little control did carry their accommodations with the Italians to the point where the matter of collaboration called for evaluation. Some of the collaborators were repudiated; but just as it is difficult at this late date to evaluate every instance of accommodation in the light of the motivation and the total military record of the "accommodators," it was sometimes exceedingly difficult for Mihailović to make judgments at a distance about commanders who had entered into accommodations with the Italians to protect their people against both the Communists and the Ustaše.

To be fair to Mihailović, it is important to note that the British officers under whose supervision he functioned did not impose a blanket prohibition on contact with the Italians. Peter Boughey, who was in charge of the SOE Yugoslav operation in London, put the matter this way in a conversation with Nora Beloff: "We certainly told Mihailović to be in touch with the Italians. We knew the situation in Montenegro and wanted him to be able to get Italian weapons when the Italians withdrew, collapsed, or surrendered." [10]

Alas, the plans of Mihailović and of SOE London were completely frustrated by the machinations of SOE Cairo. Later in this book we tell the story of how the Mihailović forces, after overcoming a large body of Germans, took the surrender of Italy's entire Venezia Division at Berane on September 13, 1943. The Mihailović officers quite naturally anticipated that in taking the surrender of the Venezia Division, they would take possession of the division's vast quantities of weapons and ammunition. But at this point SOE intervened by instructing Bailey that the Venezia Division was to be placed under Allied command—thus preventing its disarmament. A few days later a large force of Partisans entered the scene and drove off the loyalists, thus depriving Mihailović of a supply of arms that would have surpassed by far the total amount dropped to him by SOE throughout the war. What is clear from the communications quoted in a later chapter is that Bailey had no sympathy for the SOE directive, and he did not hesitate to state as much in subsequent exchanges with Cairo.

Mihailović's difficulties in making judgments at a distance on the matter of collaboration were compounded by the existence of so-called "Četnik" units, replete with the royal insignia on their hats, that owed no allegiance at all to him. Units of these false Četniks had, in fact, been organized by the Germans for frankly collaborationist purposes.

Let me illustrate some of the difficulties that confronted Mihailović by telling the stories of Dobrosav Jevdjević and Pop (Reverend) Momčilo Djujić.

Dobrosav Jevdjević was an able and ambitious lawyer from Nevesinje. As a man, he was a strange mixture of humanitarianism and ruthlessness, patriotism and opportunism. During the Ustaše massacres he raised a Četnik unit and made numerous incursions into Ustaše territory, rescuing many thousands of Serbs. As a result of the poor crop of 1942, famine was threatening in Herzegovina. Jevdjević, who until that time had made his accommodations at a distance, approached the Italians and offered to raise an anti-Communist militia under their command if they would undertake to send in enough food to avert famine. The Italians accepted the offer.

At first Jevdjević enjoyed an enormous popularity with the Serbian peasantry of Herzegovina. The food imported by the Italians in consequence of the agreement is generally credited with having saved some 100,000 lives. As for the Communists, there were very few peasants in Herzegovina, even among the anti-Italian Croats, who had not been antagonized by their methods and were not agreed on the need for combating them. But having placed himself at the complete disposal of the Italians, Jevdjević found himself caught in a quagmire into which he sank ever deeper. When the Italians collapsed, he had already lost much of his popularity, and afterward there was nothing he could do but retreat to Slovenia, where he entered into open collaboration with the Germans.

Mihailović recognized Jevdjević for a period of time but repudiated him completely in mid-1943, when reports about the scope and nature of his collaboration had been confirmed by headquarters. Jevdjević, however, was an incorrigible impostor who attempted to combine his subservience to the Italians with the aura that surrounded a commander of Mihailović's. After one particularly provocative incident, Mihailović informed Jevdjević in a note that if in the future Jevdjević even hinted that he enjoyed the authority of the Yugoslav Home Army, Mihailović would personally see to it that he was killed.

In early 1943 Jevdjević was awarded the Karadjordjević Star for his services during the Ustaše massacres. The award was never gazetted, because in the interim a communication had been received from Mihailović confirming the reports of Jevdjević's agreement with the Italians.

In the closing months of 1944 Mihailović also repudiated his commander in the Lika area, north of Split, a young Orthodox priest by the name of Pop Momčilo Djujić, who did not hesitate to accept Italian aid in defending his people from Communist incursions. When Mihailović sought to bring Djujić in for court-martial, the action divided his movement. The majority supported it, but a significant minority objected on the grounds that Mihailović was being too puritanical. Djujić was a man of charisma and great personal courage who always led his men into battle—primarily against the Ustaše and the Partisans but occasionally against the Italians, for whom he had no love.

In the closing months of the war Djujić had combined his forces with those of Jevdjević in a desperate and successful effort to fight their way through to Trieste before the Partisans closed in on them. Once they got to Italy, however, both of them went into hiding out of fear that the British would hand them back to the Tito government.

I had been greatly impressed by the account of Nedelko Plećaš, a Yugoslav operative who was dropped into Djujić's territory in 1942 and who later wrote a history of his experiences that was considered useful and objective even by unshakable supporters of Tito such as Elisabeth Barker.[11] I had also discussed his case with other Mihailović officers and political figures. There was general agreement that despite their temporary "marriage of convenience," Djujić could not be equated with Jevdjević, and that it would be a blessing if the two could be separated.

In September 1946 I managed to arrange a visit with Pop Djujić at the hiding place he shared with Jevdjević in the mountains south of Naples, Italy. This I did with the aid of Mane Vukobratović, one of the younger leaders of the Serbian Agrarian Party. We were picked up by two of Djujić's bodyguards at a restaurant in the suburbs of Naples and driven to the hiding place.

Djujić was the first to come out to meet us. I managed to say to him that his case had been greatly complicated by his association with Jevdjević, and I urged him, in his own interest, and that of his movement, to arrange for a separation. At this point Jevdjević came striding down a hill from the house he apparently shared with Djujić. Meeting him immediately confirmed the strongly negative opinion I had already formed on the basis of numerous conversations. He had the appearance of a zealot or madman, and he introduced himself to me with these words: "I am Jevdjević. I collaborated—against communism I would collaborate with the devil himself!"

Djujić emigrated to the United States. He subsequently broke with Jevdjević, apparently for personal reasons. Whether my brief intervention in the situation had anything to do with the break, I do not know.

In 1945, retreating up through Gorizia with the Partisans in full pursuit, Djujić picked up a number of American airmen who had been shot down. One of them, Lieutenant Joseph T. Harmuth, later deposed that during the final weeks of the war, despite repeated Partisan attacks, he had seen Djujić's followers clash several times with the Germans, and that with his own eyes he had counted some seventy German dead after one of these encounters.

That Djujić made accommodations with the Italians and that he sometimes fought the Partisans while they were engaged with the Germans and Italians, there can be no doubt. But neither can there be any doubt that at various times, right up until the last weeks of the war, he fought against Italians, Germans, and Ustaše; nor that while he was so engaged, the Partisans frequently attacked him on the flank or sent expeditions against his villages.

Whatever the final judgment on Djujić must be, however, his case illustrates how complicated was the mosaic of the civil war, and how difficult it sometimes can be to decide whether a man was a traitor or a patriot.

Another case in point is that of Mihailović's commander in Montenegro. Pavle Djurišić, a courageous and charismatic figure, had played a heroic role in the Montenegrin uprising of July 1941 in which the Montenegrin Serb nationalists, then coming under Mihailović's influence, had collaborated with the Communists. Within a matter of several months, however, the Montenegrin peasants, who were initially inclined to be pro-Communist out of respect for the heroism displayed by the Partisans, had turned violently anti-Partisan as a result of their personal experience with Communist rule. At this point Djurišić organized and commanded a massive offensive that drove the Partisans pell-mell from the mountains of Montenegro. Although the fighting in this offensive was done almost exclusively by the nationalist peasantry of Montenegro, there is no question that the Italians gave Djurišić weapons and ammunition, and on occasion transportation for his troops.

In the German offensive in the spring of 1943, Djurišić and several thousand of his followers were surrounded at Kolašin and forced to surrender, then taken to Austria as prisoners of war. In August 1943, Djurišić and a number of his colleagues escaped from the POW camp. After swimming the Danube, Djurišić made his way back to Mihailović's headquarters and then returned to Montenegro. In early 1945 he sought to lead some thousands of his men through Ustaše-dominated territory to Italy. It was his hope that the Ustaše, with the war obviously drawing to a close, would be willing to forget their ancient enmity with the Serbs, at least to the extent of granting a laissez-passer. Instead, his men were taken prisoner and disarmed, and he himself was executed the following day. According to widely believed reports, he was burned alive.[12]

At the end of July 1944, Djurišić had rescued some American airmen, who retreated with his forces for more than six months Finally, they were handed over to Mihailović, who in turn handed them over to the Partisans because this was the only way of evacuating them. This dramatic incident is related in the book *Eight Bailed Out*.[13]

As I have indicated, there is absolutely no question that Djurišić accepted assistance from the Italians to rid Montenegro of the Communists, and that as far as the Italians were concerned his movement enjoyed pro forma legality. The question must be asked, in his case as in others, whether men who value freedom would not have acted as Djurišić and his comrades did, first, in seeking to protect the Serbian people from the Ustaše massacres—even in collaboration with the Italians—and whether, at a later date, they would not have accepted Italian assistance in resisting the imposition of the regime of Communist terror.

In the early communications from Colonel Bailey one has the impression that he was of two minds about the relations between the Italians and several of Mihailović's commanders. In a message to SOE on April 6, 1943, he said:

> Djurišić, Baćević and Lukačević, all young officers, have distinguished themselves in the fighting [against the Partisans]. The first and last named are known

to us as excellent leaders with no serious drawbacks save their intransigent anti-Partisan attitude. We can expect vigorous action against Axis from them after Partisans are liquidated. They have satisfactory views on all internal problems and if their repeated successes strengthen their position in Mihailović's organisation we shall benefit considerably.[14]

THE ROLE PLAYED BY ITALIAN DEFEATISM

The frankly defeatist attitude of many of the Italians in Dalmatia was another factor in the calculations of the Mihailović officers who accommodated with them. The Italians had fared so badly in Greece that the spirit of defeat had got into their very bones. When the German army bogged down and was thrown back before Moscow, and when America was brought into the war by the attack on Pearl Harbor, they gave up all hope of an Axis victory.

During the latter part of the occupation the story was told of a conversation between a Dalmatian Serb of ninety-four years and two Italian officers. The officers had sat down at his table in a restaurant, and after the preliminary exchanges one of them asked him what he thought of the war. The venerable Serb thought for a while, his brows knitted. "I have heard there is a war going on," he said, "but I am an old man and my eyes no longer permit me to read. The world, moreover, is very complicated, and it is hard for an old man with a poor memory to know what is happening or who is fighting whom. I have heard that you Italians are involved in the war—you may correct me if this is not so. I do not know with whom you are fighting or against whom, and I therefore venture no opinion. But from what I have learned of history—forgive me if I am suggesting something which you already know—one thing can safely be predicted: if you are not fighting on the side of England, then you will not win the war."

The Italians laughed uproariously at the cunning of the old man, and that night, amid more laughter, they repeated the story in their mess. Soon it had spread all over Dalmatia.

When news of the Allied invasion of Italy reached Dalmatia, there were towns where the Italians demonstrated in the streets shouting, "Hurrah! The Anglo-Americans have invaded!" To them it meant the beginning of the end of a war for which they had lost all taste.

The defeatism that afflicted most of the Italian occupation troops in Yugoslavia also made it easier for the Serbs to enter into accommodations with them—not to prop up the Italian occupation but to save lives while working for the liberation of Yugoslavia.

C H A P T E R

10

The Question of Inactivity

Another charge made against Mihailović during the year preceding his abandonment is that his forces were inactive while the Partisans were engaging
in major activities. This charge, too, as a variant on the charge of collaboration, played a major role in his downfall.

Shortly after the German occupation of Yugoslavia in 1941, both Serbia
and Montenegro were swept by mighty national uprisings, which forced the
Germans and Italians out of all but the major centers. The Axis forces responded with massive reprisals, destroying hundreds of villages and executing thousands of Serbs. In these uprisings both the followers of Mihailović
and the Communists had been actively involved. In the early stages they
frequently fought shoulder to shoulder. But strains developed when it became
apparent that the Partisans were moving toward the establishment of a Communist regime, and a series of initial clashes finally evolved into full-scale
civil war.

At the close of 1941 the battered remnants of the Partisan forces withdrew from Serbia into Bosnia, where during the course of 1942 they were
able to reconstitute themselves and continue their resistance. Mihailović reacted differently after the crushing of the Montenegrin and Serbian uprisings.
In essence, he reverted to the policy that was being followed by the resistance movements in France, Poland, Norway, and the Low Countries: to lie
low, to harass the occupier with passive resistance, sabotage, and small guerrilla activities, but to avoid large-scale conflict while seeking to build up their
forces in preparation for a nationwide uprising at the appropriate moment. In
the early stages of the resistance Mihailović received precise instructions to
this effect from the Yugoslav government in exile in London. This policy, it
should be noted, had the backing of the British and the Americans: indeed,
no responsible British or American leader ever questioned the wisdom of

such a policy for any of the resistance movements in occupied Europe—
except Yugoslavia's.

Those responsible for the conduct of British policy seem to have reasoned that if the Partisans could engage in large-scale activities against the
Axis in parts of Bosnia, Croatia, and Slovenia during 1942, there was no
reason why the Mihailović forces could not engage in activities on a similar
scale in those areas of Yugoslavia where they were dominant. This simplistic
approach to the Yugoslav situation apparently came to be shared during the
course of 1943 by the chiefs of staff, the Foreign Office, and the prime
minister, as well as by SOE.

The Partisan movement must be given its due. It engaged in more activity than any other resistance movement in Europe, and the "Proletarian Brigades," which constituted the military core of the movement, were almost
certainly the toughest and most hardened guerrilla units in wartime Europe.
They endured incredible hardships and fought heroic battles. But in their
communiqués they multiplied their accomplishments astronomically; indeed,
their communiqués had Germans being killed off at such a rate that one had
to wonder where Hitler was finding troops for the Russian front. Many of
their claims of victories were demonstrably false, while many others, as the
following pages will establish, were actually stolen from Mihailović. But
even if their accomplishments amounted to only a tenth of what they claimed,
the Partisan movement would still have to be given a very high rating for its
activity and for its heroism.

All this having been said, however, the basic question must be asked:
Was the Partisan movement really a resistance movement—or was it a revolutionary movement committed to the establishment of a Communist dictatorship in Yugoslavia, using the resistance as an instrument of its strategy?
Did its activity further and protect the interests of the Free World, or did it
seek to promote its own brand of Stalinist revolution?

As Milovan Djilas put the matter in answering this question: "The military operations which we Communists launched were motivated by our revolutionary ideology . . . Although the Germans and their allies had
dismembered and partitioned Yugoslavia, it was to their advantage to rees-
tablish the old state apparatus and economic life. A revolution was not feasible without a simultaneous struggle against the occupation forces."[1]

Men with the experience of Churchill and Eden should not have needed
such an ex post facto admission from Djilas to understand this essential fact
about the Tito movement in Yugoslavia.

The reckless heroism of the Partisan guerrillas in Yugoslavia, however,
appealed to everything that was romantic in Churchill's nature. And his romantic attraction to the Partisans appeared to receive confirmation from the
first British officers attached to Tito, Captain Deakin and Brigadier Maclean,

who both repeated the stories they had heard about "Četnik collaboration" as well as the wildly inflated accounts of Partisan strength and activities. About the battle of Mount Durmitor Deakin had reported accurately; if there was exaggeration, it was not significant. But after this epic battle one has the impression that Deakin simply accepted as gospel whatever he was told by his Partisan informers.

In his book *The Embattled Mountain* Deakin speaks about taking a briefing on Četnik collaboration from Steve Serdar, the leader of the group of Canadian-Yugoslav Communists who had preceded Deakin into Tito territory. When I raised this matter with Deakin in an exchange of correspondence in late 1988, he replied, "The fact that Serdar was a communist was central to his recruitment and the others of this group . . . Why should his experience just be ignored for ideological reasons?"

What Churchill apparently did not understand was that an active resistance on this scale could be conducted only by a fanatically disciplined ideological movement like the Communist movement, and that its exclusive support by the Allies must lead inevitably to the installation of a Communist dictatorship. Any democratic resistance movement would have had to pay some heed to the desires of its own people and to the need for protecting them against the merciless reprisals that were, during most of the occupation, quick to follow every anti-German action. The Communists, however, had no such concern over reprisals. Indeed, they welcomed reprisals (when they themselves were not the immediate victims), because every mass execution and every burning of a village made hundreds and sometimes thousands of peasants take to the forests, where they could be rounded up by the Communist recruiters. Peasants who had lost their cattle and their houses and members of their own families in German reprisals made excellent recruits for the Communist battalions because they were moved by a powerful desire to strike back at the enemy, regardless of the fact that their activities might result in more mass reprisals and more burned villages.

In a number of their communications Colonel Hudson and later Colonel Bailey stressed that it was unrealistic to hope for Mihailović's landed peasantry to generate the same degree of military activity as was taking place in the Partisan area. In a report dated March 17, 1943, Colonel Hudson said:

Guerrilla warfare in an occupied country must be based on the protection it can offer to the civilian manpower threatened by occupational methods. That is why Tito failed in Serbia and succeeded in Bosnia.

. . . it was quite obvious to everyone including the Germans that the harsh reprisals the latter took at Kraljevo (4000) and Kragujevac (7000) before actually crushing the centres of revolt would inspire no one to join such bungling amateurs for either protection or revenge, but rather would induce people to resist the renewal of such folly, especially when so strongly flavoured with Communism.[2]

Here and there in the Foreign Office memoranda of the period are passages suggesting that at least a few people in the Foreign Office understood this elementary truth. But when the time for decision came, those responsible for the conduct of policy lost sight of this truth completely.

It is questionable whether the Partisans killed as many as 5,000 Germans before the Soviet Red Army entered Yugoslavia in October 1944 and, supported by a Partisan contingent, moved in to capture Belgrade. In retrospect the question must be asked whether it made sense morally or from the standpoint of Free World interests to turn Yugoslavia over to communism in return for this limited contribution to the Allied cause.

In justifying the switch to Tito, it was claimed that he was holding down twenty-four German divisions—a figure that Churchill frequently used. In fact, Nazi troop strength in Yugoslavia during 1943 never exceeded eight understrength divisions, supplemented by Bulgarian and Ustaše units, as a reading of the official German war diary, the *Kriegstagebuch*, confirms. At the time of the Quebec conference in September 1943, Churchill told Field Marshal Sir Harold Alexander that there were thirty-nine Axis divisions in Yugoslavia—seventeen Italian, nine German, five Bulgarian, and eight Croat. Walter Roberts, checking these figures against the *Kriegstagebuch*, found that all of Churchill's figures were exaggerated. There were, in fact, fourteen Italian, five German, three Bulgarian, and three Croat divisions in Yugoslavia, virtually all of them understrength.[3]

But was Tito really holding these divisions down? The chances are that even without resistance of any kind, German and satellite troop strength in Yugoslavia would have been only marginally lower. The Germans were seriously worried about the possibility of an Allied invasion of Yugoslavia, and the Allies, for their part, did their best to encourage these fears—even though it had more or less been decided by early 1943 that there would be no Balkan invasion. The "tuning up of guerrilla activities" in the Balkans called for by General Henry Maitland Wilson, commander in chief for the Middle East, in early 1943 was actually part of an elaborate "cover plan" as it was called, to make the Nazis believe that an invasion was seriously intended. The cover plan, it appears, was remarkably successful. The total Axis troop strength invested in the occupation of Yugoslavia after the great uprising of 1941 was a product of the carefully nurtured fear that the Allies were planning a Balkan invasion far more than it was of the combined activities of the Tito and Mihailović forces.

The activities of the Tito forces helped to restrain a certain number of Axis divisions. So did the more limited activities of the Mihailović forces, because their mere presence in an area compelled the local German commanders to make certain defensive dispositions against the possibility of attack. This was all the more so because of the strategic importance of Serbia. As Colonel Bailey pointed out in a message of June 12, 1943: "Most important, Serbia covers all of the north/south and north to southeast communications, vital in case of major operations anywhere in Eastern Mediterranean. Also railheads of minor east/west communications."

When the Mihailović movement is accused of inactivity, the question has to be answered: Inactive according to what standards? There is no question that Mihailović, at different times, discouraged his followers from engaging in activities against the German and Italian armies of occupation that might provoke reprisals. But although the Četniks were not uniformly active, they did engage in major activities in every year from 1941 through 1944. In 1941 they were copartners with the Partisans in the national uprisings that swept Montenegro and Serbia. In the course of these uprisings they attacked the Germans, in places with tanks, and, according to eyewitness reports, captured hundreds of German prisoners. In the fall of 1942, the on-the-spot research of Walter Roberts indicated, they had been very active fighting the forces of General Nedić, the Serbian Pétain.[4] In 1943 they engaged in numerous major and minor activities, which are detailed in the chronological compendium that appears in Chapter 15. In 1944 they were responsible for the rescue, frequently in combat, of some 500 American airmen; and despite Partisan harassment, in response to Mihailović's call for an *ustanak*, or national uprising, they attacked the Germans at many points in Serbia and cooperated with the Soviet army in the capture of several important centers. This is detailed in Chapter 28, which deals with the liberation of Yugoslavia.

Over the entire period 1941–44 the Mihailović forces engaged in more activity than any other resistance movement in Europe, with the sole exception of the Partisan army. (This, of course, does not take into consideration the final battle of Warsaw, in which the Polish Home Army suffered incredible losses but also inflicted heavy losses on the Germans.)

Returning to the charge that the Mihailović forces were inactive against the Germans, let us see what is said about this in the Operational Log; by Colonel Bailey and the other members of the British mission to Mihailović; by Captain Walter Mansfield of the first American military mission to Mihailović; and by Colonel Robert McDowell, chief of the American intelligence mission that General William Donovan, head of OSS, sent into Mihailović's headquarters in August 1944. Finally, let us examine the collective testimony of the 500-plus American airmen forced down over Mihailović territory from February 1944 on, the great majority of whom were successfully evacuated by the American Fifteenth Army Air Force, thanks to the protection and cooperation of the Mihailović forces.

11

Mihailović and the Germans

One year after Moscow had launched its campaign of character assassination against Mihailović, the bulk of the Allied press was parroting Radio Free Yugoslavia's treatment of Mihailović. It had downgraded him to the status of a collaborator and was singing paeans to the martial virtues of the Communist side in the Yugoslav civil war. For all practical purposes, by October 1943 Tito had become the monopolistic beneficiary of the greatly augmented Allied support that had become logistically possible after the collapse of Italy.

This switch in Allied policy is one of the great mysteries of World War II—all the more so because some thirty-odd British officers and seven American officers who were attached to the Mihailović forces for quite long periods of time are convinced that a grave injustice was done, and that much of the intelligence that led to the switch was false or exaggerated.

The Communists have made much of the fact that on November 11, 1941, Mihailović and three of his colleagues met with a German delegation headed by Lt. Colonel Kogard, in the town of Divci. According to the Communists, this was the beginning of Mihailović's collaboration with the Germans.

At his trial in Belgrade in the summer of 1946 Mihailović admitted that he had met with the Germans and said that he had refused their request that he surrender unconditionally. Fortunately, there exists in German war records a stenographic account of this meeting, according to which Mihailović told Kogard:

I am neither a communist nor do I work for you. But I have attempted to alleviate and hinder your terror . . . [The Communists] wish to see the greatest possible number of Serbs killed in order to ensure their own later success. No agreement can be made with them. My only purpose [in dealing with them] was to temper their terror, which is as terrible as the German terror. At this moment, innocents are suffering from the terrorist acts of both of you.

. . . As a soldier I am not ashamed to be a nationalist. In this capacity I will serve only my people . . . It is our duty as soldiers not to surrender as long as we can fight. Therefore, you cannot reproach us for not surrendering.

. . . I intend to continue the fight against the communists which began on October 31 . . . we need ammunition. This need brought me here . . . The communists have an ammunition factory and ammunition dumps in Užice. I ask you in the interest of the Serbian people, as well as in your own interest, to supply me, if possible, with ammunition this very night . . . Otherwise, if I am not given any ammunition, the communists will again obtain sway over Serbia.[1]

To this Kogard replied that his only instructions were to ask Mihailović if he was ready to capitulate unconditionally. Obviously disappointed by Kogard's reply, Mihailović said, "I do not see any sense in your invitation to come to the meeting if this is all you had to say."[2]

Let us consider some other evidence basic to an appreciation of Mihailović's and the Germans' attitude toward each other.

Colonel Bailey, an officer of outstanding ability who spoke fluent Serbo-Croat, said in a letter to the editor of *The* (London) *Times* of August 6, 1971, "I do believe that everything must now be done to give Mihailović his rightful, honorable place in history. He and his Četniks did more than is generally appreciated for the Allied cause."

An even more impressive appreciation of the role played by Mihailović—this one from an enemy point of view—was written by General Reinhard Gehlen, head of German military intelligence for eastern Europe, in a top-secret memorandum to the German General Staff, dated February 9, 1943. The memorandum underscored the truly remarkable success Mihailović had had in rebuilding his organization since his forces were defeated and dispersed by the Germans in December 1941. It read:

Among the various resistance movements which increasingly cause trouble in the area of the former Yugoslav state, the movement of General Mihailović remains in the first place with regard to leadership, armament, organization, and activity . . . The followers of D.M. come from all classes of the population and at present comprise about 80 percent of the Serbian people. Hoping for the liberation from the "alien yoke" and for a better new order, and an economical and social new balance, their number is continuously increasing.[3]

There are numerous examples of similar statements by members of the German General Staff and, for that matter, by Hitler himself. On February 16, 1943, exactly one week after the date of General Gehlen's memorandum,

Hitler wrote to Mussolini, urging the Italians to terminate their accommodations with certain Četnik commanders in the peripheral areas.[4]

Intercepts did indeed exist, proving the existence of temporary regional
understandings between the Germans and certain Yugoslav Home Army officers commanding formations in the border areas where Partisan and Mihailović forces confronted each other. (In Serbia proper, where Mihailović strength
was overwhelming, and where the Home Army did not have to fight a war
of survival against the unrelenting attacks of Partisan armies, accommodations with the Germans were a minor rarity.) But it is impossible to establish
the relative significance of these intercepts without at the same time considering the unequivocal statements repeatedly made by Hitler and his senior
staff officers.

Six weeks after the Gehlen memorandum was written, there took place
an incident that throws a new light on the charge that Mihailović was collaborating with the enemy. In March 1943 Tito sent to the headquarters of the
German commander in chief at Sarajevo a delegation consisting of Milovan
Djilas, General Koča Popović, and Dr. Vladimir Velebit, three of the top
leaders of the Tito movement. The ostensible purpose of the meeting was to
arrange for a prisoner exchange. The three Partisan leaders were subsequently flown by a special German military plane to Zagreb, where the discussions were continued. Walter Roberts, who discovered this interesting
documentation in German military archives, summarized it as follows:

> The Partisan delegation stressed that the Partisans saw no reason for fighting the
> German army—they added that they fought against the Germans only in self
> defense—but wished solely to fight the Četniks . . . that they would fight the
> British should the latter land in Yugoslavia . . . [and that] inasmuch as they
> wanted to concentrate on fighting the Četniks, they wished to suggest respective
> territories of interest.[5]

The agreement was finally vetoed by Ribbentrop at the end of March,
even though Kasche, the German minister in Zagreb, argued passionately
that the agreement was to the Germans' advantage, and that "in all of the
negotiations with the Partisans to date" the "reliability of Tito's promises"
had been "confirmed."

Kasche's language obviously implied that he was speaking not of one or
two prior agreements but of at least three or four—or more. And the question naturally arises: If the Mihailović forces were regarded as allies of the
Germans, why should the Germans have entered into written agreements with
the Partisans directed against these forces?

According to Professor Mark Wheeler, rumors of the Partisan-Nazi talks
quickly reached Mihailović, though the scope of the agenda was unknown to

him at the time. Within ten days of the meeting, Colonel Bailey, who had taken over from Hudson as chief of the British mission to Mihailović two months earlier, signaled SOE Cairo with the news. However, this news of Partisan-German collaboration seems never to have reached London.[6] Nor does London appear to have received the many references to Partisan initiatives in waging civil war that figured in the dispatches of the BLOs with Mihailović. At least, there is no reference to those matters in either Hinsley's or Foot's histories, or in the Foreign Office files.

As late as August 22, 1944, Hitler displayed his unrelenting hostility toward Mihailović. On that date he warned Hermann Neubacher, his representative in Belgrade, and Field Marshal Maximilian von Weichs that "the armament of the Četniks is out of the question." General Albert Jodl summarized Hitler's point of view as follows: "A Serbian army must not be allowed to exist. It is better to have some danger from communism."[7]

According to Mihailović's statement at his trial, he had one further meeting, in November 1944, with a Herr Stärker, who represented Neubacher. Stärker said that they had received a report that Mihailović wished to place himself at the service of the Germans. He asked whether this was true. To this Mihailović replied, "We were and still are enemies, it is a sad coincidence that I am, like you, fighting against the Partisans. This is a sad coincidence that I regret."[8]

12

"The Klugmann Period" in SOE Cairo: The Failures of British and American Internal Security

He could talk with brilliance on almost any subject, but what
he really liked to talk about was politics . . . The fact is that
politics moved in at this period, around the last months of
1942, and, unavoidably, as James said, reality came home to
roost. It could even be called the Klugmann period and it
changed a great deal.

Basil Davidson
Commanding Officer
Yugoslav Section, SOE Cairo

There were several changes in the designation and function and command of the Yugoslav Country Section of SOE Cairo and many, many changes in personnel, as the chart printed on page 102 indicates.

The office of the SOE adviser maintains, perhaps, the best available records on SOE and its personnel. The records, however, are erratic and incomplete. The several changes in command that took place at the Yugoslav desk in late 1943, for example, created a picture that SOE Adviser C. M. Woods and I had difficulty in comprehending. This personnel chart is probably not complete, but it is as complete as the records available to the SOE Adviser would permit us to make it. We are both satisfied, however, that the chart lists all significant players in the SOE Yugoslav Section drama.

During the first part of the war Yugoslav affairs were handled by a general Balkan Section of SOE. In August 1942 there was a reorganization, and the Yugoslav Country Section was separated from the Balkan Section and set up as a separate entity, known as B.1.

In the summer of 1943 SOE Cairo was redesignated "Force 133." In a letter to me dated March 23, 1988, C. M. Woods stated that he had "found a record that in February 1944 an advance headquarters of B.1 was sent to Italy under Major G. Fraser and that the final move of rear B.1 to Bari took place on April 12, 1944."

There was another change in nomenclature and function when the "Balkan Air Force" was created in mid-June 1944 and SOE's Yugoslav Country Section was placed under its operational command, as had already been done with Maclean's "37 Military Mission." Gervase Cowell, present SOE Adviser, wrote to me that "by July 1944 SOE's role became much less influential as the Partisan HQ took control and they were reduced, as it were, from senior advisors to junior suppliers."

But changes in nomenclature, function, and personnel did not affect James Klugmann. Through the numerous changes that took place, Klugmann was constantly present. It is against this background that we must view his role in guiding the transition from support of Mihailović to support of Tito.

Klugmann joined the Balkan Section of SOE Cairo as a lance corporal on February 9, 1942. While the international Communist propaganda apparatus was still supporting Mihailović at this period, the civil war in Yugoslavia had already erupted. It is worth remembering that the Soviets broke with Mihailović before the end of July 1942. Klugmann's appointment to SOE Cairo would have taken several months before it could bear fruit in the form of enhanced Soviet intelligence on Yugoslavia and on British policy toward Yugoslavia, and another several months of careful assessment before the generally cautious Stalin could be persuaded to change his policy in this highly sensitive area.

An able linguist, Klugmann soon outshone the other members of SOE Cairo in his knowledge of Serbo-Croat. The fact that he was one of the founding staff of the Balkan Section, moreover, stood him in good stead in getting his expertise accepted by superior officers. His initial duties are recorded as "looking after and keeping records of agents." [1]

Professor M. R. D. Foot in his history of SOE provides two explanations for how Klugmann managed to get appointed to that supposedly highly secret organization. First, according to Foot, it was the British "old-boy" system at work. Terence Airey, a capable and ambitious regular officer, was working in the secret Cairo office of British Military Intelligence, which went by the cover title "G(R)." One day he recognized the NCO who brought him his tea as the "cleverest boy who had ever been (after his time) at his school"—Gresham's. Airey arranged for this clever boy, who, of course, was Klugmann, to be transferred to SOE Cairo and work on the Balkan desk, not serving tea but as an embryo staff officer.[2]

Foot also says that "presumably, like all other recruits into SOE, he [Klugmann] had been handed a form to sign, which said that he was neither a Communist nor a Fascist, but as a good Communist he knew his duty to tell a lie." Foot says that when a routine check was made with MI5, they replied that they had nothing recorded against him. Why was there no record of his membership in the Communist Party, when he had held important positions in the British and European Communist student movements? According to Foot, "a chance incendiary bomb at Wormwood Scrubs had burnt the file which recorded the ex-NCO's affiliation; this was how the brilliant and devious James Klugmann, secretary of the Cambridge Communist Party in the mid-1930s, acquired a post in which he could exert leverage. Skeptics can point out that no connection between Klugmann and the *Comintern* has been proved. None was needed; a bolshevik as bright as Klugmann knew where his Party duty lay."[3]

There is, of course, another possible explanation. During the war a number of decidedly left-wing people were recruited into British intelligence, especially MI6. Their recruiters were either ideologically sympathetic to the left or else guileless conservatives who thought it might be advantageous in resistance situations to employ a number of officers who were sympathetic to—and, therefore, presumably on good terms with—the Communists. I know of no proof, one way or the other, that Klugmann lied about his previous political affiliations. Certainly, he made no effort to conceal his Communist past once established in Cairo—even less so after he was given the protection of Major (later Lt. Colonel) Basil Davidson, head of the Yugoslav desk, and Brigadier C. M. Keble, the executive head of SOE Cairo.

Bickham Sweet-Escott, a young Englishman who served in SOE, made an observation that clearly indicated that Klugmann's communism was no secret to people in SOE. Speaking about SOE Cairo, Sweet-Escott said, "There was however one cuckoo in the nest. One of the most efficient and hard-working men in the Yugoslav section was James Klugmann, now a leading member of the Communist Party of Great Britain."[4]

Klugmann's responsibilities grew steadily. On June 16, 1942, he was granted an emergency commission as second lieutenant in the General List. On May 22, 1943, he was promoted acting captain, at which date his designation was G III(i) (General Staff Officer, Grade III, Intelligence) in the Yugoslav Section. In September 1943 his designation became G III (Briefing), and on December 15, 1943, he became G II (Coordination). On March 15, 1944, by which time he had moved forward with most of the SOE staff from Cairo to Bari, Italy, he was promoted acting major as second in command of the Yugoslav Section.[5]

But this formal listing of Klugmann's promotions tells only a very small part of the story. Because of his brilliance and the assiduousness with which he applied himself to his work, and also because of the sympathy of his superiors—primarily Major Davidson and Brigadier Keble—Klugmann came to exercise an influence altogether disproportionate to his rank. The British army's staff system, of course, encourages this. Junior staff officers draft analyses and position papers for the approval of their superiors. If their work appears to be of such high quality that they gain the confidence of their immediate superiors, it will rise unaltered up the chain of responsibility and see the light of day over a general's signature.

Basil Davidson was a formidable character in his own right. A left-leaning journalist, he had been recruited early into SOE, whereupon he was sent on a mission to Hungary. He escaped through Yugoslavia, just as the Germans were invading. His next posting was a covert one in Istanbul, after which he was sent to SOE Cairo as head of the Yugoslav Section. By the time he arrived in late August 1942, Klugmann was well established as a commissioned officer, a veteran in the section who knew it all.

Time and again Davidson quotes Klugmann as a fount of oracular wisdom. "He could talk with brilliance on almost any subject," said Davidson, "but what he really liked to talk about was politics . . . The fact is that politics moved in at this period, around the last months of 1942, and, unavoidably, as James said, reality came home to roost. *It could even be called the Klugmann period and it changed a great deal.*" [6] [Author's emphasis]

These careful words reveal the immense impact that Klugmann's communism and Davidson's generally leftist leanings were soon to have on SOE Cairo's attitudes to Yugoslav resistance—attitudes that were to affect the course of Yugoslav history and the balance of power in Europe.

Klugmann's exceptional intelligence, his rare likability, and the diligence with which he applied himself to his duties all played a role in enabling him to shape SOE's intelligence data on Mihailović and Tito. If Major Kenneth Greenlees, his first boss, and Basil Davidson are to be believed, Klugmann was by far the most brilliant and prolific worker SOE Cairo had.

Klugmann came into the office early and worked late. He rarely, if ever, took time off for social activities, other than meeting with left-wing Egyptians every week for dinner. He worked obsessionally, according to those who knew him at SOE Cairo—indeed, like a man who was driven. What was he working at? What was he writing? He was producing intelligence—not raw intelligence but processed or semi-processed intelligence that would be used in preparing position papers pointing the way for future policy.

David Erskine, a junior intelligence officer who served under Klugmann beginning in September 1943, first in Cairo and then in Bari, remembers clearly that one of the functions Klugmann took on himself was the preparation of situation reports, summarizing the information received from the field on activities by the Partisans and by the Mihailović forces. In addition, he frequently briefed military VIPs and senior as well as junior officers on the situation in Yugoslavia.

Erskine thinks it highly probable that Klugmann would have been the first, or at least one of the first, to see messages as they came in from the field. The officers in charge of policy, he said, were preoccupied with other matters and only too happy to delegate such chores to a highly intelligent workaholic like Klugmann. Second, he said, the low-powered radio transmissions from the field caused most of the enciphered texts to be "corrupt" in parts, sometimes to the point of unintelligibility—certainly to someone less conversant than Klugmann with place and personal names.

But Klugmann's contribution to SOE Cairo was certainly not confined to the writing of situation reports ("sitreps"). By all the evidence, it was significant and many-sided.

Only very rarely will a commanding officer read raw intelligence from the field and write his own summations and analyses and position papers. Far more commonly he will delegate to a trusted assistant the task of writing digests of intelligence on file, periodic analyses of this intelligence, and position papers that point the way to future policy.

If he has a brilliant and trusted assistant, moreover, it is only natural that he should have this assistant at least prepare the rough draft of position papers and other documents that go out over his name. It is a tribute to Klugmann's skill in discharging these duties that his work impressed not only Davidson—which was not surprising—but also Major Greenlees, who was a staunch Catholic conservative; Brigadier Keble, who also had a conservative reputation; Hugh Seton-Watson, who served SOE as a general expert and adviser on the Balkan area (Yugoslavia, Bulgaria, Greece, Albania, and Hungary); and officers such as Captain Deakin and Brigadier Maclean, who, if they read anything at all about Yugoslavia in the course of their Yugoslav involvement, must have read a goodly quantity of papers prepared by Klugmann.

There is a saying that if one can have control of a child's education for the first six years, one does not have to worry about subsequent influences. Similarly, in an intelligence operation of several years' duration, such as SOE Cairo, it may be said that he who has control of the input for the first six months or a year after its activation inevitably controls the final shape of this intelligence and the final policy decisions.

Thus it was that Klugmann came to have a greater impact than any other officer in shaping the body of intelligence on file for the guidance of the

Foreign Office, the prime minister, the Joint Chiefs of Staff, and the British liaison officers about to be dropped into Yugoslavia. It also helped to ensure that officers who later joined SOE Cairo for six months or a year or longer were "properly" oriented on the Tito-Mihailović conflict.

Klugmann scored his greatest success in January 1943, when Churchill, visiting Cairo, was given a personal briefing on the situation in Yugoslavia. The briefing was prepared by Bill Deakin, apparently with some assistance from Basil Davidson, and administered by Brigadier Keble, with Lord Glenconner in attendance. According to Davidson, it focused heavily on recent intercepts of enemy communications. Davidson uses a number of expressions that, taken together, certainly create the impression that they were "Ultra" intercepts. He says that "there were intercepts of German regular signals decoded by a British service devoted to that work."[7] Ordinarily, intelligence officers will have access to recent intercepts of any enemy traffic. Because of its super-secret nature, however, access to "Ultra" was limited to a few carefully selected and designated people. Certainly, Davidson's description of what happened is in line with the limitations known to have been put on access to "Ultra."

Whatever the source of the intercepts, it can be taken for granted that this information was melded with the other intelligence in the files of SOE, and that in preparation for this briefing Captain Deakin must have researched the files for several weeks—this on top of his intense exposure to them immediately after joining the section. What was presented, therefore, was to a large extent a distillation of the many distillations that Klugmann had already incorporated into the files—supplemented, of course, by bits and pieces of information from other sources.

It may be true, as Deakin has written to me, that Klugmann played no direct part in preparing the briefing. But it is difficult to escape the conclusion that Klugmann was largely responsible for much of the content of the briefing, which so impressed Churchill.

About the preparation of the map that supplemented the briefing, Davidson had this to say:

> Captain Deakin at once got down to the detail, and soon we had our confidential map. I kept it on my office wall, neatly marked with information taken from the intercepts, behind a mask of paper sheets. This and the running survey confirmed in detail, from confidential German sources, what we had long guessed in outline. The Partisans were active in most regions of Yugoslavia. They were strong, effective, and aggressive. They were a formidable fighting force in constant use. Keble came in every day or so to study the map and the survey, and now one could see him at his proper stature. He was in full cry with the quarry in sight.[8]

If Klugmann was the prime architect of the British intelligence bank on Yugoslavia, he had in his immediate boss, Davidson, an eager ally. A revolutionary romantic, Basil Davidson was to devote his life as a historian to the glorification of utopian causes. In his book about World War II he devoted three pages to an explanation of why "large and serious resistance came and could only come under left-wing leadership and inspiration"[9]—a view that would hardly have been shared by the Polish resistance or, indeed, by the many non-Communist resistance organizations in Nazi-occupied Europe. But for Davidson the Yugoslav Communists under Tito represented the forces of history, while Mihailović's forces represented "beaten generals" and "ruling classes [that] had collapsed in defeat."[10] Davidson's views on the motive forces of history were further extended in several post–World War II publications that were widely construed as apologies for Marxist Black Africa.[11]

An interesting commentary on the prejudices that Davidson brought to his assignment is provided by Peter Kemp, a young British officer who was subsequently detailed for service in Albania, although Yugoslavia had been his first choice. Kemp relates that shortly after arriving in Cairo, he was introduced to Captain James Klugmann, a country section intelligence officer. "I was surprised to find Klugmann occupying such a confidential position," said Kemp, "because when I had last seen him in 1936 he had been the secretary and inspiration of the Cambridge University communists." Kemp continued:

Although it was impressed upon me from the moment of my arrival in Cairo that when I went into the field I must regard myself simply as a soldier, whose task would be the prosecution of military operations to the exclusion of politics, I could not fail to be aware of the strong political differences which divided the staff officers both in London and Cairo. Nowhere were they more evident than in the Yugoslav Section. Boughey in London had maintained that because Mihailović was the representative of the recognized Yugoslav Government he should be given every support; Major Basil Davidson, on the other hand, the head of the Country Section in Cairo, who later distinguished himself in action with partisan forces in Yugoslavia and in Northern Italy, could not conceal his antipathy to the Četniks. He wanted me to sign a declaration that I had been subjected in London to indoctrination on behalf of Mihailović; I refused, but the incident warned me of the sort of feeling that was to embitter relations between British officers in the field as well as at headquarters.[12]

Davidson recounts how Klugmann's web of influence ultimately embraced Brigadier Keble, the head of SOE Cairo, to the point where Keble, who was reputed to be a staunch conservative, protected Klugmann from British Security. On one occasion, Davidson relates, "Keble pushed James

[Klugmann] into a lavatory and said that Security was after him, but that he, Keble, would protect him."[13]

Keble was a thrusting, ambitious chief of staff, anxious to promote the reputations of SOE Cairo and Brigadier Keble. His boss was a civilian, Lord Glenconner, whose busy schedule in and out of the politico-military power centers of Cairo divorced him from day-to-day SOE policy. We shall deal later with Davidson's description of the struggle inside SOE Cairo to convert that office from support for Mihailović to support for Tito: this, obviously, was the necessary prerequisite for a wider conversion.

With the assistance of C. M. Woods, the SOE Adviser to the Foreign Office, it was possible to put together a chronological roster of all the officers who had served with the Yugoslav desk in SOE Cairo for any appreciable time. I also received assistance in finalizing some of the details from Gervase Cowell, who replaced Mr. Woods in early 1988. Running down the list of personnel, many of the names can automatically be eliminated as suspects because they were not there during all or most of the period in question. Moreover, during the critical months of August through December 1943 the top echelon of the Yugoslav Section of SOE Cairo underwent so many personnel changes that the implementation of any sustained policy simply must have been the work of a person or persons who had broad access to intelligence, recognized seniority within the section, and continued familiarity with the details, and who was in place during all or most of the six critical incidents discussed in Chapter 16, and through to SOE's final abandonment of Mihailović toward the end of November 1943.

In the interest of broadening my information, I have made a systematic effort to contact those who were in the SOE Yugoslav Section during the critical period, or, rather, those who still survive.

In the case of Denis Ionides, I received a letter from his sister, Irene Ionides, in mid-November 1978, informing me that he was dying of liver cancer, that he had read Robert Moss's prepublication review of my book *Patriot or Traitor* in *The* (London) *Daily Telegraph*, and that he would dearly love to have a copy airmailed to him. I complied with this request as soon as I received copies from the printer, which was toward the end of November, and I received a very warm letter of thanks from his sister. She indicated that Ionides, to the bitter end, was friendly to the Mihailović cause but apparently could do little about it because forces more powerful than he controlled the input to the Yugoslav Section's intelligence.

Captain J. W. Hitchen, Operations and Administration officer, departed from SOE Cairo in May 1943, before the period of the six critical incidents.

Major (later Lt. Colonel) Basil Davidson, the head of the Yugoslav Section, left in mid-August 1943 for an assignment in Hungary, hoping to go by way of Tito's Yugoslavia. For at least a month prior to that he had been

PERSONNEL OF SOE CAIRO YUGOSLAV SECTION UNDER B. 1. AND OTHER DESIGNATIONS

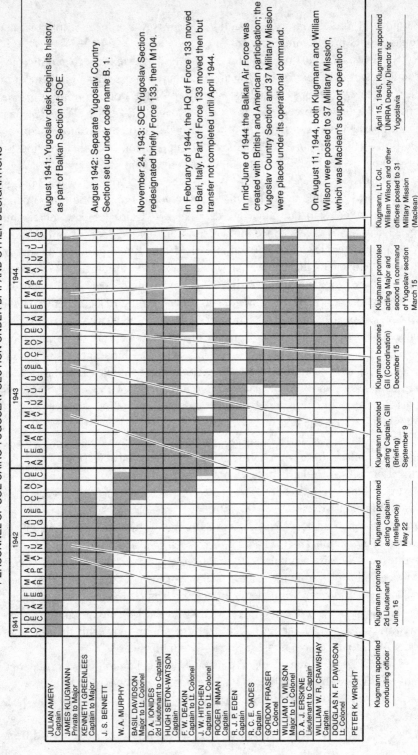

taking parachute training and preparing himself for his new mission. I wrote to Basil Davidson twice, suggesting that it might be mutually beneficial to get together. He refused point-blank, on the basis of his reading of my book *Patriot or Traitor*—unless, of course, I was sufficiently objective to accept his point of view.

In addition, I wrote to several members of SOE Cairo who figure on the personnel roster in proximity to the period in question. From Roger Inman, who briefly headed up the section, and who now lives in Sheffield, England, I received a gracious letter thanking me for the copy of *Patriot or Traitor* and saying, "I read your book with much interest. The fates were unkind to Mihailović." W. D. Wilson, who now lives in South Africa and who also briefly headed up the section, said that he had not yet found time to go through the book I had sent him but looked forward greatly to reading it. "I have not attempted to keep in touch with the literature that has come out on the controversy since the war," he said, "but I have always felt that to brand Mihailović as a traitor was vicious and wrong-headed."

Sir William Crawshay also sent me a very cordial note, saying that he was reading my book with great interest. Although he was with the Yugoslav Section as intelligence officer only through the last four months of 1943, he did recall that during September and October there was a good deal of action reported by the BLOs with Mihailović—to the "dismay" of some of the older hands in the section.

An interview with David Erskine, who now lives in Guernsey, satisfies me that he also had not been part of the pro-Tito cabal in SOE Cairo. Erskine, whose recollections were admittedly somewhat dated, was nevertheless convinced that Klugmann was the first to see messages as they came in from the field, and that it was almost certainly he who decided on the distribution of the Operational Log. Erskine also recalls that on one occasion he winced physically when Klugmann put his arm around his shoulders and addressed him as "comrade."

This leaves only a few other names yet to be accounted for. Lt. Colonel Douglas N. F. Davidson, Captain R. J. P. Eden, and Captain R. C. E. Oades served with the section for only a few months, and I was unable to run down current addresses for them.

Lt. Colonel Gordon Fraser acted as chief of the section before the end of 1943, and when the section moved to Bari in stages beginning in 1943, he served for a number of months as chief of the Bari operation. By all accounts, he was a political clone of Basil Davidson. Erskine recalls that once when he questioned the Partisans' grossly exaggerated claims, he was instructed by Fraser to include the items in his situation report exactly as worded by them. In the immediate postwar period he served at BBC as director of Yugoslav broadcasts—to the dismay of knowledgeable Yugoslavs in England, who protested that he made BBC sound like a twin brother of Belgrade Radio. After that he became a greeting card tycoon. I was going to seek an appointment with him when I was last in London, but unfortunately, he had died.

Hugh Seton-Watson is about the only other name that appears to bracket the period in question. There can be no question that Seton-Watson, at that time a typical left liberal, was friendly to Klugmann and was sympathetic to Tito. On the other hand, his position with SOE Cairo did not involve him with the Yugoslav Section as a working officer. He was a consultant on a much larger area, embracing Yugoslavia, Bulgaria, Greece, Albania, and Hungary. Unquestionably, his voice carried a fair amount of weight. But his information on what was happening in Yugoslavia was based entirely on intelligence files to which Klugmann had been the principal contributor— and this by a very wide margin. I had an appointment to see Seton-Watson in Washington just before he died. On the morning of the appointment, however, his wife called up to say that he was in the hospital with double pneumonia and would probably not survive.

Captain William Deakin, who had served in SOE Cairo as an intelligence officer, parachuted into Yugoslavia on May 27, 1943, and so could not have been involved in any of the six major incidents discussed. In an effort to better understand his sympathy for Tito, I had dinner with him in London, which, as I recall, ran for three hours.

SOE CAIRO: A STUDY IN BUREAUCRATIC KNAVERY

Bureaucratic infighting has, historically, never been characterized by adherence to the rules of sportsmanship and fairness. But according to evidence from many different sources, the SOE Cairo office was probably one of the most vindictive and unprincipled bureaus that have ever existed inside the format of a democratic government. Brigadier Fitzroy Maclean, who headed up the British mission to Tito, underscored this point in a report he made at a conference held at the University of London in July 1973.[14] The story of his personal experiences with SOE Cairo and Brigadier Keble would be almost unbelievable if it had come from a lesser person. But he confirmed this account, with several addenda, in a conversation I had with him in London on November 29, 1977.

According to Maclean, he was called back to London by Churchill in June 1943 and asked to go to Yugoslavia as commander of the British mission to Tito and as his personal representative with the Partisan command. He accepted the assignment. A short while later Churchill showed him a message that had just arrived from General Henry Maitland (''Jumbo'') Wilson, commander in chief for the Middle East. This message said that Wilson considered Maclean totally unsuitable for the job. Maclean relates that he was surprised and pained by the message because he had regarded General Wilson as an old friend. "Churchill then showed me the reply he had sent Wilson over his private link," said Maclean. "This said fairly abruptly that the commander-in-chief was to do what he was told and not to argue."

When Maclean arrived in Cairo a few days later, he went to see General Wilson. In his outer office he met two old friends. "What," they asked, "has got into the prime minister? Jumbo has just had a personal signal from him about you in reply to nothing he ever sent telling him to shut up and do as he's told." Maclean and his friends exchanged notes and quickly came to the conclusion that someone had drafted and sent off a personal message to Churchill in General Wilson's name but without his knowledge. When Maclean went in to see Wilson, the general expressed his personal anger over the incident and told Maclean to get himself gazetted brigadier and come back to him if he had any trouble.

A short while later Maclean went to see Brigadier Keble, the SOE chief of staff. Keble asked him why he was dressed as a brigadier. He replied that he wore the uniform because the commander in chief had appointed him brigadier. According to Maclean:

> He then asked me why I had been to see the Commander-in-Chief. I said because he had sent for me. He said that next time the Commander-in-Chief sent for me I was not to go. I said that, as a serving soldier, if sent for by the Commander-in-Chief, I would certainly go.

> After this brisk exchange Keble went on to say that I could take it from him that I would never go to Yugoslavia, whatever the Commander-in-Chief or the Prime Minister or anyone else might say. SOE had opposed my appointment from the start and would see to it by one method or another that I never took it up. Meanwhile he had given strict instructions that I should be shown no files, signals, or anything else concerning Yugoslavia. To this I replied, with, I hope, becoming dignity, that I saw no point in prolonging our conversation.[15]

Maclean decided to go to see Wilson at once. When he arrived, Wilson was closeted with another SOE officer, Colonel P. C. Vellacott, whose special job was to spread misinformation and rumors to confuse the enemy and otherwise serve the Allied war effort. When Maclean was ushered into Wilson's presence a short while later, Wilson asked Vellacott to repeat the information he had just given him. Vellacott said that he had received instructions from SOE to spread rumors about Maclean to the effect that he was "a hopeless drunk [and] an active homosexual," and that he had shown himself "consistently cowardly and unreliable."

Shortly afterward Maclean was dropped into Yugoslavia. "I can assure you," he told the London conference, "that I did not take the first parachute that was offered me."

SOE Cairo's opposition to Maclean's assuming command of the British mission to Tito may have been based on the parochial bureaucratic concern that they would lose control of the situation if Maclean joined Tito as Churchill's special personal representative. But one cannot exclude the possibility that SOE Cairo's unscrupulous attempts to abort the Maclean mission stemmed from concern by Klugmann and other pro-Tito elements at the Yugoslav desk over the possibility that Maclean—a staunch conservative who had been on the staff of the British embassy in Moscow at the time of the purge trials of the thirties and was known to have strong personal views about communism—might not respond affirmatively to Tito's blandishments.

In any case, Maclean did go into Yugoslavia, where he promptly revealed himself to be a pliant and effective instrument of the pro-Tito mania then sweeping through the ranks of the British government and the Western media. Indeed, he was all the more effective because he was widely regarded as a solid and knowledgeable conservative.

Did Klugmann have anything to do with SOE's campaign against Maclean? The documentation released to date provides no evidence of this, mentioning Klugmann so rarely that one almost wonders whether the man really existed.

Oddly enough, too, Deakin and Maclean do not even mention Klugmann in their books. It is, of course, possible that Maclean had no contact with Klugmann worth speaking of—indeed, after Brigadier Keble's set-to with Maclean, it is probable that before his first trip into Yugoslavia he had no access to the intelligence files of SOE Cairo. However, Deakin was on close personal terms with Klugmann, according to reports, and presumably, like most people, greatly impressed by his knowledge of everything and his industry and likability. Surely, it is not unreasonable to ask whether the fact that Deakin and Maclean did not mention Klugmann was due to the information—which probably came to them later—that he had been the subject of two investigations, sparked by suspicion that he might be a Soviet agent.

LAPSES IN INTERNAL SECURITY

The influence of pro-Communist officials in the British and US governments during World War II can in part be attributed to the appalling failure to observe the most elementary internal-security precautions.

While the slackening was uneven, in both countries there was a general tendency to regard the Communists as allies for the simple reason that the

Soviets were allies. This situation figured in a sequence of the popular British motion picture *The Tawny Pippet*: a Red Army woman sharpshooter is given an enthusiastic and emotional reception by the populace of a small English town, and the old colonel in charge of the home guard is so moved that he greets her with the clenched-fist salute. In real life the clenched-fist salute may not have been used by Englishmen and Americans sympathetic to the Soviet Union. But there were many, many people in positions of authority, and even in policymaking positions, who were as fuzzy-minded as the old colonel, and they were disposed to bring in others who saw the world as they did. Even staunch conservatives were inclined to believe that it was in the Western interest to employ a certain number of people of known Communist opinion in effecting liaison with Communist resistance groups in Europe.

On the American side, it was late 1942 when OSS began to get ready to play an active role in Yugoslavia. A number of Americans of Yugoslav origin, either the sons of immigrants or immigrants themselves, were brought together for this purpose in special training camps in various parts of the United States. Most of these Yugoslav-American trainees had no sympathy for communism. But some had fought in the International Brigade in Spain and were openly pro-Communist. Apparently, their communism was considered a plus rather than a minus from the standpoint of their impending service in Yugoslavia. This was one of the situations that moved Constantine Brown, a nationally syndicated columnist at the time, to ask General William ("Wild Bill") Donovan, head of OSS, why he had so many Communists in the organization. In reply, Donovan winked slyly and said, "It takes a commie to catch a commie." [16]

Despite General Donovan's strongly anti-Communist views and his continuing belief in Mihailović, the support of Tito resulted in much confusion and in a series of serious internal-security lapses. Almost inevitably there were a number of senior American officers in key positions who were ideologically sympathetic to Tito. For example, the OSS officers' mess in Bari in early 1944 employed seven Yugoslav refugee girls as waitresses. They made no effort to conceal their leftist politics, and each was seen in Bari in Partisan uniform. The prettiest of the seven was a Slovenian, Irene Pazdera. Toward the end of February 1944 she went to work as confidential secretary to Major Frank H. Arnoldi, the officer in charge of the Secret Intelligence desk, OSS, Yugoslav Division. Pazdera, in practice, became the actual manager of the office, with access to the most sensitive documents.

Several junior officers attached to the Yugoslav Section of OSS took their protests directly to Roosevelt's roving ambassador, Robert Murphy. As a result, in July 1944 there was a general housecleaning. Colonel Arnoldi was relieved of his command, and Irene Pazdera was dismissed. Several days after her dismissal from OSS she appeared on the streets of Bari in Partisan uniform. Her employer now was Colonel Dedijer, chief of the Partisan propaganda bureau in Bari.

But by far the most serious violations of the elementary rules of internal security were on the British side. Professor David Stafford, a Canadian academic, in his book *Camp X*[17] tells the story of the recruitment and training of the contingent of Canadian-Yugoslav Communists who were subsequently sent into Tito territory on intelligence missions.

"Camp X" was a project conceived by General Donovan in cooperation with William Stephenson, the legendary "Man Called Intrepid." A major purpose of "Camp X," according to the original conception, was to provide a training place in Canada for teams of Central European ethnics with a view to building underground resistance organizations in their native countries. It was to service the requirements of both OSS and SOE.

According to Stafford, the British government, on the basis of "Enigma" intercepts, had agreed at a relatively early stage in 1942 that "the possibility of sending a British Mission to the Communists in Croatia . . . should be explored."[18] This was the subject of a secret meeting on August 8, 1942, involving SOE, SIS (Secret Intelligence Service), and the Foreign Office.[19] Originally the goal was to find 100 Canadian-Yugoslavs of left-wing views, and to this end advertisements were placed in *Novosti*, a pro-Communist Serbo-Croat newspaper, and there were meetings with leaders of the Canadian Communist Party.

On July 22, two weeks before the August 8 meeting, the first batch of Yugoslav trainees had arrived at Camp X, near Whitby, Ontario. As Tim Buck, secretary general of the Canadian Communist Party, confirms in his memoirs, he met personally with them at a farm outside Toronto.

It is probably not an accident that the international Communist campaign against Mihailović was launched in the very week that the first Canadian-Yugoslav Communists reported for training at Camp X. After all, if the Churchill government was blind enough to recruit them for intelligence missions in Yugoslavia, Moscow can hardly be blamed for thinking that it was now safe for it to break with Mihailović.

The head of the Yugoslav recruiting mission was Colonel Bailey, later chief of the British mission to Mihailović. He was accompanied by Captain William Stuart, who had been born and educated in Yugoslavia and was recruiting separately for SIS. Stuart was dropped into Yugoslavia with Deakin on May 27, 1943, and was killed a few days later by a German bomb splinter. Stuart's place as SIS recruiter was taken by Major R. F. Lethbridge, who arrived in Canada in mid-January 1943.

It is highly unlikely that Bailey made the decision to concentrate his recruiting efforts through the Canadian Communist movement. His dispatches from Mihailović Serbia clearly indicate that he was firmly anti-Communist. It is conceivable that he was guided in this direction by Inspector George McClellan, head of the Royal Canadian Mounted Police. McClellan wanted to be cooperative—and obviously, the list of Yugoslav names in his office would have been made up primarily of those classified as subversive. It is most likely, however, that Bailey was simply carrying out orders from his superiors.

In any case, although details about some of the names have been lost, it is certain that the Yugoslavs recruited by Colonel Bailey were—with a few possible exceptions—twenty-four-karat Communists. That the leftward bent of the Yugoslav recruiting operation was part of a larger policy is suggested by the similar bent displayed in recruiting Hungarians and other ethnic Europeans.

A question that has not been answered is whether the decision to recruit identifiable Communists was in any way influenced by one of Stephenson's senior staffers, Cedric Belfrage, who was several years later identified by Elisabeth Bentley as a fellow Soviet spy, or by Stephenson's deputy, Charles Ellis, who was suspect to certain elements in British intelligence, was subjected to an official investigation, and, according to Peter Wright, took early retirement, pleading ill health, within a year after Kim Philby had fallen under suspicion.[20]

The Yugoslav government in exile and the Yugoslav ambassador to Canada were not informed of the "Camp X" project. But in light of the heavy involvement of the Canadian Communist Party in the project, it can be taken for granted that Moscow was fully informed—indeed, we have the word of Vladimir Velebit, Tito's propaganda chief, that this was so.[21] Steve Serdar, one of the leaders of the Canadian-Yugoslavs, was quoted in an interview with the prominent Yugoslav weekly *Borba* as saying that Tim Buck, the Canadian Communist leader, had informed them that Moscow had been advised of their impending departure for Yugoslavia.

According to Serdar, Buck also gave the Camp X graduates the addresses of some potentially useful contacts in Cairo.[22] It can be taken for granted that Klugmann's name was at the top of this list—but, as events demonstrated, this was an unnecessary exercise on Buck's part, because immediately on their arrival in Cairo the Canadian-Yugoslav Communists became the wards of Klugmann.

Klugmann, under Davidson, was used to brief Allied officers about to be dropped into Yugoslavia. In February of 1943, when the first group of Camp X graduates reached Cairo, they were quartered in a villa near Mena House. Before they were dropped in to Tito in late April 1943, Klugmann had charge of preparing them for their assignment. According to Davidson, Klugmann told his Canadian-Yugoslav wards, "You've got to see that this war has become more than a war *against* something, against fascism. It's become a war *for* something much bigger. For national liberation, people's liberation, colonial liberation."[23]

On April 20, 1943, a full five weeks before Deakin was dropped in to the Tito forces on Mount Durmitor, two groups of the Canadian-Yugoslav Communists who were veterans of Camp X were dropped into Yugoslavia: one into eastern Bosnia, the other into western Croatia. These two groups, quite naturally, had much to report to SOE Cairo and later to Captain Deakin when he joined them in Yugoslavia. None of it was critical of Tito. All of it was critical of Mihailović.

Such were the prime sources of British intelligence in Yugoslavia at the time the switch to Tito gathered momentum.

CHAPTER

13

Mihailović and the British Missions

The relations between the various British missions and General Mihailović had a turbulent and unhappy history.

The first officer attached to Mihailović, Major Duane T. ("Marko") Hudson, was a former mining engineer employed by the British-owned Trepča mines in Yugoslavia. Strictly speaking, Hudson did not head a mission but was part of a joint mission sent out by the British and Yugoslav governments to make preliminary findings. He was accompanied by two Yugoslav majors, Mirko I. Lalatović and Zaharije I. Ostojić. When the party was landed on the Dalmatian coast by submarine on September 18, 1941, Hudson was under vague and general instructions to contact resistance elements in Yugoslavia and report on them.[1]

The first guerrillas the Hudson party established contact with were the Partisans, whose headquarters at Užice they reached on October 23. Ostojić and Lalatović went on to Mihailović's headquarters at Brajići. Hudson, for the very good reason that he wanted to learn more about the Partisans, did not accompany them—for which, understandably, he incurred the wrath of Mihailović. Although everything had not yet fallen into place, Mihailović assumed that the British government had intended Hudson, before all else, to serve as a liaison officer with him, and he scolded Hudson for having hobnobbed with the "communist rabble."[2]

On November 29 the German 342d Division captured Užice and destroyed the bulk of the Partisan army. Tito withdrew into the Sandžak; and Hudson, who had been in Užice at the time of its fall, withdrew with the Tito forces.

The Germans then turned their attention to the Mihailović headquarters in a drive that went under the code name "Operation Mihailović." The Germans sought to pull their net so tight that Mihailović would have no opportunity to escape. On December 6 they promised any man who personally captured Mihailović six weeks' leave of absence. A few days later, on discovering that Mihailović had escaped them, they upped the offer to a substantial cash award and burned down some of the buildings in the Ravna Gora area.[3]

The manner of Mihailović's escape is worth recounting. As the 342d Division was overrunning Struganik, Mihailović jumped into a ditch and quickly hid himself in a pile of leaves. According to participants in the incident, a Serbian officer by the name of Aleksandar Mišić then stood up and identified himself as Colonel Mihailović. He was shot the next morning— but meanwhile Mihailović had been able to make good his escape.[4] Hudson returned from the Sandžak on the night of December 7–8, as the Germans were completing their encirclement of the Mihailović headquarters. In his report Hudson said, "I found no remains of Mihailović's men except himself and a few officers. Everyone else having converted themselves to Nedić men and departed, to the complete frustration of the Boche."[5]

In the eyes of Mihailović, Hudson had compounded his initial political delinquency by retreating with the Partisans; and in a fit of anger that lasted much too long, he "punished" Hudson by refusing to see him and permitting him to live in solitude for a period of almost five months. For a long time Hudson had to subsist on a diet of potatoes. Finally Mihailović relented and invited Hudson to rejoin him at his headquarters. It speaks well for Hudson as a man that he did not permit his five months of "exile" to poison his judgment of the Mihailović movement. In April 1944, when he had returned to London from Yugoslavia, Hudson attended a reception for Commonwealth leaders at the invitation of Prime Minister Churchill. When he was introduced to Field Marshal Jan Christiaan Smuts, the prime minister of South Africa, Smuts asked him whether Mihailović was a traitor. To this question Hudson replied emphatically, "General Mihailović is *not* a traitor!"[6]

It did not simplify Hudson's task that for much of his thirty months in Yugoslavia he was without radio communications of any kind. A radio transmitter he had brought into Yugoslavia apparently was retained at Tito's headquarters in Užice when Hudson joined Mihailović at his headquarters. For a period of time Mihailović permitted Hudson to use his own transmitter, but Hudson's understandable refusal to share his cipher with Mihailović resulted in much hard feeling. Hudson was without radio communication of any kind during his five-month "exile" from Mihailović's headquarters. Deakin recounts that after the German withdrawal in December 1941, Mihailović refused Hudson the use of radio communication. According to the Yugoslav-Australian historian M. Deroc, however, this was an oversimplification. Mihailović himself was off the air for security reasons for a period of several months. In any case, if Mihailović erred, it was fundamentally in his decision to suspend relations with Colonel Hudson.

In his early reports from Yugoslavia, Hudson dealt extensively and frankly with the question of the relations of certain Mihailović commanders with the Italians. This material was subsequently used against Mihailović by all of his enemies and critics, and even by his friends in the Foreign Office and SOE London. Hudson related that when he got back to SOE Cairo after being evacuated from Yugoslavia, he was so angered by the slanted manner in which his reports had been excerpted and summarized that, in a moment of supreme irritation, he tore up a sheaf of the summaries that had been passed to him for reading.[7]

In groping for political guidelines, Hudson had nothing to go by because there was no prior experience with Communist-led resistance movements, or with the many new problems involved in devising policies that would protect the area of operations from a Communist takeover at the same time as they fortified the resistance. A square-jawed and courageous officer who had held an amateur boxing championship in his native South Africa, Hudson had an excellent knowledge of the Serbo-Croat language. However, he was short on the diplomatic skills necessary to open the hearts and win the confidence of Mihailović and the other Serbian leaders with whom he was dealing. Concerned over the obvious failure to establish a rapport between Mihailović and Hudson, the Foreign Office, toward the end of 1942, decided to send in Colonel Bailey, also a former engineer in the Trepča mines and a longtime resident of Yugoslavia, to head up an enlarged British mission. Bailey was parachuted into Mihailović headquarters on Christmas Day 1942, and during the months that followed he was joined by other officers, so that by September 1943 he had under him—theoretically—some fifteen sub-missions* embracing almost thirty British officers.

I have used the word "theoretically" because, under the rules that governed his communications, Bailey could not communicate directly with any of his sub-missions. He complained of this and other matters having to do with SOE communications in a wire dated September 4, 1943. In this wire he said:

. . . Eight months [in Yugoslavia] have provided only two relevant telegrams from HMG [His Majesty's Government], one in May and one in August. I consider neither adequate . . . Although normally [nominally?] in command all sub-missions to Mihailović's forces, I was until August in practically complete ignorance of sub-missions location, plans, and activities.[8]

*In several places in the SOE documentation the number of sub-missions is given as fifteen, and in one place as seventeen. There may, in fact, be no conflict between the two, because there was sometimes a tendency for sub-missions to be divided, so that they had their own sub-missions.

A few months later Brigadier C. D. Armstrong, who succeeded Bailey as chief of mission, filed a similar complaint about the impossibility of communicating in a timely manner with his many sub-missions, when it took approximately one month's time to encode a message, send it off to Cairo, have Cairo encode it again after the inevitable bureaucratic delays, send it out to a sub-mission, have the sub-mission encode a reply and send it back to Cairo, and then have Cairo send the sub-mission's reply to Armstrong.

More the intellectual than Hudson, Bailey was a man of quite superior intelligence who after the war rose to the position of chief of the translation section of the United Nations in Geneva. He was also highly knowledgeable about Serbian politics, history, and culture. My own impression of him when we met in London in September 1946 was altogether favorable. There could be no mistaking the genuineness of his indignation over the fate meted out to Mihailović. Bailey's judgment and toughness are, however, called into question by his role in recruiting the Canadian-Yugoslav Communists later used for intelligence missions in Tito territory. (In this, however, he almost certainly was acting on instructions—against his own better judgment.) His judgment is also called into question by the fact that he permitted SOE Cairo to manipulate him in the matter of replacing Mihailović (this is discussed in Chapter 23) and by his failure to protest sooner and in more energetic terms against the serious misrepresentations by BBC that were undermining the mission's authority and effectiveness. His briefing of Churchill in March and early April of 1944 constituted perhaps the highlight of his career as a liaison officer.

But Bailey suffered from an inability to follow through on his intentions, which may have been related to his later difficulties with alcohol, about which I have heard from several people who knew him during this period. At the time of the trial of Mihailović in June 1946, for example, he told Vane Ivanović that he intended in a great hurry to write a book in defense of Mihailović. There is no question that he meant it at the time—but the book was never written. Again, in the early 1970s he told several people that he was researching his notes with the intention of writing a book on Mihailović. Nothing happened to this commitment, either.

Brigadier Charles D. Armstrong, who was dropped into Mihailović headquarters on September 25, 1943, as the new chief of the British mission, was a competent and courageous combat officer who had covered himself with glory in the evacuation of Dunkirk. However, he was without any background in Yugoslav affairs or politics in general (he even told Brigadier Keble of SOE that he did not want to go into Yugoslavia if politics was involved). His recollection also was that he was given no briefing of any kind before being sent on his mission.[9] His appointment to a country where virtually every male drank and smoked cigarettes suffered from the additional awkwardness that he was a teetotaler and nonsmoker. To top everything off, he was without influence in Whitehall, unlike Brigadier Maclean, who was a personal friend of Churchill's, with direct access to him. BLOs with whom I have discussed the matter were unanimously of the opinion that Armstrong was selected as chief of the mission to Mihailović precisely because he had no background in Yugoslav affairs and no access to Churchill—facts that reduced him to a political cipher when pitted against the eloquent and well-connected Brigadier Maclean, whose assignment it was to report directly to Churchill on the Tito resistance movement.

Though Hudson, Bailey, and Armstrong varied considerably in background and abilities, they had several disabilities in common.

First of all, they were dealing in wartime with a political situation for which no guidance could be found in past experience.

Second, they were all under orders to prod Mihailović to commit himself to aggressive action against the occupation forces, although they could offer him no quid pro quo in the form of material assistance, because at that stage of the war Britain lacked the necessary aircraft. As pointed out in Chapter 18, which deals with the sabotage of the Mihailović supply operation, from beginning to end Mihailović received pathetically limited supplies of weapons and ammunition. The excuse may be offered that until the Allies were established in Italy during the first weeks of September 1943, the aircraft for a large, sustained supply operation simply were not available. This is true. But for some six weeks after the capitulation of Italy the Mihailović forces engaged in a whole series of activities, major and minor, that would have merited a considerable expansion of the Mihailović supply operation, assuming that the letter from the Allied commander in chief, General Wilson, delivered to Mihailović by Brigadier Armstrong, was seriously intended.

"Jumbo" Wilson, though not a duplicitous person, was caught up in the duplicity of SOE Cairo, which prepared many of his statements and controlled shipments of supplies to both sides in Yugoslavia. His letter to Mihailović is worth quoting because of what it reveals about those responsible for the conduct of Yugoslav operations:

> It gives me great pleasure to have the opportunity to send you this personal message through the agency of Brigadier General Armstrong, and to inform you that it has now become logistically possible for me to send you military supplies on a much larger scale . . .
>
> I understand perfectly that the weaponry of which your forces currently dispose hardly permits them to engage in frontal attacks on forces equipped with much heavier weapons, but I believe that activity in the form of sabotage is within their capabilities, and this activity at the present stage of the war would be of immense value to our common cause . . .

> I well know the enormous sacrifices which have already been made by the heroic
> people of your country—splendid and superb sacrifices which will be appro-
> priately honored by history, and I hope that the effective assistance that we are
> now in a position to offer you will contribute materially to the liberation [of
> your country] from the yoke of German tyranny.[10]

Would the situation in Yugoslavia have been different if the Mihailović forces,
in return for their impressive record of operations from the end of August
1943 to mid-October, had received an increasing flow of supplies and been
given credit for their activities? Brigadier Armstrong was disposed to believe
that had this happened, there would have been no difficulty in persuading
Mihailović to carry out further operations against major objectives specified
by the British.

Third, at a time when his units were under constant attack by the Communists, from June 1943 until early 1944, Mihailović was reminded virtually
every day that his forces were not to fight the Partisans unless attacked by
them. Theoretically, a reciprocal restraint was supposed to be encouraged by
the BLOs attached to the Partisans. It is obvious from a reading of the record, however, that no serious effort was made to impose such restraints on
the Tito forces, either by Deakin or by the enlarged mission under Fitzroy
Maclean. Deakin does not mention any conversation with Tito designed to
promote an understanding with Mihailović. Maclean recounts only one brief
conversation with Tito on this subject: As he and Tito sat talking under the
stars, he asked Tito whether "two years after his original negotiation with
Mihailović there was any hope of reaching any agreement with the Četniks
and thus forming a united front against the enemies." Tito replied that he
had sought such an understanding but no longer regarded it as possible. And
that, apparently, was the extent of Maclean's explorations on this admittedly
tricky terrain.[11]

Fourth, there was the attitude of BBC, which had started plugging the
Partisans during the last months of 1942. During the summer and fall of 1943
BBC had repeatedly irked Mihailović by attributing to the Partisans victories
that his forces had won over the occupation forces, by announcing the Partisan occupation of numerous Home Army centers as victories over the Axis
armies, and by highlighting the defection of entire Ustaše units to the Partisans. Over and over and over again, Brigadier Armstrong, Colonel Bailey,
and other members of the British mission complained to SOE Cairo about
these inaccuracies and provocations, but to no avail. Nothing in the record
indicates that any of these protests were ever forwarded to BBC.

Fifth, although this has nothing to do with personal decency or integrity
or intelligence, the British liaison officers were a product of a culture that

inevitably gave those of less advanced nations the uncomfortable feeling that they were being treated as second-class citizens of the world. In Brigadier Armstrong's case, this projection was no doubt fed by his experience as a British officer in India. But Hudson and Bailey could also be imperious in their relations with Mihailović without realizing for a minute that they were creating profound difficulties for themselves.

To these five factors must be added a sixth, which was only partly the fault of the British. As Colonel Bailey put the matter in his report: "Effective liaison in the best sense has never been realised, because the precise function, responsibilities and rights of BLOs were never sufficiently impressed on Mihailović by the only people to whom he might have listened: namely his King and Government." [12]

Mihailović was not without his difficult side, but it is hard to believe that a statement satisfactory to both sides as to the rights and duties of the BLOs with Mihailović could not have been worked out with the Yugoslav government if SOE Cairo and the Foreign Office had made this a priority. Indeed, it is difficult to escape the conclusion that the failure in this respect was due more to the negative political attitude of SOE Cairo and the negligence of the Foreign Office than to the obtuseness of King Peter and the Yugoslav government.

Other factors contributed to the alienation. There was bad blood, for example, over the mission of Captain Charles Robertson, who in mid-1942 was sent in by SOE Cairo as a supporting officer and radio communications expert for Hudson. Robertson was a Canadian-Yugoslav whose real name was Dragi Radivojević. At one point Bailey describes him flatly as a Communist. There is no question that Robertson was a leftist, although opinion differs on whether he was a Stalinist or a Trotskyist. I am disposed, however, to credit the account of Julian Amery, then in charge of Yugoslav affairs in SOE, that Robertson escaped to the Partisans in early September 1943 and shortly thereafter was reported murdered under mysterious circumstances, by either the Partisans or the Četniks.

His Marxist sympathies could have led to his murder by the Četniks, most of whom were not sufficiently sophisticated to understand the mortal differences between Trotskyists and Stalinists, despite their common Marxist heritage. On the other hand, if Robertson did escape to the Partisans, it was a distinct possibility that he was murdered by them, because at that time the Stalinists were inclined to regard the Trotskyists as the lowest form of animal life. Apparently, Robertson, before going into Yugoslavia, had been severely beaten up by assailants who, he claimed, were Communists. He named James Klugmann as the man who had engineered the attack on him, thereby indicating rather conclusively that, whatever else he may have been, Robertson was not a follower of the Communist Party.[13] In any case, there can be no doubt that the Robertson appointment created much suspicion and bitterness among the Mihailović entourage.

There is also the matter of the conspiracy masterminded by SOE Cairo to replace Mihailović with several younger, more aggressive officers who were willing to pledge themselves to a more activist program and to cooperation with the Partisans. Communications between Bailey and SOE Cairo on this project apparently began sometime during the summer of 1943. This story is told at a later point. Suffice it to say that Mihailović found out about the conspiracy because, as was only natural, the Mihailović officers and the British mission ran intelligence operations against each other—which on occasion clearly entailed access to each other's communications.

Mihailović was deeply wounded by the involvement of several subordinate officers for whom he had genuine affection—especially Pavle Djurišić, his commander in Montenegro. Djurišić was as charismatic as he was courageous and intelligent. Mihailović demonstrated his fondness for Djurišić by always seeking him out for conversation at meetings with groups of officers. However, Mihailović took no action against the plotters, apparently confident that the SOE Cairo machinations would come to naught.

It turned out that Mihailović's confidence was justified. Officers like Djurišić, Lukačević, and Baćević may have engaged in conversations about replacing him because they believed that only in this way could the blockade on British arms shipments be broken. But from many conversations with individuals who survived the final disaster I am convinced that the so-called "dissident" officers never really had their hearts in the plot.

All these factors combined to thwart an understanding and sympathetic relationship between Mihailović and the several British mission chiefs assigned to him. Mihailović did, however, have a relationship of mutual trust and respect, even affection, with Major Kenneth Greenlees, a man of saintlike rectitude who had served as Bailey's aide since February 1943. Even when Mihailović suspected Bailey and Armstrong of being somehow involved in the campaign against him and stopped talking to them for weeks at a time, he never harbored such suspicions about Greenlees—or, for that matter, about the members of the American mission.

Still another factor had to do with the briefs given successively to Hudson, Bailey, and Armstrong, which led them to report in detail everything that even faintly merited criticism on the Mihailović side. On the Partisan side, however, weaknesses and negative features were glossed over by the British missions to Tito. As Peter Solly-Flood, who later became the first secretary of the British embassy in Washington, put the matter, the BLOs with Mihailović appeared to be operating according to one set of rules, and the BLOs with Tito according to a completely different set of rules.

The British sub-missions dropped into Mihailović territory during the last half of 1943 would report, as a matter of course, on the strength and disposition of the Mihailović forces to which they were attached, on the armament of those forces, and on the strengths and weaknesses of the officers in charge. This, of course, was priceless intelligence to the Partisan forces, which were then attempting to invade Serbia from several directions. Not very surprisingly, it occurred to Brigadier Armstrong at one point that this information might be making its way from SOE Cairo to the Partisan strategists. Alarmed by this possibility, he sent the following urgent message to SOE Cairo on November 18, 1943: "Never rpt never pass information about MVIC location, commanders, or strength to Partisans."[14]

There is no documentary evidence that James Klugmann did pass such information on to the Communists. However, there is every reason for suspecting that he did.

CHAPTER

14

Inactivity and Collaboration: The Charges vs. the Facts

. . . during the last 18 months there is no evidence of any effective anti-Axis action initiated by Mihailović.

Foreign Office Memorandum
November 19, 1943

. . . since he [Mihailović] is . . . doing nothing from a military point of view to justify our continued assistance, we should consider cutting off supplies while maintaining our political and moral support (e.g., propaganda).

Foreign Office Memorandum
November 22, 1943

Even before embarking on my research at the British Public Record Office in fall of 1976, I was convinced on the basis of what I knew that the charges of inactivity, which played a major role in the abandonment of Mihailović in the closing months of 1943, were, to say the least, very much exaggerated. In my early research I focused heavily on the period August to December 1943, because it was precisely within this time frame that the British moved from the support of Mihailović to his abandonment. The Special Operations Executive files, I had been told, were still closed. But I discovered one group of files originating in SOE that had for some reason been released, and that cast much light on the situation. This was the Operational Log of in-messages from the BLOs in Yugoslavia to SOE Cairo and out-messages to them from SOE Cairo. From many personal interviews I expected to find at least some official record of the anti-Axis activities conducted by the Mihailović forces. I was amazed, however, by the amount of information that came to light through careful examination of the Log.

Despite the obvious gaps and the terseness of the language and the maddeningly fragmentary manner in which some of the messages are excerpted—sometimes the excerpts start or terminate in midsentence—the Operational Log constitutes a priceless source of information. In it one can find a record of the BLOs' frustrations in dealing with the Mihailović commanders, as well as their exasperation with the lack of supply sorties, with SOE's obtuse handling of the situation, and with the blatant inaccuracies of BBC broadcast reports on events in Serbia. And despite the many criticisms of Mihailović personally and of his various commanders, when the bits and pieces are put together, the Operational Log also contains a truly amazing amount of evidence of activities against the Axis, including a number of major battles and many, many minor ones, of sabotage directed against the Axis communications system, and of reprisals against Mihailović followers.

To establish a clearer picture of what was actually going on in Yugoslavia at the time of Mihailović's abandonment, I decided to put together a chronological compendium for the months of August through December 1943 of reports by British and American officers dealing with anti-Axis actions and sabotage by Mihailović forces, and of reprisals by the occupation forces. In doing so, I relied primarily on the many volumes of the Operational Log and the reports of the British liaison officers in the War Office files; but in the interest of completeness I also quoted at points from the situation reports sent out at irregular intervals by SOE Cairo, from the deposition of the BLOs to the Belgrade court, from the preliminary statement of Captain Walter Mansfield to the Commission of Inquiry, and from sundry items in the War Office and Foreign Office files. Since the chronological compendium makes for heavy reading, I have decided to print it as a separate chapter, immediately following this one. But I would urge conscientious readers to make the special effort required to read or at least scan it. *What is clear is that those responsible for the political decision to abandon Mihailović in early December 1943 could not have had access to the essential facts detailed in the compendium.*

Who was responsible for keeping this vitally important information from London? One or two omissions, even important ones, might be attributed to bureaucratic carelessness. But so many omissions, including highly important ones, exceed the possibility of carelessness. Using the process of elimination, it becomes virtually unchallengeable that the person responsible must have been James Klugmann.

David Erskine was a junior intelligence officer attached to the Yugoslav

Section of SOE at the beginning of September 1943. In a letter to me he says that Klugmann was probably the first, and certainly one of the first, to have access to incoming messages from the field, and that he thought it likely that it was Klugmann who selected excerpts for the Operational Log and decided what information was to be passed on to London.

The chronological record of activities and reprisals shows that it is probably no exaggeration to call the Mihailović movement during the period in question the second most active resistance movement in Europe, ranking behind only the Partisan movement in Yugoslavia. One need only ask: Apart from the Warsaw ghetto uprising of spring 1943 and the Polish Home Army uprising in August 1944, how many battles fought by any European resistance movement resulted in 200 to 300 enemy dead? On the Mihailović ledger for the period August 15 to October 15, 1943, there were at least four such battles. Yet a Foreign Office memorandum dated November 19, 1943, could say that "during the last 18 months there is no evidence of any effective anti-Axis action initiated by Mihailović."[1] And Douglas Howard, wartime chief of the Foreign Office, Southern Department, who had been sympathetic to Mihailović as late as mid-September 1943, wrote in a memorandum dated November 22, 1943, that "since he [Mihailović] is . . . doing nothing from a military point of view to justify our continued assistance, we should consider cutting off supplies while maintaining our political and moral support (e.g., propaganda)."[2]

The chronological tabulation of Mihailović activities was shown by me, in a preliminary and far less complete version, to Howard and also to Peter Boughey, who headed the Yugoslav desk of SOE London before the abandonment of Mihailović. Both of them expressed amazement that the record contained so many references, during the final critical period of 1943, to military actions, large and small, and to sabotage and reprisals. At his home in Bedfordshire on December 1, 1977, I asked Sir Douglas the following hypothetical question (the wording here is approximate):

Suppose the Foreign Office in mid-October 1943 had received a memorandum from Bailey and Armstrong that said approximately the following:

"The past several months, despite foot-dragging in some areas, have witnessed a relatively high level of activity by the Mihailović forces. During this period they have been involved in some half-dozen major attacks on Axis forces, in each of which the enemy death toll was in the range of 200 to 300.

"At Mučanj, south of Užice, on July 31, they engaged a strong Bulgarian force and inflicted severe casualties on it.

"At Trstenik, on August 29, they derailed two troop trains and killed 200 of the enemy and captured others.

"At Prijepolje, on September 11, they attacked a German garrison approximately 1,000 strong and put it to flight after killing more than 200 enemy troops.

"At Priboj, on September 12, after a night of hard fighting, they forced the surrender of an Italian garrison of 1,800 men under Colonel Graziani.

"At Višegrad, on October 5, they attacked a German garrison some 800 strong, killing several hundred of them and driving the rest northward—after which they blew up the 600-foot Višegrad bridge, effectively disrupting the Belgrade-Sarajevo railroad line.

"At Rogatica on October 14, the Mihailović forces again attacked a strong Axis garrison, killing several hundred Ustaše.

"In addition to these actions—taken on their own initiative—they were instrumental in compelling the surrender of the Italian Venezia Division at Berane and of substantial Italian units at Kotor and other points. On top of these major engagements, there were numerous minor engagements; four important railway bridges were destroyed and tracks torn up between Višegrad and Mokra Gora on the Sarajevo-Užice line; and trains were wrecked and tracks torn up at other points.

"Finally, the period in question witnessed two large-scale attacks on Mihailović's headquarters by German forces, one on September 5 and the second on October 10. This record is all the more remarkable in view of the fact that Mihailović has received pathetically little support in terms of arms and ammunition."

"Suppose you had received such a message from Bailey and Armstrong sometime in October 1943," I continued. "Would this have affected the Foreign Office decision on Mihailović?"

Later this question was repeated to Sir Douglas Howard in a letter. The answer I received said, among other things:

> . . . If, of course, as now seems more than possible, our information re Mihailovich's activities were incomplete, to say the least, then the whole affair changes color . . . If the information contained in your work had been available to us at the time, our whole policy might and probably would, have been very different.[3]

The answer from Peter Boughey was very similar.

Most of the actions described in the compendium are relatively small ones—blowing up bridges, tearing up tracks, wrecking trains, killing 40 Bulgarians here or 16 Germans there—but there are many of them. There are also some half-dozen large-scale actions—very large-scale by guerrilla standards—where the enemy death toll ran from 200 to 300.

It is natural to assume that prime ministers and foreign ministers, when they make important decisions in foreign policy, are in possession of all the available facts. This, however, is not necessarily so—especially in the age of highly sophisticated disinformation, they can be lamentably misled by those whose duty it is to provide them with information and analytical summaries. SOE Cairo was supposed to keep London informed about the situation in Yugoslavia but, as is painfully obvious, for a long time did not do so. Was Klugmann responsible? If not, who else in the operational chain could have doctored the intelligence forwarded to London?

By the summer of 1943, Klugmann, who had joined SOE Cairo in February 1942, was the only member of SOE who had been with the Yugoslav operation virtually from the beginning. Given all that is known about his political proclivities, it is only natural to infer that he played a central role in slanting the intelligence forwarded to London so as to raise the most serious doubts about Mihailović's value to the Allied cause.

It is a tribute to Klugmann's thoroughness that even men like Hugh Seton-Watson and Bill Deakin, and Fitzroy Maclean through Bill Deakin, were heavily influenced by the slanted intelligence in the files of SOE Cairo, never even remotely suspecting Klugmann's role.

Having been won over against Mihailović, at least in part, by the built-up disinformation in the SOE files, Deakin and Maclean thereafter did much to deepen Churchill's romantic involvement with the pro-Tito mania. Their contribution to the campaign of disinformation was greater rather than smaller because they were used as tools whose personal motives could not be questioned.

Deakin relates how on the morning of December 9, 1943, he was instructed to attend a dinner that night at the British embassy in Cairo. On entering the drawing room, he found himself in the presence "not only of the British Ambassador and his staff, but of the Prime Minister, the Foreign Secretary, the British Chief(s) of Staff, and other gentlemen of formidable rank. It became obvious in a trice that the purpose of the meeting was to arrive at some urgent decisions on the situation in the Balkans." About his conversation with Churchill, Deakin said:

For nearly two hours the Prime Minister interrogated me as the officer mainly concerned with interpreting the evidence derived from captured German and Četnik documents concerning the links between Mihailović and his commanders with the Italians and Germans. It was a miserable task.

The questions were pointed and searched out every detail within the range of my knowledge, and as I talked I knew that I was compiling the elements of a hostile brief which would play a decisive part in any future break between the British government and Mihailović . . . The same evening Mr. Churchill invited me to dine at the villa of the Minister of State. The relentless questioning was resumed into the early hours.[4]

Deakin and Maclean may be accused of gullibility at a time when their gullibility was shared by the vast majority of Englishmen and Americans. Certainly, they did not belong in the same political category as Klugmann; they were patriotic Englishmen who made judgments that turned out to be dead wrong. But this is how disinformation works.

Had Deakin preceded his presentation on Četnik "collaboration" with a summary of certified Četnik activities over the previous three months, the effect on the prime minister would have been altogether different.

The chronological compendium does not complete the list of Mihailović's activities. To it must be added a whole series of items from the report filed with the War Office by Colonel Bailey after his return to England in March 1944. On his way to the Adriatic coast in an arduous trip that took from January 5 to February 6, 1944, Bailey did run into several situations that suggested, at least, the existence of some kind of accommodation between the local Mihailović commanders and the Germans. If such accommodations did exist, it is clear that Bailey was able in several cases to use them to his own advantage. These accommodations Bailey described in a detailed and forthright manner. But far more impressive as a body of evidence was his testimony concerning his many experiences with the Mihailović forces during the summer of 1943, when other sources reported them to be completely inactive. I have extracted a number of paragraphs from his report. Most of these did not describe actions of heroic scope, but at least they indicate the continuous state of hostilities between the Mihailović forces and the Germans and their various satellites. (It is to be noted that whenever Bailey speaks of a German attack on members of the British mission, this signifies an attack on the Mihailović forces with which they were then quartered.) Bailey's report included the following entries:

28. On July 14, 1943, we learned that very strong enemy forces, exceeding one division, had blocked off the area Valjevo-Kosjerići-Požega-Čačak-Milanovac-Ljig to make a full scale drive to capture Mihailović and the British Mission. [Major] Greenlees and company on Ravna Gora were in fact attacked by Germans on the morning of July 14th . . . and lost all their equipment . . .

30. Bulgar and German troops arrived in Seca Reka during the afternoon of July 15th and were engaged by our patrols while the main body took refuge in heavy forests on Jelena Gora just east of the Užice-Valjevo road. We spent July 16th in hiding in these woods, hearing much firing to the south and east, and watching Bulgarian troops patrol the road on foot.

34. Maj. Miloš Marković, commanding the Požega Corpus, under whose protection we now were, fought a delaying action while the staff retired round Mučanj to the mountain of Čemernica, 8 kms. SW of Ivanjica, reached on July 29th, 1943, (elevation 1400 metres).

38. During this period also, several actions were fought between Marković's units and Germans, Bulgarians and Quislings on both sides of the Valley of Moravica. They were finally broken off because of exhaustion of ammunition.

39. On September 5th, the eve of King Peter's birthday, celebrations were held throughout Serbia, and commemorative beacons lit on all the principal mountain ranges. This provoked the interest of the enemy, and HQ was attacked at 0600 hours September 6th. Mist and an offensive action fought by Mihailović's personal bodyguard, (the first time they had been in action during my stay in the country) compelled the enemy to retire, and HQ withdrew at leisure to the NW.

53. On October 12th considerable Bulgarian forces, sent to investigate the attack on the Sargain . . . approached Jablanica from two directions, and considerable fighting took place during the day . . . At this period, Priboj, Rudo, Višegrad and Vardište were all in the hands of Mihailović, but stronger Partisan forces were now making their way into the Sandžak from the NE.[5]

In quoting from the Bailey report, I have purposely skipped over the many paragraphs that deal with the major actions referred to in the Operational Log—the attacks on Priboj, Prijepolje, and Berane, the attacks on the four bridges at Mokra Gora, the capture of Višegrad and the destruction of the Višegrad bridge, the capture of Rogatica, and other military successes. Significantly, Bailey's account of these continuing encounters with the German and satellite forces carries the account of Četnik activities certified by the BLOs back to the beginning of July 1943.[6]

Despite this record, Bailey, at the end of one report he filed in London, poses this question: Could Mihailović himself have met with the Germans, Bulgarians, Italians, or Yugoslav quislings while Bailey was attached to the Home Army forces? In reply he points out that if such meetings did take place, "they could only have taken place when either Mihailović himself or the senior BLO was absent from Mihailović headquarters. They could hardly have taken place at Mihailović headquarters, even during the period when formal contact only was being maintained, without the facts coming to the knowledge of British officers there."[7]

Bailey's account of hostilities between the Germans and the Mihailović forces can be extended backward in time through September 1942 if one is willing to depart momentarily from a format that has up until this point limited us to the testimony of British and American officers. In one of the most carefully researched books that has appeared to date, Walter Roberts, who worked on the staff of the American embassy in Belgrade and had access to the official Yugoslav documentation, summarizes in these terms the bloody fighting between the Mihailović forces and the Nedić and German forces during the last months of 1942:

> On September 9, [1942] Mihailović called through leaflets and clandestine radio transmitters for civil disobedience to the Nedić regime. Bloody fighting broke out between Četniks and Nedić followers and as a result, the German High Command became actively involved in the persecution of Četniks, many of whom were captured and executed. There is evidence that particularly during November and December 1942, German troops were fighting Četniks if for no other reason than to bolster the Nedić regime.[8]

Taken as a whole, the compendium and ancillary information detailed above make nonsense of the charges of inactivity and collaboration and leave one wondering at the gross disparity between the field intelligence received by SOE Cairo and the repeated references in the Foreign Office and War Office files to the total inactivity of the Mihailović forces—which finally persuaded even Mihailović's friends in the Foreign Office that they had to let him go. If responsible senior officials in London could be so ignorant about Mihailović's record of activities for the period in question, one can only conclude that this information was not being transmitted to London by SOE Cairo.

15

On Doing "Nothing":
The Chronological Compendium

It must be emphasized that the following compendium is far from complete, for the following reasons:

(1) There are no log entries available for the period preceding September 1943, because the Operational Log available in the Public Record Office in London commences at the beginning of September.

(2) Many of the sheets in the Operational Log are very poor carbons. Indeed, a large number of the photocopies made by the Public Record Office for this research were completely indecipherable.

(3) Ordinarily, as indicated previously, the BLOs attached to Mihailović only passed on reports of activities that they had either witnessed or been able to confirm subsequently. The great majority of the activities described in this compendium are supported by this kind of confirmation, and in the few instances where the liaison officers reproduced unconfirmed reports from Mihailović or his commanders, this fact is noted. While allowing for some inaccuracy, there is every reason for believing that many other actions claimed by the Mihailović forces really did take place much as described.

In the following text, excerpts from the Operational Log (incoming messages) and the Signal Log (outgoing messages) are reproduced basically as they appear. In some cases, different versions of the same information appear in consecutive messages, or messages separated by several days. I have included them all in my chronological compendium to indicate what information was available from a reading of the Operational Log.

Place names frequently are garbled. Where possible, the correct name has been indicated in brackets. Garbles that cannot be deciphered are shown by a question mark in brackets. All names were in capital letters in the log.

Code names for sub-missions, for liaison officers, and for Mihailović officers are left in solid caps to indicate that they are not to be read as uncoded prose. A message was generally sent out in several parts, each part rarely exceeding five to ten typewritten lines, sometimes broken in midsentence. The Operational and Signal Logs would sometimes excerpt one part of the message, sometimes several parts. Thus, some paragraphs and even sentences appear to be incomplete.

W/T (wireless telegraph) abbreviations have been spelled out (where they could be understood) in order to make the text more intelligible. Thus, "L.C." is "lines of communication" and HMG is "heavy machine guns" (it can also mean, however, "His Majesty's Government"). The word "repeat," generally used for emphasis, has also been spelled out.

All sub-missions had code names. The code names for the Mihailović sub-missions mentioned in these excerpts include ANGELICA, ENAMEL, EXCERPT, FUGUE, NERONIAN, REPARTEE, RHODIUM, ROUGH-SHOD, RUPEES, SERBONIAN. W/T stations with Colonel Bailey and Brigadier Armstrong have the code names CAVERN TWO, RAPIER, and RAPIER UDAL. All the liaison officers, British and American, also had code names. Here the following decoding of the principal names should be sufficient: WIX—Brigadier Armstrong; OLD—Colonel Bailey; PLO—Colonel Hudson; DUTCH—Colonel Seitz; SPROC—Captain Mansfield. Other code names for British liaison officers were BIRD, CAT, DIGGER, FIELD, JILL, MEAT, PADDLE, ROBIN, STONE, TREE. (This list is not complete, but these are the names that appear in the compendium.) Michael Lees always signed his messages "Mike," obviously not a code name. Mihailović officers were sometimes also referred to by code names. Thus, JURY was Major Djurić, and NIM was Major Keserović.

CHRONOLOGICAL COMPENDIUM (AUGUST–DECEMBER 1943)
OF REPORTS BY BRITISH AND AMERICAN SOURCES
DEALING WITH ANTI-AXIS ACTIONS AND SABOTAGE BY MIHAILOVIĆ
FORCES AND REPRISALS AGAINST MIHAILOVIĆ SERBS

July 30–31

A strong Bulgarian force was engaged at Mučanj, south of Užice and severe casualties inflicted. [Deposition of BLOs to the Belgrade court.]

August

Falling Italian morale emphasizes in guerrilla news from Balkans that in Serbia the Axis is much troubled by Mihailovists. Latter's successful action against Danube shipping so worried Germans they immediately strengthened their already inhuman reprisals for this action. It is reported fifty innocent

persons including women and children shot in Belgrade by the German occupants, all within 600 yards of the Serbian side of the river being ruthlessly
evacuated, and Germans cutting down all nearby woods, frantically endeavoring to prevent recurrence of this attack on their vital Danube traffic.
[Message from the British minister of state, Cairo, to the Foreign Office,
August 4, 1943, FO (Foreign Office) 371/37589.]

August 5

From REPARTEE (37 Pt. 2): On 5 August, Kalabić killed 11 Huns and
disarmed 15 Huns. As reprisals Huns burnt village Stragari, 27 kilos from
Kragujevac, 420 houses and killed all male population who did not escape.
[WO (War Office)] 202/140, October 12, 1943.

August 28

To FUNGUS: . . . As requested here is instance known anti-Axis activity
by Mihailović troops: On 28 Aug. at Trestinic [Trstenik] they derailed 2
troop trains and killed 200, captured several troops. True that Mihailović
people not nearly as active as Partisans but strongest pressure being brought
to bear on them view speed up sabotage. [WO 202/139, September 20, 1943.]
[This message was sent to Captain William Deakin, who was in charge of
the mission at Tito's headquarters and had wired asking for "guaranteed
instances" of sabotage carried out by Mihailović.]

August

Axis forces were attacked on several occasions during the month in the
Užice-Čačak-Ivanjica area. [Deposition of BLOs to the Belgrade court.]

September 5

Witness saw and participated in fight with approximately 300 German soldiers who tried a surprise dawn attack on Gen. Mihailović's H.Q. There was
heavy fighting for over 2 hours after the Germans first succeeded in infiltrating through our patrols. Finally Germans were driven back down the mountainside. Losses were about even on both sides. Witness saw several German
soldiers taken prisoner by Chetniks and talked with one of them. After being
questioned, prisoners were killed. [Mansfield statement.]

September 6

Axis and Serb troops of General Nedić's forces were engaged at Čemernica,
near Ivanjica, casualties being inflicted and prisoners taken. [Deposition of
BLOs to the Belgrade court.]

September 8

From RAPIER CERN. I again stress imposs[ibility] conceal any ops this country from MVIC 72930 Ref. Cern 29 re Nails[?] Order No. 3778 to attack all enemy motorised columns wherever whenever poss. Kidd. [WO 202/131.]

September 9

From RAPIER: Party two German officers 14 men attempted reach Berane from Podgorica evening of 16. Their aim probably arrest Oxilia [General commanding the Venezia Division] and staff. They were ambushed by Chetniks at Trešnjevik at 23.00 hrs. 6 Km west of Andrijevica on main road to POD. [?] All Germans killed and arms equipment captured, one lorry one staff car, one NC. [WO 202/131 12473.]

September 11

A detachment of Gen. Mihailović's forces, detailed to assist British officers in securing implementation of Italian armistice as it affected local Italian forces in the valley of the Lim, attacked and captured the town of Prijepolje after its seizure by a strong German force on the 9th of September. Heavy casualties were inflicted on the Germans and a considerable quantity of booty including motor transport, captured. Without the successful conclusion of this action, the British officers could not have carried out their orders. [Deposition of BLOs to the Belgrade court.]

September 11

British Col. Wm. Bailey, with a band of 1000 Chetniks supplied by Gen. Mihailović, fought a bloody battle against a German garrison force at Prijepolje, in which over 200 Germans were killed. Col Bailey then proceeded to Berane (with Chetnik forces) where he accepted surrender of 8000 Italians at the "Venezia" Division H.Q. [Mansfield statement.]

September 12

Witness, with British Lt. Col. Duane Hudson, acting on orders from Mihailović, went with 300 Chetnik guerrillas under Lt. Novaković to Priboj, where, after one night of fighting, succeeded in effectuating surrender of Italian garrison of 1800 men under Col. Graziani. [Ibid.]

September 12–13

Upon receipt of first news of Gen. Badoglio's surrender [after the Allied invasion of Italy on September 3, 1943], Gen. Mihailović dispatched radio orders to all his field commanders to attack German and Italian occupation forces everywhere, since he believed D-day was close at hand. Witness personally read many of these orders as they were dispatched. [Ibid.]

September 14

From CAVERN 2 CERN.: Kalabić henceforth Pera Cmdr [paramount commander?] area Mladenovac to Tupolatoar and Jelovai [Topola to Arândjelovac] to Lazarevac which includes main rail and Ibad [road?] Belgrade to South now actively engaged Jerry. Anxious attack road and rail, need explosive with fuses ammo seven nine two and smgs [small machine guns]. Very keen have BLO to keep you informed. [WO 202/131.]

September 14

From CAVERN 2: Area Foča [indecipherable] Lina etc. are in hands of JUG army which defends them against Boche. Boche garrison Kalinovik 1000 and in Goražde 2000 strong. Boche column reaching Gajnica from Plevlje. Communists from East Bosnia, avoiding these Boche, intend attack JUG army in above areas. Must defend our authority and protect people from terror. Ask British mission with Partisans to demand they return and not interfere with our anti Boche action there. Ask Cairo confirm. [WO 202/131 12473.]

September 15

From ANGELICA: Reference your [message no.] 75, please confirm whether Mihailović has given him complete freedom to act as he likes. This appears unlikely in view of strict orders to Djurić to contrary. NIM now involved in heavy fighting with Ljotić and has captured considerable number arms. FIELD. [WO 202/131, September 15, 1943.]

Mid-September

Chetniks hold and administer area Bijelo Polje-Berane-Andrijevica-Mate-ševo-Kolašin. (RAPIER 767). This area is marked by brown outer line with yellow spots within, on attached map. *[This summary statement was based on a report to the War Office based on MOST SECRET SOURCES (MI6). The date on it was September 23, 1943. MI6 was generally unfriendly to Mihailović and not apt to overstate the areas occupied by his forces.]* [WO 202/162.]

September 16

Mihailović forces on 16 September ambushed 16 Germans enroute Berane. [WO 202/139, September 19, 1943.]

September 17

From CAVERN 2: Partisans overestimated. Mihailović drove Hun out of Sarkso[?] only to have Partisans now claim town. Mihailović strongly wants us to send in at least 15 American officers with own code at once to go various areas and see size, location troops to prove strength here and in North. Believes us unbiased. I feel this may be way of convincing him if he is wrong. [WO 202/131, September 17, 1943.]

September 17 (approx)

From RAPIER UDAL (762, Pt. 3): Our MT now totals 7 trucks, 4 staff cars, and 4 mc. [motorcycles]. This ambush was executed by Lašić, local commander, on his own initiative. Lašić is now committed willy nilly to fighting Hun through Gut [GHQ?] Montenegro. Pse secure BBC publicity. STONE. [Ibid., September 19, 1943.]

September 17

From RAPIER (174): 17 September Mihailović forces captured Zvornik from Huns and hold it against all counterattacks. ROBIN. [Ibid., October 5, 1943.]

September 17

From SPROC to Huot: Bosnia: Sept. 17, MVIC occupied Zvornik after fighting Hun and beat off two Hun counterattacks, thereafter taking large amount arms and ammo.

September 19

From ENAMEL (25): Following from Sinisha. On 19th Sept., railway bridge at Rabrovo on line Kučevo-Belgrade damaged. Traffic believed interrupted till end Sept. 14 Todt lorries sabotaged. On 23 Sept., 100 Nedich and Ljoticher troops disarmed at Zhabari. [Ibid., September 26, 1943.]

September 21

Unconfirmed report received that Chets under Capt. Voja Lukačević have taken Nova Varoš and that another force under Maj. Baćević have taken Dubrovnik. Will obtain confirmation. PADDLE. [WO 202/131.]

September 21

From RAPIER UDAL: Četniks have taken over civil administration Berane. Joint Četnik Itie [Italian] command for common anti-Hun ops established Berane and Rijevica [Andrijevica?] Kolašin Mateševo Ljevaroka [Ljeva Reka]. ORs [order] in other places sole responsibility Čets. Hope establish further command Priboj today. The dispositions are 1 battn Ljevarcka [Ljeva Reka]. ORs [order] in other places sole responsibility Čets. Hope establish further command Priboj today. The dispositions are 1 battn Ljevarcka [Ljeva Reka], 2 batts with light art Mateševo. 2 batts with heavy artillery at Fijevica[?]. [WO 202/131.]

September 21

From CAVERN 2: Part 2. Today at dawn we attacked one thousand Huns at Plevlje. Can hear firing but results unknown. I have been twice under fire myself. MVIC and entire staff eagerly await DUTCH [Colonel Albert Seitz, head of American mission] tonight. I have arranged reception by MVIC and all other details. Mission will be handicapped by MVIC irritation at British because British radio fosters Partisans and repeatedly announces that they are joined by Ustashi who persecuted Serbs for the Huns. [WO 202/131 12473.]

September 22

From RAPIER UDAL (766 pt. 2): Sakovici [Šahovići] Andrijevica, and Mateševo. Četniks have formally taken over administration from Itis [Italians] in all these districts. Also in Priboj and Peevlje [Plevlje] districts, and hope occupy or capture both these towns today. [Ibid., September 22, 1943.]

September 22

From CAVERN 2 [SPROC to Huot]: Fact that Marković has had to stop fighting Huns in upper Moravian valley due to lack of ammo. Can't decipher your first our[?] code but second OK. Sorry for my poor cipher but you know how I left. Message centre should realize bad working conditions here and I work day and night and often with one candle and no table. We are fired on by machine gun and mortar . . . [Ibid.]

September 23

From RAPIER (Pt. 2): . . . Sept. 23 Mihailović destroys train full of Huns and explosives in tunnel 20 kilos East of Peć by derailing in tunnel Noae[?] Mils[?]. [Ibid., October 9, 1943.]

September 23

From RAPIER (Pt. 3): Sept. 23 Mihailović attacks Hun Vandustashi [and Ustashi] near Tousla [Tuzla], inflicts losses, takes arms, ammo. [Ibid.]

September 26–27

From ANGELICA (89): Station master Mitrovica reports following sabotage. A. Collision Vučitrn 1945 hrs. 26 Sept. between trains No. 4876. [?] Eight wagons wrecked, including 2 petrol wagons which exploded. 29 Huns now in Mitrovica hospital. B. One wagon derailed Zvečan 27 Sept. C. 2 kms line wrecked at point 30 kms north of Raška, line US [?] [out of commission?] 48 hours. [Ibid., October 3, 1943.]

September 27

For Huot from SPROC: Main Belgrade defense line on Sava and Danube rivers. Many Hun aircraft arrived at Zemun and Pančevo airports. On Sep. ten MVIC attached R R station at Kremna[?]. [WO 202/131.]

September 29

From CAVERN 2 (115, Pt. 3): Railway Ljig-Lajkovac destroyed several places. Huns shot 35 hostages Užice, burnt 18 houses Bajina Bašta. [Ibid.]

September 29

From RAPIER (194 Pt. 1): On 29 Sept. Mihailović forces attacked two Hun trains on line Čačak-Požega. [Ibid., October 9, 1943.]

September 29

From SERBONIAN (Al): Completed demolition 15 hours 4 bridges destroyed at Mokra Gora message WIX. Nr one bridges three single span one triple span [all] steel girder. Two attempts derail train in tunnel unsuccessful, train jumped gap. Thirty-six Bulgars [killed] last night and seventy today. Twenty-nine on scene action surrendered without fight. See BBC credit Mihailović forces who are in good heart here. JILL and PLO helped. [Ibid., September 30, 1943.]

September 29

From SPROC to Huot: MVIC Communique Oct. 4 Rep [reports?] two nine [September 29] attacks two (t)Hun train at railroad sta of Jelendo on Čačak Požega line. Dalmatia Cln [?] railroad line Knin Drniš Šibenik still operating. MVIC says Partisans still harass his forces as they fight Hun and take as own without fight towns he took with fight from Hun. [WO 202/131.]

September 29

From SPROC to Huot: Twenty thous Italians in and near Dubrovnik made pact to fight with Huns but broke it when Huns took their arms. Now only two battns fight for Huns, rest held as Hun prisoners. Along coast from Dubrovnik to Kotor naval base Itals and MVIC men join in fighting Huns, with big fight near Gruda. Italians at Kotor want to see Allied ships land there. Would boost morale.

At Foča about two thous Ptsans, some who attacked Gacko. MVIC orders complete mobil. All his men in Herzegovina going to fight with Itals to defend Kotor. Now about seven thous his men fighting this area. MVIC men have taken Prijepolje and now surround Italian Itia [Venezia?] division which was turned back on way to Podgorica. OLD [Bailey] now treating with them. [WO 202/131.]

September 30

From FUGUE: Attacked Bulgar garrison at village Gradadnica [Gradašnica] near Pirot on 30 September. Killed 20, wounded 45. Our casualties one and one. Reprisals followed. All village burned, women and children taken away. Rest of line Gradašnica and Niš cleared of Germans except Belo Pelanka [Bela Palanka]. Give me arms quickly. BIRD. [WO 202/140, September 30, 1943.]

September 30

From NERONIAN: Djurić reports that Commander his sabotage brigade derailed train 30 September, displacing rails Tesića, twelve miles north of Niš. Forty Huns dead. Angry Huns occupy town of Vdi[?]. Believed NIM also claims this. MEAT. [WO 202/131, October 9, 1943.]

September 30

From FUGUE (69): Blew one kilo East railway night thirty [September 30]. Job done with 25 man sabotage group under English command and without Serb officer or orders Djurić. Line will be out of action for ten days. The line was passing 50 trains per day, troops, tanks, arms to Greece, mostly arms. Cont. Mike. [Ibid., October 4, 1943.]

September, end of

Attack on rail line near Gurdelica [Grdelica] about 15 kilometres south of Lescovac [Leskovac] on main line. 700 metres blown up on both rails using about 70 lbs explosive linked with primacord and fired by safety fuse. Carried out end of September. [WO 202/162, Appendix to General Report of Fugue Mission.]

September, end of

From RAPIER: Resume MVIC communique two Oct. Serbia. MVIC forces attacked Huns Arilje area and inflicted casualties, also drove Bulgars from Guco S. W. Čačak. Rly station on line Užice Višegrad attacked thirty Sept., twenty-five Bulgars captured. NIM's [Keserović] troops attacked express train from Niš Belgrade near Alexsinac twenty-nine Sept., train derailed and number of Hun victims. MVIC claims to have destroyed four locomotives and seventy wagons at Užice in area Kosovo and Metohja[?]. [WO 202/131.]

October 1

To LONDON (1957): Following resume Mihailović report 1 Oct. In action on railway Užice-Sarajevo, previously reported by WIX 161, Mihailović claims three heavy MGs, 5 LMGs, 140 rifles, 1 mortar, with amm for all . . . [WO 202/139, October 9, 1943.]

October 1

From ENAMEL (84): On 1 October Chetniks successfully ambushed Germans between Planintsa[?] and Lesicov[?] at approx. 15 kilometres S.S.W. Zaječar. Germans subsequently reinforced by Bulgars from Zaječar and Chetniks withdrew; 20 German casualties, one Bulgar lieutenant died in hospital later. Believe above accurate, as interrogated participants. [WO 202/131, October 9, 1943.]

October 1

From ANGELICA (95): Following accident arranged by station master Mitrovica 0430 hours first Oct. Vučitrn. Collision between train 5874 carrying coal to Salunar[?], train 4851 carrying its prisoners to Belgrade. Both locos, seven wagons complete wrecks, line out of order 14 hours. FIELD. (Ibid., October 8, 1943.]

October 3

From RAPIER (Pt. 2): Near Užice Mihailović destroys four locomotives and 70 freight cars by explosives. Huns take 200 hostages Užice . . . [Ibid., October 9, 1943.]

October 3

From RAPIER: Col. Ostojić hopes capture Višegrad five October and later destroy large railway bridge over Drina, approx eleven kilos West of Town. JILL [Major Jack] assisting bridge destruction. Party WIX [Brigadier Armstrong] and DUTCH [Colonel Seitz] accompany Ostojić and will report due course, Probably return H.Q. by 9 Oct. Ends. ROBIN [Captain Mansfield]. [WO 202/131.]

October 4

From RAPIER: MVIC reports four Oct: Partisans entered Zvornik thirty Sept. Town had been held by MVIC forces since seventeen Sept. On twenty nine Sept. MVIC forces attacked two Hun trains on line Čačak Požega. Hun troops reported moving from Kruševac to Užice via Kraljevo and Užice. MVIC reports actual strength his forces: DRINA CORPUS: eight thousand seven hundred and thirty men, two thousand four hundred seventy rifles, twenty seven L.M.G., three heavy M.G., one mortar. ROMANIJA CORPUS: sixteen thousand three hundred fifty men, four thousand nine hundred sixty seven rifles, seventy two L.M.G.s, twenty seven heavy M.G.s, four mortars. MAJEVICA CORPUS: fifteen thousand men, one thousand five hundred fifty rifles, forty five L.M.G.s, seven heavy M.G.s, two mortars. Figures for Dalmatia, Croatia, Slovenia not repeat not included, as considered highly controversial. Details for Serbia follow. Ends. ROBIN. [WO 202/131.]

October 5

To London, 1992: Following are repeats of messages from SERBONIAN, 191 of 4. From WIX. At Ostojić Hq for night move to attack Višegrad at 0300 on 5 Oct. All very confident. If town taken, will drink glass rakia if Ostojić will cut throat Boche commander. Don't like rakia, but like Boche less. After, move West to attack and destroy bridge, JILL assisting that operation. [WO 202/139, October 9, 1943.]

October 5

Band of 2500 Chetnik guerrillas massed together on orders from Gen. Mihailović south of Višegrad and attacked the German garrison of 800 men in that city. After 4½ hours of fighting, Chetniks took the city, killing about 200 Germans, and driving the rest northwards. Entire battle witnessed by several Allied officers, including Brigadier Armstrong (British), Col. Albert Seitz, U.S.A., and Major Jack (British) who participated in completely blowing up the famous long steel Višegrad bridge across the Drina River, with explosives parachuted into Mihailović by the Allies, and thus cutting the Belgrade-Sarajevo R. R. line for nine months. [Mansfield statement.]

October 5

SERBONIAN 191 of 4 Contd. Line at Dobrun seven kilos East Višegrad destroyed many places. My opinion for moment Boche given up any idea using line between Užice and Sarajevo at many places. Mihailović forces for present in complete control many portions. [WO 202/139, October 9, 1943.]

October 5

From NERONIAN (21 of 10 Oct.): On 5 Oct. at Jelašnic[a] and Arknjazevac [Knjaževac] Germans [were] attacked to obtain arms. Killed 14, wounded 20. One wounded was brought back, 40 rifles, 3 MGs, one maxim, 2 pistols, one binocs, good supply ammo for weapons captured and equipment from dead. Why no help from Cairo? Three planes as requested be big help. First frost today, no clothing, no money, no food. Help. Help. *[This paragraph also appears in the section dealing with the sabotage of the Mihailović supply operation.]* [WO 202/143, November 7, 1943.]

October 5

From RAPIER (174): Forces under comd JURY destroyed Tn [train] containing Tps [troops] and explosive in tunnel 20 kilos East Pec East Bosnia. [WO 202/131, October 5, 1943.]

October 5

From NERONIAN: Am sitting astride important Niš Railway D.N. lines to Sofia, Skoplje and Belgrade with Stuka aerodrome at Niš. Rolling stock and town sabotage already in full swing. Give me my planes with arms and expl. as imperative to get them now. Have strong force of three Corps to put in Field. W/T set and Operator first plane, urgent. BIRD [Ibid., October 10, 1943.]

October 5

From FUGUE: Ref. yr. 69 of 4. Cannot possibly manage with only two planes this moon. This is the most vital of all Djurić areas and embraces half his whole command. I have six local corpus commanders to supply with 1000 unarmed men in the woods. Potential reserves over 20,000. I have received only 5 planes in three months. We are the only Djurić area who have worked sabotage. This sabotage was important and I worked it without orders Djurić on promise of planes. If you grant my request for planes I can work permanent sabotage. If I do not receive planes the whole show will certainly pack up and I will be unable work anything. Please reply urgently. Mike. [WO 202/131.]

October 6

From CAVERN 2(97): Track [blown up] between Leskovac and Vranje, and 2500 metres track at station of Usepolumir[?] in Ibar Valley near Raška. Force of 7,000 near Gornji Milanovac raided 50, took 200 hostages and bombed village Trocinambrajiconsuho[?] Oct 3 enemy force [of] 3500 fights Mihailović near Kosjerić. [Ibid.]

October 6

From RAPIER: Following resume MVIC report one October in action on Railway Užice-Sarajevo previously reported by WIX. MVIC claims three heavy machine guns, five L.M.G. [light machine guns], one four zero [140] rifles, one mortar, with amo. for all, one four nine [149] Bulgar P.O.W.s. [WO 202/131.]

October 7

From RAPIER (187): Summary Mihailović report. Three miles of railway line torn up by Mihailović forces between Višegrad-Rogatica. Small bridge also demolished. (R) [road] Višegrad-Rogatica under control Mihailović. Latter also claims possession of Hun dump containing large quantity explosive at Rudo. Huns endeavouring evacuate Ljubovija, attacked by Mihailović forces and forced back. Mihailović captured one mortar, three trucks, one Hymg [heavy machine gun]. Mihailović holds Čajetina. [Ibid., October 8, 1943.]

October 7

From ROUGHSHOD: Your 52 of 4. (1) FUGUE just demolished one km. railway line. Probable delay 10 days. Expect reprisals and asks 5 sorties immediately to be followed further 5 later in month. Has given some undertaking local commander. (2) NERONIAN states ALMONER must have two sorties. (3) In view above have allotted sorties as follows: ROUGHSHOD 3, FUGUE 3, NERONIAN 1, ALMONER 1, DIPPER 1. Have asked WIX [Armstrong] try obtain 4 sorties from other areas and bring ROUGHSHOD and FUGUE to five each. Will keep you informed. [WO 202/139.]

October 8

From CAVERN ([unnumbered]: Huot Oct. 8): Mihailović reports Oct. 8. In taking Višegrad lost 18 killed and 65 wounded. Enemy 354 killed, many wounded. Mihailović took 22 prisoners, 2 guns, 3 mortars, 7 heavy, 4 light, machine guns, 200 rifles (GMA?), horses and autos. Also took bunkers and railroad bridge over Lini [Lim] near Rogatica taking train 1 [load] munitns. [WO 202/140, October 12, 1943.]

October 8

From ANGELICA (96): Ref train derailed on line Priština-Peć, 400 labourers employed for 15 days before line could work. Huns have not disclosed numbers of Huns killed and injured. FIELD. [WO 202/131, October 8, 1943.]

October 8 (Log Date)

MVIC appears definitely more pugnacious against Boche and passive resistance Partisan[s] but complains of and fears Partisan infiltration into Lim Valley. For example body Partisans appeared outside Priboj and demanded arms from Ities whom Old had previously contacted and decided to leave armed for such time as should be considered advisable. Can you get Tito to withdraw his Tps fm [troops from] this area. From WIX Ends ROBIN. [WO 202/131.]

October 9

From RAPIER (Pt. 2): Near Užice Mihailović destroys 4 locomotives and 70 freight cars by explosives. Huns take 200 hostages Užice . . . Herzegovina: Mihailović defeats large group Partisans. [Ibid., October 9, 1943.]

October 10

From ANGELICA (97): Large train load disarmed. It is being sent direction Belgrade. Fifty prisoners per truck, standing room only. Hun troop train passing, pelt them with stones. FIELD. [Ibid.]

October 10

From NERONIAN (20 of 10 Oct.): Latest encounters as follows. Between Kalna and Oiret [Pirot] attacked Bulgar force and in sweep forward drove them 15 kilos into Bulgaria. Line settled into pitched battle with reinforcements for Bulgars from Bedapaganna [Bela Palanka] and Dirot [Pirot]. Retired with no casualties. Forty Bulgars killed. Later Bugs [Bulgars] burned Kalna and killed 15 villagers. Give Ned lines quickly. See my next. [WO 202/143, November 7, 1943.]

October 10

From NERONIAN (14: BIRD via NERONIAN 222): With Shenton and Faithful, 6 Greeks, 9 Serbs, attacked railway north Leskovac. Failure, but resulted 3 Bulgars killed, 3 wounded. One Greek wounded in legs with hand grenade. Want anti-tank rifles, Solothurn trench mortars and 47 MMAT guns with as many arms you can push in. Most important of Djurić areas. [WO 202/131, October 10, 1943.]

October 10

From NERONIAN (13): Sabotage results to you in few days. Am aiming at disabling rolling stock and destroying goods. In last few days have taken from Germans 30 LMGs, 8 Schmeisers and 600 rifles with number of uniforms and equipment. These without previous arms. Help me to get more for 10,000 men this area. BIRD via NERONIAN. [Ibid.]

October 10

Witness present when Mihailović's Gen. Staff H.Q. again attacked by German forces in Ravenje Mountain near Rudo and machine-gunned by German fighter planes. Forced to retreat for two days and one night up into mountains near Višegrad. [Mansfield statement.]

October 11

From FUGUE: Very stormy interview with local sabotage commandant because I wanted to send a party to blow a train. He says that he worked first class sabotage with me on promise planes and will work no more with me without orders Djurić until he sees planes. On receipt Mx requests we will immediately blow a bridge. I must have a plane Besnica within three days.

I suggest you give me some of Djurić planes. Mike. [WO 202/140, October 11, 1943.]

October 11

From FUGUE (84): Railway line we blew up will be mended by tomorrow, eleven days after we blew it. On inf from Leskovac we stopped over half a million tons of goods. To repeat this always, I only want a few planes. Mike. [Ibid.]

October 11

A German tug and barges on the Danube at Boljetin were attacked and damaged. [Deposition of BLOs.]

October 12

From RAPIER (1: From WIX): Mihailović reports 12 Oct. Huns and Bulgars have effected blockade of Srez [County] Ljubićski, Crnogorski, Požev̌ski, Dragačevo; Mihailović estimates force 20,000 men. Thorough search of above areas being made, all males over 15 years being removed by Huns. At Čačak 150 persons were shot. [WO 202/140, October 17, 1943.]

October 12

From RAPIER: Considered opinion, destruction Drina River Rly, ten kilos West Višegrad, has cut rail communications Sarajevo to Rudo and Užice for at least three months, even if Boche commenced repairs at once. At present he is definitely neither in control of any part [of] line from and including Drina River Bridge to excluding Vardište, nor from bridge to include Rudo, nor is he yet able to carry out recce [reconnaissance] of damage to line and four bridges destroyed. Op. [operation] twenty nine Sept. near Mokra Gora between Vardište and Sandjak [Sandžak] tunnel. Boche not able re-establish through communication Sarajevo Dzice [Užice] this war . . . Ostojić assisted by Lukas [Lukačević], MVIC and Radović, preparing move west to attack Boche Croat garrison Rogatica. From WIX. Ends. [WO 202/140.]

October 14 – 15

Chetnik forces pushed on through Rogatica towards Sarajevo, chasing retreating Germans until Chetniks were attacked on their right flank by Partisans and forced to withdraw. [Mansfield statement.] At Rogatica, Chetniks attacked strong Ustashi garrison, killing several hundred. [Account of Colonel Albert Seitz in statement to New York Commission of Inquiry in the case of Mihailović.]

Middle of October

Train blown near Grabonica [Grdelica?] about 7 kilometres south of Lescovac [Leskovac]. This was a goods train and when blown slid along the track, tearing up about 150 metres of line and sleepers. Carried out middle October. [WO 202/162, Appendix to General Report of FUGUE Mission.]

October 18

From ENAMEL (17 Pt. 1): . . . Nedić guards approx 200 disarmed or come over Chetniks. Small number Bulgars disarmed, officer wounded. [WO 202/140, October 18, 1943.]

October 22

From CAVERN 2 (Pt. 1): Col. West Oct. 22. Mihailović reports 22 Oct. his forces obliged renounce attack Sokolac owing to Partisan interference. Huns now hold Bajna [Bajina] Bašta, Hun col Rfbnm [from?] Užice has arrived Novavaros [Nova Varoš]. This believed coordinated with attack 118 Div. In South Huns have reached outskirts Berane Ities [Italians] of Venezia Division. [Ibid., November 10, 1943.]

October 22

From NERONIAN (unnumbered): Your 390 and 392. No contact BIRD six days, probably forced move after heavy Bulgar reprisal activity. Rests with you whether you send to NERO or await BIRD droppings. Bombs on Niš very popular, sending Serb officers to report on damage. Četnik morale rising. Get bloody minded about Sofia. [Ibid., October 22, 1943.]

October 22

From ANGELICA: Ref raid on Skoplje. Goods station destroyed and main line out of action two four [24] hours. Serbs now fighting Albanians area Novipazar [Novi Pazar] Berane. Can see burning villages from here and hear gun fire. Bombing of Mitrovica would convince Albanians that Allies are going to win war and stop them fighting for Huns. FIELD. Ends. [Ibid.]

October 23

From ANGELICA (Immediate 123): Three Iti [Italian] officers in Mitrovica very anxious join us. Have persuaded Marković to send for them as consider they should have intelligence value and be useful for contact with Iti prisoners working on roads. Marković keen we should raise and arm a company of Itis. Please state your views on contact and arming of Itis. FIELD. [Ibid., October 23, 1943.]

October 23

From CAVERN 2 (Pt. 2): Col. West Oct. 23. Mihailović reports [October] 23 he has disarmed Ity [Italian] garrison Priboj with latter's consent. He has taken 11 Hy M.G.s [heavy machine guns] and 4 Hy mortars. [Ibid., November 10, 1943.]

October 24

From CAVERN 2: It is highly probable that Partisan attack on Mihailović forces when latter were engaging Germans and Ustashi at Sokolac in East Bosnia Oct 24 was engineered in precisely the same fashion through Partisan agents in Ustashi forces. [Bailey was talking here about the use of intelligence agents, by both Partisans and Chetniks, in units that were engaged in accommodations with the enemy, specifically for the purpose of coordinating attacks on each other.] [Ibid., December 7, 1943.]

October 27

From ENAMEL via RUPEES (44): Morning 27 October attacked German tug Centaur and Dutch tug Amsterdam each towing two barges near Boljetin. Attack failed, primary object which is sink first tug at exit narrow channel thus blocking Danube two months but when we left second tug and barges appeared stationary. Further down channel barges thought aground. One barge first tug aground outside channel. Details later. DIGGER TREE. [Ibid., October 30, 1943.]

October 28

From RAPIER (USA): West 28 Oct. Mihailović reports 28 Oct. Hun coln previously reported at Novavaros [Nova Varoš] has now entered Prijepolje, believed Huns also took Plevlje. Mihailović counterattacking Partisans at Višegrad. Unconfirmed infm indicates Partisans driven back to west bank Drina, infm still scanty owing recent moves. [Ibid., November 11, 1943.]

October 29

From ANGELICA (134): Returned today. [Track] blown 2000 hours 29 Oct. Huns have imprisoned 90 Serbs in Mitrovica as reprisals, fate not yet known. Railway workers mentioned my [message no.] 132 imprisoned. Six trucks burnt Kačanik by time incendiaries. FIELD. [Ibid., November 3, 1943.]

October 29

From RAPIER (B): Col. West 29 Oct. Mihailović reports 29 Oct. Mihailović forces now attacking Sokolac held by Huns and Ustashi. On road Višegrad-Fraca [Prača] Mihailović attacked 500 S.S. troops and captured two L.M.G.s,

20 rifles. Huns of 118 Div now attacking Partisans near Andrijevica, Kolašin and Berane. Mihailović states he has given his troops above areas strict orders not repeat not attack Partisans. [Ibid., November 12, 1943.]

October 30

Left to destroy road bridge between Mitrovica and Peć at Ketc Potol [Kacan Dol?]. 30th. Blew up bridge. Not very successful owing to bridge being of reinforced concrete. Delay action charges left in position. [WO 202/162, Report by Captain G.R.M.H. More, p. 2.]

October 30

From SERBONIAN: Tell BIRD glad read successes. MVIC confirmed to WIX full agreement all attacks railway Niš to Sofia repeat Sofia at conference twenty four Oct. On two zero Oct. MVIC said would issue orders to Radojović repeat Radojović to this affect but has not W/T to him. MVIC asked me pass signal. MVIC queried dangerous when discovered had pass through Kaiha [Cairo] resulting in six cipherings and decoding in all [indecipherable] about attack. Inform if confirmed by BLOs. [WO 202/143.]

October 30

Paraphrase message from PUB for WIX: All rail communication my district can be cut. Only need arms and ammunition to engage battle while placing charges, since every target guarded. Executions in Serbia are now carried out in Belgrade and Čačak and not as formerly in Belgrade and Kraljevo. Will therefore be able send you numbers and reasons of executions. [WO 202/139.]

October

Train blown by Serb personnel alone, across Bulgarian border near Vladicni [Vladičin] Han between Leskovac and Vranje. Personnel provided by Capt. Jovo Stefanović. October. [Ibid., Appendix to General Report of FUGUE Mission.]

October

Train blown south Grdelica about 20 kilometres from Leskovac—October. [Ibid.]

November 7

From NERONIAN (A., 22): Following burnt as reprisal Kalna expedition. Gabrovnica, Tatrasica [Tatrašnica], Crni Vrh[?], Chucitza [Kustica], Ravna Buci [Ravno Bučje], Janja, Chugrin[?], Milcovzia[?] Tovarnica[?], Croval[?], Htanjanci[?], Dagovic[?], Orjilja[?], Miranovac[?], Chestigava[?], Gorjnja[?]

Kamenica. And nine others. Villagers irrespective age and sex shot at all places. See my next. Ends. BIRD. [WO 202/140, November 7, 1943.]

November 7

From NERONIAN (A., 23): Surviving villagers seek weapons. Victor plans expedition total force on eighteenth. Am doing best holding check pending arrival weapons etc. from you. Give all help possible now. Would remind you read previous messages this month. Here is live wire Cmdr. Why waste him? Give me all assistance requested now. This area needs more than presence British personnel to prove British interests. [Ibid.]

November 10

From ROUGHSHOD: Near thing. Bulgars tried surround us eight Nov. Four regiments including Cavalry M.G.s, mortars, from Bosingrad [Bosiljegrad?] Vranje and Grivo Balanka [Kriva Palanka]. Majority Bulgars began taking us for themselves and nightfall saved us. Twelve hour night march took us well away for time being. Ready sorties eleven repeat eleven Nov as per my one three of six. (Log X.138.) CAT. [WO 202/140.]

November 19

From CAVERN TWO (21): Armstrong reports "two Hun aircraft shot down Mihailović forces near Foča." [Ibid., November 19, 1943.]

November 20

From ANGELICA: Of four time bombs placed in wreckage of bridge road Mitrevica Pic only one exploded. No repairs yet undertaken for fear of their explosion . . . One more white Russian has deserted from bunkers. [WO 202.]

November 24

From CAVERN 2 CERN: Tell TREE MVIC agreed at conference twenty-four Oct all attacks suggested Homolje area. Understand rly being completed and new road made Azjeca repeat Azjeca Bor to Požarevac for winter use. If correct want TREE repeat TREE attack this. Want TREE use Tire Bursters against convoys from Bor repeat Bor. Tell TREE if cannot sabotage power station Bor, do best disrupt evacuation of metals mined. [WO 202/143.]

November 24

From CAVERN 2 SBN: Following is my suggested programme for supply arms to MVIC forces in forty four. In absence directive for forty-four and inf. on sorties I can expect monthly or number specialist teams available for me, and with MVIC and staff in ignorance of and contd steadfast refusal to produce any accurate details numbers armaments, I have worked on plan I consider feasible.

In each area with BLO I plan to equip one Bn as effective striking unit with supporting weapons and to supply proportion rifles and amm for other compys and bns in same area as named H.Q. Proposed supply certain heavier supporting weapons to six known Jug Comds without BLOs who have from time to time taken action against Boche and areas lie in flanks important comms and same who also form western flank. I propose as second priority to supply lower scale of small arms and amm but not supporting weapons and teams.

If you want us to take effective share in fighting next year, MVIC forces must be suitably repeat suitably armed for this purpose. Their standard of training is so low that I cannot repeat not expect efficient employment of supporting arms if they are expected to supply teams. [WO 202/143.]

November 25

From ROUGHSHOD (27): German troop train head on collision between Vranje and Kumanovo. Sixty killed. Peasants report that German Lieut. shot all seriously injured. Station Master has run away. From CAT. [Ibid., November 25, 1943.]

November 26

From NERONIAN: LAKE cannot repeat cannot receive aircraft till night fourth Dec. FUGUE reports demolition of one kilo line Leskovac area thirteenth Nov. and requests BBC will not again attribute this to Partisans as they have on two previous occasions. Pse send three MT inspection lamps six volt as lighting facilities here nil. Have you contacted FUGUE yet? HORSE. [WO 202/143.]

November 27

From RHODIUM (25): 27th Nov., eighty Ljotić in Hun uniform well trained and armed blockaded Brus, shot 21, took three away and beat up others, also took three civilian wireless sets. Heard all Bulgars have left Kruševac. No exact news NIM's whereabout for 15 days when last saw him. PADDLE. [Ibid., December 1, 1943.]

November

Line blown 1000 metres on same method as on first occasion near Grabonica [Grdelica?] south of Leskovac—November. [WO 202/162, Appendix to General Report of FUGUE Mission.]

November

Train blown by Serb personnel alone, north of Lescovac [Leskovac] about five kilometres. Men provided by Capt Milc Andreović[?]—November. [Ibid.]

November

Captain Stefanović with a party of 150 men ambushed a Bulgarian company over the Bulgarian border. He completely wiped them out, about ten men only escaping. He captured their equipment. This occurred in November. With his men he also attacked small parties of Bulgars crossing the frontier to loot farms in Serbia. I accompanied Captain Stefanović on one of these operations. He appeared to be a capable commander. [WO 202/162, Report of Major Michael Lees, BLO Reports.]

December 8

From EXCERPT (16): Sabotage by railwaymen caused two headon collisions main line from Belgrade. One at Malakrstna [Mala Krsna] one at Topčider. Three locos destroyed, one damaged. Type trains amount rolling stock damaged unknown. [WO 202/140, December 8, 1943.]

December, early

Trains blown across Bulgarian border, first between the two tunnels immediately north of Vladicni [Vladičin] Han, the other two days later near Mitvice (Mrtvica) about 8 kilometres further north. Carried out early in December. This was the last operation before the break. The next operation planned for the 14th was cancelled by the break on the 12th. [WO 202/162, Appendix to General Report of FUGUE Mission.]

December 15

From SEIZURE: Lt. Col. Djurić has already carried out attack on Dec fifteen nineteen four three on rly station of Tabanovce[?] north of Kumanovo, at which time three Hun troop trains were in station. Station was captured, water tower and installations and switches destroyed, one truck derailed and track torn up for distance seven kilometers [eight six of two six part five]. [WO 202/136.]

This was the last entry in the Operational Log dealing with military activities by the Mihailović forces during the last part of 1943. Again it must be emphasized that the Operational Log was incomplete in many respects and that even major activities by Mihailović were either ignored or dealt with in obtuse language.

CHAPTER

16

SOE Disinformation: The Six
Critical Incidents

*We do not know whether the Partisan reports about actions
are accurate, exaggerated or utterly untrue. This is because
for the most part we have taken the Partisan word for what
went on since we seldom had our own observer with them . . .*

Major Richard Weil, OSS

In the period preceding the abandonment of Mihailović, from the end of May
until the end of November 1943, six incidents in the relationship between
SOE Cairo and Mihailović were characterized by such apparent malevolence
or inaccuracy that they simply could not have been the product of accident
or error. The six incidents are discussed in the order in which they occurred.

1. THE DIRECTIVE OF MAY 28, 1943

On May 28, 1943, SOE Cairo sent to Colonel Bailey a lengthy message that,
in retrospect, marked the formal turning point in SOE's relations with the
Mihailović movement. The message, which bore the signature of General
Henry Maitland Wilson, Allied commander in chief for the Middle East, was
ostensibly designed to prevent hostilities between Home Army forces and
Partisans by delineating their respective territories of operation. Actually, it
asked, in insulting terms, that Mihailović pull back all his forces to a small
area in eastern Serbia, leaving all the rest of Yugoslavia to Tito. The message said:

149

General Mihailović does not represent a fighting force of any importance west of Kopaonik. His units in Montenegro, Herzegovina, and Bosnia are already annihilated or else in close cooperation with the Axis; it is also difficult to say that his units exist in Croatia, Slovenia, and Slavonia.

The Partisans represent a good and effective fighting force in all parts, whereas only the quislings represent General Mihailović . . . You will advise General Mihailović that he immediately go to Kopaonik with all his faithful officers and men; if necessary, he is to break through by armed force . . . In the future the Supreme Command will consider the districts under his command and influence to be bordered on the west by the fighting elements already existing on the right bank of the Ibar River and toward the south to Skoplje.[1]

Colonel Bailey had no alternative but to show the text of the directive to Mihailović, although he had the most serious misgivings about its wisdom. Mihailović's reaction, as could have been predicted, was immediate and explosive. His reply to the directive said, among other things:

The statement . . . that my forces are not of any importance west of Kopaonik, is absolutely without foundation. It is not true that the units of the Yugoslav Army in Montenegro, Herzegovina, and Bosnia are annihilated, and there is even less truth in the same statement that they are in close cooperation with the Axis. It is not true that it cannot be said that Yugoslav Army units exist in Slovenia and Slavonia. On the contrary, the Yugoslav Army exists in all parts, and it will prove its existence to the entire world. *I will not tolerate such insults any longer . . .*[2] [Emphasis in original]

It developed that the message to Colonel Bailey had been sent off without the knowledge or approval of the Foreign Office. The Foreign Office, indeed, strongly disapproved of the message and asked that it be rescinded. Commenting on Mihailović's reaction to the May 28 directive, Douglas Howard, head of the Foreign Office, Southern Department, wrote to his superiors on June 15, 1943:

In one way or another, SOE have excelled themselves in the handling of this question. First, Lord Glenconner goes and sends Bailey a telegram off his own bat and completely at variance with our own policy . . . we have suggested to the Chiefs of Staff that the disastrous telegram should be rescinded . . . even if it is withdrawn, so much bad blood will have been spilled that it may be very difficult to come to terms.[3]

How did the May 28, 1943 directive come to be written? Obviously, it could not have been based on any direct intelligence, because the Deakin mission did not arrive in Yugoslavia until May 27, and the directive was probably a week or more in the drafting and processing. Who wrote the directive? In a long interview in England in September 1946, Colonel Bailey told me flatly that Basil Davidson was the person responsible for the message. This I recounted in my book *Patriot or Traitor*.

In a letter to the editor of *The South Slav Journal* (March 1980) Basil Davidson challenged the credibility of my book in several respects but not on any of the basic facts about the May 28 directive nor my information from Colonel Bailey that Davidson had himself formulated this directive. This I pointed out in a letter published in the June 1980 issue of the *Journal*. To this letter Davidson did not respond.

Colonel Bailey had given me this information in a manner indicating that he was absolutely certain of his facts. However, in a letter to me dated November 30, 1987, Davidson denied categorically that he had written the directive. He wrote:

> The memorandum in question could only have been sent—that is, authorized for despatch if not actually written by—Lord Glenconner; and, if not written by him, then it must have been written by one of his senior staff officers or advisers such as the late Colonel G. Taylor. As you know, the SOE archives are not accessible.

So there the matter must rest until the SOE files are open to researchers.

After the episode of the unauthorized directive, incidents prejudicial to sound relations between the Mihailović movement and the British government succeeded each other with such relentless regularity that it was mathematically inconceivable that they were due to simple bureaucratic stupidities.

2. BBC'S TREATMENT OF THE REWARD FOR TITO AND MIHAILOVIĆ

A scant two months after the incident of the directive, BBC, basing itself on reports it had received via SOE Cairo, announced internationally that the Germans had offered 100,000 gold marks for the head of Tito. This was one of those half-truths that are equivalent to total falsehoods. The significance of the story as reported was that Tito was the resistance leader whom the Nazis really feared and were unconcerned about Mihailović. The only trouble with this was that the original announcement, printed in *Novo Vreme* and other Yugoslav newspapers on July 21, 1943, offered identical rewards in virtually identical words and in identical space—exactly one-quarter of a page each—for the heads of Tito *and* Mihailović. The matter was called to the attention of BBC by the Yugoslav government in London and by the conservative MP Mr. Kenneth Pickthorn.[4] But no correction was ever made.

Of course, the people in Yugoslavia knew that the BBC broadcasts were dishonest, having seen the original offers of reward. This was one of the many glaring dishonesties that gave birth to the expression, widespread in Yugoslavia during the last phase of the war, "You lie like London."

3. THE CAPTURE OF PRIJEPOLJE AND BERANE

On September 11 there took place the most spectacular action in which the Mihailović forces engaged during the last half of 1943. SOE's handling of this incident constituted the third major affront to Mihailović.

On September 8, as soon as the capitulation of Italy had been announced, Colonel Bailey was instructed to proceed to the town of Berane with a contingent of Mihailović forces to take the surrender of the Italian Venezia Division before the Germans could get to them. Colonel Bailey set out immediately, accompanied by several well-known Mihailović officers, including Major Voja Lukačević and Lt. Colonels Milan Lašić and Rudi Perhinek, all three highly respected professional military men. (The details of the account that follows were provided by Colonel Perhinek in an interview in Cleveland. It has been accepted as valid, first, because Perhinek was an impressive and highly intelligent Slovene career officer, and, second, because in all fundamentals it is corroborated by the brief statement Bailey and other BLOs gave to the Belgrade court at the trial of Mihailović in the summer of 1946 and by the text of several messages sent from the field.)

In between the Mihailović forces and Berane there lay the town of Prijepolje, now garrisoned by a force of some 1,000 Germans.

On the question of Prijepolje, the statement of the BLOs to the Belgrade court said:

> 11th September 1943: A detachment of General Mihailović's forces, detailed to assist British officers in securing implementation of the Italian armistice as it affected local Italian forces in the valley of the Lim, attacked and captured the town of Prijepolje after its seizure by a strong German force on the 9th of September. Heavy casualties were inflicted on the Germans and a considerable quantity of booty including motor transport, captured. Without the successful conclusion of this action, the British officers could not have carried out their orders.[5]

According to Colonel Perhinek, the movement of Bailey and his Mihailović cohorts toward Berane was slow because they were on foot, and the entire project was placed in jeopardy by the existence of a German garrison, about 1,000 strong, in the town of Prijepolje, approximately eighty kilometers north of Berane. The Mihailović officers, who had hastily mobilized some 1,500 Home Army irregulars from the surrounding areas, proposed a night attack on the German garrison. Colonel Bailey expressed doubts about the feasibility of the project but was won over by the confidence of the Mihailović officers.

The Mihailović irregulars waited until midnight before they went into action. Phase I of the attack involved knocking out the German perimeter defenses and guard positions. This was accomplished without a shot being fired, by combining stealth with the practiced use of knives. Then the Home Army irregulars launched their attack on the German garrison. One way or another, the German munitions magazine went up in a great explosion. When the battle was over, the Mihailović forces had killed some 200 of the German defenders, put the rest of them to rout, and captured a very large quantity of war booty. After resting for a day, Colonel Bailey and his Mihailović forces, now motorized with captured German equipment, started moving toward Berane on September 14. Bailey and Perhinek were driving together in the captured car of the German commander, with Bailey at the wheel, when they heard BBC announce that "the Partisans have captured Prijepolje from the Germans." Perhinek turned to Bailey in consternation and asked how BBC could say this. In painful embarrassment, Bailey replied, "I can only tell you that I reported events exactly as they happened."

There can be absolutely no doubt that Colonel Bailey reported in detail about the battle of Prijepolje—a truly major engagement by any guerrilla standards and by far the largest single engagement he had witnessed in eight and a half months in Yugoslavia. But apart from a few fleeting references, which give no idea of the magnitude of the battle, the Operational Log does not mention Prijepolje. A detailed description of the battle by Bailey does appear, however, in an appendix to the omnibus report he filed in April 1944 on his return to London. When BBC credited the capture of Prijepolje to the Partisans, it was almost certainly acting on the basis of information received via the SOE Yugoslav desk in Cairo—it was *not* acting counter to information received from this source.

When Colonel Bailey and the Mihailović column arrived at Berane, General Antonio Oxilia, the commander of the Venezia Division, was completely prepared to offer his submission. At this point Bailey said to Colonel Perhinek and Colonel Lašić and Major Lukačević that he would like, with their permission, to meet privately with General Oxilia. There was nothing that the Mihailović officers could do but accede to this request.

Five minutes later Bailey came out of General Oxilia's office and said to the Yugoslav officers, "Gentlemen, I am happy to inform you that General Oxilia has agreed to place his division under Allied command. We are now Allied forces." The jaws of the Mihailović officers fell. They had been hoping to take over the armament of the 7,000-man Venezia Division—an acquisition that would have enormously strengthened their position. But with the division under Allied command, it would no longer be possible to disarm them.

On September 12, the day after Prijepolje was assaulted, a Mihailović task force, accompanied by Hudson and Captain Mansfield, took the surrender of a large Italian garrison at Priboj after a night-long shoot-out. Again, things were arranged in a manner that prevented the Mihailović forces from disarming the Italians.

The order to bring the Venezia Division under Allied command had been sent to Bailey by SOE Cairo. That he did not relish implementing this order is apparent from the bitter reminder he sent SOE on October 13, 1943:

> No mention was made by Mihailović of the BBC broadcast on the evening of the 13th October re Berane and the disarmament of the Venezia Division by the Partisans. Although Berane Mts. are ringed off on Mihailović's map as being in Partisan hands, we have feeling this silence unnatural and that Mihailović intends to pursue his own policy vis-a-vis Partisans without disclosing his intentions to this Mission. But would state on his behalf, that he has received grave provocation in the Berane case, because at *your* instigation, [emphasis in original] Col. Bailey managed to persuade Mihailović *not* to disarm the Italians in the Lim Valley, and to avoid all conflict with the Partisans, with the result that his forces have now been driven out of the Lim valley.[6]

(Although the signature on this was Armstrong's, it is obvious from the style that Bailey composed this communication.)

Deprived by SOE of the wealth of Italian arms they had hoped to take over from the Venezia Division, and hard pressed by the Partisans, who were seeking to take over control of the Lim Valley, Perhinek told me that, as a matter of self-preservation, he and Lukačević entered into a nonaggression pact with the local Bulgarians.

4. THE BRIDGES AT MOKRA GORA AND VIŠEGRAD

The fourth major incident that embittered relations between SOE and Mihailović was the false attribution to the Partisan forces of the destruction of five bridges, which, in fact, had been accomplished by the Mihailović units in early October 1943. Brigadier Armstrong and Colonel Albert Seitz, as heads of, respectively, the British and the American mission, had been greeted on their arrival by a minor bridge-busting orgy in the region of Mokra Gora. In addition to knocking out the four fair-sized bridges in the area, the Yugoslav Home Army forces killed some 100 Bulgarian soldiers. On the night of October 4 the same Home Army forces, under the command of Major Ostojić, stormed the town of Višegrad, overcoming a strong garrison of German and Ustaše troops and killing several hundred of them. Major Archie Jack of the British mission set the charges under the Višegrad bridge, a 150-meter-long steel span, which, with Brigadier Armstrong and Colonel Seitz as spectators, was sent toppling down into the gorge. This was probably the biggest single bridge-busting operation carried out by Balkan guerrillas during the war.

Brigadier Armstrong, elated over the success of the expedition, sent in a report to SOE Cairo, together with a request that BBC make a little fanfare and pat the Mihailović forces on the back for a job well done. Every day at the appointed hour they tuned in on BBC. But no announcement came. Some ten days later, back at Mihailović's headquarters, Colonel Seitz, Brigadier Armstrong, and three other members of the British mission were sitting in front of their tent, warming themselves at a log fire and chatting away against the background of the daily broadcast from BBC. Suddenly they caught the word "Višegrad." "The Partisans," said the announcer, "have destroyed the five bridges of the railway Užice-Višegrad."

There was a moment of stunned silence.

"Brigadier, this is a terrible thing," said Colonel Seitz.[7]

The Brigadier agreed that it was a terrible thing. He immediately dispatched a message to Cairo informing them that he had personally witnessed the blowing of the Višegrad bridge by Mihailović forces. And he added some words that he had never used before in an official communication.[8]

BBC made no rectification. Nor has it ever been explained how it came about that when a British brigadier in the field requested that BBC broadcast an account of an action to which he had been an eyewitness, this request was ignored; while when a Partisan communiqué described an action which had not been witnessed by any Allied officer and was in complete contradiction of intelligence already on file, BBC reproduced the Partisan communiqué, thus endowing it with apparent authenticity.

A letter from the research division of BBC informs me that any communications from SOE Cairo would not have come directly to BBC but would have been forwarded via the Political Warfare Executive (PWE). Perhaps PWE was negligent in forwarding to BBC the numerous protests from Brigadier Armstrong and other BLOs about the unbroken series of quite spectacular inaccuracies in the British broadcasts to Yugoslavia. It is far more likely, however, that SOE Cairo never forwarded these protests to PWE.

Unfortunately, the military laurels won by the Mihailović forces at Višegrad were tarnished by the wanton killing of Višegrad Moslems by some of the Home Army soldiers who took part in the operation. I have heard several stories from both British and American officers bearing on this aspect of the capture of Višegrad. Colonel Seitz, who was with the forces of Major Lukačević, saw a sergeant throwing an elderly Moslem woman over the railing of a bridge. He protested in very strong terms to Lukačević, who promptly stood the sergeant up against a tree and shot him. Later Lukačević told Seitz that the man had been his best sergeant, and that shortly after the Nazi invasion he had seen members of his own family massacred by the Moslems in an anti-Serbian pogrom.[9]

This episode was an illustration of the complicated emotional situation that Mihailović inherited. Živko Topalović, who was elected head of Mihailović's Central National Committee in January 1944, and who also served as the leader of the Social Democratic Party of Yugoslavia, pointed out in a memorandum he sent to the British government that "massacres beget countermassacres," and that Mihailović was doing his best to bring this difficult situation under control.

One year later, when Colonel Robert McDowell's mission retreated with Mihailović through areas under his control in western Bosnia, McDowell was greatly impressed to find a large body of pro-Mihailović peasants—Serbs, Croats, and Moslems—living together harmoniously under the leadership of a venerable Serbian priest, Pop Sava Božić. Actually, as early as 1943 the Moslem community gave indications of growing support for the Mihailović movement. Before his death in 1984 I had a number of meetings with Alija Konjhodžić, a highly intelligent and dedicated Yugoslav Moslem who was the editor of a pro-Mihailović Moslem publication in Toronto, Canada.

Each instance of disinformation cited here had a long-term effect. The Anglo-American press had been won over to Tito's side by Moscow's remorseless propaganda and even more by the apparent confirmation from BBC. Even when the communiqués of Mihailović quoted responsible British and American officers as witnesses of Mihailović actions, the press ignored them. The story of the blowing up of the Višegrad bridge is a case in point. On October 16, 1943, the following cable was received by Yugoslav Ambassador Constantin Fotitch in Washington from Mihailović:

Woods and Mountains of Yugoslavia: The communist radio station Free Yugoslavia informed the world, and this information was reproduced by the London radio, that the Partisan formations destroyed the bridges on the railway Užice-Višegrad-Sarajevo, frustrating thus for a long time the use of this important railroad linking Serbia with Bosnia and the Adriatic Sea. A representative of the Democratic Yugoslav News Agency saw General Miroslav Trifunović, Commander of Serbia in the Yugoslav Army commanded by General Mihailović, from whom he received the following statement concerning the above communist propaganda:

I can tell you only this—the four bridges of the railroad Užice-Višegrad were destroyed by our units under my own command and in the presence of Brigadier

Armstrong, Chief of the British Military Mission . . . This happened at the beginning of October 1943. On the seventh of the same month we took a 150-meter-long railway bridge over the Drina River after thirteen hours of hard fighting because the bridge was guarded by one German and two Croatian quisling companies, protected by twenty-five blockhouses on both sides of the river. The bridge was taken by assault, and using only hand grenades. We lost twenty-one dead and thirty wounded. This operation and the complete destruction of the bridge was executed in the presence of Brigadier Armstrong and Lieutenant-Colonel Seitz, Chief of the American Military Mission.[10]

Though this communiqué was circulated to the press, not a single American paper saw fit to print it. This was six weeks before Teheran. After Teheran the situation became a hundredfold more difficult. The British press, needless to say, was at least as resistant as the American press to correcting the numerous pro-Tito misrepresentations of this period.

5. THE CAPTURE OF ROGATICA

The fifth major incident to exacerbate relations between Mihailović and SOE Cairo was the false attribution to the Partisans of the capture of the important Bosnian town of Rogatica in mid-October 1943.

No Allied officer witnessed the capture, but by careful interrogation an experienced intelligence officer can satisfy himself that an action has taken place much as described by the guerrillas he is attached to. Rogatica was garrisoned by the mortal enemy of the Mihailović forces, the infamous Ustaše. The fighting was bitter, and available accounts more or less agree that in taking the town, the Yugoslav Home Army Forces had succeeded in killing over 200 of the enemy. Not surprisingly, the capture of Rogatica was attributed by BBC reports to the Partisans.

Having endured many such misrepresentations, Brigadier Armstrong, in desperation, fired off the following message to SOE Cairo on November 18, 1943:

If you want to get the best out of Mihailović you must give him fairer press and broadcasts. Bailey was with Mihailović forces when [they] took Priboj and Prijepolje and Berane. I saw capture Višegrad, destruction bridges, and know Ostojić took Rogatica. Mihailović never credited with any [of] these, although reported to you. On other hand, when Partisans drove his forces out, Partisans credited on BBC [with capture of these places from enemy]. Show this to comrade Fitz [Fitzroy Maclean].[11]

On August 20 Captain Deakin, who was at Tito's headquarters, at one point wired SOE Cairo asking for "guaranteed instance" of sabotage carried out by Mihailović forces. The manner in which Deakin recounts the incident strongly suggests that he felt confident Cairo would confirm that there had, in fact, been no such "guaranteed instance" in recent months. On September 20, 1943, SOE Cairo wired back to Deakin, informing him that on August 28 at Trstenik the Mihailović forces had "derailed two troop trains and killed 200, captured several troops."[12] However, the message to Deakin said nothing about the Yugoslav Home Army's major victory at Prijepolje, or about the capture of Berane and the surrender of the Venezia Division, or about the capture of Priboj.

In November, Home Army forces attacked and overcame two sizable Bulgarian garrisons at Kalna and Nova Varoš. As was invariably the case, the credit went to the Partisans.

6. THE NOVEMBER 1943 ALLEGATION OF COLLABORATION WITH NEDIĆ

Sir Douglas Howard observed angrily that every time the British mission and the Foreign Office appeared on the verge of a satisfactory understanding with Mihailović, SOE Cairo had responded by throwing a monkey wrench into the works. This was never more apparent than in the charges of intended collaboration with Nedić that surfaced toward the end of November 1943, just a few weeks before the decision to recall the BLOs with Mihailović.

On November 21, just about the time the anti-Mihailović forces in SOE Cairo were moving in for the kill, the Foreign Office received from Ralph S. Stevenson, the British ambassador to the Yugoslav government in Cairo, a copy of the following wire from Major Cope, the senior BLO with Djurić:

> Just obtained this information from Djurić. Mihailović has ordered Djurić to co-operate with Nedić Government in action against Partisans. This is confirmed by report from Nedić officer recently at this headquarters that this news proclaimed to Nedić's troops in Nish.[13]

Major Cope, who had no background in Yugoslav affairs, had been in the country only a month when he sent out this message. It was immediately (November 22) challenged by Armstrong and Bailey, who pointed out that since Mihailović was not a fool, it seemed unlikely that he would order Djurić, in writing, to collaborate with Nedić—all the more so when Djurić was already under suspicion of seeking a settlement with the Partisans. Bailey and Armstrong asked whether Major Cope could persuade Djurić to show him the actual order he had received from Mihailović and have it translated by a reliable interpreter. They also asked what a Nedić officer was doing at Djurić's headquarters.

Cairo's apparent agitation over Major Cope's report is all the more difficult to understand in the light of a very strongly worded message SOE had received from Mihailović only a week previously, on November 13. The message stated:

> The Germans and Ljotić are spreading rumours about an alleged agreement between Nedić and myself. The aim of this is to cause confusion in our ranks at a moment when the Germans are feeling threatened and when our ranks should be most firm. I most categorically refute this base lie. I have never and at no place either attempted nor am I attempting, nor shall I attempt to come to any agreement with Nedić or with the Germans . . . It is not enough that I must defend myself against the Germans, Ustashi and communists, but now apparently also against our Allies. I ask you to see that this ceases once and for all.[14]

For twelve days messages flew back and forth between the British mission and SOE Cairo regarding Mihailović's alleged collaboration with Nedić. Cairo never thought it necessary to ask Cope to demand that Djurić show him the actual directive or to suggest that he have it translated by a person whom he knew to be reliable. Instead, it accepted the assessment of a neophyte BLO with all of one month's experience in Yugoslavia against the assessment of Colonel Bailey, who was without question the most mature and knowledgeable of all the BLOs who served in Yugoslavia during World War II. Finally, on December 3, Ambassador Stevenson wired to London that Cope had reported that, according to Djurić, all Mihailović commanders had received orders not to have any contact with Nedić or the Germans, without Mihailović's express order. Djurić had no explanation for Mihailović's apparent reversal of policy.[15]

This should have been the end of Djurić's allegations about Mihailović and Nedić. But months later both SOE and Foreign Office papers still talked about Mihailović's collaboration with Nedić and the Germans. In this way the anti-Mihailović pot was kept boiling right up to the very end.

The misrepresentations during the period in question were not limited to centers taken by the Mihailović forces. Captain Mansfield of the American mission reported that he was repeatedly present with Mihailović troops in towns that BBC had declared delivered from German control by the Partisans—but there would be no Partisans or Germans in evidence.[16]

The chronological compendium of reports by British and American sources dealing with anti-Axis actions by Mihailović forces that was part of my book *Patriot or Traitor,* and which I have expanded in the previous chapter, lists excerpts from numerous reports dating from the end of August until the end of November 1943. It was this compendium that moved Sir Douglas Howard to express his anger and amazement in his letter to me.

Although reports from the British and American liaison officers with the Partisans suggested that the Tito forces were engaging the Germans throughout the length and breadth of Yugoslavia, the fact is that only a handful of these officers were eyewitnesses to the actions they reported. Colonel Linn Farish, chief of the first American mission to Tito, went into Yugoslavia at the same time as Brigadier Fitzroy Maclean. He came out again in late October and went in once more in January 1944, this time accompanied by his deputy, Lieutenant (later Captain) Eli Popovich, the son of Serbian immigrant parents. But after four tours in the country, extending through most of 1944, Popovich reported that he had not once been permitted to witness a Partisan action against the Axis.[17]

An OSS operational officer, Major Richard Weil, who, as a liaison officer with the Tito forces, had only a number of months previous reported in glowing terms about the accomplishments of the Yugoslav Partisans, sent a much more sober communication to his superiors in early 1944:

We do not know whether the Partisan reports about actions are accurate, exaggerated or utterly untrue. This is because for the most part we have taken the Partisan word for what went on since we seldom had our own observer with them . . .[18]

17

The Briefing of Winston Churchill
and the History of SOE Maps

Brigadier Keble, by a staff accident, retained throughout his stewardship of SOE Cairo access to "Ultra" intelligence because he had earlier worked at the source. The "Ultra" intelligence communiqués were based on the greatest British code-breaking success of World War II. Early in the war the Germans had developed a supposedly foolproof encoding machine known as "Enigma." The only trouble was that the Polish underground managed to smuggle out of the country a copy of this machine—which gave the British blanket access to top-secret communications within the German high command. These communications were received and processed at Bletchley Park, not far from London. The information contained in the coded messages was forwarded to a very limited number of recipients in the Allied command, in heavily altered language so that if the Germans should by chance decipher the British codes, they would still not realize that their entire "Enigma" operation was a washout.

As Basil Davidson tells the story, it was shortly before New Year's Day 1943 when Keble burst in on him, closed the door, and produced some papers that, he said, were "enemy traffic." He said he would be receiving more of them and he wanted Davidson and Deakin, who in the month of May was to become head of a British mission to Tito, to go through them carefully with a view to seeing what light they threw on the fighting in Yugoslavia. "Otherwise, full secrecy."

When Churchill visited Cairo at the end of January 1943, Keble was able to present to him a briefing paper, and a map, the details of which had been compiled by Davidson and Deakin.[1] I had originally surmised that Klugmann, as Davidson's most knowledgeable and most assiduous aide, would

have been assigned to assist Deakin in this operation—all the more so because Deakin had only recently arrived in Cairo from the United States and
had no serious background in Yugoslav affairs. Deakin has assured me that
Klugmann played no direct part in the operation.[2] This was probably unnecessary because of Klugmann's preeminent role in the distillation of intelligence over the previous year. From the time of his arrival in Cairo in mid-
November 1942, Deakin, an avid scholar, had devoted himself to mastering
details of the intelligence files to which Klugmann had made so singular a
contribution. This process of self-education was abetted by frequent personal
contacts with Klugmann, who was a most impressive briefer and very sim-
patico as a human being.

To judge from what has been published, little of the new material given
to Deakin was not already known in London. It confirmed Colonel Hudson's
reports of accommodations with the Italians in Montenegro and Dalmatia by
certain Mihailović commanders. As for the secret intercepts that were added
to this information, Professor Ralph Bennett, in his book *Ultra and Mediterranean Strategy*,[3] makes the point that during the last months of 1942 and
the first months of 1943 the Balkan situation produced very little "Ultra"
traffic. He says that "Ultra" did not provide a great deal of information
about Yugoslavia until the middle of 1943. He speculates that the decrypts
that Keble showed to Deakin and Davidson "were of Abwehr, Police, or
Sicherheitsdienst hand-cipher intercepts (exactly which is not clear, but the
balance of opinion favours SD)." Bennett asks whether hand-ciphers were
classed as "Ultra" in Cairo or whether confusion has resulted from the fact
that Keble formerly had access to "Ultra," and "that it was not Ultra which
Keble showed to Deakin and Davidson."

Whatever the nature of the intercepts Keble gave Deakin and Davidson,
Bennett does not question that they showed the Partisans involved in sub-
stantially more activity than the Mihailović forces. This limited assertion
Mihailović himself would not have challenged. However, speaking about
decrypts that became available later in 1943, Bennett said that a decrypt of
May 5 described plans for action against Mihailović by the Italians.

No briefing is complete without a map. Because of the totally uncritical
attitude SOE displayed in putting together some of its subsequent maps, one
is justified in asking whether Prime Minister Churchill was not seriously
misled by the estimates of Partisan and Mihailović strength inevitably conveyed as a first impression by the briefing map. Let me point to several case
histories that justify such skepticism.

On June 2, 1944, two days after the personnel of the British mission
were evacuated to Bari, Italy, from Yugoslavia, two of the BLOs who had
been with Mihailović, Majors Jasper Rootham and Archie Jack, visited the
SOE operations room in Bari. On the wall was a map of Yugoslavia with

little flags marking the positions of Partisan, Mihailović, and German forces. All over Serbia there were Partisan pins—with here and there some isolated Mihailović pins. Rootham turned to the young captain in charge of the operations room and said to him that the map was wrong, explaining that he had spent the better part of a year in Serbia, that he had been there "only the day before yesterday." He said that the situation portrayed by the map was completely false: huge areas where he and other Mihailović BLOs had moved freely in recent months, and which were 100 percent pro-Mihailović, were depicted as being held by Tito's Partisans. The young officer blandly told Rootham that he was misinformed.

"Are you calling me a liar?" Rootham shot back angrily. "I said you're misinformed," repeated the young officer.

At this point Rootham, despite a professional training that made for restraint under stress (he had served as secretary to Prime Minister Neville Chamberlain), was unable to contain his anger. He walked up to the map, swept his sleeve over the offending pins, and "wiped the whole bloody lot" off the map of Serbia. After that, as Rootham relates, no member of the British mission to Mihailović was ever permitted to enter the SOE Yugoslav operations room.[4]

Rootham's explosion was understandable given the map's flagrant inaccuracy. Among the towns shown as under Partisan control was the town of Pranjani in Serbia, from which the British mission had been evacuated by air only a few days previously. When an American Air Crew Rescue Unit went into Pranjani in early August 1944 to evacuate several hundred American airmen who had been rescued by the Mihailović forces, the SOE map showed Pranjani as being under Partisan control.[5] And when Colonel McDowell was flown into Pranjani a few weeks later to head up an American intelligence mission in Serbia, the pins on the map still showed Pranjani under Partisan control.[6]

We come back to the question posed earlier: Was the map used to brief Churchill in Cairo in January 1943 put together from the same sources of information used in compiling the wildly inaccurate maps maintained by SOE in the middle of 1944? Churchill himself may have given a partial answer to this question at the end of his second conversation with Colonel Bailey: "I now realize that on this subject I have been badly informed" (as recounted shortly afterward by Bailey to his friend and colleague Major Archie Jack).

The impact of Bailey's briefing was apparent in Churchill's speech in Parliament of May 24, 1943, in which he said:

> We do not know what will happen in the Serbian parts of Yugoslavia . . . It must, however, be remembered that the question does not turn on General Mihailović alone. There is a very large body, amounting to perhaps 200,000, of

Serbian peasant proprietors, who are anti-German but strongly Serbian, and who naturally hold the view of a peasant ownership community in regard to property. They are not as enthusiastic in regard to communism as are some of those in Croatia and Slovenia . . .[7]

Obviously, Bailey had at least succeeded in convincing Churchill that, contrary to what he had been told by Deakin and Maclean, Serbia was solidly pro-Mihailović.

There is every reason to believe that the map used to brief Churchill in Cairo on January 30, 1943, was the forerunner of all the grossly inaccurate maps subsequently prepared by SOE Cairo. For example, toward the end of 1943 Maclean, Keble, and Deakin authored a series of memoranda that put Mihailović's strength in Serbia at 20,000 under arms and another 50,000 in reserve. In comparison, the Partisans were credited with an armed strength of some 220,000 men, of whom 30,000 were in Serbia and Macedonia. As Michael Lees, one of the most active of the BLOs and onetime head of the FUGUE mission in southern Serbia, points out, this estimate of Partisan strength in Serbia "was vital to the decision to can Mihailović. Without Partisan strength in Serbia, the decision was in no way justified."

One year later both Deakin and Maclean had radically changed their estimates of Partisan strength in Serbia at the close of 1943. Instead of 30,000, they now said there were approximately 1,700. In September 1944 Maclean wrote: "At the beginning of this year, 1944, Partisan forces in Serbia were limited to a few scattered, ill-equipped detachments of a few hundred men each, who were all that had been left to carry on the struggle after the Partisan defeat and withdrawal of 1941 . . ."[8]

But the gross overestimation of Partisan strength in Serbia in the fall of 1943 had been of critical importance in justifying the decision to abandon Mihailović.

Leaving aside for the moment the question of the accuracy or inaccuracy of the map used to brief Churchill in January 1943, the important thing was that, since Glenconner and Keble were both involved in the briefing, the entire senior staff of SOE Cairo was henceforth committed to denigrating Mihailović—because the oracle cannot be mistaken.

By a complex process, certainly conscious on the part of Klugmann, not at all conscious on the part of the other players, SOE Cairo had become a vital part of the Communist disinformation transmission belt.

Basil Davidson was personally elated by the effect of this briefing. He relates that news of the briefing "exploded around the corridors of the Rustem Building with the scattering effect of shrapnel. The Cairo 'partisans' had won."[9]

And so, on the issue of Mihailović, the senior officers in the SOE Cairo

Yugoslav desk operation came to be united in a coalition cutting across ideological lines. On the far left there was James Klugmann, a committed Communist. Somewhere left of center was Basil Davidson, the revolutionary romantic who somehow managed to equate effective anti-Axis resistance with a willingness to accept Tito as the leader of the Yugoslav resistance movement. Next to him there was the impulsive bureaucrat, Brigadier Keble, who saw in the Tito movement an opportunity for self-promotion. And finally there was William Deakin, the bright young Oxford historian, who, though cut of more conservative cloth than Klugmann and Davidson, got caught up in pro-Tito hysteria like so many other British conservatives during World War II.

In October 1977 I had a three-hour dinner conversation with Deakin in London. I asked to know his personal reading of my assumption that, all Foreign Office records to the contrary, Mihailović had for all practical purposes been abandoned by the beginning of September 1943. Deakin told me that he agreed with this assessment—although this left open the questions of who had engineered the abandonment at this early date, and how.

As I recount in Chapters 14 and 15, the Mihailović forces were never more active than they were from the end of August to mid-October 1943— that is, just before Mihailović's abandonment. During this period members of the British and American missions with Mihailović witnessed a number of quite important—indeed, by guerrilla standards, spectacular—actions by the Mihailović forces. In four of these alone—at Trstenik, Prijepolje, Višegrad, and Rogatica—the enemy dead count was somewhere between 200 and 300. One need only ask how many actions of similar magnitude were realized by the resistance movements in other occupied European countries. The British and American missions also witnessed a large number of minor actions, all of which were reported in detail by the liaison officers to the Yugoslav desk SOE Cairo. But practically none of this information was passed on to London, with the obvious result that the Foreign Office and Winston Churchill were under the impression that the Mihailović forces were doing nothing.

On December 30, 1943, in a fervent plea to London, via SOE Cairo, to reconsider its decision to abandon Mihailović, Brigadier Armstrong said:

> I would strongly advise we take big and long view, it will pay us in end. Mihailović undoubtedly commands superiority in areas of vital North and South Commands. In months ahead you will want these constantly under attack. The Partisans will not repeat not command sufficient support to be able to do this. Mihailović does and will.[10]

This was the substance of numerous messages sent to SOE Cairo in November and December 1943 by Brigadier Armstrong and Colonel Bailey. Bailey was by all odds the most knowledgeable liaison officer the British had on either side in Yugoslavia. Apart from having headed the British mission since Christmas 1942, he had lived for many years in the country, was familiar with its culture and politics and fluent in the language—unlike Deakin and Maclean, who had no prior Yugoslav background. Bailey, it is obvious, did not believe the Mihailović forces had been finished by the battle of Neretva.

Because even Deakin had been kept in ignorance by the one-sided intelligence reporting from SOE Cairo, the final briefing he gave Churchill on December 9, 1943, was anything but two-sided. On December 10 the Foreign Office files carried a notation that Churchill wanted to move immediately to break Britain's ties with Mihailović. Two days later SOE Cairo instructed the Mihailović BLOs to abandon their posts and join the Partisans.

18

The Sabotage of the
Mihailović Operation

*After the BLOs were evacuated at the end of May 1944, we
dispersed, virtually all of us, I believe, angry, disappointed,
and confused, not only at the treatment meted out to the Četniks but at the conviction that we too had been deceived and
had been pawns in a very big dirty tricks campaign. This
impression was heightened by the devious manner in which
we were treated and by the arrogant shut-minded attitude of
the staff at base.*

Major Michael Lees
in a letter to the author

*"For KLUGMANN from PIERRO. We are still living. You
seem to have forgotten us."*

ALKALI sub-mission to SOE
Cairo, November 4, 1943

British relations with Mihailović were strained on a continuing basis by SOE
Cairo's performance in providing him with supplies and by its performance—or nonperformance—in communicating with Colonel Bailey. During the course of 1942 and even 1943 there were elements in SOE Cairo who
were friendly to Mihailović, but because of the shortage of planes and the
long distances to be flown from North Africa, the supplies sent to him came
to no more than a nominal aggregate. When Bailey was dropped into Mihailović territory on Christmas Day 1942, he brought with him a brief demand-

ing a substantial increase in anti-Axis activities by the Mihailović forces. At that point the record suggests that Bailey was himself impressed by the glowing accounts of Partisan activities that BBC had begun to publicize during the latter half of 1942. He was, at least for a while, disposed to agree with the official line then taking shape, which in essence said, "If the Partisans can do it, why can't Mihailović?" In one of his early messages to the Foreign Office he wrote:

> The time has come to treat Mihailović firmly. He must be made to realize that we can make or break him. In return for former we demand frank and sincere cooperation.[1]

But while Bailey, in accordance with his instructions, was constantly pressing Mihailović for more activity against the enemy, he was in no position to respond affirmatively to Mihailović's demands for weapons and supplies to conduct a more aggressive program. On top of that, the few supplies sent in during the first half of 1943 corresponded to nothing that had been requested, and were, indeed, infuriatingly worthless. Bailey himself has given this account of the supply difficulties he ran into with Mihailović during that period:

> . . . I found myself in difficulties with Mihailović, who had not unreasonably taken my arrival as an indication not only that material support would in future reach him on a greatly increased scale, but also that what he regarded as the monstrous publicity being given by the BBC to Partisan activities would cease. Regrettably the continued necessity for allocating long-range aircraft in the Mediterranean theatre to anti-submarine warfare and to the support of land operations in Libya made an increase in air sorties to Yugoslavia or other parts of the Balkans impossible. In fact, during the ten weeks following my arrival at Mihailović's headquarters we received only two sorties. The few tons of supplies dropped included thirty million Italian occupation lire, overprinted in bright red "Ethiopia," and several hundred boxes of tropical anti-snakebite serum. Mihailović's rage was matched only by my own when I got instructions from Cairo to the effect that I was to count the lire myself, then have them checked independently by Hudson and the other officer on the mission, before formally acknowledging receipt. This was but one of many foolish demands from Cairo to which I turned a deaf ear.[2]

In a message sent out of Yugoslavia on September 4, 1943, Bailey said, "There was no real improvement in air sorties to this country until May 1943, five months after my arrival. Subsequent improvement in monthly sorties flown has not repeat not kept pace with development of organization and rapid introduction of sub-missions."[3]

When Brigadier Armstrong was preparing to be dropped into Yugoslavia to assume command of the mission to Mihailović, General Wilson gave him a cordial personal letter to Mihailović, written in French, which held forth the promise of vastly increased aid. (Excerpts from this letter are to be found on pages 115–116.)

On his arrival in Yugoslavia, Armstrong received from Bailey an account of the quite impressive activities carried out by the Mihailović forces, primarily on their own initiative, during September, and he also found that Mihailović had given the necessary orders and made the necessary preparations for the Mokra Gora–Višegrad operations, which took place over the ensuing week. On October 3 and 4, on the eve of the night attack on Višegrad, Armstrong sent two optimistic wires saying that "Mihailović appears definitely more pugnacious against Boche," and that the attack was about to take place.[4]

The Mihailović forces performed in a highly creditable manner in this series of operations. Brigadier Armstrong strongly believed that had there been an affirmative British response at this juncture—had Mihailović, instead of the Partisans, been given credit for these operations, and had he received an increased flow of supplies in recognition of his performance—he would have carried out further operations against major objectives specified by the British. Instead, as is documented in the preceding pages, the Partisans received credit for all of Mihailović's major actions, while the flow of supplies was reduced practically to nil, and most of those received could only be considered an insult by Mihailović. For example, Captain Mansfield reported that he was present when the Mihailović forces received a large quantity of uniforms and boots. The fact that they were leftovers from some quartermaster operation was beside the point—what really appalled the Allied officers present was that all of the uniforms and boots were sized for men approximately 5′2″ in height.[5]

Commenting on this situation in a letter to *The* (London) *Daily Telegraph* on January 24, 1977, Brigadier Armstrong said that it became apparent to him shortly after his arrival at Mihailović headquarters that there was no intention to supply arms to him. He quoted Sir Winston Churchill as saying, "We support those who fight for us." And then Armstrong went on to say:

. . . Poor Mihailović had not got the weapons to fight the Germans with all their modern weapons; his supply depended on what his forces could capture. I remember particularly two air-drops at my HQ, one consisted mainly of gumboots [rubber boots], the other of office equipment!

. . . [Tito,] assisted by missions from the British, Americans and Russians, eventually drove the Germans out of Yugoslavia. If Mihailović had had similar support, perhaps the political situation in the Balkans today would be very different.

Theoretically, at that time it was British policy to send arms to both Tito and Mihailović, and entries by Douglas Howard in the Foreign Office files indicate that as late as mid-November Howard was under the impression that Mihailović was still receiving supplies and therefore could be penalized for his "inactivity" by the withholding of further air sorties.[6] Howard's impression of the quantity of supplies received by Mihailović was sadly mistaken. A message to the British mission at Mihailović headquarters on September 24, 1943, said that thirty-five air sorties had been allotted for the period October 5 through November 3 inclusive; a parallel message to the TYPICAL [Deakin] mission at Tito headquarters promised an allotment of sixty-five sorties for the same period.[7]

Fitzroy Maclean complains at one point in his report that the Partisans received only half the air sorties that had been promised for the month of October. The Partisans, however, also received very substantial quantities of arms and ammunition in the seaborne operations conducted at various points along the Adriatic coast. These shipments compensated many times over for the air sorties they had not received. But very little of what was promised to Mihailović ever got through to him, and what did get through frequently appeared to consist of the most senseless, miscellaneous rubbish that SOE could find in Cairo—rusty rifles and waterlogged ammunition, office lighting equipment, and canisters of toilet paper.

The in-message Operational Log for October, November, and December 1943 is filled with pathetic pleas from the British liaison officers in various parts of Serbia asking for arms, ammunition, and supplies, and with complaints about the quality of the few supplies they did receive. Many of the messages said bluntly that certain Mihailović officers had promised to carry out sabotage and other activities against Axis forces if they received the necessary weapons and ammunition but they could not act unless they received the promised supplies.

An early message sent by Armstrong shortly after the victory at Višegrad said that the Mihailović forces were "brave when attacking" and had "dash and enthusiasm" but "grievously lacked supporting weapons . . . Urgently recommend K.M.G. teams [British machine-gun teams] as well as mortars and anti-tank [weapons] sent as soon as possible repeat as soon as possible." Continuing his message, Armstrong said:

Strongly represent necessity for W/T sets for communications. Alternative by Courier too slow in Hills . . . If we had three W/T sets, two mortars, two H.M.G. and anti-tank guns with us, no Boche would have got away and our casualties lighter. Mortar team orders were, quote: On line centre my back, aim, unquote. Number one held a string from end of barrel to get line. [The mortar being used by the Četniks had no sights. To sight it, a string was pulled from the end of the barrel in the direction of the target and the barrel was sighted along the string.][8]

A message from Major Michael Lees with the FUGUE mission in the Priština area on October 21 said:

Understand from yours, am to receive five repeat five planes this moon. This is very inadequate but will ease position if you send at once. We have had four good nights but have not received a plane. It is in your interest to support me, and fail to understand your attitude. If you support me fully you will get all sabotage you want. We are only interested in sabotage, not sitting here and sending through information from doubtful sources.[9]

Another message from one of the Priština sub-missions dated October 21 read:

Marković [commander of Mihailović's 2d Kosovo Corps] very worried at having no sorties and has bargained for three sorties before the end of the month. If this agreed, will allow me forthwith to wreck train near Mitrovica which should put line out of order fifteen days. If you will agree, shall be able to carry out job at once. FIELD.[10]

Complaints to SOE about the quantity and quality of the supplies received also abound in the Operational Log. A message from the REPARTEE sub-mission on October 22 read:

Raković [commander of the 2d Ravna Gora Corps in central Serbia] is willing to fight Occupator immediately repeat immediately if I give the order. If impossible to send arms, please send only seven nine two German ammo for two thousand rifles already with me. Do not repeat not send seven nine two ammo as sent with English rifles, as it does not fit German or Serb rifles. Has there been a mistake? Perhaps I have received material not intended for me and my sortie dropped in another area. If so, will exchange at once. If not, please repeat please send some ammo as NO repeat NO more explosive required. From PUB.[11]

On the same day, October 22, Armstrong wired another protest over the inventory foul-up on a sortie just received:

Well flown and otherwise excellent sortie completely spoilt by fact you [have] not complied our requirements (see CERN one two eight) What Hell good [are] twelve hund [hundred] lbs explosive? We ask for 170 [lbs] only. You send gelignite; we ask [for] plastic or 808. You send no incendiaries, no Williams toys [weapons] except one zero seven stores.[12]

Some of the BLOs with Mihailović thought that SOE's supply operation was handicapped by the poor quality of the personnel (including Italian POWs) used to pack the canisters at Derna. Allowing for the most generous interpretation, however, I still find it difficult to believe that the events documented in this chapter were completely without motivation and direction.

I wish to make it clear again that I do not have firm evidence that Klugmann was personally involved in the sabotage of the Mihailović operation. SOE Cairo, in addition to having a directing officer corps, also embraced numerous rank and file types, civilians, and even Italian POWs. These performed either technical duties or more physical and less sophisticated chores. Supplies to be dropped into Yugoslavia, for example, were packed and loaded at the Derna airfield. I have heard from an authoritative source that Klugmann was able to arrange the employment of personnel in every sector of SOE Cairo. If that was the case, then it is easy to see how he could have masterminded the sabotage of the Mihailović supply operation.

Snafus and delays are inevitable in any major supply operation. Unquestionably, there were some on the Tito side as well. But on the whole the Tito supply operation for this period functioned massively and efficiently, whereas on the Mihailović side, as demonstrated by the handful of quotations above, snafus and inexplicable delays were the general rule. This dual consistency points to a general policy being pursued by SOE Cairo or elements in it.

As the weeks dragged on, the supply situation for the Mihailović sub-missions became progressively worse instead of better. On November 4 the ENAMEL sub-mission in the Homolje area wired this protest to SOE Cairo over the cutback in sorties:

In view small number sorties November must press with emphasis that no further bodies be sent [i.e., that no additional BLOs be dropped in] unless heavy increase sorties. Shortfall three sorties October plus new total two November without explanation will be last nail BRITISH COFFIN here. As repeatedly told by you, we have in good faith told YUGOSLAVS here position will improve. Monthly it has got worse. What explanation can we offer SERBS?[13]

On November 11 the ANGELICA sub-mission, after receiving an indication that there would probably be no further support, wired:

Bitterly disappointed your one six one [message number 161] . . . as must now explain Marković why sorties promised now cancelled and no further likelihood of support . . . Biggest chance of getting action is always promise of support if action produced. This lever you have effectively removed from me. FIELD.[14]

Even when reports of activities against the Germans contained urgent requests for personal supplies from members of the British mission, these were, with rare exceptions, ignored by SOE. A message of October 10 from NERONIAN said:

On 5 Oct. at Jelašnica and Knjaževac Germans [were] attacked to obtain arms. Killed 14, wounded 20. One wounded was brought back, 40 rifles, 3 MGs, one maxim, 2 pistols, one binocs, good supply ammo for weapons captured and equipment from dead. Why no help from Cairo? Three planes as requested be big help. First frost today, no clothing, no money, no food. Help. Help.[15]

An even more bitter message from the NERONIAN sub-mission on November 7 read:

Things very precarious here. After a month of waiting with last few days of frost and snow you still ignore our existence. Planes here will give you full returns. We English here are living like wogs with no clothing to keep out the cold, no decent food, no money. If you send no help before twenty this month you only support the German propaganda which says Britain cannot help with winter. For the love of Mike and all the saints do something to support me here. I will not be responsible after the twentieth. Ends, almost in despair.[16]

On November 9 Armstrong wired the following protest to SOE:

Must represent again most unsatisfactory state existing re sorties flown to Mihailović forces. Yesterday was informed Mihailović said WIX [Armstrong] promised thirty-five aircraft and only nine arrived. Took matter up at conference with Mihailović last night when matter sorties came to a head again. Emphasized for second time [I] never promise aircraft, the flying of which I exercise no control.

You refuse to give dates between which sortie may be expected, probably not realising many drop areas are many hours journey from H.Q. and are on top of windswept mountains: peasant carts or pack horses requisitioned from villages night after night for no result. The cumulative moral effect of this is becoming bad, besides being exceedingly bad propaganda for us and RAF.

. . . still maintain my suggestion made that block of four or five days only be allotted for standing by for YUG [Yugoslav] sorties. If no success, a second block be allotted. I say frankly present attitude CAIRO or RAF not helpful and definitely doing harm, especially on top monumental BBC gaffs which senior cmdrs here now receive with laugh, if trifle hollow![17]

On November 18 Lt. Colonel Cope (HORSE) added his complaint to the chorus:

> Lack of Aircraft my area last two moons in spite of excellent met conditions here has considerably lowered British prestige. Slogan more anti-Axis damage, more planes, no longer holds water. After my own experiences TOCRA consider RAF system needs considerable improvement. No fun sitting in snow all night waiting. Players please.[18]

On December 1 ALMONER, an officer with the NERONIAN sub-mission in the Priština area, wired: "Still waiting planes. Have no W/T, no money, only summer clothes. What do you intend doing about it?"[19]

To these numerous complaints of the Mihailović BLOs, SOE Cairo replied with polite evasions and excuses and vague promises that were never kept. For example, on September 27 SOE sent identical excuses to the ROUGHSHOD, NERONIAN, and RHODIUM sub-missions: "Most deeply regret no more this month possible, but plane shortage and Bizerta failure has rendered inevitable. Doing utmost pep up average in October."[20] In answer to a complaint from the ENAMEL sub-mission in eastern Serbia, SOE Cairo wired on October 8:

> Much appreciate work you are doing under very difficult circumstances (your message number 81 of 6 October). Do NOT be discouraged. We have to divide inadequate number of sorties among many applicants. Principle is to allot most sorties to areas which have shown best results but inadequate even for this. East Serbia is considered important.[21]

Such excuses were endless.

Some supplies of acceptable quality were delivered at various points to the Mihailović forces during this period, but the major part of what was sent in appears to have been scavenged from the most antique sources available to the Cairo SOE. A report by Major J. Sehmer, who served with the British mission in the Priština area, gave this description of his experience with the supplies received from Cairo:

> Sorties: The percentage casualties of WT equipment dropped was inordinately high: I should put it at 70% of WT equipment dropped. This was due in many instances to the static lines of bundles being attached to the plane, and also to insufficient packing material being used.
>
> Arms and ammunition generally arrived in a deplorable state, red with rust and the ammunition sodden with water.
>
> Loading lists were invariably incorrect, a great waste of time as one never knew how many packages to look for.

At least 40% of the cartridge type of container with linen chutes arrived smashed due to either the chutes not opening fully, or the rigging lines tearing off.[22]

The petty vindictiveness of SOE Cairo toward Mihailović carried over into its relations with the British and American officers assigned to him. This is dramatically highlighted by the experiences of Colonel Hudson and Captain George Musulin. These experiences strongly suggest that they were not the product of momentary aberrations of judgment or acts of forgetfulness but of a sustained policy carried out over many months.

Colonel Hudson set forth his own personal grievance against his treatment by SOE Cairo in the following wire dispatched on September 22, 1943:

I have been waiting one and half years for battle dress blouse size 6 ft, waiting at least 7 months for boots size 11 and riding breeches size 6 ft and large great coat. All repeatedly asked for. It was not funny last year when in lieu of above you sent me my tennis trousers and silk pajamas, nor this year when you sent your stunted five foot five outfits. In fact ever since you sent me in from Cairo with bum W/T equipment your supply dept has been just plain lousy.[23]

Even cruder was SOE Cairo's treatment of Captain Musulin, who was dropped into Mihailović's headquarters in mid-October 1943 to reinforce the American component of the Allied mission, which at that time consisted of Colonel Seitz and Captain Mansfield. Musulin remained in Yugoslavia until the end of May 1944, when he was evacuated to Bari, Italy, together with Brigadier Armstrong and the personnel of the British mission. Especially during his first months with Mihailović, he sent out some dozens of messages via SOE Cairo addressed to his OSS superiors. To these Musulin never received replies or even acknowledgments—so that his fiancée and his mother, who he had asked be notified of his safe arrival in Yugoslavia, did not know whether he was alive or dead until he got to Bari. When Musulin checked his personal file at the OSS office in Bari, none of the messages he had sent out of Yugoslavia were in it. They had not been forwarded by SOE.[24]

Why was Musulin treated in this way when messages from Colonel Seitz and Captain Mansfield apparently were being forwarded—although with some delays—on a fairly regular basis? Suppressing messages from Seitz and Mansfield (who was known to be a protégé of General Donovan) would have been a very risky business. But Musulin was a junior officer without any important personal connections. He was, moreover, an American of Serbian parentage who was known to be strongly pro-Mihailović. Therefore, Musulin was both a safe and an inviting target for the dispensers of personal vindictiveness in SOE Cairo.[25]

As November 1943 came to an end, it became increasingly apparent that

British policy was moving toward a break with Mihailović. At this point SOE Cairo in its messages to Armstrong had dropped its hollow pretense about the possibility of support. On December 1, commenting on a request for arms received from the ANGELICA sub-mission, SOE Cairo wired to Armstrong as follows:

> Following is signal from ANGELICA quote Must again put forward Marković proposition. Marković refuses destroy bridges unless he can prevent local reprisals by Hun. Ten sorties and Marković guarantees action within seven days, to include blowing of rail and road bridges near Raška and Mitrovian [Mitrovica]. Action to be taken without order Mihailović . . . unquote. This number of sorties impossible to send. Your comments.[26]

On December 8 SOE wired to the NERONIAN sub-mission:

> Your 13 (312) of 30 [Your message number 13 (312) of 30 November]. 1. Most unlikely anything more than stores for maintenance mission will reach you next few months. 2. Hope send you full explanation next few days. 3. Continue efforts obtain action against lines of communication but state frankly bad weather will make sorties negligible. No repeat No plans should depend on their arrival.[27]

The situation of the British liaison officers was further complicated by the fact that Mihailović's intelligence every day brought fresh reports about the massive quantities of supplies being air-dropped and shipped to the Tito forces. These reports the BLOs were not in a position to either confirm or deny, and their repeated queries to SOE Cairo on this subject produced no enlightenment. The record that is now available, however, establishes that Mihailović's intelligence, if anything, seriously underestimated the scale of deliveries to the Partisan forces during the final quarter of 1943. According to a report in the files of the Prime Minister's Office, sea-lifted supplies alone to the Yugoslav coastal islands during October 1943 totaled 650 tons, and included almost 10,000 rifles, 171 light and medium machine guns, 3,372,000 rounds of small ammunition, 4,800 mortar bombs, and many other items.[28]

The story of the sabotage of the Mihailović supply operation would be incomplete without a reference to the strange case of Major Radoslav Djurić, the officer in charge of the Mihailović forces in southeastern Serbia. For some strange reason, which had nothing to do with any request from Brigadier Armstrong, Djurić received the bulk of the limited quantities of supplies sent to the Mihailović forces during the fall of 1943. Indeed, there is some evidence in the Operational Log that Djurić continued to receive supplies as late as January 1944, while all supplies for Mihailović units elsewhere in

Serbia came to a dead stop by the end of November 1943. All of this made no sense at all, in the light of the many negative reports filed by the British liaison officers to the effect that Djurić was given to dissolute living and had been almost completely inactive against the Axis. One report expressed the opinion that he had almost certainly been in contact with the enemy. It also described him as a completely unscrupulous person, unpopular with his men and hated by his subordinate officers. Indeed, in a communication to General Mihailović through Colonel Bailey, the British command had in August 1943 asked Mihailović to dismiss Djurić together with several other officers.

There are also dramatic reports in the British files dealing with the relationship between Djurić and Vera Pešić, a woman who had been the mistress of Reichswehr General Paul Bader and was suspected by some of being a Gestapo agent, by others a double agent who was ultimately working for the Communists. In early September 1943 Djurić informed Major Rupert Raw of the British mission that he had succeeded in kidnapping Vera from her mother's house and that "it was his intention to give her a summary trial followed by immediate execution." Major Raw reported that not only was nothing done to Vera Pešić, but when he returned to Djurić's headquarters on November 1, it was obvious that Pešić had become Djurić's mistress and, according to officers on Djurić's staff, was "the dominating influence in all his decisions."[29]

Even SOE Cairo was disturbed about Vera Pešić. On October 17 they wired to Armstrong:

VERA PEŠIĆ, ex mistress of GENERAL BADER and GESTAPO agent, was captured and now in hands DJURIĆ. We sent important questionnaire for interrogation Vera. DJURIĆ now feeds and goes for walks with VERA in spite of saying he will have her executed. Local rumors state VERA has some control of DJURIĆ. Please ask Mihailović order DJURIĆ allow British interrogate VERA and then execute her.[30]

Vera Pešić was not executed by Djurić. In early June 1944 Mihailović sent a platoon of soldiers to arrest the two of them. According to the Mihailović version of what happened, Pešić was killed in a Partisan attack, while Djurić was arrested but escaped and joined the Partisans. However, that is not part of this story.

By the beginning of November 1943 Djurić had become a favorite of SOE Cairo. The miraculous reversal in attitude toward him must have stemmed from the fact that he appeared to have turned against Mihailović and now talked, in confidence, to some of the British liaison officers about negotiating an agreement with the Partisans and organizing other Mihailović officers to depose him. A voluminous exchange between SOE Cairo and Lt. Colonel

Cope and Major Raw, who were attached to Djurić, and with Brigadier Armstrong, centers on the prospect of working out an agreement with the Partisans through Major Djurić.

Armstrong appeared to have had serious doubts about Djurić; certainly, it was not he who recommended that the bulk of the limited supplies delivered to Mihailović's terrority be sent to Major Djurić. It is difficult to escape the impression that SOE Cairo made Djurić its favorite recipient of supplies because it believed both that this would encourage him to pursue his negotiations with the Partisans and break with Mihailović and that the arms thus delivered would soon be taken over by the Partisans. Actually, as matters turned out, Djurić did defect to the Partisans after his arrest in June 1944—and was immediately appointed deputy chief of staff at the Partisan headquarters for southeastern Serbia. The Partisans made a big play of the Djurić defection, claiming that he had come over to their side with many of his men. Actually, we have the eyewitness testimony of the American mission (Colonel Farish and Captain Popovich) that Djurić walked into Partisan headquarters all by himself.[31]

As I stated at the outset, nothing available at the Public Record Office documents Klugmann's role in all this, despite the fact that he was "Mr. Continuity." But the details given above would suffice to persuade any reasonable person that SOE Cairo, or elements in it, consistently sabotaged the Mihailović supply operation, especially during the latter half of 1943.

The operations of the Mihailović forces were also sabotaged in other ways. Repeatedly, proposals for operations that were made by the British and American liaison officers with Mihailović were either ignored or flatly prohibited.

On September 9, 1943, Michael Lees of the FUGUE sub-mission wired to Cairo that he had established contact with an impressive group of conservative Albanians who supported King Zog, all of them armed and keen to work. He hoped "to raise 300 men within three days, with possible reserves 30,000, all armed." The British mission in Albania at that time was working with resistance forces that were dominated by the Communists. Julian Amery and other members of that mission were disturbed about the situation, but they were handicapped by an apparent shortage of Albanian resisters for Zog. Conceivably, the information that Michael Lees conveyed to Cairo had a critical potential. Just conceivably, it might have prevented a Communist takeover of Albania when the war ended. Lees asked for one planeload of supplies—machine guns, ammunition, cigarettes, etc., to demonstrate British seriousness and to test his Albanians. He never got the supplies.[32]

Early in December 1943 Captain George Musulin had his first meeting with Mihailović. The general complained bitterly that the attitude of the British was making it impossible for him to work with them. He assured Musulin that he and his forces were willing to carry out any reasonable assignment under Allied direction. He further expressed the hope that the Americans would play a somewhat more independent role than they had done up until that time.

At this meeting Mihailović personally approved and pledged his unconditional cooperation for an attack on the important Lisa antimony mine near Dragačevo, entailing the complete destruction of the power plant, the compressors, and the smelters. This operation would for some time have deprived the Germans of a principal source of antimony, which is used in tempering steel for shells and bombs and other weapons. Major Jack of the British mission, before he left for Yugoslavia, was given a paper by SOE that placed the production of the Lisa mines at 120 tons per month, out of a total of 420 tons available to the Nazis from all sources. Musulin radioed the project to Cairo and asked for permission to proceed. SOE replied immediately, instructing him *not* to proceed.

How disappointing the break with Mihailović was to liaison officers who had spent months developing sabotage forces is apparent from a report by Captain Robert Purvis of the ROUGHSHOD mission on the Bulgarian frontier. Purvis's record of sabotage activities was very impressive, all the more so because, like all the sub-mission commanders, he had been starved of supplies. His report said:

> The break was a great disappointment to us all, as we had raised the Corpus from less than 50 men to a good 700 with whom we were always on the best of terms. There was also no question of their not carrying out sabotage which they were keen to do. Given the proper supplies we could, I am sure, have managed to be more of a nuisance, and, with experience, have tackled larger targets.[33]

Finally, there was a matter of communications. We have already quoted Colonel Bailey's complaint that in eight months in Yugoslavia he had been virtually ignored by Cairo, and that he could recall only one or two communications he would consider substantive. Even more appalling was the handling of Mihailović's communications with his own government, which were transmitted by the British mission via Malta, in British ciphers, under the code name "Villa Resta." At one time there were some 200 Villa Resta communications from Mihailović to the Yugoslav government awaiting transmittal to London. One transmittal to the Yugoslav prime minister in London, received on March 31, 1943, dealt with the differences in strategy between Mihailović and the Communists. The message, as received, bore the notation: "This message, although dated in March last, has only just been received."[34]

19

The Deakin-Maclean Reports
and Afterward

It is characteristic of Communist disinformation operations that identifiable Communists at the core of the operation are masked by involving people whose background makes it impossible to suspect them of being Communist sympathizers. It is questionable whether Churchill was even aware of the existence of James Klugmann. But Klugmann's brilliance, his expertise, and his quite exceptional personality enabled him to win the support of other officers in SOE, from the frankly radical Basil Davidson to the reputedly conservative Brigadier Keble. Thus it was that Klugmann was able to shape the intelligence on file with SOE Cairo. From Davidson and Keble it was only one more step to Captain William Deakin and Brigadier Fitzroy Maclean, who served successively as the senior officers of the British mission to the Partisan forces. And from Deakin and Maclean it was only another small step to Winston Churchill.

Captain Deakin, as was previously pointed out, was responsible for putting together the information for the Churchill briefing in Cairo in January 1943. At the end of May 1943 he was dropped into Yugoslavia to head up an expanding British mission to Tito. From a Partisan standpoint, he could not have been dropped in at a more providential time or a more opportune place. The Partisan forces, or what was left of them, were at the time fighting heroically to extricate themselves from a tightening German encirclement on Mount Durmitor near the Neretva River. A bomb that exploded near the line of march wounded both Tito and Deakin, who from that moment on tended to regard each other as "blood brothers."

When he came out of Yugoslavia, after spending only six months with Tito and the Partisans, Deakin spoke with the utmost emotion of the heroism he had witnessed. In his memoir, *The Embattled Mountain*, Deakin said frankly, "I had taken on in stages a binding and absolute identity with those around me."[1]

Deakin also spoke of Četnik "collaborators," reporting that he had been invited to interrogate captured Četniks but had declined to do so. At another point in his memoirs Deakin reported that he had received a briefing on Četnik collaboration from Steve Serdar, the leader of the group of Canadian-Croatian Communists who had preceded him into Yugoslavia. Deakin was aware that Serdar belonged to the international Communist movement—but apparently he saw no reason for questioning Serdar's objectivity on ideological grounds.

At the end of August 1943, when he was asked to comment on the proposal that certain Četnik commanders charged with collaboration should be denounced by name over BBC, Deakin replied, "I feel that to attack the collaborationist Četniks on the B.B.C. would be a definite step forward, but to do so without implicating Mihailović would be a subtlety which would neither be appreciated nor understood here."[2] It is obvious that Deakin's mind was made up by this time.

Deakin's reports from the Tito mission carried much weight because, as I have related, he had, as a young Oxford history don, assisted Churchill in writing his life of Marlborough. His messages from the field therefore received Churchill's personal attention, whereas those from Colonel Bailey did not.

Although British officialdom in August 1943 still remained divided on the question of Tito and Mihailović, it was decided on the basis of early reports from Deakin to send in Fitzroy Maclean, a conservative MP who had once served in the British embassy in Moscow, to head up an enlarged British mission. It is clear from the record that Maclean was Churchill's personal choice. To underscore the mission's seniority and the importance that the British attached to it, Maclean was to have the rank of brigadier. In an effort to simulate an even-handed approach to the two Yugoslav resistance movements, Colonel Charles D. Armstrong was promoted to brigadier and sent in to head up an enlarged mission to Mihailović. But in retrospect it is difficult to escape the impression that the entire Armstrong operation was a political charade.

As we have seen, the letter to Mihailović that Armstrong was given by General Wilson was ignored or violated from the beginning. This fate met the explicit clause written into the directives of Allied Command Middle East that Bailey was to be the senior political officer for Yugoslavia, serving both the mission to Mihailović and the mission to Tito.[3]

Maclean relates that before leaving England, he was given a copy of the directive issued by the prime minister concerning his appointment. "What we want," Churchill had written, "is a daring ambassador-leader to these hardy and hunted guerrillas."[4] This passage and others in the directive strongly suggest that Churchill was already the victim of a strong romantic attachment to Tito and the Partisans.

The official brief that Maclean was given before his departure spoke in more balanced and less emotional terms. It said:

> Our first aim is to endeavour to bring about the co-ordination of the military activities of Mihailović and Partisans (and any other resistance elements in Yugoslavia) under the direction of the Commander-in-Chief, Middle East.
>
> . . . At the same time, the ultimate aim of His Majesty's Government is to endeavour to reconcile all such groups to each other and persuade them to subordinate the racial, religious and ideological differences which separate them today, so that Yugoslav unity may be preserved and the political, economic and constitutional problems which today confront the country may be settled by the free will of the people.
>
> . . . We would like to know much more about the composition of such resistance movements—i.e. to which parties they originally belonged and to what extent they still consider themselves as members of such parties.
>
> . . . We are particularly anxious to have your report on the way in which King Peter, Mihailović and the existing Yugoslav Government are regarded in the above mentioned parts of Yugoslavia.
>
> . . . We should like to know to what extent they [the Partisans] are under the influence of Moscow, whether they are in W/T communication with them, and whether Moscow has sent them any emissaries or material or financial support of any form.
>
> . . . You will be under the orders of the head of S.O.E. Cairo either directly or through his staff officers.[5]

As matters turned out, certain key terms of this brief fell into immediate disuse because its authors were not aware of Maclean's embittered relations with SOE Cairo and his low opinion of the SOE operation, nor of the difficulty of raising, let alone discussing, the issue of cooperation with the Mihailović forces. Maclean distrusted SOE so completely that he categorically refused to subordinate himself to it and insisted that his communications be directly with the commander in chief.

In his first meetings with Tito, Maclean did not bring up, as his brief directed, the possibility of a reconciliation with Mihailović. In a message dated October 8, 1943, Maclean reported that the Partisan leader had invariably expressed the opinion "that Mihailović is a traitor whose active collaboration with Axis and hindrance to Partisan efforts have forced them to unalterable conclusion that his liquidation is necessary." Given this attitude, Maclean said, he was convinced that it would do no good and might conceivably do much harm if he were to pursue the matter with Tito.

Having entered Yugoslavia on September 19, Maclean made a time-consuming trip to the Adriatic coast and then left the country on October 26. He had been working on a lengthy report that he intended to file upon arriving at Bari or Cairo. At the time he wrote the report he had been in Yugoslavia for less than a month, and if he saw any significant military action then, his book *Eastern Approaches* does not mention it. It is obvious that he accepted at face value, as Deakin—with somewhat more justification—had done before him, Partisan claims of their strength and military achievements. That he also took the Partisans' word for everything about the Mihailović forces and collaboration is reflected in his lengthy "top-secret" report—the so-called "blockbuster" report—which was filed on November 6, 1943, promptly printed, and distributed to Parliament and the press.[6]

Maclean's report is characterized by superlatives and an almost total lack of criticism, only occasionally punctuated by realistic appraisals. He said that "from the outset, the Partisan movement has been based on a common front, directed by the Communist party in the person of Tito . . . As a leader he enjoys the undivided devotion of his followers for whom he has become a legendary figure."[7] The Partisans, he said, "get virtually all their arms and ammunition from the enemy . . . They count on not losing more than one man killed for five of the Germans and 10 against Ustaše or Četniks."[8] They had, said Maclean, an army of twenty-six divisions, numbering 220,000 men, of whom 30,000 were in Serbia and Macedonia. They were holding down a force of fourteen German divisions throughout Yugoslavia.

Maclean said that "religious toleration prevails" and "there are no signs of class warfare." While the Partisan movement was essentially revolutionary, he added, the Yugoslav Communists "have not found it necessary to persecute and thereby alienate whole sections of the population, but there can be no question of a return to the old order."[9] (Compare this to the frank admission of Milovan Djilas that the Partisans killed "far too many people" and that this resulted in massive popular alienation!)

The Partisans, Maclean said, "look forward to friendly collaboration after the war with all neighboring countries including their former enemies. They seek no territorial aggrandisement beyond their pre-war frontiers, with the exception of the former Italian territories of Slovene and Croat populations, already for the most part in their hands."[10] Within six months after this was written, the Partisans were up to their ears in support of the attempted takeover by the EAM revolutionaries in Greece and had moved their forces into Venezia Giulia with the manifest intention of annexing the territory.

The exaggerated rhetoric of the Maclean report aroused the suspicions of some who read it. For example, a Southern Department memorandum of November 16, 1943, says, "The Chief of the Air Staff inquired whether Brigadier Maclean was a reliable observer, or, like many people who go on similar missions, a fanatic."[11] Anthony Eden, in a communication to Churchill on January 19, 1944, expressed similar reservations about the Maclean report. "Naturally," he said, "to Maclean Tito was all white and Mihailović all black. I have a suspicion that grey is a more common Balkan color."[12]

Douglas Howard reacted strongly to Maclean's central recommendation that Britain sever all relations with Mihailović. In a memorandum dated November 22, 1943, he noted that according to a recent telegram from Brigadier Armstrong, Mihailović was still dominant in Serbia proper and had the backing of the people, not only as a Serbian patriot but also in his stand against the Partisans. In light of Mihailović's strong position in Serbia, it appeared to be impossible to agree to throw him over entirely at that moment and give undivided support to the Partisans. But Howard and others in the Foreign Office, including Eden, who urged caution, were outclassed and overruled by the enthusiasm that Prime Minister Churchill displayed on receiving the Maclean report.

Maclean's estimate of Partisan strength was clearly not supported by the evidence. Even if one concedes that the Partisans had the twenty-six divisions they claimed, this would not have justified an estimate of 220,000 enlisted men, because the Partisan divisions at this juncture were closer to 2,500 or 3,000 men than to 9,000. It has been pointed out in the introduction that a guerrilla army of 220,000 in 1943 in Yugoslavia would be the equivalent to the United States fielding a guerrilla army of over 4 million in the event that it was ever overrun by a foreign nation. As for Partisan strength in Serbia, geographically and strategically the heartland of Yugoslavia, Maclean himself later admitted that it was limited to a few isolated pockets from the time they were driven out by the Germans in early 1942 until well past mid-1944. But Churchill took Maclean's figures of Partisan strength from the November 6, 1943 report and enlarged upon them in reporting to the British public.

Maclean and the other Allied officers who went into the Tito-controlled areas of Yugoslavia could not prevent themselves from being used for propaganda purposes by the Partisans. Indeed, their mere presence invited such exploitation. After delivering his "blockbuster" report in London, Brigadier Maclean, along with Colonel Farish, the head of the American mission, returned to Yugoslavia on January 20, 1944. Their party jumped into Tito's territory near the village of Bosanski Petrovac, roughly four hours by foot from Tito's headquarters. The party included Randolph Churchill, who came to Yugoslavia obviously as a representative of his father. A Partisan commander, Colonel Slavko Rotić, made a speech of welcome (in Serbo-Croat) and introduced them to the Partisan troops and the local villagers. In his speech he was careful to emphasize that this was Winston Churchill's son who stood before them. There could be no better evidence than this, he said, that Britain and America were now supporting Tito and considered General Mihailović a traitor. Whenever the mission came to a village, the Partisans would organize a mass reception for them, taking great pains to point out that this was Prime Minister Churchill's son. The simple villagers were enormously impressed.

The Yugoslav peoples, Serbs, Croats, and Slovenes, felt only the utmost friendliness for Britain and America. The peasants always turned out to cheer the Allied officers on their visits to villages, regardless of who was escorting them. At first the members of the Anglo-American mission interpreted these demonstrations as indications of the popularity of the Partisans. Soon, however, some of them learned that many of the peasants who were cheering them were really violently anti-Partisan.

Those officers who did not speak Serbo-Croat had no means of discovering the true state of village opinion, and the few who did speak the language were so carefully watched that only very rarely were they able to speak in confidence to individual peasants. When they protested against being constantly accompanied by guards, the Partisan commander replied that there were many Četniks around—"It's for your own safety," he insisted.

Despite the best precautions of the guards, however, the officers who knew Serbo-Croat soon discovered that all was not as it seemed on the surface. Peasants to whom they spoke in twos or threes all appeared to be Partisans. But when they were able to find a few moments away from their guards to speak to peasants individually and in confidence, the peasants would almost invariably whisper to them words to this effect: "These are the Communists. They aren't the true people of our village. The true people have all been killed."

Despite the peasants' hostility to the Partisans, the presence of American and British officers with them and the receipt of tangible Allied aid inevitably helped the Partisans to maintain their authority and enlarge their forces.

In January–February 1944 Colonel Bailey made a hazardous trip to a secret embarkation point on the Adriatic coast, in the hope that he would be able to return to England and report to Churchill personally before it was too late. He finally met with Churchill in mid-March and early April. As Bailey reported subsequently to his colleague Major Archie Jack, Churchill said to him at the end of their conversation, "I see now that I was badly informed." We have already quoted Churchill's May 17, 1944 letter to Tito (see page xxix), which substantially bears out this account of his reaction to the Bailey briefing and which completely contradicts the information he had received earlier from both Deakin and Maclean on the situation in Serbia. That he

would venture to incorporate such contentious information in a personal letter
to the arrogant Marshal Tito, written only a few weeks after his meeting with
Colonel Bailey, certainly suggests that the briefing had an enormous impact.
Clearly, the information in the letter was not based on anything he had received from Deakin or Maclean—although both of them did change their
estimate of the situation in Serbia only a few months later.

Further confirmation of Churchill's changed appreciation of the situation
in Yugoslavia after his meetings with Colonel Bailey is also apparent from
his second note to Tito, sent August 12, 1944, three months after the first.
In the second note he wrote:

> The desire of His Majesty's Government is to see a united Yugoslavia Govern-
> ment, in which all Yugoslavs resisting the enemy are represented, and a recon-
> ciliation between the Serbian people and the National Liberation Movement.
>
> . . . His Majesty's Government, while regarding Marshal Tito and his brave
> men with the utmost admiration, are not satisfied that sufficient recognition has
> been given to the power and rights of the Serbian people, or to the help which
> has been given, and will be continued, by His Majesty's Government.[13]

Again it must be noted that the language here resembles none of that
contained in the Deakin-Maclean reports. At this late hour Churchill seems
to have backtracked, in the sense of recognizing that the Serbian people and
Tito's National Liberation Movement constituted two distinct entities. For
this reason he indicated that the British government was not satisfied that
significant recognition had been given to the power and rights of the Serbian
people. Alas! At this juncture these remonstrations had as little impact on
the Yugoslav dictator as did Churchill's efforts to persuade him that
Yugoslavia's international position would be enhanced by retaining King
Peter.

Churchill's many misgivings about the continued support of Tito and
about the policy urged on him by some of his closest friends in SOE are
also apparent from his conversation with Colonel Hudson at his Chequers
residence in May 1944. Nora Beloff quotes Hudson as telling her that
Churchill "knew that Cairo had cooked the books, destroyed records and that
the SOE office was 'a nest of intrigue.' " But changing course was very difficult. The course could probably have been altered in the wake of Tito's
near-disaster at Drvar at the end of May 1944. Four months after this event
it was too late, because the Soviet army was already in Yugoslavia. One
can only speculate on what would have happened if Bailey had been
brought out of Yugoslavia in time to brief Churchill before a final decision
was made.

THE DESTRUCTION OF TITO'S HEADQUARTERS

On May 24, 1944, Churchill gave the House of Commons one of his several romantic and inflated reports on the accomplishments of Tito and the Partisans. The next day, 600 Nazi paratroopers, in a surprise attack, were dropped into Tito's headquarters at Drvar. Stojan Pribićević of Time-Life-Fortune, John Talbot of the Associated Press, and several other Allied personnel were captured. Pribićević, however, succeeded in getting away from the Germans.

Tito personally escaped the first onslaught, went to the Partisan airfield nearby, boarded an Allied aircraft, and was flown to Bari. There a group of SOE officers of the Yugoslav desk, having heard of the attack, were waiting to receive the Marshal in their car, parked at the upwind end of the runway. But the aircraft landed downwind, and at that end of the runway Tito entered a Russian jeep and was driven to the offices of the Russian mission, where the British subsequently contacted him.

The battle at Drvar lasted for five days. An AP report of May 29 (delayed) quoted an American colonel as saying, "It certainly looked as if the Germans knew what they were doing. It is my guess that the whole headquarters area had been photographed and mapped down to the smallest detail." Rhona Churchill, writing in *The Daily Mail* for March 2, 1945, quoted an account of the capture of Drvar from the interrogation of Helmuth Kleber, an SS trooper who had been taken by the British:

> We took the Yugoslavs completely by surprise, although they knew that we were planning such a landing. Tito knew that we were coming, but expected us the next day. He drove out of his camp as our planes were dropping us. The first thing I saw when I reached his headquarters were the bodies of two Yugoslav girls, fanatical Nazis, whom we had trained as spies and sent to his camp equipped with Morse radio transmitters. We had been in constant communication with these two girls who had done valuable work for us. They made the whole attack possible . . . We fought in Tito's camp for four days before our own forces relieved us. By the time they came only 120 of our original 600 were still living . . .

Tito's flight from Drvar presented the Allies with a delicate problem. The Partisans had suffered so heavily in the attack on Drvar and in the simultaneous attack on other sectors that, desirable as it might have been, it was impossible at the time to reconstitute Tito's headquarters on the Yugoslav mainland. Instead, it was set up on the island of Vis in the mid-Adriatic, which the British had taken and then used to build up a large military establishment for the Partisans. (Interestingly, it was King Peter, months previously, who had suggested to Eden and Churchill seizing Vis as an ideal locale from which to conduct resistance operations in Yugoslavia.) Tito remained on Vis until he took off secretly for the Soviet Union on the night of September 18–19.

Much of the Partisan propaganda concentrated on the theme that King Peter had fled the country and abandoned his people, whereas Tito had not left the country for an instant since the beginning of the war. The Partisan movement, moreover, suffered from the brittle weakness of all movements that adhere to the cult of the führer: as soon as they lose their leader, or feel abandoned by him, their morale collapses. The Partisan staff was anxious at all costs to conceal the news that Tito was no longer in the country. The British authorities understood their difficulty and endeavored to assist them.

The Partisan communiqué of May 25, the day of the attack on Drvar, reported that "the irregular Yugoslav front has erupted into a mass of flashing guns and raging battles, with many Germans slain . . . 6,500 Germans and Četniks have been destroyed in a single battle." The Partisan communiqué of June 1 announced that Marshal Tito had ordered a general offensive. On this day the German paratroopers, with Wehrmacht reinforcements, were mopping up the remnants of the Partisan army at Drvar. Weeks later Partisan communiqués continued to speak as though Tito were still in Yugoslavia.

The first reports of the attack on Drvar, which appeared in the Allied press on June 3, made no mention of Marshal Tito's whereabouts. The Axis radio announced that he had flown to Italy, but Allied Headquarters could not confirm the news when queried by the press. On June 8 BBC announced that Tito, with Allied aid, had shifted his headquarters from one part of Yugoslavia to another. Finally, on June 18, the press was told that Tito had flown to Italy because there was no airfield available in Yugoslavia, but that he was now back on the Yugoslav mainland. The fact that Tito was now on an island in the mid-Adriatic was still not admitted. A. F. Voigt, the respected editor of *The Nineteenth Century and After*, told the story of Tito and the island of Vis on the basis of private information and was called on the carpet for violating security regulations. He was able to acquit himself by proving that Vis had already figured in Partisan communiqués.[14]

In America Constantin Fotitch, who was dismissed as Yugoslav ambassador when the Tito-Šubašić government took over in June 1944, also conveyed the story of the attack on Drvar to the press. On June 17 the New York afternoon daily *PM* ran an article from its Washington correspondent, Blair Bolles, headlined thus:

Fotitch Invented News In Effort
To Poison U.S. Against Tito

"As a characteristic last-moment gesture of hatred," said the article, "Fotitch planted a newspaper story that Tito, the Partisan leader, had suffered an overwhelming defeat and had been forced to flee to Italy. Fotitch is an old hand at inventing news he would like to happen . . .''

Despite the utmost efforts to conceal Tito's disappearance from the Yugoslav mainland, the news got around to Yugoslav peasants through the grapevine. Had it not been for the tremendous flow of Allied supplies and the support of the Allied missions, the Partisan movement at this stage might have undergone a fatal disintegration. As it was, it lost heavily. Indeed, it was reported that after the attack on Drvar the Russian mission had so poor an opinion of the potentialities of the Partisan movement that they were seriously considering a rapprochement with Mihailović.[15]

THE WORM TURNS

The story of Churchill's personal relations with Marshal Tito during August and September 1944 makes for depressing reading. Here are two paragraphs from Churchill's description of his meeting with Marshal Tito on August 12 in Caserta, Italy:

> On the morning of August 12 Marshal Tito came up to the villa. He wore a magnificent gold and blue uniform which was very tight under the collar and singularly unsuited to the blazing heat. The uniform had been given him by the Russians, and, as I was afterwards informed, the gold lace came from the United States. I joined him on the terrace of the villa, accompanied by Brigadier Maclean and an interpreter.

> I suggested that the Marshal might first like to see General Wilson's War Room, and we moved inside. The Marshal, who was attended by two ferocious-looking bodyguards, each carrying automatic pistols, wanted to bring them with him in case of treachery on our part. He was dissuaded from this with some difficulty, and proposed to bring them to guard him at dinner instead.[16]

Tito assured Churchill that he had no intention of introducing the Communist system into Yugoslavia. Churchill asked him if he would make this statement in public, but Tito objected that he might appear to be doing so under pressure from the British. On the question of King Peter, Tito was completely evasive.

The next important event in the relationship between Churchill and Tito occurred on September 18, 1944. On that date, as Churchill related, "Tito, having lived under our protection for three or four months at Vis, suddenly levanted, leaving no address, but keeping sentries over his cave to make out that he was still there. He then proceeded to Moscow, where he conferred, and yesterday M. Molotov confessed this fact to Mr. Eden.''[17] Actually, the deception was carried a number of degrees past the point indicated by Churchill. The British and American missions, which found it inconceivable that Tito would take off for Moscow without notifying them of his plans, searched high and low for him on the island of Vis. A variety of excuses were offered by the guards and junior officers still stationed outside his quarters. Some said that Tito had gone for a walk, others that he was sick, still others that he was overwhelmed with work and would be available again in the very near future.

Eden, indeed, put the matter far more bluntly than did Churchill. In a wire to the Foreign Office from Moscow after meeting with Molotov, he said:

> We took the strongest objection to Marshal Tito's behavior and to the fact that we had not been told about the visit. If he had had the courtesy to tell us that he was going to Moscow we should have wished him bon voyage . . . Molotov hurriedly put all the blame on Marshal Tito. He said he was a peasant and did not understand anything about politics . . . I told Molotov that he must understand the effect that events of this character must have on our relations. There were many people in England who said that the Soviet Government was pursuing its own policy in the Balkans without the slighest regard to us . . . More explanations about ignorance of Yugoslav peasants followed.[18]

Tito reentered Yugoslavia with the invading forces of the Soviet army on October 12, 1944.

CHAPTER

20

The Armstrong-Bailey
Recommendations

Both the Foreign Office and War Office files contain copies of a 7,000-word telegraphic report that Brigadier Armstrong and Colonel Bailey dispatched to London in the first part of November 1943. It was almost without question the longest telegraphic message sent off by any Allied officer from occupied Europe during the war. Remarkably enough, it was drawn up at roughly the same time as Maclean's "blockbuster" report of November 6, 1943. The Foreign Office copy of the report is headed "Telegraphic Report Received from Brigadier Armstrong and Colonel Bailey Dated 18 November 1943." This is almost certainly the date of transmission from SOE Cairo. From the copy in the War Office files it is clear that Armstrong and Bailey began transmitting their report and recommendations on November 7. For a message of this magnitude, the task of encoding and transmission alone must have required several days' labor. The message was received in London on November 27.

The text of the communication says: "This signal is in 43 paragraphs. Most important it should not be read or discussed by you London or high level authorities until all parts have been received." It was addressed to Lord Glenconner and Brigadier Keble for transmission to London.[1]

In essence, the report constituted an appeal to the British government for a frank recognition of Mihailović's legitimate grievances and of the pressures with which he had to contend, and it proposed that the Yugoslav civil war be held in check by dividing the country into Tito and Mihailović zones of operation, with a no-man's-land in between. "In our opinion," said the wire, "the only way to bring Mihailović to satisfactory collaboration is by a combination of pressure applied through the *proper* channels and a recognition

191

by us of Mihailović's difficulties and cost to him and to the Serbs of work
we wish done, plus recognition of our own obligations in the latter regard.''

It said the paucity of supplies had convinced Mihailović and those around
him that this was another attempt by ''perfidious Albion'' to purchase strategic benefits with Serb blood, without any intention of giving an adequate
quid pro quo. The wire continued:

> Greatest mistrust and apprehension, however, derive from the conviction of all
> Yugoslavs here that the present one hundred percent support of Partisans by
> BBC, including gross misrepresentation of known facts, plus minimum mention
> of Mihailović's activities, plus greater material support he believes we give the
> Partisans, plus fact that it is clear to him that a BLO with Partisans is always
> believed in preference to a BLO with his forces, all add up to mean that British
> have completely sold Yugoslavia down the river to the Russians.

The wire further said:

> Armstrong now batting on worse wicket than Bailey before Armstrong came in
> . . . Mihailović rarely raises any matters at our conferences, never gives Arm-
> strong his confidence and always leaves the initiative with us.

The wire spoke of the need to offer sufficient incentive for a change of
attitude to that of ''willing cooperation.''

With such a solution in view, Armstrong and Bailey made a series of
recommendations to His Majesty's Government. First of all, they recommended that the government publicly recommit itself to the statement made
in the House of Commons by Anthony Eden in July 1941, pledging Britain
to work for the restoration of Yugoslavia's prewar frontiers. Second, the
report called for the holding of free elections to determine Yugoslavia's future form of government. Third, it proposed an agreement on separate zones
of operation for the Tito forces and the Mihailović forces, with a neutral
zone in between. Fourth, it called for equal moral and propaganda support
for both groups. Fifth, it recommended placing both groups under the operational command of the commander in chief for the Middle East. Sixth, it
suggested that punitive sanctions be established—that either side failing without
reasonable cause to carry out orders of the commander in chief must forfeit
all support. Seventh, in order to achieve adequate liaison with both sides,
the report called for the evacuation forthwith from Yugoslavia of one senior
officer from the Mihailović mission and one from the Tito mission, each
officer to bring with him one ''reliable Yugoslav.''

The Armstrong-Bailey wire said:

We do not think Partisans should find the plan against their interests. Operations zones would be based on the present de facto territorial situation. Their public recognition by King and Government and Mihailović's tantamount reduction should please them and aid them in extending their popular appeal in their area. If their hold on the people is as strong as they maintain, temporary renunciation their peculiar political and propaganda activities and acceptance of dynasty cannot harm them, and victory at the elections would allow them to introduce their own political system.[2]

The opening sentence of paragraph 34 says, "The decision on this proposal must be taken on highest level." By "highest level" Armstrong and Bailey clearly meant Churchill and Anthony Eden and the War Cabinet.

As matters turned out, by the time SOE Cairo had finished recoding and retransmitting the report, it was already November 27. The dates given make it clear that SOE Cairo did not break its back to expedite the transmission of this critically important message. The indications are that when it arrived in London, it was seen only by junior officials.

There is no indication that the report was ever seen by Churchill or Eden or other members of the War Cabinet, for whose attention it was clearly intended.

CHAPTER

21

Britain Abandons Mihailović

In July 1943 Fitzroy Maclean was called to Winston Churchill's residence at Chequers to discuss his forthcoming assignment in Yugoslavia. Maclean recounted his conversation with Churchill in these terms:

> After he [Churchill] had finished, there was only one point which, it seemed to me, still required clearing up. The years that I had spent in the Soviet Union had made me deeply and lastingly conscious of the expansionist tendencies of international Communism and of its intimate connection with Soviet foreign policy . . . If, as I had been told, the Partisans were under Communist leadership, they might easily be fighting very well for the Allied cause, but their ultimate aim would undoubtedly be to establish in Jugoslavia a Communist regime closely linked to Moscow. How did His Majesty's Government view such an eventuality? Was it at this stage their policy to obstruct Soviet expansion in the Balkans? If so, my task looked like being a ticklish one.
>
> Mr. Churchill's reply left me in no doubt as to the answer to my problem. So long, he said, as the whole Western civilization was threatened by the Nazi menace, we could not afford to let our attention be diverted from the immediate issue by considerations of long-term policy. We were as loyal to our Soviet Allies as we hoped they were to us. My task was simply to find out who was killing the most Germans and suggest means by which we could help them to kill more. Politics must be a secondary consideration.[1]

This conversation, it is to be noted, took place a full five months before the decision to abandon Mihailović.

At the end of November 1943, just before the Teheran conference, Maclean, who had spent five weeks in Yugoslavia—this including an overland trek of about two weeks to the Adriatic coast—met with Churchill in Cairo. This time the prime minister justified his growing commitment to Tito in even more cynical terms. As Maclean has recounted it:

I now emphasized to Mr. Churchill the other points which I had already made in my report, namely, that in my view the Partisans, whether we helped them or not, would be the decisive political factor in Jugoslavia after the war and secondly, that Tito and the other leaders of the movement were openly and avowedly Communist and that the system which they would establish would inevitably be on Soviet lines and, in all probability, strongly orientated towards the Soviet Union.

The Prime Minister's reply resolved my doubts. "Do you intend," he asked, "to make Jugoslavia your home after the war?" "No, Sir," I replied. "Neither do I," he said. "And, that being so, the less you and I worry about the form of Government they set up, the better. That is for them to decide. What interests us is, which of them is doing most harm to the Germans?" [2]

From these conversations and other fragmentary statements it would appear that Churchill was under no illusion as to the outcome of support for Tito. However, he was bound to have misgivings over the prospect of a Communist Yugoslavia, and it was these misgivings, no doubt, that prompted him to engage in futile exercises which, in retrospect, made him appear almost schizophrenic at times. Prominent among Churchill's episodes of wishful thinking was his conversation with Stalin at the Moscow conference of October 1944.

Let us settle about our affairs in the Balkans, [said Churchill to Stalin]. Your armies are in Rumania and Bulgaria. We have interests, missions, and agents there. Don't let us get at cross-purposes in small ways. So far as Britain and Russia are concerned, how would it do for you to have ninety percent predominance in Rumania, for us to have ninety percent of the say in Greece, and go fifty-fifty about Yugoslavia? While this was being translated I wrote out on a half-sheet of paper:

Rumania	
Russia	90%
The others	10%
Greece	
Great Britain	90%
(in accord with U.S.A.)	
Russia	10%
Yugoslavia	50–50%
Hungary	50–50%
Bulgaria	
Russia	75%
The others	25%

I pushed this across to Stalin, who had by then heard the translation. There was a slight pause. Then he took his blue pencil and made a large tick upon it, and passed it back to us. It was all settled in no more time than it takes to set down . . .

After this there was a long silence. The pencilled paper lay in the centre of the table. At length I said, "Might it not be thought rather cynical if it seemed we had disposed of these issues, so fateful to millions of people, in such an offhand manner? Let us burn the paper." "No, you keep it," said Stalin.[3]

Anthony Eden, to his credit, although he finally went along with the abandonment of Mihailović, never addressed the matter in the cynical terms of Prime Minister Churchill. From beginning to end, he and his colleagues in the Foreign Office (Sir Alexander Cadogan, the permanent undersecretary; Sir Orme Sargent, Cadogan's deputy; and Sir Douglas Howard, the head of the Foreign Office, Southern Department) were disposed to think in terms of ultimate political consequences rather than temporary advantages. And that is why they acceded to the abandonment of Mihailović only with reluctance and extreme misgivings.

In December 1942, although the British government was already discussing the possibility of establishing contact with Tito, Anthony Eden wrote in a memorandum to Churchill: ". . . on the long view . . . we should be wise to go on supporting Mihailovich in order to prevent anarchy and Communist chaos after the war."[4]

Months after the formal abandonment of Mihailović was a fact, some Foreign Office documents continued to give evidence of the same hard-headed realism. For example, a top-secret Foreign Office paper on "Soviet Policy in the Balkans," dated June 7, 1944, said:

[The] Russians are, generally speaking, out for a predominant position in S.E. Europe and are using Communist-led movements in Yugoslavia, Albania and Greece as a means to an end . . . If anyone is to blame for the present situation in which the Communist-led movements are the most powerful elements in Yugoslavia and Greece, it is we ourselves. The Russians have merely sat back and watched us doing their work for them. And it is only when we have shown signs of putting a brake on their movements (such as our continued recognition of King Peter and Mihailović, and more recently the strong line taken against E.A.M. . . .) that they have come into the open and shown where their interests lay . . .

Similar belated appreciations came, both before and after the formal abandonment of Mihailović, from elements in the War Office, the Cabinet Committee on Yugoslavia, and the chiefs of staff.

THE ROLE OF SOE CAIRO

While these things were happening at the level of Churchill and Eden and the Foreign Office, other events at lower levels were moving Churchill and Eden, slowly but unerringly, to the final abandonment of Mihailović.

That outrageous things happened under the auspices of the Yugoslav desk of SOE Cairo during most of 1943 is unchallengeable. By itself this does not prove that Klugmann was the person responsible (even though it would be reasonable to assume that he used his influence on behalf of Tito). After all, there were other people, too, who were members of the small military bureaucracy that operated as the Yugoslav desk. But obviously, the person or persons responsible would have had to be part of the operation at least from May 1943 until the end of the year.

As indicated previously, there was, for a time, a left-to-right coalition in the Yugoslav Section of SOE Cairo that supported Tito—ranging from Klugmann on the extreme left to Brigadier Keble, a conservative bureaucrat committed to the embellishment of his own reputation.

If SOE Cairo, or elements in it, could play the game of disinformation so successfully vis-à-vis BBC and the British government in London, it is virtually impossible to avoid the conclusion that Klugmann was somehow implicated. He was the only officer attached to the Yugoslav Section of SOE Cairo from May to December 1943, when the six major incidents occurred. He had exercised much influence before Basil Davidson's departure in August 1943 and even more during the period of confused succession, during which British policy moved relentlessly from support of both Tito and Mihailović to all-out support for Tito.

Would Klugmann have lent himself to this kind of disinformation? Michael Straight told me, without reservation, that Klugmann would have considered such tailoring of information to flow automatically from his total dedication to communism. Nor can there be any doubt that Klugmann had ample opportunity to engage in such tailoring, thus, in effect, depriving the prime minister, the Foreign Office, the chiefs of staff, the minister of state, and the ambassador to the Yugoslav government of the opportunity to weigh seriously the advisability of keeping the Mihailović option open.

The Foreign Office, during the first part of this critical period, leaned strongly toward continued support of Mihailović. For example, on September 9, 1943, Sir Douglas Howard, the head of the Foreign Office, Southern Department, wrote a scathing memorandum in which he said:

> The fact is, I am sure, that SOE Cairo . . . do not want us to come to a satisfactory arrangement with Mihailović. We have been on the verge of doing

so many times, but on each occasion a spanner has been thrown in to prevent us . . .[5]

Sir Orme Sargent, the deputy undersecretary for foreign affairs, minuted his agreement with this evaluation.

Two and a half months later, on November 22, 1943, Howard took a completely contrary stand in a second memorandum:

> Since he [Mihailović] . . . is doing nothing from a military point of view to justify our continued assistance, we should consider cutting off supplies while maintaining our political and moral support (e.g., propaganda).[6]

This memorandum reflects what information was reaching the Foreign Office in communications from the field through SOE Cairo—and what information was not.

In November 1943, when arrangements were being made to bring Brigadier Maclean and a Partisan delegation to Cairo to meet with a panel of British VIPs, Sir Orme Sargent wired to Sir Ralph S. Stevenson, who in August 1943 had replaced George Rendel as ambassador to Yugoslavia:

> We think it would be useful if Brigadier Armstrong and Colonel Bailey were both summoned to Egypt to arrive at the same time as Brigadier Maclean and the Partisan delegation and to be available for consultation during negotiations between Commander-in-Chief and delegation.[7]

(The proposal that Bailey be brought out of the country to report on the situation there was made independently in the impressive 7,000-word summary that Bailey and Armstrong sent to Cairo at the end of the first week in November.[8]) The Foreign Office files show no reply to Sargent's proposal, nor was there any reply to the several other proposals made by Bailey and Armstrong between September and November.

Diplomatic and political openings did exist that would have made it politically realistic to retain relations with Mihailović.

On November 4, 1943, the Foreign Office had written to Ambassador Stevenson concerning the possibility of bringing out of Yugoslavia Dr. Vladko Maček, the enormously popular president of the Croatian Peasant Party, who was under house arrest in Zagreb. Mihailović at this time was already thinking of an approach to Maček with a view to creating a broad, popular all-Yugoslav resistance to both the Germans and the Partisans. Had Maček been brought out of Yugoslavia at this stage, it is quite conceivable that a Mihailović-Maček coalition, promising free elections under Allied supervision after the liberation, could have persuaded many of those who were leaning to Tito that there was a viable democratic alternative. The proposal presented many difficulties, but it deserved serious consideration. This it did not receive.

In addition, at the Teheran conference in December 1943 a Foreign Office document reported that Molotov, the Soviet foreign minister, had raised "the possibility of sending a Soviet mission to Mihailović." The document, after reporting that Mihailović would accept a Soviet mission if offered, concluded with these words:

> On the other hand, since at the present we are trying to eliminate Mihailović not only from the government, but also from Yugoslavia, this is obviously the wrong moment to take this proposal any further.[9]

Having failed to respond affirmatively to Orme Sargent's request to bring Bailey and Armstrong out of Yugoslavia for consultation at a meeting between Allied notables and a Partisan delegation in early December, Ambassador Stevenson apparently had some qualms of conscience about the haste with which Mihailović was being abandoned. When the Special Operations Committee met on December 3, 1943, he proposed that a decision on the break with Mihailović "be deferred until Lt. Colonel Bailey could be evacuated and consulted." However, the committee found no reason to defer a decision on the break because it was unlikely that Bailey "would be able to add very much to our knowledge of the situation in Serbia about which we have recently received such voluminous telegraphic reports."[10]

The negative attitude of SOE Cairo to Mihailović's repeated requests that Allied correspondents be attached to his forces—with a promise of complete freedom of movement—was another example of its opposition to the publication of any non-SOE opinion. The dispatch of correspondents would have established that Tito's society, even at that early stage, was a closed one and Mihailović's society was an open one. This should have said something to those in charge of Yugoslav policy.

As has been emphasized before, Klugmann's operation in SOE received valuable assistance from pro-Tito elements in other sectors of the wartime bureaucracy. Foreign Office files contain copies of a number of messages received from "Most Secret Source" (as MI6 was referred to in interoffice communications) that displayed a consistent pro-Tito and anti-Mihailović bias. One such memorandum, dated September 24, 1943, said:

> RAPIER 776 [message No. 776 from Bailey] requests that the BBC give publicity to the occupation, "not capture" by Četniks of BIJELOPOLJE [this is almost certainly a reference to Prijepolje, to which Bailey and the other BLOs testified

in their statement to the Belgrade court], KOLAŠIN, BERANE, MOJKOVAD [MOJKOVAC], SEKOVICI [ŠAHOVIĆI], ANDRIJEVICA and MATEŠEVO. These places were abandoned by the Italians, and taken over by a mixture of ex-Djurišić and other Četniks, without having to fight anyone. Their attitude to the Germans, should the latter appear in force, is highly doubtful. They are men with a long record of collaboration with the Axis, and have executed Partisans, killed many in battle, and made themselves hated by the anti-Axis part of the population. To give their "success" publicity on the BBC would be a disastrous error, especially as the Partisans are again fighting the enemy in Montenegro.[11]

Every single point made by "Most Secret Source" in this commentary gives evidence of a reckless and unrelenting prejudice.

First of all, while it is true that many towns occupied by the Italians fell into the hands of the Mihailović forces without a fight, this was also true of an even larger number of towns garrisoned by the Italians that fell into the hands of the Partisans. If it was considered appropriate for BBC to announce the occupation of such places by the Partisans, precisely the same criterion should have been applied to the Mihailović forces. Second, the suggestion that the Mihailović forces would not fight the Germans was in cavalier contradiction of hard intelligence already on file dealing with the battle of Prijepolje and other anti-German actions by the Mihailović forces, major and minor, during September. Third, with a civil war going on, it was pointless to talk about the Home Army executing Partisans or killing them in battle, because the converse was equally true. Fourth, the statement that the Mihailović forces had "made themselves hated by the anti-Axis part of the population" reeks of the peculiar political idiom found in the writings of ideological Marxists.

What did "Most Secret Source" mean by "the anti-Axis part of the population"? The Serbs were by far the largest national group in prewar Yugoslavia. They were also, by common consent, one of the most passionately anti-German peoples in Europe. The point that Mihailović enjoyed virtually universal support in Serbia proper and very wide support in Montenegro, Bosnia, Herzegovina, and the other Serbian-inhabited areas of Yugoslavia was made over and over again, not only in Bailey and Armstrong's reports but also in those of German intelligence. Indeed, it was even conceded in Foreign Office documents after the decision to abandon Mihailović had been reached.

Exactly when was the decision to abandon Mihailović reached? This is not an easy question to answer. Clearly, those who were pulling strings to promote the abandonment had made their decision long before it actually took place. The first indication that Churchill himself had reached this decision came in early December 1943. The Foreign Office hung on for a bit longer. However, the first unambiguous recommendation from SOE calling for the abandonment of Mihailović was contained in a policy paper dated November 19, 1943, and entitled "Appreciation Regarding the Military Situation in Serbia So As to Determine What in the Future Should Be Our Military Policy." This paper, which was in all probability drafted by Klugmann, repeated all the most outrageous lies about the Mihailović movement and the most outrageous exaggerations about the Partisan movement.

It said that reports from British BLOs with Mihailović placed his armed strength in Serbia at 15,000 to 20,000 men with a possible quick mobilization of 50,000. (Actually, the British and American officers attached to Mihailović generally estimated his strength at 35,000 under arms in Serbia and a mobilized strength of 150,000 to 200,000.)

It said that "during the last 18 months there is no evidence of any effective anti-Axis action initiated by Mihailović commanders. In this entire period two minor attacks on Danube shipping and four minor attacks on railways have been initiated by British officers, in most cases against the wishes of the Mihailović commanders." It said further that the Mihailović forces "are hated and feared by Croats, Slovenes, and Moslems inside Yugoslavia," and that its movement is "associated in the minds of the majority of the Serbs with the corrupt and pro-fascist circles who brought their country to disaster."

It reiterated the Maclean estimate (subsequently reduced by Maclean) that 30,000 armed Partisans were already operating in Serbia and Macedonia, and that the Partisan movement disposed of a total armed strength of 220,000 men.

In its closing sentences the report recommended
1. To discontinue support of Mihailović.
2. To evacuate British missions with Mihailović by making the necessary arrangements with Tito.

THE ULTIMATUM

On December 9, 1943, Mihailović was given an ultimatum to blow up two key railway bridges as a final test of his loyalty to the Allied cause. Specifically, he was asked to blow up the bridge over the Morava River at Cerovo, eight kilometers southeast of Stalać, and the bridge over the Ibar River at the road junction for Jošanička Banja, fourteen kilometers north of Raška.

The directive gave Mihailović until December 29 to assent to both bridge operations.* Although it did not use the word, the directive was clearly intended as an ultimatum. In effect, the British government was saying to Mihailović that if he did not agree to carry out the operations within the time specified, he would be abandoned as a collaborator and a traitor.

At the time the ultimatum was delivered, relations with Mihailović had deteriorated to the point where—for different reasons—various people in the Foreign Office, including Anthony Eden, felt constrained to question whether the ultimatum had been made in good faith. This matter is still the subject of historical debate.

In an interview in London in 1977 I asked Brigadier Fitzroy Maclean whether, in his opinion, the bridge ultimatum was not part of a glorified cat-and-mouse game that the British government appeared to be playing with Mihailović. He assured me that the ultimatum was honestly intended, and that Mihailović would, in fact, have received continued support had he lived up to his side of the bargain. But a number of facts in the history of this period argue otherwise.

In a communication to Brigadier Armstrong dated December 1943, Ambassador Stevenson, who was from the beginning outspokenly anti-Mihailović, said, "Wish to make it clear to you that decision to break is being considered on its own merits irrespective of Mihailović's attitude towards these operations." [13]

A series of interoffice memoranda that preceded delivery of the ultimatum suggested that the political-military bureaucracy was deeply divided on the wisdom of presenting the ultimatum to Mihailović. A War Office memorandum from a brigadier with an indecipherable name, dated November 20, said:

> We have a draft instruction to MO4 telling them to request Mihailović to carry out certain operations against railways in areas adjoining those occupied by his troops. These will require some 25 sorties carrying arms, ammunition and explosives. With the evidence that we have available, we can only doubt whether such arms and ammunition would be used against the enemy. It appears much more likely that they would be used against the Partisans. [14]

A memorandum from Anthony Eden to Prime Minister Churchill dated December 28, 1943, said in its final paragraph:

*From a reading of the record it is obvious that some of the people in various British government offices who dealt with the Mihailović matter were under the impression that the actions themselves were supposed to be carried out by December 29; the references on this point are admittedly confused. However, the original message from General Wilson that Armstrong conveyed to Mihailović said very explicitly, "Your agreement requested by 29 December." [12]

You will bear in mind that G.H.Q.M.E. [General Headquarters, Middle East] have themselves asked Mihailović to carry out an operation which he is likely to regard as a test of his good faith on the 29th. If he carries this out do you propose to ignore the fact and adhere to your advice of breaking with him at once?[15]

Brigadier Armstrong received the directive on December 9 and passed it to Mihailović, who, however, pleading preoccupation with other matters, did not meet with Armstrong to discuss the matter until December 23. Meanwhile, a message to SOE Cairo from FIELD, one of the BLOs with Mihailović, noted that on December 15 he had personally seen a signal from Mihailović to Keserović, one of his more effective commanders in southern Serbia, instructing him to prepare for the move against the bridges.[16]

On December 13, 1943, four days after the ultimatum was received and sixteen days before the deadline set for Mihailović's agreement was to expire, and while communications about the operation were flying back and forth between Cairo and Yugoslavia, SOE Cairo signaled all the BLOs with the seventeen Mihailović sub-missions to leave their positions and escape to the Partisans. The message read as follows:

During next few days, His Majesty's Government may decide to drop Mihailović which would involve evacuation all British personnel from Mihailović HQ and areas. Burn this signal after reading. Only method evacuation is through PARTISAN territory . . . Be prepared to move 15th if journey to PARTISANS considered possible.[17]

Commenting on this directive, Armstrong, during the ensuing weeks, fired off several angry communications to SOE Cairo. In a long message on December 14 he opposed the planned method of withdrawing the personnel of the British mission from Mihailović in these words:

Note you have informed sub-Mission Comds with whom in W/T contact provisionally prepared to move to nearest Pzn unit if considered practicable, your twelve of twelve Dec. My opinion most dangerous any sub-missions try rpt try join Pzn Forces in Serbia. Also existence impossible and intolerable if Missions remain jobless and unsupported.

My opinion, borne out by OLD, no British member sub-Mission has least chance moving through Serbia to Bosnia or leaving MVIC Forces without guide or unescorted. Certain be picked up due course so consider most inadvisable any British rank should be allowed consider possibility trying to escape.

If desire withdraw Missions from MVIC Forces, strongly rpt strongly advise should be arranged with MVIC through me.

Consider only arrangement for sub-Mission personnel, if desired to withdraw
them, is to arrange for this to be done through MVIC and for them to concentrate at my H.Q. Unless special facilities granted by MVIC to Americans will
treat them exactly as British personnel.

Do not intend take any steps re evacuation until receive orders from you to do
so. Then I will only do so in full consultation with MVIC. Consider only hope
success is to deal quite openly with MVIC and try get him arrange evacuation,
any other method I assure you will fail.[18]

When there was no indication that SOE Cairo had rethought its position,
Armstrong reinforced his arguments in a message on December 21:

I wish to point out in strongest terms the very serious mistakes you are making
in your method of breaking Mihailović. Every day you make it more and more
difficult for me to deal with Mihailović. I know the man, you don't.

I am most disturbed at the information your twenty one (X.390) [your message
of December 21]. Even if ALKALI, ANGELICA and RHODIUM [sub-mis-
sions] make good their escape what am I to say to Mihailović please? I ordered
my officers to run away? It is perfectly maddening. Same old attitude: the fellow
sitting at nice desk invariably knows more than man on spot.

Do you fondly imagine that NIM, MATT [code names for Mihailović com-
manders] and STOJANOVIĆ will not tell Mihailović their BLOs have fled?
Probably Mihailović had heard about PADDLE [code name for BLO], that was
why in such a temper when he saw me on seventeenth. What do you imagine is
now going to be attitude of JUGS to all my Officers who remain their posts,
implicit trust put?

Do you imagine JURY will think everything is normal when BIRD and WAY
[BLOs] turn up? Do you imagine Mihailović will trust me after all this underhand business when I have to go to him to break off relations and try to arrange
evacuation of those who have remained on?

It is just plumb crazy. Here I am supposed to be commanding a Mission and
you make vital decisions without even consulting me. You ask officers not fluent
in language to sound [Mihailović officers] re Mihailović removal; you tell young
inexperienced officers in isolated sub-Missions to run away if they think they
can.[19]

Finally Armstrong's determined and earthy language carried the day.
Armstrong *did* consult Mihailović, who pledged his complete cooperation in
the withdrawal of the British mission. The personnel of the mission *did*
concentrate at Armstrong's headquarters as he had proposed, and at the
end of May they were airlifted out of Yugoslavia without any casualties or
difficulties.

Not because of the December 12 directive but because he considered it his duty to get back to London and try to set Churchill straight, Colonel Bailey, with a Home Army escort party, left for the Adriatic coast on January 5. From there he was evacuated to Bari on February 6 and ultimately to Cairo and England. Colonel Hudson, shortly after receiving the December 12 wire ordering the BLOs to evacuate themselves via Partisan territory, moved to comply with the order by striking out for the Adriatic coast. He took with him another BLO, Major Robert Wade, and the chief of the American mission to Mihailović, Colonel Albert Seitz.

Even though it was, or should have been, obvious that at this late date reversing the abandonment of Mihailović would be extremely difficult, if not impossible, Armstrong and Bailey both put up a stubborn rearguard battle. In reply to a message they had received on December 12, indicating that the government was on the verge of breaking with Mihailović, Bailey sent the following reply:

> While realising we may not be in full possession all relevant facts, I state emphatically that I consider action foreshadowed your signal would be most disadvantageous at present.
>
> This statement is made solely in interests our immediate programme of action against enemy lines of communication in SERBIA. Full argumentation on which my views are based has been given in recent signals to you.
>
> We shall thus be faced hostile Mihailović forces and civilian population, which will preclude any possibility attacking railway lines BELGRADE, SOFIA, SKOPLJE either from within or from without country.
>
> In these circumstances, I consider PARTISANS will not repeat not succeed in penetrating SERBIA or south SERBIA north of SKOPLJE. Neither do I consider PARTISAN forces already existing in SERBIA strong enough to do our work for us in face constant attacks from GERMANS, quislings, and Mihailović forces . . .
>
> I presume His Majesty's Government has taken into consideration fact that on December 9th WIX gave Mihailović in writing C-in-Cs directive. This gave Mihailović until December 29 to carry out certain specific operations for us.* His Majesty's Government now apparently proposes to drop Mihailović before expiration this term—that is without giving him full term in which prove his readiness collaborate. I do not repeat not suggest Mihailović likely to comply, but that should not relieve us from ONUS of honouring our own ultimatum.[20]

Twice, on December 26 and 30, Armstrong renewed the plea for reconsideration. His message of December 30 said:

*See footnote on page 202.

I would strongly advise we take big and long view, it will pay us in end. Mihailović undoubtedly commands superiority in areas of vital North and South Commands. In months ahead you will want these constantly under attack. The PARTISANS will NOT repeat NOT command sufficient support to be able to do this. Mihailović does and will.

At present he is committed to cooperation. If you seize opportunity and support with sorties, the dividends you gather will be greatly increased. If you hesitate to provide material support and continue propaganda attacks you will relapse to old spirit of preservation SERB blood—the British want all but will give us nothing in return. As a result, work BLOS out here will be wasted and useless.[21]

Despite Mihailović's delay in responding to the December 9 ultimatum, Armstrong argued passionately in favor of giving him a chance to prove himself, once he had agreed to the essential terms of the directive from Middle East Command. Apparently, he was completely, or almost completely, convinced of the sincerity of Mihailović's reaction in affirming his willingness to undertake the operations. In his message of December 24, 1943, the day after his meeting with Mihailović, Armstrong said:

(From SEIZURE:) In continuation of my eight one of two three Dec [message No. 81 of December 23] we have recd a gift horse as Xmas present, so for heaven's sake don't examine its teeth too closely. Please give it a run before you say spavined and broken winded. You and I both have thoughts as to reason for this volte face but as I have said before, give MVIC a fair deal. At conference MVIC only touched lightly [on] lack arms and then got to business broad lines telling me which Cmds detailed main attacks. Also ordered MATT carry out attacks at once against all lines Ibar Valley and JURY carry out attacks also, despite fact not rec'd supplies [or] money agreed purpose.

Again MVIC said could not complete arrangements by two nine [December 29] but said would carry out attacks during first fortnight Jan. I requested attacks be coordinated to take place same day but MVIC doubtful if he could arrange that. It all sounded fine. I of course realize there will probably be delays and disappointments but MVIC will anyhow stick to his orders. I most strongly recommend you give him a chance. Give me a stick that is sorties and supplies and the horse will go—perhaps not at full speed, but I stand by my assertion and faith that it will go.

You have got us in a queer street despite my beseeching you to tell my BLOs not to run without my orders. The country is now littered with them. What MVIC thinks of me heaven only knows as he has not said a word.[22]

This improved cordiality between Mihailović and the British mission continued into the first part of January. Under the new timetable agreed to, Mihailović was to blow both bridges by January 14.

The improved cordiality, however, was in part a mask. Mihailović was seething with anger and bitterness that had been building up since early 1943. The depth of this bitterness was dramatically conveyed in a message from the British mission to SOE dated January 9, 1944:

> At conference two Jan at which he reported progress in preparations for attacking targets specified in C-in-C's directive, Mihailović made following request Quote ONLY repeat ONLY reward I ask for carrying out these Ops is that, if successful, there should be NO repeat NO mention whatever of them over BBC Unquote.
>
> Mihailović explained that by its complete reversal of policy over the past year, by its indiscriminate fulsome support, first, of him, and now of TITO, and its recent veiled attacks on King PETER and JUG Govt, BBC had irremediably compromised itself with people of SERBIA.
>
> Mihailović finally said Quote I would be most happy if BBC would in future simply ignore me and my movement. In view of the unjust and disloyal attacks which have been made on me by the ALLIES over the BBC in the past, I could NOT repeat NOT in future accept its support should this again be offered. I therefore again ask that there be no mention, either favourable or unfavourable, of my activities by BBC Unquote.
>
> Mihailović added a protest against the anti-dynastic tendency of two recent BBC broadcasts. This will be separately reported. Please ask at once that Mihailović's request regarding favourable publicity will be granted and indicate what are prospects that request Re. unfavourable mention will also be granted. WIX [Armstrong] considers Mihailović is making serious error in resenting BBC report. OLD [Bailey] does not agree as he considers BBC is compromised in SERBIA and Mihailović's arguments on this basis are valid.[23]

Over the last days of December and the first part of January, messages concerning the bridge ultimatum flew thick and fast from one government office to another, including the Foreign Office, the Prime Minister's Office, the Joint Chiefs of Staff, the Office of the Supreme Command Middle East, the British mission to Mihailović, and finally Mihailović himself. On December 26 Mihailović, through Brigadier Armstrong, radioed the following message to General Wilson, commander in chief for the Middle East:

> Dear General, I fully appreciate the importance of the railway communication in the valleys of the Southern Morava and Ibar [rivers]. We will undertake attacks on objectives recommended for purpose by General Wilson.
>
> Have undertaken necessary preparations for actions. I can say at once, having regard to the serious nature of Ops. and circumstances under which we must

operate, also magnitude of preparations, the term set is too short. I understood at conferences attacks [were to] be made first fortnight Jan.

I also wish remark targets exceptionally well defended as result of importance enemy attaches to them. Although we have at our disposal only very limited quantity of ammo and are short of special weapons for attacking pillboxes, am prepared do everything execute these ops.

If it is desired guarantee success, besides a well thought out plan, actions ought be well supplied with necessary equipment and material and, insofar as allies prepared to help with adequate supply of ammo, prospect of success would be enhanced.[24]

Brigadier Armstrong strongly supported Mihailović's request for supplies with which to undertake the projected missions. Despite the previously quoted statement in the War Office memorandum of November 20, 1943, that these operations would require "some 25 sorties carrying arms, ammunition and explosives," SOE Cairo now changed its tune and argued that Mihailović already had adequate supplies—and further hardened its position just before the operation was supposed to take place when it took the stand that "There can be no question of replenishment after the battle. Sorties are too scarce."[25]

Meanwhile those government bureaucrats who opposed Mihailović became more vocal and more militant, and even those who had been friendly to him now backed away. "The sooner we can get on with the job of replacing both Mihailović and the present Yugoslav government, the better," wrote P. L. Rose, an assistant to Douglas Howard in the Foreign Office, Southern Department.[26] And Ambassador Stevenson offered the following formula for a response in case Mihailović should raise the question of Britain's bad faith:

[Mihailović] can say that we have treated him exceedingly badly in asking him to carry out an operation and at the same time starting with our preparations for abandoning him. The answer is (1) that the operation is highly desirable from a military point of view and that is the reason why he was asked to carry it out; (2) that the decision to withdraw our support from him was taken because of his attitude of non-co-operation over a long period and because of his approval of the collaboration of his subordinate leaders with the enemy; and (3) that it is impossible in an occupied country, when the freedom and perhaps the lives of our officers are at stake, to behave with strict punctilio.[27]

The Foreign Office and SOE Cairo stopped pushing for the bridge-busting project in early January 1944, apparently fearful that Mihailović might put them on the spot by complying with the ultimatum. It is obvious that the BLOs who remained with him must have been embarrassed and demoralized by the knowledge that he was going to be abandoned anyway. It is only natural, too, that Mihailović's motivation should have waned, in face of the growing evidence that the British government had, for all practical purposes, already abandoned him.

Indicative of the views and manners of the military bureaucrats who administered Yugoslav policy in Bari was the pointless vindictiveness with which Mihailović associates passing through Bari were treated.

In January–February 1944 Major Voja Lukačević, Mihailović's commander in the Sandžak, escorted Colonel Bailey to the coast and out of the country. The courage and resourcefulness he displayed on this trip was highly commended by Bailey. He took advantage of his sojourn in London to attend King Peter's wedding on March 20. In May he set off on the return trip to Yugoslavia. At Bari he was about to board an airplane that was to bring out members of the British mission still in Yugoslavia, when the British authorities took him in tow. They disarmed him and took away his personal papers, letters that he was bearing from the king to people in Yugoslavia, a bag of gold that the king had sent as a personal contribution to the Četnik movement, his revolver, and finally his wristwatch. To Lukačević's protests they replied that everything would be returned before his aircraft took off. But just before takeoff they shoved him aboard, minus papers, letters, gold, revolver, and watch. As soon as the plane landed at Pranjani, he leapt out, bellowing like a wounded bull and swearing by every Serbian oath that Armstrong and his fellow officers would not depart until Bari had restored his property to him. After Lukačevic's temper had cooled off a bit, Mihailović prevailed upon him by pointing out that Armstrong personally had had nothing to do with the confiscation of his property, and that it would do no good to hold him hostage.[28]

When now Colonel Živan Knežević and Major Bora Todorović left Washington for Yugoslavia in September 1944, bearing letters of authority from General George Marshall and Ambassador Robert Murphy, they were placed under close arrest by the British in Bari and released only after energetic protests from the American authorities.[29]

Again, when Živko Topalović and Adam Pribićević—the former, head of the Socialist Party of Yugoslavia and a member of the Executive Committee of the Second International; the latter, perhaps the most universally revered man in Serbian politics—were evacuated to Italy at the end of May 1944 together with the members of the British mission, the authorities in Bari held them incommunicado, Topalović for several days, Pribićević for almost one month.[30]

Somehow the arbitrariness and meanness of these actions provided a fitting conclusion to the entire sordid story of the abandonment of Mihailović.

For more than five and a half months after the BLOs were told to abandon Mihailović, and for several months after the abandonment had been formally announced in Parliament, the Mihailović forces took care of the members of the British mission, sometimes clashing with the enemy to protect them. Jasper Rootham recounts one such clash when he and a small group of other BLOs were being escorted to the concentration point from which they were to be evacuated. Their escorting officer, Captain Pavlović, had under him 23 of his own men and 30 more of the local militia. On March 28, 1944, in the early morning, they ran into a Bulgarian unit. Not knowing how many Bulgarians he faced, Pavlović went over to the counterattack. After briefing his men, he screamed at the top of his voice, "Number one company on the right, number two company on the left, number three company in the center!"—and then ordered his bugler to sound the charge for this imaginary force. His small force opened up with all the weapons they had. And the Bulgarians—some 200 strong—broke and ran.

About Pavlović, Rootham said:

> He knew that we were being evacuated, that we were ordered to leave him and those who thought as he did, and that he had nothing to expect from us. He went out at the head of his men to cover our retreat. It is perhaps unwise to argue from the particular to the general, but we cannot forget that it was the so-called collaborationist organization of Mihailović which, with less than no inducement and no motive but honour and chivalry . . . saved us British in Eastern Serbia on March 28, 1944.[31]

Over a period of three nights beginning May 31, 1944, Brigadier Armstrong and some twoscore British personnel of all ranks were evacuated by air to Bari. With them they took 30 to 40 American airmen who had been forced down or shot down over Yugoslavia. Over the ensuing months the grand total of American airmen rescued and evacuated from Mihailović territory exceeded 430. In addition, it is estimated that a minimum of eight to ten aircrews (approximately 100 airmen) were picked up by the Mihailović forces but turned over to the Partisans because at the given time and place an air evacuation from Mihailović territory was not practical.

Jasper Rootham wrote a moving account of Mihailović's dignified parting with the British officers on May 31:

> We drank *rakia*, and conversed desultorily for a whole. Finally we rose to go. We said, and I see no reason to apologize for it, that we were sorry that we had to leave, but that we should try, if we got safely out, to confine ourselves to the facts as we had seen them, whether they were favourable or the reverse.
>
> Mihailović replied. He said that whatever anybody might say or think, he and those who fought with him regarded themselves as the friends and allies of the Western Democracies, and for that reason, if for no other, he regarded it as his

duty by all means in his power to ensure that, since we had been ordered by our High Command to leave, our evacuation was successfully carried out. We shook hands, saluted, and left.[32]

The bulk of the mission was evacuated by American, not British, planes. On the first night the RAF did fly in two planes. The runway was very short. The first plane, which was heavily loaded, had considerable difficulty in clearing a nearby hilltop and clipped off some of the top branches of a tree, which became jammed in its undercarriage. The second plane, not so heavily loaded, had no difficulty in taking off. At this point there was a pause in the British operation for reasons of safety. On virtually no notice the US Army Air Force took over from the RAF and completed the evacuation over the next two nights.

CHAPTER

22

The Mansfield Report:
An American Appreciation

Captain Walter Mansfield was the first American officer dropped in to Mihailović's headquarters. He arrived on August 18, 1943. On his return to Washington after spending five months with Mihailović, he filed a forty-page, single-spaced report with OSS, which is credited with greatly impressing both General Donovan and President Roosevelt.

Mansfield's report is remarkable for the understanding it displays of a very complex situation and for its meticulous weighing of the facts. His report deals successively with Mihailović and his policy, Mihailović's army, the Partisan-Četnik war, collaboration between Četniks and Germans, and Mihailović's communications with his government.

Mansfield was a bright young lawyer who after the war became a junior partner in the law firm headed up by General Donovan. In 1966 he was appointed a federal judge for the New York First Circuit. In 1971 he was elevated to the Federal Court of Appeals for the First Circuit, a position he held until his death in 1987.

Although he was in Yugoslavia for only five months, Mansfield and his superior officer, Colonel Albert Seitz, saw much more of the Mihailović movement than did most liaison officers. Toward the end of October they obtained Brigadier Armstrong's approval for a tour of inspection of the Mihailović forces in central Serbia. Armstrong assigned Colonel Hudson of the British mission, who was completely fluent in Serbian, to accompany them as interpreter.

At the time of the Italian surrender Mansfield reported that Mihailović had sent out a general order to his men throughout Yugoslavia to attack German troops and lines of communication. Mansfield said that he had the order translated and wired a copy to OSS in Cairo. "Thereafter," he reported, "for several days, Mihailović was showing me radio reports from all of his Korpus commanders reporting extensive sabotage and attacks on small German columns throughout Serbia, Herzegovina, Bosnia, and Dalmatia; that several trains were derailed in south Serbia; that a large number of German lorries were destroyed, and several villages and towns taken. Mihailović commanders in Bosnia and Dalmatia were complaining bitterly about being attacked in the rear by Partisans while Četniks were fighting Germans. For example, they stated that after taking Gacko and driving the Germans toward Bileće, the Partisans walked into Gacko and claimed that they had taken it from the Germans."

Mansfield reported that "Mihailović still has a great grip on the Serbian peasants. Everywhere Colonel Seitz and I traveled on our tour through north-central Serbia the people in villages who turned out to see us cheered him madly. In private conversations they talk of him as one would of the Messiah. Četnik troops and peasants alike sing romantic songs about him, and Ravna Gora, his original hideout, has become very sacred to the Serbian people. To them, Mihailović still stands as a symbol of their spirit of resistance against the occupator. He also stands for the things they want, the King and democracy." Mansfield reported that he saw no collaboration between the Mihailović forces and the Germans in Serbia, that on the contrary he witnessed many clashes between them. However, he said, the Mihailović troops in north Sandžak, Herzegovina, and Bosnia were devoting virtually all of their efforts to the fight against the Partisans. He quoted one Home Army officer, Captain Bora Todorović, as informing him that Mihailović was allocating 65 percent of his weapons and ammunition to the war against the Partisans and 35 percent to the war against the Germans.[1]

His report contains some highly interesting paragraphs on the subject of accommodation. In north central Serbia he inspected the forces of Captain Nikola Kalabić, who told him frankly that he maintained a friendly relationship with some fifteen Nedić gendarmes in Arandjelovac—but also that it was they who had tipped him off in August 1943 that a German truck convoy, carrying machine guns and ammunition, would be passing through the town of Stragari. Kalabić had ambushed the column, killed more than a score of Germans, and captured forty Zorka light machine guns with much ammunition. Mansfield said that when he visited Stragari, the entire village of some 150 houses had been destroyed by the Germans in reprisal for Kalabić's attack.[2]

Even though all Mihailović soldiers served without pay and were told not to expect pay in the future, and despite their obviously grim living conditions in the field, Mansfield said that many thousands of young Serbs volunteered for the Home Army. He said that he saw 1,600 recruits sworn in at one ceremony in October and a similar contingent of some 1,500 in late December. The one difficulty, he said, was in finding arms and ammunition for these men—there was no problem with food and lodging, since the Serbian peasants gladly shared what they had with them.

About the hardships of life in the Mihailović army, Mansfield had this to say:

> During the past 2½ years their uniforms have worn out and there has been very little replacement of clothing, with the result that the troops are now in an extremely ragged condition. While the peasants can supply food and shelter, clothes and shoes are almost impossible to obtain. They must be purchased on the black market at sky high prices, and without funds this is impossible. The only source of clothing is an attack on enemy troops, and I have heard troops planning such an attack to get themselves some clothes. At present Mihailović's troops wear all kinds of oddments, including peasant garb, and Italian, German, Bulgar, and British uniforms. The great majority wear native opankes [moccasins] for shoes, and these afford little protection against rain, rocks and snow. Perhaps the most extreme example of raggedness was in Vučković's area, where we saw 25 soldiers of the Second Takovska Brigade, who had walked without shoes eight hours in the snow to appear for inspection. Yet one rarely hears them or their commanders complain about lack of proper clothes. All they ask is arms and ammunition.[3]

Mansfield said that the rifle of the average Mihailović soldier in Serbia was pitted and worn and looked more like a museum piece than a weapon that could be used on the battlefield. In the bitter Serbian winter, he said, "the Četniks live under conditions which I would have considered it impossible for them to stand if I had not seen it with my own eyes, often marching many hours with heavy equipment through deep snows."

The report was frank in discussing the weaknesses of the Mihailović movement. Mihailović himself came in for criticism because of his resistance to delegating authority. While some of his officers were impressive, others were not. (Most of the regular army officers, taken prisoner in the capitulation to the Nazis, spent the rest of the war as POWs in Germany.) His political entourage also did not receive high marks. (The entourage changed dramatically after the congress at Ba in early January 1944—but on this Mansfield had no information when he wrote his report.)

Mansfield's report also dealt with the troubled relations between Mihailović and the British mission. This section, obviously, must have been based on information from Colonels Hudson and Bailey. According to Mansfield, Hudson, the first British officer to join Mihailović (October 1941), had been intent on stopping the civil war between the Četniks and the Partisans. Believing that most of the material sent to Mihailović would be used against the Partisans, he had tried to stop Cairo from sending aid to Mihailović. In the winter of 1941–42 this resulted in Hudson's "exile" to a hut on a mountainside, where for five months he lived the life of a hermit. In the case of Bailey, too, Mansfield reported instances of serious friction with Mihailović, which resulted in long periods when Mihailović, on one pretext or another, would refuse to speak to him. Mansfield said that Bailey had tried to persuade Mihailović to permit the British BLOs to witness planned operations, and that Mihailović initially had resisted this proposal but finally consented and reestablished relations with Bailey.

He also reported on the strained relations between the British mission and SOE Cairo. This was based in part on the lack of communication with Cairo and the inordinate time that Cairo took to respond to communications. Mansfield said that in early September he had repeatedly wired Cairo for orders to accompany Bailey to the Venezia Division surrender, but that no reply was received. The British mission was obviously irritated, in addition, by SOE Cairo's overall failure to send in supplies for the Mihailović forces and by the quality of the few supplies that were sent in. As an example, Mansfield said that he himself had seen airdropped canisters filled with shoes and overcoats for men approximately 5'2" in height.

Mansfield dealt frankly with the irritants that plagued relations between Armstrong and Colonel Seitz, especially during the initial period. Armstrong apparently had been briefed by SOE Cairo that the American mission was not to be accorded coequal status with the British mission, and that Colonel Seitz and Mansfield would have to send all of their communications with OSS in British code, via SOE Cairo. It is not clear whether Armstrong was, again, following orders or else acting on his own initiative when he barred Colonel Seitz from some of the early conferences with Mihailović. What is clear, however, is that Klugmann and company, who were at that time closing in for the kill, were apprehensive about any increase in American influence in the Mihailović area.

Mansfield said that Mihailović was most affable in his relations with Colonel Seitz and himself, and he recommended increasing the size of the American mission, apparently convinced that Mihailović would then deliver more consistently on anti-German actions. He was also convinced that Britain and the United States had an obligation to try to stop the civil war in Yugoslavia.

On January 6, 1944, Captain Mansfield joined up with Colonel Bailey in a forced march to the Adriatic coast and evacuation. When he returned to Washington in early March 1944, he immediately wrote his lengthy, balanced, and persuasive report. (See Appendix No. 3.) Colonel Seitz did not get back to Washington and file his report for another several weeks, so his report was eclipsed by Mansfield's, although the two agreed on all essential points.

Even before receiving the Mansfield report, Donovan, as head of OSS, had favored a position that kept the Mihailović option open. He was opposed to the exclusive support of either side in Yugoslavia. Accordingly, in February 1944 he decided to send in a somewhat more substantial mission to Mihailović with a total personnel of forty, divided into six teams of six, with four auxiliary members. No matter what the truth about Mihailović, Donovan felt it was important that American teams be scattered throughout Serbia for the purpose of gathering intelligence. The personnel were selected, brought together in a villa near Brindisi, Italy, and briefed in preparation for their departure to Yugoslavia. At the last minute the British government intervened, and the entire mission was called off.

When the Mansfield report was submitted, Donovan sent copies to President Roosevelt and the State Department. Both were so impressed by the report that toward the end of March 1944 it was decided to dispatch immediate Lend-Lease aid to Mihailović. Preparations were made. A telephone call came from Churchill. The plans for the Lend-Lease shipments were canceled.

In the opinion of Colonel Seitz and Captain Mansfield and several members of the British mission, it was not unrealistic to think in terms of denying Yugoslavia to the control of the Communist sphere. This opportunity probably remained open until the month of July or, conceivably, August. Had Britain and America taken political advantage of the destruction of Tito's headquarters at Drvar on May 25, there is reason to believe that a Yugoslav compromise could have been pulled off. By early October, however, with the Soviet army massed on the Bulgarian frontier in preparation for its invasion of Yugoslavia, it was almost certainly too late for any realistic compromise.

CHAPTER

23

The Plot to "Dispose of" Mihailović

Before [the] Allied Missions finally withdraw from Mihailo-
vić's H.Q., the dissident officers [should] be unofficially en-
couraged to take the law into their own hands, [and] remove
Mihailović . . . Mihailović [should] be disposed of within the
country by his own followers.

Colonel S. W. Bailey
in a report filed in London
on March 14, 1944

It is appropriate at this point to say something about the report that Colonel Bailey filed in London on March 14, 1944, in which he clearly called for the assassination of Mihailović. What motivated him it is difficult to say, because this recommendation runs completely counter to the views he expressed in my only interview with him, in London in September 1946. It is also at odds with the views expressed in his letter to *The Times* of London (see frontispiece) and in his communications from the field—especially the 7,000-word message he cosigned with Brigadier Armstrong on November 7, 1943.[1]

Since Colonel Bailey left no notes[2] that might throw light on this rather amazing contradiction, one can only surmise that he was motivated by the desire to get a settlement that would prevent a complete Communist takeover in Yugoslavia, and that, to the end of saving something of the Serbia he knew, as well as the many thousands of Serbs who belonged to Mihailović's organization, he was prepared to offer up Mihailović himself as a blood sacrifice.

As has been pointed out previously, SOE Cairo had for some time been pushing for the elimination of Mihailović in the name of making a rapprochement with the Tito forces possible. I found only one message from SOE to the BLOs that dealt with this matter, but that a number of such messages were sent is clear from Armstrong's stinging rebuke to Cairo in late December 1943 for asking young, inexperienced officers to sound out the Yugoslav commanding officers in their areas on the possibility of replacing Mihailović. This is also clear from Colonel Bailey's lengthy communication to Cairo in early September 1943 reporting on a secret meeting he had had with Pavle Djurišić, Mihailović's commander in Montenegro, who had just escaped from a German POW camp in Austria and had made his way back to Mihailović's headquarters.

The report that Bailey filed in London on March 14, 1944, started out by making the point that "although Tito is supreme both in a political and military sense, in the greater portion of the country, Mihailović is firmly established in Serbia proper, where Tito has only isolated groups of followers." He also made the point that "the area which Mihailovíc dominates covers all roads and rail communication from Belgrade to Skoplje and to Niš and Sofia, and controls Belgrade itself." Then he recommended that "before Allied Missions finally withdraw from Mihailović's H.Q., the dissident officers be unofficially encouraged to take the law into their own hands, remove Mihailović, his immediate staff, and political advisers, and put the policy outlined . . . into immediate effect."

Somewhat later in the same paper Bailey recommended that "Mihailović . . . be disposed of within the country by his own followers" and his movement be reoriented so as to make for more activity within the country and compromise with the Partisans.[3] In a second memorandum of the same date, Bailey repeated that "the problem is for Mihailović to be disposed of within the country by his own followers."[4] Commenting on Bailey's recommendations, a Major D. Hohner, in a memorandum found in the War Office files, said that he did not consider them "very inviting, because they contain what is in effect an incitement to the dissidents to murder Mihailović. Even in this war, the Allies would presumably feel some scruples in trying to dispose of a former associate by such shady means."[5]

The fact that Bailey now talked about "disposing of" Mihailović instead of "replacing" him, as he had done in previous communications, may have been due to the realization that Mihailović's enormous popularity made any effort to "replace" him without "disposing of" him extremely precarious. Even more precarious, however, was the situation that would have resulted if Mihailović had been assassinated. In the absence of a single unifying figure, his movement would inevitably have collapsed, making more probable an imminent and complete Communist takeover.

How far up did involvement in the plot to "dispose of" Mihailović go? There is reason to believe that both Churchill and Eden were aware of this approach to the problem of Yugoslavia. A draft of a paper dated December 11, 1943, prepared for Eden for presentation to the entire cabinet, starts out by saying that he has recently had under consideration Britain's entire policy toward the resistance movements in Yugoslavia. Reports from the BLOs with both Tito and Mihailović, says the paper, have led him "to the conclusion that the interest of the United Nations as a whole will be best served by the elimination of General Mihailović . . ." When the draft was passed around for comment, Eden encircled the word "elimination" three times on the first page of the draft and wrote the following note in the margin: "I am not quite sure what this word means in this context. We aren't going to bump him off?"[6]

On March 20, 1944, SOE Cairo received from the British mission—it was obviously a personal wire from Armstrong—a message that said, "The dissident group at MVIC HQ is incapable rpt incapable of removing MVIC or inducing him to change his policy." This message put an end to the fatuous and unworthy speculation about "eliminating" or "disposing of" Mihailović.

CHAPTER

24

The Farish Reports

Of all the reports filed by British and American liaison officers with the resistance forces in Yugoslavia, none is more sensitive or moving than the final report filed by Major (later Lt. Colonel) Linn M. Farish, who was in charge of the American mission to Marshal Tito.

Farish was by profession a petroleum engineer, with a degree from Stanford University. According to officers who knew him, he was one of those rare people who instantly command admiration and affection. He was one of the handful of Americans who acted on the conviction that civilization was at stake in World War II, and went to England to join the RAF. Brigadier Maclean refers repeatedly and with obvious affection to "Slim" Farish.

Farish was dropped into Tito's headquarters on September 17, 1943, at the same time as Brigadier Maclean. Like all the fledgling British and American liaison officers who went into Yugoslavia at this period, he had first been pumped full of crude pro-Tito propaganda. This is reflected in his first report, which, like Maclean, he wrote five weeks after being dropped into Yugoslavia. The report also reflects the political naïveté of the average British and American liaison officer sent in to Tito. Among the opening paragraphs of his report we find the following:

The Partisans have created solely by their own efforts in the face of the Germans, Italians, Ustashe, and Četniks, a free community of no mean size entirely encircled by enemy forces. Within this area, Mohammedans, Christians, Serbs, Croats, Communist Party members, any person of any religion or political belief can express an opinion concerning the way in which he believes the affairs of the community should be conducted. The above situation is probably unique in all of Occupied Europe.

The Communist Party failed in its initial attempt to organize the movement strictly along party lines and sensibly decided to concentrate every available force of any character against the common enemy. Thus, the Communist Party is in theory only one element within the Partisan movement, but it is a very active one, and there is every evidence that strongly indoctrinated Party members are working hard to shape the structure of this newly born state according to their social, political, and economic beliefs.

In view of the facts stated above, it seems quite evident that, if an atmosphere of free and enlightened discussion can be maintained, there is a wonderful opportunity for the Partisans to select for themselves those portions of all forms of government and ways of life which they believe would be suitable to their temperament and environment; in such a case, it seems quite probable that a state will emerge which will be a meeting ground between political beliefs which are now widely separated in their extreme phases.[1]

Farish was carried away by rhetoric in describing the heroic accomplishments of the Partisans. From the beginning, he said, they had "dedicated themselves to the fight against the Axis, that they have always fought them, and will fight them to the end. The story of this struggle is at times almost beyond the imagination. It is so immense that only a suggestion of it can be given in this short report."

His report dealt with the Mihailović forces curtly and in a manner that would have won the complete endorsement of the Klugmann cabal in Cairo. "The Četniks under Colonel Mihailović and other officers of the Yugoslav army," he said, "fought for a time against the occupying Axis troops in conjunction with the Partisans. But Mihailović made the fatal mistake of allowing his political beliefs and his plans for the future to overcome his better judgment. He feared Communism more than he feared the common enemy."[2]

Farish said that the Partisans estimated their strength at 180,000 men, organized in eighteen divisions, and that these forces controlled very large areas in Yugoslavia, which he enumerated.[3] (The Maclean report, written roughly at the same time, credited the Partisans with 220,000 men, organized in twenty-six divisions.)

Farish entered repeated and passionate pleas for increased military assistance to the Partisans and for air support to their combat operations. "The primary factor in the matter of supply must be speed," he said. ". . . cold, hungry, and inadequately armed men will surely remember from whence aid came when they were fighting for their very existence."

The report ended with these words: "Personalities are of no importance in a matter of this kind. Our sole object must be to correctly assess the potentialities of the Partisan movement. The observer sincerely believes that the most serious mistake which could be made would be to underestimate it."

When Farish came out of Yugoslavia in June 1944, after several tours of duty in the country, his views had altogether changed—perhaps because his last tour before writing the report was in southern Serbia, where for the first time he met up with the reality of the Mihailović movement. In any case, as is apparent from the report, he was now confused and ill at ease, and he expressed serious doubt about his ability to carry on in his Yugoslav assignment unless Britain and the United States made a determined effort to stop the civil war.

One exposure that altered his judgment of the situation in Yugoslavia was his experience as a liaison officer with a Partisan recruiting mission in southeast Serbia. Anticipating the entry of the Red Army, the Partisans were anxious to build up their hitherto negligible forces in this area and asked that an Anglo-American mission be attached to a small group operating near Kumanovo in the Siroka Mountains. And so on April 15, 1944, a small mission headed up by Major John Henneker-Major, on the British side, and Major Farish was dropped into the Sirokas.

When the mission arrived in the first village in the area, all the villagers refused to speak to them for four days. On the fifth day a few peasants approached some members of the mission who could speak the language. Henneker-Major had a tolerable command of Serbo-Croat, but most of the time it was Farish's deputy, Eli Popovich, who spoke for the group.[4]

"Is it true," the peasants asked, "that Americans and the British are sending in all these supplies for the Communists?"

The members of the mission replied that the Allies were, in fact, doing so, in the belief that the Communists were offering effective resistance to the Nazis.

"Then is it true that America and Britain are supporting the Communists?"

Popovich, who answered the question, again asserted that it was Allied policy to support those who fight the Nazis.

The peasants scratched their heads. This was more than they could understand. "But why are you supporting the Communists?" they asked. "Don't you know they're your worst enemies?"

A few days later the village magistrate, at the head of a parade of villagers, came up to the members of the Anglo-American mission and took off his hat.

"Before you came here," he told them, "we didn't believe the Communists when they told us that the British and Americans were supporting them. Now we see that it was true. But tell me—is it really true that America and Britain want us Serbs to join the Partisans?"

Though some of the mission already felt uneasy, they could do nothing under the circumstances but answer "Yes."

"Then, if both Britain and America want us to join them," replied the peasant magistrate, "we must join them."

That day he reported with the entire adult male population of the village, some 270 in all, for service with the Partisan army.

Wherever the mission went in eastern Serbia, the attitude of the peasantry was one of dismay, mixed with friendliness for the Anglo-Americans and hatred for the Partisans. More than half the equipment dropped to the mission was picked up by the peasants to keep it from the Partisans.

One day the mission was proceeding with a unit of Partisans along a road near the village of Ravna Rijeka. At the bend of a hill they were ambushed by a band of several hundred local villagers armed with ancient rifles. The Partisans were armed with tommy guns, automatic rifles, and hand grenades. Deploying themselves in soldierly fashion, they routed the villagers and returned to the mission with a number of prisoners, among them the village magistrate. When this sturdy, middle-aged peasant with a patriarchal beard was brought before the British and American officers, he broke down and wept. Over and over again he implored their forgiveness. He knew that he had very little time to live, and he spoke his heart.

"If we had known that there were American officers with the Communists, I swear that we wouldn't have fired a single shot—I swear by everything I hold holy. But how were we to know? These people have been our worst enemies. We've always been told that Britain and America are democratic, that they're against communism. If you are democrats, then they're your worst enemies, too. Tell me, why is it—why is it that you British and Americans are supporting the Communists now, when only a few months ago you were supporting Mihailović?"

Popovich, translating for Farish, groped for an answer. In the presence of this weeping patriarch who was shortly to die before a Partisan firing squad he felt more uneasy than he had ever felt in his life.

"Gospodine Pretsedniče," Popovich finally said, "I'm not a politician. All I can tell you is that the Allies are supporting the Partisans because they believe that the Partisans are fighting the Germans, whereas the Četniks aren't. The authorities also believe that the Četniks are collaborating with the enemy."

From where they were near the peak of the hill they could see far out over the valley on either side. The peasant swung his arm out in a semicircle and drew their attention to the columns of smoke spiraling up from burning villages.

"Look at our villages," he said. "The Bulgars were through this morning and set fire to eight of them. Why do you think they are taking these reprisals? Does that look like collaboration—or does it look like resistance?

Why, then, do the Allies say that we are not fighting? Why do they support the Communists?''

There was nothing that Popovich or Farish or Henneker-Major could say.

With the aid of British and American supplies, and employing the moral authority of British and American recruiting officers, the Partisans were able in two months' time to build up a force of 10,000 in southeast Serbia. The force consisted for the most part of Serbian peasants who were anti-Communist. It included, in addition, one Bulgar battalion, which was accepted into the Partisan army intact. Some of the Serb peasants who were now in Partisan uniform said to the American officers, "Until now the Bulgars have been massacring us and burning our villages. Now we must address them as *drug* [comrade].''

A highly sensitive man, Farish was greatly impressed by these several experiences with the peasants of Serbia. He would have rejected the idea that he was serving as a recruiter for the Partisan army, but certainly, the Anglo-American mission was being used to this end. Other things impressed Farish, too. In his second report he said:

> The situation in Yugoslavia has, from the beginning, been terribly confusing, and almost beyond the comprehension of an impartial outside observer. The deep rooted causes of the internecine strife are contained in racial, religious, and political disputations which are of such long standing that the people themselves do not understand them. The same applies to the present civil war, or war being waged by the various factions. In the case of the forces of Marshal Tito and General Mihailović, both sides tell exactly the same stories of incidents which occurred at certain places on the same dates, the only difference being that each side places the blame on the other.

> . . . On 1 June Lt. Popovich, of my party, Lt. Comdr. Macphail, a British doctor, and his orderly, and myself, arrived in the Kukavica Mtns in search of three wounded American airmen, whom we found in a former Četnik hospital in the area where the fighting had taken place. These airmen informed us that they had been rescued by the Četniks, that Četniks doctors had treated them as best they could, and that the people of the so-called "Četnik villages" had done everything possible to make them comfortable. They stated that a Četnik doctor came back through the fighting for three nights to dress their wounds. They further stated that this Četnik doctor had photographs of a great many American and British airmen whom he had treated and helped to escape from the country.

> What a very peculiar set of circumstances these facts bring out! Rifles stamped "U.S. Property" firing W.R.A. Ammunition, flown [in] by American airmen in American aircraft, being fired at people who have rescued other American airmen and who were doing everything to make them comfortable and to return them to safety.

If I am confused, what must be the state of mind of the people of Yugoslavia
. . . Is it any wonder that hundreds of them have taken us aside and asked us
to tell them what to do, which way to turn?

. . . They are a simple peasant type of people, strong willed, hot-blooded with
tremendous powers of endurance and great personal courage. They love intrigue
and gossip, and are the most profound liars I have ever met. I do not believe
there is any tremendous urge for Revolution among them. They love their mountains, their small homes, their farms, and their flocks. They want something
better, but, measured by our standards, what most of them ask is not a great
deal, a good government, their King and their church, schools, more roads,
shoes, clothing, a few modern conveniences, better modern farming equipment
and some better livestock.

. . . I, personally, do not feel that I can go on with the work in Yugoslavia
unless I can sincerely feel that every possible honest effort is being made to put
an end to the civil strife . . . Under any conditions, two things stand out, every
effort must be made to end the conflict among the people of Yugoslavia, and
the United States has a very definite interest in seeing that it is ended as soon as
possible.[5]

On September 11, 1944, a short time after writing this report, Colonel
Farish was killed in an airplane accident in Greece. The copy of his reports
in the National Archives bears the notation that copies were sent to President
Roosevelt, the secretary of state, and the chief of staff of the US Army,
General George C. Marshall.

25

Under the Enemy's Nose:
The Rescue of the American Airmen

Unfortunately those of us who lived with these people are few and far between, but believe you me, never will we forget how the men and women of Serbia unquestioningly risked their very lives for us, clothed us, and gave us shelter when they themselves were ill-clad, cold and hungry.

First Lieutenant John E. Scroggs
Rescued American airman

The Ploesti oil complex in Rumania was Hitler's most important source of oil during World War II. Shortly after the Allies installed themselves in Italy in the fall of 1943, they embarked on a sustained campaign of bombing sorties directed against Ploesti—many hundreds during the first part of 1944 alone. The casualties were heavy. Since the route back to Italy led across Serbia (Yugoslavia's largest state), and since rural Serbia was solidly under the control of General Mihailović right up until the entry of the Red Army in October 1944, hundreds of American airmen forced to bail out over Yugoslavia found themselves picked up by men wearing the royal insignia on their caps. In this way they became eyewitnesses to one of the most bitterly disputed issues of World War II.

In the summer and fall of 1944 the American Air Crew Rescue Unit evacuated from Mihailović's territory 432 American airmen who had been shot down at various times and in various parts of Yugoslavia, had been rescued by the Home Army, and had been brought together at several concentration points where American aircraft could land. In addition to the 432

Americans, the rescue unit evacuated 4 British airmen, 2 Canadians, 2 Belgians, 30 Russians, and 76 Italians.

In a wire sent to Ambassador Fotitch in Washington in early August, Mihailović complained that he had radioed the British several times to inform them that he had with him many American airmen who had been rescued by his forces and who could be evacuated safely if planes were flown in. He asked the British to notify the American air force. This apparently was not done.

Was Mihailović's radio link with the British no longer operative? Apart from the fact that it would only be natural to assume that the British kept on monitoring signals received from Mihailović's headquarters, the author received unchallengeable confirmation of this assumption while in England in the fall of 1944. I was taken by a Yugoslav friend to a "safe house" in the British countryside—a beautiful house with a thatched roof and modernized plumbing—to meet an "interesting person" just arrived from Yugoslavia. This turned out to be Dr. Ivan Popov, brother of the celebrated double agent Duško Popov (*Spy and Counter-Spy*).

Ivan Popov, also a double agent, had walked into Četnik headquarters at Pranjani and asked to be evacuated with the airmen. Captain George Musulin, commander of the Air Crew Rescue Unit, had difficulty in restraining some of the Mihailović men from cutting Popov's throat, because they had seen him in Belgrade in Gestapo uniform. Musulin urgently notified Bari of Popov's arrival and asked for instructions. Back came a wire the following morning instructing him that Popov was to be flown to Italy immediately.

Incidentally, I found it impossible to believe Popov when he told me that Mihailović had rescued some 400 American airmen later flown out of Yugoslavia. But I simply had to believe him when he produced some half-dozen photographs of their evacuation. This is how I came to be the first Allied journalist to tell the story of the rescue of the airmen. (I had been a journalist before I joined the Royal Canadian Air Force in England in the summer of 1942. The article was written under the nom de plume de guerre of R. V. Elson in *World Review* for February 1944.)

The rescued airmen, not surprisingly, formed some very strong opinions on the subject of Mihailović. What one or two or three or four airmen observed in Yugoslavia during a brief sojourn with the Mihailović forces might not disprove the charge of widespread collaboration between Mihailović and the Germans. But when 500 American airmen drop in unexpectedly all over Yugoslavia; when many of them are rescued in pitched battles with the Germans; when scores of Mihailović peasants are executed in public reprisals by the Germans for failure to turn over American airmen who had parachuted to safety; when all of the airmen praise the sacrificial efforts made by the followers of Mihailović, both soldiers and peasants, in rescuing them, caring for them, concealing them, and treating their wounds; when they report that they were given complete freedom of movement during sojourns in Mihailović territory sometimes lasting four to six months, that they witnessed numerous clashes between German and Četnik forces and saw absolutely no evidence of collaboration—all of this testimony taken together creates an intelligence mosaic so panoramic and so detailed that its validity is beyond any reasonable challenge.

The American airmen rescued by the Mihailović forces may not have been trained intelligence officers, but it does not require such training to see collaboration. Fundamentally, it is a matter of whether you shoot with the Germans or against them. With the exception of one man, all of the 500 rescued airmen reported that at no time during their stay with the Četniks did they witness anything suggesting collaboration—that, on the contrary, they witnessed many acts of resistance directed against the German forces of occupation. To quote the words of Staff Sergeant Gus T. Brown of Luling, Texas, member of the first American crew to be shot down over Yugoslavia: "In five and a half months I witnessed not a single friendly encounter with the Germans. The only encounters I ever witnessed were shootin' encounters."

Most of the airmen bailed out at 10,000 to 20,000 feet in broad daylight. Frequently it happened that by the time they hit the ground, both the Germans and the Četniks were racing up to get them, and their possession was decided only after Germans and Četniks had fought it out. Staff Sergeant Leland Porter of Lexington, Kentucky, who was shot down near Belgrade after a bombing raid on September 9, 1944, made the following deposition: "The Germans who were garrisoned at a nearby railroad station tried to take us from the Četniks. A battle followed. One Četnik and four Germans were killed. Six Germans were captured." Lieutenant Merrill L. Walker of Compton, California, told a similar story. Walker was in a plane that crash-landed on June 6, 1944, near the town of Rudnik, forty miles south of Belgrade. His deposition said: "On the day we crash-landed two men were trapped in the plane. Before we could get them free, a German patrol attempted to capture us but they were held off by the Četnik forces until we got the two men free. There was some fierce fighting . . . and I know that the Četniks suffered some casualties . . . The Germans were in half-tracks and on motorcycles . . ." Staff Sergeant Mike McKool of Dallas, Texas, said that because the peasants refused to reveal the whereabouts of the ten American airmen who were seen to have parachuted into the area, the Germans executed ten hostages and issued a warning that if Allied airmen were sheltered in the future, more drastic measures would be taken.

The more detailed case histories that follow are characteristic of the hundreds of statements given to debriefing officers after the rescue and to the American press at a later date.

It was the morning of June 6, 1944. As Lieutenant Donald J. Smith[1] banked his Liberator bomber into a final approach to his Ploesti target, the sky was alive with ack-ack fire. The plane shuddered as a round exploded underneath it—and one engine conked out. Lieutenant Smith readjusted his rudder to keep his plane heading for target through the storm of bursting shells. Over target he dropped his bombs—and as he did so, his Liberator was hit again and a second engine went dead. Reversing course for his base in Italy, he ordered his men to dump every possible excess item to lighten the plane. Since it seemed highly doubtful that they could get back to Italy, the crew was also ordered to stand by for bailout. They were flying over mountainous terrain about seventy miles southwest of Belgrade when a third engine exploded in a ball of fire. Smith ordered his crew to bail out immediately.

Smith hit the ground hard—and was greeted almost immediately on landing by a bearded man on a horse. The man could speak no English and Smith knew no Serbian, but somehow they managed to converse. Smith's ankle was dislocated and enormously swollen, so the bearded man dismounted and beckoned to him to get on his horse. In the valley below they could hear a heavy rat-tat-tat of machine guns and the bursting of grenades— and it took only a few words in Serbian from the bearded man for Smith to understand that a battle with the Germans was going on nearby. The rest of Smith's crew had come down nearby, but none of them was visible. The bearded man—a Mihailović officer—instructed Smith to round them up as rapidly as possible by shouting to them from a rise of ground. Smith bellowed at the top of his lungs—and before many minutes had passed, the other nine members of his crew had all been rounded up.

The Mihailović officer, on foot, led Lieutenant Smith and his crew along a riverbed until they came to a little farmhouse. At that point Smith discovered that he and his crew had dropped into Yugoslavia virtually smack on top of General Mihailović's secret headquarters. The general personally greeted the American airmen and invited them to share lunch with him, sitting on the ground.

A few officers in the general's headquarters party understood some English, so from here on the conversation moved more easily. The Americans learned that the Germans had seen them bail out and had initiated an intense search for them in the area. Because of this, General Mihailović had to move his headquarters out of the area. As soon as it became dark, Mihailović and his headquarters group, accompanied by the American airmen, moved out toward the north. Sleeping by day and moving at night, they traveled together for three days. During this time, as a result of constant companionship and many hours of conversation, Smith and his fellow airmen felt that they had come to know General Mihailović intimately. They had dropped into Yugoslavia knowing very little about the general, and the little they had been told had inclined them to be suspicious. But like all the American airmen who had met Mihailović personally, they felt they were in the presence of a truly great man—a man who bore himself with humility despite his rank, was without rancor despite his abandonment by the Western Allies, and whose humanity was apparent in his relations with his peasant followers. The charges of collaboration with the enemy simply could not be reconciled with the extremely hard life led by their peasant rescuers, their lack of ammunition and even medical supplies, and the frequent sounds of battle wherever they traveled.

After the third day Mihailović parted company with the American airmen and assigned a company of troops under the command of Lieutenant Mike Panović to escort them. For the next sixty-three days Smith and his crew, with their Mihailović escorts, traveled from village to village, never remaining in one place longer than four or five days. Finally, on August 9, they were evacuated together with 240 other rescued airmen from the secret airfield that the Mihailović units had prepared near the village of Pranjani.

Lieutenant Richard L. Felman,[2] the navigator aboard a U.S. bomber bearing the suggestive name *Never a Dull Moment,* vividly recalls the briefing he and his buddies received before setting off on a raid on the Ploesti oil fields in July of 1944. In effect they were told that the Partisans were the good guys and the Četniks were the bad guys, and that they had a nasty habit of cutting off the ears of American airmen and then turning the airmen over to the Germans.

Never a Dull Moment lived up to its name in the skies over Ploesti. The plane took a terrific pounding, and although the pilot turned in the direction of its home base, the crew members realized that they would probably have to bail out over Yugoslavia. This is exactly what happened.

Felman recalls that at the moment he hit the ground he realized that he had been wounded and couldn't move his leg. In an article which he later wrote about his experiences, Felman said:

> At that moment I was surrounded—by about 20 peasants, men, women, and children. The bearded men kissed me. The women and children kept an awed distance. No red stars. Četniks! Instinctively the words of the briefing officer came to mind. I reached for my ears to protect them. They didn't want my ears.

They raised me on their shoulders and carried me about 500 yards to a group of three cabins and laid me comfortably in a small room.[3]

The overwhelming majority of the airmen evacuated from Mihailović's territory had nothing but praise for the attention that the Serbian people, both peasants and soldiers, lavished on them. William T. Emmett, the US Army Air Force intelligence officer responsible for debriefing the rescued and evacuated airmen, told the Commission of Inquiry in New York in June 1946 that of the 200-plus airmen he had debriefed, not a single one reported an instance of any airman being turned over to the Germans or suffering maltreatment nor of collaboration between the Mihailović forces and the Germans.

THE DECISION TO SET UP THE HALYARD MISSION

When the tail end of the British mission left Yugoslavia on June 1, 1944, George Musulin, the last of the American liaison officers with Mihailović, was evacuated with them. So were some forty American airmen who had been forced down at various points in Yugoslavia and assembled at the makeshift airfield near Pranjani. Shortly afterward the British, whose radio link was still receiving Mihailović's transmissions, began to get message after message informing them that his forces had rescued many American airmen and urging that arrangements be made to evacuate them by air. There should have been nothing implausible about these messages, because Allied airmen had been dropping out of the skies over Mihailović territory at an increasing rate beginning February 1944. However, for some reason these messages were never passed on to the Fifteenth Air Force as Mihailović had requested.

The official British position at that time was that the Četniks were handing Allied airmen over to the Germans. Those British authorities who accepted this position found it difficult to believe that the Četniks had actually rescued as many Allied airmen as Mihailović claimed. What made them even more suspicious was that some of the messages were being sent "in the clear," i.e., uncoded. A few British officers even suggested that the whole thing was a German come-on. It is difficult to believe that James Klugmann, who had since March 1944 been ensconced as deputy commander of the Yugoslav Section of SOE in Bari, did not know the real facts about the rescued American airmen or did nothing to encourage the British military in their negative attitude toward the proposed evacuation of the airmen.

Impatient over his failure to receive any reply to his several radioed messages, Mihailović in the summer of 1944 had begun to send messages directly to Ambassador Fotitch in Washington. For this purpose he used a more powerful transmitter, built by several enterprising radio men. His message of July 12 read:

> Please advise the American Air Ministry that there are more than one hundred American aviators in our midst . . . We notified the English Supreme Command for the Mediterranean a long time ago . . . The English replied that they would send an officer to take care of the evacuation.

> Meanwhile, to date this has not been done . . . It would be better still if the Americans, and not the British, take part in the evacuation.[4]

The message was picked up by a coast guard station and delivered to Fotitch through the courtesy of the State Department and the United States Navy, which also offered him assistance in replying to it. The growing volume of messages back and forth that followed this first one led to a request that Fotitch commercialize them. This he did, having first been granted a license to receive them, required because they emanated from a country under hostile occupation.

These messages, sent in the clear, were picked up by arrangement with RCA and delivered to Fotitch, who paid for them at the rate of sixteen cents per word. Several of the telegrams contained long lists of names and serial numbers of rescued airmen, as well as messages to their families. The longest of these, which was received on August 4, conveyed messages from more than 100 American airmen. Sometimes Ambassador Fotitch would be able to notify the airmen's families that their sons were safe in Yugoslavia only forty-eight hours after they had been shot down. This was the only "service" of its kind in any occupied country during World War II.

At the urging of SOE, the British government on several occasions brought pressure to bear on Washington to terminate Mihailović's "Station YTG" messages to Fotitch. One memorandum on this point even stated that the PWE had evidence that Station YTG was under German control!

Meanwhile, back in Bari, George Musulin succeeded in persuading the Fifteenth Air Force that the messages were genuine, that there were, indeed, rescued American airmen waiting to be evacuated, and that the proposed operation was feasible. When the Fifteenth Air Force proposed sending in a rescue mission, the Yugoslav Section of SOE, now established in Bari, responded with skepticism and even outright hostility. Some of the British officers frankly argued that Tito might not like it.

Moreover, the British maps showed the proposed landing field at Pranjani to be in solid Partisan territory. The Fifteenth Air Force insisted that it try to arrange the evacuation of the rescued airmen. The British countered with the proposal that they themselves would undertake the operation. This the Fifteenth Air Force refused: the airmen in question were Americans, and even though the Fifteenth was under British operational control, it made no sense to prohibit the Americans from undertaking the rescue operation.

By mid-July, despite British objections, the decision had been made to send in an Air Crew Rescue Unit, code-named "the Halyard Mission," under Musulin's command. (Musulin was told that, because of the strongly negative British attitude, the matter had been bucked all the way up to President Roosevelt, who personally made the decision.) But when the unit sought to go into Yugoslavia, it encountered a whole series of exasperating delays.

Three successive sorties, attempted on the basis of arrangements made by the British radio link, ended in failure. For some mysterious reason Pranjani, the target area, always seemed to elude them. Two other sorties were aborted. In one case, the rescue unit was already aboard the plane and ready to take off, when Musulin routinely asked the pilot if he could look at the map coordinates for the drop. The pilot showed him the map—and the coordinates were not at Pranjani but at a point that Musulin knew to be right in the middle of Partisan territory. He told the British officer in charge of the operation that the map was wrong, and that it would mean almost certain death for the members of the unit if they fell into Partisan hands. Although only a captain, he aborted the mission on his own authority, and he was strongly upheld by his American commanding officer.

On the second occasion the Air Crew Rescue Unit was on the plane, about to take off, when Musulin saw a soldier wearing the red-starred cap of the Yugoslav Partisans sitting in the plane. When Musulin asked the British officer overseeing the operation what the Partisan soldier was doing there, he was told that the soldier was coming along to serve as their "dispatcher." (The function of the dispatcher is to check on rip cords and give each jumper a push as he leaves the plane.) In an angry exchange Musulin told the British officer in charge that "no sonuvabitch of a Communist" was going to push him and his team out of a plane. When the British officer refused to give ground on this point, Musulin again aborted the mission on his own authority—and again had to invoke his commanding officer's support.

Musulin stopped short of using the word "sabotage" in speaking about his five unsuccessful efforts to take the Air Crew Rescue Unit into Yugoslavia when the British radio link was handling communications. Of Klugmann's existence he knew vaguely, but it was enough to worry him. He could not help feeling that "something is rotten in the state of Denmark," and that the failures had more than a little to do with Klugmann's machinations and the pro-Tito bias of the small clique of British officers who were running Yugoslav operations.

AMERICAN INGENUITY TO THE RESCUE

Musulin's exasperation was echoed by that of the American airmen who were awaiting evacuation. Instinctively they felt that the many messages sent via the Mihailović-British link were somehow not getting through. Apprehensive about their chances of getting out of the country, they borrowed a transmitter from some friendly Mihailović radio men and decided to try their hand at establishing an "all-American" link. The problems were formidable. Since they had no code, they would have to send in the clear or devise a code that would be proof against German ingenuity but understandable, with effort, to the Americans. The genius behind this all-American operation was a Lieutenant (later Lt. Colonel) T. K. Oliver.

The message that was finally sent via the all-American link was a source of so much bewilderment to the Americans that one can only wonder about the consternation of the German intelligence officers who read it. Among other things, the message said:

(1) Mudcat Driver to CO, APO 520 (2) 150 Yanks are in Yugo (3) Shoot us workhorses. Ask British about job. (4) Our challenge first letter of bombardier's name, color of Banana Nose Benignos Scarf.[5]

Lt. Colonel Charles L. Davis USAF (Ret.) recalls that Oliver also transmitted the serial numbers of the officers and men in his own crew and Davis's crew, adding to them the geographic coordinates of their location in Yugoslavia so that when the serial numbers were canceled out, the remaining numbers would reflect their position.

One can only sympathize with the Air Force intelligence officer whose job it was to put together all the pieces of this strange puzzle. According to Charlie Davis, the officer in question finally locked himself in his room and left word with his secretary not to disturb him—unless it was to see someone who outranked him.

For some time, the officer assigned to the task of solving the riddle sat looking at the message. An earlier transmission had contained some names and mysterious groups of digits. After a few hours, it occurred to him that, if the correct serial numbers could be confirmed, the extra digits attached to each group must convey some message—which, he correctly assumed, must be the latitude and longitude of the airmen. He got together with Major Christi, commander of the 459th Bomb Group. Major Christi looked at the communication for a while—and suddenly he realized that "Mudcat Driver" and "Banana Nose Benigno" and the other strange names used in the message were men under his command. At the moment of realization he cried out to his fellow officer, "That's Oliver's crew and Buckler's crew. My God, go get them!"

On August 2, 1944, using Lieutenant Oliver's all-American link, the Halyard Mission carried out a successful sortie—*on the first attempt.*

Apart from Musulin, the other two members of the Halyard Mission team were Master Sergeant (later Lieutenant) Michael Rajachich, who had joined OSS for hazardous duty after being told that he was too old to be drafted, and Arthur Jibilian, a featherweight radio operator recruited from the US Navy, who had seen earlier service in Yugoslavia on the Partisan side.

THE EVACUATION OF THE AIRMEN

Musulin, Rajachich, and Jibilian left the plane in a tight vertical formation. Big "Gov" Musulin, despite his outsize thirty-two-foot parachute, was the first to hit the ground. He landed on top of a chicken coop, utterly demolishing it. Mike Rajachich came down next. He landed in a tree near the chicken coop and shouted for Musulin to help him get untangled. Jibilian was the last to touch down.

They were hardly out of their harnesses when the peasant woman on whose property they had landed came charging up. Not stopping to notice her demolished chicken coop, she bestowed repeated kisses on the embarrassed Americans, called them "liberators"—apparently, she thought they were part of a parachute invasion—and insisted they have something to eat. Musulin gave her 15,000 dinars (about $10) to cover the cost of her chicken coop, and then she pointed them to the nearby Mihailović unit.

The trio set off along the road in the direction shown by the old woman, and around a bend they ran straight into a group of bearded men wearing the royal insignia on their caps. There were cheers and more kisses. Some of the Home Army who knew Musulin from his previous stay with Mihailović actually wept for joy; although Musulin emphasized that they were to attach no diplomatic significance to his arrival, they could not help believing that it meant the return of Allied backing.

Some of the American airmen almost wept for joy, too. There were roughly 250 airmen in the district, of whom 26 were sick or wounded. The airmen told the mission how wonderful the Serbian peasants had been, how they had given them their own beds while they themselves slept on the floor and had insisted on the airmen eating first while they ate what was left over. But despite the kindness of the peasants, all of the airmen were fed up with waiting. They knew that the Mihailović radio had been sending out repeated signals, and could not understand why the Allied authorities had not acted sooner on them.

That day the mission held a council of war with a committee of several airmen and representatives of the Mihailović command. The airmen were divided into six groups of forty to fifty men, each quartered in a separate village and under the command of its own officer, so as to minimize danger in case the Germans staged a surprise attack. Each group was assigned to a specific wave of aircraft: they were not to report to the field until shortly before that wave was due in.

The Mihailović forces, for their part, had taken the most comprehensive security measures. The projected airfield at Pranjani was guarded by the First and Second Ravna Gora Corps under the command of Captain Zvonimir Vučković and Major Marko Muzikravić. The troops, numbering some 10,000 men, were distributed through all the villages within a radius of ten to fifteen miles. They blocked all of the roads and even the cow paths, and they enforced a total ban on movements to and from the operational area. Two thousand of the best-armed men were distributed in the immediate vicinity of the airstrip.

The airstrip itself was a natural plateau, extremely level and some 700 yards long. This was a bit on the short side for C-47s, and it was therefore decided to extend it about 75 yards to bring it up to the minimum for safety. Three hundred peasants with 60 carts were mobilized, and they went to work carting gravel and filling in. For this work they refused to accept any pay.

To offset the possibility of a surprise attack by the Germans, teams were sent out to reconnoiter two auxiliary airfields, each within one day's trek.

There was plenty of reason to fear a German attack. Several hundred American airmen would be a major prize in the eyes of the Germans. Moreover, within a radius of twenty to thirty miles there were some half-dozen important centers—Čačak, Kraljevo, Valjevo, Kragujevac, Gornji Milanovac, Užice—with German garrisons ranging from several hundred to several thousand men. At Kraljevo, some thirty miles away, there was an airfield that housed a Luftwaffe unit. Officers who participated in the evacuation operation are divided on why the Germans failed to attack. Some felt that the Germans had a fairly good idea of what was going on but were too dispirited at that time to venture an attack on an army of 10,000 determined men. Others felt that the extraordinary security measures taken by the Home Army completely baffled German intelligence.

The first evacuation was scheduled for the night of August 9, 1944. There were two anxious moments before it took place. The night before the evacuation, members of the mission who were sleeping in Pranjani suddenly awoke to the sound of machine-gun fire. They slipped into their trousers on the double and got ready to move. Minutes later Captain Vučković came around and informed them that the guard had challenged a moving object; the object had not answered, and the guard had fired—killing a cow.

On the morning of the ninth, Musulin and Rajachich were out on the airstrip supervising the final touches. From the direction of Belgrade two specks began to approach. Everyone ran for cover. The specks came closer. They grew into German hospital aircraft and flew, almost loiteringly, right for the field at a height of 1,000 feet. Several hundred hearts sank at the same time. Just then a small herd of cows, noticing the meadow deserted for the first time in a week, sauntered onto the field, munching at the turf. It was probably this little act of providential camouflage, more than anything else, that prevented the Germans from noticing the field.

That night at 11:00 the first wave of four C-47s arrived. The ground crew flashed the letters of the day. The aircraft flashed back. The gooseneck flares, improvised out of oilcans, were lit. The aircraft came in. The peasants from all around Pranjani had congregated to witness the sight. If Ringling Brothers and Barnum & Bailey had come to this little Serbian village, it could not have caused more excitement. The peasants garlanded the rescued airmen and arriving aircrews, they threw flowers at them, they brought them bottles of the potent Serbian brandy known as rakia, they embraced, they sang.

Before they took off half an hour later in the C-47s, the airmen said goodbye to those who had rescued them and cared for them. They took off their shoes, they took off their jackets, some of them even took off their socks and shirts, and left them with their benefactors. The planes were airborne to the cheers of the assembled peasants.

At 8:00 the next morning a wave of six C-47s came in with a fighter cover of twenty P-51s. The fighters shot up the field and put on a real aerial rodeo for the entertainment of the local populace—which could hardly contain its pride. "Well, whatever you say," remarked one octogenarian, "this is the only American airfield in Serbia." The commander of the airfield guard strutted around with his chest puffed out a yard. "Tell me," he asked one of the Americans, "is LaGuardia Field anything like this?"

Half an hour later another flight of C-47s with a fighter cover of twenty came in for the balance of the airmen. When the roll call for the last craft was taken, one airman was missing. The C-47 was just taxiing up for the takeoff when the missing airman came stumbling onto the field. He had been overindulging in rakia.

Captain Nick Lalich, who came in on the first aircraft on the night of August 9, took over as commanding officer of the Halyard mission when Musulin returned to Italy under orders on the evening of August 26. With every passing day new batches of rescued airmen kept arriving at Pranjani. One week after the big evacuation of August 9–10 there was another small one. Mihailović arrived at Pranjani on August 20 and helped plan the evacuation of another fifty-eight American airmen on the nights of August 26 and 27 and subsequent evacuations, which are detailed below.

In exchange for the 350 American airmen turned over by Mihailović up to the end of August, the Home Army received one and a half tons of medical supplies—half of an aircraft load. Certain British and American circles at Bari expressed much opposition to sending in even this small quantity.

One incident that took place on August 27 Mihailović, who was present, never forgave. The first of the six American aircraft came in directly and landed at Pranjani. The other five, loaded with munitions for the Partisan army driving into Serbia, and carrying Partisan dispatcher crews, dropped off their cargo and then came in to land at nearby Pranjani. One of the Partisan dispatchers, perhaps not realizing where he was, hopped out of the aircraft. "Well, comrades," he said, "we've just had a successful drop." If the American officers had not intervened and bundled him back into the aircraft, the Home Army soldiers would have slit his throat on the spot.

At the time of this incident the Partisan invasion of Serbia was already underway. Within a week scores of wounded soldiers were being brought back to Pranjani from the front. With the few materials they had, the Mihailović doctors coped as best they could. Only those wounded who had a fighting chance of surviving were hospitalized or given drugs.

At the direction of General Donovan, OSS had sent Major Jacques Mitrani and Colonel Walter T. ("Doc") Carpenter into Pranjani to look after the health of the evacuees and tend to the wounded. Dr. Carpenter had just come from the Partisan hospital on the island of Vis, where Allied medical supplies were so plentiful that the commissars were able to commandeer sheets and towels and blankets and special foods for themselves. Arriving at Pranjani, Drs. Mitrani and Carpenter found the polar extreme of the situation at Vis. The local hospital was being administered by two Serbian doctors and one Italian doctor, with the aid of several villagers. The doctors were capable—the Home Army was relatively well off in that regard because few doctors gravitated of their own volition to the Partisan movement. But the Mihailović doctors were working without anything. They had no medicines, no anesthetics, no soap, no sheets, no proper surgical instruments, not even a decent first-aid kit. The patients slept on straw on the floors. Major operations were performed without anesthesia.[6]

In early September the Partisan "Serb" Lika Brigade broke through Mihailović's weak southern flank, bypassing the German garrisons at Višegrad, Užice, and Požega, and made straight for the Mihailović headquarters at Pranjani. On September 9 Mihailović broke camp and moved northward through the region of Semberija to Bosnia.

On September 17 the Air Crew Rescue Unit evacuated twenty-odd

Americans from an airstrip near Koceljevo, on the Valjevo-Šabac highway. While a battle between Partisans and Četniks was raging no more than four miles away, two DC-3s came in with a cover of six fighters and took off the American airmen.

Captain Lalich and Lt. Colonel Robert H. McDowell, who arrived at Mihailović headquarters August 26 as head of an OSS intelligence mission authorized by General Donovan, traveled with Mihailović up into eastern Bosnia. Toward the end of October another evacuation of American airmen took place from an airstrip at Boljanić, eight miles east of Doboj, under the protection of the troops of two heroic Orthodox clergymen, Pop Sava and Pop Miloš, who commanded Mihailović forces in the area.

Continuing his travels with Mihailović headquarters, Captain Lalich picked up another nine airmen near Višegrad, seven more (all of them injured) near Srednje, twenty kilometers north of Sarajevo, and a few at other points. Captain Lalich, with the twenty-four airmen he had accumulated by that time, decided to return to the airstrip at Boljanić.

On December 10, the day before Mihailović and the Americans left Srednje for Boljanić, the villagers staged a big dance in honor of Mihailović and the Americans. People came from as far as Sarajevo to attend the celebration. Mihailović made a speech and led the kolo, the national Serbian dance. The following day Mihailović and Lalich shook hands for the last time. To the amazement of all the Americans, Mihailović appeared optimistic. "The Allies have made a mistake," he said. "But some day they will come back to us."

At the time these events took place the Partisans, with the aid of Red Army bayonets, had been in control of Belgrade for almost two months.

Before he made this statement, Mihailović had refused an American offer to be evacuated to safety in Italy with the American airmen, because he considered it a compelling moral duty to remain with his people.

Mihailović headed south into the Sandžak, and Lalich, with his wounded airmen mounted on horses, headed north for Boljanić under Home Army escort. The final evacuation took place from Boljanić airstrip on December 27. At that time reports had arrived of the rescue of several groups of airmen in other parts of Serbia. In view of the diplomatic impossibility of continuing evacuations from its territory, the Mihailović command agreed to forward these airmen to Partisan units.

The central facts about the rescue were not made public at the time, even though security played no role once the Halyard team had completed its mission.

On March 29, 1948, President Truman, on the recommendation of General Dwight D. Eisenhower, awarded the Legion of Merit in the Degree of

Chief Commander to General Draža Mihailović in recognition of his services to the Allied cause. Among other things, President Truman's citation said about Mihailović, "Through the undaunted efforts of his troops, many United States airmen were rescued and returned safely to friendly control."

But for the first and only time in American history, the award of the Legion of Merit was classified and kept secret. The facts about the award were not made public until Congressman Edward J. Derwinski of Illinois intervened in 1967—almost twenty years after the event—to oblige the State Department to make public the text of President Truman's citation.

It was letters from the rescued airmen that led General Eisenhower to recommend the award to General Mihailović—but the airmen did not expect the award to be swallowed up in the conspiracy of silence that followed.

In 1974 the airmen petitioned Congress for permission to erect a monument on public land by way of expressing their gratitude to the man who had saved their lives. Legislation to this end has been introduced in every session of Congress since that time. It has had as many as ninety cosponsors in the House of Representatives. Hearings have been held on it, and it has twice passed the Senate by voice vote. It has been approved by the AFL-CIO, by the Convention of the American Legion, and by the Senate Rules Committee. But each time it has been flagged down by the Department of State, with the argument that the Yugoslav Communist government might not like it. The rescued airmen, whose ranks are becoming thinner with each passing year, persist in their efforts because they feel they owe an inescapable moral debt to General Mihailović.

The spirit that animated and still animates the airmen was spelled out in a letter written to Ambassador Fotitch by one of the rescued airmen, First Lieutenant John E. Scroggs, of Kansas City, Missouri, at the time of the Mihailović trial. It said:

> Those of us who know the real circumstances in Serbia are enraged at the unfair attacks on the Četniks and their leaders. If only someone could open the poor blind eyes of the spoiled American public, a wonderful group of people might receive their due recognition. Unfortunately those of us who lived with these people are few and far between, but believe you me, never will we forget how the men and women of Serbia unquestioningly risked their very lives for us, clothed us, and gave us shelter when they themselves were ill-clad, cold and hungry . . . I vowed to myself that if I could ever possibly begin to repay these people for all they had done for me, I wouldn't hesitate to do so. Unfortunately, what little I might be able to do would not even pay the interest on my debt to the Serbian people. I suffer with them in their present plight, and in the injustice rendered to them by the American press as well as the American and British Governments.[7]

C H A P T E R

26

The Tito-Šubašić Minuet

The military abandonment of Mihailović was thus completed by early January 1944. The public and political abandonment required more time to consummate. It was characterized by much wishful thinking on Churchill's part and somewhat less on Eden's part.

On his return from the Teheran conference in November 1943, Churchill called in King Peter and Prime Minister Božidar Purić to inform them of the change in British policy. "Today, Tito is the only one fighting the enemy," he told them, "while Mihailović remains passive and his inactivity borders on treason." Churchill and Eden sought to persuade King Peter and Dr. Purić to drop Mihailović, assuring them that the Partisan movement was a truly national movement that united Yugoslavs of all political opinion. In vain Purić sought to argue that the Partisan movement was completely dominated by a militant Communist minority. The meeting broke up without agreement.

In the ensuing months there were repeated sessions, initially with Purić and the king. When it became obvious, however, that Purić was adamantly opposed to the Churchill-Eden formula, the leaders of the British government presented the king with a modified proposal. They now proposed that the king dismiss the entire Purić government—which, of course, included Mihailović as minister of war—and replace it with a new government headed by Dr. Ivan Šubašić, the former *ban,* or governor, of Croatia.

In reporting about Yugoslavia to the House of Commons on February 22, 1944, Churchill credited Mihailović with having started the Yugoslav resistance but said that he had drifted into a position "where some of his commanders made accommodations with the Italian and German troops." He was lavish in his praise of Tito. The Tito army, he said, "was at this moment holding in check no fewer than 14 out of 20 German divisions in the Balkan Peninsula." He wound up his eulogy with these words: "In Marshal Tito, the Partisans have found an outstanding leader, glorious in the fight for freedom.''

In the weeks that followed, Eden and Churchill had repeated meetings with Purić and King Peter. Towards mid-March there was a letup in the bludgeoning process to accommodate the king's marriage to Princess Alexandra of Greece on March 20. The presence at the ceremony of both Eden, representing His Majesty's Government, and Major Voja Lukačević, who had arrived in London with Colonel Bailey in early March representing the Mihailović movement, suggested to some that there might have been an easing of the hostility toward the Mihailović movement.

When the king returned from a brief honeymoon, Eden called on him on April 6 and a second time on April 13. This time, according to Ambassador Fotitch, "Mr. Churchill made his demand almost in the form of an ultimatum." Unless the king complied, he was informed, Churchill "would accuse Mihailović publicly of collaboration with the enemy and . . . would treat the King and his government accordingly." [1]

In desperation King Peter wrote a letter of appeal to President Roosevelt, who had, ever since their meeting in 1942, displayed a paternal attitude toward him. He closed his letter with these words:

> In these times, so difficult for my people, being fatherless, I address myself to you, Mr. President, asking you to be good enough to send me without delay your advice and your opinion. [2]

Having failed in their approach to Purić and King Peter, Churchill and Eden turned to Dr. Šubašić. Šubašić was considered a moderate pro-Yugoslav Croat rather than an extreme Croatian nationalist but had publicly taken a stand against Mihailović and for Tito.

On May 24, 1944, Churchill reported to the House of Commons that he had "received a message from King Peter that he has accepted the resignation of Dr. Purić," and that he understood that Šubašić was to be the next prime minister. According to Purić, King Peter, and Ambassador Fotitch, Purić never submitted his resignation and the king had not dismissed him at the time Churchill made his speech. [3] Apparently, what happened is that Churchill informed King Peter that he planned to address the House of Commons on May 24 and expected the resignation of Dr. Purić before noon of that day. But he did not resign, nor did the king dismiss him. Churchill, it seems, went ahead and made the announcement as though Purić's resignation were a fait accompli.

The effort to create a "coalition" government under Dr. Šubašić was, of course, doomed from the outset. The whole exercise was like a minuet in which the dancers performed with feigned cordiality, each side being careful to take no initiative that it felt would be unacceptable in Churchill's eyes. When it was all over and Dr. Šubašić, very disappointed, left Belgrade for his home in Zagreb, it was obvious to everyone that Tito, employing orthodox Communist "salami tactics"—eliminating his opposition a slice at a time—had made himself the unquestioned master of Yugoslavia. In doing so, he had conceded nothing to Šubašić and the few Yugoslavs who had been persuaded to take part in the minuet with him.

On June 6, 1944, Dr. Šubašić left London for Italy. From there he was taken to the island of Vis, where Tito had been set up by the British after the Nazi destruction of his headquarters at Drvar on the Yugoslav mainland on May 25. According to reports, the meeting that took place between Šubašić and Tito was cordial. After three days of negotiations Tito and Šubašić reached an agreement that accepted Tito's position on all essential points. Šubašić's principal concession was to accept the provisional administration established by the Anti-Fascist Council (AVNOJ) and the National Liberation Committee of Yugoslavia. As Ambassador Fotitch noted, in doing so, Šubašić, who had just been installed as prime minister of "the legal government of Yugoslavia, ratified the revolutionary changes made by Tito's AVNOJ on November 29, 1943."[4] This affected the whole constitutional organization of Yugoslavia. On July 7 Šubašić announced the composition of a new Yugoslav government in exile, which did not contain a single Serb minister.

On September 12, 1944, the king, in an act that tormented him until his last days, succumbed to Churchill's pressures and called upon "all Serbs, Croats, and Slovenes to unite and join the National Liberation Army under the leadership of Marshal Tito." But the king's ordeal was not yet over. In another speech on October 20, 1944, obviously scripted for him by some Churchillian speechwriter, the king paid tribute to "the glorious liberation struggle of the National Liberation Army, under Josip Broz Tito, intrepid Marshal of Yugoslavia."

Mihailović and the great mass of the Serbian people were thrown into painful consternation by King Peter's apparent abandonment of the nationalist cause and by his support for Marshal Tito. Simple Yugoslav peasants argued that the king was obviously a prisoner of the British government and doing their bidding under compulsion. More sophisticated Serbs correctly diagnosed the situation by speculating that their youthful monarch had finally caved in to Churchill's "unremitting exertions." Ambassador Fotitch notes, "The impression the speeches gave was that they had not been originally written in Serbian but had been translated from another language."

On September 28, 1944, Marshal Tolbukhin, the commander of the Soviet army about to invade Yugoslavia, issued a communiqué stating that Marshal Tito had authorized the Red Army to cross Yugoslavia. At the moment the communiqué was issued, Tito was about to enter Yugoslavia himself with the forces of Marshal Tolbukhin. The situation was farcical, but it served to make the point that no army, however powerful, could enter Yugoslavia without Tito's permission. And, in fact, when two British detachments landed in the Boka Kotorska region in late October, Tito, with his right to grant permission confirmed by the Soviet precedent, ordered the detachments to reembark immediately.

The British government all agreed that the issue of the monarchy should be decided by plebiscite after Yugoslavia had been liberated. The question then arose of appointing a regency council to act for the king until the plebiscite could be held. Immediately both sides were once again at loggerheads. The king insisted, quite understandably, on appointing the regency council himself, since it was supposed to act in his behalf. Tito would have none of this. Finally Šubašić and the British government gave in and agreed to a regency council whose members were acceptable to Tito.

The farce had not yet played itself out. On March 6, 1945, the British government gave tacit approval to the formation of a provisional government in Belgrade under the chairmanship of Tito. It called itself "the Federal and Democratic Government of Yugoslavia." Šubašić was appointed foreign minister, and, under British urging, Milan Grol, leader of the Serbian Democratic Party and a prominent member of the government in exile, joined the government as vice-premier. Tito had performed his role in the farce by promising to observe freedom of speech and of the press and to allow opposition political parties.

Grol resigned on August 18, 1945, after less than six months of being bullied and frustrated. In his letter of resignation he said that despite his position in the government, he had had no say in any of its decisions. When he tried to publish a newspaper, it was suppressed. When he tried to organize a committee of his old party, the secret police intervened. Grol was even threatened with physical harm or imprisonment.

A scant two months later Šubašić resigned from the government, and the Tito-Šubašić minuet came to an end.

On August 8, 1945, King Peter withdrew his grant of authority to the regents, saying that "they have ignored their oath and their obligations to me."

In January 1946 a new constitution was adopted, guaranteeing freedom of the press, freedom of speech and assembly, freedom of religion, and all other freedoms in language closely modeled after the langauge of the Stalin constitution in the Soviet Union.

CHAPTER

27

From the American Side:
The McDowell Report and OSS

Did the operations of James Klugmann and company in any way impinge on or affect American policy toward Tito? The indications are that they did— and in a very basic sense. When OSS set up its Yugoslav Section in Cairo in early 1943, it was new to the operation and had no agents of its own in Yugoslavia, with either Tito or Mihailović. It was therefore entirely dependent on SOE Cairo for intelligence. Contact between the two Yugoslav sections was frequent and continuous—and all the evidence is that by the end of June 1943 Major Louis Huot, who was in command of the OSS Cairo operation, had been won over completely to the Klugmann-Davidson assessment of Tito and Mihailović. From that time on, OSS was to be plagued— on an even larger and perhaps more active scale—with the same division of opinion as SOE on the Tito-Mihailović controversy. Papers supporting both movements were written by OSS officers up to the rank of colonel. Sometimes American policy appeared to favor Tito, at other times—especially near the end—Mihailović. Churchill had to intervene personally on three occasions when the agency appeared to be leaning toward Mihailović.

In mid-1942, on General Donovan's instructions, OSS had begun training a group of young Americans of Yugoslav parentage in anticipation of their being dropped in to Mihailović. On arriving in Cairo during June 1943, however, they were told that the plans had been changed and they would be dropped in to Tito instead. Only one member of the group, Captain George Musulin, risked the ire of his commanding officer by insisting that he be dropped in to Mihailović—a goal he was finally able to achieve in October 1943, thanks to the energetic intervention of Lt. Colonel Albert Seitz, chief of the American mission to Mihailović.[1]

In the fall of 1943 Major Huot was able to mount a massive sealift of weapons and supplies to Tito, using Bari as the chief port of loading. This operation Major Huot memorialized in his book *Guns for Tito*.[2] Huot was no Marxist, but his book was written with a fervor that became standard baggage for most of the non-Communist supporters of Tito, and which was soon to cost him his command.

Dissatisfied with the rate at which shipments of arms to Tito were being stepped up, Huot obtained permission from General Donovan and General Eisenhower to mount a trans-Adriatic seaborne supply operation in early October 1943. He begged, borrowed, and contrived the diversion of military and medical equipment and food from every available source for his supply operation—with the result that over a three-month period he and his team of American officers managed to ship in to the Partisans almost 6,000 tons of supplies, evacuating sick and wounded Partisans on their return trips. Huot exceeded his authority by going into Yugoslavia to meet Tito without the authorization of his American superiors or Brigadier Maclean. There was also a good deal of talk in Bari about irregularities in obtaining equipment for his crash supply program to the Partisans. In any case, in early November he was transferred out of the theater by Colonel John E. Toulmin, the new OSS chief in the area.

At this late date it may be difficult to document the contacts that took place between the Yugoslav sections of OSS and SOE Cairo. It stands to reason that these contacts were numerous—and it is a matter of record that they had considerable impact on OSS officers, especially the fledgling officers who were about to be dropped into Yugoslavia. Certainly, they had a lot to do with the paralyzing division on Yugoslav policy that afflicted OSS until the end. General Donovan strongly favored continued aid to Mihailović. At the intermediate level, however, the OSS officer corps was divided and pulling in two directions. This accounts for many of the apparent contradictions in US policy toward Yugoslavia in 1943 and 1944.

American policy with regard to Mihailović was far from parallel to British policy. Indeed, the record is clear that both President Roosevelt and General Donovan were gravely disturbed by Churchill's stubborn insistence on swinging Allied support to Tito. But since there was an agreement that Britain would have priority in determining Allied policy in the Balkans, it was Churchill's view that prevailed.

The evacuation of the rescued American airmen started General Donovan thinking again. As he told me in the course of several interviews in late 1946, it was his opinion that wherever there was intelligence to be gleaned, American intelligence officers should be present. He did not approve of the British policy which effectively denied the Allies a direct intelligence-gath-

ering capability in Serbia proper—which until the end was Mihailović territory, and which, despite Tito, was still the heart of Yugoslavia.

Taking advantage of the evacuation of the American airmen in August
1944, Donovan ordered an intelligence team of four officers, under the command of Lt. Colonel Robert McDowell, into Yugoslavia. The officers were
Lieutenant Ellsworth Kramer, Captain John Milodragevich, and Lieutenant
Michael Rajachich. (Rajachich had originally entered the country as part of
the Air Crew Rescue Unit.)

McDowell, who later served for many years as senior Soviet analyst at
the Pentagon, was by far the most qualified intelligence officer to go into
Yugoslavia for either Britain or the United States. The son of American
missionary parents, he had grown up in the Middle East, had learned to
speak a half-dozen Middle Eastern languages, had served with British intelligence during World War I in the Armenian areas of Turkey, and afterward
had served again with British intelligence, attached to anti-Bolshevik guerrillas in the Caucasus. After that he taught history at the University of Michigan, specializing in modern Balkan history in the period before his enlistment.
He was generally considered to be a left liberal and was sympathetic to Tito
at the point of being posted to the Middle East.

Captain George Vujnovich, the OSS operations officer in Bari, who was
a son of Serbian immigrants, vividly recalls his spirited arguments with
McDowell at that time on the question of support to Tito or Mihailović. On
the basis of his initial contacts with McDowell, Vujnovich was inclined to
look upon him as just another starry-eyed liberal sympathizer of the
Partisans.[3]

For a number of months before McDowell was dropped into Yugoslavia,
he compiled intelligence reports based on information coming out of the
country. This experience made him extremely skeptical about the validity of
Partisan communiqués, and he set up a group of personnel to evaluate them
in a long-range study. This study, he said, "revealed that Communist claims
of territory liberated in Yugoslavia and of defeats of Axis forces *were consistently contradicted by subsequent communiques*. It was evident that they
were put out as propaganda, and they put in serious doubt all Yugoslav
Communist claims of contribution to the Allied cause other than those actually witnessed by Allied officers."[4]

The British were furious when they learned of the dispatch of the Mc-
Dowell mission. Even though it was made clear to both Tito and Mihailović
that the function of the mission was limited to gathering intelligence, and
even though Donovan had previously spoken to General Wilson about the
matter, Churchill raised the issue with Roosevelt in early September 1944,
just before the Quebec conference. Again Roosevelt agreed to call off a Don-

ovan plan which appeared to keep the Mihailović option open. McDowell, however, remained in Yugoslavia until the end of October before he could be evacuated.

In his report McDowell said that hatred of communism by the Yugoslav masses derived not only from the still basically conservative and individualistic character of the country's peasants but also from the record of Partisan collaboration with Axis and quisling forces, their attacks upon Mihailović forces engaged in battle with the Germans, their failure to attack Axis forces, their falsification of communiqués, and their atrocities against Nationalist civilians, including women and priests.[5]

The four-officer McDowell mission saw a good deal during its more than two months in Yugoslavia because the way McDowell had his subordinates fan out made them eyewitnesses to much that happened in Serbia and Bosnia. Among the other points made by the McDowell report were the following:

• The Yugoslav Nationalist Movement (McDowell always used this designation in referring to the Mihailović movement) was the sum total of a large number of local movements, each of which developed in 1941 and 1942 as a spontaneous local uprising against Axis occupation and atrocities. "General Mihailović is nominal head of the Yugoslav Nationalist Movement . . . He leads the movement only insofar as the local district leaders and the people are willing to follow . . ."

• The term "Četnik" had resulted in a good deal of confusion. Historically it meant, in Serbia, a Serb who engaged in irregular warfare. The term was also used by the pre–World War II Četnik association led by Kosta Pećanac, which openly collaborated with the Germans and against which the Mihailović units fought many bitter battles. It was also used by other formations that were completely outside the Mihailović organization or only nominally a part of it. General Mihailović and most of his lieutenants did not apply the word to their own troops.

• "It was clear to the mission that today in Old Serbia the feeling of the peasants for the General approaches adoration, while the intellectual leaders and students proclaim him the only one of the ranking leaders in whom they have complete confidence."

• Yugoslav Nationalists said to the McDowell mission: [paraphrased quotation] "The Partisans lie, and the British believe them. The British send officers, but they see and hear nothing. We will be persecuted and killed, and the outside world will know nothing of it . . . We have been sealed off as thoroughly as Jews in a gas chamber—and for the same end."

• The members of the McDowell mission repeatedly witnessed Partisan attacks on Mihailović forces engaged at the time in actions against the Germans. These instances are described in detail in the McDowell report and in the supplementary reports by the other members of the mission.

• McDowell personally interviewed a number of Partisan prisoners taken by the Mihailović forces. Among them were Croats, Serbs, Slovenes, Italians, and one Russian. *Though they had fought against the Mihailović forces in "Dalamatia, Herzegovina, Montenegro, and Serbia, not one of them had seen action against the Germans or Ustashi"* [emphasis added]. (The picture that emerges from the McDowell report is reinforced by the account of Captain Eli Popovich, deputy to Colonel Farish, commander of the American mission to Tito. Popovich, also the son of Serbian immigrant parents, spoke fluent Serbo-Croat. He interviewed many wounded Partisans who all told him, in approximately the same words, that although their wounds hurt them, what hurt even more was the knowledge that these had been suffered in combat with fellow Serbs.)[6]

• It was McDowell's "considered judgment" that during September and October 1944, until the final drive on Belgrade, the Mihailović forces did more than the Partisans to kill, capture, and disrupt the Germans.

• Rather sadly, in the light of developments, McDowell reported that despite British support to the Partisans, he was astonished by the strength of pro-British feeling among the Nationalists and by the hopes still entertained that "Britain and the Serb Nationalists would eventually resume their traditional friendly relationship."[7]

The McDowell report received close and sympathetic attention from Donovan and Roosevelt and other key players in the American war effort, but by the time it was written and filed, Tito and the Red Army had occupied Belgrade and the deadline for exercising options in Yugoslavia had passed.

Colonel McDowell, who had been dropped into Mihailović's headquarters on August 26, arrived back in Bari on November 1. On November 9 he submitted a thirty-page, single-spaced preliminary report, which was immediately wired to General Donovan. Donovan must have been greatly impressed by it, because he sent it off immediately to Roosevelt's secretary, Grace Tully, with a little covering note asking her to bring it to his attention. McDowell's final report, which ran thirty-nine typewritten pages, single-spaced, was submitted on November 23, 1944. A copy of it was sent immediately to President Roosevelt.

Tito and Churchill were both alarmed by the decision to send in the McDowell mission to Mihailović's headquarters: Tito out of his Stalinist hatred for American and British imperialism, Churchill for fear that the presence of the mission might undermine British diplomacy vis-à-vis the Partisans. President Roosevelt wired to General Donovan on September 3, 1944, that "in view of British objection, it seems best to withdraw the mission to General

Mihailović.''[8] Donovan, in his reply, agreed to withdraw the McDowell mission but argued that since the Air Crew Rescue Unit had already succeeded in evacuating over 200 American airmen, that operation should continue as long as there were airmen to be evacuated.

It was also pointed out to the president that "at a meeting on August 11 with Tito, General Donovan informed him and Brigadier Maclean of the dispatch of an OSS rescue intelligence team to Mihailovich. At that time Tito nodded his head and voiced no objection." In defending Donovan's action, his deputy, Charles S. Cheston, said that "the lives of American airmen and the military advantage gained by their recovery overrides any objection the British might have on political grounds."[9]

On September 1 Donovan had wired the president, defending his action, while agreeing to withdraw the McDowell mission. He noted that although the Americans had established a mission with Tito, they had made no promise to send in arms or equipment or supplies; they made it clear that "we will not support either side in internal political strife, although the fact of delivery of supplies by the British in which our supplies to the British were included may be considered a refutation of this," and that OSS personnel were still needed in Yugoslavia for finding, assembling, and evacuating American aircrew.[10]

In a continuing defense of Donovan's action in sending in the McDowell mission, Cheston said in a wire dated September 11 to the US Joint Chiefs of Staff:

> In June, General Wilson told General Donovan that no intelligence was being received from the Četnik areas and that it was urgently needed by the Allies. He not only agreed with the basic principle of independent American secret intelligence operations and approved General Donovan's proposal to dispatch an intelligence team to the Četniks, but he urged that this be done. General Donovan wrote the president of this talk on July 4 and on the 6th of July discussed the matter with him in person.[11]

In the OSS files there are numerous such communications that indicate dramatically how Donovan and his senior lieutenants felt about Tito and the Yugoslav situation in general.

CHAPTER

28

The Agony of a Nation:
How Yugoslavia Was Liberated

When Colonel Robert McDowell and his mission arrived at Pranjani in late August 1944, Mihailović went over with them his plans for the long-promised *ustanak*, or national uprising. The general mobilization was to be the signal for a series of attacks on minor garrison towns in northern and northeastern Serbia for obtaining arms. Once armed, major concentrations were to be thrown against key centers like Kruševac, Čačak, Kraljevo, and Valjevo, and an all-out offensive was to be opened on the German railway network. Finally, Belgrade was to be completely isolated and then taken by attack from both without and within. The necessary troop dispositions for executing this plan were almost complete.

There were, however, a number of imponderables in the situation. Mihailović contemplated no difficulty in arranging for collaboration with the British and American forces that, he seemed confident, would soon be landed in Yugoslavia. But the entrance of the Red Army was imminently expected, and no one was sure what its attitude would be. Mihailović hoped—indeed, he seemed to believe—that the Russians would accept the active cooperation of his forces. But though he professed to be optimistic, the attitude of the Russians toward the Warsaw uprising, in progress at that time, boded ill for the possibility of any compromise with the Mihailović forces. The Red Army had stopped on the outskirts of Warsaw, and it remained there for weeks while the Nazi artillery mercilessly shelled the Polish Home Army. The Red Army refused to provide any assistance at all, even refusing landing facilities requested by the British government so that the RAF could fly supplies in directly to the Home Army Poles. As Churchill put it in a statement to the House, it was clear that the Russians wished to see them "killed to the full."

The greatest problem, however, was the Partisans. Tito was intent above all on the annihilation of the Mihailović movement—on this score Mihailović harbored no illusions. Since the destruction of Tito's headquarters at Drvar by a German paratroop raid on May 25, 1944, the Partisans, with British and American aid, had been able to recoup some of their losses and in several respects had improved their position vis-à-vis the Mihailović forces. In late August—again, operating with British and American airborne support—they had succeeded in driving the forces of Keserović from the mountain bastion of Kapaonik. And with the assistance of American and British recruiting officers they had built up an army of some 10,000 in southeast Serbia, and Kapaonik was now being used as a staging post for the infiltration of additional troops.

The purpose of this concentration in the southeast, quite obviously, was to link up with the Red Army. Mihailović's intelligence reported further concentrations of Partisan troops, which suggested an impending invasion from the west and southwest. Despite the fact that in so doing he was leaving himself vulnerable to Partisan attack, Mihailović deployed his troops for the general assault on the German positions in northern and northeastern Serbia.

"When the undersigned reached Mihailović headquarters in August, 1944, a general Nationalist mobilization had already been ordered," said Colonel McDowell in his official statement to the Commission of Inquiry of the Committee for a Fair Trial for Draja Mihailovich. His statement (which, incidentally, had to be submitted to the Pentagon for approval) continued thus:

> The undersigned was shown the plans and orders issued for an allout attack on Axis forces and, along with the other U.S. officers, personally witnessed the troop dispositions made for this offensive. The evidence was unmistakable that General Mihailović had disposed his forces properly for a major effort against the German garrisons, depots, and lines of communication, but in doing this had been obliged to leave his rear and left flank exposed to major Partisan concentrations which only recently had been attacking the Nationalists.

> Insofar as the small group of American officers were able to cover the front and make observations, during September the Nationalist forces engaged German and Bulgarian forces to the extent of their capability and equipment. Axis movements were thoroughly disrupted and considerable quantities of munitions and prisoners were taken.

On September 1 Mihailović issued an order for general mobilization. "In the name of Peter the Second," read the translation wirelessed to former Ambassador Fotitch in Washington, "in accordance with our great coalition, and on the base of the permissions given to me, I proclaim with the day of

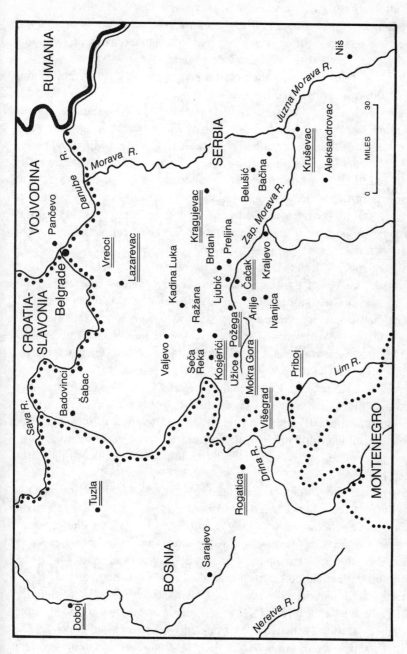

Areas (underlined) of confirmed activities of the Mihailović forces at the time of the national uprising, beginning September 1, 1944

First September, 1944, at 0 o'clock, total mobilization of the whole nation against all enemies. [It is obvious that Mihailović was calling for a mobilization against both the Nazis and the Communists.] I order that the action must be executed under directives given by the headquarters of the Yugoslavian Army in the country and by menace of death." [1]

At midnight on August 31 the prearranged signal was given. The church bells rang out in every village in Serbia.

When day broke on the morning of September 1, only old men, women, and children were to be seen in the villages of Serbia. All those who had arms or were able to carry arms had reported to the nearest Mihailović commander. The total number answering the call was in the neighborhood of 150,000, only half of whom, however, had rifles. In the pages that follow, the members of the McDowell mission recount the many military actions to which they were eyewitnesses, and a Mihailović officer, Captain Vojislav Ilić, presents an account of the several actions in the Čačak area in which he took part.

On September 2 Lieutenant Mike Rajachich of the McDowell mission arrived in the village of Kadina Luka at a railway junction near Lazarevac. Rajachich, the son of immigrants, was a graduate of the University of Belgrade. He had originally entered Yugoslavia as a member of the Air Crew Rescue Unit but was transferred to the McDowell intelligence operation at the point where McDowell parachuted into Pranjani. When Rajachich arrived at Kadina Luka, a battle was in full progress. Some 3,000 Home Army soldiers of the Kolubarski Corps under Captain Grga Topalović had surrounded the village, and after tearing up the rails for two kilometers on either side of the junction and cutting all telegraph and telephone lines, they had sent a fifteen-minute ultimatum to the commander of the German garrison. The commander had refused it, and at 4:30 in the afternoon the opening shots had been fired. [2]

The Home Army soldiers were pathetically armed. Only one in three had a rifle. Some of the others carried homemade hand grenades. The remainder went into battle without arms of any kind, either waiting to pick up arms from fallen comrades or else hoping to seize weapons from dead or captured Germans. For the 3,000 men they had only one machine gun—a 20mm cannon, which they had taken from a crashed American bomber at Ljig and had affectionately nicknamed "Saint Eli" after the Serbian saint of thunder.

The Germans had a force of some 350 men concentrated in the environs of the railway station, which was surrounded by six steel-and-concrete pillboxes. A picked squad of Home Army machine-gunners crept in between the pillboxes. Before the Germans realized what was happening, there was Saint Eli perched on top of the railway station, dominating the entire scene of battle. While the Germans concerned themselves with the "Saint," Mihailović grenadiers snaked Indian-style up to the pillboxes and knocked them out one by one.

A train coming up from Sarajevo to the assistance of the beleaguered garrison was derailed, and the complement of several hundred Germans was wiped out. Toward midnight a Panzer train came up from Belgrade, stopped at the track break three kilometers outside the village, and opened up with its artillery in a futile endeavor to assist the German garrison. By 1:30 the following morning the battle had been decided.

In this engagement the Home Army took over 150 prisoners. In Kadina Luka alone Lieutenant Rajachich personally counted 86 German bodies. The Home Army losses were one man killed—a member of the crew of Saint Eli—and a dozen wounded. "If I hadn't seen it with my own eyes," said Lieutenant Rajachich, "I wouldn't have believed it possible."[3]

The following day the Kolubarski Corps moved on to the town of Lazarevac, which was garrisoned by a contingent of similar size. They attacked at dusk, taking the Germans by surprise. One group of Germans succeeded in getting through to the Serb Orthodox church and mounted their machine guns in the belfry. Another group fortified themselves inside the town hospital. After three hours of sharp fighting, Lazarevac was in Mihailović hands. Nine Germans were killed and 200 were taken prisoner for a total loss of 4 Home Army lives. The prisoners from both engagements were taken to the village of Belanovica and placed under guard in the schoolhouse.

In the morning the victorious Mihailović forces staged a triumphal parade through the streets of Lazarevac. The people were delirious—the day of liberation had come! The proceedings culminated in a victory dinner in the house of the local priest, Pop Petrović, who said a prayer for the Allies before all sat down to eat.

The radio was tuned in on BBC. The announcer began reading off the Partisan communiqué for the day. "The Partisans," said the announcer, "have just taken the town of Lazarevac." A Mihailović officer exploded and slapped hard at the offending radio so that for a second or two it teetered on its little table. Lieutenant Rajachich hung his head.

After the capture of Lazarevac the Kolubarski Corps turned around and headed toward Ljig. At this point Rajachich parted with them. When they said good-bye, Captain Topalović was optimistic. "Soon we'll be liberating Belgrade," he said.

Traveling up nearer Belgrade, Lieutenant Rajachich came across signs of action in almost every village he visited. At Vreoci, for example, the Mihailović forces had wiped out the local garrison and destroyed the power plant, the source of one-third of Belgrade's electricity. The large towns were still controlled by the Germans, but in the villages the Mihailović forces were everywhere in control.

During the first days of September the Partisans launched their long-expected invasion of western Serbia. The only enemy in which they showed any interest was the Mihailović army. They made no effort to engage the Germans during this period or to disrupt German communications. Mc-Dowell and the other American officers saw with their own eyes how the Partisans bypassed the German garrisons at Užice and Čačak and drove straight for the flank of the Mihailović deployment. They saw, too, how the German traffic between Čačak, Kraljevo, and Užice, which had been brought to a dead stop by the Mihailović units operating in the area, was reopened by the Germans as soon as the Partisans had driven off the Mihailović units.

By September 9 the Partisan invasion had reached a line passing through Požega-Kosjerić-Razana. To meet the threat, Račić's Cer group of corps and Kalabić's Oplenac group were diverted from their original deployment. Kalabić made contact with the Partisans on September 10. Within several days he had driven the Partisans out of Požega and hurled them back almost forty kilometers to the banks of the Drina.[4]

Allied officers will testify that man for man, other things being approximately equal, the soldiers of the Mihailović forces outfought the Partisans almost every time they met them, especially in close-range combat. There is nothing very surprising in this. As has been pointed out before, the Home Army soldiers were fighting on their own soil, whose every inch they knew. But what was more important, they were fighting for their own homes. The Partisan army, in contrast, was a migratory army composed of a hard core of seasoned Communist troops surrounded by a softer mass of Bulgarian, Hungarian, Albanian, and Italian conscripts, ex-Ustaše quislings, and conscripted Serb peasants who had little heart for fighting against Mihailović Serbs.

But there is a limit to how much human courage can do without ammunition and without modern weapons. The troops of Kalabić and Račić went into battle with no more than ten to fifteen rounds per rifle. Some of Mihailović's units, indeed, were down to one or two rounds per rifle at that time. They had pitifully few automatic weapons, next to no machine guns, and no mortars. (Surely, no group of men ever "collaborated" with the Germans for so poor a return!) Their only source of supplies was what they could capture from the Germans and the Partisans.

The day after the Kalabić troops had captured Seca Reka a flotilla of American transport aircraft dropped supplies to the Partisans. The Kalabić units had taken up positions on a hill overlooking the town. The next morning, the Partisans opened up a devastating mortar fire on the Kalabić positions. The Kalabić soldiers had no entrenching implements, and there was no effective natural cover available. But what was most demoralizing of all was that they had no means of replying to the Partisan mortars. Yet for hours they held on while their ranks were being decimated. Finally they broke and plunged back over the far side of the hill into the ravine. The ravine proved worse than the hilltop. The Partisans, using their mortars expertly, lifted their fire. There was frightful carnage before Kalabić's men were able to disperse and get themselves out of range. Leaving a holding unit to cover his retreat, Kalabić withdrew northeast into Maljen Planina.

Captain John Milodragovich, a member of the McDowell mission who happened to be at the scene of battle, brought back from the encounter a number of American 88mm mortar firing tables left behind by the Partisans.[5]

It would have been bad enough from the standpoint of the Mihailović forces if they had simply had to contend with a much stronger enemy continuously being air-supplied by the so-called "Balkan Air Force." But now they had to contend with the agony of hearing their king openly endorse the Tito movement and brand as traitors all those who refused to join the movement. After months of being pressured and browbeaten by Churchill, and despite intense personal misgivings, King Peter on September 12 broadcast a message to Yugoslavia in which he called upon "all Serbs, Croats and Slovenes to unite and join the National Liberation Army under the leadership of Marshal Tito." He said that all those who remained deaf to this appeal would not escape "the brand of traitor" before their people and their history. He concluded:

> By this message I strongly condemn the misuse of the name of the King and the authority of the Crown by which an attempt has been made to justify collaboration with the enemy and to provoke discord amongst our fighting people in the very gravest days of their history, thus solely profiting the enemy.[6]

With heavy hearts the Serbian peasants and soldiers who followed Mihailović continued their struggle against the Partisans and against the Germans and their various quisling forces.

THE RED ARMY ENTERS YUGOSLAVIA

Despite his involvement with the Partisans, Mihailović continued to hope that it would be possible to arrive at an understanding with the Red Army. To this end he dispatched a mission under Major Piletić, which crossed the Danube near Kladovo in the first days of October, and established contact with the advance units of the Red Army. Major Piletić presented them with a position map of eastern Serbia together with a plan of joint operations that Mihailović had worked out. Piletić was arrested by the Russians (the Partisan version was that he had "surrendered"), but he later succeeded in escaping and came to Paris.

Other attempts were made by prominent Mihailović commanders to achieve an entente with the Russians. The Belgrade judge Puniša Vasović took it upon himself to negotiate after Piletić's failure. He was disarmed, handed over to the local Partisans, and executed the same day. Major Vesić, commander of the Deligrad Corps, also went to meet the Russians. He was disarmed by them and placed under arrest but succeeded in escaping.

The Red Army reached the Yugoslav frontier at Turnu Severin on September 28. They asked Tito, then at Marshal Tolbukhin's headquarters, for permission to enter Yugoslavia, promising to leave civilian administration entirely in Partisan hands. Tito, to the surprise of no one, granted the requested "permission."

The Red Army offensive took three main directions. The first was directed from the Rumanian border toward Pančevo. The second was pointed from Bulgaria toward Zaječar and Knjaževac. The third branch of the offensive, in which a number of Bulgarian divisions participated, headed for Niš. Had the Red Army been intent on destroying the German Balkan armies, it would probably have cut across the more northerly reaches of Yugoslavia. The purpose of its strategy, however, was political rather than military: to capture Belgrade and establish Tito in power.

KRUŠEVAC

After being driven from Kopaonik before the end of August, Major Keserović and his Toplica Corps had held their own against the Partisan armies supplied by Allied transport aircraft. Whenever Allied aircraft came over at night, the Partisans would let loose on the Mihailović positions in the morning. For almost two months a ding-dong battle raged in the reaches of the Zapadna Morava River. Both sides were so completely engrossed in fighting each other that there was little time for fighting the Germans. Sometimes, indeed, the Germans drove nonchalantly along roads within gunshot of battles between the two Yugoslav factions. The Partisans pushed Keserović across the river as far as Baćina and Belušić. Keserović turned around and drove them pell-mell back over the river to Aleksandrovac and Brus.

When Lieutenant Ellsworth ("Bob") Kramer of the McDowell mission, who was then attached to Keserović, sent a message to the Partisan command asking for collaboration against the common enemy, his courier was killed. A second courier was abused and sent back with an insulting reply.[7]

In the first week of October it became known that the Russian army was approaching Kruševac, an important communications city on one of the main German lines of retreat. Major Keserović, while holding his own against the Partisan drive in the Zapadna Morava Valley, had strong forces deployed in the area. Lieutenant Kramer found himself confronted with a number of delicate problems. Some of the Home Army officers were uneasy. "The Russians will let the Partisans take over and slaughter all of us," they said. Kramer assured them that the Russians were allies and that they would be only too glad to have the cooperation of the Mihailović forces. Despite his personal misgivings, Keserović pronounced himself in favor of attempting an understanding.

Meanwhile, the Germans in Kruševac had sent a delegate to Keserović and Lieutenant Kramer to discuss surrender. Like the German troops everywhere in Europe, they wished to surrender to the Americans and British rather than the Russians. The German delegate indicated that, provided he was given a guarantee of American custody, he would be able to arrange the surrender of the German garrisons at Kraljevo, Kragujevac, and Kruševac, and conceivably of all the German forces right down to the Greek frontier. Since Kramer was in no position to guarantee American custody, there was nothing he could do about the offer.

Kruševac was held by a garrison of 700 Germans and 1,000 White Russians, supported by thirteen tanks. When Keserović heard that the Russian spearhead was within twenty kilometers of the town, he dispatched an envoy to meet them. At dawn the next day the envoy came back with a Russian lieutenant. In the presence of Kramer, Keserović and the lieutenant embraced each other in the manner of the Slav peoples, called each other *moy brat*—"my brother"—and drank each other's health. Keserović explained how he could take the town with a minimum of hurt to the civilian population. The Russian delegate accepted his plan. Keserović immediately ordered his men into the attack. The Home Army soldiers fought as they had fought at Lazarevac—with a medley of ancient rifles and homemade hand grenades. The Germans offered little resistance, but the White Russians were somewhat more difficult to subdue. In three hours the fighting was over and the Yugoslav flag was flying from the town hall.

At this point the Russian spearhead entered the town. The major in command came up and greeted Keserović and Lieutenant Kramer. There were more *moy brat*s. On behalf of the Royal Yugoslav Army, Keserović turned the town and his prisoners over to the Red Army. Then the three of them—the Russian major, Keserović, and Lieutenant Kramer—mounted the balcony in front of the town hall. They greeted the delirious townspeople demonstrating below them.

"*Živela naša ruska braća!*" roared the crowd—"Long live our Russian brothers!"

The Russian major acknowledged the salute. *"Živeo Roosevelt!"* he shouted—"Long live Roosevelt!"

"Živeo!" responded the crowd.

"Živeo Churchill!"

"Živeo!"

"Živeo Staljin!"

"Živeo!"

"Živeo Kralj Pera!"—"Long live King Peter!"

"Živeo! Živeo!" The crowd went mad. The Russians apparently were going to be good brothers.

The German radio's version of Kruševac was that Keserović had gone over to the Russians, who, in recognition, had appointed him mayor. No such rosy fate befell Keserović.

Half an hour after the joint celebration Lieutenant Kramer was under arrest and the Home Army troops were being disarmed. Lieutenant Kramer was finally released after a brief detention in Bulgaria.[8]

Keserović himself succeeded in escaping from Kruševac with the better part of his forces. He was subsequently captured by the Partisans and tried for treason together with five other Mihailović commanders. In one of those macabre orgies of self-condemnation that passed for trials wherever Stalinist jurisprudence held sway, Keserović, tears streaming down his cheeks, spoke brokenly of his "guilt." Of the capture of Kruševac he said not a word.

ČAČAK

The Germans were evacuating the bulk of their troops from the southern Balkans along the railways and highways of the Morava Valley. One of the key communications centers along this route was the town of Čačak.

On October 4, at a meeting of Mihailović army corps commanders in the village of Umka, it was decided to undertake a major operation against Čačak. The chief commanders were Major Smiljanić, Major Pelivanović, Major Račić, and Captain Raković. The attack was launched on October 6. Four times during the ensuing fortnight the Home Army succeeded in fighting their way into Čačak, and four times they were driven out by the arrival of large German convoys.

Toward the end of October the Red Army and units of the Partisan army arrived in the region of Čačak. The manner of the first contact between the Russians and the Mihailović forces has been described by Captain Vojislav Ilić, commander of the First Ljubić Brigade, who was responsible for the capture of the railway village of Preljina:

On October 24, 1944, I was engaged in fighting the Germans for Preljina. I had under my command two brigades of 1,100 men. We succeeded in taking the town, thus cutting off the German line of retreat. While our attack was in progress we found ourselves being shelled by the Russians and Partisans from the direction of Gornji Milanovac.

I at once sent a courier to them to explain the situation and to request that the shelling be stopped. The Russians accepted our request: in fact, they even helped us by sending two Katusha shells into the German lines. When the Russians finally met up with us, they expressed great surprise at finding Četniks fighting against the Germans: the Partisans apparently had succeeded in convincing them that we were all collaborators. They were somewhat more surprised when I turned over to them 700 German prisoners (among them some White Russians) in the village of Brdani. For this delivery my delegate received a signed receipt from them.[9]

A meeting was arranged between the Mihailović commanders and the Russian commanders in the captured village of Preljina, and a joint plan of attack was worked out. According to this plan, the Russians were to attack Čačak from the left side of the Morava, deploying their artillery along the line Brdani-Preljina-Konjević. To assist their operations, two Mihailović brigades were to remain on the left side of the river under the direct command of Russian officers. The other Mihailović units were to attack from the right side of the Morava. Five Russian liaison officers were attached to these units, while Captain Ceković was appointed liaison officer with the Russians at Gornji Milanovac. Under the agreement the Home Army was to turn over all prisoners and all captured war materiel to the Russians, who in return would supply the Home Army with rifles and ammunition.

The attack was launched immediately upon conclusion of the agreement. As a result of a heavy influx of retreating troops, the German garrison in Čačak had grown to a force of over 20,000 men. The fighting was bitter and protracted: Home Army losses alone were 2,500 killed and wounded. While the Mihailović units were engaging the Germans, they were attacked in the rear five times by Partisan units from the direction of Ivanjica-Arilje-Požega. The Russian liaison officers observed these attacks but did nothing to prevent them.

After the battle the Home Army turned over to the Russians 4,500 German prisoners, 200 vehicles, and much other booty.

The following day the Russians began to disarm the Home Army soldiers. Some of them succeeded in escaping, some did not. In early December the Partisans managed to locate Captain Raković in his hideout and surrounded him. Either they executed him or he committed suicide. In any case, his body was placed on display in the marketplace in Čačak.

DOBOJ

When Mihailović's headquarters party, together with members of the Air Crew Rescue Unit, reached eastern Bosnia in early October, they came upon one of the most remarkable jobs of railway wrecking of the entire war. The end of the track had been torn up, ties and all, at Doboj; and then, by using the deadweight of the rails for leverage, the ties had been spiraled all the way down the line almost thirty kilometers to Tuzla. But German traffic was still moving normally along the parallel line ten to fifteen miles to the south— a key escape route—in territory that was supposed to be firmly held by the Partisans. That did not prevent BBC from crediting the destruction of the Doboj-Tuzla line to the Partisans.

The most important towns in Serbia proper were liberated by the forces of General Mihailović, acting either on their own or else in conjunction with the Red Army. But the world heard nothing about this. So far as the Allied press was concerned, his followers were traitors who were collaborating with the enemy.

The unexpected Partisan-Russian advance,'' wrote Stojan Pribićević, in *The New Statesman and Nation* for January 27, 1945,

> . . . seems to have caught Mihailović by surprise. In October he fled with a small detachment to Bosnia and then to Northern Dalmatia . . . leaving confusion among his units in Serbia. Some of his commanders in Serbia (Keserović, Kalabić, etc.) continued to fight the Partisans and even the Russians; others, such as Piletić and Stanković, surrendered to the Russians to avoid being captured by the Partisans; yet another fraction of Mihailović's units roamed the Serbian forests, not knowing whom to fight; still another faction disbanded and filtered back to their homes. I have met Mihailović officers who last August and September reported to fight the Germans and returned clandestinely to Belgrade, weeping; while the Wehrmacht was retreating from Serbia they had been sent to fight the Partisans. *At no time has any Mihailović unit been reported attacking a German position in the battle for the liberation of Serbia.* [Author's emphasis]

At the time this article appeared, I was in London and so was Pribićević, and Captain Vojislav Ilić had recently arrived in England. I had been so impressed by Ilić's account of the fighting for Preljina and Čačak that I set up a luncheon meeting with Pribićević and Ilić. As a *Time-Life-Fortune* correspondent, Pribićević had played a central role in selling Tito to the British and American public and depicting Mihailović as a collaborator. It was obvious from the beginning to the end of our luncheon conversation that Pribićević was as impressed as I had been by Captain Ilić's account—which

Ilić reinforced with a series of rough maps drawn in pencil on the Hotel Dorchester napkins. In fact, Pribićević maintained an embarrassed silence, chain-smoking endlessly, not once challenging Ilić's account with questions.

The importance of the role played by Pribićević in shaping British and American public opinion on the Tito-Mihailović controversy cannot be overstated. However, history will more probably accept the account of Colonel McDowell and the other American officers who saw with their own eyes how the Mihailović forces attacked position after position in the battle for the liberation of Serbia.

THE MEETING WITH THE GERMANS

In mid-September the German commander in Belgrade, through a Serbian emissary, established contact with Lt. Colonel McDowell at Mihailović's headquarters to discuss surrender. Two meetings took place between Colonel McDowell and a Herr Stärker, representing Herr Neubacher, Ribbentrop's deputy in Belgrade. The German position was that they wished to surrender to the Americans and the Mihailović forces rather than to the Russians and the Partisans, and that if the Americans could guarantee custody with a force of 1,000 paratroopers, the surrender of most of the German Balkan armies could, they believed, be effected. The discussions were duly reported to Allied headquarters. For obvious reasons it was decided that nothing could be done about the German proposal—although, after the flagrant Soviet betrayal of the Warsaw uprising, it can be argued that we were fools to play by the old rules governing our conduct. It is something to reflect upon that had this offer been accepted, the war might have ended by October 1944 and several hundred thousand lives might have been saved.

Somehow the Partisans got hold of a few details of the meeting. "I possess the eye-witness testimony of high Četnik officers," wrote Stojan Pribićević, "that on September 16, 1944, with the Russian Army already in Serbia, Mihailović had a meeting with Herr Stärker, chief adviser to Neubacher, Ribbentrop's deputy in Belgrade, in the village of Badovinci near the town of Šabac, west of Belgrade—and that a week later the Germans supplied Mihailović's headquarters with 5,500 rifles. According to the Partisans, Mihailović is a traitor and an enemy of the people . . ." [10]

THE ROLE OF THE PARTISANS

Just how prominent a role the Partisan army played in the liberation of Serbia it is difficult to say. They did attack the Germans at certain points, especially after their junction with the Red Army, approximately October 10. But the claims they put out for public consumption were so preposterously inflated, and so frequently in conflict with those of their Russian and Bulgar allies, that it is virtually impossible to sort out fantasy from reality. What makes a serious assessment all the more difficult is the fact that very few of the actions claimed by the Partisans were witnessed by British or American liaison officers. After the entry of the Red Army into Serbia, the British and American liaison officers were treated more like enemies than like allies who had provided the Partisan army with the bulk of its training and materiel and with hospitalization for its wounded.

The most cursory study would justify a healthy skepticism about Partisan communiqués. *The Daily Worker* for September 15, 1944, quoted Tito's communiqué: "The link-up between the Red Army and the National Army of Liberation was announced yesterday in a special communique from Marshal Tito. His troops had captured Negotin, 28 miles south of Turnu Severin and their left wing is in contact with Soviet troops."

The communiqué issued by the Soviet Information Bureau on September 30, a fortnight later, carried the following information: "In the wake of reconnaissance parties which several days ago infiltrated into Yugoslavia, Soviet troops yesterday crossed the Yugoslav frontier south of the Russian town of Turnu Severin, and in the very first clash of arms overwhelmed the German troops, capturing the following places: Tekia, Kladovo . . . and *Negotin*!" [Author's italics]

A number of other towns figured similarly in the communiqués of the Soviet and the Bulgarian armies and the Army of National Liberation. We list two of many examples.

On November 14 the Bulgarian Home Service announced that the important railway junction of Skoplje had been taken by the Second Thracian Infantry Division under General Stoychev. On November 15 Radio Free Yugoslavia announced that Skoplje had been liberated by units of the Forty-second and Fiftieth divisions of the Army of National Liberation. On November 15 Radio Free Yugoslavia announced that Partisan units had "encircled Uroševac and then immediately captured the city by storm." On the same day, Sofia Radio announced that Uroševac had been captured by the Bulgarian army under the command of Generals Stanchev and Atanasov.

Add all these contradictions to the numerous incidents witnessed by American officers, in which the Partisans claimed to have occupied towns actually occupied by the Mihailović units—and the question is: How much can one believe of the entire Partisan saga?

About the two Partisan armies that drove into Serbia from the west and southwest it can definitely be stated that they made little or no effort to combat the Germans until they met up with the Russians outside Belgrade.

Recent Partisan conscripts, captured in the fighting with the Mihailović forces around Užice, told Colonel McDowell that they had not engaged in a single battle with the Germans. They had fought only Četniks.

The statistics of the Partisan army, as well as its activities, are subject to a degree of conjecture. Mihailović's headquarters, in making preparations, estimated that they were up against a Partisan army of 65,000 men. Of this number a minimum of 10,000—possibly 15,000—were ex-Ustaše troops who had come over since the fall of Italy. Hungarians, Bulgars, Rumanians, and Albanians accounted for another 10,000. And there were a minimum of 10,000—some say 20,000—Italians. The number of Italians in the Partisan army was substantial enough for Mihailović to maintain a separate Italian propaganda bureau, which was run by a sympathetic Italian socialist. After one collision with the "Serb" Lika Brigade, the Mihailović units came back with thirty captives, whom they showed to American officers. All of them were Italians.[11]

According to Mihailović sources, of the 50,000 to 60,000 Yugoslavs behind Tito, some 15,000 were real Partisans—hardened Communists and fanatical fighters. The balance were simple peasants whom the Partisans in regions under their control had either conscripted or else recently recruited, exploiting the presence of the Anglo-American missions. There was no ideological conflict between these peasants and the peasants of the Mihailović movement. Both groups were profoundly attached to their farms and their flocks; they were kindly, great-hearted, God-fearing individualists desiring some improvements and a better government than they had had before the war, but they were opposed to radical change, and certainly opposed to Soviet communism. Now they found themselves caught up by forces over which they had no control, and fighting one another to the death.

"We are being liberated," said the peasants of Serbia, "by the Communists together with the Ustaše, the Bulgars, the Albanians, the Hungarians, the Italians. In short, we are being 'liberated' by all those who massacred us during the war."

THE LIBERATION OF BELGRADE

The Red Army, with the ex-quisling Marko Mesić at the head of its auxiliary Yugoslav contingent, advanced toward Belgrade in early October. A brief digression at this point on the record of Colonel Mesić will throw valuable light on the history of the period. The most appropriate title for his story would be "The Apotheosis of a Quisling."

The Moscow correspondent of *Soviet War News* for January 10, 1944, said this of Mesić:

One of the most active organizers of the Independent Yugoslav Volunteer Unit in the U.S.S.R. was a seasoned officer of the Yugoslav Army, Lt. Colonel Marko Mesić. He, too, had been forcibly mobilized by the Germans. While still a prisoner of war, he rallied round him the Yugoslav officers and men in the camp, and expressed his desire to fight the Germans in the way he fought them in Yugoslavia in 1941, when he was in command of an artillery regiment. When the question arose as to who was to be the commander of the unit, all the officers were unanimous in their choice of Lt. Colonel Marko Mesić.

In a letter to *The* (London) *Times* dated March 18, 1944, two Royal Yugoslav Army officers, Colonel Dragutin Savić and Major Vladeta Bogdanović, both of whom played a prominent role in the revolution of March 27, presented the following biographical facts on Mesić, which have never been challenged. Their letter said that Mesić, who held the rank of major before the war, deserted from the Yugoslav army during the invasion and joined the ranks of the Croat quisling Ante Pavelić. According to the Ustaše organ *Hrvatski Narod* (June 27, 1943), Mesić was one of the Croat officers who, "although stationed on the Serbo-Bulgarian frontier, not fearing even the gravest dangers, arrived by land to the territory of liberated Croatia, being one of the first to place himself at the disposal of the Croat armed forces."

In recognition of his services to the "liberated" fatherland, Mesić was promoted to the rank of colonel and awarded the order of Knight Companion of the Croat Iron Clover and the German Iron Cross, Second Class.

"In September 1941," said the letter, "Mesić was appointed commander of the artillery section of the Croat volunteer legion which was sent to the Russian front. In January 1943 he was placed in command of all Croat forces fighting against the Russians at Stalingrad; in this capacity he was taken prisoner by the Russians at Stalingrad on February 2, 1943. For his bravery . . . against the Russians he was awarded the order of Knight Grand Commander of the Croat Iron Clover, and the German Iron Cross, First Class."

During the last fateful days in Stalingrad, Mesić sent a message to Pavelić informing him that the members of the Croat Legion in Stalingrad would fulfill their duty to the *poglavnik* (the Croat equivalent of "führer"), the Croat state, and to Hitler. In captivity Mesić ruminated and became converted to the Communist cause.

What a commentary it is on the nature of Tito's regime that this "seasoned officer" who received most of his "seasoning" in fighting against the Russians; who "fought against the Germans" in 1941 by deserting for the quisling army of Pavelić; and who, though "forcibly mobilized," fought bravely enough for the Germans to win the highest awards for himself, and what is more, fought to the end—what a commentary it is that this "democrat" should have entered Yugoslavia with the Red Army and then become

Commander of the Guard of the Chief of State, occupying the office of the former Commander of the King's Guard!

The Red Army fought its way into the suburbs of Belgrade on October 14. It had paused for five days on the outskirts of the city in order to give the Partisan army—whose commanders had made the most extravagant predictions—an opportunity to establish their prestige by "liberating" the capital city of Yugoslavia. Finally, realizing the complete inability of the Partisans to engage the Germans in major combat, the Red Army acted on its own.

In Paris, in Antwerp, in Brussels, in Rome, in Florence, in almost every major city that the Allies liberated during the war, they were aided in great or small degree by the populace of the liberated cities. In Belgrade, although the fighting went on for almost two weeks, neither Tito's communiqués nor the Red Army's made any mention of active assistance by the people of the city. From the past record of the Serbs one would have expected another Warsaw in Belgrade. Instead, not an ink bottle was thrown to assist the liberating armies. The powerful Belgrade underground, which could have mobilized the city to a man had the liberating armies consisted of British, American, and Mihailović troops, had no alternative but to remain inactive. Warsaw and Kruševac had taught them that assisting the Russians meant merely exposure to the Partisan executioners. Weeks after the liberation, when the first Allied correspondents were permitted to make a cursory visit to Belgrade, even the uniformly sympathetic Hubert Harrison of Reuters, who had been in charge of BBC broadcasts to Yugoslavia, described a populace that seemed dazed and indifferent. According to Stojan Pribićević, when the Partisans entered the city, 80 percent of the people were anti-Tito.[12] To cope with the situation, the Partisans were compelled to introduce an 8:00 P.M. curfew—a measure far more severe than any imposed during the German occupation.

Thus was Belgrade liberated, on October 20, 1944.

THE BRITISH BRIGADE AT DUBROVNIK

On October 28, 1944, it was announced that a British artillery brigade, acting on a request from Marshal Tito, had landed at Dubrovnik on the Dalmatian coast. The force was commanded by Brigadier Sir Henry Floyd, and was known as Floydforce. The news was widely interpreted as an indication that the British were preparing to land a substantial force in Yugoslavia that would collaborate with the Partisans in a drive to the north. The agreement, however, did not go this far.

Though the assistance of the British artillery brigade had been requested by Marshal Tito himself, the day after the announcement appeared in the

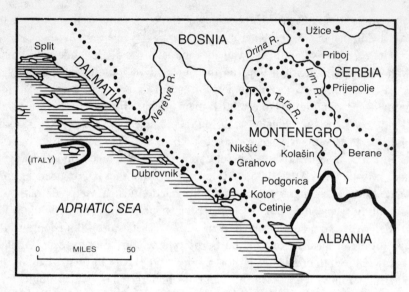

Area of maneuvers of the British brigade at Dubrovnik October–November 1944

British press Partisan headquarters issued a statement saying that it was untrue that British troops were operating in Yugoslavia.[13]

The Partisans had made the request because they badly needed immediate artillery support. The German garrison at Dubrovnik had withdrawn to Kotor; and around Kotor, Cetinje, and Podgorica there were now substantial German concentrations, obviously preparing for an escape northward via Nikšić. The Partisans, who had moved into Dubrovnik when the Germans moved out, feared such an attempted breakthrough because they knew they did not have enough artillery to cover the German escape routes.

Without the support of the British artillery brigade and the RAF, the Partisans would have been able to do nothing, or, if they had attempted action, would have sustained a serious setback. The artillery performed with particular brilliance, first driving the Germans out of Kotor, Cetinje, and Podgorica and then forcing them to abandon their planned retreat via the main highway through Grahovo. In desperation the Germans took the secondary highways, which were little more than cow paths through the inhospitable Montenegrin mountains. Here they were decimated by the RAF and the Fifteenth US Army Air Force.

The operation is described in some detail in *Grand Strategy*, the official British history of World War II. *Grand Strategy* says that while the British, over the previous year, had been able to count on the full cooperation of the

Partisans, they were "disappointed" and surprised at the marked change in their treatment in November 1944. "The disappointment was greater because it was provoked by the first occasion on which British land forces had operated on the mainland of Yugoslavia. Air support had been provided continuously since the summer and had increased substantially from September."[14]

Allied air operations in Yugoslavia were on an enormous scale and were given a number-one priority. To step up air support to the Tito forces, in June the Allies had pooled their strength to create a special "Balkan Air Force." Mitchells and Mustangs and Hurricanes and rocket-firing Typhoons destroyed hundreds of locomotives and wagons and scores of bridges. They strafed enemy columns, blew up enemy munition dumps, and generally harassed the enemy at their leisure. In the opinion of allied officers, the Balkan Air Force, which combined the Fifteenth US Army Air Force and the RAF, was by far the most serious obstacle the Germans had to contend with. Apart from the beating it took from the Allied air arm, the Wehrmacht's retreat from the Balkans was orderly and without serious difficulty.

Having occupied Kotor, Cetinje, and Podgorica with very minor losses, the Partisans made a tremendous fanfare about their victories. In their communiqués they claimed the glory entirely for themselves and ignored the part played by the British brigade because it would have damaged their prestige at home.

So keen were the Partisans on preventing the British from playing too prominent a role in the fighting around Dubrovnik that they controlled all movements of British artillery, sometimes even forbidding those ordered by the British officer commanding artillery. The Partisans simply could not understand the complicated business of indirect fire. What little artillery they had they fired over open sights at a visible enemy. When the British started moving their artillery hither and thither, with no enemy in sight anywhere, it aroused their suspicion.

The Partisans also interfered with British operations in various other ways. For example, after the capture of Kotor the British suggested that it would be much easier to bring in supplies if the Gulf of Kotor were swept of mines. The Partisans apparently agreed. Minesweepers, then at an extreme premium, were ordered up to Kotor, and two British vehicles with signaling equipment set out for a point on the coast to bring them in. The vehicles were held up by the local Partisan commander, who insisted that he could not let them proceed without orders from "Comrade Tito." The British officers remonstrated, but to no avail. The minesweepers hung around off the coast for two days and then were compelled to leave because their services were required elsewhere. About a month later a Partisan vessel struck a mine near Kotor and blew up, with a loss of over 100 lives.

British officers were amazed to find how strong the followers of Mihailović were in Montenegro, despite Partisan repression. The peasants with whom they were quartered—naturally, considered to be loyal Partisans— frequently came creeping up to them at night, made a sign, and then in whispers told them about the Mihailović units in the area or conveyed a message from a local Mihailović commander. Generally, these messages ran something like this: "We know that you must collaborate with the Partisans for political reasons, but we also know that you are much closer in ideology to us than to the Communists, and that ultimately the Communists are your enemies as well as ours. We beg you to try to find some means of arranging for collaboration with us."

Relations between the British forces at Dubrovnik and the Partisan forces were uniformly bad from top to bottom. Under orders from the Partisan command, the British rank-and-file were forbidden to speak to the populace or to Partisans. This alone created enormous ill-feeling. British officers with the brigade sent many reports to headquarters complaining of their treatment by the Partisans—of their duplicity, their restrictions on British movements, their obvious hostility.

In the second half of November, *Grand Strategy* notes, the atmosphere changed:

The British artillery, which by then was operating inland, was ordered to withdraw at once to the neighbourhood of Dubrovnik, on the patently artificial excuse that the Germans were threatening to attack the town; and on the 25th, the Partisans stated over the wireless that no agreement had been signed authorizing the entry of British or American troops into Yugoslavia, 'such as has been signed between Yugoslavia and the Soviet High Command.' Floydforce thereafter found itself in an unenviable position. Despite occasional hints that its services would be required, it was not used again; and after a period of uncertainty, punctuated by complaints of its behaviour or existence, was withdrawn in the middle of January, 1945.[15]

After the landing at Dubrovnik, Field Marshal Alexander obtained permission from Marshal Tito to land a much more substantial force for a joint drive on the retreating German armies. When the British tried to put this agreement into effect, the Partisans refused. Since the Russians had already set a precedent in acting only with Partisan "permission," there was little the British could do but abide by the refusal.

THE FINAL PHASE

Once Tito had been firmly installed in Belgrade, the Red Army brought its offensive to a standstill and shipped its surplus troops to other parts of Europe where they were urgently needed.

The fact that Tito, despite his vaunted following of 400,000 men, had had to call upon the Red Army to liberate Serbia for him was in itself compromising, both nationally and internationally. Realizing this, Tito may well have been anxious to dispense with the aid of the Red Army at the earliest possible opportunity.

What happened after this point is something that the foreign historian must piece together from odd scraps of information. For a brief period after the liberation of Belgrade, Stojan Pribićević, Hubert Harrison, and a few other sympathetic Allied correspondents were allowed into Yugoslavia, under restrictions. But toward the end of November a complete blackout on news coverage was imposed that remained in force for several months, notwithstanding energetic protests from the British and American governments. Why were no foreign journalists allowed in Yugoslavia for this period? Tito had work to accomplish that was better accomplished without witnesses. By the hundreds and thousands, by platoons and companies, "enemies of the working class" were marched out of Belgrade, never to be seen again. It was widely believed that 50,000 to 60,000 residents of the city perished in this way.

As for the British and American military missions still in the country (most of them had been asked to leave before or just after the entry of the Red Army), they were permitted to see even less than previously. Relations between the Partisan and British enlisted men were so strained that it sometimes required a determined effort by the British officers to keep their men from shooting.

CONFIRMATION FROM VESELIN DJURETIĆ

Within the past several years the basic thesis of the McDowell report has received unexpected support from a Yugoslav academic source. In June 1985 Veselin Djuretić, a researcher at the Institute of Balkan Studies in Belgrade, published a book, *The Allies and the Yugoslav War Drama*, which he had originally written as a doctoral thesis. Djuretić's research included access to the files of the Yugoslav government, the Public Record Office in London, and Soviet sources as well. Among other things, Djuretić points out that the Partisan situation reports sent to Moscow made no mention of German expeditions against the Mihailović forces, especially their Montenegrin units, during the late spring and early summer of 1943. He produces a mass of facts to support his contention that during the final phase of the fighting the Partisans invaded Serbia from several directions, bypassing German strong points because their enemies were the Mihailović forces and they were under strict order to avoid anti-German actions.

According to Fitzroy Maclean, "Ratweek" was conceived by the Partisans to harass the German retreat in Serbia. Two entire chapters of Maclean's book *Eastern Approaches* are devoted to portraying the operation in this light. Actually, says Djuretić, its purpose was to make possible an all-out Partisan attack on the Mihailović formations in Serbia. Indeed, the very name "Ratweek" suggests that the operation was meant to destroy domestic military formations that the Communists regarded as traitorous.[16]

Speaking about his motivation in writing the book, Djuretić said, "Historical facts are not set down once and for all. The essence of scholarly research is to question and revise. Speaking up for my book, I speak for the dignity of scholarship and the honor of man."

With the supplies received from Britain and America, and with the muscular backing of the Red Army, Tito was able to retain control of Yugoslavia despite the hostility of the overwhelming mass of the people. In the areas brought under Partisan government, conscription was immediately introduced. In this way Tito was able to build up his army to an estimated figure of 200,000 by the end of 1944 and to 350,000–400,000 by April 1945. The figure officially claimed was 500,000.

The Partisans have offered no official explanation for the failure of this much-vaunted army to budge any significant distance against the Germans for almost six months after the fall of Belgrade. During this period not a single major center was liberated from the Germans, nor was there a single indication of a pro-Partisan uprising in German-held territory. When the Red Army had surrounded Berlin and the German capitulation was a matter of weeks away, the Partisans finally announced the "capture" of Sarajevo. Actually, the German army had vacated Sarajevo as part of a planned general evacuation. After Sarajevo there were a number of sharp clashes between Partisans and Germans, but on the whole the final act of liberation was little more than a route march in the wake of a rapidly retreating and vanquished enemy.

One aspect of the "liberation" of Yugoslavia by the Partisans has been studiously avoided by all those who fawned on Tito during the war and whose writings enjoyed currency both during and after the war: the massacre of Yugoslavs by Tito's forces.

As the war came to an end, tens of thousands of Yugoslavs—men, women, and children, Ustaše, Croatian and Slovenian *domobranci*, followers of Mihailović, and anti-Communist Russians—filled the roads of northern

Yugoslavia, fleeing the Communist hordes behind them. Some of them entered Italy; most of them entered Austria, where they were given refuge near the town of Klagenfurt in Carinthia. The episode has been recorded for history in a chapter aptly called "The Flight of a Nation" by Count Nikolai Tolstoy in his book *The Minister and the Massacres*.

As a result of bureaucratic indifference, timidity, and plain stupidity, the great majority of these refugees were forced back across the Austrian frontier into Yugoslavia and the waiting hands of the Tito forces. This, despite solemn assurances that they would not be sent back, and despite the generally sympathetic attitude of many high-ranking British and Americans. There then took place one of the most brutal massacres of World War II—one in which 26,000 Yugoslavs perished at the hands of Tito's "liberators." Asked about this matter when he was interviewed by George Urban for *Encounter* magazine, Milovan Djilas said:

> The great majority of the people the British forced back from Austria were simple peasants. They had no murders on their hands. They had not been Ustashis or Slovenian "Home Guards." Their only crime was fear of Communism and the reputation of the Communists. Their sole motivation for leaving the country was panic. If the British had handed over to us "Quisling" leaders such as Nedić, and police agents who had collaborated with the Nazis in torturing and killing people, or had done it on their own, there could be no question of the morality of the British action. But this is not what they did. They forced back the lot—and this was profoundly wrong.[17]

The manner of the massacres has been described by Count Tolstoy in a gruesome chapter entitled "The Pit of Kocevje." It is based on the experience of Milan Zajec, a Slovenian *domobran*. According to Zajec, the victims were led out to a pit on the outskirts of Ljubljana, where they were riddled with bullets or dynamited. For five days "sheaves of bodies" fell screaming down into the abyss. "Further dynamiting took place . . . ."[18]

Massacres on a smaller scale also took place. Several thousand anti-Communists, Italians as well as Slovenians, were reported to have been executed and thrown into a pit outside Trieste when the Partisans occupied the city briefly at the end of May 1945. And in every Yugoslav city liberated, just as in Belgrade, platoons and companies of anti-Communist suspects were marched away, never to be seen again.

29

Stations of the Cross

On March 25, 1946, one year and five months after the fall of Belgrade, the Yugoslav press proudly announced to the world that General Mihailović had been taken captive. For one year and five months the Partisan army of 500,000 had been moving heaven and earth to capture Mihailović. Six whole divisions had been assigned to the task. In the course of this manhunt—perhaps the most gigantic in history—many bloody engagements were fought and Tito lost one of his favorite officers, General Drapšin. But the odds against Mihailović were so great that it was a miracle he was able to hold out as long as he did. Certainly, he could not have done so without the active assistance of the Serbian peasantry.

On June 10 he was brought to trial in Belgrade, and on July 15, after a hearing that violated all the rules of civilized legal procedure, Draža Mihailović, together with several of his associates, was sentenced to death. Less than forty-eight hours later, on July 17, he fell before the firing squad.

In the fall of 1945, during an epidemic that gravely affected his troops, Mihailović had contracted typhus. Although he was ill to the point of death, his followers carried him on a stretcher from village to village and mountain to mountain, always on the move to avoid the Partisan army. In early 1946 friends wrote to him from Switzerland, urging that he leave Yugoslavia for a while to recover his strength. His letter of reply, dated February 2, 1946, is worth quoting:

Under no conceivable circumstances will I leave my country and my people. "You cannot carry your country with you on the soles of your shoes," said Danton when he was urged to leave France. I can do no more than repeat those very words today. For I am not Josip Broz Tito, who has nothing in common with this land and these people, so that I should run away at the first sign of danger and seek refuge on some isolated island. On several occasions I have been in desperate straits, surrounded on all sides and without any apparent means of escape. With God's help we have always succeeded in escaping.

You know my strategic purpose: to maintain myself at all costs for the great task which lies ahead. It may be that I shall fall in our sacred cause. But you all know well that this would not mean that the righteous cause for which our nation is fighting would fall with me. For I am only carrying out the will of the people—that is why I commenced the struggle against the occupying forces and later against the communists. I do not doubt for one minute that the sunshine of freedom from Ravna Gora will soon brighten our troubled and suffering motherland.[1]

THE TRIAL OF MIHAILOVIĆ

On April 2, 1946, the State Department addressed a note to the Yugoslav government, informing them that the American officers formerly attached to Mihailović and numerous airmen rescued by him had approached the State Department with a view to giving evidence for Mihailović at his scheduled trial. The note pointed out that Mihailović had "remained in his native land and, without adequate supplies and fighting under the greatest hardships, contributed with his forces materially to the Allied cause." The reply of the Yugoslav government was: "The crimes of Mihailović are too great and too horrible to permit of discussion." When the State Department on May 7 sent a second note along the same lines to the Yugoslav government, the Yugoslav foreign minister informed the press that the note would be "ignored."

In the United States a group of airmen who had been rescued by Mihailović came together and set up "the National Committee of American Airmen to Aid General Mihailović and the Serbian People." Within a fortnight they had succeeded in locating and in obtaining depositions from over 100 of their fellow airmen who had been evacuated from Mihailović territory. On Sunday, April 28, a delegation of 22 airmen left Chicago for Washington, D.C., in a specially chartered plane, rebaptized for the occasion—*Mission for Mihailović*. In their meetings with the State Department the airmen declared that they considered the Mihailović case an affair of both personal conscience and national honor, and they asked that the American government insist on their right to testify in Mihailović's defense.

At the same time, a group of distinguished American citizens came together and formed a "Committee for a Fair Trial for Draja Mihailovich." Their appeal, publicly addressed to the State Department, was signed by five state governors, six senators, and many top-ranking members of the House of Representatives, as well as by jurists, clergymen, and educators of international reputation. Listing the contributions of Mihailović to the Allied cause, the appeal declared that these made his case an inter-Allied rather than an exclusively Yugoslav concern, and called upon the American government to urge that the case be turned over to a special international tribunal and to urge, further, that American personnel be permitted to testify at his trial.

At the request of the Committee for a Fair Trial, four eminent American jurists, Arthur Garfield Hays, Adolph Berle, Charles Poletti, and Theodore Kiendl, constituted themselves into a "Commission of Inquiry." Since it was already apparent that the Belgrade tribunal would refuse to accept the testimony of Allied personnel, the Commission set itself the task of taking the evidence of the American airmen who had been rescued by Mihailović and of American officers who had been attached to either the Partisans or the Home Army forces. For an entire week the Commission sat as airmen and officers testified before it. On May 24 it issued its report, which said in its introduction:

> We are convinced . . . that the testimony given before us is material to the question of the guilt or innocence of General Mihailović as a war criminal and that under standards of justice which have been recognized by civilized nations throughout the years the exclusion of such testimony from the trial of the charges against General Mihailović would be so highly prejudicial as to prevent the possibility of his obtaining a fair trial.[2]

The report of the Commission of Inquiry, together with the 586 pages of testimony taken by it, were forwarded to the Yugoslav government by the State Department. The Belgrade tribunal, as had been foreseen, ignored the report and the mass of evidence accompanying it. But the precedent set by the distinguished jurists, who, in the best tradition of the American bar, voluntarily devoted so much of their time to the cause of historic truth, will live long in the annals of civilized jurisprudence.

The movement for a fair trial for General Mihailović was not as massive in Britain as it was in the United States, but nevertheless it did exist, and it attracted the support of many people of consequence.

In a letter published in *Reynolds News* on May 19, 1946, Winston Churchill said, among other things, that he had "no sympathy with the Communists and crypto-Communists in this country who are endeavoring to deny General Mihailović a fair trial. He it was who took the lead in making the revolution in Yugoslavia which played a part in delaying the German attack on Russia by several weeks."

The (London) *Times* on June 3 published a letter signed by thirteen prominent Britons, including Bernard Cardinal Griffin, Air Chief Marshal Arthur Longmore, John McKinsey, moderator of the Church of Scotland, Gilbert Murray, and Rebecca West.

Although the news was not given publicity at the time, the Foreign Office did transmit to the Belgrade court a deposition on Mihailović's behalf signed by Colonel Bailey and six other British liaison officers who had served with the forces of General Mihailović.

It was freely predicted by those familiar with Moscow techniques that the trial of Mihailović, like previous Moscow trials, would be a political exhibition directed against supposedly unfriendly governments—in this case, Britain and the United States. The prediction was completely borne out by events. "It has become clear," said the Yugoslav prosecutor in summing up, "that British and American military representatives who were at Mihailović's headquarters instigating Mihailović's struggle against the Communists, really supported the collaboration with the occupier in his struggle against the liberation movement of the peoples of Yugoslavia."

The charge that Britain and the United States, while ostensibly supporting the Partisans, were in reality giving underhanded support to the Mihailović forces in their struggle against the Partisans is fantastic to the point of impudence. It is a simple matter of record that Britain and the United States provided the Partisans with 95 percent of the supplies that they received from abroad. It is a matter of record, too, that BBC and The Voice of America converted themselves into virtual propaganda agencies for the Partisans and from early 1943 onward openly waged propaganda warfare against Mihailović. Indeed, when Britain and the United States decided to withdraw support from Mihailović, they bent over backwards to assure the Partisans that Mihailović had, in fact, been completely and finally abandoned: to such grotesque extremes did these countries carry their endeavors that they forbade their own intelligence officers to enter Mihailović territory even for the purpose of gathering vital information on Axis communications.

Colonels Bailey and Hudson of the British mission were accused by the prosecution of encouraging Mihailović to "liquidate" the Partisans. But the official reports of Bailey and Hudson, which are on file with British intelligence, reveal that they strove at all times to bring about an understanding between the two Yugoslav factions, and that their final recommendations envisaged a delimitation, to be enforced by Allied control, of spheres of activity between Mihailović and the Partisans.

Colonel McDowell, chief of the final American mission, was accused by the court of assuring Mihailović that the American government would support the Mihailović command and the Četnik movement exclusively. According to the court, he also assured Mihailović that American troops would occupy Yugoslavia, that there would be an election under Allied control, and that "with Roosevelt's blessings he [Mihailovic] would surely prevail." As Colonel McDowell himself said in a statement under oath to the Commission of Inquiry:

I definitely did not tell General Mihailović that the United States would aid him and his government exclusively. To have done so would have been to convict myself as both liar and fool. It was painfully obvious to all of us around the General that no American nor British aid was available for his cause, while nearly every night we could see or hear American planes coming over to drop supplies and munitions to the Communists.[3]

The pattern followed in previous Moscow trials was confession, confession, confession, without a single variation in motif. The sheer incredibility of this pattern made even the least politically minded Westerner suspicious.

In the Soviet trial of General Okulicki and his associates of the Polish Home Army, it was noted that although the defendants pleaded not guilty in general to the charges against them, they admitted guilt on most specific details. This more subtle pattern of confession and denial endowed the entire trial with an aura of plausibility not enjoyed by previous confessional trials. Only those who had made an intense study of the situation were in a position to know that certain of the specific crimes to which the defendants admitted could not possibly have been committed by them.

The trial of Mihailović followed a somewhat similar pattern. Mihailović pleaded not guilty in general but confessed responsibility for so many of the detailed charges against him that his plea of not guilty lost all meaning. In general, it would appear that while the prosecution permitted him a good deal of latitude in defending his own person, it extracted from him confessions that damned all of his subordinate commanders and the London government, and that simultaneously implicated Britain and the United States.

A standard technique employed in all Moscow trials up until that time was to arraign before the same court as codefendants an amalgam of political opponents who were to be tried for treasonable crimes they never committed and real traitors and quislings who actually were guilty of some of the charges against them. The Belgrade trial did not deviate from this pattern.

On trial at the same time, and therefore arraigned as codefendants, were (1) Mihailović and several other military and political leaders of his movement, (2) members of the Nedić administration and the Nedić State Guard, and (3) sundry other people who had been guilty of collaboration. The purpose of this technique, even where it failed to show any direct connection between Mihailović and his "codefendants," was to associate him in the public's mind with the crimes to which they had confessed.

This technique found its most farcical expression in the evidence of two Belgrade gravediggers, who, testifying for the prosecution, informed the court that during two and a half years of the German occupation they witnessed the execution and burial of almost 20,000 Yugoslav citizens. The inescapable implication here was that Mihailović and his codefendants were in some way jointly responsible for these executions. However, the vast majority of these citizens were executed by the Germans, either for being followers of Mihailović or else in reprisals against the Mihailović movement. This fact is borne out by the many proclamations in the Axis press at the time. One of the gravedigger-witnesses told the court that he had seen 6,000 to 7,000 people shot to death at a concentration camp near Belgrade. This event, which took place on Christmas Eve 1942, was a massacre of Mihailović personnel—as was admitted by so staunch a pro-Tito publicist as Stojan Pribićević. In short, employing the method of the amalgam, the prosecution was attempting to prove that the Mihailović followers had been indirectly responsible for the massacre of 20,000 Mihailović followers!

One of the prosecution witnesses, Jovanović, testified that he had acted as interpreter for four American airmen picked up by the Četniks; that these airmen had been stripped to the waist and deprived of their revolvers and watches; that they had been compelled to join the Četniks against their will; and that they were now listed as missing by the US Air Force. Jovanović did indeed act as interpreter for the four Americans named by him. But on every other point he perjured himself. The four American airmen—Sergeants O'Connell, Hunt, Leber, and Wink—were alive and happy in the US, and they testified that they had not been stripped to the waist or deprived of their possessions, and that they had voluntarily joined the Četniks, from whom they had experienced only the best of treatment. How many other prosecution witnesses perjured themselves in this manner we have no way of knowing.

The meeting between Colonel McDowell and Herr Stärker has been dealt with in Chapter 28. On this point Mihailović maintained stoutly that it was McDowell who had arranged the meeting, and that the sole purpose was to discuss a German surrender. He denied point-blank the declaration of a prosecution witness that he and Colonel McDowell had met with the Gestapo and Herr Neubacher, Hitler's special envoy, and that Colonel McDowell had urged Neubacher to give arms to the Četniks. In the United States Colonel McDowell testified that the story of the meeting between himself, Mihailović, and Neubacher was a complete fabrication. He pointed out that although he would have liked to meet with Neubacher to pursue his discussions with Stärker, the meeting never took place for the simple reason that he did not receive a green light for it. But despite Colonel McDowell's testimony, the court ruled that the evidence had definitely established the facts of the meeting between Mihailović, McDowell, and Neubacher.

The Mihailović who testified against himself in the Belgrade court spoke in a confused, contradictory, utterly abnormal, and sometimes cryptic manner, so that many of those who knew him well expressed the opinion that he simply did not sound like the old Mihailović.

Frequently he complained of extreme weariness. At one point he said,

"I wish you would not torture me with rhetoric. I am a soldier and too weary mentally to remember." On another occasion he said, "I am very tired. Sometimes I am so tired that I say 'yes' when I mean 'no.' Even now I might say 'yes.' " It is impossible to accept as rational and voluntary Mihailović's declaration that he disapproved "in principle" of having American airmen and liaison officers testify in his behalf, even though he knew that "they could add much to my defense."

The procedure followed by the Belgrade court was an obscene parody of juridical procedure as it is understood by the civilized world.

When Dragić Joksimović, counsel for Mihailović, attempted to read a cable from nine American officers and airmen offering their testimony, the presiding judge stopped him with this admonition: "It is absolutely unnecessary to read the cable." When Joksimović persevered, the judge rang the bell and admonished him again, "I warn Mr. Joksimović that he must adhere to the order of the court." Approving the attitude of the judge, the prosecution said that "for proof of collaboration so many documents and witnesses are available in Yugoslavia it is unnecessary to call for others." In short, according to the presiding judge of the court, *there were so many witnesses for the prosecution that it was pointless to call any witnesses for the defense*!

When Joksimović requested that Mihailović be permitted to read the British, American, and Russian press in order to follow his case better, the prosecution opposed this with a sneering remark: "Next we shall be asked that Mihailović be allowed to go walking in the streets of Belgrade." The presiding judge of the court, it goes without saying, upheld the prosecution.

When Joksimović protested against the court president's decision to exclude General Mihailović from the court while his codefendant, Stevan Moljević, was giving evidence, the judge replied, "This is not a normal case!"

The presiding judge spoke more truly than he knew.

Mihailović was tried for the "crime" of opposing the Communist Party by a court that was subject to the discipline of the Communist Party. He was tried by a court that had no hesitation about inducing witnesses for the prosecution to perjure themselves in order to build up a case against Mihailović. He was tried under a totalitarian regime whose previous declarations would have made it a state crime for any Yugoslav citizen to testify for the defense.

Mihailović's closing statement greatly impressed the corps of foreign correspondents who covered the trial. The special correspondent for *The* (London) *Times* reported on Mihailović's closing statement in these terms:

At last the deserted man, who for 30 days has seemed so incoherent and indeterminate, acquired clear character. He spoke for over four hours without oratory, without rancor towards political opponents or private enemies, lucidly and in detail. It was the professional soldier presenting a military report, compelling because of its simplicity.

Throughout, General Mihailović's care for detail was astonishing . . . He went through action after action, place by place, until the time when the British mission left him [in 1944].

What he said had the ring of truth, and at least it will be among the documents which history must sift. It was pitch dark when he ended. Quietly folding his papers, he said: "I wanted nothing for myself . . . I never wanted the old Yugoslavia, but I had a difficult legacy . . . I had against me a competitive organization, the Communist Party, which seeks its aims without compromise. I was faced with changes in my own Government, and accused of connections with every possible secret service, enemy and allied. I believed I was on the right road and called on any foreign journalist or Red Army mission to visit me and see everything. But fate was merciless to me when it threw me into this maelstrom.

I wanted much, I started much, but the gale of the world carried away me and my work.[4]

Among the most important contributions of the testimonies by the Allied officers and rescued airmen before the Commission for a Fair Trial were the many accounts of the reverence and affection with which Mihailović was regarded by the Serbian peasants. The Serbs were, without challenge, one of the most stubbornly anti-Nazi peoples in Europe. This is why Mihailović himself refused to surrender to the occupiers in April 1941, and why he enjoyed such a widespread popular allegiance. His followers not only hated the Nazis; with equal passion they hated the Serbian collaborators, the followers of Ljotić and Pećanac; and they regarded General Milan Nedić with pity and contempt. As to who was collaborating and who was resisting, the Serbian peasants could not be fooled. In their eyes, as the British and American liaison officers and rescued airmen have attested, Mihailović became the personification of national resistance to both the occupiers and the Communists. To those who lived through this time and who still survive in Yugoslavia or abroad, he will always be *Chicha Draža*—"Uncle Draža"—a national leader in the mold of Serbia's legendary heroes. Nobody has expressed this more eloquently or courageously than did Dragić Joksimović, Mihailovic's counsel, when, on July 12, before the end of the trial, he described Mihailović to the court as "the mountain czar of the Serbian people." The policies he pursued, with all their strengths and all their weaknesses, constituted a true reflection of the aspirations and desires of the Serbian masses. To a very large degree they also reflected the aspirations of the Yugoslav peasant masses generally.

Epilogue

It is an irony of history that Tito should have been the creation of the capitalist democracies, Great Britain and the United States.

His movement, even at its height, was a minority movement that had won for itself the active hostility of the mass of the Serb, Croat, and Slovene peoples. By arming this movement, by providing it with the services of BBC and American radio, by converting the democratic press into a propaganda agency for it, by sending Allied officers into Yugoslavia to be used as propaganda exhibits in its recruiting efforts, and finally, by cloaking this movement in their own enormous moral authority, Great Britain and the United States made themselves directly responsible for Tito's rise to power.

COULD THE ALLIES HAVE ENFORCED A COMPROMISE?

There is good reason to believe that by pursuing a different policy the Allies could have forced a truce in the civil war in Yugoslavia and then imposed conditions to ensure democratic elections after the liberation.

By the fall of 1943 Mihailović was more disposed than before to compromise. In December 1943 Mihailović appealed to Brigadier Armstrong, chief of the British military mission, asking British intervention to arrange a meeting between his delegates and Tito's somewhere in the Sàndžak for the purpose of terminating hostilities and arranging cooperation between the two movements. In January 1943, after the congress of Ba, Dr. Živko Topalović, the new chairman of Mihailović's Central National Committee, addressed an impressively reasoned memorandum to the Allied authorities, arguing in favor of separate operational zones of activity for the Mihailović and Partisan armies. He said it was the duty of the Allies to impose such an agreement.

Once it was signed, he said, the agreement could be fitted into a general plan of action for the Balkans.

It may be said that the recommendations of both the British and American military missions with Mihailović were substantially along the lines suggested by Dr. Topalović. The British and American officers were convinced of the feasibility of the proposal. If operational zones for the two armies had been delineated, with a neutral area in between; if a sufficiently large corps of observers had been attached to each army to keep tabs on the activities of all major units; if both sides had been informed that the first side responsible for hostilities would receive no further Allied assistance—given these conditions, the Allies might have succeeded in regulating the Yugoslav civil war. This position could have been further reinforced by an agreement for a joint Anglo-American-Russian occupation for a specified period after the liberation, ending with national elections supervised by an Anglo-American-Russian commission. Logistically, such a solution would not have been feasible before the Italians surrendered. But afterward, in October and November 1943, the Allies did have the means to move a substantial body of observers into Yugoslavia. Had they made a serious effort to enforce such a solution, the civil war might have been terminated and Yugoslavia saved for democracy. The Great Powers, however, saw fit to do otherwise.

One argument offered against this approach to the Tito-Mihailović problem appeared plausible, on the surface. Whatever merits the proposal may have had earlier, it was argued, the Mihailović movement was so weakened by the battle of Neretva and the Partisan movement so strengthened both by the outcome of that battle and by its gains from the Italian capitulation that Tito could not realistically be expected to come to terms with the proposal.

The myth that the Partisan movement inflicted a fatal wound on the Mihailović forces at Neretva constituted a favorite theme of the Partisan propaganda machine, and it was widely believed. William Deakin expressed this conviction in the course of a long conversation I had with him over dinner in London. I was not surprised, because Deakin had had no contact with Mihailović's Yugoslavia.

That the battle of Neretva was anything but a fatal wound was demonstrated by the remarkable record of anti-German activities put together by the Mihailović forces from late August to October 15, 1943 (see Chapter 15). The loss of a battle is not the loss of a war, and there can be no question that the best of the Mihailović officers regarded Neretva as a lost battle—a serious loss, to be sure—but certainly not decisive for the outcome of the war. The argument that Neretva was catastrophic for the Mihailović forces was also challenged by the repeated statements of Brigadier Armstrong and Colonel Bailey toward the close of 1943 that in Serbia the Mihailović forces were everywhere paramount and the Tito forces amounted to nothing. The final argument against the thesis that Neretva constituted a fatal wound was that the Mihailović forces, although starved for supplies, were able to hold the Partisan army at the gates to Serbia up until the invasion of the mighty Red Army.

The enforcement of a compromise would have required some very hard-nosed negotiations for the British and Americans, but at that time a more hard-nosed attitude on the part of the Western Allies would certainly have been in order; moreover, we had the means at that time to make a tougher approach feasible. For all practical purposes this window of opportunity was finally closed when, in quick succession, we did nothing to oppose Moscow's blatant betrayal of the Warsaw uprising; nothing to oppose Moscow's invasion of Bulgaria at the end of August 1944, when Bulgaria had already declared war on the Axis powers; and nothing in Yugoslavia to assist those forces that were committed to saving their country from a Communist take-over. Although our record of assistance should have entitled us to a major say in Yugoslav affairs, we slavishly kowtowed to Tito even when his movement had been greatly weakened by the Nazi capture of his headquarters at Drvar.

But all this is water over the dam, reflections on things that could have been done but for some reason were not. Churchill's blunder in Yugoslavia condemned the peoples of that country to more than forty-five years of Communist rule—leading to nothing but impoverishment and demoralization and the sharpening of national antagonisms. This is a fact that the most inveterate pro-Titoites in the Western nations would have to admit. Indeed, Yugoslavia has now been caught up in the same kind of tumultuous change as the rest of Communist Europe. If Tito had been alive in 1989, the chances are that he would have been the object of the same kind of popular uprisings that brought about the downfall of Erich Honecker in East Germany and Nicolae Ceauşescu in Rumania.

It is not merely that the people in Yugoslavia are openly anti-Communist, but they are becoming increasingly anti-Tito. The de-Titoization of the country is well advanced. The Serbian media, in particular, have been merciless to what little remains of the Tito legend. Critical articles are being written by an army of "revisionists," including noted historians, investigative journalists, former party and state officials, and even Tito's official biographers, such as Vladimir Dedijer. Legislative proposals have been offered that would retroactively put an end to all aspects of the Tito personality cult. The few "defenders of the faith" who remain are clearly on the defensive. Almost pathetically, they argue that all controversies about the life and work of Josip Broz Tito should now be left to history's judgment—as though almost fifty years after the events we were not in a position to make historical judgments.

In reflecting on the tragedy of Mihailović it is, of course, a source of comfort to know that the monstrous injustice of which he was the victim is, many years after his trial and execution, giving way to a new appreciation of the honored role he played in World War II.

The final nail in Tito's historical coffin was driven home at the Fourteenth Extraordinary Congress of the League of Communists of Yugoslavia, which convened in Belgrade from January 20 to 22, 1990. Ten years after his death the meeting of the once monolithic party he bequeathed to his country broke up in complete disorder. The gathering dispersed in gloom, leaving unanswered the question of whether it will ever reconvene. The authoritive daily newspaper *Borba* said on its front page that the Communist Party of Yugoslavia "no longer exists."

There is a lesson to be learned from the tragic story of General Mihailović. Although the international situation we confront today is far less ominous than it has been for several decades, no one has yet suggested that we have now reached the promised land and that we can therefore safely do away with all internal security. It is my firm hope that this story of the Klugmann operation in SOE Cairo will result in a wide-ranging investigation to establish what was fact and what was myth in the legend of Josip Broz Tito, how much influence Klugmann actually had in SOE Cairo, what papers he wrote for others, what views he expressed in them, who cooperated with Klugmann and how, and whether there was any international coordinating machinery. Only in this way can the uncertainties be eliminated and the future integrity of Western intelligence operations be served.

But there is a more basic lesson to be learned. There can be no doubt that recent events in Yugoslavia have been like ashes in the mouths of the many men of intelligence and goodwill who supported Tito at the time because, like Churchill, they were carried away by stories of martial valor. Martial valor by itself is all very good, but it says nothing about the nature of the cause for which it is exercised. The Nazis in their attacks on Western countries, and in their long retreat from the Soviet Union, displayed great martial valor. But no one will question that they served a profoundly evil purpose.

One can only pray that divine providence will protect the free nations of the world from the kind of coalition of revolutionary extremists and utopian conservatives, bewitched by demonstrations of martial valor, that resulted in the imposition of the Tito dictatorship on the Yugoslav peoples.

Bibliography

Amery, Julian. *Approach March: A Venture in Autobiography.* London: Hutchinson of London, 1973.

Auty, Phyllis, and Richard Clogg, eds. *British Policy towards Wartime Resistance in Yugoslavia and Greece.* London: The Macmillan Press, 1975.

Barker, Elisabeth. *British Policy in South-East Europe in the Second World War.* London: The Macmillan Press, 1976.

Beevor, J. G. *SOE: Recollections and Reflections 1940–45.* London: Bodley Head, 1981.

Beloff, Nora. *Tito's Flawed Legacy.* London: Victor Gollancz, 1985.

Bennett, Ralph. *Ultra and Mediterranean Strategy.* New York: William Morrow and Company, 1989.

Blunt, Anthony. "From Bloomsbury to Marxism." *Studio International*, vol. 186, no. 960. November 1973.

Boyle, Andrew. *The Climate of Treason.* London: Hutchinson & Co., 1979. Rev. ed. London: Coronet Books, Hodder and Stoughton, 1980.

Churchill, Winston S. *The Second World War.* Vols. 5 and 6 of 6 vols. Boston: Houghton Mifflin Co., 1948–1953.

Clissold, Stephen, ed. *Yugoslavia and the Soviet Union 1939–1973: A Documentary Survey.* London: Oxford University Press, 1975.

Davidson, Basil. *Special Operations Europe.* London: Victor Gollancz, 1981.

Deacon, Richard. *'C': A Biography of Sir Maurice Oldfield.* London: Macdonald, 1984.

Deakin, F. W. D. *The Embattled Mountain.* London: Oxford University Press, 1971.

Deroc, M. *British Special Operations Explored: Yugoslavia in Turmoil 1941–1943 and the British Response.* Boulder, Colo.: East European Monographs, 1988. Distributed by Columbia University Press, New York.

Djilas, Milovan. *Wartime.* New York: Harcourt Brace Jovanovich, 1977.

Eden, Anthony. *The Memoirs of Anthony Eden.* Vol. 3 of 3 vols. Boston: Houghton Mifflin Co., 1965.

Ehrman, John. *Grand Strategy.* Vol. 6 of 6 volumes, October 1944–August 1945. London: Her Majesty's Stationery Office, 1956.

Felman, Richard L. "Mihailovich and I." *Serbian Democratic Forum*, October 1972.

Foot, M. R. D. *SOE: An Outline History of the Special Operations Executive, 1940–46.* London: BBC, 1984.

Ford, Thomas Kirkwood, Jr. *Pawns and Powerbrokers: OSS and the Yugoslav Resistance During the Second World War.* Ann Arbor, Mich.: University Microfilms International, 1980.

Fotitch, Constantin. *The War We Lost.* New York: The Viking Press, 1948.

Hinsley, F. H., et al., eds. *British Intelligence in the Second World War.* Vol. 3. London: Her Majesty's Stationery Office, 1988.

Hitler[, Adolf, and Benito] Mussolini. *Lettere e documenti.* Milan: Rizzoli, 1946.

Huot, Louis. *Guns for Tito.* New York: L. B. Fischer, 1945.

Inks, James M. *Eight Bailed Out.* Ed. Lawrence Klingman. New York: W. W. Norton & Co., 1954.

Ivanović, Vane. *LX: Memoirs of a Jugoslav.* New York: Harcourt Brace Jovanovich, 1977.

Jukić, Ilija. *The Fall of Yugoslavia.* Trans. Dorian Cooke. New York: Harcourt Brace Jovanovich, 1974.

Karchmar, Lucien. *Draža Mihailović and the Rise of the Četnik Movement, 1941–1942.* 2 vols. Ann Arbor, Mich.: University Microfilms International, 1973.

Kardelj, Edvard. "The Struggle for Recognition of the National Liberation Movement of Yugoslavia." *Macedonian Review,* Skoplje, Macedonia, vol. 11, no. 2, 1981.

Kemp, Peter. *No Colours or Crest.* London: Cassell, 1958.

Kisch, Richard. *The Days of the Good Soldiers.* London: Journeyman Press, 1985.

Knezevich, Zhivan L. *Why the Allies Abandoned the Yugoslav Army of General Mihailovich.* N.p. Mimeographed documentation. Washington, D. C.: Library of Congress, 1945.

Kriegstagebuch des Oberkommandos der Wehrmacht, 1940–1945. Frankfurtam Main: Bernard & Graefe, 1965.

Lawrence, Christie. *Irregular Adventure.* London: Faber & Faber, 1947.

Lees, Michael. *Special Operations Executed.* London: William Kimber, 1986.

Maclean, Fitzroy. *Eastern Approaches.* London: J. Cape, 1949. Reprint. New York: Atheneum, 1984.

Malaparte, Curzio. *Kaputt.* Translated from the Italian by Cesare Foligno. New York: E. P. Dutton & Co., 1946.

Martin, David. *Ally Betrayed.* New York: Prentice-Hall, 1946.

———. *Patriot or Traitor: The Case of General Mihailovich.* Stanford: Hoover Institution Press, 1978.

Neubacher, Hermann. *Sonderauftrag Sudost, 1940–1945.* Gottingen: Musterschmidt-Verlag, 1956.

Pavlowitch, Stevan K. *Yugoslavia.* New York: Praeger Publishers, 1971.

———. "London-Moscow through the Fog of Yugoslavia's Wartime Drama: Djuretić's Controversial History." Two-part article in *Storia delle relazioni internazionali.* Italy. Issues 2 and 3, 1987.

Peter II, King of Yugoslavia. *A King's Heritage.* London: Cassell, 1955.

Pincher, Chapman. *Their Trade Is Treachery.* London: Sidgwick & Jackson, 1981.

Rendel, Sir George. *The Sword and the Olive.* London: John Murray, 1957.

Ritter, Harry Ray, Jr. *Hermann Neubacher and the German Occupation of the Balkans, 1940–1945.* Ann Arbor, Mich.: University Microfilms International, 1969.

Roberts, Walter R. *Tito, Mihailović and the Allies, 1941/1945.* New Brunswick, N. J.: Rutgers University Press, 1973.

Rootham, Jasper. *Miss Fire.* London: Chatto & Windus, 1946.

Seton-Watson, Hugh. "Reflections of a Learner." *Government and Opposition.* London: fall 1980.

Stafford, David. *Camp X.* New York: Dodd, Mead & Co., 1987.

Straight, Michael. *After Long Silence*. New York: W.W. Norton & Co., 1983.

Sudjić, Milivoj J. *Yugoslavia in Arms*. London: L. Drummond, 1942.

Sweet-Escott, Bickham. *Baker Street Irregular*. London: Methuen & Co., 1965.

Tito, Josip Broz. *The Yugoslav Peoples Fight to Live*. New York: The United Committee of South-Slavic Americans, 1944.

Tolstoy, Nikolai. *The Minister and the Massacres*. London: Century Hutchinson, 1986.

The Trial of Dragoljub-Draža Mihailović. Belgrade: Union of the Journalists' Associations of the Federative People's Republic of Yugoslavia, 1946.

Urban, George. Interview with Milovan Djilas. *Encounter*. London, December 1979.

Vitou, Maurice. "The Truth about Mihailovich? IV." *World Review*. London: Hulton Press, August 1945.

Warlimont, Walter. *Inside Hitler's Headquarters, 1939–1945*. New York: Frederick A. Praeger, 1964.

Wheeler, Mark C. *Britain and the War for Yugoslavia, 1940–1943*. Boulder, Colo. East European Monographs, 1980. Distributed by Columbia University Press, New York.

Woodward, E. L. *British Foreign Policy in the Second World War*. London: Her Majesty's Stationery Office, 1962.

Wright, Peter. *Spy Catcher*. New York: Viking Penguin, 1987.

Notes

British sources identified in the following notes as the Foreign Office (FO), the Prime Minister's Office (PM) or the Premier (PREM) and the War Office (WO) are available in the British Public Record Office, Kew, Richmond, Surrey, England.

OSS documentation on Mihailović was received in unindexed form in response to the author's Freedom of Information Act (FOIA) request for copies of all documents pertaining to Mihailović. The World War II section of the National Archives several years ago received hundreds of linear feet of World War II documents from the CIA. These are still being indexed and catalogued.

Thesis and Introduction

1. Vane Ivanović, *LX: Memoirs of a Jugoslav* (New York: Harcourt Brace Jovanovich, 1977), p. 247. A similar observation was offered by Sir George Rendel, British ambassador to the Yugoslav government in exile until August 1943, in his book *The Sword and the Olive* (London: John Murray, 1957), p. 228, in which he describes "the full weight of left-wing influence in England [that in 1943 was] being thrown on Tito's side."

2. Winston S. Churchill, *The Second World War*, 6 vols. (Boston: Houghton Mifflin Co., 1948–1953), vol. 5, p. 293.

3. WO 208/3103. Appendix A, p. 4.

4. WO 202/155, p. 1.

5. Interview with Major Archie Jack in La Collanche, Thorens-Glières, France, October 1984.

6. Churchill, *The Second World War*, vol. 5, pp. 477–478.

7. Churchill, *The Second World War*, vol. 6, p. 92.

8. E. L. Woodward, *British Foreign Policy in the Second World War* (London: Her Majesty's Stationery Office, 1962), p. 346.

9. Christie Lawrence, *Irregular Adventure* (London: Faber & Faber, 1947), p. 147.

Chapter 1

1. Andrew Boyle, *The Climate of Treason* (London: Hutchinson & Co., 1979; Coronet Books, Hodder and Stoughton, 1980), p. 510.

2. Boyle, *The Climate of Treason*, p. 75.

3. Richard Kisch, *The Days of the Good Soldiers* (London: Journeyman Press, 1985).

4. Richard Deacon, *'C': A Biography of Sir Maurice Oldfield* (London: Macdonald, 1984), p. 37.

5. Chapman Pincher, *Their Trade Is Treachery* (London: Sidgwick & Jackson, 1981), pp. 127–141.

6. Michael Straight, *After Long Silence* (New York: W. W. Norton & Co., 1983), pp. 72–73.

7. Straight, *After Long Silence*, p. 73.

8. Anthony Blunt, "From Bloomsbury to Marxism," *Studio International*, vol. 186, no. 960, November 1973, p. 164.

9. Hugh Seton-Watson, "Reflections of a Learner," *Government and Opposition* (London: fall 1980), p. 520.

10. Kenneth Greenlees, letter to the editor, *Special Forces Club* (London) *Newsletter*.

11. Interview with Kenneth Greenlees in London, November 1976.

12. Interview with Michael Straight in Bethesda, Maryland, November 1987.

Chapter 2

No notes.

Chapter 3

1. Julian Amery, *Approach March: A Venture in Autobiography* (London: Hutchinson of London, 1973), p. 227.

2. Amery, *Approach March*, p. 227.

3. Stevan K. Pavlowitch, *Yugoslavia* (New York: Praeger Publishers, 1971), pp. 108–114.

Chapter 4

1. Stephen Clissold, ed., *Yugoslavia and the Soviet Union 1939–1973: A Documentary Survey* (London: Oxford University Press, 1975), p. 127.

2. Milovan Djilas, *Wartime* (New York: Harcourt Brace Jovanovich, 1977), p. 244.

3. Djilas, *Wartime*, p. 149.

4. Djilas, *Wartime*, p. 149.

5. Edvard Kardelj, "The Struggle for Recognition of the National Liberation Movement of Yugoslavia," *Macedonian Review* (Skoplje, Macedonia), vol. 11, no. 2, 1981, p. 190.

6. *The Economist*, London, May 29, 1943, p. 1.

7. For much of the information contained in this chronology I am indebted to Walter R. Roberts's heavily documented study *Tito, Mihailović and the Allies, 1941/1945* (New Brunswick, N. J.: Rutgers University Press, 1973).

8. Constantin Fotitch, *The War We Lost* (New York: The Viking Press, 1948), p. 184.

Chapter 5

1. Milivoj J. Sudjić, *Yugoslavia in Arms* (London: L. Drummond, 1942), p. 74.

2. Nora Beloff, *Tito's Flawed Legacy* (London: Victor Gollancz, 1985), p. 62.

3. Amery, *Approach March*, pp. 179–180.

4. The author was a close friend of Dr. Dimitrov's in Washington and met with him frequently.

5. The author saw a good deal of Michael Padev in Washington in the post–World War II period, when he served as a foreign-affairs writer for the Copley Press. He was always apologetic for his wartime biography of Tito, admitting frankly that he knew next to nothing about the subject.

6. Lucien Karchmar, *Draža Mihailović and the Rise of the Četnik Movement, 1941–1942*, 2 vols., Ph.D. dissertation (Ann Arbor, Mich.: University Microfilms International, 1973), vol. 1, p. 73.

7. Karchmar, *Draža Mihailović*, vol. 1, p. 77.

8. M. Deroc, *British Special Operations Explored: Yugoslavia in Turmoil 1941–1943 and the British Response* (Boulder, Colo.: East European Monographs, 1988, distributed by Columbia University Press, New York), pp. 192–193.

Chapter 6

1. Ilija Jukić, *The Fall of Yugoslavia*, trans. Dorian Cooke (New York: Harcourt Brace Jovanovich, 1974), p. 107.

2. *Kriegstagebuch des Oferkommandos der Wehrmacht, 1940–45* (Frankfurt am Main: Bernard & Graefe, 1965), vol. II, 991ff., as quoted by Roberts in *Tito, Mihailović and the Allies*, p. 331.

3. FO 371/37582, p. 80.

4. FO 371/37582, p. 52.

5. Jasper Rootham, *Miss Fire* (London: Chatto & Windus, 1946), p. 144.

6. Rootham, *Miss Fire*, p. 206.

7. *Jugoslavja Turisticka Enciklopedija* (Belgrade: State Publishing House, 1959), p. 150.

8. FO 371/37584.

9. Beloff, *Tito's Flawed Legacy*, p. 75.

10. Harry Ray Ritter, Jr., *Hermann Neubacher and the German Occupation of the Balkans, 1940–1945* (Ann Arbor, Mich.: University Microfilms International, 1969), p. 203.

11. Ritter, *Hermann Neubacher*, p. 204.

12. Ritter, *Hermann Neubacher*, p. 218.

Chapter 7

1. Interview with Lieutenant Joe Veselinovich, Chicago, January 1946.

2. Curzio Malaparte, *Kaputt*, translated from the Italian by Cesare Foligno (New York: E. P. Dutton & Co., 1946), p. 266.

3. Josip Broz Tito, *The Yugoslav Peoples Fight to Live* (New York: The United Committee of South-Slavic Americans, 1944), p. 30.

4. The author interviewed Ante Jerić for the first time after he arrived in London. He later talked with him on a number of occasions in London and New York.

5. WO 202/131, September 18, 1943.

6. The author interviewed Dr. Živko Topalović in Rome in 1946 and recieved some key documents from him.

7. The author interviewed Vladimir Predavec for the first time in Geneva in September 1946 and subsequently in London and New York.

8. Article in *The Manchester Guardian*, October 16, 1945.

Chapter 8

1. Deroc, *British Special Operations Explored*, pp. 175–177.
2. This information was confirmed in an interview with Zvonko Vučković in Chicago in June 1979.
3. Maurice Vitou, "The Truth About Mihailovich? IV," *World Review* (London: Hulton Press, August 1945), pp. 31–37.
4. Remarks of Colonel Duane Hudson at a conference at St. Anthony College, Oxford, December 1962.
5. Tito, *The Yugoslav Peoples Fight*, pp. 13–14.
6. Tito, *The Yugoslav Peoples Fight*, p. 14.
7. Tito, *The Yugoslav Peoples Fight*, p. 23.
8. WO 208/2018A.
9. WO 208/2018A.
10. Interview with Joe Veselinovich in Chicago, January 1946.
11. Vitou, "The Truth about Mihailovich? IV," pp. 31–37.
12. Conversation with Dr. George M. Dimitrov in Washington, D. C., in January 1970.
13. Reports of Lt. Colonel Linn M. Farish, OSS documentation on Mihailović, "Operation Balkans," National Archives, Washington, D.C.

Chapter 9

1. Pavlowitch, *Yugoslavia*, p. 114.
2. Tito, *The Yugoslav Peoples Fight*, p. 18.
3. Tito, *The Yugoslav Peoples Fight*, p. 19.
4. Records of the German Foreign Office in the National Archives, Washington, D. C., Microfilm T-120, Roll 615(245–266), as quoted in Roberts, *Tito, Mihailović and the Allies*, p. 104.
5. Roberts, *Tito, Mihailović and the Allies*, p. 105.
6. Interview with Colonel Duane Hudson in London, October 1977.
7. David Martin, *Ally Betrayed* (New York: Prentice-Hall, 1946), p. 215.
8. Martin, *Ally Betrayed*, p. 216.
9. Fotitch, *The War We Lost*, p. 222.
10. Beloff, *Tito's Flawed Legacy*, p. 78.
11. Conversations with Elisabeth Barker on October 1 and October 15, 1984, in Kew Gardens, England.
12. One of the last people to see Pavle Djurišić before his execution was Predrag Cemović, today an engineer in Chicago. The author has tape-recorded an interview with Cemović describing Djurišić's capture and execution.
13. James M. Inks, *Eight Bailed Out*, ed. Lawrence Klingman (New York: W. W. Norton & Co., 1954).
14. FO 371/37584, April 6, 1943, p. 2.

Chapter 10

1. Djilas, *Wartime*, p. 4.
2. WO 202/162, March 17, 1943, p. 2.
3. Roberts, *Tito, Mihailović and the Allies*, p. 131.
4. Roberts, *Tito, Mihailović and the Allies*, p. 67.

Chapter 11

1. Deroc, *British Special Operations Explored*, pp. 188–189.
2. Deroc, *British Special Operations Explored*, p. 189.
3. Quoted in *Trials of War Criminals before the Nuremberg Military Tribunals*, vol. XI (Washington, D. C.: U. S. Government Printing Office, 1950), p. 1016.
4. Martin, *Ally Betrayed*, p. 149; from *Il Momento*, Milan, September 30, 1945, translated version.
5. Roberts, *Tito, Mihailović and the Allies*, p. 108.
6. Mark C. Wheeler, *Britain and the War for Yugoslavia, 1940–1943* (Boulder, Colo.: East European Monographs, 1980), distributed by Columbia University Press, New York, pp. 227–228.
7. Hermann Neubacher, *Sonderauftrag Sudost, 1940–1945* (Gottingen: Musterschmidt-Verlag, 1956), p. 170; Walter Warlimont, *Inside Hitler's Headquarters, 1939–1945* (New York: Frederick A. Praeger, 1964), p. 469; and Records of Headquarters, German Armed Forces High Command, National Archives, Washington, D.C., Microcopy T-77-781-5507576.
8. *The Trial of Dragoljub-Draža Mihailović* (Belgrade: Union of the Journalists' Associations of the Federative People's Republic of Yugoslavia, 1946), p. 268.

Chapter 12

1. For this information about Klugmann and other facts about the personnel of SOE Cairo, the author is indebted to C. M. Woods, previous SOE Adviser, Foreign and Commonwealth Office, London, letter dated November 9, 1984.
2. M. R. D. Foot, *SOE: An Outline History of the Special Operations Executive, 1940–46* (London: BBC, 1984), p. 9.
3. Foot, *SOE: An Outline History*, p. 46.
4. Bickham Sweet-Escott, *Baker Street Irregular* (London: Methuen & Co., 1965), p. 172.
5. Letter from C. M. Woods, SOE Adviser, November 9, 1984.
6. Basil Davidson, *Special Operations Europe* (London: Victor Gollancz, 1981), p. 86.
7. Davidson, *Special Operations Europe*, p. 116.
8. Davidson, *Special Operations Europe*, p. 117.
9. Davidson, *Special Operations Europe*, p. 93.
10. Davidson, *Special Operations Europe*, p. 93.
11. Basil Davidson, *The Liberation of Guiné: Aspects of an African Revolution* (Harmonsworth: Penguin, 1971); *Black Star: A View of the Life and Times of Kwame Nkrumah* (London: Allen Lane, 1973); and *Southern Africa: The New Politics of Revolution* (with Joe Slovo and Anthony R. Wilkinson) (Harmonsworth: Penguin, 1976).
12. Peter Kemp, *No Colours or Crest* (London: Cassell, 1958), p. 74.
13. Davidson, *Special Operations Europe*, p. 123.
14. Comments made by Brigadier Fitzroy Maclean at a conference sponsored by the History Department of the School of Slavonic and East European Studies at the University of London in July 1973, as quoted in *British Policy towards Wartime Resistance in Yugoslavia and Greece*, edited by Phyllis Auty and Richard Clogg (London: The Macmillan Press, 1975), pp. 223–227.
15. Auty, *British Policy towards Wartime Resistance*, p. 224.
16. Conversation with Constantine Brown, syndicated columnist, in Rome, November 1961.

17. David Stafford, *Camp X* (New York: Dodd, Mead & Co., 1987).

18. Stafford, *Camp X*, p. 170.

19. Stafford, *Camp X*, p. 170.

20. Peter Wright, *Spy Catcher* (New York: Viking Penguin, 1987), p. 326.

21. Stafford, *Camp X*, p. 174.

22. Stafford, *Camp X*, p. 174.

23. Davidson, *Special Operations Europe*, p. 100.

Chapter 13

1. F. W. D. Deakin, *The Embattled Mountain* (London: Oxford University Press, 1971), pp. 130–131.

2. Deroc, *British Special Operations Explored*, p. 207.

3. Deroc, *British Special Operations Explored*, p. 212.

4. Deroc, *British Special Operations Explored*, p. 211.

5. Deroc, *British Special Operations Explored*, p. 214.

6. Interview with Colonel Duane Hudson in London, November 1977.

7. Interview with Colonel Duane Hudson in London, November 1977.

8. FO 371/37590.

9. Interview with Brigadier Charles D. Armstrong in Camberley, Surrey, November 1977.

10. FO 371/37591.

11. Fitzroy Maclean, *Eastern Approaches* (New York: Atheneum, 1984), p. 313; reprint of book (London: J. Cape, 1949).

12. WO 208/2018A. Appendix 3, p. 6, to report of Colonel S. W. Bailey, April 1944.

13. Information from the Right Honorable Julian Amery, MP.

14. WO 202/145, November 18, 1943.

Chapter 14

1. WO 202/132A.

2. FO 371/37616.

3. Letter to author from Sir Douglas Howard, May 31, 1978.

4. Deakin, *The Embattled Mountain*, pp. 263–264.

5. WO 208/2018A.

6. WO 208/2018A.

7. WO 208/2018A. Appendix 3, p. 7, to report of Colonel S. W. Bailey, April 1944.

8. Roberts, Tito, Mihailović and the *Allies*, p. 67.

Chapter 15

No notes.

Chapter 16

1. Zhivan L. Knezevich, *Why the Allies Abandoned the Yugoslav Army of General Mihailovich*, mimeographed documentation (Washington, D. C.: Library of Congress), April 25, 1945, p. 11.

2. Knezevich, *Why the Allies Abandoned the Yugoslav Army of General Mihailovich*, p. 11.

3. FO 371/37588, message of June 12, 1943.

4. Conversation with Kenneth Pickthorn, London, November 1944.

5. David Martin, *Patriot or Traitor: The Case of General Mihailovich* (Stanford: Hoover Institution Press, 1978), p. 50.

6. WO 371/37615.

7. Interview with Colonel Albert Seitz, New York, January 1946.

8. Interview with Colonel Albert Seitz, New York, January 1946.

9. A number of entries in Foreign Office documentation mention efforts to enlist the aid of the Turkish government in restraining the participation of Yugoslav Moslems in anti-Serbian pogroms.

10. The papers of Ambassador Fotitch and the Yugoslav embassy in Washington, D. C., are available to the public in the Archives of the Hoover Institution of Stanford University.

11. WO 202/140.

12. WO 202/139, September 21, 1943.

13. FO 371/37616, message no. 102 from Stevenson, November 19, 1943.

14. FO 371/37591.

15. FO 371/37617.

16. Captain Walter Mansfield, preliminary statement to the Commission of Inquiry of the Committee for a Fair Trial for Draja Mihailovich, June 1946.

17. Interview with Eli Popovich in Washington, D. C., January 1989.

18. Richard Weil, OSS documentation on Mihailović, "Operation Balkan," (Washington, D. C.: National Archives).

Chapter 17

1. Davidson, *Special Operations Europe*, p. 116.

2. Letter from F. W. D. Deakin to author dated September 28, 1988.

3. Ralph Bennett, *Ultra and Mediterranean Strategy* (New York: William Morrow and Company, 1989), pp. 325, 345, 395.

4. Tape-recorded interview of author with Jasper Rootham, London, October 1976.

5. Interview with Captain George Musulin in Washington, D. C., January 1946.

6. Interview with Colonel Robert H. McDowell in Washington, D. C., January 1946.

7. *Parliamentary Debates* (Commons),   ser., vol.   (1944–45), col.

8. WO 202/155, report of Fitzroy Maclean, September 29, 1944, p. 1.

9. Davidson, *Special Operations Europe*, p. 119.

10. WO 202/140, sheet 490, December 31, 1943.

Chapter 18

1. FO 371/37582.

2. S. W. Bailey, "British Policy towards General Draža Mihailović," in Auty and Clogg, eds., *British Policy towards Wartime Resistance in Yugoslavia and Greece*, p. 75. This book consists of reports presented at a conference at the University of London in July 1973 under the same name.

3. FO 371/37590.

4. WO 202/139, sheet 45.

5. Preliminary statement of Walter R. Mansfield to the Commission of Inquiry of the Committee for a Fair Trial for Draja Mihailovich.

6. FO 371/37616.

7. WO 202/139.

8. WO 202/140.

9. WO 202/140.

10. WO 202/140.

11. WO 202/140.

12. WO 202/143, sheet 60.

13. WO 202/143, sheet 130, November 5, 1943.

14. WO 202/143.

15. WO 202/143, November 7, 1943.

16. WO 202/143.

17. WO 202/143, sheet 146.

18. WO 202/143, sheet 221.

19. WO 202/143, sheet 293.

20. WO 202/139.

21. WO 202/139, sheet 61.

22. WO 202/162, BLO Reports: Major J. Sehmer, *War Diary April 19, 1943 – December 13, 1943*.

23. WO 202/131.

24. Interview with Captain George Musulin in Washington, D.C., January 1946.

25. Interview with Captain George Musulin in Washington, D.C., January 1946.

26. WO 202/139.

27. WO 202/139.

28. Prime Minister/PM 3, 510/13, December 1, 1943.

29. WO 202/162, "Report on Vera Pešić," by Major Rupert Raw.

30. WO 202/145, sheet 30.

31. Interview with Eli Popovich in Chicago, January 1946.

32. Letter from Michael Lees to the author. Lees was commanding officer of the FUGUE sub-mission to Mihailović.

33. WO 202/162, BLO Reports: Report of Captain Robert Purvis, dated June 1, 1944, p. 6.

34. FO 371/37584, telegram no. 1400 of March 31, 1943, to the Yugoslav prime minister [London] from General Mihailović.

Chapter 19

1. Deakin, *The Embattled Mountain*, p. 76.

2. Deakin, *The Embattled Mountain*, p. 76.

3. WO 208/3202.

4. Maclean, *Eastern Approaches*, p. 294.

5. WO 208/3102, FO "Brief for Captain Fitzroy Maclean," September 11, 1943.

6. WO 201/1581, Fitzroy Maclean Report, November 6, 1943.

7. WO 201/1581, Maclean Report, 2.

8. WO 201/1581, Maclean Report, 1.

9. WO 201/1581, Maclean Report, 9.

10. WO 201/1581, Maclean Report, 12.

11. Prime Minister/PM3/511/2.

12. PREM 3/511/2.
13. Churchill, *The Second World War*, vol. 6, p. 92.
14. Conversation with A. F. Voigt in London, December 1944.
15. Conversation with Captain George Musulin in Washington, D.C., January 1946.
16. Churchill, *The Second World War*, vol. 6, p. 88.
17. Churchill, *The Second World War*, vol. 6, p. 230.
18. Anthony Eden, *The Memoirs of Anthony Eden*, 3 vols. (Boston: Houghton Mifflin Co., 1965), vol. 3, *The Reckoning*, p. 559.

Chapter 20

1. FO 371/37617, pp. 53–63.
2. FO 371/37617, pp. 53–63.

Chapter 21

1. Maclean, *Eastern Approaches*, p. 291.
2. Maclean, *Eastern Approaches*, p. 403.
3. Churchill, *The Second World War*, vol. 6, pp. 227–228.
4. Prime Minister/PM/42/308.
5. FO 371/43646. Abbreviated quotation taken from Auty and Clogg, eds., *British Policy towards Wartime Resistance in Yugoslavia and Greece*, p. 48.
6. FO 371/37616.
7. FO 371/37616.
8. FO 371/37616, message of November 11, 1943.
9. FO 371/37167.
10. FO 371/37591, minute of P. L. Rose, December 15, 1943.
11. WO 202/162.
12. WO 202/139.
13. WO 202/144.
14. WO 201/1581.
15. WO 201/1599.
16. WO 202/140, December 16, 1943.
17. WO 202/145, sheet 355, December 13, 1943.
18. WO 202/140.
19. WO 202/140.
20. WO 202/140, sheet 424, December 19, 1943.
21. WO 202/140, sheet 490, December 31, 1943.
22. WO 202/140, sheet 446.
23. WO 202/140.
24. WO 202/140, sheet 475.
25. WO 202/136.
26. WO 202/136.
27. WO 202/138.
28. Interview with Captain George Musulin in Washington, D.C., January 1946.
29. Interview with Major Bora Todorović in New York, February 1946.
30. Interviews with Major Bora Todorović in New York, February 1946, and with Živko Topalović and Adam Pribićević in Rome, September 19, 1946.

31. Rootham, *Miss Fire*, p. 207.
32. Rootham, *Miss Fire*, p. 218.

Chapter 22

1. Walter R. Mansfield, *Report on Mission to General Draga* [sic] *Mihailović*, dated March 1, 1944, OSS documentation: Cairo-OSS-OP-7, Entry 154, Folder 565, Box 39, Record Group 226 (Washington, D.C.: National Archives), p. 17.
2. Mansfield, *Report on Mission to Mihailović*, pp. 38–39.
3. Mansfield, *Report on Mission to Mihailović*, p. 25.

Chapter 23

1. FO 371/37617, telegram from the British embassy to Yugoslavia to the Foreign Office, November 23, 1943, pp. 53–63. See full report in Appendix 2.
2. I had been hoping to learn something about the status of Colonel Bailey's notes when I met with Colonel Deakin in London in November 1977. Bailey and Deakin had been near-neighbors in France and had seen a good deal of each other on a friendly basis, despite their disagreement on Yugoslavia. I was amazed, therefore, when Deakin told me that "Colonel Bailey left no notes." Efforts to track down Colonel Bailey's notes through other individuals also bore no fruit. I am personally certain that Bailey did leave notes, all the more so because he tended to wordiness in his reports. Hopefully, the missing notes will someday show up.
3. WO 208/2018A.
4. WO 208/2018A.
5. WO 208/3103/64578, April 1, 1944. Commentary on memorandum on Yugoslavia by Colonel Bailey dated March 14, 1944.
6. FO 371/37591, note initialed by Anthony Eden on a draft of a cabinet paper on "Policy towards Mihailović."

Chapter 24

1. Linn M. Farish, "Preliminary Report on a Visit to the National Army of Liberation, Yugoslavia," dated October 29, 1943, OSS documentation on Mihailović, "Operation Balkans" (Washington, D.C.: National Archives), p. 1.
2. Farish, "Preliminary Report," p. 2.
3. Farish, "Preliminary Report," p. 2.
4. Interview with Eli Popovich in Washington, D.C., January 1946; also interviewed in January 1989.
5. Linn M. Farish, "Summary Report on Observations in Jugoslavia for the period 19 September 1943 until 16 June 1944," dated June 28, 1944, OSS documentation on Mihailović, "Operation Balkans" (Washington, D.C.: National Archives), p. 7. For full texts of the two Farish reports, see Appendix 4.

Chapter 25

1. In the final years of his career as a US Air Force pilot, Major General Donald J. Smith became commander of the Air National Guard for the state of Illinois. He retired in 1986.
2. Major Richard L. Felman now lives in Tucson, Arizona.

3. Richard L. Felman, "Mihailovich and I," *Serbian Democratic Forum*, October 1972, p. 18.

4. The papers of Ambassador Fotitch and the Yugoslav embassy in Washington, D.C., are available to the public in the Archives of the Hoover Institution, Stanford University.

5. I am indebted to Thomas Kirkwood Ford, Jr., for the copy of the text of the wireless message sent to Bari by Lt. Colonel T. K. Oliver. Oliver is now a resident of Los Angeles.

6. Interview with Dr. Walter Carpenter in New York, January 1946.

7. Letter to Ambassador Fotitch from First Lieutenant John E. Scroggs, American airman, at the time of the Mihailović trial, spring 1946.

Chapter 26

1. Fotitch, *The War We Lost*, p. 247.
2. Fotitch, *The War We Lost*, p. 249.
3. Fotitch, *The War We Lost*, p. 251.
4. Fotitch, *The War We Lost*, p. 257.

Chapter 27

1. Interview with Captain George Musulin in Washington, D.C., January 1946.

2. Louis Huot, *Guns for Tito* (New York: L. B. Fischer, 1945).

3. Telephone interview with George Vujnovich, wartime director of OSS operations, Bari, spring 1989.

4. Statement of Colonel Robert H. McDowell to Commission of Inquiry into Case of Draja Mihailovich [sic], in Martin, *Patriot or Traitor*, p. 492.

5. Robert H. McDowell, "Report on Mission to Yugoslavia, Ranger Unit," dated November 23, 1944, OSS documentation on Mihailović, "Operation Balkans" (Washington, D.C.: National Archives), p. 4.

6. Interview with Eli Popovich in Chicago, January 1946.

7. McDowell, "Report on Mission to Yugoslavia," p. 38.

8. OSS documentation on Mihailović (Washington, D.C.: National Archives.)

9. OSS documentation on Mihailović (Washington, D.C.: National Archives.)

10. OSS documentation on Mihailović (Washington, D.C.: National Archives).

11. OSS documentation on Mihailović (Washington, D.C.: National Archives).

Chapter 28

1. The papers of Ambassador Fotitch and the Yugoslav embassy in Washington, D.C., are available to the public in the Archives of the Hoover Institution, Stanford University.

2. Interview with Lieutenant Michael Rajachich in Washington, D.C., January 1946.

3. Interview with Lieutenant Michael Rajachich in Washington, D.C., January 1946.

4. Interview with Captain John Milodragovich of the McDowell mission in Washington, D.C., February 1946.

5. Interview with Captain John Milodragovich of the McDowell mission in Washington, D.C., February 1946.

6. Fotitch, *The War We Lost*, p. 277.

7. Interview with Lieutenant Ellsworth Kramer in Washington, D.C., February 1946.

8. Interview with Lieutenant Ellsworth Kramer in Washington, D.C., February 1946.

9. Written statement given to the author by Captain Vojislav Ilić in person, December 1944.

10. Stojan Pribićević, article in *The New Statesman and Nation*, January 27, 1945.

11. McDowell, "Report on Mission to Yugoslavia."

12. Pribićević, article in *The New Statesman and Nation*, January 27, 1945.

13. Interview with Major Davidson of Floydforce in London, January 1945. Davidson, who had run over a land mine in his jeep, had a badly broken hip.

14. John Ehrman, *Grand Strategy*, 6 vols. (London: Her Majesty's Stationery Office, 1956), vol. VI, October 1944 – August 1945, p. 53.

15. Ehrman, *Grand Strategy*, p. 54.

16. Stevan K. Pavlowitch, "London-Moscow through the Fog of Yugoslavia's Wartime Drama: Djuretić's Controversial History," two-part article in *Storia delle relazioni internazionali*, Italy, issues 2 and 3, 1987.

17. George Urban, interview with Milovan Djilas, *Encounter* magazine, London, December 1979.

18. Nikolai Tolstoy, *The Minister and the Massacres* (London: Century Hutchinson, 1986), p. 184.

Chapter 29

1. Martin, *Ally Betrayed*, p. 343.

2. Report of Commission of Inquiry of the Committee for a Fair Trial for Draja Mihailovich, in Martin, *Patriot or Traitor*, p. 480.

3. Colonel McDowell's reply to interrogatory no. 27, in Martin, *Patriot or Traitor*, p. 475.

4. "Mihailovitch Ends His Defence," *The* (London) *Times*, July 12, 1946.

Appendices

1. The Maclean Report (November 6, 1943)

2. The Armstrong-Bailey Recommendations (November 1943)

3. The Mansfield Report (March 1, 1944)

4. The Farish Reports (October 29, 1943; June 28, 1944)

5. The McDowell Report (November 23, 1944)

Note: Except for "The Armstrong-Bailey Recommendations," the text of each appendix is an exact copy of the original document. Errors in spelling, punctuation, grammar, syntax, and diction have not been corrected. The text for "The Armstrong-Bailey Recommendations" is taken from a slightly edited War Office copy that was based on an original telegram sent to the Foreign Office. Errors in this copy have not been corrected.

1. The Maclean Report
(November 6, 1943)

THE PARTISAN MOVEMENT IN YUGOSLAVIA

I

The Partisan Movement, which now dominates the greater part of Jugoslavia and disposes of an Army of some 26 divisions and an efficient political and administrative system, had its beginnings in the summer of 1941 in a few handfuls of determined men scattered in the woods and mountains. For arms and equipment, the Partisans relied on what they could capture from the enemy. They followed traditional guerrilla tactics of attacking and harrassing the enemy wherever possible, while never allowing themselves to be forced on to the defensive. By these means, they were successful in keeping their own casualties to a minimum, while inflicting heavy losses on the enemy. (They count on not losing more than one man killed for five of the enemy against Germans and ten against Ustasi or Cetniks). They have received the whole-hearted support of the civil population. The savage reprisals of the enemy are not taken into consideration. All share the same dangers and are equally careless of death. Quarter is neither given or expected. As Lawrence wrote of the Arab revolt: "We had won a province when we had taught the civilians in it to die for our ideal of freedom. The presence or absence of the enemy was a secondary matter." As their successes became known and their supply of arms increased, they were joined by large numbers of fresh volunteers. These came from all over the country and from all walks of life, and were of widely differing political opinions and creeds. They joined the Partisan movement because they saw in it their best chance of striking a blow for freedom.

The fortunes of the Partisans have varied. The enemy soon realised the danger, and, in the course of two years, have launched against them no less than five major offensives. These culminated in the Montenegrin campaign this summer, when the main body of the Partisan forces came near to being completely encircled and wiped out by a combined force including, in addition to seven German and four Italian divisions, Bulgarian, Ustasi and Domobran troops and the Cetniks of General Mihailovic, backed by strong artillery and air support. The enemy failed, however, in their object, and the Partisans emerged from the ordeal stronger and more confident than ever. The collapse of Italy has brought further benefit by greatly increasing their stock of arms and weakening the German position in Jugoslavia.

From the outset, the Partisan movement has been based on a common Front, Directed by the Communist party in the person of Tito, the Commander in Chief of the Partisan Forces, and his principal political and military advisers. Tito's identity is kept a secret. He is known to be a man of the people and to have worked underground as a Communist agent ever since the last war. It seems likely that he is, in fact, Joseph Broz, a Zagreb metal worker, who, after passing some years in the Soviet Union, was sent back to Jugoslavia by the Comintern in 1937 to reorganize and assume the leadership of the illegal Jugoslav Communist Party. Although primarily a politician, with no previous experience as a military commander, he has from the start personally directed and assisted at the operations of his forces, his Chief of Staff and other military advisers playing a secondary role. In political and administrative matters, though he holds no office save that of leader of the Communist party, he is the dominating personality. As a leader, he enjoys the undivided devotion of his followers for whom he has become a legendary figure. In appearance, he is a sensible looking man of 45 to 50, clean shaven and tidy, with grey hair, and giving an impression of intelligence and determination. In conversation, while he leaves no doubt as to his views on a subject, I have always found him reasonable and friendly, with a wide comprehension of military and political problems and a well developed sense of humour.

The military and political structure built up by Tito and his followers in two years, from nothing, in enemy occupied territory, with no outside help, is an impressive one. Much of what has been achieved, is due to the traditional love of liberty of the people of Jugoslavia and much to the leadership and ability of Tito and of the many younger men placed by him in positions of responsibility, but perhaps most of all is due to the immense enthusiasm of all concerned for the new Jugoslavia which they are building and to their unshakable confidence in the future. It is this enthusiasm and this confidence that first strike an observer and convince him, as much as any of the material achievements of the Partisans, that here is something more considerable than is generally suspected in the outside world.

II

The National Army of Liberation (N.O.V & P.O.J.) does not, as generally supposed, consist of scattered guerrilla bands living in the mountains and woods and carrying out haphazard raids on the enemy's communications, but is in fact a well organised force, which completely controls large areas of Jugoslavia and has, unaided, forced the Germans to withdraw into the main towns and confine their activities to keeping open the roads to the towns which they occupy. It is now organised into brigades, divisions and corps, though this is not a rigid organisation, the size of the different formations varying according to circumstances. Moreover, it must be realised that their armaments consist of infantry weapons with but few supporting arms. The latest information gives the number of divisions as 26 and the total number of troops as 220,000. Of these 50,000 are said to be in Bosnia, 15,000 in the Sanjak, 20,000 in Croatia, 10,000 in Slavonia, 60,000 in Slovenia and Istria, 25,000 in Dalmatia, 10,000 in the Vojvodina and 30,000 in Serbia and Macedonia. Formations possess properly organised staffs, which, in spite of occasionally deficient communications, exercise complete control over units under their command. Similarly, the Partisan General Staff completely controls the whole. In the case of the more remote formations, such as those in Slovenia, Slavonia and Macedonia, the policy is laid down by Partisan G.H.Q. and it is left to the formations concerned to interpret it in detail. In all cases, in spite of difficult conditions, morale seems high and discipline good.

Communication between G.H.Q. and certain of the more important outlying formations is by wireless, and, wherever possible, formations have established telephone communication to neighbouring localities within the liberated areas. Otherwise all communication is by courier, a slow and often uncertain method. The provision of more wireless sets would, by improving communications, make possible more complete control, and is thus of the first importance.

An impressive feature of the National Army of Liberation is its administration, which by making full use of the limited means available and by intelligent improvisation succeeds in supplying and feeding very considerable forces. The distribution of material captured from the enemy or supplied by the Allies is methodical, rapid and well planned. The large quantities of stores and equipment recently taken from the Italians, including a certain number of trucks and even a few small tanks and armoured cars, have been valuable and have made it possible to arm and equip numbers of fresh volunteers; but they are far from meeting the Army's requirements.

The need for the rapid organisation and despatch of supplies by the Allies cannot be emphasized enough. In particular the despatch of supplies by sea is of the greatest urgency. Air supplies, although of assistance, are really no more than a token that we are prepared to help. Thus, despite our promise of seventy sorties for September and sixty for October, no more than eleven sorties were flown to the whole of the National Army of Liberation in September and thirty in October, making together approximately eighty tons of material in two months, or the equivalent of the cargo of one small schooner. During the three months previous to this, going back to the date when we first started helping the Partisans, supplies were on an even smaller scale and it is doubtful whether, in all, we have supplied more than one hundred and fifty tons of material by this means. For nearly two months the Partisans have now controlled the Islands and large stretches of coast but little or no use has so far been made of this opportunity and it is essential that an efficient system of sea supplies on a large scale should be set up without further delay. Almost equally important, both strategically and from the point of view of morale, are attacks by the Allied Air Forces on targets in Jugoslavia. The first signs of Allied air support have been greeted with great enthusiasm by the partisans.

In spite of the great development of the Partisan forces the fundamental principles of Tito's strategy have remained unchanged. He well realises that, although his troops are ideally suited to the semi-guerrilla warfare in which they are now engaged, they are neither trained nor equipped for normal modern warfare, and that if they attempted a pitched battle with the Germans, they would undoubtedly be heavily defeated. His policy has therefore been to attack the enemy wherever the enemy is least prepared to meet an attack, and to avoid being forced into positions which it would be costly to defend. This does not mean that he confines himself to small scale raids or isolated attacks on lines of communication, though the Partisans have been particularly successful in this sphere (see Railway Map). If the opportunity offers he will and does occupy towns and large areas of country, and exploit the resources which they contain, but he is never tempted, either by these resources or by considerations of prestige, to risk his valuable troops in a last man-last round defence of them. Many parts of the country have been captured, evacuated and recaptured two or three times in the past two years. Similarly the Partisans will use, when they can, captured artillery and transport and even tanks, but they do not allow the fact of their possession to lead them into changing their basic mode of warfare, and they are always ready to abandon them and revert to the hills and to classical guerrilla tactics at a moments notice, should circumstances demand it.

The attacks of the National Army of Liberation are causing ever graver embarrassment to the Germans, who, with an enemy who presents no targets against which they can strike back decisively, with unreliable allies, and without enough troops of their own to occupy the country effectively, have been obliged to confine themselves to garrisoning the larger towns and trying to keep open communications between them, while leaving the rest of the country to the Partisans. This much the Partisans have achieved practically unassisted. Were they to be provided with sufficient arms and equipment, the embarrassment caused to the Germans would be enormously increased, and it might well be that in time the National Army of Liberation could force the Germans to withdraw from the country altogether. At present the number of Reichswehr Divisions in Jugoslavia is estimated at about fourteen.

There is, of course, no question of any Allied officer or other outside authority conducting the operations of the National Army of Liberation or in any way directing its strategy. Tito has however agreed that it would be useful if I would, in accordance with the terms of my charter laid down in General Wilson's message to him, keep him informed of the main lines of Allied military policy, and he has undertaken to do what he can to further Allied plans. I have no doubt that his readiness to accept our guidance and suit his strategy to our plans will be in direct proportion to the amount of material help that we are able to give him.

III

As the areas controlled by them grow larger, political and administrative problems are becoming of increasing interest to the Partisans. A foundation has existed from the start. The Communists, officially accepted as the directing force of the movement have, needless to say, never lacked in political consciousness and have sufficient experience to be able to work underground in any circumstances. The Administrative and political unit adopted by the Partisans is the Odbor, corresponding to the Russian Soviet, and constitutional *arrangements* are roughly on Soviet lines. The town or village Odbor is elected by universal suffrage and its delegates in turn elect from their numbers the members of the District Odbors, whence the chain goes on through Area and Regional Odbors, to the Committees of the various Nationalities (e.g. ZAVNCH, the Croat Anti-fascist Committee of National Liberation) and, finally, to Avnoj, the Jugoslav Anti-fascist Committee of National Liberation, which is the supreme civil authority. Each Odbor is divided into various sections dealing with different subjects. It also has a plenum, an executive committee and a President. The President of Avonoj is Dr. Ivan Ribar, the former Speaker of the Jugoslave Parliament, who is nominally the political head of the movement, though in fact he and his colleagues are completely overshadowed by Tito. Elections to the various Odbors have been held under the occupation, regardless of the presence of the enemy, with the result that, when Partisan forces capture a town or village, the necessary local administrative and political machinery is already in existence and is able to take over the administration forthwith. Liaison between the political and military authorities is undertaken locally by the Political Commissars of units and formations, who, like their former Soviet counterparts, are also entrusted with the ideological welfare of the troops. Political Commissars are all picked men and take an active part in military operations. I have been most favourably impressed by all those I have met.

The elections are nominally on non-party lines, the Partisan political system being based on a common anti-fascist front under Communist leadership. In fact, however, all key posts are held by members of the Communist Party and policy is dictated by them. Provided that they are prepared to accept Communist hegemony and follow the Party line, other parties and institutions, though ultimate Gleichschaltung doubtless awaits them, are tolerated and encouraged to join the common front. In Croatia a section of the Croat Peasant-Party has joined the Partisans and, under their austices even publishes its own newspaper, "Slobodni Dom". (Most of the remainder of the Croat Peasant Party have thrown in their lot with the Ustasi, and Macek, though imprisoned by the Germans, is denounced by the Partisans as a traitor). In Slovenia the common front comprises several of the former political Parties.

Religious toleration prevails. The movement includes numbers of Catholic and Orthodox Priests, as well as Moslem Imams, and even has its official chaplains to the Partisan Forces. In Jajce the Partisans have restored and formally reopened the Orthodox Church destroyed by the Ustasi, and services are also held in the Catholic church and in the numerous mosques. This policy has won over many who had expected of the Partisans an anti-God attitude on out of date Soviet lines.

Nor are there any signs of class warfare. Numbers of the military and political leaders of the movement come from the well-to-do classes, and there is a strong sprinkling of intelligensia, including many technical experts. Many regular officers have also joined the Partisans, some after they had been disappointed by General Mihailovic.

The question of private property and private enterprise has conveniently been left in abeyance. Amongst the Partisans themselves all assets are paid into official funds, whence they are redistributed as required. Looting or violence against the civil population is punished by death, nor have I been able to find evidence of mass arrests or executions on the lines of those perpetrated by the Ustasi and Cetniks.

Partisan policy is in short constructive rather than destructive. To this bears witness the rapidity with which, throughout the liberated areas, factories, power stations and even railways are set working, while on the cultural side corresponding activity is shown, newspapers are produced, and schools, youth associations, women's institutes and other similar societies are set up, all, needless to say, on strictly Party lines. In particular a determined effort is being made to combat illiteracy. In all these activities an increasingly active part is being played by the women whose emmancipation is an important plank in the Partisan platform.

The Movement is none the less essentially revolutionary. The Jugoslave Communists have profited by the experience of others; they have begun where their Russian counterparts left off, and have not found it necessary to persecute and thereby alienate whole sections of the population, but there can be no question of a return to the old order.

In particular great emphasis is laid on the need for a new solution of the problem of nationalities within Jugoslavia. To quote Tito: "The struggle for National freedom and the question of nationalities in Jugoslavia are closely connected. Our efforts to liberate our country would not be so determined or so successful if the peoples of Jugoslavia did not see in them to-day, not only a victory over Fascism, but a victory over the old regime and over those who once oppressed the different races of Jugoslavia and hope to oppress them once again." A federal scheme is envisaged under which Serbs, Croats and Slovenes will enjoy equal rights and good mutual relations under a central government, and no one race dominate the rest. At the same time, the Partisans strongly discourage separatist tendencies and point to the unity and harmony prevailing in their own ranks, where all the different nationalities are well represented, Serbs actually predominating.

In contrast to their attitude towards the parties and organisations who have joined their common front against the Axis, the Partisans have sworn undying hatred against Nedic, Pavelic, Macek and Mihailovic. With Mihailovic, they sought to reach an understanding in 1941, when he still showed some signs of resisting the invaders. According to Partisan accounts, negotiations between Tito and Mihailovic for the unification of their forces under Mihailovic's command broke down when the Cetniks joined the Germans in an attack on the Partisans at Uzice. After the Cetniks had explained that this was due to a mistake, negotiations were resumed, but a repetition of the incident, followed by further acts of treachery, including the wholesale murder of Partisan wounded and medical personnel, caused the Partisans to put aside for good any hope of an understanding with Mihailovic, whom they now regard as a traitor to his country and one of their bitterest enemies, and whom, as such, they are bent on exterminating. Ever since, evidence of Cetnik collaboration with both the Germans and Italians has been steadily accumulating. Particulars of this have already been given by signal and a detailed report is now under preparation). General Mihailovic may possibly deny that he himself has acted in direct collaboration with the Axis, but he cannot deny the open and active collaboration of many of his principal Commanders, of which there is irrefutable evidence. To take only one example, Djuic, Commander of the Cetnik Dinaric Division of 3,000 men, representing approximately one quarter of the total Cetnik forces, has steadily collaborated first with the Italians and now with the Germans. Mihailovic cannot disown him, for it was on his recommendation that Djuic was awarded the Karageorge Star over the B.B.C. by the Royal Jugoslav Government, an award which, according to an Italian Officer whom I met, he celebrated at the table of the local Italian Divisional Commander. In any case, if he disowns only the most notorious Collaborationists among his Commanders, it leaves him with practically no forces at his disposal. If, on the other hand, he admits to having so little control over his Commanders that, instead of fighting the enemy, they place themselves under enemy command, it says very little for his powers as a leader.

By their support of their Minister of War, the Royal Jugoslav Government, or Government of Traitors and Deserters, as they are known in their own country, have earned the same degree of hatred as is felt for Mihailovic himself. This hatred is continually expressed in articles, speeches and informal conversation by Partisans of all kinds, whether Serb, Croat or Slovene. In particular the Government are regarded as sharing Mihailovic's violently Pan-Serb and anti Croat views and as aiming at the restoration of the old regime with all its abuses. To this must be added the contempt felt for a Government, who, while the Partisans have been fighting and building up a new Jugoslavia, have been living comfortably in London, proclaiming over the B.B.C. that "The time has not yet come to start the fight for Freedom".

Unfortunately, King Peter's public support of Mihailovic has also caused deep offence and has served to strengthen the belief that a return of the Dynasty would mean a return to Pan-Serb policy and to the old order of things. Nor do the Partisans feel that they have much in common with a King who has taken no part in their struggle for liberation and who, even if he joined them at this juncture, would in their estimation arrive two years too late. Partisan propaganda has however scrupulously refrained from attacking His Majesty and it is clear that the Partisan leaders do not wish the question of the Monarchy raised at this juncture, their attitude being that it is a matter which must in due course be freely decided by the people of Jugoslavia.

IV

Their struggle against the invader has left the Partisans but little time for Foreign Affairs. Towards foreign countries in general, their attitude is one of universal benevolence on Soviet lines, attributing any lapses from virtue to the inherent wickedness of most Governments, and based on the assumption that, if left to themselves, the workers of the world would be only too glad to unite. On this basis, they look forward to friendly collaboration after the war with all neighbouring countries including their former enemies. They seek no territorial aggrandisment beyond their prewar frontiers, with the exception of the former Italian territories of Slovene and Croat population, already for the most part in their hands.

At the same time, certain aspects of the world situation loom very large on their horizon. First and foremost comes Soviet Russia. The liquidation of the Tsars did not put an end to Pan-Slavism, nor has the liquidation of the Comintern cut off Moscow from all contact with Communist Parties in other countries. Both these factors play an important part in Jugoslavia to-day, and to them must be added the superiority of Soviet propaganda to that of most other countries. To the Partisans, Soviet Russia appears variously as their political mentor, as the traditional protector of all Slav races and, finally, as the only country taking any part in the war besides themselves. Everywhere Comrade Tito's portrait is balanced by that of Comrade Stalin; the latest Russian songs are sung in preference to Jugoslav ones; Soviet institutions and jargon are copied, and praise of the glorious Red Army and the "Great Russian people" (in the classical phrase, "Veliki ruski narod") is on everyone's lips. In fact, with political slogans on every wall and Red Star, Hammer and Sickle on the cap badges of the troops, an observer familiar with the Soviet Union might, at times, imagine himself in one of the Republics of the Union. How far the Soviet Government actively intervene in Partisan affairs is another matter. There is not as yet any official Soviet representative with the Partisans, nor have the Soviet Government given them any material support. On the other hand, the Free Jugoslavia broadcasting station is unofficially admitted to be on Soviet territory, and Partisan G.H.Q. is in wireless touch with Moscow. Events will show the nature of Soviet intentions towards Jugoslavia, much will also depend on Tito, and whether he sees himself still in his former role of Comintern agent, or as the potential ruler of an independent Jugoslav state. Much, finally, depends on the part played by other Powers in the liberation of Jugoslavia.

At present Great Britain comes a long way after Russia in the estimation of the Partisans. For one thing, as a Capitalist and non-Slav state, we are at a certain disadvantage. Further, the Partisans are puzzled by our continued support of Mihailovic, despite his collaboration with the Axis and failure to use the arms sent him against anyone except the Partisans themselves. Although Tito, at any rate, understands the nature and extent of our obligations towards the King and the Royal Jugoslav Government, and has readily accepted my assurance that it is the desire of His Majesty's Government that the Jugoslav people should freely choose their own type of Government, many of the rank and file undoubtedly suspect us of wishing to impose on them by force the former regime, with all its evils and Mihailovic thrown in. Suspicion and resentment have also been caused by the misguided broadcasts of the B.B.C. which, though an improvement is now noticeable, over a long period consistently extolled Mihailovic and ignored or attacked the Partisans, or, worse still, attributed to the former the exploits of the latter. This served to discredit British propaganda in Partisan eyes, while lack of suitable information has led them greatly to underestimate the British share in the war. Grave disappointment has also been felt at our prolonged failure to give the National Army of Liberation any substantial material aid or active support, particularly since the way has been open for supplies by sea. On the other hand, there is to my mind in Jugoslavia a deepseated liking and admiration for Great Britain which could easily be developed. Everywhere, my Mission has been given a most friendly reception, and overwhelmed with requests for information about Great Britain and the British War effort, as well as for Union Jacks and portraits of the Prime Minister to take their place alongside those of Tito and Stalin. Finally, the Partisans cannot but realise that, unlike the Russians, we dominate the Mediterranean and are in a position at this juncture to give them the active help and support they so urgently need.

Most of these considerations apply also to the United States. Here again, the same factors have damped the enthusiasm and admiration which undoubtedly exist. For instance the news, of the recent gift of the United States Government of four liberators to the Royal Jugoslav Government was very badly received, while Columbia Broadcasts are a perpetual source of annoyance.

V.

For his Majesty's Government, the choice lies between continuing, as long as circumstances permit, the present policy of giving an approximately equal measure of moral and material support to both the Partisans and Mihailovic, or, on the other hand, dropping Mihailovic, and giving our wholehearted support to the Partisans. Of recociliation, or of dividing the country into two spheres of influence, there can be no question.

In reaching a decision, there are two main aspects of the problem to be considered: The immediate Jugoslav contribution to the Allied war Effort, and our standing in Jugoslavia and in the Balkans after the war. In the matter of military effectiveness there can clearly be no comparison between the Partisans and the Cetniks. The Partisans are between 10 and 20 times as numerous, infinitely better organised, better equipped and better disciplined. Moreover, they fight the Germans, while the Cetniks either help the Germans or do nothing. It might, of course, be argued that it is worth continuing to support the Cetniks in the hope that they may eventually turn against the Germans and thereby contribute something to the united war effort. This argument would carry more weight if the Cetniks were more numerous, less disorganised and less set in their collaborationist ways. As it is it seems likely that they are only kept going by our moral and material support, and that, if we were to drop them, the leaders would fade away and the rank and file join the Partisans, as many of them have done already. Apart from relieving the Partisans of a constant source of annoyance, we should, by withdrawing our support from the Cetniks, release arms of which the Partisans could make the best possible use.

Taking a long view, the case for wholehearted support of the Partisans is equally strong. There seems little doubt that nothing short of large scale armed intervention will prevent them from taking power in Jugoslavia as soon as the Germans are finally driven out. In fact, they effectively control large areas already. Furthermore, they can count on the powerful backing of our Soviet allies. Mihailovic, on the other hand, is thoroughly discredited in the eyes of most of the population and, even in the most favourable circumstances, would have no prospect of uniting the country. His policy is, in any case, Pan-Serb, anti-Croat and violently reactionary, and is therefore apposed to our own aims. The support which we give him can only serve to prolong existing internal dissensions and by it, we are, in return for no corresponding advantage, prejudicing our position with the Partisans and driving them more and more to the conclusion that the Soviet Union is their only friend.

On the other hand, were we to drop Mihailovic and at the same time substantially increase our material aid to the partisans, we should not only further the Jugoslav contribution to the Allied War effort, but we should establish Anglo - Jugoslav relations on a firm basis which would do much to consolidate our position in the Balkans after the War.

In these circumstances my recommendations are as follows:

(1) That support of Mihailovic should be discontinued.
(2) That our aid to the Partisans should be substantially increased.
(3) That, in particular, an efficient system of supply by sea should be organised on a large scale without further delay.
(4) That suitable targets in Jugoslavia should be attacked from the air whenever possible.
(5) That B.B.C. broadcasts and other publicity should be kept in line with the policy of His Majesty's Government.

F.H.R. MACLEAN, Brigadier,
Commanding Allied Military Mission to
the Partisan Forces.

6th November 1943

2. The Armstrong-Bailey
Recommendations (November 1943)

SAVING TELEGRAM FROM THE BRITISH EMBASSY TO YUGOSLAVIA TO THE FOREIGN OFFICE.

No. 7 Saving
23rd November, 1943.

Following is text of report from Brigadier Armstrong of the 18th November, received in full on the 23rd November.

Begins:

This signal is in 43 paragraphs. Most important it should not be read or discussed by you London or high level authorities until all parts have been received.

1. Have now reached tacit deadlock with Mihailović. Brigadier Armstrong's efforts here restricted to badgering him operation by operation into doing absolute minimum with which he thinks he can regain our nominal support. If Armstrong is to do job for which you sent him here, Mihailović must be brought to abandon present attitude for one of willing and loyal collaboration so that Armstrong can co-ordinate Mihailović's own desire to carry out extensive operations with requirements of Commander-in-Chief and exercise necessary technical control to make operations efficient and successful. Absolutely essential Armstrong do this in role of accepted expert adviser rather than of nuisance who must be placated as now.

2. In view recent falling off in sorties flown and current B.B.C. propaganda all we could hope for by threatening to withdraw our support would be a grudging temporary increase of activity, precisely adjusted to keep us playing, at minimum expense to Mihailović forces and Serb civilian population.

3. In our opinion only way to bring Mihailović to satisfactory collaboration is by combination of pressure applied through proper channels and recognition by us of Mihailović's difficulties and cost to him and Serbs of work we wish done, plus

315

recognition of our own obligations in latter regard. This signal suggests a detailed course of action which we believe will meet all requirements.

4. To make this proposal clear it is essential to set out in detail factors which confirm Mihailović in his present un-cooperative attitude.

5. The elements common to all factors are fear and hatred: -

A. Fear of Partisans, partly as a hostile operational force in action now, but chiefly as a post-war rival for control of the country.

Anti-dynastic, anti-social and anti-constitutional emphasis of Partisans' activities, as illustrated by their declaration of the Uzice and Bihac republics, is completely opposed to everything on which such popular support as Mihailović now commands rests, while Milhailović's own anti-Partisan record, deriving from his training and career as a regular officer, not only intensifies his personal hatred of Partisans but introduces an acute personal fear of them.

Above remarks are made without prejudice to Mihailović's justifiable complaints re Partisans, such as recent Lim Valley episode.

B. Fear of incurring reprisals on Serb population by executing operations for us:

(i) because they will reduce the total Serb population, as compared with Croats and, to lesser degree, Slovenes. Mihailović and company envisage a post-war Yugoslavia on federal basis but somewhat enlarged territorially (see D. below). This is therefore a most important point. Sekulić's report of September 1941, with its figure of 700,000 Serb deaths in Croatia, another subsequent support of this report by the Church of England, and Pan-Serb section of Yugoslav language press in America have had most unfortunate results here. Mihailović and Central National Committee are now unshakeably convinced of accuracy this figure, and believe total Serb casualties in this war exceed 1,000,000. It is useless to attempt to shake this belief by propaganda. Sources of any alternative figures given by outside world and deriving from Croat or Catholic sources would be rejected without consideration by Serbs in country, and particularly so if proceeding from British Liaison Officers with Partisan forces now operating in territory where alleged massacres took place, especially in view of recent Partisan-Ustashi collaborations. Constant emphasis on these exaggerated figures of Mihailović's international propaganda have spread this conviction to 95% of those Serbs who support him. In 1941 there were approximately 6½ million Serbs to 5 million Croats. Since Mihailović and general Serb conception of their war casualties, coupled with fact that Croats have suffered much more lightly, makes a guarantee by United Nations of free post war elections less attractive to them than we might think, since Croats might in their view achieve numerical superiority at such elections if reprisals continue at present rate. Any such guarantee must, therefore be coupled with some practical assistance which will re-assure Serbs on this point. See paragraph 32 below. Further, since the majority of the alleged casualties occurred in what is now Free Croatia, and caused wholesale immigration to Serbia of such Serbs as escaped, Mihailović and company expect complete Croat domination throughout Bosnia. This is territory to which Serbs lay violent national claim and was the subject of continual internal dispute throughout the inter-war period. This factor is much magnified by the circumstance that Moljević is a Chauvinistic

Serb of provincial outlook and a bigot from precisely that area of Croatia where atrocities were worst, namely, Banja Luka.

(ii) because they weaken Mihailović's position vis-à-vis Nedić.

(iii) from a genuine desire to conserve Serb blood or at least sell it at the best possible price. In all this matter of reprisals Mihailović is naturally a good Serb and a bad Ally.

C. Fear of Nedić who, thanks to his persistent if hypocritical emphasis on loyalty to the King, has not completely lost face in Serbia.

The Serb peasant is by character and interest anti-communist and, by result of years of controlled propaganda, largely anti-Croat. Nedić takes astute advantage of these factors and, by basing his appeal to the country on them, is able to profit by the points made in paragraph A and part (i) of paragraph B above.

There is thus real competition between Mihailović and Nedić for Serb popular support, and although Nedić's prestige is much inferior, Mihailović is not inclined to take any action which might strengthen Nedić at his expense unless it is made well worth his while.

D. Fear that operations carried out before final rising will prejudice his own future by depriving him of man-power and popular support which at that moment would enable him to realise his personal plans based on his conception of his duty and responsibility as deputy Commander-in-Chief of the Yugoslav Army. These plans envisage not only the regaining of pre-1941 frontiers but also occupation of certain extraneous territories to which Yugoslavia has always aspired.

These are Istria, Gorizia, Carynthia and the lowland section of northern Albania around Scutari. Such loss of man-power and popular support would also hamper him in dealing with Croats who he considers must be punished for their military betrayal of April 1941 as well as political misdemeanours of the inter-war period, and with the Church of Rome whom he considers the instigator of the Serb massacres in Croatia.

E. Fear and hatred of both Albanians and other Moslems of Serb origin for the advantage taken by them of enemy occupation to terrorise the Serb population and pay off old scores, and for the active military assistance they have given and are giving to Axis forces in this country, and finally for the large part they have played in Ustashi activities.

Here again it is unfortunate that Moljević's interests are central in an area where the Serb-Moslem issue is acute, long-standing and persistent. This factor also is recorded without prejudice to such attempts as Mihailović has made to pacify and establish active co-operation with certain Moslem elements.

6. To summarise, the anti-German activities of Mihailović, his staff and advisers and the Central National Committee, which has taken over the active control of political affairs, are nullified by their anxiety to deal with Partisan, Croat, Moslem and Catholic affairs now.

7. This elucidates Mihailović's pre-occupation with post-war political horizon, and Ustanak military activity already commented on by us several times, and explains why the gap between him and Nedić is sometimes narrower than that between him and other elements of resistance in the country.

8. We are faced with question, why cannot you and we force a change of attitude by means already tried. The answer lies partly in Mihailović's old belief that he is indispensable to us, at any rate in Serbia, and that we are to this extent at his mercy, but by far the most important reason is that he profoundly mistrusts the British:

(A) because of the paucity of material support. It is "perfide Albion" attempting to purchase strategic benefits with Serb blood without any intention of giving an adequate *quid pro quo*. This mistrust is enhanced by his conviction that the British merely transport funds and material aid on behalf of Yugoslav Government on whom the full financial burden falls. This makes British cynicism more reprehensible.

(B) because few instructions reach him through what he considers proper channels of King and Government. There is a very strong feeling here that earlier Yugoslav Governments in exile were broken by British because Serbs in them would not agree to our policy of unequal support for Partisans and execution of demolitions and military operations now, regardless of cost to Serbs, and that present Government of puppets was chosen for its subservience to British policy and interests.

Mihailović also believes that not content with this G.H.Q. has attempted to force him into taking direct orders from British without knowledge of Yugoslav Government. He firmly believes also that we have not scrupled to employ underhand methods to persuade his local commanders to take orders direct from us, regardless of their duty towards Mihailović as Deputy Commander-in-Chief, Yugoslav Army.

Examples of the incidents which give rise to such convictions are G.H.Q.'s attempt to make Mihailović move east and restrict his territory, which accompanied directive from Yugoslav Government in May and allegations against Lake and Bought's actions during July which have been reported and commented on by us both. All this confirms Mihailović in his auto-hypnotic martyr's role of the sole defender of the Serbs, and makes him an even better Serb and worse Ally.

(C) Greatest mistrust and apprehension, however, derive from conviction of all Yugoslavs here that present 100% support of Partisans by B.B.C., including gross misrepresentation of known facts, plus minimum mention of Mihailović's activities, plus greater material support he believes we give the Partisans, plus fact that it is clear to him that a British Liaison Officer with Partisans is always believed in preference to a British Liaison Officer with his forces, all add up to mean that British have completely sold Yugoslavia down the river to the Russians.

He is convinced that we have agreed that Yugoslavia shall fall within Russian sphere of influence after war, but will not say so now so that we may callously extract maximum advantage from his forces now. Consequently he will have to fight his own battle with the Partisans after war without material, moral or political support from us.

These apprehensions are enhanced by the rapidity of the Russian advance in the Ukraine, the slowness of the Allied advance in Italy, and the lack of any indication of an Allied invasion of the Balkans, and the consequent fear that Russians may reach Danube or Bulgar-Serb frontier before Allied troops set foot in Yugoslavia. Apprehensions are particularly marked at the moment, as it is feared Moscow conference may have resulted in increased favouring of Partisans at Mihailović's expense.

9. Armstrong is encountering great difficulties because Mihailović hoped he would

bring reassurances on some of the above points. Fact that we took no advantage of arrival of a senior officer to do so, plus clear indication that Armstrong has no control whatever over B.B.C. broadcasts, volume of sorties and supplies, or, via you, over Partisan activities in disputed areas, has caused sharp reaction in direction of doing nothing operationally and restricting contact with this mission to a minimum.

Mihailović rarely raises any matters at our conferences, never gives Armstrong his confidence and always leaves the initiative with us. Armstrong now batting on a worse wicket than Colonel Bailey before Armstrong came in. King's message Armstrong brought has produced no effect so far and will not do so until we receive original signed script, and, in any case, is likely to increase Mihailović's passive resistance to our demands since it recognises Partisans without giving Serbs and Mihailović any corresponding *quid pro quo.*

10. On the other hand, we have the problem of Mihailović's character and the deficiencies of his organisation. He is a career officer, narrow-minded and stubborn, very Pan-Serb, wily and a master of evasion and procrastination. He has a strong sense of duty and loyalty to his King and people, but does not hesitate to manipulate or even ignore this to gain his own ends or secure respite in negotiation. His good qualities are offset by his exaggerated idea of his importance as deputy Commander-in-Chief and Minister.

Two years divorce from modern warfare and pre-occupation with pure H.Q. political considerations, plus attractive possibilities of a post-war career in statesmanship, plus influence of second-rate staff and advisers, have greatly impaired his military efficiency. Same applies to many of his local commanders whose organisation, planning and tactical ability leave much to be desired.

11. We have therefore to devise means: -

(a) of reassuring Mihailović on points in paragraphs 5 and 8;

(b) of modifying his present official position so that he can no longer evade carrying out our instructions;

(c) of offering sufficient incentive to make a change of attitude to willing co-operation attractive. Without this no advantage will be gained from (b);

(d) of safeguarding our interests generally and obtaining friendly operational control over him so that we can improve efficiency of his operations;

(e) of effecting an immediate, even if temporary, agreement between him and Tito.

12. Please appreciate that we are not making these proposals in any spirit of concession to Mihailović. They are designed to check his constant procrastination and evasion and make our collaboration profitable. But we cannot expect success unless we are prepared to face our own responsibilities and give them unambiguous expression. To attempt to secure (b) and (d) of paragraph 11 without considering (a) and (c) will be useless.

13. For our part we realise our suggestions may conflict with high level policy, political or military. Being ignorant of these we cannot foresee snags, neither can we foresee from here wider political implications of my proposal.

14. Negotiation of an agreement in the first place between the Yugoslav Government and H.M. Government as the Government most closely concerned with Eu-

ropean Governments in exile. The question of whether either or both the American and Russian Governments should be parties in a trilateral or quadrilateral agreement, or whether either or both should simply recognise the agreement with H.M. Government depends on diplomatic expediency and on the time required to realise each possibility, since the essential requirement for the success of this plan is speedy execution.

But if the maximum benefit is to be gained in this country it is highly desirable that both America and Russia should approve the agreement in a way which would make wide publicity practicable. Diplomatic expediency and policy consider Allies must also determine the actual form of the agreement. Whatever the final form, it must consist of three parts.

15. *First,* an overt agreement as short as possible containing all the following:

(a) Reiteration of statement made in Commons July 1941 by Foreign Secretary that restoration of pre-1941 Yugoslavia is a British war aim.

(b) Guarantee that free elections to determine future form of Government of the country will be held as soon as practicable after liberation under control of the Government in exile in power at the time. The Government in exile to be considered as provisional during the time between liberation and elections.

(c) Recognition by the King and Government of Yugoslavia:

1. That the general strategic interests of the United Nations demand they subordinate their interests and activities to the policy of H.M. Government and Allies as long as the agreement is in force.

2. That in the military field all elements of resistance in Yugoslavia must come under direct military command of the Allied Commander-in-Chief or Commanders-in-Chief in whose theatre or theatres the Balkans fall.

(d) Undertaking by H.M. Government that it will, in conjunction with other Allied Governments, secure to the resistance elements and to Yugoslav Government the necessary and corresponding body of material, moral and propaganda support. In addition, if possible, some indication of sympathetic consideration by United Nations of Yugoslav territorial aspirations beyond the pre-war frontiers should be included.

16. *Second.* Two secret protocols to the agreement, one for Partisans, and one for Mihailović forces, to be negotiated between SUU? Yugoslav Government, Mihailović and Tito via Armstrong and his opposite number. These must be specific and explicit, one for

(a) operational areas allotted to each resistance group;

(b) extent of neutral zone and obligations and responsibilities of each group towards it;

(c) our general strategic requirements both long and short term;

(d) on our *quids pro quo* in shape of

1. material support and sorties;

2. equal moral and propaganda support for both groups.

(e) propaganda which each group will be permitted to carry out in country and its control by us;

(f) exact status, function, rights, responsibilities all British Liaison Officers from heads of missions down, deriving from their position as Commander-in-Chief's representatives for transmission of his orders plus location and composition of missions;

(g) relation between resistance groups and H.M. Government in respect of financial burden of supporting them;

(h) security considerations such as use of safe uncompromised cyphers, possibly under our control, and secure organisation of internal communications.

17. Protocols must also include sanction clauses providing for forfeiture of all support and privileges by any group failing to respect provisions of agreement, particularly in respect of operational areas and neutral zone.

18. Protocols should also, if practicable, include provision for utilisation of Mihailović and Partisan forces after liberation and before elections:

(a) for further operations based on Yugoslavia against enemy. We consider it essential to divert mutual hatred to enemy if we are to avoid an immediate outbreak of civil war after liberation, which may well involve unprofitable use of British troops, whereas use of forces in manner proposed might prove advantageous;

(b) for maintenance internal order strictly within their operational areas.

We realise this raises thorny problem of future of Partisan forces in Mihailović area and *vice versa,* but so does any other plan for allocation of operational areas. We believe, if plan outlined in this signal be realised, general progress could be made which would obviate this particular problem before liberation.

19. After conclusion of agreements and protocols, King to make an appropriate personal broadcast. This to be followed immediately by authorised declarations by Tito and Mihailović, and such publicity regarding support of H.M. Governments and other Governments as is expedient.

20. In the statements both Mihailović and Tito would:

(a) renounce political activities for duration of occupation;

(b) renounce all propaganda activity except that essential for securing support of population in their respective areas and maintenance morale of their troops. Such restricted propaganda to conform to our general policy and to be carried out under our supervision and control;

(c) renounce military operations against one another;

(d) pledge 100% direction their energies to prosecuting war against Germany and satellites. In addition Tito would be asked formally to recognise dynasty for present, and Mihailović would be required to renounce all activities against Croats, Moslems and other minorities;

(e) assist in negotiations in Cairo and provide latest detailed information from the country.

21. One senior British officer from each Brigade to be evacuated forthwith, accompanied by one reliable Yugoslav. In view absence such Yugoslav our side, suggest Zujović might fill this role. He is comparatively up to date on conditions in country, enjoys Mihailović's full confidence and is, we believe, well disposed to us and reasonable in outlook. Grateful your comments in light your own dealings with him.

22. After conclusion of agreements, these Officers to return to their respective

H.Q. with copies of agreement and protocols and full written instructions from King, Government and C-in-C. Each to be accompanied by Senior Jugoslav Staff Officer and Jugoslav Political Representative, all to be acceptable to H.M.G. and C-in-C.

23. Instructions from Commander-in-Chief would embrace orders based on urgent military necessity for an immediate conference between Mihailović, Tito, Armstrong and opposite number, at which operational plans both sides would be coordinated and arrangements made for maintenance of internal contact. Meanwhile our own comments on plan are: -

24. We realise this plan is on highest level. We do not pretend it is an infallible remedy for present ills. We do contend

(a) It is only level on which we can really force issue with Mihailović as it turns his insistence on functions as Deputy Commander-in-Chief and Minister into channels for coercing him.

(b) True it will force Mihailović to display true colours beyond recall and so crystallise situation (?) for all our relations and prospects of getting operations done on scale we require. We personally feel plan will succeed, but even if it fails, we shall be able to cut our losses or make alternative arrangements for carrying out operations in Mihailović area.

25. Essential factor is to get Yugoslav King and Government to play. Now they are in Cairo personal influence and pressure of Minister of State and Commander-in-Chief can be brought to bear. As regards the King, dismissal of court clique of Pan-Serb officers should make him more amenable to our demands, particularly if he can be relieved of anxiety as to immediate Russian intentions in Balkans. It must be clear to the present Government that they have little chance of returning to country, either officially and collectively, or individually, without British support, and presumably their diplomatic and civil service pacts make them immune from personal political ambitions. In these circumstances feel you should be batting on a good wicket.

26. Non-political nature of the present Government should also help assure Mihailović and Tito that it could be entrusted with control of post-war elections, but we must be certain they have in fact no political axe to grind.

27. Agreement would be automatically terminated on completion of elections.

28. King's broadcast would kill Nedić's appeal to Serbs, and terms of overt agreement coupled with the declarations by Tito and Mihailović would remove doubts among people as to possibility of either resistance group instituting its own dictatorship after war. This would increase popular support for resistance groups throughout the country.

29. Mihailović himself in his letter to Commander-in-Chief stated:

A. He is ready for complete military collaboration.

B. He is now devoting his whole time to military operations.

C. The Central National Committee was founded because of the absence of King and Government. It is therefore by implication acting only as their representative here.

If Mihailović and company, despite British assurances and instructions from King and Government, refuse to accept the Agreement and protocols, or, after acceptance, refuse to obey orders from Commander-in-Chief, or attempt to evade their responsibilities, and continue to follow their present line, they make themselves insubordinate servants of King and Government, and can be dealt with accordingly. We shall know precisely where we stand.

30. We do not think Partisans should find plan against their interests. Operational zones would be based on present *de facto* territorial situation. Their public recognition by King and Government, and Mihailović's tantamount reduction, should please them and aid them in extending their popular appeal in their area. If their hold on people is as strong as they maintain, temporary renunciation of their peculiar political and propaganda activities and acceptance of dynasty cannot harm them, and victory at the elections would allow them introduce their own political system.

If they are unwilling to make these concessions they cannot expect Mihailović to make parallel ones and must bear their share of responsibility for the continuance of the civil war. These arguments apply to Mihailović with equal force.

31. Nevertheless Partisans' attitude to this proposal will be largely determined by attitude Russian Government. This is written in ignorance of result of Moscow conference, but if Comintern was dissolved in good faith we see no reason why Russians should oppose. But an essential condition of the agreement being accepted by Mihailović and his continued observance of its terms would be the maintenance by Russia of an attitude similar to our own.

There must be no future favouring of the Partisans by the Russians, and should they later take an active interest in operations in Yugoslavia they must send representatives and supplies and provide propaganda to both sides equally, imposing the same safeguards as we do. We believe in fact that a suggestion to send a Russian representative to this H.Q. even now would not be rejected out of hand.

32. For our part, we must squarely face fact that there is a moral responsibility on us to offer immediate rewards to all resistance groups for the burdens imposed on both troops and civilian population by the execution of operations for us. If we ignore this responsibility we defeat our own ends. (a), (b), and (f) of paragraph 15, and (2) of sub-paragraph (d) of paragraph 16 provide moral *quid pro quo*.

This is not sufficient to produce immediate action and would be considered by most Serbs as no more than their just reward for services rendered in April 1941. Neither as far as Mihailović is concerned does it provide satisfaction on the vital point of reprisals mentioned in (ii) of sub-paragraph B. of paragraph 5.

For this we must be prepared to give a substantial material *quid pro quo* which we can represent to him as aid intended to enable him adequately to defend the civilian population from reprisals provoked by operations and so ensure that the disparity between Serb and Croat losses in the war will not further be increased. Technical considerations also demand material assistance on a much larger scale as we cannot hope to bring off successful operations with troops inadequately equipped with supporting arms.

We believe the support stipulated in (1) of sub-paragraph (d) of paragraph 16 must be of the order of 300 sorties per month, per side, to demonstrate to the Yugoslavs beyond doubt our good faith, and dispel misgivings about "perfide Albion".

We do not suggest we should depart from our present policy of giving the bulk of supplies after successful operations, but it is manifestly impossible to insist on this condition when the number of sorties available per month is decreasing as rapidly as our demands for action are increasing.

The Partisans are given the whole Adriatic seaboard in your proposal for the neutral zone. It should be possible to supply them in part by sea from bases in Italy. This would relieve pressure on aircraft and render the increase in machines demanded by your proposed expanded programme less formidable.

33. If it is decided to act on paragraph 18, preparations should also be started now for large scale supply of arms by normal sea and land routes after liberation.

34. The decision on this proposal must be taken on highest level. To reach it a balance must be struck between the cost to us of political assurances and material support and the maximum contribution we estimate Mihailović and Tito can make to the war effort. Such an estimate can only be based on reports from our own observers.

We are not including such information in this signal, but we now have enough British Liaison Officers on either side to provide ample data insofar as not already collected, and "Dutch" 's [an American officer] proposed tour of western Serbia and possibly Sandjak and Montenegro will fill outstanding gaps in our knowledge of Mihailović's forces.

35. If decision is that it will not pay us to give assurances and support on scale we suggest, it would be better to say so frankly and seek other means or basis for carrying out essential operations in this country.

But we must cease raising constant hopes as in the directive received from Yugoslav Government of May, 1943, and the letters from King and Commander-in-Chief which Armstrong brought, in that material support will increase, even when coupled with provisos as to Mihailović's attitude if in effect sorties flown per month show considerable and progressive decrease.

We must also avoid such gaffes as General Eisenhower's decision that no aircraft could be diverted from present operations in Italy over Yugoslavia, or ourselves pleading diversion of aircraft for pamphlet raids and bombing in Italy, and following this up almost immediately with bombing of Nis and Skoplje. Incidentally this bombing was completely uncoordinated with any activities by Mihailović's forces despite his constant pleas for combined operations.

36. If decision is favourable, then Americans could be of great assistance in helping to secure necessary new aircraft to make the expanded sortie programme possible and also perhaps in securing supplies of weapons, ammunition and equipment, particularly W/T sets and material. Please therefore read this signal in conjunction with my Udal 50 of October 30th.

But "Dutch" 's scheme should not be automatically dropped if the decision on my proposal is unfavourable. On the contrary it should be proceeded with as any increase of aircraft would be invaluable.

37. Mihailović will of course be required to show good faith during progress negotiations by continuing to carry out operations on present scale, particularly those planned for Vardar Valley and Kacanik. Both parties would also be expected to suspend needless mutual slaughter and to respect one another in the neutral zone

pending conclusion of agreement. Your plan for delineation of neutral zone is not affected by your proposal.

38. We are assuming that there will be no major change in the Balkan situation before spring, and that without prejudice to the importance of present operations maximum activity will be most valuable then. We thus have about three months to realise this proposal, and two months to give it full implementation. We believe this can be done.

If the problem of evacuation is tackled energetically, the British officers could reach Cairo by mid-December. That would leave at least five weeks for the negotiations which could be put in train before the arrival of the officers.

39. If your decision is favourable, Armstrong will evacuate Bailey as his representative. Apart from his qualifications to assist in the negotiations, he could also put you completely in the picture regarding conditions in the country and clear up many of our present misunderstandings. In his absence "Noah" [one of the British Liaison Officers] could interpret.

40. If the plan fully materialises King Peter might be put into country after meeting between Tito and Mihailović. It is most important that[/]does not come earlier as his identification with either side at present would compromise him with the other and might endanger his personal safety.

Consult Serb history from 1813 to 1903. We have at moment inestimable advantage of no dynastic trouble to complicate our problems here. We must avoid creating a second Greek situation, but on conditions suggested his presence would be most valuable.

41. Despite emphasis at certain points on "liberation", this telegram is prompted essentially by military necessity - how we can best get our essential operations done. If we want extensive action from Mihailović we must be prepared to think and act on big lines ourselves. If we aren't so prepared, let's say so and readjust our tactics.

The present situation is largely due to the fact that our efforts to coerce Mihailović during the past nine months have resulted in one lukewarm directive from the Yugoslav Government, which entirely begged the essential issue of placing Mihailović under Commander-in-Chief's command and in a moderate and temporary increase in number of sorties.

42. It may be possible to realise the essence of this plan without the degree of diplomatic obligation proposed. The Moscow conference may have solved some of the difficulties which the proposal is intended to remove. If so, well and good. But the essence itself must be achieved if there is to be a change here for the better. It is:

(a) Exercise of pressure on Mihailović on the right level and through the proper channels.

(b) Recognition of our obligations to Yugoslavs, not abstractly, but as a material pre-condition of successful execution of our operations.

43. Please repeat to London and advise me when this done.

3. The Mansfield Report

(March 1, 1944)

SUMMARY

1. I was in Yugoslavia for a period of six months, i.e. from 18 August 1943 to 15 February 1944 with Mihailovic's forces. The first three months were spent with General Mihailovic at his General Staff Headquarters; the last three months on a tour of inspection of his troops. I travelled through the entire area of West and North Central Serbia on the inspection tour, going north from the Drina and Lim Rivers to a point just south of the Sava River at Sabac, west to a point 40 miles south of Belgrade, and south almost to Raska, in the Ibar Valley. I got out of Yugoslavia by going overland with small Cetnik bands through Herzogovina and Southern Dalmatia to a point on the Adriatic Sea a few miles south of Dubrovnik.

I had many talks with General Mihailovic and various members of his Staff and gathered information about him, his policies, his staff, army, communications system, operations, and relations with the British Mission attached to him.

On the inspection tour I personally inspected about 4,000 Cetnik troops with arms, and 10,000 without arms. I gathered statistics and information in each area inspected on the number of men mobilized, number mobilizable, number and types of arms and ammunition on hand, communications, personal histories of commanders and their officers, number and disposition of the enemy in the area, operations executed and planned, reprisals, hostages, propaganda (both Cetnik and enemy), morale of troops and people, attitude of troops and people toward the Partisans, living conditions and food situation, potential airdromes, etc. However, all of my pencilled notes and most propaganda collected were turned over to my superior, Lieutenant Colonel Seitz, whom it was thought would get out first. But I took out complete statistics furnished by Mihailovic on his army, letters from Mihailovic to President Roosevelt and General Donovan, and I have tried to reconstruct what I could from memory. I also have a substantial number of photographs.

2. Mihailovic has a fairly well organized army mobilized in Serbia. It is composed mostly of former Yugoslav army officers and men who had two years military training before the war. It is organized on a geographical basis with separate commanders and brigades in each "Srez" or political subdivision and a chain of command from the Minister himself down to the smallest platoon. Mihailovic claims he has 57,440 men mobilized and could mobilize over 400,000 if he had arms. Based on numbers of men seen, I estimate he has 35,000 men mobilized with arms but can give a better estimate when Lieutenant Colonel Seitz returns with our figures which can be spot-checked against Mihailovic's figures.

3. Most arms seen were in very poor condition and area commanders claimed they desperately needed arms and ammunition. Most rifles were old Yugoslav army type, pitted and worn. There are substantial numbers of German machine pistols and Barettas. Light machine guns were Zorkas or Holland type. There were very few mortars or heavy machine guns, and practically no artillery pieces. I would estimate each soldier has an average of about 25 to 40 rounds per rifle, and 150 to 200 rounds per machine gun. About every other soldier carries a hand grenade.

4. Mihailovic states he has 90,739 rifles, 321 HMG's, 1149 LMG's, 65 Mortars, and 294 Machine Pistols. The excess of arms over number of men mobilized does not exist in that part of Serbia inspected, however, but in such areas as Herzogovina and Southern Dalmatia, where it should be noted most fighting has been against the Partisans.

5. Most troop commanders impress me as capable soldiers. Mihailovic himself, while in good health and obviously having considerable ability as a leader, has surrounded himself with a second rate General Staff, with a political adviser, Dr. Moljevic, who is an extreme Pan-Serb. Mihailovic lacks ability to delegate.

6. The average Cetnik soldier is extremely poorly clothed and has been living a hard, rugged, and miserable life for three years in the woods, suffering many hardships, living in dirty peasant huts and eating what the peasant will give him. Many troops have not seen their families for nearly three years, or have lost them through German reprisals. Considering these factors, the morale and discipline of the troops in Serbia is very good; in Herzogovina rather poor.

7. The Army has a poor communications system, with a sprinkling of homemade, weak radio transmitters and relies mainly on couriers who take hours or days to deliver messages which should be received at once.

8. Military Intelligence generally is very poor.

9. The people in that part of Serbia inspected are 100% for King Peter II and very strong for Mihailovic, whom they revere because he led the resistance in 1941 when all other nations were losing, and because he stands for King and democracy. They do not seem to want communism or Partisans. In Herzogovina I was unable to get such a strong impression.

10. Morale of Serbian troops and people would be tremendously increased by even a token Allied invasion. They would then probably want to rise up in revold at once.

11. The Serbian people are tremendously enthusiastic for Americans. They refer to America as the only nation which has no ultimate designs on them.

12. Mihailovic is now doing very little fighting against the Germans, although he did have a month of considerable activity after the Italian capitulation in September 1943, when he cut the Belgrade-Sarajevo Railroad by destroying two important bridges, took many towns, and obtained personal surrender of the Italian "Venetzia" Division at Berane.

Mihailovic's policy is to hold up operations until "D-Day" (or "Justanek" as the Serbs call it) when he expects an Allied invasion and states that he will throw all he has into one all-out effort. He refuses to start operations now, stating (1) he wants to avoid heavy reprisals on the people, and (2) that he does not have enough arms and ammunition. He is determined to preserve the Serb population ethnically and numerically against the Croats. He also claims the he has only a "one-shot" army which will be wiped out by German reinforcements if he undertakes operations before "D-Day." He claims willingness to undertake continuous operations against the Germans if he is given a steady stream of supplies which would enable him to do it and thus counteract attempted reprisals. On the other hand, his record shows that while he promised to cut the main Belgrade-Nis-Skoplje Railroad lines in the Ibar or Vardar vallies (which are most valuable to the Germans as supply lines and avenues of retreat from Greece), he failed to keep his promise after his commander for this area received substantial arms by plane from the British. He also has failed to destroy the Bor and Trepsa Mines, important sources of copper and lead to the Germans.

Mihailovic complains that the British have failed to assure him that requested operations have been coordinated with general Allied strategy elsewhere.

13. Most Cetnik commanders and troops seen in Serbia would like to fight, but ask for more arms and ammunition which they claim they need in order to carry the fight to the Germans and prevent heavy reprisals.

14. There is complete distrust of the British by Mihailovic and his leaders, who feel the British have now sold them down the river to Stalin. They are particularly irritated at the British because of the BBC London Yugoslav news (which is their main Allied news source. Station WRUL, Boston, is too weak to be heard regularly). They point out that since September 1943 it has devoted its time almost exclusively to Partisan news and ignored Mihailovic despite the fact that he carried out substantial anti-German operations; and that in many instances BBC falsely credited the Partisans with many operations in fact carried out by the Cetniks, such as the driving of Germans out of Rogatica. There was evidence corroborating this.

15. I saw no Partisans in the area of Serbia inspected except a band of 800 to 1000 near Ivanica in January which had been pushed from the Sanjak into Serbia and was fighting Cetniks there. I saw small numbers of Partisans in the area of Herzogovina through which I traveled.

16. Cetniks in the north Sanjak, Herzogovina, and Bosnia are devoting virtually all of their efforts to the fight against the Partisans. The Cetnik attitude is that the civil war against the Partisans is now primarily racial, secondarily ideological. Cetniks claim that over 75% of the Partisans are Croats, many of whom are former German Quisling Ustachi who deserted the Yugoslav Army in 1941 to join with the Germans when German victory appeared inevitable, and who now have joined the Partisans when it appears that the Allies may win after all; and that these Croats,

carrying over their earlier racial and religious discontent, first decimated the Serb population in their blood purge of 1941–42, and are now determined to build up Croat control at all costs.

17. I saw no collaboration between Cetniks and Germans in Serbia, other than a liaison with the Nedici at Belanovica, east of Valjevo and at Aranjelovac, south of Belgrade, allegedly for the purpose of getting information on German movements. It was claimed that in one instance this enabled the Area Commander to make a successful attack on a German column and capture arms.

Cetniks in Southern Herzogovina and Southern Dalmatia are in some places collaborating with the Germans to the extent that the Germans are not fighting them there and are allowing them to travel unmolested so that they can fight Partisans. In one instance a local village commander admitted knowing the Germans there and assisting to billet 640 German troops. One Cetnik soldier showed me a legitimacia issued to him by the German Army at Dubrovnik, which described him as a "Cetnik" entitled to go into Dubrovnik to visit the hospital. I saw no evidence, however, that the Germans were giving arms to the Cetniks, or that Mihailovic knew about this collaboration.

18. I gathered there is a feeling on the part of both Cetnik troops and people that, while they are all for the King, they would not favor the government in exile.

19. There is no famine in parts of Serbia visited. Germans are collecting only a portion of the requisitions demanded, and then only in the plains regions where they can come and get it.

20. I cannot state what "line" Cetnik propaganda to the people is taking because it was too voluminous to be translated. A large batch of Cetnik pamphlets, newspapers and mimeographed material collected in the various areas inspected has been sent to Washington for translation.

1 March 1944

REPORT OF CAPTAIN W. R. MANSFIELD, USMCR ON MISSION TO GENERAL DRAGA MIHAILOVIC

I. CHRONOLOGICAL OUTLINE OF PERSONAL ACTIVITIES

On the night of 18 August 1943 I was dropped by parachute from a Halifax bomber to the General Staff of General Mihailovic on a mountain near Ivanica, Serbia, after a five hour trip from Derna, Africa. We spotted the signal fires almost immediately and made a pass at the field, during which I could see the fires from the hole through which I jumped. As soon as we checked our flash signal with the one seen on the ground, we did a circle of about ten miles, and came back. Then I shook hands with the RAF dispatcher, gave our "thumbs up" signal, and when the light went green, shoved off. When the chute blossomed I immediately saw the fires, realized I was a way off to one side, and landed in a pile of rocks, hurting my hip slightly. I found myself on a cool mountainside and in a few minutes was surrounded by a group of big bearded Cetniks who tried to smother me with kisses, yelling "Zdravo. Purvi

Amerikanec!'' (Greetings, first American) I lit my Very Light, signalling the pilot all was okay and was led to the dropping ground where I met many more Cetniks, Colonel William Bailey, Chief of the British Mission, and Major Greenlees, his Chief of Staff. In a little while the plane returned and nearly beaned us with about 15 containers, dipping its wings as it disappeared in the night. They were immediately taken away in oxen carts.

I learned that Mihailovic's ''Starb'' was less than one hour away and that he was waiting to see me. We walked over the mountain, noticing Cetnik guards posted on all surrounding hills as we passed them in the darkness. The ''Starb'' (or General Staff Headquarters) proved to be a few makeshift parachute tents grouped together and camouflaged in a copse near a few ''kolibars'' (mountain huts used by shepherds). There was nothing but the roughest equipment lying about, and a fire burning with logs around as benches.

A few minutes later the Minister appeared out of the darkness with some members of his Staff and personal bodyguard. We met and were able to converse in French. I found him to be a man of about 50 years, medium build, heavy gray beard, glasses, a friendly smile, and a sharp sense of humor. He introduced me at once to General Trifunivic, his Chief of Staff, Lieutenant Colonel Laladevic, his Operations Officer, and others. We then sat around the fire, drinking ''rakia'' (prune whiskey, similar to vodka) and discussing people we knew. Most men present were bearded and showed the effects of nearly three years ''in the woods''. They were dressed in all kinds of oddments, some wearing remnants of their old Yugoslav uniforms. Colonel Bailey broke the ice for me in getting to know them.

After an hour I went to the British Camp, about a half mile away, which I found to be a crude peasant hut and two parachute tents. Here I met Lieutenant Colonel Duane Hudson, the first British officer sent in, who landed blind by submarine on the Montenegran coast in September 1941, and two Royal Marine sergeants who had been captured on Crete in 1941 and jumped a prison train in Yugoslavia. We had a little more ''rakia'', then went to bed on some hay in one of the tents. In the meantime the oxen teams arrived and were being unloaded by the Cetniks.

I spent the next few days getting used to a new life, which was fairly rugged, and learning something of the current situation. We paid an official visit to the Minister and his Staff on the following day. Thereafter I had dinner several times with the Minister around his campfire, and engaged in long talks with Colonel Bailey, Colonel Hudson, Mihailovic and his Staff members. Only ''faux-pas'' committed to my knowledge was toasting to the Minister with the phrase ''Tvrd, sa mnoge godine'', the meaning of which I will not explain here. Much of what I learned was sent home over Bailey's radio. Before leaving Cairo I was told by Major Huot that I should use the British cipher because there was an understanding that all of our messages would be seen by the British. I was also given a poem cipher for emergency use only. When I arrived in Yugoslavia, Colonel Bailey advised me Cairo had sent a signal stating that I should use my own private code, showing all messages to him before sending them. Both he and I understood this to mean that my wires would be seen only by him. He advised me that I should feel free to send anything I liked. I therefore used my poem cipher until Lieutenant Colonel Seitz later arrived.

Life here was fairly rugged. We were located on the plateau of Cermernina Planina, with Germans about three hours away by foot. I immediately bought pack and riding horses and several quick-packing drills were held so that we could be up and away in a hurry if necessary. We slept on the ground and ate out of a common pot. Each day I spent some time with a Cetnik officer learning the language. Our Cetnik guard of about 30 men were raggedly clothed, dirty, and very curious but rugged looking and willing to help us in every way. They mostly carried old Yugoslav rifles, pitted and worn.

We were not starved, however. There was plenty of black bread, kimak (a kind of butter made from the top of the milk), pig, lamb, potatoes, plums and a little tea and sugar which came with me.

Colonel Bailey was most helpful to me upon my arrival. He impressed me as a capable, broad minded, intelligent, and patient officer who was far more familiar with the problems faced in dealing with Mihailovic than officers with whom I had talked in Cairo. He speaks the language like a native and knows all of the personalities involved, having been in Yugoslavia for many years before the war. He advised me that while I was part of the British Mission I should feel free to visit Mihailovic and his Staff whenever I liked, without reservation. He stated that he was very glad American representatives were coming, and hoped that there would be more.

Both Colonels Bailey and Hudson outlined to me their activities as British Liaison Officers, and the history of their relations with Mihailovic. At this time Bailey was engrossed in trying to get Mihailovic to undertake more extensive operations against the Germans. Mihailovic was balking, on the ground that he had insufficient arms, and that the reprisals would be too heavy. A few days after my arrival, Bailey sent Mihailovic a written ultimatum, pointing out how Mihailovic had failed on certain operations, and requesting that orders be given for execution of these operations. Bailey's one strong point was the failure of Mihailovic to carry out sabotage on the north-south communication lines in the Ibar and Vardar valleys where the area commandant, Djuric, had received a substantial number of planes. Mihailovic replied by letter, agreeing to issue orders for more action, and specifically agreeing to order Djuric to start operations in his area.

I found a situation on arrival, where there was some friction between Colonel Bailey and Cairo, because of alleged lack of cooperation by Cairo in not sending planes with arms for operations, which Cairo was insisting that Mihailovic carry out immediately. When planes did arrive they contained a great deal of defective or wrong equipment. I, myself, saw containers filled with nothing but undersize shoes and overcoats which would fit people only five feet, two inches high. Despite repeated wires to Cairo giving exact pin points, times, requests, etc., wires from Cairo indicated that they were paying no attention to Bailey's requests. For example, quite aside from the question of arms and equipment, the personal needs and necessities of the Mission were being neglected, and some members lacked proper clothes, boots, etc.

In my daily talks with Mihailovic and his Staff, I received considerable information about his army, organization, and communications. I also studied living conditions for the purpose of giving my prospective commanding officer some idea of what he would face, and what he should bring in with him in the way of supplies.

Everyone, both in the British Mission, and in Mihailovic's Staff were interested in knowing what was to be the status and functions of the American Officers, whether more Americans were coming; whether the Americans would send in arms and supplies; what was our attitude toward the Partisans; whether we would have our own private radio to Cairo; and similar questions. Mihailovic was, of course, particularly interested in knowing whether the Americans would be under the British, or would set up separate missions with him. Before leaving Cairo I had repeatedly asked for instructions on our functions, and had been told that I was going in simply to prepare the way for a senior officer who would be fully briefed; that I should acquaint myself with the personalities and general situation, and send home over the British radio, such information and intelligence as might be of use to my senior officer coming in, particularly on the question of what supplies he should personally bring in. Answers on the question of our functions were always very general and to the effect that my senior officer would be able to instruct me upon arrival. I had one briefing conference with Major Inman, head of the Yugoslav desk at M.O.4, Cairo, in which he advised that the Partisans were doing much more fighting against the Germans than Mihailovic; that Bailey was having great difficulty getting Mihailovic to undertake operations, and was, in fact, not seen by Mihailovic; that it would be necessary to send in a new man with a firm hand, Brigadier Armstrong, who would bring pressure to bear on Mihailovic to carry out these operations; and that the most important operations were destruction of lines of communication in the Ibar and Vardar Valleys, i.e., the main railroad lines into Greece and Bulgaria.

I, therefore, answered the many queries by stating that I was merely sent in to prepare the way for my superior, who would be in a better position to answer; that I did not know how many more Americans would come in, but I hoped many; that we were working in full cooperation with the British in all respects; and that for the present I would be simply an American military observer.

Without knowing exactly what our functions would be, it seemed to me that we might possibly serve in any of the following capacities:

(1) *Military Observers*, reporting home military intelligence. But for this function, we would need at least 30 or 40 representatives throughout areas occupied by Mihailovic's troops, with radios, in order to report first-hand intelligence. No fighting is done by Mihailovic's G.H.Q., except when it is attacked. American representatives there could only serve as a conduit, transmitting home such day-to-day unconfirmed reports as Mihailovic's Chief of Intelligence might offer. One officer could easily handle this job for both British and Americans.

(2) *Military Liaison* to advise Mihailovic on strategy, and coordinate his operations with general Allied strategy in Europe. This function would require that the officer have some knowledge from Cairo as to what advice could be given regarding general strategy.

(3) *Supply Liaison*, checking on Mihailovic's needs and requirements for operation, handling negotiations with Cairo for supplies, administering the distribution of

supplies to Mihailovic's forces, and checking on their use in the field. This would depend on whether the U.S.A. was going to send in any supplies.

(4) *Operations*. American representatives could furnish American technical operational personnel such as demolition experts, radio operators, etc.

The last three of the above would depend, of course, on whether Mihailovic's operations were going to be extensive enough to warrant them.

For the first two weeks life was relatively calm. Two Musselmen spies were captured and I had the unpleasant experience of seeing them get their throats slit. An average of about two German transports, and one light bomber flew over every day, but we were well camouflaged. The local Korpus commander gave us a tremendous dinner out in the open under the trees (about four miles away) at which I stuffed myself, drank "rakia", and even gave a speech of thanks with what little Serbian I knew. Cetniks and peasants came and gaped at me while I ate. I was initiated into the "kola" (national dance) to the music of a harmonica, and had to heave the shot-put a bit. At this point it seemed like a damn good war with no bang and plenty of pleasant people who were obviously lionizing me right and left.

On 4 September we heard of the Allied invasion of Italy and immediately hoped we would be in Belgrade by Christmas. So did the Serbs. There was much celebrating, and on 5 September fires were lit in honor of King Peter's birthday.

On the following morning, 6 September, the Germans let us have it and I had my first taste of combat. In the early morning mist a force of about 200 Germans came up the mountain side on our side of the General Staff, while we were asleep. All of a sudden all hell broke loose, with heavy machine fire "dum-dumming" and light machine rat-tating in all directions, right close by. Bailey and I threw on our pants and shoes, grabbed our rifles and "quick-packs", slit a hole through the back of our tent and jumped into the woods. We could see the Jerries coming up over the hills at about 400 yards in their blue-green uniforms with rifles, and opened up fire ourselves. But there did not seem to be any front. Machine guns, Sten guns were being fired from all directions, both in front and in back of us, and were cutting branches in the trees overhead. Bailey suggested we back further into the woods, which we did. Finally we did a semi-circle about a half-mile back and were near the Starb. The firing continued another hour and a half. We learned that the Germans had been driven back down the mountain. We then went back, got our horses and things and returned to Mihailovic.

Several were killed on both sides and some prisoners taken. I saw one prisoner being alternately questioned and then kicked and beaten. Later I was told that he had had his throat cut.

We immediately left on a long day and night march in the rain over the steep mountains for two days to Zlatibor, with Mihailovic, his Staff and a guard of about 150 soldiers. Here we pitched camp near the Uvac River. Mihailovic and Staff were located about two miles from us, spread out in different kolibars. His radio stations were located about one mile from us on the other side. It was the usual custom for us to spread out in this fashion, for security reasons, and to have some privacy. On the march we always traveled in a single column, with about 250 people, and 40 to 50 horses.

We were now in the area of bushy-haired Captain Radovic, local commander, who became a close friend when I gave him some film. He gave me a considerable amount of intelligence on German disposition in his area, which I wired to Cairo. That week four of his soldiers created a mild sensation by dressing up in the uniforms of some Germans they had killed, going into Uzice (where there was a large German garrison) and machine gunning a notorious Quisling leader in his home.

On the night of 8 September we heard over the BBC, the announcement that Italy had signed a capitulation on 3 September. We were at the time, not far from a garrison of about 2,000 Italians at Priboj, and were surprised that we had not received some advance notice from Cairo, which would have enabled us to place Mihailovic's troops near the Italian garrison and obtain their personal surrender, as well as their arms, before the Germans stepped in. On the following day, Colonel Bailey received a wire from Cairo, instructing him to do everything possible to obtain surrender of the Italians in the area, but not to take their arms and ammunition away from them if they would agree to fight with the Cetniks against the Germans. At Berane, was located the Italian "Venetzia" Division, command post for Italian troops there and at Priboj. The "Tauranese" and "Emilia" Divisions were reported to be in the area from Podgorica and Bokor Kotor north to Dubrovnik. Bailey immediately set out with Major Lukasevic and a band of Cetniks for Berane to try to obtain surrender of the "Venetzia" division. I repeatedly wired Cairo for orders to go with him, thinking that it would be helpful to have an American representative at any talk with the Italian commandant, but received no reply for over a week.

On 11 September, Colonel Hudson and I went to Priboj to try to obtain personal capitulation of the Italians there, whom we could hear all night, fighting the Cetniks who were attacking their garrison. We arrived that night close to the Italian garrison, but when our peasant courier tried to make contact with the Italians inside, they opened heavy fire on us, which lasted three hours. We retreated up the mountain, and received word on the following day from the Italian commandant that he was under orders from his command post at Berane, and that he would not surrender until he received instructions to do so from his General. We then proceeded back to the British Mission.

In the meantime, Mihailovic had sent out a general order to his troops throughout Yugoslavia to attack lines of communication, and German troops. I had a copy of this order translated and sent home a signal about it. Thereafter, for several days, Mihailovic was showing me radio reports from all of his Korpus commanders reporting extensive sabotage and attacks on small German columns throughout Serbia, Herzogovina, Bosnia, and Dalmatia; that several trains were derailed in south Serbia; that a large number of German lorries were destroyed, and several villages and towns taken. Commanders in Bosnia and Dalmatia were complaining bitterly about being attacked in the rear by Partisans, while Cetniks were fighting Germans. For example, they stated that after taking Gacko and driving the Germans toward Bileca, Partisans walked into Gacko and claimed that they had taken it from the Germans.

While this was all going on, BBC London, on its Yugoslav news program, began an extensive program of Partisan news, devoting its attention almost exclusively to reports that the Partisans were fighting the Germans everywhere, and taking numerous cities and towns from the Germans throughout the region of Bosnia, North Herzogovina, and Dalmatia. Mihailovic was never mentioned, despite the fact that his intelligence reports were to the effect that he had taken many towns, such as Berane, Priepolje, and Gacko; and had carried out the above mentioned operations. The American station WRUL was reporting both Cetnik and Partisan operations at this time, but it was so weak that it could be heard only infrequently.

At this time Mihailovic asked me to see him at a conference with his Staff. He was furious at the British because of the BBC news, and showed me intelligence reports from his own commanders indicating that some of the BBC news was false. He asked me whether it would be possible to have a group of American observers come in solely for the purpose of going out with his troops to see for themselves the operations which he was conducting and report back intelligence to my government. He stated that he felt further talk with the British on the subject would be useless because it was quite apparent to him that the British had sold him down the river to Stalin. I told him that I would report the matter home for consideration by my chief. I immediately revealed our entire conversation to the British Mission and sent home a signal.

From this point on there was complete distrust of the British by Mihailovic, his staff, and his area commanders. The feeling toward the Americans, on the other hand, was one of intense friendship. Time and again, both Mihailovic and his officers stated that they felt that America was the only democracy left which would take a fair and unbiased view of what was going on in the country.

I had now been in the country one month, sent home over 90 signals, and received four replies. One congratulated me on my safe arrival. The second was not decipherable. The third advised me to keep each message under 300 letters, rather than 350 letters, the British limit, and to stay with Mihailovic rather than join Bailey on the trip to Priboj. I received no replies to several questions submitted to Cairo during the month. A fourth had to do with the Theater Command.

On 20 September, Colonel Bailey returned from Berane. He and the British enlisted personnel with him reported that on the way down to Berane, Lucasevic and his troops had taken Priepolje from the Germans in an all day attack, driving the Germans toward Plevlje and killing, I believe, over 100; that he had obtained complete personal capitulation from the Italian commanders at Berane and Priboj and entering into an agreement for joint coordinated action against the Germans; that in view of this agreement he had not disarmed the Italians, but had left a skeleton Cetnik force in each town. About two weeks later, Mihailovic reported that the Partisans had attacked Berane, and disarmed the Italians.

On 23 September Colonel Seitz and Brigadier Armstrong were dropped to us on Zlatibor. Armstrong brought with him Major Flood, Intelligence Officer; Major Jacks, Operations Officer; Lieutenant Colonel Howard, Chief of Staff; two enlisted wireless operators; and one batman. Both Seitz and Armstrong lost a great deal of their equipment upon landing, either through theft or dropping too far from the landing ground.

Colonel Seitz was unable to answer many of the above questions regarding our functions, which I had faced the first month. There was a strong difference between him and Brigadier Armstrong on these matters. At the first meeting with the Minister and his Staff, Brigadier Armstrong presented letters to Mihailovic from King Peter II, General Wilson, and Colonel Putnik, head of the Yugoslav legation at Cairo. Seitz stated that he had not been advised of these letters. After the initial greetings, the Brigadier obtained a private audience with the Minister for himself and Colonel Bailey, to which Seitz was not invited, and on the following day, at the first official staff conference with Mihailovic and his staff, the Brigadier excluded us in front of all personnel present, including the Yugoslavs. The Brigadier also took the position that while we must show him all of our wires, he need not show us all of his wires to Cairo. Shortly thereafter, he also forbade Colonel Seitz's going to Priboj to purchase a horse, and to see the Italians who had surrendered, although his own Intelligence Officer, Major Flood, was allowed to go there.

The American members of the Mission were now relegated to the position of doing practically nothing. We submitted a signal to Cairo on the above, and received a reply that we were under the Brigadier's command; that the only persons allowed to see the Minister would be Brigadier Armstrong, or, in his absence, his next in command, and Colonel Seitz or, in his absence, his next in command, in the presence of an interpreter selected by Brigadier Armstrong; and that the Brigadier's messages would be subject to scrutiny at his discretion.

Soon after his arrival, the Brigadier stated that we could expect very few planes all winter, because the RAF was allowing only a very small number for these operations; that Mihailovic would only get supplies by plane for specific operations, which he hoped to persuade Mihailovic to undertake, such as the blowing up of bridges on the Ibar and Varda valley railroad lines.

During his first week, the Brigadier went with Colonel Hudson to blow up a bridge on the Belgrade-Sarajevo narrow gauge railroad line near Vardiste. This job was a success, and they returned six days later. During this period there had been a complete mix-up with Cairo on whether arms would be sent in for the job. Cairo had refused a plane load to Zlatibor, on the ground that it was located too near Partisans in the Sanjak, but eventually agreed to send arms to Cermernica. Lieutenant Kolarovic sent a large group of men two days travel time to this latter spot which was now dangerous because it had been compromised when we were attacked by the Germans there on 6 September. They waited several nights in the cold but no plane came. This only served to increase the strain between Mihailovic and the British, especially since Mihailovic had already sanctioned this rather important job which would cut the supply lines by railroad from Belgrade to Dubrovnik. Despite repeated clear wires from the British Mission on pin points for landing grounds on Zlatibor, signals received from Cairo indicated either a complete misunderstanding, or ignorance of our signals.

On 2 October, Brigadier Armstrong, Colonel Seitz, Colonel Hudson, and Major Jacks went with a large number of Cetniks to attack Visegrad and destroy the large railroad bridge on the Belgrade-Sarajevo near Rogatica. The operation was a success. The Germans were driven out of Visegrad and the Cetniks gained control of the railroad line. The bridge was blown up a couple of days later. During this period, I was attending intelligence meetings daily with Major Flood and Lieutenant Colonel Novarkovic, the Minister's Chief of Intelligence. Daily Intelligence bulletins were sent home by Flood and myself, in the American cipher, for the reason that the British deciphering branch at Cairo reported that they had such a back-log of undeciphered messages that we could expect quicker transmittal if we used our own cipher which was jointly held with the British.

The Brigadier, upon his return from the Visegrad job, would have a daily conference with the Minister, to some of which Colonel Seitz was now being invited. At these conferences, the Brigadier would try to get the Minister to undertake new operations, but Mihailovic would continue to stall action, raising such questions as whether the British would give him arms for the jobs, whether the cost in reprisals was too high, and how the job fitted into General Allied strategy. Many conferences were held, for instance, on a plan for Djuiric in the south to attack the main railroad lines north of Skoplje with a mobile striking force which would then move south toward Macedonia and cut the Salonika line. After much haggling Mihailovic agreed to authorize the job, provided certain special weapons were sent in to Djuric by the British. Not much hope was held out for completion of the operation, however, because Mihailovic had already reneged on a previous order to Djuric, who had stated that he had received no previous orders to carry out an attack on the railroad lines.

Relations were becoming more and more strained, however, and the Brigadier's position was getting more and more difficult because we were receiving virtually no supplies, and each day BBC London was devoting its time entirely to the Partisans.

In October we received one plane at the General Staff, containing two bodies and some explosives. Thereafter I believe that no planes were sent in to Mihailovic anywhere. Mihailovic at the same time was incensed because after his troops had taken Rogatica from the Germans in early October, and had assembled a large number of his forces for an attack on Sarajevo, he was attacked in the rear by Partisans. Simultaneously, BBC announced that the Partisans had taken Rogatica from the Germans, although the Cetniks had control of the town at the time.

In view of these circumstances I suggested to Colonel Seitz that we make an appreciation of the situation to determine how the American members might be of use in this theater. I then prepared a basic estimate which reached the conclusion that Allied control of Mihailovic operations was necessary; that such control could be obtained only if the Allies were in a position to feed him with supplies; and that we should make a general inspection of Mihailovic's army in Certral Serbia and report our findings to Cairo and Washington. Colonel Seitz took the report up with the Brigadier, who sanctioned the inspection tour. The substance of the report was sent in signals to Cairo. The Brigadier then took up the proposed inspection tour with Mihailovic, who agreed with our plan and assigned Captain B. Tovorovic, Yugoslav officer with the General Staff, as our Liaison Officer. Colonel Hudson was assigned as interpreter from the British Mission. It was anticipated that we would try to get out of the country at the conclusion of the tour after we had obtained all the statistics on Mihailovic's army.

In the meantime we were attacked by Germans near Rudo, on the Lim River, and moved north for several days close to Ljubovija, which is on the Drina River, southwest from Valjevo, North Serbia.

Our itinerary was selected to enable us to see the largest number of areas and troops in Central Serbia that could be inspected in about one month and a half. These areas included those under the following commanders: Major Racic, Major Milovanovic, Captain Ninkovic, Captain Kalabic, Major Smiljanic, Major Vuckovic, Major Cvetic, and Major Lucavsevic. Maps showing the routes followed, places where we stopped and the troops and people viewed are attached hereto as Exhibit "B". This itinerary would also permit us to see troops both in the plains in North Serbia and the mountains in the south.

On 7 November 1943, we left on the tour with Major Racic, went north toward Sabac, going east through Vladimirci, south to a point below Valjevo, east to a point near Topola, then south near Gornja Milanovac, Cacak, Guca, ending up in Cvetic's area near Raska.

The procedure followed in each area was about the same. We first had a long conference with each Area Commander, in which we obtained general information about his staff, troops, arms on hand, men mobilized, men mobilizable, communications, enemy disposition, operations executed and planned, reprisals, medical supplies, potential airports, enemy movements, and other information. Such information as was tabulatable we obtained on a form of questionaire for each Srez from the commander interviewed. The balance was recorded in pencilled notes. At the same time, Captain Todorovic had requested the Minister to obtain the same information from all Area Commanders whom we would be unable to visit and to forward the same to us in Cvetic's area where we expected to be in the middle of December.

Following is a list of troops and people actually seen by us on the entire tour:

Area Commander	Location	Date	Unit	No. of men with Arms	No. of people without Arms
Major Racic	Dornja Oravica		Azhukovaska Brigade	350	900
"	Stave		Radjevska Brigade	125	125
"	Gornje Sipula		Cerska and Jaduska Brigades	400	250
"	Sinocovic		Pocorski Brigade	40	300
"	Svilenva		?	50	
Major Milova- novic	Tulari	—	1st Tamnavsha Brigade	50	2,000
"	Dupljaj and vicinity	—	?	200	2,000 (including women and children)
"	Struganik	—	Valjevska Brigade	70	350
Captain Ninkovic	Ivanovci	—	?	190	200
Captain Kalabic	?	—	Kreiljeva Gardia	600	300
"	Vlackca	—	Orasacka Brigade	80	500
"	Stragari	—	?	100	750

Area Commander	Location	Date	Unit	No. of men with arms	No. of People without Arms
Major Simljanic	Kamenica	24 Nov.	?	100	400
Major Simljanic	Ljljaci	25 Nov.	2nd Kruzanka Brigade	250	250
Major Vuckovic	Bielo Polje	26 Nov.	2nd Takovska Brigade	300	400
"	Brusnica	27 Nov.	—	—	300
"	Pranjani	28 Nov.	1st Takovska Brigade	140	630
Markovic	Kamenica	30 Nov.	?	50	
Vuckovic	Krstac	1 Dec.	—	—	70
"	Kotraze	3 Dec.	?	120	200
"	Luke	4 Dec.	—	—	200
Major Cvetic	Rudno	5 Dec.	Staff Cos. of 1st & 2nd Ltudenica Brigades	89	100
"	"	7 Dec.	?	200	
"	Golija Mtn.	19 Dec.	Bazervska Brigade	300	
					1,200 recruits
			Total	3,804	9,625

We arrived in Cvetic's area in the first part of December near Raska. At this time the Brigadier was still up north in Racic's area. The information requested from the Minister had not arrived and we had no radio contact with the General Staff because Cvetic's radio was not working. When the radio was repaired we sent some messages to the Brigadier through Mihailovic's General Staff, but had no replies.

After waiting several more days we decided to try to make for the Adriatic coast as soon as we had obtained the balance of the information from the Minister, in order to present this information which we thought would be of some importance to our Government in deciding its policy toward Mihailovic.

On 23 December while we were hiding away in the little village of Krljani in Cvetic's area, we received a penciled note via Celjak courier from Captain John Wade, British Liaison Officer attached to Kesserovic. He stated that he was with a group of six enlisted men located about three hours from us, and that pursuant to orders received from Cairo, he was on his way to cross over to the Partisans in order to leave the country. We immediately went over and found him. He stated that relations between the Allies and Mihailovic were almost broken off because Mihailovic was refusing to fight the Germans, and that Mihailovic was accused of collaborating with Germans in his fight against the Partisans; and that he was ordered to join the Partisans if he felt that he could make his way over with a reasonable degree of safety. He had been given a pin point near Berane, but since the intervening territory was heavily populated with Germans and Cetniks, he decided to try to make his way through Zlatibor, then cross the Drina, and work his way down south until he could make contact with the Partisans. He was told to ask for the commander of the 2nd

Partisan Korpus and was advised that safe passage to Italy had been guaranteed by the Partisans.

Colonels Hudson and Seitz decided that we would join Wade at once. Colonel Seitz felt that if we waited any longer the information which we had collected would become stale and that it was better to get out with part of the information rather than lose all. Hudson stayed with Wade, who went to Srednja Reka, where we joined him the next day. That night Colonel Seitz and I talked the matter over further, and decided that it would be better if he went on with the information already collected while I waited, obtained the balance of the information, and follow him as soon as possible. I gave him all of my penciled notes and statistical data collected from various Area Commanders on our tour of inspection. Early on the morning of 24 December, the entire party left in a westerly direction toward Stitkovo, while I remained at Srednja Reka.

On the afternoon of 24 December, Major Cvetic and Captain Todoravic arrived at Srednja Reka, and I explained to them what had happened. On Christmas day we received a message from the Minister to the effect that Major Lukasevic was leaving in a few days with all information, and would escort us to the coast through Bacevic's area where a canal was now open. On 1 January, having seen nothing of Lukasevic, I decided to push on toward Novo Varos, in Lukasevic's area, in the hope that I could establish liaison with him and save time. On 2 January I arrived in Stitkovo and found that we were surrounded on three sides by Germans and Partisans who had come over from the Sanjak, and that it would be impossible to hide away in a small village, for the reason that small groups of Partisans had been infiltrating into the area for several days. I also found that Lukasevic and Kalaitoic were both near Novo Varos, but separated from us by German and Partisan troops. We therefore made a hasty fifteen hour retreat back to the area of Srednja Reka. Enroute, we bumped into Captains More and Stock, British Army, who said they were following Wade. I advised them of the situation, and they decided to wait while I went back to try to establish liaison with Mihailovic. We were then separated by very heavy two day snow fall, after which I found that they had pushed on.

After eight days I went forward again as far as Bratljevo, and found that about 1000 Partisans had been pushed from the Sanjak into the Stitkovo area, and were now between us and Novo Varos, our objective. On the night of 13 January we attempted to sneak through their lines but were unsuccessful when our two guides were captured by the Partisans. On the following day we circumvented the Partisans by going over Javor Mountain, and arrived safely in Stitkovo, where we saw Kalaitovic, who told us that the canal to the sea was now open, and that we should proceed in the direction of Priboj to meet Lukasevic.

From then on we continued our march to the sea, in the course of which we had a few brushes with Partisans and Germans. Briefly, our route was from Stitkovo to Novo Varos, Priboj, Rudo, Gorazde, Kalinovik, Ulog, Kifino Selo, Lubinje, Stare Slano, and the region south of Dubrovnik. We crossed the Lim River at Priboj, the Drina River at Gorazde, and the Trebisnjica River at Stare Slano.

At Priboj we met Lieutenant Colonel Ostojic, who advised that Lukasevic had left with a party of 16 Yugoslav naval officers for the coast. He gave us letters from

Mihailovic to Roosevelt, Donovan, and Eisenhower, which I sewed inside of my jacket. At Priboj the route of the canal was outlined to us, and we followed it with some variations depending upon whether we met Partisans or Germans enroute. We traveled with armed escorts ranging from five to 60 men, depending upon how many we could obtain from the local Cetnik commander in each area. We made several forced marches, one for twenty-two hours, without stopping, and several during the night time to avoid conflict with the Partisans. When we arrived south of Kifino Selo we found ourselves blocked by large numbers of Partisans in the surrounding mountains and after traveling six hours to try to make a path through, our guard of 50 men balked, and were forced to retreat back near Kifino Selo. On the following morning we learned that Colonel William Bailey and Major Lukasevic were not far away, and we joined their party.

I learned immediately from Colonel Bailey that he was doing the same thing as myself and hoped to get out of the country by giving a pin point by radio to the British, and having a naval craft pick him up. He invited me to join him, and I did so.

Previously my plans were to try to capture or buy a small boat on the coast and see if I could make my way across the Adraiatic. I heard that tow parties had done this successfully.

Our party now numbered about 180 men. We succeeded in pushing through the Partisan area to a spot near Lubinje, where we found ourselves blocked by several hundred Germans on one side, and a brigade of Partisans on the other. After almost bumping into the Germans, we decided to change our route and go between the Partisans and the Germans. We had proceeded only one half hour when I, at the head of one of the columns, bumped into a German patrol at about fifty yeards. Here it was Lukasevic's quick thinking which saved us. He advanced with some men as if he were looking for the Germans, and told us to go back. I later learned that he demanded to see their commandant, stating that he was the Commandant of the Cetnik Nevisinje Brigade, and that he had important information to give the Germans; that he was escorted into the village, met the German commandant and advised him that he was out scouting for Partisans and that a large band of Partisans were intending to attack the Germans that night, and that he, Lukasevic, hoped that the Germans would be on the alert. The Germans allowed him to go for the purpose of fighting the Partisans. In a little while the local Cetnik Srez commander arrived. He stated that he was acquainted with the German commandant, that he had found living accommodations for 640 of the German troops in the area and was expecting another 640 the next day. That night we went in the dark through the area, not far from where the Germans were billeted. On the following day we crossed the Trebesnjica, and made contact with Lieutenant Colonel Bacevic's Headquarters. Thereafter, we remained in the vicinity of Dubrovnik, while Colonel Bailey made contact by radio with Cairo.

We were then about five hours from the coast. Bacevic had advance notice of our coming, and a young Yugoslav navy lieutenant in his area who knew the coast very well had made a survey for the purpose of trying to find a pin point. He finally selected a point about five kilometers south of Cavtat where the rocks descended abruptly into the Adriatic Sea and there was a deep water cove from which we could flash a signal without its being seen by Germans. The only difficulty was that there were several villages between us and the point which harbored a number of Ustachi. Between us and these villages was a large range of mountains descending to a plateau which in turn descended to the sea.

Another difficulty was that Bailey's batteries needed to be charged. We had been told that Bacevic would do this at his headquarters which were about eight hours inland, but when we arrived we found he had no gasoline. We therefore sent a courier into Trebinje, where the batteries were charged by a local concern. We finally made contact with Cairo and received word a day or so later to stand by for three days at the pin point, the coordinates of which we had signaled to Cairo, and to signal certain letters by Morse code with our flashlight each night for three hours.

Up to this point the weather had been excellent. On the night we started down to the coast, a big storm blew up. After sneaking down the mountainside through several villages, in rubber-soled shoes, we arrived at the pin point without much difficulty. There was an angry sea and we knew that we could not embark, but we kept flashing the signal for three hours. When no boat showed up, our Celjak guide, who lived about three quarters of an hour on the pin point, agreed that we could hide out up in his bedroom the next day, so we returned and stayed there all that night and the next day. There were now ten of us, and we stayed in this room without moving out, the landlord bringing us food during the day. Again we tried the next night, but without success, because the weather was still unsettled, and we stayed one more night and day in the same house. When the boat did not show up the third night we made a long hard retreat up over the mountains for five hours back to the Knezevic family, who hid us for the following day. On the following night we returned to the little safe village from which we had originally started.

By this time we were pretty discouraged because we found out that the Gestapo knew that we were in the general vicinity, but did not know exactly where we were. We received this word through one of Bacevic's spies in the local Gestapo office at Dubrovnik. Furthermore, our batteries had run out, and we had no way of getting them charged except at Trebinje. When we sent a peasant there with the batteries to be charged, he found that the Germans were getting their batteries charged, and had left a soldier to watch their batteries. The soldier became interested in our batteries which were of a different type, so that we had to get the batteries out of there that night. Finally we managed to get another battery.

The weather continued to be bad and we had a heavy snow storm. We finally established contact with Cairo and tried to arrange that we would not proceed again to the pin point until Cairo gave us a signal that the ship had already left Bari. This we did because we felt the canal was good for only two more days and we did not want to compromise it. The signal finally came through from Cairo and we again proceeded on the night of 14 February over a slightly different route to the pin point. The trip down the mountainside was extremely difficult because of the snow which made our boots slip on rocks and roused several dogs in the neighborhood. We were only twenty minutes at the pin point flashing the letters R N when we heard the low hum of the motor. About fifteen minutes later the ship slowly pulled up and slung a dingy overboard. In 26 minutes we had embarked all nine of our party. The ship was a British Navy type ML, about 75 tons, bristling with nine machine guns. We arrived in Bari at 0900 the following morning.

While in southern Dalmatia I was advised by everyone, both Yugoslav officers and peasants, that there were no Partisans south of Dubrovnik. I did not run into any on our trip to the coast through this area.

II. MIHAILOVIC AND HIS POLICY

Mihailovic's general policy is the same as that of any other guerrilla force in an occupied country, i.e. resistence based on ultimate Allied victory. His order of battle, however, as expressed both by himself and many of his leaders, is based upon saving up his offensive for "D-Day" or "Justanek", as it is called by the Yugoslavs. This policy is based upon the assumption that the Allies will invade the Balkans, or if they do not, that he will be called upon to make one grand effort to throw the Germans out of Yugoslavia without Allied help. Mihailovic's position is that he does not have enough arms to engage in extensive operations before this great "D-Day" and still have enough left for the great day. He bases this upon the tremendous reprisals and German counter offensive which followed his "justanek" in the fall of 1941. He also wishes to avoid any further extensive reprisals which he believes will only serve to further reduce the numbers of the Serb population which he states has already been decimated by the Croats, Ustachi and Germans. He is determined to preserve the Serb population ethnically and numerically to avoid Croat domination after the occupator is thrown out.

For the above reasons his policy as expressed personally and in operational orders to his area commanders is to cut down operations against the Germans and Bulgars before "D-Day" to a minimum, unless he receives sufficient arms from the Allies to wage a continuous war against them. His present orders allow each commander to engage in small attacks against the German forces where his own forces are numerically superior in the particular instance to those of the enemy and gain from the operation (either in arms captured or damage done) will more than offset the subsequent cost in reprisals.

The only major departure from the above policy during the past year came immediately after the Italian capitulation, in September 1943, when for a period of one month Mihailovic issued general orders to his leaders to attack communications and enemy forces wherever possible.

At the same time, Mihailovic continues extensive fighting against the Partisans, insisting, however, that his orders are that commanders will fight Partisans only when attacked. In January I was advised by Captain Todorovic, who had sat in on secret meetings of Mihailovic's Staff, that Mihailovic allocates percentages of arms to be used in certain areas against the Germans and Partisans; and that everywhere he is allocating a greater percentage (estimated at about 65%) to the Partisan War. This is borne out by Mihailovic's own figures which show he has an excess of arms over men in certain areas, such as Herzogovina, where he is fighting the Partisans.

The above policy reduces the Cetnik army in Serbia (where there is little or no conflict with Partisans, because there are very few Partisans in Serbia) to a static condition where everybody is waiting for "D-Day". Many of the leaders and men would probably like to do more fighting because they are sick of being in the woods for three years. Mihailovic thus only serves the purpose of keeping immobilized a certain number of German troops who must be on hand to check the threat of a general uprising by his troops.

The following is Mihailovic's history as related to me by Colonels Bailey, Hudson, and others: Mihailovic personally is a regular career officer in the Yugoslav army, born near Ivanica, Central Serbia, of Serbian parents. Before the war he had served in several different capacities in the Yugoslav army. For a time he was Military Attache at Prague, Czechoslovakia, and Military Attache at Sofia, Bulgaria. He speaks good French. When the war with Germany broke out he was a General Staff Colonel on the extreme left wing in Bosnia, near Sarajevo. When the army began collapsing in his area he immediately retired to the hills with several of his officers and men. Gradually he was joined by others and found himself to be the highest ranking officer. At that time his immediate policy was not to fight the Axis until he was supported by the Allies, thereby precluding heavy reprisals upon the Serbs. He planned to wait until "D-Day", when he would make one great effort to throw out the Germans. He soon found that the Musselmen in Bosnia were being appealed to by the Croat anti-Serb population to join with the Ustachi in the purge of the Serbs, so he went from Bosnia in May 1941 to Ravne Gora, north of Cacak. At this time the country was in a virtual state of anarchy because the Germans had not yet organized their control. It was being run by Belgrade commissars and gendarmes who were too weak and demoralized to keep order for the Germans. Mihailovic got considerable backing from the local people around Ravne Gora by putting local bandits in the hills. He was also joined by large numbers of Yugoslav officers and men who had escaped the Germans and did not want to go into the cities where they would be taken prisoner and sent to prison camp.

In June 1941 Russia entered the war against Germany. Prior to this the Communists had been outlawed in Yugoslavia. Now a small group who call themselves Partisans and who were strongest in the vicinity of Montenegro (where the poverty of the land has always caused the population to take more to Communism and to produce more artisans who showed Communistic feelings) began organizing. Their chief appeal was that now *the people*, and not the army and politicians who had let them down, would do the fighting. The Partisans were therefore fairly popular because they promised everything, didn't go against the King, and were all for getting rid of the old politicians.

Mihailovic's position at this time was not strong, because he came from an army which had been compromised. The Serb peasant who formed over 80% of the population of Serbia, was extremely disappointed at the showing made by his country's army of 1,500,000 men, which he had supported by the sweat of his brow for many years. The Serb felt that he had paid for a fight and that he hadn't received a fight.

In the fall of 1941 the Germans left a very small force to occupy Serbia, mainly because they had drawn most of their forces to the Russian front. The Partisans, finding the Germans weak, began making successful attacks on communications, railroads, and small German columns.

Mihailovic was now forced to take a different position, because he found himself with a competitor appealing to the Serbian people who were getting excited over the successes of the Partisans. In August 1941 he therefore issued a general statement that he realized the temper of the people, that he had been appealed to as a responsible leader, and that he was now going to come down and lead a general revolt against the occupator. This he did, with considerable success for two months, working with the Partisans jointly part of the time. Uzice, Pozega, Cacak, and many other towns in Central Serbia were taken, and Valjevo was besieged.

The joint offensive did not last very long, however, because of the many differences between the Partisans and the Cetniks. Peace was made for a while, but did not last long. Then the Germans mustered their strength, made a drive south into Serbia and crushed both the Partisans and Mihailovic with a full scale offensive with tanks and infantry. Mihailovic went into Montenegro. The Partisans first went into Herzogovina and were pushed from there into Bosnia. This spelled the end of the Partisan appeal to the Serb people because the Partisans were defeated and now Nedic and the collaborators became popular. The general feeling was that a German victory was inevitable and that the people might as well follow the Nedic slogan, "Work, and order. Let the big nations fight out the issues which the Serbs cannot settle, and from which the Serbs can only get futile bloodshed". Now the people wanted peace and no reprisals—particularly those who would lose the most.

Mihailovic now sat in Montenegro where he reorganized his army with orders that it should stay under cover until it could be strengthened. He was able to stay in Montenegro from September 1942 until May 1943 because of collaboration between his local leaders there and the Italian occupators to whom control of Montenegro had been given by the Axis after the defeat of Yugoslavia. Mihailovic justified the receipt of Italian arms which he used against the Partisans on the ground that he would subsequently use them against the Italians themselves.

Today Mihailovic still has a great grip on the Serbian peasant. Everywhere Colonel Seitz and I traveled on our tour through north-central Serbia the people in villages who turned out to see us cheered him madly. In private conversations they talk of him as one would of the Messiah. Cetnik troops and peasants alike sing romantic songs about him, and Ravne Gora, his original hideout, has become very sacred to the Serbian people. To them, Mihailovic still stands as a symbol of their spirit of resistance against the occupator. He also stands for the things they want, King and democracy. They feel that he did not desert them in their greatest hour of need, immediately after capitulation, but stayed to organize their resistance and fought against the Germans in 1941 when the big nations were losing the war everywhere else. One must remember that the Serb peasant is a simple man, uneducated, and bound to grasp firmly to simple ideas.

As far as qualities of leadership are concerned, Mihailovic seems to lack the ability to delegate authority. For example, he personally sees and answers every telegram and letter from his various commanders and other representatives throughout the country. This wastes valuable time which could be used for important matters, and delays answers which must be sent off immediately. Even on minor matters such as arrangements for movement of his GHQ to another location he personally supervises everything.

Colonel Bailey has also reported that Mihailovic fancies himself as a very clever politician and diplomat who has attempted in relations with the British to get help without making commitments binding upon himself, with the result that he hurts his own position because he only encourages hard dealing and lack of complete frankness on both sides. For example, he refused to accept as a condition to the receipt of British aid, that he would permit British liaison officers to witness the operations which he said he would carry out if the aid were forthcoming, and he isolated himself from Colonel Bailey, after Bailey had made this request. Bailey's position was that if Mihailovic was actually going to carry out the operations as requested, he would lose nothing by allowing British officers to witness them and would in fact probably help himself because the British could render first-hand reports to Cairo. Later, Mihailovic withdrew from this position and reestablished relations with Bailey.

In his dealings with the British missions sent in to him, Mihailovic, (according to Bailey) has unfortunately adopted an attitude that they are only glorified quartermasters. He has limited his discussions primarily to making requests for arms and ammunition, and that the British broadcast certain propaganda submitted by him. No attempt was made at the outset to enter into complete and frank joint discussions or agreements on proposed operations, and whether they would tie in with Allied policy. This may partly be due to early action of the British. At the outset of their relations with Mihailovic, in the fall of 1941, they sent Mihailovic a plane load of arms over the objection of their own British liaison officer, Colonel Hudson, who pointed out that the aid would be used in the civil war which was beginning to brew with the Partisans. When Mihailovic learned of this he adopted the attitude that the British mission was relatively unimportant because he could get aid in spite of it. During this same period BBC London, regardless of messages from Hudson, was making a world wide figure of Mihailovic. This only tended to inflate Mihailovic's superiority complex in his early dealings with Hudson, and in his later dealings with Bailey. Mihailovic also showed evidence of smallness in his treatment of Colonel Hudson. When he found that Hudson had tried to stop Cairo from sending aid, he kept Hudson virtually incommunicado for almost six months. More recently Bailey reports that Mihailovic tried in several ways to keep him from getting out of the country.

Toward Colonel Seitz and myself, Mihailovic has always been most affable, but we have never had dealings with him involving American supplies or requested operations.

Mihailovic has a very second rate general staff, probably in part due to his inability to delegate authority. His next highest ranking officer is General Trifunivic, who appears to be his Chief of Staff. Actually he seemed to me to be nothing but a rubber stamp. Rumor has it that Mihailovic kept Trifunivic constantly at his side to prevent potential rivalry for control of the Yugoslav army. Before leaving, however, I heard that Trifunivic has been placed in charge of a group of Korpuses. Mihailovic's Chief Operations Officer, Lieutenant Colonel Laladevic is reported by the British to be rather narrow minded and inefficient. Mihailovic's political advisor, Dr.

Moljevic, is an extreme pan-Serb, anti-Croat, a former lawyer who lived and practiced in Banja Luka, which was purged mercilessly by Ustachi in 1941 and 1942. Major Tersic and Captain Slepcovic, other assistants to the Minister, are pleasant and friendly but seem to lack ability and force. The only staff officer who appears to have ability suited to his position is Lieutenant Colonel Novarkovic, Chief of Intelligence, who is a hard worker, but he is hampered by poor communications system and lack of operational orders regarding intelligence.

As distinguished from the General Staff officers, Mihailovic's Area and Korpus commanders are on the whole, fairly capable leaders, when one takes into consideration the paucity of officer material available after capitulation, and that the cream of the officers, numbering about 12,000, are in German prison camps. The Cetnik commanders are, with few exceptions, former regular Yugoslav Army officers, averaging about 35 years of age. Nearly all of them have been with Mihailovic since his early days in Ravne Gora, and are used to many hardships after three years in the woods. These commanders must almost of necessity be fairly capable men, because they must lead groups of volunteers serving without pay, without adequate equipment or arms, and under most rugged living conditions.

Idealogically Mihailovic stands for King, and democratic principles of representative government. As Minister of War of the only Yugoslav Government politically recognized by the Allies, Mihailovic takes the position that he is the legal head of all men of legal fighting age throughout Yugoslavia, and that upon receipt of orders from him they should mobilize under his banner. This may color his thinking on the number of men he can actually mobilize because he may be under the impression that they will mobilize merely because they are legally mobilizable.

III. MIHAILOVIC'S ARMY

The information which follows is based upon a personal inspection made by Colonel Seitz and myself of Mihailovic's troops in North Central Serbia, the areas of which have already been listed above. While each area commander suggested a route through his area which would permit us to see the greatest number of his troops, we were given free choice to choose our own routes if we so desired. Maps showing our exact route are attached hereto as Exhibit "A". Scarcely a day was passed without an inspection and review of some unit of Mihailovic's forces. Photographs were taken of nearly all Brigades inspected and are attached hereto as Exhibit "B".

In nearly all areas large numbers of villagers and towns people collected to greet us. In fact, our daily receptions by the people in some areas were almost overwhelming. For instance, in Milovanovic's area, north of Valjevo, people lined the roads for miles, showering us with flowers and fruit, and stopping us for brief visits. It was possible to make this trip without running into the enemy because we always kept on the move.

Under the above conditions we had an excellent opportunity to study the condition of the men, their arms, morale, age, etc. We also had a chance to gain some impression of the type and ability of their leaders and the morale and attitude of the people.

We first obtained from each Area Commander, detailed information from his area on each of the following topics: (1) Names and short personal history sketches of his officers: (2) Disposition of enemy in his area, with reasons why they are so disposed; (3) Disposition of his own troops; (4) Description of targets in area; (5) Communications System; (6) Supply; (7) Reprisals; (8) Hostages; (9) Potential Airdromes; (10) List of operations to date; (11) Plan of operations; (12) Relations with Nedici; (13) Propaganda, including enemy, Cetnik, Partisan, and Allied; (14) Economic Intelligence. Pencilled notes taken by me on the above were turned over to Colonel Seitz.

Each Area Commander also gave us a schedule prepared by him showing for each Srez in his area, the following: (1) Population; (2) Number of men already mobilized and under arms; (3) Men mobilizable in all three branches; (4) Arms and ammunition on hand; (5) Arms and ammunition requested. In addition to the above, Mihailovic gave me his own schedule giving the same information for all Areas, including those visited by us. This schedule is attached as Exhibit "C". A glance will show the painstaking work to which Mihailovic has gone in order to set forth the numbers for each Srez, or political district.

It was our plan to check the figures personally collected by us, and spot-checked in the field, against those received from Mihailovic. This will be impossible, however, until Colonel Seitz returns, for the reason that I turned over all schedules to him except the one received from Major Cvetic. The latter checks very closely against Mihailovic's figures.

Since Colonel Seitz has all of the notes, schedules, and propaganda collected in the figures, the information set forth below is reconstructed entirely from memory, and hence is very incomplete.

(a) *Organization of the Army*

Mihailovic states that he has 57,440 men mobilized, and that he could mobilize 472,900 for the first group (active mobile combat troops, 18 to 40 years); 169,600 for the second group (saboteurs, men between 40 and 55 years of age); and 58,520 for the third group (homeguard, over 55 years of age).

I believe that Mihailovic now has mobilized about 35,000 men with arms. This figure, which must of necessity be a pure guess, is based upon the fact that in the very, very limited area of Serbia inspected by us we saw at least 3,000 men with arms. In many areas we were unable to see all of the Brigades, for many different reasons. Some were doing guard duty. Others were stationed too far from us to appear. In some areas we showed up as a total surprise to the Korpus commander, so that he was unable to muster all men from the different parts of his area during the very short period when we were with him.

The army is organized geographically. Each Srez in Serbia (political division of area comprising a small section of yugoslavia) has at least one Brigade depending upon its population, of which an average of about 250 men are constantly mobilized in the woods. There are also many more recruits without arms in each area who are called together frequently for a period of training. If completely mobilized, each brigade would number between 2,500 and 5,000 men, depending upon the population of the area.

The army is organized as follows:

(1) Vod (troop or platoon)

(2) Ceta (company - 2 or more vods

(3) Brigade - 2 or more cetas

(4) Korpus - 2 or more brigades

(5) Area or Call - 2 or more korpuses

The commander of each unit is responsible to the commander of the next highest unit, and each Area Commander is responsible directly to General Mihailovic. Korpuses and Srezes are shown in a map attached hereto as Exhibit "D".

Until very recently Mihailovic made no promotions of officers in the army, who continued to hold the rank which they had at the time of capitulation. While korpus commanders tried as much as possible, for the sake of discipline, to have junior officers who were subordinate in rank, it was not uncommon to find a Lieutenant in command of a Brigade, with a Captain under him, the Lieutenant having proven himself a more capable leader of troops during the past two years. Of late, however, Mihailovic has promoted some officers, and there now appears to be a hierarchy of command. Of course, all troops serve without pay, and are told not to expect pay in the future.

Korpus commanders are responsible for all operations within their areas and enter the areas of other Korpus commanders only upon orders of their Area Commander or Mihailovic.

Guerilla warfare (requiring men to organize where cover is best and to live mostly in the woods) requires that any organization of forces be flexible and adaptable to changed circumstances. In general, however, each Area and Korpus Commander has a Chief of Staff, Intelligence Officer, Intendant, Adjutant, Propaganda Officer, and a Staff Company or Personal Guard. Each officer and soldier is issued a personal Cetnik legitemacia, and a roll is kept of membership in each area.

Each Korpus Commander advised that figures showing the number of men whom he could mobilize in his area were based upon secret rolls kept by the Cetnik Mayors of the villages in the areas; that they could rely upon the loyalty of the people in these villages, and that periodically, organizational meetings were held for the purpose of testing the morale and willingness of the people to serve. In some areas troops mobilized for active duty are constantly kept in rotation so that large numbers of the population eventually see service at some time or another in the Cetnik ranks.

In most areas visited there was always a large number of men without arms, who turned out for inspection. For instance, in Vuckovic's area at one inspection we saw over 600 such men.

(b) *State of Army, Morale, and Fighting Ability*

When the troops originally rallied around Mihailovic on Ravne Gora in 1941, many had their uniforms, rifles, and ammunition; a great deal of which was depleted by the unsuccessful revolt in the fall of 1941. During the past 2½ years their uniforms have worn out and there has been very little replacement of clothing, with the result that the troops are now in an extremely ragged condition. While the peasants can supply food and shelter, clothes and shoes are almost impossible to obtain. They must be purchased on the black market at sky high prices, and without funds this is impossible. The only source of clothing is an attack on enemy troops, and I have heard troops planning such an attack to get themselves some clothes. At present Mihailovic's troops wear all kinds of oddments, including peasant garb, and Italian, German, Bulgar, and British uniforms. The great majority wear native Opankas for shoes, and these afford little protection against rain, rocks and snow. Perhaps the most extreme example of raggedness was in Vuckovic's area, where we saw 25 soldiers of the Second Takovska Brigade, who had walked without shoes eight hours in the snow to appear for inspection. Yet one rarely hears them or their commanders complain about lack of proper clothes. All they ask is arms and ammunition.

About half the Cetniks are heavily bearded, carry their ammunition on their persons, with one or two hand grenades hooked onto their belts, and look like "tough hombres".

The average Cetnik soldier in Serbia has a Yugoslav rifle which is pitted and worn, and shows the marks of having been buried for some time after capitulation. The leather sling has been worn out completely, and is now replaced with rope or rag. There are no supplies, soap or oil for cleaning these rifles, so that it is impossible to keep them in first class condition. In short, the average rifle often looks more like a museum piece, than an instrument ready for use on the battlefield.

Mihailovic's figures show that for 57,440 men mobilized, he has on hand the following arms and ammunition:

> 90,739 Rifles
> 321 Heavy Machine Guns
> 1,149 Light Machine Guns
> 65 Mortars
> 294 Machine Pistols

Some of these figures seem out of all proportion to what we found on inspection. For instance, Mihailovic's report states that he has over one and one-half times as many rifles as men mobilized. Upon inspection, we found everywhere in North Serbia, that there were insufficient arms. Each Commander advised that if he had more arms he would mobilize more troops.

Mihailovic's own figures show that the excess of arms over men mobilized does not exist in the part of Serbia inspected by us, but in areas like Herzogovina where he is fighting the Partisans. This ties in with my own observation. Lieutenant Colonel Bacevic did state, for instance, that in his area (Herzogovina and South Dalmatia) he had plenty of arms taken from the Italians, and did not want anything except shoes and clothing for his men.

As for ammunition, the amount varies in different areas in Serbia. An individual soldier may have from 10 to 100 rounds for his particular rifle, or at best, enough for about one day's fighting. There is a small sprinkling of automatic weapons and light machine guns in every korpus, and each korpus usually has two or three mortars with sufficient bombs to last not more than an hour in battle. There are practically no heavier weapons such as light mountain artillery pieces (seventy-five milometers), Howitzers, or the like.

There are, of course, exceptions to the above. For instance, Kalabic's area, where the King's guard is located has a substantial number of light machine guns captured from the Germans in August 1943.

The best way to test all of Mihailovic's figures will be to check them against those personally obtained by us when Colonel Seitz returns.

When one considers that for two and a half years these men have been serving without pay, living in the woods under most difficult conditions, suffering reprisals upon their families, and that they are poorly equipped, poorly clothed, and poorly housed and fed, their morale is excellent. Their clothes are often so ragged that they look more like tramps than soldiers. In the bitter Serbian winter, without any clothes, other than thin jackets and pants, without gloves, and without shoes other than thin "opancies" they live under conditions which I would have considered it impossible for them to stand if I had not seen it with my own eyes, often marching many hours with heavy equipment through deep snows.

The discipline in the Serbian Cetnik is also amazingly good. I have seen men ordered by their commanders to carry out long marches under most difficult conditions without a murmur. In fact, on the road they keep up spirits by singing peasant songs. Breaches of orders are, however, dealt with rather drastically. Men may be shot by their commanders for violations which incur a lesser penalty in our army. Minor infractions are punished by 25 blows on the back with a stick in front of the platoon.

It is difficult to gage the fighting ability of the Cetnik soldiers. The majority, i.e. all men over 25 years of age, went through two years of compulsory training required by the Yugoslav government before the war, and hence have a basic knowledge of infantry weapons. There seems to be a noticeable lack, however, of capable junior tactical officers.

Brigade commanders and junior tactical officers do not go in for any extensive training before making an attack on the enemy or carring out a sabotage operation. Their combat intelligence before attack is very poor. They rely mainly upon the element of surprise for success, but they are apt to be surprised themselves by factors which were not properly briefed before the attack, such as the length and construction of a bridge, the housing of the enemy forces, the number of the enemy in the neighborhood, the length of time to get to and from the point of attack, and the deployment of their own forces. Usually, however, the Cetnik has an advantage over superior numbers of the enemy because he knows the terrain better, and gets information from natives concerning the enemy. Hence, the German sticks mostly to the towns and main roads, and rarely ventures up into the hills.

The tactics used by Cetniks in attacks on the enemy are crude. The forces usually assemble in the woods close to their target. If the target is a moving column, they strike heavily by surprise from the woods, and the attack is either a success or failure within the first hour. In attacking towns they tried to strike by surprise during the night or at dawn, stealing up within striking distance. If they have success they invade the town, kill as many of the enemy as possible, destroy targets, and take off what food and equipment they can lug. If the general area is held by Cetniks they stay in the town until they are ousted by the enemy.

Mihailovic's army obtains its food from the Serbian peasants who seem to give both food and lodging willingly to the Cetniks. Most commanders advised that it was rarely if ever necessary to requisition food from the peasants, and that the peasants were only too glad to give it. When a commander finds it necessary to ask for large amounts for a concentrated group of his soldiers, he sometimes gives a receipt to the peasant, which it is hoped will entitle the peasant to payment after the war. The problem remains as to how the army would be supported if it were fully mobilized, since nearly all the peasants would then be taken off the farms and put in the army. Most commanders feel that women and children could work the farms during this period.

The above information applies only to that part of Serbia inspected by us. In Southern Herzogovina and Dalmatia, through which I went on my trip out of the country, the situation differed considerable from Serbia. The troops in these areas seemed to have more arms and ammunition, which Lieutenant Colonel Bacevic, commander for the area, stated that he had taken from the Italians after they capitulated. But the morale, fighting spirit, and discipline of these forces does not compare with that of the Cetniks in Serbia. For example, one band of 60 Cetniks refused to continue with us through one area south of Nevisinje because they were afraid of running into Partisans who blocked off the area. On the retreat back to our starting point, about 50 of these men disappeared. There was a great lack of junior officers with the result that 100 men would often be under a sergeant only. In one instance, a soldier sent off on a most urgent mission as a courier was found two hours later still waiting around for a rest, and something to eat before he left. Major Lukasevic nearly ordered him to be shot. This lack of morale may in part be due to the collaboration with Germans in this area, and in part to the fact that the people are war weary.

(c) *Communications*

Mihailovic's army has a very poor and inadequate communication system, with the result that it depends almost entirely upon couriers, who take days to deliver a message which should be delivered at once. At the General Staff there are five central radio transmitters, each one of which maintains daily liaison with about seven Korpus commanders. Each of these commanders in turn has a small home-made, low powered primitive radio transmitter which is usually only capable of operation during the day time, and is often out of commission. Some of the Korpus commanders have a few similar transmitters within their areas for the purpose of keeping liaison with distance Brigade Commanders.

When Colonel Seitz and I were on our tour of inspection we saw how frustrating it can be to try to operate an army with such an inadequate system. For instance, when I was in the southern part of Cvetic's area I made a two day trip over mountains through heavy snow to Stikovo to try to find Lukasevic or Kalitovic, who had radio transmitters, so that I might establish liaison with GHQ by means of their radio. I arrived to find that both commanders had left the vicinity two days before and that we were surrounded on three sides by Germans and Partisans. All of this would have been avoided if Cvetic's Korpus commander had had radio liaison with GHQ or with Lukasevic. The result was that we did not know whether to take a chance and go on from Stitkovo, or to retreat. The approach of German forces finally led us to make a thirteen hour retreat back to the point from which we started.

Mihailovic's army would be tremendously improved with just a moderate amount of radio transmitters properly placed. With his present inadequate system, important combat intelligence often fails to arrive on time. It also means that when a certain brigade is ordered to action in an area, action cannot be commenced until it is too late, because word is not received on time. It further results in divorcement of Brigade Commanders from their Korpus commanders, with the result that there cannot be coordination of activities in different areas, and forces are trapped by the enemy because word cannot be gotten to them in time.

Mihailovic presently works his primitive radio system to the extreme, and accomplishes the most he can, but he is tremendously handicapped by lack of equipment.

(d) *Intelligence*

Mihailovic has the facilities for an excellent intelligence system in Serbia, because in every village and town there are Cetniks who want to help him. The results obtained, however, are very poor. Each Korpus commander seemed to us to know the enemy disposition in his area pretty well, and most operations are reported in to the Korpus commander, but most Korpus commanders showed an appalling lack of knowledge about targets in their areas or about other strategic information of interest to the Allies. For instance, they could give only rough estimates on lengths and construction of railroad bridges and tunnels, the nature and extent of enemy protection of targets, the times of movements of trains, the daily movements and habits of enemy garrisons, the locations and sizes of potential airfields, the equipment and operation of strategic factories and mines, etc. This ignorace is in part due to probably a lack of appreciation, and in part to sheer laziness. It is mostly due, however, to lack of proper organization and orders from the Minister and his Chief of Intelligence. It was only recently, and after much hammering that we were able to get Mihailovic to direct commanders to collect details on railroad traffic, enemy aviation activities, etc.

Good target intelligence is still lacking. For example, before our attack on Visegrad and the destruction of the Rogatica bridge, we received three different estimates on the size and structure of this bridge, all of which varied greatly, and all of which were wrong. It would have been a simple task for the Area Commander to make an accurate and complete reconnaissance of the bridge. We likewise received only the roughest information from Vuckovic and Cvetic on bridges and factories in their areas.

No plausible excuse was offered by Area Commanders for not providing excellent intelligence on all matters within their areas. The men who are now standing by in the woods waiting for arms and ''D-Day'' could easily be put to work to provide the Allies with top-notch intelligence. Such activity might also improve their morale. I feel that good results will not be obtained unless Mihailovic issues a forceful directive making it clear to everybody that he considers the matter to be of vital importance. At the same time, each commander should be given the categories into which such intelligence must be divided, such as (1) Target intelligence, (2) Enemy movements and disposition, (3) Disposition of Mihailovic's forces, (4) Operations, (5) Enemy propaganda, (6) Miscellaneous matters, such as word received concerning enemy plans or enemy letters intercepted. Each commander should also be impressed with the fact that this is a continuous job and that details are important.

(e) *Operations to Date*

On the subject of operations generally, my impression is that prior to the Italian capitulation in September 1943, Mihailovic was conducting nothing but minor operations against the Germans. In September and October, a substantial amount of operations against the Germans were reported from all areas, some of which were witnessed by Allied personnel. Several trains were wrecked. A large amount of railroad track was torn up. The Belgrade-Sarajevo Railroad line was broken by destruction of the Vardiste and Rogatica bridges (the latter a very long one). Many towns were taken after attacks on Germans, such as Priepolje, Bielo Polje, Berane, Priboj, Visegrad, Rogatica, Gacko, Bileca, etc. The Italian "Venetzia" Division surrendered. A large number of German cannons were destroyed, and a substantial number of Germans killed. Since October, activity seems to have gone down almost to its former level.

The fact remains, however, the Mihailovic (despite promises) has failed to cut the main railroad lines north and south through the Ibar and Varda vallies. These are most important both as present supply lines and as the principal means by which Germans would retreat from Greece and Macedonia. Mihailovic has also failed to destroy the Bor and Trepca Mines, important sources of metal to the Germans.

From each Area Commander visited, Colonel Seitz and I obtained a statement of his operations to date against the enemy, showing the time and place of the operation, the numbers involved on both sides, with the results. Colonel Seitz now has the pencilled notes on all of this data, so that it is impossible for me to list the details. My only recollection is that most of the Area Commanders claim to have carried out several small operations a month during the past year, a small operation being one in which a band of 100-200 Cetniks attacked a larger number of Germans, Lotishevci, Nedici, Bulgars, or Arnauts. In some areas much larger operations are reported. Two typical lists of operations received from Area Commanders, which I happened to retain, are attached as Exhibits "E" and "F".

Since there were no Partisans in the areas visited by us on our inspection tour, the question of operations against the Partisans did not come up.

(f) *Operations Planned*

Each Area Commander expects that there will be a "D-Day" when he will receive an order to conduct all-out operations against the enemy within his area. His plan of attack is to deploy his available manpower in such a way that he can wipe out enemy garrisons within the area and cut enemy lines of communication. For instance, Kalabic showed us in some detail how he would deploy his troops to attack the enemy if the enemy disposition is the same on "D-Day" as it is now. Colonel Seitz has our pencilled notes on these plans.

For operations prior to "D-Day" each commander operates under an order from the Minister, directing that he may in his discretion, carry out minor operations where the number of his forces is greater than the enemy, and the results gained will be worth the cost in reprisals.

(g) *Medical Attendance and Supplies*

Mihailovic's army is woefully lacking in medical officers and supplies. Each area has one or two medical officers at best, and no supplies other than a few bandages and battle dressings. In some regions, such as Cvetic's area, there are no military doctors, but the Commandant has an arrangement with certain doctors in the towns that they will render assistance when called. This, of course, would prove most unsatisfactory during any large scale operations, because the assistance would come too little and too late.

One of the most pitiful instances of lack of medical attendance and equipment was reported by two British enlisted men who were present when Major Lukasevic attacked Priepolje in September 1943. They stated that several men with bullets in the chest or stomach, finding no medical assistance in the rear lines, returned to the front line and continued firing until they died.

(h) *Training and Recruitment*

Mihailovic's commanders have no difficulty in finding recruits in Serbia. We have witnessed many Cetnik recruitment ceremonies, in which thousands of Serbian peasant youths showed up to be sworn in to the Cetnik Army. In Zlatibor I saw 1600 recruits at one ceremony in October, and in Cvetic's I saw about 1,500 at another in late December. The only difficulty is in finding arms and ammunition for these men.

Serbian youths who wish to join the Cetnik ranks are accepted by the local commanders if found physically fit. They do not, however, become Cetniks until they take the oath. This is administered by a local Orthodox pope, at an impressive ceremony usually held in the woods under the supervision of the commandant and his officers. All youths assemble, and prayers are first read by the pope. Under the guidance of the pope recruits then raise their right hand, swear allegiance to the King, country, and Cetnik army. Then there are many speeches by the local commander and members of his staff, and many cheers for King Peter, Yugoslavia, and Draga Mihailovic. Thereafter, the men go into a period of training which varies according to their areas. The next step is to provide them with arms. If there are no arms, they may be returned to their homes until called to active duty or placed on active duty without arms, such as courier duty.

The training in most areas consists of the Yugoslav manual of arms and infantry tactics. There is very little close order drill, because guerrilla warfare does not call for it. There is, however, a large amount of deployed infantry tactics; which are used most of the time in the woods. We have seen recruits going through this training.

In nearly all districts there is a "youth movement". Youths from 12 to 18 years of age are recruited and trained in infantry tactics, using wooden rifles and machine guns which they make themselves.

The living conditions of the recruits and active soldiers are most rugged. The recruit enters without pay or equipment (other than his rifle) and carries his own food with him to the recruitment ceremony. Thereafter, he must live as best he can on the generosity of the peasants.

In some areas soldiers are considered to own the rifles which they bring with them into the service, so that it is impossible to have a rotating army. In other areas, however, (such as Kalabic's area) all arms are treated as community property. Soldiers are then kept on active duty for a period of several months, and are then permitted to return to their farms, being replaced by new recruits who are given their arms. This system seems to work out better and permits the area commander to have a larger number of mobilizable combat troops available in his area.

(i) *Propaganda*

By far the chief source of Allied news to the people of Yugoslavia is the radio, and the only Allied station which most radios can always get without interference is BBC London. The Boston station, WRUL, is too weak to be heard regularly.

In the country areas where we lived there are very few radios, mainly because these people cannot afford a radio and would have difficulty getting an accumulator periodically charged for its operation. Each Srez probably has not more than three radios, one of which is usually owned by the Brigade Commander for the area.

The peasant receives his news, therefore, by word of mouth from those who hear the radio, or through mimeographed news sheets and propaganda issued by the Cetnik Commander in his area, who has a radio. The only other source of news are the German controlled newspapers, such as "Novo Vreme" or magazines, such as "Signal" which is published in the Serbian language.

Each Korpus has its Propaganda Officer, who is responsible to the Chief of Propaganda with Mihailovic. There is no uniform type of propaganda leaflet issued for all Serbia. In some areas, newspapers are printed, such as "Ravne Gora" and "Gardist", (published in Kalabic's area). Elsewhere, there are mimeographed pamphlets issued daily in some areas, weekly in others.

I am not prepared here to answer questions on the "line" taken by Mihailovic's propaganda. Colonel Seitz and I collected a great volume of material, but we were unable to get it translated for us because there was not enough time. When this is all translated here, we will be in a better position to see what the general trend, appeal, and arguments are. My present impression is that, even though there are few Partisans in North Central Serbia, Mihailovic still issued a great deal of anti-Partisan propaganda there.

The BBC which, since September 1943, has devoted most of its time to Partisan news, has caused a tremendous anti-British sentiment in all Cetnik ranks. This is shared to a lesser extent by the peasants who are more perplexed than antagonistic. They cannot understand how this radio station, which praised Mihailovic so highly in 1941 and 1942, is now backing their civil enemy so strongly. At first the local propaganda officers tried to explain the BBC news to the people by stating that BBC did not reflect the views of the British people. Since December, however, when Law, in the House of Commons, stated that the British Government was giving far more aid to the Partisans, because they are doing more fighting against the Germans, they have ceased this explanation.

The Germans, in addition to controlling the newspapers, issue propaganda pamphlets and place placards in most of the cities and towns. I turned many of these over to Colonel Seitz, and upon his return they can be studied.

The only Allied pamphlet I saw was one dropped by plane in Herzogovina in January. It showed a picture of Roosevelt, Churchill, and Stalin at Teheran, and gave a Serbian text of the statement issued by them there.

On the whole, the Serbian peasant seems to learn important news events quickly. Of course, the fact that both Mihailovic and the German controlled newspapers attack the Partisans, may class them together in the eyes of the peasant.

The Cetniks like the Boston radio station, WRUL very much, stating they believe it tries to give an impartial statement of the news, but are disappointed because it is very weak and cannot be heard regularly. As for discussions on the radio from the United States, however, whether over WRUL or rebroadcast over BBC, the criticism generally was that they did not go enough into the deeper problems. The Serbs, while glad to hear broadcasts from friends of their own race in America, are not very impressed when sister Divna from Pittsburgh gets on the radio and sends best wishes to everybody in some town in Ivanica where she used to live. They want something more serious.

(j) *Food Situation*

There is no famine in Serbia. The peasant still eats and lives almost as well as he did before the war, except that he lacks white flour, sugar, and such delicacies, which are so expensive that they are in most cases entirely beyond his reach. There is plenty of black bread, corn, "kimak", pig, lamb, "rachia", chicken, and the like. The only scarcity is found in those mountainous areas which always were poor.

The Germans requisition from each village, a certain percentage of its crops and livestock, and require that the food be delivered to a receiving station periodically in some central town. If it is not delivered as ordered, the Germans go on punitive campaigns, burning houses, etc. In the northern plains the peasant delivers on the average about 50% of his requisitions, because the flat country enables the Germans to go out and collect easily. But in the mountainous regions, the peasant delivers only about 10% of his requisitions (if this much) because the Germans do not have the forces or inclination to go up into the mountains and collect.

The situation in Southern Herzogovina is quite different. Here there are areas where food is very difficult to obtain.

Colonel Seitz and I collected extensive data on prevailing prices of food and commodities in Belgrade and other cities and towns of Serbia, which I turned over to him.

(k) *Reprisals - hostages - potential airdromes - targets - personal histories of Cetnik officers - German disposition.*

Colonel Seitz has our pencilled notes on each of the above topics, showing for each area the number of reprisals and hostages, location and description of potential airdromes, location and description of military targets in each area, and personal histories of Cetnik officers. Since, without these notes I could furnish only a hazy general recollection of the facts, I suggest we wait until he arrives with the data.

IV. THE PARTISAN-CETNIK WAR - ATTITUDE OF CETNIKS

In North Central Serbia we saw no Partisans, and were advised everywhere that there were no Partisans in the area, with the exception of a small band of two or three hundred who had crossed the Sava River between Sabac and Obrenovac and had penetrated a short distance southward. It was also reported that there are a small group of Partisans in the Kaponik Mountains and in the south near Pristina. When I arrived near Raska in late December I found that a band of 800 to 1,000 Partisans had been pushed over from the Sanjak, through Stitkovo. On 10 January they had penetrated almost as far as Ivanica, but were being surrounded on all sides by Cetniks. Later I heard that there were also Partisans in the Zlatibor region.

My impression is that the *people* in Serbia do not favor the Partisans, and that they are against communism. Every peasant wants only his King and a democratic form of government. We heard this expressed thousands of times. The peasants fear and hate the Partisans, whom they represent as an enemy which will burn down their houses and take away all of their food.

The general feeling on the part of Cetnik commanders in the area of Serbia inspected seemed to be that they were not worried about Partisans trying to establish a foothold. The chief enemy in Central Serbia still seems to be the Germans.

On the march to the sea through the Sanjak and Herzogovina, I found an entirely different situation. Here the chief interest of the Cetnik commanders, their men, and the Serb peasants were the Partisans. By far the greatest part of the military effort here is devoted against the Partisans, and there is a bitter civil war raging everywhere. For instance, I have personally seen many houses alleged to have been burned down by Partisans in Herzogovina, and have listened to many local pro-Cetnik Serb peasants describe bitterly how badly they have been treated by the Partisans. For instance, when I have asked to buy food from peasants, they have replied that they would only be too glad to give me something if they had it, but that the Partisans had been in the village and had taken everything. I have personally, from a hill near Kalinovik, seen the Partisans, through my field glasses, burning down the houses of the local Cetnik commandant and his leaders.

Both the attitude of Mihailovic, as expressed in his letters to Generals Donovan and Eisenhower, and that of his Area Commanders, shows that they consider the war against the Partisans to have primarily a racial basis, and only secondarily a ideological basis. Several Yugoslav officers explained the situation to me as follows:

"In 1941 the Partisans under Tito comprised mostly poor Serbs from Montenegro and the Sanjak, to whom communism appealed, because it gave these people a chance to share the wealth. At the same time, the Partisans appealed strongly to those Serbs who felt that rich politicians and bureaucrats were responsible for the sudden defeat of their large army. The Serbs feel, however, that the real reason for the army's fiasco was the treachery of a large percentage of Croat officers and men who, being strongly Germanophil, and believing that Nazi domination of Continental Europe was inevitable, were willing to surrender without resistance. After the capitulation, the Germans brought in Pavelic, and the Ustachi and these traitorous Croats joined the Ustachi. At this time both Tito and Mihailovic had the same objective, i.e. to defeat the occupator, and the only difference between them was that Tito stood for communism. Meanwhile, the Ustachi and treacherous Croats began their blood purge of Serbs in Croatia,

Bosnia, Herzogovina, and Dalmatia, believing firmly that permanent German domination of Yugoslavia was inevitable, since the Allies were losing heavily on every front.

"After the Germans crushed both Tito and Mihailovic in the fall of 1941, Tito was eventually forced up in to the region of West Bosnia, his main stronghold. During the year 1942 it became apparent that the Allies might possible win the war after all. Rommel was pushed back out of Egypt. The Allies landed in North Africa. Russia continued to have success on the Eastern Front. The Ustachi then realized that if the Allies were successful, they would be shot as war criminals. Mihailovic had vowed that for every Serb life taken by the Ustachi and Croats, a Croat life would be taken in reprisal, and BBC London was broadcasting this announcement. The Ustachi could not, therefore, make peace with Mihailovic, and their only hope of saving themselves was to go over to the Allied side by joining the Partisans.

"Inspection of Partisan bodies and prisoners taken in battle shows that the Partisan army is now comprised of more than seventy-five percent Croats and former Ustachi. The Cetniks claim that they are fighting the ~~Serbs~~ Croats to preserve themselves ethnically and numerically, and to insure for themselves postwar control of Yugoslavia. At the beginning of the war there were about 4,800,000 Croats in Yugoslavia, 6,000,000. Serbs, 1,000,000 Slovenians, 750,000 Musselman, and 1,000,000 of other minorities.

"Before the war, the Croats both feared and resented any Serb domination of Yugoslavia. They felt, on the contrary, that since their population, together with that of the Slovenians, was almost equal to that of the Serbs, the capital of Yugoslavia should be at Zagreb, especially since they were closer to the centers of European culture. While willing to accept the benefits of a Yugoslav state, the Croats, under Dr. Macek, were constantly agitating for an independent state, and an independent king, not a Kara-George. Dr. Macek had aspirations for the throne.

"The Serb-Croat antagonism was further increased by the fact that the Croats are overwhelmingly Catholic, and the Serbs, Orthodox. In 1937 there was nearly a religious war between the Serbs and Croats, when the Yugoslav Government's Concordat gave more rights to Catholics.

"The Serb officers feel that the Croats are the politicians, whereas the Serbs have, in the course of history, done all the fighting. They point to the country's history in the last world war, when the Serbs on the Salonika front were the spearhead which eventually liberated their country with a tremendous loss of life.

"The Cetnik officers maintain that Tito is now devoting by far the greater amount of his forces, arms, and ammunition against the Cetniks in this civil war."

The above expression of attitude shows how bitterly the Cetniks feel against the Partisans, whom they consider as comprising the overwhelming percentage of Croats and former Ustachi. They cannot forgive the Croats for their purge of the Serb population in 1941 and 1942, which they claim took 700,000 lives. They cannot understand why Britain, which formerly backed Mihailovic against the Ustachi, in the days when the Allies were losing the war on all fronts, is now sponsoring an army alleged to consist mainly of these Ustachi. On the other hand, many Cetnik officers believe that there should still be a Yugoslav nation after the war is over, based upon a federation of states, which would include an independent Croat state, and an independent Serb state. They seem to favor a structure patterned after the federal and state governments in the United States, with a king at the head of the new Yugoslav federal state. Other officers are Pan-Serb in their attitude and believe in having a Yugoslavia in which Serbia will be the dominating influence.

Some Cetnik officers favor a truce with the Partisans until the war against Germany is finished. A notable example is Major Lukasevic, who states that much as he hates the Partisans he would be willing to have a truce, provided a geographical line could be established dividing Yugoslavia into two areas, on the understanding that the Partisans would fight the Germans in the north, and the Cetniks would fight the Germans in the south. Other Cetnik officers believe that peace is impossible.

V. COLLABORATION BETWEEN CETNIKS AND GERMANS

In North-Central Serbia I saw no evidence of collaboration between Cetniks and Germans, with two small exceptions. One instance was at the town of Belanovica, east of Valjevo, in the area of Captain Ninkovic, a Cetnik Korpus commander. Here there were about 50 Nedici gendarmes under one lieutenant whose function is to keep order in the town. Ninkovic advised that the Lieutenant and most of the men were loyal to the Cetniks, and stated that if they were called upon, they would immediately join the Cetniks in the woods; that he could disarm them at any time, but that they were more useful to him in their present capacity because they gave him valuable information on German movements in the area. After we had passed near the town, Colonel Seitz and I met the Nedici Lieutenant, who had followed us for the purpose of meeting us in the woods. He professed to be loyal to the Cetniks, and willing to help them in any way that he could, but surprised us all and infuriated Ninkovic and the other Cetniks present when, in answer to my question as to how the people in the town felt toward the Nedici, he stated that he thought that they were sympathetic, because the Nedici saved them from heavy reprisals which the Germans would otherwise have taken.

Likewise, Kalabic admitted that he maintained friendly contact with about 50 Nedici gendarmes in Aranjelovac, about 50 kilometers south of Belgrade, who were assigned there by the Germans to guard the railroad station. He stated that he maintained this relation for the same reason as Ninkovic, and also for the reason that they were a source of arms. He pointed out, for example, that they had tipped him off in August, 1943, that some German lorries were traveling south through Stragari with a lot of machine guns and ammunition. As a result of this information he was able to attack the column, kill 80 Germans, and capture 40 Zorka light machine guns with a considerable amount of ammunition. I saw Stragari. The entire village, including over 150 houses, was destroyed by the Germans in reprisal for this attack.

In southern Herzogovina and southern Dalmatia I saw collaboration between the Cetniks and the Germans for the purpose of fighting the Partisans. On one afternoon while I was at the head of a column I bumped into a German patrol and made a hasty retreat. Major Lukasevic went forward with some of his troops while we retreated to a nearby village. I later learned that Lukasevic, upon being brought down to the local German commandant, stated that he was the commander of the Cetnik Nevisinje Brigade; that he had come down purposely to make contact with the Germans, in order to advise them that there was a large band of Partisans advancing toward their position, and that he, Lukasevic and his men, were taking up positions in the woods to fight these Partisans. The German commandant thanked him very much for this information and allowed him and his men to escape in order to fight the Partisans. We later met Lukasevic about six hours south of this point.

While we were waiting for Lukasevic, the local Cetnik Srez commander advised us that he was friendly with the German commandant for the Lubinje area; that on the previous day he had found living accommodations for 640 of the newly arrived German troops, and that he was expecting another 640 shortly. We could see many of these German troops from the mountainside.

While we were hiding out near Dubrovik, south of Trevinje, one of Bacevic's soldiers showed me a German legitimacia issued to him by the German authorities at Dubrovik. The paper had on it the printed letterhead of the German Army headquarters at Dubrovik. In the Serbian language it described him as a "Cetnik" fighting the Partisans, and allowed him the right to go to the hospital at Dubrovik. He advised me that it had been issued to him by the German authorities at Dubrovik.

When faced with such evidence of collaboration, Lieutenant Colonel Bacevic tried to justify it on the grounds that it was necessary to know what the Germans were knowing in his area. I expressed the opinion that such activities would constitute espionage against the Germans, but that this was not espionage because the Germans knew that these men were Cetniks. He replied that all persons of Orthodox religion in the area are described as "Cetniks" by the Germans.

My own impression is that there is very little collaboration in Serbia, where the German is still the primary enemy, but that there is collaboration in Herzogovina, because Mihailovic's leaders, much as they hate the Germans, feel that they must collaborate against the Partisans in order to save themselves from losing the civil war against the Partisans. This collaboration does not seem to bother their conscience any. They point out that they are, in fact, fighting former Croat Ustachi, many of whom are presently collaborating with Pavelic; and that the British are feeding arms to the Partisans, which are being used by the Partisans against the Cetniks. This all plays into the hands of the Germans, who are taking advantage of the fact that the civil war is foremost in the minds of the Cetniks.

The above collaboration in the area of southern Herzogovina seems to be just a continuation of the collaboration which existed earlier in 1942 and 1943 between the Cetniks and the Italians against the Partisans.

VI. MIHAILOVIC'S COMMUNICATIONS WITH HIS GOVERNMENT

When I arrived in Yugoslavia, the British Mission advised that Mihailovic's only method of communication with his government in Cairo was by radio to Malta, in a cipher known to the British. In January 1944, Colonel Bailey advised he thought Mihailovic probably had established direct radio liaison with his government, but that his messages were undoubtedly monitored.

As far back as October, Mihailovic advised me that he had direct liaison with America through a radio he kept in the woods; that he could send messages via this method to Fotich, Yugoslav Ambassador at Washington; and asked if I wanted to send a message direct to anyone in Washington. I politely declined and reported the matter to Bailey, who took it up with Cairo and London. I later learned he had a young Serb-American, Robert Marjonovic, working at this secret station.

4. The Farish Reports
(October 29, 1943; June 28, 1944)

Bari, Italy
29 October, 1943

SUBJECT: Preliminary Report on a visit to the National Army of Liberation, Yugoslavia

TO: Major Louis Huot, OSS Advance Base, Bari

1. The following conclusions were formed as the result of personal observation in the field with the National Army of Liberation during the period from 17 Sept; to the 27 Oct., 1943.

2. The Partizan movement is of far greater military and political importance than is commonly realized in the outside world.

3. The Partizans have created solely by their own efforts in the face of the Germans, Italians, Ustasha, and Chetniks a free community of no mean size entirely encircled by enemy forces. Within this area, Mohammedans, Christians, Serbs, Croats, Communist Party members, any person of any religion or political belief can express an opinion concerning the way in which he believes the affairs of the community should be conducted.

4. The above situation is probably unique in all Occupied Europe. The Partizans are in contact with liberation groups in all the adjoining countries. A considerable number of Italian troops are fighting with them as organized units. It seems quite certain that the manner in which the movement develops, the way of life which they decide to adopt, will have a great effect upon all the Balkan States and probably upon the greater portion of Europe.

5. The initial resistance against the occupying Axis forces and their native Quislings after the defeat of the regular Yugoslav army stemmed from the indominatable

will of various isolated groups to remain free. Peculiarly favourable geographic conditions aided these bands to presist in the face of utterly overwhelming odds.

6. The Communist Party especially after the German attack on the Soviet, actively recruited resistance groups, but their principal initial function in the Partizan movement was to supply the underground organization whereby the isolated groups could communicate with each other and weld themselves into a common body.

7. The Communist Party failed in its initial attempt to organize the movement strictly along party lines and sensibly decided to concentrate every available force of any character against the common enemy. Thus, the Communist Party is in theory only one element within the Partizan movement, but it is a very active one, and there is every evidence that strongly indoctrinated Party members are working hard to shape the structure of this newly born state according to their social, political, and economic beliefs.

8. The average Partizan soldier and civilian was undoubtedly pleased to meet the members of the Allied Mission. As an American, the observer was at times embarrassed by the enthusiastic reception which he received and the implicit faith of the people that the United States would come to their aid. This was especially true in the case of those who had relatives or friends in America, and there was never a village, a unit, or group of any kind visited that there were not people in this category. This is a factually true statement concerning which the observer paid particular attention.

9. In view of the facts stated above, it seems quite evident that, if an atmosphere of free and enlightened discussion can be maintained, there is a wonder opportunity for the Partizans to select for themselves those portions of all forms of government and ways of life which they believe would be suitable to their temperment and environment; in such a case, it seems quite probable that a state will emerge which will be a meeting ground between political beliefs which are now widely separated in their extreme phases. The Partizans are very favourably placed in this regard due to the fact that they can directly incorporate into their way of life those portions of these divergent beliefs which they think would be good for them without going through the slow and cumbersome processes of any exidting legislative system. It was in such an environment and under similar conditions that the beginnings of the United States were established.

10. There can be no question of a doubt that the Partizan forces dedicated themselves to the fight against the Axis from the beginning; that they have always fought them; that they are fighting them at this time, and will fight them to the end. The story of this struggle is at times almost beyond the imagination. It is so immense that only a suggestion of it can be given in this short report. The observer must content himself with the statement that if ever a movement had the background of indomitable will and courage with thich to build to great things, it is to be found in Yugoslavia. It may not take place, but, nevertheless, all of the necessary elements are there, and it will be to the eternal discredit of the leaders of the Partizan movement if they do not build wisely and unselfishly upon the solid foundation of this tremendous human effort. We have sent representatives to the Partizans and have been

supplying them with weapons and materials. If the Partizan movement should fail, and if such failure could be directly attributed to our improper appraisal of the situation or lack of effective material support, then we, also, must accept our portion of the responsibility.

11. Whereas the Partizans have fought steadfastly against the Axis occupying forces, other Yugoslav groups have not done so. *Ustasha* are the Himmerlite terrorists of the Croatian puppet state and the evidences of their ferocious treatment of Partizan communities can be seen on all sides. The *Domabrands* are the conscripted soldiers of the puppet state. They have never fought effectively and never attempted to do so. The *Chetniks* under Col. Mihailovich and other officers of the Yugoslav army fought for a time against the occupying Axis troops in conjunction with the Partizans. But Mihailovich made the fatal mistake of allowing his political beliefs and his plans for the future to overcome his better judgment.

He feared Communism more than he feared the common enemy. He and his leaders were more concerned with their plans for themselves after the war than they were with the actual ending of the war by defeating the Axis. Acting upon these misconceptions, Mihailovich ordered his Chetnicks to attack the Partizan forces, and thus commenced the bitter civil war which has become so savage that it is difficult to see how a reasonable understanding can be brought about.

Not all the Chetnick leaders obeyed the order to attack the Partizans and some of them came over to the Partizans. Since then more have come and are coming over every day. The above is the story they tell. Unquestionably it will not be the story of Mihailovich, but that the Chetnicks are now fighting the Partizans is a fact to which the observer can personally testify. Furthermore, the Allied Mission has numerous captured Chetnick documents including routine correspondence, orders, pay books, pay rolls, etc. which afford ample concrete evidence that the Chetnik forces have been fighting with the Germans and Italians against the Partizans.

12. The presence of this civil war in Yugoslavia is unfortunate. As in any civil war, it is extremely difficult for a foreign observer to understand the no quarter ferocity with which it is being fought. But these facts stand out from a military standpoint:

    a. Repeating, the Partizans have always fought the Germans and are doing so now.

    b. They are a more potent striking force at this time than they have ever been before. They are better trained and equipped, and there is every evidence that, provided they can obtain the necessary arms and supplies, their army will constantly increase in size and efficiency. Their present strength is given by them as 180,000 men which are included in 18 divisions, garrison troops, and detachments guarding the lines of communication.

    c. These forces control one large mountainous area extending from the Montenegro-Serbian border northwest through Herzegovina to Western Bosnia. Other mountainous portions of Croatia, Slovenia, Slavonia, and the Pola Peninsula are also in their hands.

    d. All of the Adriatic Coast, with the exception of the principal seaports, such as, Zara, Sibenik, Split, Makaraka, Dubrovnik, and Kotor, is controlled by the Partizans, as well as the costal islands, with the possible exception of Peljesac where fighting is now taking place.

e. The Germans and their Ustasa Quislings hold all of the principal cities but outside of a few miles radius of these points their control of the country ceases. The observer does not have accurate information at his disposal concerning the strength of the German, Ustasha, and Chetnik forces but he does know from personal experience that it is in no way sufficient to prevent the Partizans from travelling almost at will throughout the length and breadth of the country, from Albania to Austria, from the Dalmatian Coast to Belgrade. The observer states without hesitancy that, provided the Partizans are efficiently and immediately supplied with food, clothing, medical equipment and supplies, transport, weapons, and other materials which are needed to properly equip their present forces and the recruits which are available, Allied personnel can in comparative safety be conducted to any point from the Adriatic Coast to the Danube Basin. A communication system to the outside world can be established, airfields constructed, supply dumps established, and any other projects of military importance accomplished.

But in all this it must be remembered that this report could not be written and these plans could not be envisaged if it had not been that a comparative handful of men, betrayed and harassed by a portion of their own countrymen, had the courage and faith to stand up to what was at that time the most powerful military power the world had ever seen. These few people have made such things possible. Now they compose the backbone of the National Army of Liberation and they are justifiably proud of the fight they have made. It is time they received full credit, and we must work directly through them and with them in this strategically important gateway to the Danube Basin and the Northern Balkans.

13. Their favourable geographical position, knowledge of mountain warfare, and great courage enabled the Partizans to defeat a sustained, well-planned German offensive against them in Montenegro during the first six months of 1943 in which several divisions of German, Italian, Chetnik, and Ustasha troops encircled 8,000 fighting troops of the Partizan army. Led by Tito himself, this force fought its way out to the north through successive enemy positions, passing within a few miles of Sarajevo. By their tenacity, their resourcefulness, and their ability to withstand extreme hardships, these people discouraged the German High Command. The Partizans broke through and established themselves in the easily defended Vrbas Valley by taking the towns of Mrkonic Grad, Jajce, Donji Vakuf, and Bugojno. We, of course, can feel a certain satisfaction in the thought that perhaps these events were influenced by the offensives which the Allies were conducting against the Germans on several fronts, but, nevertheless, a lesser people than the Partizans could not have withstood the hardships and apparently hopeless positions in which they often found themselves.

One extremely important point is that the Italians had fought themselves clear and had established themselves in the Vrbas Valley before the capitulation of Italy.

Following the Italian surrender, the Partizan First Division occupied the Adriatic seaport of Split, capturing a large amount of Italian equipment and recruiting 9,000 men, a considerable contingent of Italian troops joing them as well. At that time they asked for Allied air support against the garrison towns of Sinj, Knin, Imotski, Zara, and Gospic, signifying their intention of attacking Sinj, Knin, and Gospic with the idea in mind of severing the coastwise communication system of the Germans, isolating the ports of Zara and Sibenik, thus establishing themselves firmly on the Dalmatian Coast with free access to the interior mountainous regions of Herzegovina and Bosnia. They also asked for the delivery of essential war materials to Split, the evacuation of Italian prisoners and seriously wounded Partizans.

The Partizans received no response to these requests except that some 3,000 Italian prisoners were evacuated. The Germans attacked Split from Knin, Sinj, and Imotski in such numbers that the Partizans were forced to fight their way out and retreat into the mountains of Bosnia taking with them as much of the Italian equipment as possible. Merely as a matter of incident, they overran the strongly garrisoned Ustasha towns of Livne and Kupres in order to clear a way for the transport, field guns, and tanks which they had been able to bring out of Split. These events took place during the latter part of September and early October. The bulk of the captured equipment arrived at Bugojno during the second week of October. It can never be determined whether the Partizan plans for the occupation of the Dalmatian coast were too ambitious for the resources of the Partizan army, but two things are important as far as the Allies are concerned, namely, (1) the military strategy was sound, and (2) no Allied air assistance was forthcoming.

14. It is hoped that from this brief outline the military position of the Partizan forces can be roughly established. Their potentialities are great, but their position can be improved. The observer believes that two factors are of great importance; (1) immediate delivery of supplies by sea and air, and (2) a limited amount of air support along the Dalmatian Coast in order to protect the supply lines, as well as at the German-held town of Travnik in Central Bosnia.

Travnik is not a natural German position. This enemy position is only 22 miles airline to the southwest of Jajce, the GHQ of the Partizan forces where Tito is in residence. Travnik is well into the mountains and is not an integral portion of any enemy supply line. The observer obtained private information that it is strongly fortified and garrisoned by 2,600 well-equipped German troops with tanks. There are Ustasha troops there also. This position was attacked by the Partizans in mid-October, and possibly in the earlier part of the month, but they could not take it.

The importance of Travnik may be summarized as follows:

a. It constitutes a direct threat to the very heart and GHQ of the Partizan positions.

b. At least two of the best Partizan divisions must be held in the mountains to guard against this potential threat. In the Central Bosnian area there cannot be over three Partizan divisions sufficiently well-equipped and trained to stand up to the Germans.

c. The observer believes that an attack on the Partizan communications and garrisons on the Dalmation Coast and islands would be logical German strategy as soon as the snow blocks the mountain passes. If this attack if forth-coming, the Partizans will be faced with the problem of reinforcing the Dalmation forces, but if they withdraw troops from Bugojno or Donji Vakuf they will expose themselves to the threat from Travnik.

The Partizans have asked for air support for an attack upon Travnik, and the observer believes that this support should be offered to them as soon as it is possible to do so. From a military standpoint it will be nothing more than a bombing and strafing attack in preparation for a ground operation by Partizan troops. The distance from Bari to Travnik is approximately 300 miles. A courier can proceed to the Par-tizan GHQ, offer the air support and obtain all the necessary information relative to timing, objectives, enemy positions, A/A defenses, air strength, etc. This journey can be made in something in the order of four days. The observer cannot express to strongly the great moral effect that such air support would have on the situation in Yugoslavia. The Germans, of course, would not be seriously affected except by the manner in which their military position is weakened. The Ustasha, whose moral is deteriorating rapidly, would be thoroughly shaken. This would be particularly advan-tageous if the Germans have left them as garrison troops following the repulse of the Partizan attack. The Chetniks would also be shaken, as they have been spreading the rumour and no doubt believe that no Allied support will be given to the Partizans. The Partizans themselves will be the most affected. Even if the military operation attains no great success, the effect will be tremendous. They have been subjected to enemy air attacks for over two years without once seeing a friendly aircraft. Anyone who has been in an area of complete enemy air control will know what this means. A great many Partizans have completely lost faith in the possibility of any Allied air support and have asked the observer some rather embarrassing questions about the leaflet load of the Halifax and the Liberator.

For moral effect the flight in and out should be over as many Partizan head-quarters as possible with the aircraft flying low in order that the markings can be clearly seen. These are also the safest routes. These Partizan positions are, the island of Vis, Brac, and Hvar, and the inland towns of Livno; Kupres; Bugojno, Donji Vakuf, Jajce, and Mrkonic Grad. Localities to avoid are Metkovic, Makarska, Split, Sibenik, Zara, Mostar, Imotski, Sinj, Knin, Gospic, Bihac, and Banjaluka. Attacks may come from enemy airfields at Mostar, Knin, Gospic, Bihac, and Banjaluka, but it is not believed that they will be heavy. The Partizans should be asked for detailed information concerning the nember of types of aircraft at these or any other adjacent enemy airfields.

The observer believes this offer of air assistance to be of prime importance. As to the moral effect, the observer can only state what it would have meant to him to have seen one of his aircraft during his short stay in Yugoslavia. What it would mena to men who have stood two years of defenseless attack can only be conjectured.

15. The one most important factor in regard to the military effectiveness of the Partizans is that of supply. The needed materials may be roughly classified as cloth-ing, food, medical supplies, transport, weapons, (rifles, light machine guns, anti-tank rifles, mortars, and ammunition), light tanks, mines and explosives, grenades,

signal equipment, and other miscellaneous articles. Considering the scale and complicated nature of modern warfare, these supplies are simple in character, small in quantity, and not of any great value.

The primary factor in the matter of supply must be speed. Winter is fast approaching, when the roads through the mountains will be blocked by snow just at the time when the materials will be the most acutely needed. The supply line passes within a few miles of enemy held towns which are peculiarly non-resistant at this time. A portion of the route is actually used by both the Partizans and the enemy. The observer feels that the apparent indifference of the enemy to an obvious situation is due to the fact that he has plans for the future when the snows have blocked the high mountains and he will have an overwhelming advantage on the Dalmatian Coast.

The observer has never believed that supplies can be dropped from the air in quantities proportionate to the needs of the Partizan army. Airborne supplies are, however, of vital importance in connection with isolated areas or where hard pressed troops are in need of immediate supply. It seems probable that instances falling[?] within these categories will increase during the Winter months.

From personal experience, the observer believes that the efficient despatch of supplies by air depends to a great extent upon a completely adequate communication system. Those who are within the country and aware of the situation must be able to transmit to the supply base the lists of materials needed together with the exact location and time when they can be received. It is then the duty of the base organization to see that these conditions are met precisely as laid down. If there is any discrepancy whatsoever, those who are working internally must be immediately advised in order that they can make their plans accordingly.

This, then, is the observers conception of the problem of delivery of supplies to the Partizans; (1) bulk supplies landed by sea transport on the Dalmatian Coast, and (2) airborne supplies, necessarily in smaller and more exact quantities, to isolated internal areas; or to hard pressed troops. These are actually two separate operations under very divergent conditions and involving correspondligly different transport methods and equipment, personnel, and stores. The first involves stores, ships, and personnel for the movement across the Adriatic of large quantities of supplies of general categories. This operation requires a minimum of personnel and communication within Yugoslavia, but necessitates a maximum of bulk stores in Italy. The second operation is exactly the reverse. It requires a maximum of personnel and communication within Yugoslavia, and a minimum of carefully chosen stores at the operational base. These operations are of equal importance and at the present time the Partizan army cannot be adequately without the efficient operation of both.

The actual policy of supply to the Partizans has not actually been a matter of debate for some months. When the first airborne supplies were dropped to the Partizans, that policy was established insofar as they were concerned. Our only problem now is whether we supply them adequately, inadequately, or not at all. Thus, by force of circumstance, we are forced to supply them efficiently, rapidly, and in proportion to their needs.

Cold, hungry, and inadequately armed men will surely remember from whence aid came when they were fighting for their very existance. The observer feels certain that one modern, efficiently staffed field hospital will be equal to all the most eloquent words which can be written or spoken in a lifetime.

16. A situation such as exists in Yugoslavia is not easy to assess. It is even more difficult to place these assessments on paper in a coherent manner. The following are a few facts which seem to stand out, no matter from what angle the situation is viewed:

    a. The Partizan movement is of far greater magnitude and military importance than is commonly known in the world outside.

    b. The Partizans are fashioning themselves a way of life which will surely have a great effect upon the Balkans and probably upon all Europe. It can be a meeting place between divergent political beliefs.

    c. The Communist Party has played a leading role in the organization of the movement, but has not been able to indoctrinate it along strictly party lines.

    d. The average Partizan is very sympathetic to the U.S.A. and is steadfast in his belief that we will come to their aid.

    e. The Partizans have steadfastly fought the common enemy from the beginning, while other factions within Yugoslavia have not.

    f. The Partizan forces have control of a militarily strategic area and travel almost at will in a much larger area.

    g. Air support should be offered to the Partizan COS in an effort to eliminate a dangerous enemy position at Travnik.

    h. By dropping supplies from the air to the Partizan forces for some months, we have commited ourselves to the policy of aiding them. We must, therefore, send them the supplies they need, efficiently and promptly, in order that they may continue their fight against the enemy with increasing intensity, and so that they will feel sympathetically inclined toward us.

    i. The supply problem consists of two distinct operations, (1) the transport by sea of bulk supplies across the Adriatic from Italy to the Dalmatian Coast.

    j. Speed, efficiency, and complete cooperation between all Allied services is essential.

17. The writer served in Yugoslavia in the dual capacity of an American observer and as a member of the staff of the Allied Military Mission headed by Brigadier Maclean. He wishes to thank the other members of the Mission, all British but one, for their comradship and complete courtesy and consideration. Yugoslavia is obviously a country where it would be most difficult to conduct efficient operations without complete British and American cooperation toward a common end.

18. The issues in Yugoslavia are confusing and the feeling is so intense that is is almost impossible to obtain and unbiased opinion. The conclusions set forth in this report are based solely upon the writers personal observations and such other information as he believed to be authentic. There are other reports which must be taken into consideration, notably those from our Mission to the GHQ of Mihailovich. There are also the reports of other members of the Allied Mission, some of whom have been in Yugoslavia much longer than the writer.

19. Personalities are of no importance in a matter of this kind. Our sole object

must be to correctly assess the potentialities of the Partizan movement. The observer sincerely believes that the most serious mistake which could be made would be to underestimate it.

(s) Linn M. Farish,
Major, AUS
Bari, Italy,
29 October, 1943.

SUMMARY REPORT ON OBSERVATIONS IN JUGOSLAVIA FOR THE PERIOD
19 SEPT 1943 UNTIL 16 JUNE 1944.

Prepared by Linn M. Farish, Lt. Col. AUS
Senior American Officer, Anglo-American Military
Mission to the Jugoslav Peoples Army of National
Liberation.

I have been asked by Lt. Comdr. Green, USNR Commanding Officer, Strategic Balkans Services (OSS), Bari, Italy, to prepare a report on conditions in Jugoslavia.

The basis for this report is approximately six months spent in the field during the periods 19 Sept to 3 Nov. 1943, 20 Jan to 19 Mar. 1944, and 16 April to 16 June 1944. Entrance to the country was effected by three parachute descents, on 19 Sept. 1943, between Banja Luka and Mrkonic Grad, Bosnia; on 20 Jan., 1944 at Bosanski Petrovac, Bosnia; and on 16 April, 1944 at Shiroka Planina, South Serbia, near Vranje, between the Morava River and the old Bulgarian border.

During these periods I served as a staff officer under Brigadier F. H. Maclean, who commanded the Anglo-American Mission. In the first period Capt. Benson and myself were the sole American members of the mission. In the second period the American members were Capt. Selvig, Capt. Goodwin, Lt. Green and Lt. Popovich. During the third period, the personnel and conditions remained the same, with exception that Lt. Popovich and myself were in direct radio contact with S.B.S. base in Bari. Our radio operator was Arthur Jibilian, SP(X) 3c USNR.

Lt. Col. Seitz, Capt. Mansfield, and Lt. Musulin, who were in liaison with the forces under the command of General Mihailovich, are all known to me. Col. Seitz is a friend of long standing, and I have perfect confidence that any report or statement he has made has been honest and sincere. Although not so well known to me, I am positive that the same applies to Capt. Mansfield and Lt. Musulin.

All of the above mentioned officers and men have, to my knowledge, conducted themselves admirably under the most difficult conditions. The hardships they have undergone, the physical courage they have shown, and the mental distress they have experienced due to the confused position in which they have been placed, will probably never be known. I can only attest that their conduct in the field has brought credit to America and the Armed Forces of the United States. Placed in a perplexing whirl of external and internal politics, they have endeavoured to maintain their balance and to report objectively on conditions as they saw and experienced them.

Severe cases of mental and physical exhaustion are certain to develop among those officers who have taken their work seriously. It is a known fact that the mental powers of certain British officers who have undergone slightly more have been definitively impaired.

The work which the American personnel in combination with the British personnel, both through the aid of the Jugoslav people, have performed in the rescue and evacuation of Allied airmen, especially American, has in itself been outstanding and a direct contribution to the war effort.

The situation in Jugoslavia has, from the beginning, been terribly confusing, and almost beyond the comprehension of an impartial outside observer. The deep rooted causes of the internecine strife are contained in racial, religous, and political disputions which are of such long standing that the people themselves do not understand them. The same applies to the present civil war, or wars being waged by the various factions. In the case of the forces of Marshal Tito and General Mihailovich, both sides tell exactly the same stories of incidents which occured at certain places on the same dates, the only difference being that each side places the blame on the other.

Both sides proclaim as their aim a Free, United, and Democratic Jugoslavia with a form of government determined by a free electorate of the people after the country has been freed of the occupier. Both sides tell the people that the other side is not sincere. The Chetniks say, and undoubtedly believe, that the aim of the Partizans is to force the indoctrinated communism of a minority on all the people. The Partizans say that the Chetniks are fighting to return the government of a few, which they claim is corrupt, fascist and dictatorial. At the same time, as stated above, both sides proclaim almost identical aims for the future of Jugoslavia.

Both sides attribute to the other the lack of effective resistance to the Germans. The Partizans say that they were betrayed by elements of the Government which are now included in the government-in-exile and the forces of General Mihailovich. The Chetniks claim that the Communists many of whom are now the leaders of the Partizans, particularly the Croats, commited acts of sabotage and prevented the effective mobilization of the Jugoslav Army.

Both sides claim that they have been attacked by the other in collaboration with the Germans and will cite time and places as evidence.

Both sides claim that they have not been supported by the Allies, and that in order to fight the enemy they have had to first face arms in the hands of traitorous countrymen place there by the Allies.

Both sides believe that their first enemy is the other, with the Germans and Bulgarians second.

We have in our possession direct orders from Mihailovich Headquarters to that effect. Many Partizans have told us that their first enemy is the traitor at their [?]. I am inclined to believe that in this case both sides are speaking the truth. They are their own worst enemies. When we were with the Partizans, our actions were more hampered by the Chetniks and other native elements that they were by the true enemy, the Germans and Bulgarians. Both the Chetniks and the Partizans are composed of men of unquestionable fighting qualities, men of terrific endurance and perfectly at home in the rugged mountains where no outsider could possibly find his way about.

On 21 May we watched 3000 men of the Partizan First Serbian Division march south from the Rodon Mountains into the Kukavicu Mountains where they engaged and defeated the Chetnik forces under the command of Major Djuric composed of 2000 men. The Partizans forces were 70% armed by recent sorties received by the British mission, of which at least 50% were American manufactured and of all aircraft received at least 90% were American and flown by American crews.

From a strictly military point of view, the Partizan attack on the Chetniks was absolutely necessary. The Partizan position in the Rodan Mountains was not secure, The Bulgarians and German positions protecting the railway were in the oper[?] valley to the North. The Chetnik troops occupied the mountainous areas to the South, which were admirably suited for an attack on the railway. If the Partizans attacked the Bulgarians and Germans to the North, they would have been forced to advance across oper country, while the Chetniks could infiltrate into their rear leaving the Partizans no place to return when forced to withdraw by superior enemy strength.

So the Partizans attacked the Chetniks first, drove them out of a portion of the Kukavica Mtns., regrouped their forces, and on the night of 19 June attacked the large city of Leskovac, where they inflicted great damage on the enemy garrison and the railway center which they were guarding.

On 1 June, Lt Popovich, of my party, Lt. Comdr. Mac Phail, a British doctor, and his orderly, and myself, arrived in the Kukavica Mtns. in search of three wounded American airmen, whom we found in a former Chetnik hospital in the area where the fighting had taken place. These airmen informed us that they had been rescued by the Chetniks, that Chetnik doctors had treated them as best they could, and that the people of the so-called "Chetnik villages" had done everything possible to make them comfortable. They stated that a Chetnik doctor come back through the fighting for three nights to dress their wounds. They further stated that this Chetnik doctor had photographs of a great many American and British airmen whom he had treated and helped to escape from the country.

As we carried our wounded through villages which a few days before had been "dangerous Chetnik territory," it was heartrending to witness the treatment which they received. Peasants supplied carts, oxen, and straw. They lined the roads with food and drink, wreaths of flowers, presents of all kinds. Women stroked the brows of the wounded men they cried and prayed over them. Men offered them strong drinks of rakija and called them brother but they cursed the Germans.

We saw both Chetnik and Partizan wounded. To me they were only poorly clothed, barefoot and hungry peasant farmers, some of them badly wounded, who had born their pain with a forebearance one would hardly believe possible. I could not see any dangerous characters among them. I couldn't tell who was Left or who was Right, who was Communist or Reactionary. Somehow those terms that one hears used so glibly on the outside did not seem to fit the actuat circumstances.

What a very peculiar set of circumstances these facts bring out! Rifles stamped

"U.S. Property", firing W.R.A. Ammunition, flown by American airmen in American aircraft being fired at people who have rescued other American airmen and who were doing everything to make them comfortable and to return them to safety.

If I am confused, what must be the state of mind of the people of Jugoslavia. Add to what has already been mentioned as controversial between the Partizans and the Chetniks the strong propaganda of the Germans, Bulgarians, Italians, Nedic, Leotic, White Guard, Ustasi and so on. Is it any wonder that hundreds of them have taken us aside and asked us to tell them what to do, which way to turn.

In all of this welter of confusion, of conflicting reports and misunderstandings, a few pertinent facts stand out:

1. The vast majority of the people in Jugoslavia, and we have seen them in Bosnia, Herzegovina, Dalmatia, Sandjak, Montenegro, Serbia, Macedonia, and the Dalmatian Islands, are neither Right, Left, Communist, Reactionary, or anything else. They are a simple peasant type of people, strong willed, hot blooded with tremendous powers of endurance and great personal courage. They love intrigue and gossip, and are the most profound liars I have ever met. I do not believe there is any tremendous urge for Revolution among them. They love their mountains their small homes, their farms, and their flocks. They want something better, but, measured by our standards, what most of them ask is not a great deal, a good government, their King and their church, schools, more roads, shoes, clothing, a few modern conveniences, better modern farming equipment and some better livestock.

2. These people quite unique in Europe, have the will and the environment with which to effectively fight the enemy. Despite the confused state of their affairs they have caused him great difficulty and have killed large numbers of his troops. Retaliations against them by various enemies have never stopped them and is not stopping them today. Rather it has made them more determined and increased their hatred of the enemy.

3. The senseless killing of these people by each other must be stopped. It is usless now to endeavour to decide which side first did wrong. Too much blood has been spilt, the feeling is too bitter, and too many men on both sides have uttered rash accusations and performed rash acts.

4. It does not seem to me that the Allies have done well in Jugoslavia. We have never presented an united front to them. I have always believed in Allied cooperation, that there should have been one Military Mission composed of duly constituted high ranking officers of at least Great Britain, the Soviet Union, and the United States, who could have called all the conflicting parties together and taken such steps as were necessary in the form of a provisional government and military command to the end that the civil war was stopped and the maximum effort directed against the enemy. I have always opposed, as far as possible independent missions of the various Allies and have always worked to present at least an Anglo-American front to the Partizans.

However, as in the case of the primary issues between the Chetniks and the Partizans, it does no good to report what we believe should have been done. What we must decide is, what shall we do in the face of conditions as they exist today.

It is too late to draw all the factions together into one group directed against the enemy under the guarentee of a free election without violence after the war? As far as the great mass of the people are concerned[?], it can be done, because they are weary of fighting each other, but eager to fight the enemy. There are thousands who have buried their rifles and refuse to march with any group. There are thousands more who would volunteer if they could decide which side to support.

Only a few people on each side prevent a union from being formed - a few defeatists among the Nedic group who believed it was hopeless to oppose the German Army - A few Croats who hated the Serbs worse than the Germans - A few communists who would see their brothers killed to further their political aims - A few Serb Nationalists who classed as X Communists all those who did not agree with them - A few politicians who did not think of anything except to retain their power after the war. - A few clergymen who forget their teachings - only a handful of misguided people, in comparison to the millions who have suffered as a result of their misguidance, either honest or dishonest.

5. In all of this terrible story of misguidance, of rape and death and destruction, the one great power that I feel might have prevented it, or have stopped it, has never been used. The United States of America is mentioned in the same breath with God in Jugoslavia. We were the one nation on earth to whom the people believed they could turn for unbiased, unpolitical aid and advise without having to pay something in return. I am speaking now of the common man, not of Marshal Tito, General Mihailovich, or any one of the members of the government or the leaders of the various factions. How many hundreds of homes did we enter in which the people crossed themselves and thanked God when they found that we were American officers. I have previously reported at length concerning these facts. Other of our officers, as well as British officers, have reported similar experiences. It would be difficult to express the utter sense of helplessness and frustration which we felt in the face of such complete faith in the ability of our country to right the wrongs which were so evident on all sides.

There is in the records of the 15th Ariforce evidence from returning airmen that practically every faction in Jugoslavia has aided in the rescue and evacuation of our men forced to descend in that country. This applies to Nedic troops, even Ustasi and Bulgars. But it is wrong to say that the people who have aided our men were Nedic, Chetnik, Partizan, and so forth—it is more proper to say that they were the common people of Jugoslavia, a people confused and suffering, suffering under the heel of the occupying enemy and then at the same time torn by internal strife. They saw in us and those airmen of ours the representatives of a powerful democratic nation in which people of all racial extraction, religions, and political beliefs live side by side in harmony, free to speak openly and to discuss their mutual problems without fear. In comparison to their own pitiful condition, it is not hard to realize why the free and abundant life of America, where we have at least partially solved the identical problems which now confront Jugoslavia, has taken on a more rosy hue that it perhaps deserves.

All this is not rhetoric, it is based upon hundreds of conversations with people all over Jugoslavia. It has been the experience of all the American officers with whom I have talked. The question that morries all of us is, how long can a great nation continue not to pay attention to the obligations contained in such trust and respect? How long can a great nation continue in this manner and still remain great?

6. I do not ask for aid to the Partizans, as I am confident that the officers who have been with the Chetniks will not ask for aid to the Chetniks. An exact, literal translation of our reports could be interpreted in this manner but we are not Chetniks or Partizans, we are American offers who have been with opposing factions composed of the same people. When I have called for aid to the Partizans, and officers with the Chetniks have called for aid to their group, we have had the same person in mind - a barefoot, cold, and hungry peasant farmer, a man whose courage and endurance must be observed to be understood. To us they were not Communists or Reactionaries, Partizans or Chetniks, they were merely brave men who looked to us for aid with great confidence that it would be forthcoming. We would have been strange people if we had not responded - we could not have done otherwise and been American.

7. It is not now a question of whether the United States should send aid and representation to the Partizans - - We have been sending them aid and have had representation with them for a long time.

During Jan., Feb., and March of this year, we saw and received in Bosnia numerous night sorties, two mass daylight drops with fighter escort, one daylight glider sortie with fighter escort, and several night landings.

During April, May and June, we saw and helped receive in Serbia approximately 100 night sorties and one night landing.

Out of all these aircraft, something in the neighborhood of 300 with 60 in the air at one time, I have only identified 50 which were not American.

The Russian Mission to the Partizans was landed by gliders, American gliders towed by C-47's flown by American pilots and escorted by American fighters. The Russian Mission rode in the gliders and British pilots landed them. We have seen "Russian" aid dropped to the Partizans from "Russian" planes, yet the planes were again the old C-47's and the goods were largely American packed in American containers dropped by American Parachutes.

We have helped to collect hundreds of tons of American radio equipment, drugs, foods, clothing, arms and ammunition, again dropped with American parachutes from American planes flown by American pilots. The first motor vehicle landed in Jugoslavia was an American Jeep and trailor - again with the faithful C-47.

Nothing stated here should be construed as anti-British, anti-Russian, or anti-Anything. They are merely statements of facts intended to point out that we do have a very direct interest in what is taking place in Jugoslavia. It does no good to say that we are not interested in Jugoslavia and are not participating in the situation there, because we are, in a most material and effective manner.

I, personally, do not feel that I can go on with the work in Jugoslavia unless I can sincerely feel that every possible honest effort is being made to put an end to the civil strife. It is not nice to see arms dropped by one group of our airmen to be turned against men who have rescued and protected their brothers in arms. It is not a pleasant sight to see our wounded lying side by side with the men who rescued and cared for them - and to realize that the bullet holes in the rescuers could have resulted from American ammunition, fired from American rifles, dropped from American aircraft flown by American pilots.

At one time I worried because America was not getting the proper recognition for her participation in supply operations. Now I wonder - do we want it. I can only hope that the small round holes which I saw in those simple peasant boys in the guerilla hospital in Lipovica village were not caused by cartridges stamped W.R.A., or fired from rifles marked "U.S. Property."

It is inconceivable that the combine strength and influence of the Soviet Union, Great Britain, and the United States could not put an abrupt end to the civil wars in Jugoslavia and guarentee the people a free electorate after the occupying troops have withdrawn and the hot blood has cooled. That it has not been done is, in the eyes of many, not a good portent for the future. The issues in Jugoslavia are ones which will have to be faced in many parts of the world. The Jugoslavian's with their wild, turbulent, strong willed nature, have abandoned Reason and resorted to Force. Is this the shape of the things to come? Are we all of us sacrificing to end this war only to have dozens of little wars spring up which may well merge into one gigantic conflict involving all Mankind?

I posed the above questions in a report written last November. They are even more apparent now. It appears to me that there are indications in the past few months that there has been less emphasis placed on the fight against the enemy and more preparation for the political struggle to follow the ending of the war. Under any conditions, two things stand out, every effort must be made to end the conflict among the people of Jugoslavia and the United States has a very definite interest in seeing that it is ended as soon as possible. This is furthermore a test of the ability of the United Nations, especially the three Great Powers interested in the war in Europe, to cooperate unselfishly toward a common end, that end being that the people of Jugoslavia shall be free to select the form of government and manner of living which the majority of them desire, free from undue external political pressure and the fear of armed internal minorities.

Linn M. Farish
Lt. Col. AUS.
Bari, Italy
28 June, 1944

5. The McDowell Report
(November 23, 1944)

RECEIVED IN CODE OR CIPHER

#12514. From McDowell to Donovan.

1. Since my return, have talked with Generals McNarney and Rooks, Colonel Sloan of G-2, British Minister Resident MacMillan, and other officials at AFHQ. They all appear satisfied charges brought against me by Partisans and German propaganda use of my mission are false. MacMillan suggests I should go to Washington via London to see MacLean. McNarney interested in possibility I proposed of securing surrender Germans in Yugoslavia through special Anglo-U.S. Mission.

2. Will require 5 days finish my reports. In brief my conclusions as follows: real Serb Nationalist leadership vested less in Mihailovich more in local district leaders in Serbia and Bosnia. Latter have been almost continuously fighting Axis forces since 1941 and their troops better armed and disciplined than those directly under Mihailovich. These leaders give nominal allegiance Mihailovich and violently oppose Partisans as Communist but almost equally hate old Belgrade ruling class. Despite 1941 massacres by Ustashi local Serb leaders Bosnia cooperate closely with Moslem and Croat Nationalists. Latter 2 groups now arming heavily in preparation joint campaign with Serbs against Partisans. In pending civil war Partisans will win formal battles owing superiority arms and munitions, but Nationalists will outnumber Partisans and guerrillas;[?] war with heavy bloodshed inevitable for at least 2 years unless Allies make effective military occupation all Yugoslavia. I have concrete evidence of continued failure of Partisans to seriously attack retreating Germans and of Partisan massacre of Nationalist civilians including women in areas occupied by them. We personally observed Partisans attacking Nationalist troops when latter engaged fighting Germans. To entrust Yugoslav Government to Tito is to insure civil war. The local leaders and masses among both Partisans and Nationalists will quickly

agree and unite if Allies will cease all support of small Communist group on one side and small reactionary group on other.

TOR: 11/7/44 4:16 p.m.

9 November 1944

Miss Grace Tully
The White House

Dear Grace:

I believe the President would be interested in the attached report on Yugoslavia. Will you kindly see that it is brought to his attention? Thank you.

Sincerely yours,

William J. Donovan
Director

Enclosure.

HEADQUARTERS
2677 REGIMENT, OSS (PROV.)
APO 512, U. S. ARMY

23 November 1944

Subject: Report on Mission to Yugoslavia, Ranger Unit

To: The Commanding Officer
         2677 Regiment, OSS (Prov.)
         APO 512, U. S. Army

1. The undersigned was sent into Yugoslavia as head of an Intelligence unit to contact the Yugoslav Nationalist Forces. The party reached Serbia on 26 August and arrived back in Bari, Italy, on 1 November 1944.

2. The attached report deals primarily with the principal problem assigned to the unit - the status and significance of the Nationalist movement in Yugoslavia.

3. The undersigned has relations with G-2, AFHQ, and with JICA, USAFIME. He would appreciate it if copies of this report will be furnished promptly to these two organizations. He believes, also, that copies would be appreciated by the U. S. Political Adviser to General Wilson, and by the British Minister Resident.

Respectfully submitted,

ROBERT H. McDOWELL
Lt. Col., M.I.

Attachment

HEADQUARTERS
2677TH REGIMENT
OFFICE OF STRATEGIC SERVICES (PROVISIONAL)
APO 512. U. S. ARMY

23 November 1944

SUBJECT: Yugoslavia - An Examination of Yugoslav Nationalism
A. Introductory

1. Sources and Degree of Reliability

The following observations represent the principal conclusions reached by the undersigned as a result of his mission to Yugoslavia during the period 26 August - 1 November, 1944. Prior to this war the undersigned taught the history of the Balkans at the University of Michigan and has spent twenty-five years in the Near East and the Balkans. In the U. S. Army since November, 1942, he has been engaged in the study of military and political developments in the Balkans with particular emphasis on Yugoslavia. Though untrained in Serbo-Croatian he speaks French, German, and Turkish, all of which were found most useful inside Yugoslavia. Three of the four other members of his mission speak Serbo-Croatian.

The members of the mission travelled almost constantly during their stay in Yugoslavia. The undersigned personally as well as most of his staff covered Western Serbia and East Bosnia, that is, the area from the Morava to the Bosna. One member of the mission spent several weeks in East Serbia and another reached the suburbs of Belgrade and stayed there for several days. Officially the mission maintained relations with General Mihailovich and the Yugoslav Nationalist organization, but in practice each member of the mission sought the broadest and most frequent contacts with the general population.

Particular significance attaches to this basic aim of the mission. British and American officers with the Yugoslav Partisan formations have consistently found their contacts with the general population either limited or forbidden except through specified Partisan channels. With few exceptions officers previously attached to Nationalist formations, either through ignorance of language or personal choice, have limited their relations largely to the principal officers serving under General Mihailovich. It has been the unvarying experience of the undersigned and his staff that no restraint whatsoever has been placed on their efforts to establish direct contacts. With only rare exceptions the mission lived apart from Nationalist officials. Though travelling in the general company of the Nationalists, local stops were made when and where the American officers desired, and only by chance and rarely were Nationalist officers present at conversations with the population.

Owing to the above freedom of contact and to the great response of the general population to the interest shown by the American officers in their local conditions and problems, the mission was able to converse with dozens of people in each local community and with literally hundreds during the whole period. These comprised, besides Nationalist soldiers and Partisan prisoners, rich and poor peasants, shop keepers, professional men, intellectuals and students, including Bosnian Moslems and some Croats and Slovenes as well as Serbs from all parts of Yugoslavia who had moved into free Nationalist territory during the war years. In view of the number and variety of the sources, plus the fact that the members of the mission already possessed a good background in Yugoslav affairs, it is the judgement of the undersigned that the conclusions reached in this study as to past events and the current thought of the people in the areas covered are factual and fairly presented.

In addition to these personal contacts the mission received the daily radio reports from Nationalist commanders in all parts of Yugoslavia and had numerous conversations with Nationalist military and civilian leaders not only from the areas visited but from numerous districts in East Serbia, West Bosnia, Slavonia, Herzegovina, and Montenegro whose delegates were present at Nationalist Headquarters. Material from these sources, though not accepted as necessarily authentic, was of considerable value.

2. Summary of Examination

a. Yugoslav Nationalism is the movement supported by those Yugoslavs - Serbs, Croats, Moslems, Slovenes - who on the one hand have opposed the Axis occupation and on the other, the attempt of the Yugoslav Communist Party to gain control through its present domination of the Partisan movement.

b. The Yugoslav Nationalist Movement is the sum total of a large number of local movements each of which developed in 1941 and 1942 as a spontaneous local uprising against Axis occupation and atrocities. The Movement was created by the Yugoslav masses, and it is only the numerous local Nationalist leaders, chosen by the people, who exercise real power in the movement. General Mihailovich is nominal head of the Yugoslav Nationalist Movement. In no sense did he create it or its program nor is he essential to its survival. He leads the movement only in so far as the local district leaders and the people are willing to follow. But he is admired and trusted by the peasants and students - the two principal elements in the movement - as is no other single Nationalist leader.

c. The Yugoslav Nationalist movement was created as a ''home guard'', a series of local defense units, against Axis and quisling occupation and atrocities; it has continued resistance to the Axis to the extent of its capacity; but the unremittant efforts of the Yugoslav Communist Party to destroy Nationalism since 1941 has increasingly forced the movement to devote its principal strength to self defense against the Communists and the Partisan Army which the Communists control. Though solely military and defensive in its inception, Yugoslav Nationalism through force of circumstances has become in addition a political movement. This political phase has increasingly imbued the whole movement with a more positive, dynamic, even revolutionary tone.

d. The Yugoslav Nationalist movement is devoted to the liberation of the country from domination by Germans or any other foreign power, by Yugoslav Communists, and by the old Parties and leaders who controlled the country during most of the past twenty-five years. It seeks genuinely free elections, preferably under control of the three Allies, which will enable all the National and political groups, including the communists, to express and implement their wishes as to the future government and society of Yugoslavia in proportion to their numerical strength. The movement includes conservatives who perhaps pay only lip service to this program. But its strongest supporters and its all important local leaders are peasants, intellectuals, and students who are determined to achieve a legal revolution and a more realistic democracy.

e. The great majority of both Nationalists and Partisans, about 85 per cent of the total population, share common hopes for the future political and economic life of the country. They are divided by fear of reaction on the part of the Partisan masses and fear of Communism on the part of the Nationalist masses. To purge Nationalism of reaction presents no great problem, but the Communists control the Partisan movement.

f. Hatred on the part of the Nationalist masses as well as leadership against the Communist leadership of the Partisans has become implacable. It derives not only from the still basically conservative and individualistic character of the majority of Yugoslavs. It has been created in large measure by the record of this communist leadership in its attempts to destroy the Nationalist movement. Much of this record has been personally checked by the undersigned, and includes Communist collaboration with Axis and Quisling groups; attacks upon Nationalist forces while the latter were engaged against the Germans; Partisan failure to attack German forces; falsification of Partisan communiques; and atrocities against Nationalist civilians, including women and priests, on a recently increasing scale.

g. Nationalists made up of Serbs, Moslems, Croats, and Slovenes heavily outnumber Partisans throughout Yugoslavia, but the latter, due to better organization and especially Allied military support, represent a stronger military force.

h. A long and bloody civil war is inevitable between Partisans and Nationalists unless the Allies intervene and set up effective machinery for genuinely free elections and free expression of democratic rule by the majority of the population.

3. Definition of Terms

It has become the common practice to employ the term Cetnik in reference to the followers of General Mihailovich and to equate the General's name with the whole of the movement with which he is associated. Both of these practices are incorrect and misleading.

Inside Yugoslavia it is universally recognised that traditionally a Cetnik has been simply a Serb engaged in irregular warfare, though a very few Moslems and Slovenes have adopted the term. Some irregulars who give their allegiance to Mihailovich, especially in Western Yugoslavia, call themselves Cetniks, but the General and most of his lieutenants have never accepted the word in application to their troops. Indeed the term has been definitely unpopular among patriotic Serbs and its widespread use outside the country in reference to Mihailovich was due in the first instance to romantically inclined American and British writers and more recently to Partisan sympathizers who have deliberately attempted to smear the General with the ill repute attached to some Cetniks. For, in fact, though traditionally possessed of patriotic associations, during this war the term has been officially sponsored in large measure by Quislings, and even prior to the war the official Cetnik Association had too frequently served as the tool of reactionaries. Pechanatz, at the outbreak of this war the head of the Cetnik Association, became an open Quisling in 1941, and his followers either joined Mihailovich or entered the Fascist organization of Ljotic. The latter was a known Fascist prior to the war and the Ljotic Cetniks in Serbia have proved the most ferocious of all the enemies of the Mihailovich men.

The most characteristic use of the term, however, has developed in Dalmatia and parts of Herzegovina and Montenegro where first the Italians and later the Germans raised armed bands from among the homeless and desperate local Serbs who then adopted the name of Cetnik. Ample substantiation of this development is to be found in Italian (and doubtless German) documents and in Croat and Serb newspapers. The fact that in these same areas some patriotic Serbs have continued to use the traditional term has led to both honest confusion and malevolent misuse of this confusion.

Misunderstanding outside Yugoslavia of the relation of General Mihailovich to the resistance movement has developed through faulty liaison on the part of the British and through deliberate fostering of a myth by certain Serb emigres. The fact is, as the General himself consistently points out, that Mihailovich was only one among many patriotic Serbs who after April, 1941, set themselves the task of rousing the people against the occupants. Since that date he has in no sense been either the inspiration or the controlling genius of the Serb resistance movement in Yugoslavia as a whole. His role will be discussed further below. Here it is sufficient to insist that the use of the General's name to denote a widespread political movement leads only to misunderstanding of the significance of the movement.

All who are concerned with Yugoslav affairs require a term which can properly be used to denote those who, whether Serb, Croat, Slovene or Moslem, are connected with neither the occupants on the one hand nor the Partisans on the other. To fill this requirement the undersigned has always used the term Yugoslav Nationalist or simply Nationalist, and the present study conforms to this practice. Only in a few instances, notably in Montenegro, has the word been adopted by collaborationists, and more than any other term it expresses that which distinguishes a large part of the Yugoslav population from Quislings and Partisans. This will be discussed in detail below, but the reader should understand that in the judgement of the undersigned General Mihailovich and those who work with him or along parallel lines constitute the Yugoslav Nationalist Movement.

The term Ustashi also requires special consideration..The undersigned has long suspected that there were "good" as well as "bad" Ustashi, and personal observation in Bosnia has borne this out. In that part, at least, of the puppet state of Croatia many Croat villagers and some Moslems have avoided active military service for the

Axis by accepting membership in village home defense units whose members are called Ustashi and in part at least wear the Ustashi uniform. The Serb population unanimously testifies that these home defense units have indulged in none of the atrocities with which the word Ustashi is generally associated. Though originally organized by the puppet government they have ceased to recognize its representatives in the towns and constitute in fact the local governing body in the Croat village communities of Bosnia. Their recent role in the Nationalist Movement will be discussed below.

Any consideration of Bosnian affairs requires appreciation of still another element in the military and political situation - the "Green Cadre". This is a loose Moslem organization composed principally of deserters from the German SS Division originally formed from Bosnian Moslems under the auspices of the Grand Mufti. Today these deserters are organised in village home defense units whose members not only employ full German equipment but from necessity continue to wear their German uniforms, though they are bitterly hostile to both Germans and the Quisling forces by whom they are frequently attacked. Their future significance will be discussed later.

B. Examination of the Yugoslav Nationalist Movement.

1. Genesis of the Serb Nationalist Movement

The Serb Nationalist Movement was generated during 1941 as a result of three principal stimuli, and these stimuli have in large measure continued to determine its development since 1941. In chronological sequence they are (a) National self defense against the Axis invaders, (b) self defense of individual life and property against the atrocities and exaction of the Germans and the Ustashis, (c) self defense against the threat, first to the social structure later to life and property, which developed out of the organization of the Partisan movement by the Yugoslav Communist Party. The essentially defensive - and hence to a degree the passive, even negative - character of the Serb Nationalist Movement is fundamental and the source of much of its past weakness as well as its basic strength. However these same stimuli have contributed to the development within the Serb Nationalist movement of a dynamic, even revolutionary, spirit which is extremely significant for the future.

a. Reaction to Invasion

In April, 1941, immediately upon the collapse of formal Yugoslav resistance, numbers of Serb officers and men collected in the forests in obedience to the traditional Serb patriotic impulse. This instinctive movement was wholly military in character but, contrary to popular legend, gives no indication of having been previously planned or of possessing centralized control. General Mihailovich has told the undersigned that, after the capitulation when he disobeyed orders and broke through the German lines with his unit, he was anticipating further organised resistance by the Yugoslav Army as such rather than recourse to irregular warfare in the forests. By his own repeated statements it is clear also that the resistance movement which he organised from his hideout in Ravna Gora was initially purely local and was only one of several similar centers independently developed in various regions of Serbia by Army officers. This initial phase of the Serb Nationalist Movement was largely limited to Old Serbia, though a few centers developed in Montenegro and Herzegovina. All the evidence strongly supports the conclusion that each local leader at this period was blindly following patriotic instinct for National defense and the movement possessed neither a broad strategy nor even the slightest political program. Nor, as yet, was it a popular movement.

b. German Atrocities

By May and June of 1941 the Germans in Serbia had begun to reveal the savage ruthlessness that was to characterize their occupation throughout the war. The mission devoted a great deal of time to careful investigation of German atrocities by an indirect approach which would tend to minimize the opportunity for exaggeration on the part of the contacts. In addition, of course, a great many prepared statements on atrocities were received. It is clear that atrocities began not as reprisals but as a technique of discouraging the thought of resistance. As resistance developed, the reprisals made the initial terrorism appear as moderation. In each community, in almost every home visited by the mission, the story was the same - one or more of the male members of the family murdered in 1941 or 1942 by German troops. The undersigned on the evidence is completely convinced that the Serb claims concerning their treatment at the hands of the Germans are essentially accurate, and that only in Poland was there more wholesale and barbarous treatment of the civilian population. It is worth noting that the high German official with whom the undersigned held conversations in Serbia admitted that German conduct had been worse in Serbia than in any other part of the Balkans including Greece.

c. Ustashi Atrocities

German savagery was of the same quality in Bosnia but there the massacres of Serbs by Ustashi were still more brutish and on a larger scale than those carried out by Germans directly. In Bosnia the mission collected evidence of current as well as past savageries on the part of Ustashi. The record is only too clear that whereas the Germans were primarily concerned with simply killing males, the Ustashi made a general practice of killing by torture women and children as well as men. During 1917-19 in the Caucasus and Turkey the undersigned became very much accustomed to massacre and torture, but the carefully checked stories from Bosnia revealed a sadism, an insanity, much beyond the worst of the last war's atrocities. It is to be presumed that the Ustashi record has been equally bad in Herzegovina, Croatia, and Dalmatia.

d. Reaction to Atrocities

The Serb Nationalist movement gained popular support as a result of these excesses rather than of the Axis occupation as such. For, to the undersigned, it appears clear that in Yugoslavia as in France the mass of the population had suffered domestic mis-Government too long to enable it to effectively rally around traditional symbols. It was only the instinct of self-preservation that led the mass of the Serb peasants and intellectuals to join with the small groups of officers and men already in the forests of Old Serbia, or, as in Bosnia, to organise their own defense forces. During this second phase, the emphasis was again on self defense, this time of the individual and local community. It was during this period - the second half of 1941 - that the various Serb "Corps" were organised which remain today the basis for Serb Nationalist military activity. They were, and still are, essentially militia for home defense, raised entirely through local initiative, officered largely by local men locally chosen, and in the long run responsible only to local ideas as to strategy and tactics.

e. The role of Mihailovich, 1941 - 42.

It is difficult to assess exactly the significance of General Mihailovich during this phase. It was clear to the mission that today in Old Serbia the feeling of the peasants for the General approaches adoration, while the intellectual leaders and students proclaim him the only one of the ranking leaders in whom they have complete confidence. At the same time he appears to be genuinely accepted as at least nominal head of the Yugoslav as well as Serb Nationalist movement by all leaders with whom the mission had contacts. On the other hand the undersigned found no evidence, and certainly the General made no claims, that the growth of the Nationalist movement during 1941 was in any significant respect due to any action or influence of the General. It is the present judgement of the undersigned that the degree of eminence among Nationalist leaders which Mihailovich has attained is due in the first instance to the support and publicity which he received from the King and the British Government through Liaison officers and the British Broadcasting Corporation during 1942. In short, the Serb Nationalist movement was created, and developed certain basic characteristics, through spontaneous popular reaction towards self defense expressed primarily in terms of local community interests and loyalties. It had, and still has, its roots in the people. It was not created by leaders; it has created its own local leaders.

The undersigned wishes in no way to detract from the qualities of General Mihailovich, for whom he has sincere respect and admiration. Today he fills a position of great significance in the Nationalist movement and his role in the future may be still more important. Though in a sense the creation of BBC, he has won the respect and confidence of the great majority of the Yugoslavs who have come to know him. But his influence over the people is not that of a creator but of an interpreter of their own basic instincts.

2. Serb Nationalists and the Partisan Movement.

The third stimulus to the development of the Nationalist movement—reaction of the people to the Communist created Partisan movement—has become so significant that it must be examined in detail. Throughout his mission the undersigned has taken the position that particular importance attached to the task of ascertaining the reaction of the masses to the Partisan movement and to Yugoslav Communism. This reaction has proved to be complicated and superficially contradictory. Briefly stated

there is almost complete disdain and hatred for Communists, with whom are brack-
eted all Partisan leaders; the Partisan political program receives mingled sympathy
and distrust; the Partisan social and economic program as it exists on paper meets
with entire sympathy; the rank and file of Yugoslav Partisans are recognised as brothers, misled but generally forgiven.

a. The Role of Local "Reds".

Great significance must be attached to the fact that to most of the population of
Old Serbia and East Bosnia, at least, the Partisans are known primarily as invaders
and occupants by military force who hitherto have never remained for long in a given
community. Each community, on the other hand, has long known its own local Communists or Communist sympathisers and the local attitude towards these "Reds" has
been that characteristic of Americans from the Midwest. The "Red" is always represented as the local intellectual who became a social misfit or the local ne'erdowell,
too lazy to work or a thief. Invariably contacts stated that whenever Partisan forces
arrived in a given community these local "Reds" showed up clothed with authority
and eager to use it at the expense of his former fellows.

b. The Role of the Communist Party, April-May, 1941

Among intellectuals and officers contacted a principal charge brought against
Yugoslav Communists was to the effect that they were traitors in a double sense -
they had served both Russia and Germany. Specifically there were two charges: (a)
attempts to induce soldiers and civilians not to resist the Germans on the grounds
that it was not a "people's war" (until Germany attacked Russia in June, 1941), (b)
cooperation with the Gestapo and denunciation of Nationalist resistance leaders.

Details on the first charge have been given to the undersigned by at least six
individuals covering incidents in Belgrade, the Banat, Ljubljana, Mostar, and Berane. The informants appeared to be respectable and reliable characters and each
claimed to have been an eye witness. In the Belgrade incident the informant was a
girl, a student at the University who took part in street demonstrations in favor of
Yugoslavia's entrance into the war. She alleged that Belgrade communists organised
a counter demonstration denouncing the war during which she was severely beaten
by Communists; leaving scars which are still visible. The other informants included
a Socialist engineer from Ljubljana, a chemist from Berane, and a Moslem doctor
from Mostar. General accusations of a similar sort were made by numerous contacts,
and it is clear that the charge is sincerely believed by Serb Nationalists. In view of
the facts that Communists in America and Britain pursued the same line and that the
Yugoslav Communists have produced no evidence that Tito, then Secretary-general
of the Party, took any part in resistance to the Germans until after the attack on
Russia, considerable credence must be given to this charge.

The charge that Yugoslav Communists have assisted the German Gestapo in
tracking down under cover agents of General Mihailovich in Belgrade is widely made
in Nationalist circles. Leaders of the Nationalist underground movement in Belgrade
told one member of the mission that they could furnish the names of Communists
now serving the Gestapo in this respect. Several individuals who had been held in

the German concentration camp for Nationalists at Belgrade related to the under-signed numerous stories supporting the charge. Finally, the German representative with whom the undersigned held conversations, as a part of his denunciation of the Gestapo and the SS officers, stated that these German elements in Yugoslavia and throughout southeastern Europe maintained relations of this sort with the local Com-munists whom the Germans were supposed to be eradicating. In view of past known instances of collaboration between Nazis and Communists this statement justifies fur-ther investigation. On the basis of the evidence available the undersigned does not consider the charge substantiated, but for the purposes of this study it remains sig-nificant that the Nationalists sincerely believe the Yugoslav Communists to be double traitors who have sent patriotic Yugoslavs to death at the hands of Germans.

c. The Break Between Nationalists and Partisans, Summer of 1941

Everywhere the mission found evidence of the uneasy collaboration between Nationalists and Partisans during the summer of 1941. In each community visited the story was essentially the same. After the German attack on Russia, strangers from the cities would arrive at local Nationalist headquarters in the forests and ask to join in the struggle against the Germans. The local Communists and sympathizers would soon gravitate around these strangers, communist propaganda was started, stories were circulated against the local leaders, and finally would come a demand for share in the leadership or, in some instances, the assassination of local leaders. These infiltration tactics were distinct from the direct formation of independent Communist led bands in certain districts. In Bosnia this infiltration of Communists came later than in Serbia and in this early period there were no local Partisan bands. In Bosnia, too, the break came after, and in a measure as a result of, the break in Serbia be-tween Mihailovich and Tito. Up to this point, in the judgement of the undersigned, the evidence is ample and unmistakable that the Nationalists were first in the field, actively fighting the Germans, Bulgars, and Ustashi; that the communists first be-came active only after Russia came into the war; that initially the principal Partisan endeavor was to infiltrate and take over the already existing resistance groups, that failing this they organised their own "Popular Front" or Partisan movement; and that from the very beginning of the collaboration, the local Communists displayed a desire to disrupt and destroy the Nationalist organization and local leadership.

The question as to who first gave the famous "stab in the back", Mihailovich or Tito, has been disputed. The undersigned had heard the story from authoritative Partisan sources prior to his visit. Inside the country he was given all details, with dates and places, by the Nationalist leaders and by several participants of no rank. The date on which the Nationalists allege they were attacked by Partisans is earlier than the date given by Partisans for the alleged initial attack on them by Nationalists.

The undersigned here would like to call attention to a pamphlet published by G-2, AFHQ., *The Cetniks, A Survey of Cetnik Activity in Yugoslavia*, Sept., 1944. This document has been edited in a spirit of hostility towards the Nationalist move-ment, and fails to cite any of the several Allied Liaison officers who supported the Nationalists. Yet one of its principal witnesses against the "Cetniks", a German named Mueller, states (p. 10) that the Partisans were the first to break the agreement and gives the details and dates of the attacks on Nationalists by Partisans prior to the first attack on the latter by the Nationalists. His evidence, that is, completely supports the story given the undersigned by the Nationalists and contradicts that of the Partisans.

d. Falsification of Information by Partisan Headquarters

It should be borne in mind that one of the most common complaints of the Nationalists against the Partisans, and the basis for much of their complete distrust of Partisan leaders and their promises for the future is the alleged dishonesty revealed in Partisan documents and in their radio emissions through BBC and "Voice of America". The undersigned had become interested in this matter prior to his trip as a result of the daily situation map and sheet maintained in his office at Cairo during the period April-July, 1944, based exclusively on the official Partisan communiques. This study revealed so many serious contradictions in Partisan claims as to require rejection of the communiques as serious military documents. Further studies by the undersigned reported to Washington during the summer of 1944 revealed gross exaggeration in the totals claimed for the Partisan Army. There was the further evidence of Capt. Mansfield, American Liaison officer with the Nationalists in 1943. Capt. Mansfield in company with a British Liaison officer witnessed the capture of a town by Nationalist troops and then heard the BBC announce capture of the same place by the Partisans.

When the undersigned was about to leave for Serbia he examined a situation map prepared by the British from Partisan sources. This showed much of Western Serbia where the mission was expected to land as Partisan "liberated territory". After landing, the undersigned diligently sought for evidence of Partisan liberated areas between the Morava and the Drina but found that there were none and had been none.

During the last days of August the Partisan radio emission was heard stating that the liberation had been accomplished of the area in north central Serbia around the towns of Lazaravać, Belanovica, and Ljig. The undersigned at once ordered one of the mission to the area. He left on 2 September and visited each center named in the Partisan emission. In each he found the Nationalists in complete control and busy destroying and driving out the German garrisons. Of Partisans there was no trace though he examined both the German dead and prisoners.

During the period 26-29 September the undersigned was in the district of Semberija in East Bosnia. While there he heard the English broadcast of a Partisan announcement that this district had risen for the Partisans. The undersigned spent several days travelling through the area engaging in conversations with local Serb and Moslem Nationalist leaders and in inspection of Serb Nationalist schools and hospitals. There was absolutely no trace of a local Partisan rising. On the contrary all adult males seen along the roads wore Nationalist insignia, and the Serb Nationalists controlled not only the military situation but the civil administration outside the principal towns held by Axis garrisons. The only Partisan activity in the area was the sporadic infiltration of "troikas" (groups of three to five men) from Srem and their passage through the area towards South Bosnia. In one hospital the undersigned talked with three civilians who had been attacked and wounded by such transient marauders.

Around the middle of October the Partisan radio emission announced the liberation of Gracanica in East Bosnia and the destruction of the railway between that town and Doboj (on the West bank of the Bosna River). The undersigned was in the area at the time and lived for some ten days within about ten miles of Gracanica. He took daily walks along the railway in question. Actually the Partisans raided the town but held it for only two days, while the railway had been thoroughly destroyed by the Nationalists of Ozren many months previously.

During September the Partisan Headquarters made the official claim that Keserovich, one of the Mihailovich commanders in Serbia, had broken with the General and denounced him as a collaborationist. The undersigned received orders to check this claim and despatched Lt. Kramer to the headquarters of Keserovich. Lt. Kramer found the officer in question vigorously defending himself from the Partisans while attacking the Germans. As late as 24 October Keserovich was still in the field under the command of Mihailovich and still actively engaged against Germans and Partisans.

In September, again, a Partisan communique announced that members of the staff of Mihailovich had been captured during the latter's retreat in Serbia, along with important archives. Every member of the staff was personally known to the mission and all were still accounted for as late as 24 October. During the retreat in question the archives of the General's headquarters were carried on pack horses, and in the line of march were always immediately in front of the mission party. No attack was ever made on them.

Throughout the stay in Yugoslavia the mission received numerous detailed accounts by apparently reliable sources of similar false statements on Partisan radio emission regarding Partisan strength and achievements. In view of the evidence for which the undersigned can personally vouch, in his judgement there can be no doubt but that the Partisan leaders follow a deliberate policy of falsification of news and documents to suit their needs. This cynical attitude has convinced the Nationalists not only that no confidence can be placed in the promises of Partisan leaders but that the Allies have shown themselves naive in accepting Partisan claims. It has contributed materially to the complete break between Nationalists and Partisans and to the elevation of the latter to the status of most dangerous enemy.

e. Status of Allied Liaison Officers with the Partisans

In many communities visited which had at one time or another experienced occupation by Partisan troops, conversations with the Mission staff turned to the presence of Allied Liaison officers with the Partisans. No question was raised as to the reason liaison was maintained. But invariably in communities which had been visited by such liaison officers the question was raised as to why there were so few, or no, contacts on the part of these officers and the local population. Invariably the story was told of efforts to meet and talk with such officers which were frustrated by the Partisans around them. The free manner in which the present mission mingled with the local population emphasized in their minds the apparent fear on the part of the Partisan leaders of the results of free contacts. In some communities there was a conviction that the officers in British uniform were actually only Partisans trying to pass as British, and that this explained the barrier. There is ample evidence, of course, from both British and American officers that the Partisan commanders in most instances do discourage or forbid personal investigation by liaison officers of the local situation and sentiments. To the undersigned, indeed, it is truly astonishing that this practice on the part of the Partisans - and the contrasting freedom consistently enjoyed by liaison officers attached to the Nationalists - is not given the significance which it deserves. For only those who fear and mistrust public sentiment seek to throttle its free expression. But the point the undersigned wishes to make here is that the Nationalists *do* recognize the significance of this Partisan practice, and it serves to complete their mistrust of Partisan leaders and their unwillingness to come to terms with them. Repeatedly Nationalists of all classes have insisted to the undersigned - "If we accept a government by Tito we are lost. The Partisans lie, and the British believe them. The British send officers, but they see and hear nothing. We will be persecuted and killed, and the outside world will know nothing of it". This conviction on the part of Nationalists is sincere and deep, and it again explains the elevation of the Partisans to the status of most dangerous enemy.

f. Nationalist Charges of Partisan Atrocities

During the stay in Yugoslavia the mission was offered a great deal of information concerning alleged atrocities committed by Partisans on Nationalist civilian populations. This fell into three classes - prepared official compilations of former incidents, information concerning individual incidents brought out in conversations with the population, radio reports of current incidents received at Nationalist Headquarters from district and field commanders. Because of extensive past experience with atrocity charges, and the natural tendency to exaggerate, the undersigned hesitated to devote much time to this phase of intelligence. In the case of one current incident he reported the names and requested that liaison officers with the Partisans be ordered to investigate. He also requested that he be advised whether or not he should continue to accumulate data of this sort. As these requests were ignored he has not brought out from the country extensive material on this subject.

Despite this, the undersigned wishes to emphasize the seriousness of these charges. They involve execution, beatings, "disappearance" of individuals under Partisan custody, burning and looting of property. In the case of charges of individual incidents brought up in conversation, the mission staff made every effort to check the story and seek evidence of other witnesses. In the case of some of the charges brought in official Nationalist documents it was possible in some instances to secure independent witnesses. No member of the mission personally saw any act of atrocity, though numbers of alleged victims of attacks were interviewed and examined. In the light of considerable past experience in the investigation of atrocity stories the undersigned is convinced that there is no common standard in this matter among Partisans. It was freely admitted that on some occasions of Partisan occupation the attitude has been correct - beyond the natural seizure of cattle and other food supplies. On the other hand the mass of evidence and the extent of corroboration require the undersigned to believe that in many instances civilian Nationalists, including women and priests, have been murdered, while many others have been carried away. The majority of charges involve two classes of Partisan troops, the ex-Ustashis who have been accepted so freely in Partisan ranks, both Croats and Moslems, and the foreign troops which have been so conspicuous in the recent Serbian campaign - Bulgars, Rumanians, and Hungarians. There appears, further, to have been a marked increase in such terroristic practices during the past two months, involving in particular Serbia and the Dalmatian Coast.

Whether mistaken or not, there is a sincere and deep conviction on the part of the Nationalist leadership and rank and file that the deliberate intention of the Partisan leadership is to exterminate at least the local Nationalist leaders in each community in the hope that the masses may be persuaded to accept the Partisan movement. Paralleling this is the conviction that the Partisan-Ustashi combination in Western Yugoslavia is now engaged in the extermination of the whole Nationalist Serb population. These convictions must be considered in connection with the Nationalist realization that the Allied Liaison officers with the Partisans are not permitted to observe conditions for themselves. The two together engender desperation and a desperate hatred for the Partisan leadership which has provoked this situation. Whether mistaken or not, that it is a sincere conviction on the part of a large portion of the population of Serbia is proved by what the mission witnessed during the retreat in Serbia - old men, women, and children streaming over the hills in flight before the advance of the "liberating" Partisans; and the population which stayed behind lining the roads with tears running down their cheeks as they passed out water and bread to the retreating Nationalists.

g. Partisans and the Nationalist Isolation

Nationalist hatred and distrust of Partisan leadership spring also from the conviction these leaders have from the beginning pursued a deliberate policy of isolating Nationalists and especially Serbs from their traditional friends, Britain and America. They are convinced that the Communist leadership of the Partisans intends to bring all the Balkans under Russian domination. They see that Allied officers with the Partisans are screened from the people. They hear on the radio that the desperately needed food, clothing, medicine, and measures for rehabilitation are not to be administered directly by British and American officers but through the Partisans. Today the Partisans are known to have an abundance of medical supplies, whereas the Nationalist hospitals lack both drugs and instruments, and operations and amputations are performed without anesthetics. They realize that in this blockade food and medicine from Britain and America are to be used as a weapon to strike down Nationalism.

Still more horrifying to the Nationalist consciousness is the undoubted fact that they have been sealed off not only from official contacts but from the voice of public opinion in Britain and America. They know that the British and Americans will no longer permit Nationalist representatives to leave the interior and present their case nor may British or American officers or newspaper men visit Nationalist held territory. As they phrase it, they have been "sealed off as thoroughly as Jews in a German gas chamber - and for the same end".

At present, resentment at this catastrophe is not directed against Britain and America nor even Russia. The Nationalists as yet cannot bring themselves to believe that with the long Serb record of democracy and readiness to fight for freedom, a great segment of the Serbs can be deliberately destined by America and Britain for destruction. Rather, to the Nationalist mind today, it is Yugoslav Communist trickery which has brought them - and the conscience of Britain and America - to this pass.

h. Alleged Partisan Failure to Fight the Axis

In all communities visited the mission found a wide spread belief among Nationalists that Partisan troops rarely if ever seriously attacked German troops or installations. It was freely admitted that the Partisan rank and file had joined with the intention of actively fighting the Axis, and some individuals admitted under pressure that in the early years of the struggle even some Communist leaders may have been animated by similar emotions. But the general conviction was that the Communist leadership of the Partisan movement had taken advantage of the willingness of the masses to fight and of the readiness of the Allies to supply arms for this purpose, simply in order to create an armed force that could eventually be used to enforce their mastery of Yugoslavia and the Balkans. It was insisted that from 1941 on the principal military objective of the Partisans has been to attack and destroy Nationalist resistance among Serbs, Croats and Slovenes.

To support these charges a great mass of evidence was offered the members of the mission, much of which, of course, could not be checked in the time available. In many instances, however, corroborating testimony was secured from individuals whose character and honesty could not be lightly impugned. In addition, of course, members of the mission personally observed sufficient instances of Partisan avoidance of German troops and installations in Serbia during August and September to require the conclusion which the undersigned unhesitatingly accepts - that during this period at least the Partisan Army made no serious effort to fight Germans or hinder their retreat, but concentrated on attacking Nationalist troops who in some instances were occupied in attacking Germans.

When the mission reached Serbia, Nationalist mobilization was already under way and a series of attacks had been initiated on German and Bulgar garrisons and lines of communication. General Mihailovich explained to the undersigned that he intended first to clean out German garrisons in Northwestern Serbia, between the Drina and the Sava, and in Northeastern Serbia along the Danube. In these operations his primary objective was the seizure of certain known German depots of munitions which the Serbs badly needed. The second operation was to cut the German lines of communication between Belgrade and Sofia, Belgrade and Kraljevo, and Belgrade and Uzice, to be followed by the clearing of the line Uzice-Kraljevo. He planned, that is, to put his Serbian forces right astride the main German line of retreat from the South to Belgrade. The troops at his command in this area numbered about 40,000 by the first of September, but were deficient in automatic weapons, mortars, and ammunition. He estimated that a maximum of six German divisions would come up the Morava from the South, but that owing to communications no more than two could be deployed against him simultaneously. He anticipated that in the immediate future no more than two and one-half divisions could be concentrated against him in the Belgrade area. He had hoped that Allied air support would be made available as well as supplies of ammunition. He possessed reserves of from 50,000 - 60,000 trained soldiers who had no arms. Negotiations with certain high Bulgar officers gave him reason to believe that the latter would turn over important depots of arms and ammunition in return for safe passage of Bulgar personnel to the frontier. To this Mihailovich was prepared to accede on the basis of Bulgar parole to take no later part in the war, and it was his intention to handle German prisoners in the same way in case no means were provided by the Allies for disposing of prisoners. He himself was in no position to feed or secure large numbers of prisoners.

In part the above plan was disturbed by the impetuosity of the Nationalist field commanders. Disregarding the planned schedule, Nationalist formations began to attack both German and Bulgar garrisons and communications all over North Serbia during the last week in August and the first week in September. Though there is ample proof that these operations resulted in significant losses and disrupted the German and Bulgar lines of communications, their piecemeal character delayed the concentration of Nationalist troops at key points and led to the breakdown of negotiations with the Bulgars who found the Partisans more ready to facilitate their retreat.

Disaster came, however, on the heels of victory when the Partisans unleashed a sudden offensive northwards over the Zap Morava, accompanied by the use of American fighter planes in strafing operations which resulted in much more harm to the Nationalists than to the Germans. At this period the mission was staying just north of the Zap Morava and roughly midway between Kraljevo and Uzice, and the members of the mission had ample opportunity to observe the character of the Partisan offensive. The German garrisons at Kraljevo, Cacak, and Uzice were carefully avoided by the Partisans. German traffic between these points had already been severed by the Nationalists, and the three towns had been partially invested. The first phase of the Partisan offensive was limited exclusively to driving the Nationalist north away from these towns and communication lines. The undersigned vouches for the fact that German traffic was then renewed between Uzice and Kraljevo and the German garrisons were attacked or forced to retreat only in October.

The second phase of the Partisan offensive comprised a supreme effort to push the Nationalist troops north into German arms. To accomplish this concentration in the north the Partisans evacuated most of the territory along the Zap Morava - interesting evidence of their numerical weakness. Mihailovich in turn sent most of his field forces south through the Partisan lines where they again began to harry German communications in the Ibar Vallery as well as along the Zap Morava. With less than 400 men around him Mihailovich, by his clever use of knowledge of the country, evaded capture by greatly superior Partisan forces which pursued him as far as the Drina River. In the third phase, again, the mission was able to observe in the Valjevo and Sabac areas the careful abstention of the Partisans from any attack on German held towns.

Early in September one member of the mission had been sent to the Krusevac area in East Serbia. Here throughout September and part of October he witnessed the Partisan concentration of forces against the Nationalists while at the same time a steady stream of German traffic from Greece followed the Ibar vallery route to Kraljevo. Though the Partisans held positions in strength along much of this route throughout most of September and October, nothing significant was attempted to disrupt this line. In fact its use was discontinued only because of the approach of Russian troops late in October.

In the light of all the evidence which the undersigned has been able to gather regarding the fighting in Serbia during September and October, it is his considered judgement that up until the final drive on Belgrade, for which he has no details, the Partisan forces killed, captured, or disrupted fewer German forces than did the Nationalists, despite the Partisan disruption of the General's plans. Yet throughout this period the Partisans regularly received supplies of ammunition from the British by American planes while Nationalist troops went into battle with as few as ten cartridges and accompanied by unarmed men who hoped to acquire a weapon during the engagement.

Further direct evidence of Partisan unwillingness to attack the Germans was observed by the mission in Bosnia, while stopping in the district of Ozren near the Bosna River. On the West bank of the river, where the Nationalists were poorly organized, Partisan forces were constantly attacking and harassing the Nationalists. Meanwhile a principal German escape route, the railway and highway from Sarajevo to Doboy, ran along the river, and the steady stream of German personnel and materiel was never interrupted by the Partisans. On the Ozren side the potentially equally important escape route from Visegrad through Tuzla to Doboj, had for months been completely blocked by the Nationalists despite repeated German efforts to open it.

Another source of direct evidence were Partisan prisoners of the Nationalists with whom the undersigned talked - Croats, Slovenes, Italians, and a Russian. They were asked by the undersigned to give an account of their marches and engagements during the current year. Though each had been repeatedly engaged against Nationalists in Dalmatia, Herzegovina, Montenegro, or Serbia, not one had seen any action against Germans or Ustashi. They also testified that they had never seen any British or American officers in the vicinity of any engagement, though some of them knew that there were liaison officers at rear headquarters.

These examples of evidence supporting the numerous detailed charges brought by Nationalists of Partisan failure to attack Germans must be associated with the known instances of Partisan falsification of communiques. To this should be added the testimony of British and American liaison officers attached to Partisan units, given in official reports as well as orally, to the effect that they have not been permitted to observe Partisan activity and they suspect the Partisans of failing to seriously attack Germans while hoarding the arms and munitions received from the Allies in order to use them in a civil war. The sum total of the evidence requires the objective observer to give serious consideration to the Nationalist charge that the principal concern of the Partisan leadership has been, not to destroy Germans, but Nationalists and Nationalism in Yugoslavia and the Balkans.

i. Partisan Collaboration with Ustashis

The mission received a great deal of information charging that the Ustashi and Partisans were collaborating in attacks on Nationalists in Dalmatia and that in Bosnia Ustashis in large numbers were joining the Partisan ranks. It was charged in particular that known Ustashi criminals, who had been active in the terrible killings of 1941, had taken this means of escaping punishment. Since coming out from the country the undersigned has been told by a competent source that this last charge has been recognized as true by the British and that unsuccessful representations have been made to Partisan Headquarters on the subject. The Nationalists, both Serbs and Moslems, have collected a mass of detailed reports on Ustashi crimes, with names, places, and dates. They also have the names of the better known criminals who have joined the Partisan Army or civil administration or who have been accepted by the Partisans as collaborators against the Nationalists.

The undersigned was not in a position to obtain direct proof of these charges, but their specific character and the varied character of the sources give the impression of veracity. It is certainly true that the charges are believed by Serb Nationalists and encourages them to believe that the Partisan leadership, in addition to its Communist character, has inherited the program of Pavelich and the Ustashis which sought the destruction of the Serb population in Western Yugoslavia. The latest reports from Dalmatia received by the undersigned prior to leaving the country, covering the second and third weeks in October, do strongly suggest that a bloc of one half million Nationalist Serbs in that general area are being harried by both Partisans and Ustashi, that many civilians are being murdered, and that large numbers of civilians are fleeing into the higher mountain districts despite the winter and lack of food. Since this area lies so close to the British and Americans in Italy, at Nationalist Headquarters it was felt that Dalmatia would serve as a test case. If in this area the British and Americans do nothing to stop the civil war and bring security and relief to the civilian population, then Nationalists generally throughout Yugoslavia must be prepared to fight the civil war to the bitter end.

j. Defensive Character of Nationalist Combat with the Partisans.

In any attempt to estimate the influence of the Partisan movement on the development of Serb Nationalism, it must be borne in mind that in the struggle with the Partisans, as with the Axis, the strategy and the psychology of the Nationalists has been basically defensive - the defense of many different local communities, never a coordinated offensive to destroy the enemy. Ever since the 1941 effort of the Yugoslav Communists to destroy the budding Nationalist Movement by infiltration, followed by the Partisan "stab in the back" in the fall of 1941, each year of the war has seen either one or two major Partisan offensives from Western Yugoslavia directed against Old Serbia and Bosnia, the principal strongholds of Nationalism. Since 1942 these offensives have been sustained by British and American munitions, food, hospitalization, clothing, and air support. Though Allied authorities gave supplies and support in the belief that they were being employed to defeat Germany, it has been only too evident to the Nationalist troops that this aid has been turned against them.

To each member of the mission this American participation in the internal strife of a supposedly friendly country became a most painful subject. During the Partisan offensive in Serbia the members of the mission were obliged to watch American planes strafing area held not by Germans but by Nationalists. They heard American pilots who had been shot down state that in their briefing they have been told that everything was "enemy" North of the Partisan lines in the Zap Morava valley - though in fact it was entirely and exclusively Nationalist held. After a day spent in watching Nationalist troops go into battle with rifles and scant ammunition to face American and British mortars and automatic weapons, the mission each night had to listen, alongside these Nationalists while American transport planes circled overhead while preparing to drop further weapons and munitions into the Partisan lines for the morrow's battle.

The psychological effect on the Nationalists of this continuous defensive struggle against bitter enemies who are aided by those whom the Nationalists count their closest friends, has been very significant. Only to a moderate extent has it lessened the determination to continue the Nationalist struggle, but it has sown a spirit of frustration, of self-pity, and even of hopelessness regarding all the future which is leaving its impress on the Nationalist Movement.

k. The Nationalists and the Partisan Political and Social Programs

In the preceding sections the undersigned has attempted to draw a picture of the Nationalist hostility towards the Partisan movement. In later sections the political and social programs of Serb Nationalists will be discussed in detail. But at this point the undersigned wishes to draw further attention to his observations concerning Nationalist-Partisan relationships.

All Nationalists, of course, draw a distinction between professed and real Partisan intentions. To them it is inconceivable that Communist Party members of long standing, of proved discipline and loyalty, as are Tito and his closest associates, can sincerely work for the success of a movement with the professed political and social aims hitherto sponsored by the Partisans. These professed aims fall far short of socialism, to say nothing of Communism, and constitute individualism as well as capitalism. The Nationalists correctly insist that the world has yet to see a Communist of Tito's rank sincerely support such a program. They correctly point out the known fact that the Yugoslav Communist Party, of which Tito was chief, down to June, 1941, held to Communist dogma much more radical than that of Russia, and that repeatedly since that date Tito has been obliged to reprove his Communist followers for failure to cover up that program, but has never renounced it.

The above are facts. The Nationalists add to these generalities a long list of specific incidents which allegedly prove that the Communists in the Partisan movement continue to preach communism and to assert that communism is to be installed in the Balkans. During September handbills were circulating in parts of Partisan occupied Serbia which denounced capitalistic and plutocratic Britain and America, attacked Churchill and Roosevelt specifically, and proclaimed the coming of communism to Yugoslavia. Such bills have been seen by American officers, but the undersigned believes that they may well have been distributed by German agents to create trouble between Russia and the Anglo-Saxons.

Another source of these charges is constituted by Serbs who have left Partisan ranks and joined the Nationalists. The undersigned has met some of these, and was much impressed by the apparent honesty as well as intelligence of one in particular, a Montenegrin, a reserve officer who had been an officer in the Partisan Army and is now an officer in the Nationalist army. He was and still is extremely sympathetic towards the professed Partisan aims and doesn't conceal his respect for certain of the Partisan leaders and his dislike of certain conservatives among the Nationalists. Yet he gave members of the mission detailed and specific accounts of statements and practices of Communist Partisans which showed a determination to enforce Communism in Yugoslavia.

To the undersigned the most significant source of information along this line came from the incidental conversation of peasants with whom the mission stayed and who had previously been hosts to Partisan officers during passage of Partisan forces through their districts. Several such occasions presented themselves, and the undersigned stakes his judgement that there was no opportunity for the concoction of false stories. The incidents related by these peasants were based on either conversations among Partisan officers - in one instance a quarrel - or statements made by them to the peasants. The whole tenor of the remarks pointed to the sincere belief on the part of these Partisans that the aim of their movement was to install communism in Yugoslavia.

In any case Nationalists believe that the professed political and social aims of the Partisan movement will not be carried out by its present, largely Communist, leadership. On the other hand they freely admit that numbers of the non-Communist Partisans are sincerely working for these aims. Numbers of younger Nationalists have told the undersigned of the struggle that went on in their minds during 1941 as to whether they should join the Partisans or Nationalists. Most of these younger men related that some of their camerades had turned Partisan. The question that divided them was whether a greater threat to their common hopes for a better Yugoslavia came from the left wing of the Partisans or the right wing of the Nationalists. Repeatedly Nationalist leaders have told the undersigned that the only factor which separated Partisans and Nationalists was Communism. No leader among the Nationalists would question the professed Partisan social aims.

The political program of the Partisans had a mixed reaction; was definitely greeted with considerable misgivings. This was due primarily to the very prevalent belief among Serb Nationalists that the Partisan leaders, whether Communists, or ex-Ustashi, or Croat politicians, were aiming to weaken Serbdom. In the judgement of the undersigned this belief is being skillfully spread by right wing elements from Old Serbia, and by men including some intellectuals whose lives are wrapped up in the position of Belgrade as the center of Yugoslav life. Among Montenegrin and Bosnian Serb Nationalists the undersigned found a healthy readiness to place a regional loyalty alongside their sentiments as Serbs. Further, throughout his stay, the undersigned was very much impressed by the prevalent and sincere Nationalist devotion to the concept of a united federated Yugoslavia.

The question naturally arises whether Serb Nationalist political and social thinking has been significantly influenced by the impact of the Partisan movement, especially in view of the facts that in its inception the movement was almost entirely devoted to armed self defense and has remained essentially defensive in character. At this period, so close to the events, a final answer cannot be given. But, on the evidence available, the judgement of the undersigned is that a positive, dynamic, and revolutionary character has developed within the Serb Nationalist Movement primarily as a result of convictions held by the mass of its supporters prior to 1941. That is, the common elements in the Nationalist and Partisan movements - a deep desire for political and social reform - in neither movement spring from the upper leadership but from the people, especially the peasants and students. In the Partisan movement the high leadership was itself dynamic, politically minded, and positive, and was quick, therefore, to grasp and make use of the popular sentiment. In the Nationalist movement, however, the high leadership was conventional, overly mature, prevailingly military, and defensive in its strategy to the point of passivity. General Mihailovich and many of his top collaborators had long recognized the necessity for profound changes in the Yugoslav political and social structure, but it has required pressure from beneath to make the demand for these changes the vital element in the movement which they have become.

The significant stimulus to the Nationalist Movement which derives from Partisan sources lies in the pressures created by the Partisan political strategy which in self defense have forced the Serb Nationalist leaders to stress the political as well as the military character of their movement. Through this move the dynamic qualities of popular sentiment on political and social questions have been rallied to the service of the Nationalist military program. The Nationalist masses, and their local leaders, are today more willing to entrust their local fighting forces to the command of Mihailovich, the political leader and crusader, than they were previously to Mihailovich, the General and Minister of War. It is not too much to say that now in this second half of 1944 the Nationalists have begun to fight not only *against* hated enemies, but *for* a positive program of their own. In the judgement of the undersigned it is largely to the Partisans that - perhaps too late - the Nationalists owe their new maturity as a political movement and Mihailovich personally, the discovery of his true role as a leader.

3. Serb Nationalists and Charges of Collaboration

Charges are frequently brought against the Serb Nationalists that they have collaborated with the Axis, or that, at least, they have failed to support the other Allies in attacking the Axis. These charges should be considered separately.

a. Alleged Collaboration

In the introductory section of this paper it was explained that the term Cetnik is used to denote a variety of classes of Serbs, and that Partisan propaganda has made use of foreign misunderstanding of the term in order to convict General Mihailovich of collaboration. The Partisan leadership, with its patent hatred of Mihailovich and its record in respect to the falsification of information, should not be taken too seriously in its role of accuser. However, one must face the fact that certain Serbs have collaborated with the Axis forces in varying degrees. The question at issue is, can General Mihailovich, or, more properly, the Serb Nationalist Movement, be held responsible?

Prior to his stay inside Yugoslavia the undersigned was inclined to believe that a degree of collaboration was in effect between the Germans and certain Serb Nationalist leaders and that General Mihailovich tacitly accepted this situation. During the stay in the country no evidence whatsoever was obtained which supported the suspicion that the General in any way connived with the Germans to maintain or prolong their occupation of the country. On the contrary, there was ample evidence that the General, the field commanders, and the Nationalist political leaders were filled with a burning hatred for the Germans much beyond that held by British and Americans. There was further, an intense distress that Serbs were playing so minor a role in the defeat of Germany.

On the other hand it was clear that in Serbia, the immediate and most formidable enemy of the Nationalists had become not the Germans but the Partisans. After 1942 the Germans had limited themselves to a defensive role in Yugoslavia - they attacked only when seriously pressed - and these tactics were applied to both Nationalists and Partisans. Nationalist pressure on German forces had dwindled in proportion as Partisan attacks on the Nationalists increased. The relative passivity of General Mihailovich in Serbia during 1943 and the first half of 1944 in part sprang from his unwillingness to expose the people there to German reprisals. But the evidence is unmistakable that during this same period the tempo and weight of Partisan attacks on Serbian Nationalists had increased to the point where they engaged all of the troops whom the General could adequately supply with ammunition. These Partisan offensives were successfully stood off. The Partisan attack of September, however, which caught the Nationalists deployed against the Germans, proved the inability of the Nationalists to fight simultaneously both Partisans and Germans. In East Bosnia, where the Partisan attacks on the Nationalists have been intermittent and on a smaller scale, the Mission found ample evidence that the German and his henchman, the Ustashi, had remained the principal Nationalist enemy against whom operations have been carried on throughout the war years.

In the light of the evidence the undersigned is inclined to believe that a semblance of collaboration has made its appearance wherever the Partisan attacks on the Nationalists have been most intense and have constituted a potential danger to the Germans as well as a menace to the Nationalists. Without having any evidence to prove it, he is inclined to believe that under such circumstances some but not all, Nationalist officers would accept aid from the Germans and would seek to attack Partisan forces already engaged against Germans. This is collaboration of sorts, and the undersigned doubts that officers practicing it would be disciplined by the Nationalist Headquarters if their record was otherwise clear. In fairness, however, this must be viewed against the background - the all out Nationalist resistance to the Germans in 1941, the continued struggle in East Bosnia, the sincerity of Nationalist hatred for the Germans and love for democracy and freedom, the bitterness of the Partisan attacks on the Nationalists, and the instances of Partisan attacks timed to catch the Nationalists engaged against the Germans. All the evidence, including much collected earlier by British and American liaison officers, cries out against the hypocrisy and dishonesty of the Partisan effort to destroy the Nationalist movement by labelling it collaborationist or quisling. By this attack they have only succeeded in depriving the Allies at this moment of the services of well seasoned troops, eager to attack the Germans if only relieved of the pressure of Partisan attacks.

b. The passivity of General Mihailovich since 1941.

As has already been stated, in the face of the terrible German reprisals for the Nationalist attacks in 1941, General Mihailovich informed the Allies that no useful purpose could be served by further major acts of resistance until the Allies were ready to invade the Balkans. When that day arrived he would throw all the manpower of the country into active service. This attitude was completely in line with the policy laid down by the British and American Governments for all patriots in occupied countries. Disagreement arose between the British authorities and General Mihailovich over the matter of sabotage and other minor acts of resistance. The undersigned has heard the story from the Nationalist point of view, but does not believe that it would be useful to discuss this matter in this report. He wishes to point out here simply that passive resistance and sabotage have both been carried on by the Nationalists in Serbia and especially in Belgrade throughout the period of German occupation, and that in East Bosnia active resistance has been the rule rather than the exception. Throughout this period the Nationalists have continued to bear German reprisals through execution and imprisonment in concentration camps. When all of the evidence is evaluated, it is the considered judgement of the undersigned that only the Poles in all occupied Europe will be able to equal the record of Serb Nationalists in respect to losses suffered at German hands. They still stand ready to renew their attacks on the Germans whenever the Partisans agree to cease civil war.

4. Yugoslav Nationalism in Bosnia

Bosnia is well known as the home of mixed populations of Orthodox Serbs, Roman Catholic Croats, and Moslems. In 1941 Croat and Moslem elements under Ustashi leadership carried out major massacres of Serbs. In 1942 in a few instances, Serb Nationalists conducted counter massacres of Moslems. Outside the country much has been written about the deep hatred and chaos that has developed as a result.

During four weeks the undersigned covered most of East Bosnia and was in touch with Serbs, Croats, and Moslems from the west and south. The evidence thus collected in his judgement constitutes the greatest contribution made by the mission. For the evidence clearly demonstrates that the peoples of Yugoslavia have within themselves the capacity to compose their differences and to join in the reconstruction of their country. The composition of the differences between Serb, Croat, and Moslem has been a part of the program of General Mihailovich for at least the past two years. But the credit for what has been accomplished in East Bosnia must go to the people themselves and to the local leaders, particularly to Father Sava, Orthodox priest and Serb Nationalist leader.

East Bosnia, of course, is part of the Puppet State of Croatia, but the latter has been completely unable to establish a local administration. The Germans control the principal towns with forces which include both SS troops and Ustashi. Outside these towns, with the exception of small areas controlled by Partisans, the administration is in the hands of Nationalists. Outside the towns the Axis forces move only in convoys, and trade between towns and countryside is largely at a standstill. Axis forces are constantly subject to attack, and only a limited number of roads are used by their convoys. The Royal Yugoslav emblem is openly worn throughout the countryside.

The Serb Nationalists, as the best organized, have been the prime movers in this development. But increasingly Moslems and Croats have been consolidating their own strength and ridding their communities of pro-Axis elements. Complete harmony exists among Serb, Moslem, and Croat Nationalist leaders. A joint staff has been set up to coordinate all military operations whether involving Axis forces or Partisans, and joint operations are undertaken on an increasingly large scale. On the civilian side each of the three National groups handles its own affairs, and disputes involving two or more of the groups are handled by joint committees. The sincerity of the friendship and cooperation developed on all levels is unmistakable. The significance of this development lies in the fact that it emphasizes both its Bosnian and its Yugoslav character. In the interests of each of the local communities it has been proved by sad experience that they must first unite as Bosnians and then work as a unit of Yugoslavia. This of course, is the antithesis of Great Serbism or of Great Croatism, both of which deny the existence of Bosnian entity, and supports the Partisan contention that Bosnia, along with Hercegovina, should constitute one of the federal units of the future Yugoslavia. Not only is this correct but, in the judgement of the undersigned, the Bosnian Serbs and Croats are in a position to influence powerfully the promotion of a closer understanding between the main bodies of Serbs and Croats.

For the purposes of the present report the particular importance of the Bosnian situation lies in the fact that Bosnia rather than Old Serbia has become the principal stronghold of Nationalism. All three elements in the population appear to be overwhelmingly opposed to the Partisan movement because of the Communist influence and republican tendencies which characterize this movement. Nationalism in Bosnia is positive and dynamic, the population, warlike and well armed. Nationalist refugees from both Serbia and Dalmatia have already begun to stream into Bosnia. In the approaching civil war the principal formal engagements will be fought on its borders and it will remain the center from which Serbs, Croats, and Moslems irregular bands will strike out into the surrounding areas to keep the struggle alive.

5. The Program of Yugoslav Nationalism.

The undersigned has discussed Nationalism with all Yugoslav elements, Slovenes, Croats, Moslems, and Serbs from all the centers of Serbdom. Yugoslav Nationalism in one sense is heterogeneous. Each of the National and religious elements composing it have their own fears and ambitions. In terms of ideologies it embraces all political parties from Right to Left except for the Communists. It has not been created by a small group seeking to impose their blueprints on a whole country. Rather, it was first a series of local movements, which, under pressure, have coordinated - or are coordinating - their programs and interests to achieve certain common aims.

The common aims of Yugoslav Nationalism may be summarized as follows:

a. The freeing of the soil of Yugoslavia from all foreign domination.

b. The complete defeat of the present attempt of the Yugoslav Communist Party to win National control through its control of the Partisan movement.

c. The purging from all political parties of all individuals who have played any significant role in the various Yugoslav Governments of the past fifteen years, and the punishment of certain leaders either for collaboration with the Axis or for anti-democratic actions prior to the war.

d. The creation of a completely new political constitution for Yugoslavia that will re-define the rights of both national groups and the individual citizen; this to be accomplished through a series of elections, perhaps under control of the Great Powers.

e. A new orientation of the economic life of the country with all emphasis on the employment of Yugoslav wealth to create better living conditions for the people as a whole rather than for favored classes; to be accomplished with a minimum of permanent government regulation, a maximum adoption of the principles of Cooperatives.

f. Reform of the educational system to place the greatest emphasis on the base rather than the apex.

g. A policy looking towards the creation of a Balkan Federation.

h. A policy of friendliness towards all the Great Powers, specifically including Russia, but refusal to recognize any part of the Balkans as the sphere of influence of any one power.

i. Reorganization of the Army, with forced retirement of all officers of General grade.

The largest group within the Nationalist movement are the peasants. They reject any Communist associations for Yugoslavia, but they show almost equal hatred for all of the old political leaders and parties, including the Agrarian Party. Their basic feeling is one of determination to free themselves from strict government control of their economic life - whether from Right or Left. They believe in cooperatives managed by the farmers themselves. They believe that they must be represented in the government by actual "dirt farmers", not by politicians who used to be farmers. The vast majority of these peasants are mildly Royalist, in certain areas royalism is intense, but as a whole the question of the monarchy is less important than that of reform.

The most dynamic group in the Nationalist movement are the students, who have furnished so many of the best Nationalist fighters. For the most part their program is that of the peasants, in fact they believe in a peasant government, but they are more revolutionary, less individualistic, than are the mass of the peasants. Their hatred for the "old order" reaches the point of a demand for the trial and execution of many of the old political and capitalistic leaders. Yet their hatred for Communism is intense. The students are probably more royalist than are the peasants today.

The third element of significance in the Nationalist movement comprises older intellectual and professional men, ex-politicians, and former government employees. Some of these are undoubtedly idealist and reformist, but many of them, in the judgement of the undersigned, are riding the Nationalist wagon primarily because they have no other alternative. Some of this element is called "the Belgrade group", and is viewed with considerable distrust by peasants and students, as well as by many local leaders who dislike the past influence of the capital in national affairs.

The role of General Mihailovich places him in a special category. In Serbia he is adored by both peasants and students; Bosnian and Slovene leaders appear to have great respect for him; but his influence appears to be very slight among Croat Nationalists in Croatia proper. His admirers among the students blame him for being unwilling to place more young men in positions of responsibility, and numbers of Serbs from outside Old Serbia feel that the influence of the Belgrade group has tied him too closely to Serbia. But General Mihailovich accepts the revolutionary character of the Nationalist movement, and apparently sincerely supports all the programs of the peasants. Only second to his devotion to the peasants is his keen interest in the subject of Balkan federation. It is probably true that he is essentially a compromiser - the one significant link uniting the conservative Nationalists with the students and peasants, and he may increasingly serve to unite the various national elements of Yugoslavia and the Balkans.

To any one who seriously studies both the Nationalist and the Partisan movements it becomes clear that the announced programs of both agree, or diverge only slightly, on most points. The rank and file in both movements certainly share the same hopes for the future, but have separated over the point of their fears - the one group fearing most the power of reaction, the others, the power of communism. In the judgement of the undersigned at least 85 per cent of the peoples of Yugoslavia share common fundamental aspirations as to the future political, economic, and social life of their country. The differences which do divide this great majority are not vital, but latent. Potentially they remain a menace to future unity, but only if small groups of willful men are permitted to stir up, to over-emphasize, these differences.

The above optimistic appraisal of popular sentiment must not be misunderstood. If the approximately 15 percent of the Yugoslav population which comprises both the Communists and the overly Conservative element in Nationalism could be removed from all positions of power in the two movements, within a very few months the very great majority would unite under new leadership drawn from both Partisan and Nationalist ranks. The Communist Party members and the ultra-Conservatives could, of course, be given their share in this leadership in proportion to their numerical strength. But the above is theory. The actuality is bloody civil war and increasing anarchy. The ultra-conservatives have little influence in the Nationalist movement, particularly in respect to control of active resistance. But on the Partisan side the National Army of Liberation is completely dominated by officers who are devoted Communists.

C. Conclusions and Recommendations.

1. Strength and Weakness of the Nationalists and Partisans

a. Popular and Proportional Strength.

It has long been the conviction of the undersigned, only strengthened by recent experience, that in evaluating the sentiments of any large groups of people one must

distinguish between active and passive proponents or opponents of any given sentiment. That is in considering Yugoslavia he would distinguish between active and
passive supporters of Nationalism and of the Partisan movement.

At the most, only 5 percent of the total population can be labelled as pro-Axis,
and these must be classed as almost entirely passive - they serve the Axis only
because of force of circumstances. For practical purposes, aside from a few individuals, they can be ignored as a distinct group, and considered as either Nationalist or
Partisan. Thus, numbers of active Ustashi leaders are joining the Partisans and Nedich followers are certain to be assimilated by Nationalists.

Not more than 10-12 percent of the Yugoslav population are Communist Party
members or aspirants for membership. Of these a majority are Serbs from all centers
of Serbdom but particularly from Western Yugoslavia, followed, in numerical order,
by Slovenes, Croats, and Moslems. This includes, of course, women and youth. A
large majority of this total have been attracted to Communism only since the outbreak
of war and the consequence, upheaval of Yugoslav society.

Not more than 3-5 percent of the Yugoslav population are ultra-Conservatives,
almost entirely male and in the upper age brackets. It is not unfair to class them all
as either plutocrats (men whose political thinking is determined by their economic
intents) or politico-religious leaders (political thinking determined by clerical interests). They are well distributed among Serbs, Slovenes, Croats and Moslems.

Of the remaining large majority of the population, and including both active and
passive, it is the considered judgment of the undersigned, based on all available
evidence, that Nationalists heavily outnumber Partisans, probably not less than the
ratio of 3 to 1. That is, throughout Yugoslavia there are at least three individuals
whose principal fear is Communist domination for every individual whose great fear
is directed at reaction.

The strongest factors supporting Nationalism among Serbs, Croats, Slovenes,
and Moslems are:

(1) The conservative and individualistic character of the peasants, a large majority of whom own their own land.

(2) The influence of the three religious faiths and the fact that a heavy majority
of the clergy insist that Communism is anathema to God, and actively support Nationalism.

(3) The tradition of National patriotism combined with the conviction that Communism is alien and works to subject the country to alien influence.

(4) Intense hatred for the Partisan leadership engendered by the record of that
leadership during the past four years, in particular, atrocities.

The strongest factors supporting the Partisan movement are:

(1) Dislocation produced by the war, in particular the atrocities by Germans in
Slovenia, by Ustashi in Croatia, West Bosnia and Dalmatia, which drove large numbers of desperate men into the forests and mountains, ready to welcome any leader
who could promise food and arms.

(2) Conditions of poverty in Montenegro, Dalmatia and Western Bosnia even
prior to the war.

(3) Disgust with the regimes which have governed Yugoslavia throughout most

of the period between 1920 and 1940, and the consequent spread of pro-Communist sentiment among intellectuals, idealists, and some peasants in nearly every Community.

(4) Excellent discipline and organization of the Yugoslav Communist Party; its training in Partisan tactics prior to the war on the battlefields of Spain, in France, and above all, in certain schools in Moscow. Particularly skillful has been the training in propaganda.

(5) The economic and military support contributed by Britain and America.

If one turns to consideration of active supporters of the two movements, the ratio becomes more favorable to the Partisans. Among the latter nearly all are perforce active because of both Communist discipline and the highly organized character of the movement. Among Nationalists, as has already been explained, loyalty and discipline are based primarily on small local groups; the organization is loose, and the high leadership cannot impose its will. Nationalists who are active are exclusively volunteers, whether as fighters or political workers.

It is the considered judgement of the undersigned, indeed, that the Partisan movement today has come to comprise in large measure simply a military machine placed at the disposition of its leaders, whereas the Nationalist movement has become primarily political.

In terms of numerical strength among the Yugoslav population, there are probably at least two active Nationalists to every one active Partisan, but in terms of practical military and political strength, their present organization and the Allied resources available to the Partisans give them effective superiority.

b. Current military strength of Nationalists and Partisans on the basis of careful studies based largely on material from Partisan and British sources gathered since April, 1944, the undersigned estimated that as of last July the Partisan military effectives numbered no more than 100,000 for all of Yugoslavia. All evidence gathered during the stay in the country corroborated this conclusion and further demonstrated the numerical weakness of the Partisans through their inability to effectively hold territory which they had over-run. For each new advance they were obliged to evacuate territory formerly held.

Since August of this year, the Partisan Army has received significant accretions from Bulgarian, Rumanian, and Ustashi sources, and they have been joined by about one half of the Domobran, the army of the Puppet state of Croatia. One must assume, though the undersigned lacks evidence, that recruits have been secured from among the population of Old Serbia, in particular, Belgrad. On the other hand, there was good evidence as of mid-October, that the average Partisan division - of the large number concentrated in or near Old Serbia - totalled closer to 2000 than to 3000 men. The average strength, of the division, that is, was less in October than that estimated by the undersigned for July. There is certainly no basis for estimating current Partisan army strength at more than 150,000 effectives. These are concentrated principally in Old Serbia and Dalmatia and Western Croatia. They effectively control only small parts of Slovenia, Bosnia, Hercegovina and the Sandjak.

As of the first week in September, Serb Nationalist troops in the field numbered close to 100,000, but were widely scattered throughout Old Serbia, East and West

Bosnia, Dalmatia, Hercegovina, and Montenegro. As of the third week in October, this field strength had been reduced to between 60-70,000, mostly in Bosnia, Hercegovina and Dalmatia. Some 10,000 additional Nationalist troops have gone underground in Partisan-occupied Old Serbia.

All Serb Nationalist units are effectively handicapped by lack of ammunition and of mortars and artillery. About half of their units have serious shortages of automatic weapons. The soldiers and the non-commissioned officers are of good quality, adequately trained, and, of course, exclusively volunteers. In the judgement of the undersigned there is a serious deficiency in field grade and, especially, staff officers. In this connection it must be borne in mind that most Yugoslav officers are prisoners in Germany, as well as over 100,000 enlisted men mostly Serbs. A very serious additional handicap is the point already made, that Nationalist troops are still essentially a homeguard militia, effectively at the disposal of the commanding general only in so far as local sentiment concurs with his objectives.

In addition to Serb Nationalist military strength, one must consider the potential contribution of Nationalist Moslems, Croats, and Slovenes. In East Bosnia the Moslem homeguard, the Green Cadre, as of 20 October, numbered not less than 20,000. These men, before desertion from Axis formations, had been trained by German officers, and are well armed and supplied. As further inevitable disintegration overtakes the Moslem SS units, recruits and supplies will continue to flow into the Green Cadre. Within the next few months it is expected that Green Cadre strength in Bosnia will total about 50,000. These Moslems have a fine military tradition, and the enlisted men and junior officers appear both well-trained and possessed of high elan. Owing to the ease with which they have been able to rob German depots - guarded by other Moslems planning to desert subsequently - they are well-equipped with all weapons save field artillery, and possess a considerable reserve of ammunition. As hitherto primarily a village home defense force, the Green Cadre has functioned only through small units. With the aid of Serb Nationalists during October considerable progress was made in the organization of battalions and brigades, and the Moslem leaders at that time were planning integration of all Moslem forces in Bosnia into a group of "Corps" on the model of the Serb Nationalists. General Mihailovich assisted these leaders in procuring the services of certain Yugoslav Regular Army officers of Moslem extraction. It is hoped, later, to secure the services of Turkish officers. The Moslem Nationalist forces, in short, are weak in the present organization of larger units, but for defensive purposes and irregular warfare their contribution to the Civil War will be very significant - especially in view of the strong antipathy felt by most Moslems towards Communism. In addition to Bosnia, as of 20 October in the Sandjak a force of about 4000 local Moslems was cooperating with the Serb Nationalists.

As has already been noted in Bosnia the Croats have organized Nationalist home defense forces by taking over certain elements in the Ustashi organization. About half of the Domobran has either deserted to swell these village units or has formed Nationalist bands under command of Peasant Party leaders in the forests of Western Bosnia and Slovenia. Here, too, General Mihailovich and the Serb Nationalists have been of considerable assistance. But, in the judgment of the undersigned, the Croat

Nationalist military movement, at least in Bosnia and Slavonia is still weak. Up to 21 October, their numbers cannot have exceeded 10,000. All the men have had some military training, and they possess an adequate number of officers, but organization and equipment are still very deficient.

All who are familiar with Croats will agree that Croat Nationalist resistance to the efforts of the Partisans to establish domination over Croatia will be intense, perhaps fatal to the Partisan cause. But whether they will make a significant military contribution to the Civil War will depend in large measure on the energy which may, or may not, be displayed by Machek and the other Peasant Party leaders. If Machek retires from active leadership there is some reason to fear an internal dispute among Nationalist Croat leaders over the succession. However, if the Partisans continue their recent practice of persecuting and killing Croat Nationalists - as established by British sources - this internal dispute will probably be postponed.

Prior to his visit to Serbia, the undersigned had managed to establish rather satisfactory sources of information on the Slovene Nationalist movement. About 10,000 Slovene Nationalists fled to Serbia and Bosnia during the first two years of the war, and most of these have actively joined in the Serb Nationalist movement. General Mihailovich has maintained close relations with the leaders in Slovenia, and has been formally recognized as in command of all Slovene Nationalist troops. Slovene Nationalists claim two military bodies. The homeguard organized by General Rupnik and recognized and armed by the Germans last summer possessed a total of about 12,000 men, well-armed save for artillery, and fairly well-trained and officered. It is claimed, and the undersigned believes, correctly, that with the exception of a small number of senior officers, including of course Rupnik, this force is thoroughly anti-German. It definitely is Nationalist and strongly anti-Communist. Upon the retirement of the Germans this force is certain to put itself at the disposition of the Nationalist cause in any Civil War with the Partisans. The illegal Slovene Nationalist force in Slovenia numbered last summer approximately 6,000 men actually under arms. They were neither well-armed nor well-trained, but increasingly they were being joined by Slovene deserters from the German army. The military strength of Slovene Nationalism is, thus, not insignificant, but presently largely potential. But Slovene Nationalism is as intense and dynamic as Slovene Communism, and, numerically, enjoys a ratio of at least 4 to 1. It must be borne in mind that much of the Partisan strength in Slovenia has come from the Italian minority.

c. Estimate of Future Strength or Weakness of Nationalists and Partisans.

The present strength of the Partisan movement, political and military is the result of war, more specifically, the result of British and American military and propaganda support. The present strength of the Nationalist movement derives solely from popular sentiment and conviction. Given normal peacetime conditions, it is the considered judgement of the undersigned that the Partisan movement as now constituted would disappear. It would become a political influence in proportion to its popular support. The Partisan Army today is largely conscript. The best of its troops are drawn from the displaced elements of the population. If peace should bring the opportunity for these elements to return to the rebuilding of their homes and their normal life, a large majority would renounce their military service. If Allied military and economic assistance and propaganda support should be withheld from the Partisan Army as such, the present movement would collapse in a few months. Marshal Tito, that is, can retain his present position and power only through continuation of both Allied support and at least the semblance of conditions of war.

Nationalist military strength is incapable of standing in formal war against the Allied supported Partisan Army. Notwithstanding, whenever the expected full dress Civil War breaks out, the Nationalists - Serbs, Moslems, Croats, and Slovenes - are likely to make, initially, a resistance based on formal warfare. Assuming continued Allied assistance to Marshal Tito, they will meet defeat owing to shortages in armament and to the ability of the Partisans to make rapid concentrations.

This defeat will inaugurate a period of irregular warfare for which the Nationalists are already laying plans. Their extended strategy is that already so successfully applied by both Mihailovich and Tito against the Germans - infiltration through and behind the enemy lines. They calculate that to successfully crush organized irregular resistance, Tito will need a numerical superiority of 4 to 1, that is, a field force of at least 400,000. With a Partisan force of no more than 200,000, they believe the Partisans will be unable to effectively occupy a major part of Yugoslavia, and the irregular warfare can be continued for at least two years. They believe further that if Tito attempts to raise an army large enough to crush the Nationalist movement in from six months to a year, he will overstrain the resources of the country and bring about his own destruction.

The Nationalist leaders anticipate bloody repression of the type which has already been inaugurated by the Partisans against the Serbs. But they count on the very broad base of the Nationalist movement, and in the large number of trusted local leaders, to render such repression ineffective. On the other hand, they anticipate that the Communist leadership of the Partisan movement will be unable to find any large number of Yugoslavs willing for long to act as executioners of their own people. What they perhaps most fear is that the Yugoslav Partisan movement will be integrated with the Partisan movements of neighboring countries; that Yugoslav Partisans will be conscripted to repress Nationalism in those neighboring countries, while Yugoslavia is being terrorized by a conscript army of Hungarians, Rumanians, Bulgarians, and Albanians under Tito's command.

The undersigned cannot too strongly emphasize that these Nationalist preparations are being made in deadly seriousness. Though they still hope that the Allies will desist from seeking to impose Partisan domination by force, and will instead impose genuinely free elections, as realists the Nationalist leaders - Serbs, Moslems, Croats, and Slovenes - recognize that their peoples have survived previous blood baths. If these leaders did not so plan, their place would be taken by other leaders.

It is the firm conviction of the undersigned that a Communist led and dominated Partisan movement can *in the long run* neither win over Yugoslav Nationalism nor effectively crush it. Due to its present effective military strength, it will win temporarily a measure of success, but it lacks the possibility of winning a broad basis of popular support under its present leadership. If, on the other hand, the Allies would insure genuinely free elections, and if a government should be set up representative of all the elements in the population, both the Partisan movement and the Communist Party have sufficient vitality to make a significant and beneficial contribution to the future of the country.

2. Russians, British and Americans in Yugoslavia

a. Russia in Yugoslavia

Prior to the entrance of Russian armies into Yugoslavia, the undersigned found no evidence of any Russian activity among either Partisans or Nationalists except for radio broadcasts. Once the Russian armies crossed the border, reports began to come in from Nationalist field commanders indicating that no fixed policy had been laid down by the Russian High Command. Contacts between Russians and Nationalists were established by General Mihailovich's command wherever possible. In numbers of instances, the Partisans were able to prevent such contacts, or to stultify them. In some instances, the Nationalist officers and men and civilian leaders were imprisoned by the Russians, in others, by Partisans operating with the Russians. But in certain instances Russian commanders established friendly relations with the local Nationalists, assured them that Russian occupation was purely military and temporary. In a few instances, liaison officers were exchanged and the Russians accepted Nationalist offers to cooperate in attacking the Germans. In some towns, Russian discipline was reported as excellent; in others, excesses of a regrettable nature were reported.

Among Nationalists the undersigned found no hostility towards Russia except insofar as it was feared that she would support the Yugoslav Communists. There is considerable evidence to suggest that the Nationalist leadership would welcome any move towards cooperation that might be made by Russians on the basis of recognition of Russia as a protector and obstention by Russia from interference in local affairs.

b. Britain in Yugoslavia

Despite the support given by Britain to the Partisans, the undersigned was astonished at the strength of pro-British feeling among Nationalists. Bitterness was developing, and may become general, but for the most part there was still a belief that Britain and the Serb Nationalists would eventually resume their traditional friendly tradition.

c. America - Yugoslavia

After making allowances for the natural tendency of a friendly people to demonstrate in the presence of visiting officers, the undersigned was left with the impression that American decision to assume no responsibility for Balkan developments is not accepted by thinking Nationalists. Baldly their position is that American power in the world is such that though she may seek to avoid responsibility in this quarter, she will, nevertheless, be saddled with it. If the sentiment of the people should turn against Britain, America will in large measure be viewed in the same light. In optimistic moments, Nationalists speak often of increased American participation in Yugoslav economic life. Otherwise, all they expect of America is a share in the alleged joint Allied responsibility to insure free elections after the German retreat. They would welcome American occupation along with that of Britain and Russia, but do not consider this essential.

In general, all Nationalists are convinced that the best and only effective way of preventing Civil war is for the Allies to occupy all of Yugoslavia, to oversee the elections, and recognize a responsible Yugoslav Government only after such elections.

3. Recommendations

a. The undersigned recommends that the Allies jointly inform both Nationalist and Partisan leaders that civil war and all acts of organized violence must cease immediately; that failure to comply will insure withdrawal of Allied support - military, economic, and political - from that group.

b. The undersigned recommends that Allied missions be established in all provincial centers of Yugoslavia, attached to no local group, but charged with the duty of establishing temporary zones of local administration, recognising temporarily in each area the local group now exercising the powers of administration.

c. The undersigned recommends that a provisional National Government be set up on the following basis: One third of the members to be nominated by Partisan authorities, one-third, by Nationalist authorities, and one-third by the Allies from among Yugoslav personalities. The duties of this provisional government would be, (1) to accept the dissolution of the present Partisan and Nationalist armies and incorporate them in a Yugoslav Army which would be placed under Allied command for use against Germans; (2) set up the machinery for elections for a National Convention which would determine the future political organization of Yugoslavia. Failure of any group to carry out this program would insure withdrawal of Allied support from that group.

Obviously the policy above recommended is feasible only if supported by the three Allies. Whether or not such joint action is possible is unknown to the undersigned. If possible, however, the undersigned is convinced that after preliminary outbursts of protest, a large majority of both Partisans and Nationalists would accept the policy. The undersigned is convinced further that the enforcement of this policy would require only tactful firmness, not the employment of large bodies of Allied troops to maintain order.

Failure of the Allies to enforce their joint will on all groups in Yugoslavia will inevitable lead to bloody and prolonged civil war which may spread and eventually require a much more grave involvement of the Allies than that envisaged in the above recommendations.

ROBERT H. McDOWELL
Lt. Col, M. I.

Index

413

A Note About the Author

DAVID MARTIN was the organizer and executive director of the Committee for a Fair Trial for Draja Mihailović, which was set up in New York in 1946 after it was announced that General Mihailović had been captured by the Tito forces and would be brought to trial. The committee set up a panel of four distinguished American jurists (Arthur Garfield Hays, head of the American Civil Liberties Union; the Honorable Charles Poletti, former governor of New York; Adolf A. Berle, Jr., former assistant secretary of state; and Theodore Kiendl, an eminent Wall Street lawyer) to take the testimony of the American officers who had been attached to Mihailović and of the American airmen who had been rescued by him. Despite representations to the contrary by the State Department, this testimony had been specifically refused by the Belgrade court.

Mr. Martin is the author of two previous books about Mihailović: *Ally Betrayed* (Prentice-Hall, 1946) and *Patriot or Traitor: The Case of General Mihailovich* (Hoover Institution Press, 1978).